PURE
Java™ 2

Kenneth Litwak

SAMS

Copyright © 2000 by Sams Publishing

All rights reserved. No part of this book shall be reproduced, stored in a retrieval system, or transmitted by any means, electronic, mechanical, photocopying, recording, or otherwise, without written permission from the publisher. No patent liability is assumed with respect to the use of the information contained herein. Although every precaution has been taken in the preparation of this book, the publisher and author assume no responsibility for errors or omissions. Neither is any liability assumed for damages resulting from the use of the information contained herein.

International Standard Book Number: 0-672-31654-4

Library of Congress Catalog Card Number: 99-63646

Printed in the United States of America

First Printing: December 1999

02 01 00 99   4 3 2 1

Trademarks

All terms mentioned in this book that are known to be trademarks or service marks have been appropriately capitalized. Sams Publishing cannot attest to the accuracy of this information. Use of a term in this book should not be regarded as affecting the validity of any trademark or service mark. Java is a trademark of Sun Microsystems, Inc.

Warning and Disclaimer

Every effort has been made to make this book as complete and as accurate as possible, but no warranty or fitness is implied. The information provided is on an "as is" basis. The authors and the publisher shall have neither liability nor responsibility to any person or entity with respect to any loss or damages arising from the information contained in this book.

ASSOCIATE PUBLISHER
Angie Wethington

EXECUTIVE EDITOR
Tim Ryan

ACQUISITIONS EDITOR
Steve Anglin

DEVELOPMENT EDITOR
Jon Steever

MANAGING EDITOR
Lisa Wilson

PROJECT EDITOR
Gayle Johnson

COPY EDITOR
Mary Lagu

INDEXER
Sandra Henselmeier

PROOFREADER
Jill Mazurczyk

TECHNICAL EDITORS
Alexandre Calsavara
David R. Chung
Ethan Henry

TEAM COORDINATOR
Karen Opal

MEDIA DEVELOPER
Dan Scherf

INTERIOR DESIGNER
Karen Ruggles

COVER DESIGNER
Aren Howell

COPY WRITER
Eric Borgert

LAYOUT TECHNICIANS
Darin Crone
Lizbeth Johnston

PRODUCTION
Dan Harris

Overview

Introduction 1

PART I CONCEPTUAL REFERENCE 5

1. What Is Java? 7
2. New Features in Java 2 17
3. Java Program Features 27
4. Data Types 33
5. Methods 63
6. Interfaces 79
7. Syntax 85

PART II TECHNIQUES REFERENCE 103

8. GUI Programming I: Applications 105
9. GUI Programming II: Applets 165
10. Exceptions 189
11. Multithreaded Programming in Java 203
12. I/O in Java 223
13. Reflection 245
14. Java Network Programming 257
15. RMI 279
16. Java Security 309
17. JDBC: Java Database Programming 331
18. Text 365
19. Utility Classes 379

PART III SYNTAX REFERENCE 405

20. java.applet 407
21. java.awt 413
22. java.beans 529
23. java.io 541
24. java.lang 583
25. java.lang.reflect 615
26. java.math 625

27	java.net	**629**
28	java.rmi	**647**
29	java.rmi.server and java.rmi.activation	**653**
30	java.security	**665**
31	java.sql	**679**
32	java.text	**691**
33	java.util	**701**
34	java.util.jar	**725**

INDEX   733

Contents

INTRODUCTION 1

PART I CONCEPTUAL REFERENCE 5

1 What Is Java? 7

Java Overview 7
   Java Is Platform-Neutral 8
   Java Is Object-Oriented 8
   Java Is Network-Ready 10
   Java Is Extensible 10
   Java Is a Better C 11
   Java Is Secure 11
   Java Is Multithreaded 13
The Java Virtual Machine 13
Garbage Collector 14
The Java 2 SDK 14
   Classes 14
   Tools 15
   Versions 16

2 New Features in Java 2 17

Swing/Java Foundation Classes 17
   Swing 18
   Pluggable Look and Feel 18
   Accessibility 19
   Java 2D Classes 19
   Swing Design Philosophy: MVC 20
   Drag and Drop 20
The Policy-Based Security Model 21
RMI Enhancements 21
JDBC 2.0 Enhancements 22
   Package Versioning 24
   Reference Objects 24
   Extensions 24
   Collections 25
   Sound 26
   Other Enhancements 26

3 Java Program Features 27

Basic Layout 27
   Class Definition 28
   Package Statement 28
   Import Statements 28
   Comments 30

Names 30
Punctuation 31
Required Methods 31

4 DATA TYPES   33

Primitives 33
    boolean 34
    char 34
    byte 35
    short 36
    int 36
    long 36
    float 36
    double 37
Classes 37
    Defining Classes 38
    Inheritance: Extends 39
    Creating Instances of Classes: Constructors 40
How Objects Are Created by the JVM 45
Initialization of Data Members 46
Abstract Classes 47
Final Classes 50
Some Important Common Classes 50
    String 51
    Date 53
    Object 54
    Class 54
    System 55
    Runtime 55
    Vector 56
    Properties 57
    Calendar 57
    Thread 58
    Wrapper Classes for Primitives 59
    Arrays of Objects 59

5 METHODS   63

Method Signatures 63
Parameter Names 63
this 64
Modifiers 65
    Final 65
    Static 65
Access Modifiers 67
    Public 67

vii

  Protected 68
  Private 68
  Package-Level Default 70
 Other Modifiers 70
  Native 70
  Synchronized 71
 Overloading Methods 74
 Polymorphism: Overriding Methods 75

6 INTERFACES 79

 An Example from GUI Event-Handling Interfaces 79
 Interface Contents 83

7 SYNTAX 85

 Punctuation 85
 Keywords 86
 Operators 87
  Logical Operators 87
  Arithmetic Operators 87
  Increment/Decrement Operators: ++ and -- 88
  Relational Operators 89
  The ?: Operator 90
  Bitwise Operators 90
 Control Flow 96
  if-else 96
  do-while 98
  while 98
  for 99
  switch 100
 Modifying Control Flow: break and continue 101

PART II TECHNIQUES REFERENCE 103

8 GUI PROGRAMMING I: APPLICATIONS 105

 Basic GUI Application Programming 105
 Layout Managers 107
 Absolute Positioning 107
  Using Absolute Positioning (No LayoutManager):
   Code Example 107
 Leaving Positioning to Layout Managers 110
  FlowLayout Code Example 111
  BorderLayout Code Example 113
  CardLayout Code Example 117
  GridLayout Code Example 120
  GridBagLayout Code Example 122

	Java Foundation Classes 125
	Basic Swing Code Example 127
	Using Accessibility in a Java GUI Application 131
	Using Delegation Event Handling 136
	Adapter Classes 137
	Using Drag and Drop in Java 148

9 GUI Programming II: Applets   165

An Applet Overview 165
Applet Security Considerations 166
Main Applet Methods 167
Running Applets 168
    Using the AppletViewer 170
    The Java Plug-In 170
Applet Programming 171
    A Simple Applet: Code Example 171
    Parameters in an Applet: Code Example 172
    Sound in an Applet: Code Example 175
    Using Images in an Applet 177
    A Single Image in an Applet: Code Example 178
    Multiple Images in an Applet: Code Example 180

10 Exceptions   189

The Throwable Class 189
    Handling Exceptions: try-catch-finally 190
    try-catch Code Example 191
    Handling Specific Exceptions 194
    finally Clause Code Example 195
    Declaring a Method That Throws Exceptions: Code Example 197
    Creating Your Own Exception Classes: Code Example 198
    Handle or Declare? 201

11 Multithreaded Programming in Java   203

Thread States 203
Creating Threads 204
    Creating Threads with Runnable Objects: Code Example 204
    Creating a Thread Subclass: Code Example 206
Primary Thread Methods 207
Using Synchronization 209
    Synchronization Code Example 213
Avoiding Deadlocks with wait() and notify() 217
    wait() and notify() Code Example 218

12 I/O in Java   223

A Quick Overview of Stream 223
An Overview of the Main Stream, Reader, and Writer Classes 224

Using Files in Java 225
    File: Code Example 226
    RandomAccessFile Code Example 229
Performing I/O in Java 231
    Performing I/O Using FileInputStream and FileOutputStream:
    Code Example 231
    Performing I/O on Java Primitives Using DataInputStream and
    DataOutputStream: Code Example 234
    Reading and Writing Lines of Text: Code Example 237
    Reading and Writing Objects 240
    Object Serialization 240
    ObjectOutputStream and ObjectInputStream: Code Example 241

13 REFLECTION 245

Discovering the Name and Attributes of a Class 246
    Using Reflection to Retrieve Class Information:
    Code Example 246
Getting Constructor and Method Information with Reflection 249
    Reflection of Constructor and Method Information:
    Code Example 249
Discovering Interface Information 251
    Interface Reflection: Code Example 251
Modifying Data Members and Calling Methods 253
    Class Manipulation: Code Example 253

14 JAVA NETWORK PROGRAMMING 257

Core Networking Concepts 258
Working with Host Names and IP Addresses 259
    Host Information Using INetAddress: Code Example 260
Creating a TCP Client and Server Application 261
    TCP Socket with Socket and ServerSocket: Code Example 262
Using Datagram Packets and UDP Sockets 269
    UDP Using DataGramPacket and DatagramSocket:
    Code Example 269
Working with URLs in Java 273

15 RMI 279

RMI Architecture Overview 279
Parameters for Remote Methods 280
Finding Remote Objects 281
Calling a Remote Object's Methods 282
    Create a Remote Interface: Code Example 282
    Implement a Remote Object Class Definition: Code Example 283
    Create a Remote Factory on a Server: Code Example 285
    Implement a Client Program: Code Example 288
    Generate a Stub and Skeleton 291

        Start the RMIRegistry 292
        Start the Remote Factory Program Using a Policy File 292
        Run the Client 292
        Calling a Remote Object with a Remote Object Parameter:
           Code Examples 292
        Creating a Remote Object from a Client: Remote Activation
           Code Examples 298

16 JAVA SECURITY 309

        Using Policy-Based Security 309
        Creating a Policy File 312
        Sample Code for Digital Signing 314
        Procedure for Digitally Signing Code 318
        Creating Custom Permissions 323
           User-Defined Permission Code Example 324
        Message Digests 326
           MessageDigest Code Example 327

17 JDBC: JAVA DATABASE PROGRAMMING 331

        Creating a Database Connection 332
           Database Connection and Table Creation: Code Example 334
           ResultSet and ResultSetMetadata: Code Example 341
           PreparedStatement: Code Example 345
        Using Callable Statements 348
        JDBC 2.0 Techniques 349
           Scrollable ResultSet 350
           Scrollable ResultSet: Code Example 350
           Batch Updates 355
           Modifiable ResultSets 355
           Updatable ResultSet: Code Example 356
        Other Important Points to Remember 361
           Limit ResultSet Size 361
           Turn Off Auto-Commit 362
           Set the Isolation Level 362

18 TEXT 365

        Basic Internationalization in a Java Application 366
           Locale and ResourceBundle Classes: Code Example 367
        Formatting Text 369
        Formatting Numeric Data 370
           Numeric Formatting: Code Example 370
        Formatting Dates and Times 373
           Date and Time Using DateFormat: Code Example 373

19 UTILITY CLASSES 379

        The Collection Framework 379
        Collection Interfaces 380

Collection Implementations 382
　　Set Implementations 384
　　HashSet Code Example 384
　　List Implementations 387
　　List Code Example 387
　　Map Implementations 391
　　Map Code Example 391
GregorianCalendar 394
　　GregorianCalendar Code Example 395
Using Properties 399
　　Properties Code Example 400

PART III SYNTAX REFERENCE 405

20 JAVA.APPLET 407

Package Name: java.applet 407
　　Interfaces 407
　　Class 408
Interface and Class Details 408
　　Interface AppletContext 408
　　Interface AppletStub 408
　　Interface AudioClip 409
　　Class Applet 409

21 JAVA.AWT 413

Package Name: java.awt 413
　　Interfaces 413
　　Classes 413
　　Exceptions 415
　　Errors 415
Package Name: java.awt.datatransfer 415
　　Interfaces 415
　　Classes 415
　　Exceptions 415
Package Name: java.awt.dnd 415
　　Interfaces 415
　　Classes 415
　　Exceptions 416
Package Name: java.awt.event 416
　　Interfaces 416
　　Classes 416
Package Name: java.awt.font 417
　　Interfaces 417
　　Classes 417
Package Name: java.awt.geom 417
　　Interfaces 417

Classes 417
Exceptions 418
Package Name: java.awt.print 418
Interfaces 418
Classes 418
Exceptions 418
java.awt Interface and Class Details 419
Interface ActiveEvent 419
Interface Adjustable 419
Interface Composite 419
Interface CompositeContext 420
Interface ItemSelectable 420
Interface LayoutManager 420
Interface LayoutManager2 420
Interface MenuContainer 421
Interface Paint 421
Interface PaintContext 421
Interface PrintGraphics 421
Interface Shape 421
Interface Transparency 422
Class AWTEvent 422
Class AWTEventMulticaster 423
Class BorderLayout 426
Class Button 427
Class Canvas 428
Class CardLayout 429
Class Checkbox 430
Class CheckboxGroup 431
Class Choice 432
Class Color 433
Class Component 435
Class Container 439
Class Cursor 441
Class Dialog 442
Class FileDialog 444
Class FlowLayout 445
Class Font 446
Class Frame 449
Class Graphics 451
Class Graphics2D 453
Class GridBagConstraints 455
Class GridBagLayout 457
Class GridLayout 458
Class Image 459
Class Insets 460

Class Label	461
Class List	462
Class MediaTracker	464
Class Menu	465
Class MenuBar	467
Class MenuItem	468
Class MenuShortcut	469
Class Panel	469
Class Point	470
Class PopupMenu	471
Class PrintJob	472
Class Rectangle	473
Class ScrollPane	475
Class TextArea	476
Class TextComponent	477
Class TextField	478
Class Toolkit	479
Class Window	483
java.awt.datatransfer Interface and Class Details	484
Interface ClipboardOwner	484
Interface FlavorMap	484
Interface Transferable	484
Class Clipboard	485
Class DataFlavor	489
Class StringSelection	490
Class SystemFlavorMap	491
java.awt.dnd Interface and Class Details	491
Interface Autoscroll	491
Interface DragGestureListener	492
Interface DragSourceListener	492
Interface DropTargetListener	492
Class DnDConstants	493
Class DragGestureEvent	493
Class DragGestureRecognizer	494
Class DragSource	495
Class DragSourceEvent	496
Class DropTarget	497
Class DropTargetEvent	498
Class MouseDragGestureRecognizer	499
java.awt.event Interface and Class Details	500
Interface ActionListener	500
Interface AdjustmentListener	500
Interface FocusListener	501
Interface InputMethodListener	502
Interface ItemListener	502

Interface KeyListener 503
Interface MouseListener 503
Interface MouseMotionListener 503
Interface TextListener 504
Interface WindowListener 504
Class ActionEvent 504
Class AdjustmentEvent 506
Class FocusAdapter 507
Class FocusEvent 507
Class InputEvent 508
Class ItemEvent 509
Class KeyEvent 510
Class MouseEvent 517
Class PaintEvent 519
Class TextEvent 520
Class WindowAdapter 521
Class WindowEvent 522
java.awt.print Interface and Class Details 523
Interface Pageable 524
Interface Printable 524
Interface PrinterGraphics 524
Class Book 524
Class PageFormat 525
Class PrinterJob 526

22 JAVA.BEANS 529

Package Name: java.beans 530
   Interfaces 530
   Classes 530
   Exceptions 531
Package Name: java.beans.beancontext 531
   Interfaces 531
   Classes 531
java.beans Interface and Class Details 532
   Interface AppletInitializer 532
   Interface BeanInfo 532
   Interface Customizer 532
   Interface PropertyChangeListener 533
   Interface PropertyEditor 533
   Interface VetoableChangeListener 534
   Class BeanDescriptor 534
   Class Beans 535
   Class IndexedPropertyDescriptor 536
   Class Introspector 537
   Class PropertyChangeEvent 537

Class PropertyDescriptor 538
Class SimpleBeanInfo 539

23 JAVA.IO 541

Package Name: java.io 541
　Interfaces 541
　Classes 542
　Exceptions 543
Interface and Class Details 543
　Interface Externalizable 543
　Interface FileFilter 544
　Interface FilenameFilter 544
　Interface Serializable 544
　Class BufferedOutputStream 546
　Class BufferedReader 547
　Class BufferedWriter 548
　Class ByteArrayInputStream 549
　Class ByteArrayOutputStream 550
　Class CharArrayReader 551
　Class CharArrayWriter 552
　Class DataInputStream 552
　Class DataOutputStream 554
　Class File 555
　Class FileInputStream 557
　Class FileOutputStream 558
　Class FilePermission 559
　Class FileReader 560
　Class FileWriter 561
　Class InputStream 561
　Class InputStreamReader 562
　Class LineNumberReader 563
　Class ObjectInputStream 564
　Class ObjectOutputStream 566
　Class OutputStream 568
　Class PipedInputStream 569
　Class PipedOutputStream 570
　Class PrintStream 571
　Class PrintWriter 572
　Class RandomAccessFile 574
　Class Reader 576
　Class SequenceInputStream 577
　Class StreamTokenizer 578
　Class StringBufferInputStream 579
　Class StringReader 580
　Class StringWriter 580
　Class Writer 581

24 JAVA.LANG 583

Interfaces 583
Classes 583
Exceptions 584
Errors 585
Interface and Class Details 585
    Interface Cloneable 585
    Interface Comparable 585
    Interface Runnable 586
    Class Boolean 586
    Class Byte 587
    Class Character 588
    Class Class 590
    Class ClassLoader 591
    Class Compiler 592
    Class Double 593
    Class Float 594
    Class Integer 595
    Class Long 597
    Class Math 598
    Class Object 599
    Class Runtime 600
    Class RuntimePermission 601
    Class SecurityManager 602
    Class Short 604
    Class String 605
    Class StringBuffer 608
    Class System 609
    Class Thread 610
    Class ThreadGroup 612
    Class Throwable 613

25 JAVA.LANG.REFLECT 615

Interfaces 616
Classes 616
Interface and Class Details 616
    The Interface Member 616
    Class AccessibleObject 616
    Class Array 617
    Class Constructor 618
    Class Field 619
    Class Method 620
    Class Modifier 621
    Class ReflectPermission 622

26 JAVA.MATH 625

Classes 625
Class Details 625
Class BigDecimal 625
Class BigInteger 627

27 JAVA.NET 629

Interfaces 629
Classes 629
Exceptions 630
Interface and Class Details 630
Interface ContentHandlerFactory 630
Interface SocketImplFactory 631
Interface SocketOptions 631
Class ContentHandler 631
Class DatagramPacket 632
Class DatagramSocket 633
Class HttpURLConnection 634
Class InetAddress 636
Class JarURLConnection 637
Class MulticastSocket 638
Class PasswordAuthentication 640
Class ServerSocket 640
Class Socket 641
Class SocketImpl 642
Class URL 643
Class URLConnection 644
Class URLStreamHandler 646

28 JAVA.RMI 647

Interfaces 647
Classes 647
Exceptions 647
Interface and Class Details 648
Interface Remote 648
Class MarshalledObject 648
Class Naming 649
Class RMISecurityManager 650

29 JAVA.RMI.SERVER AND JAVA.RMI.ACTIVATION 653

Package Name: java.rmi.activation 653
Interfaces 653
Classes 653
Exceptions 654

Package Name: java.rmi.server 654
   Interfaces 654
   Classes 654
   Exceptions 654
java.rmi.server Interface and Class Details 655
   Interface RemoteRef 655
   Interface RMIClientSocketFactory 655
   Interface RMIServerSocketFactory 655
   Interface ServerRef 656
   Class RemoteObject 656
   Class RMIClassLoader 657
   Class RemoteServer 657
   Class UnicastRemoteObject 658
java.rmi.activation Class Details 659
   Class Activatable 659
   Class ActivationDesc 660
   Class ActivationGroup 661
   Class ActivationGroupDesc 662
   Class ActivationID 663

30 JAVA.SECURITY   665

Package Name: java.security 665
   Interfaces 665
   Classes 665
   Exceptions 666
Package Name: java.security.cert 667
   Interfaces 667
   Classes 667
   Exceptions 667
java.security.cert Interface and Class Details 667
   Interface Key 667
   Class AllPermission 668
   Class CodeSource 669
   Class KeyPair 669
   Class KeyStore 670
   Class MessageDigest 671
   Class Permission 672
   Class Policy 673
   Class ProtectionDomain 674
java.security.cert Class Details 674
   Class Certificate 674
   Class CRL 675
   Class X509Certificate 676
   Class X509CRL 677

31 JAVA.SQL 679

Interfaces 679
Classes 679
Exceptions 680
Interface and Class Details 680
Interface Blob 680
Interface CallableStatement 680
Interface Connection 681
Interface Driver 683
Interface PreparedStatement 683
Interface ResultSet 685
Interface Statement 688
Class DriverManager 689
Class Timestamp 690

32 JAVA.TEXT 691

Interfaces 691
Classes 691
Exception 691
Class Details 692
Class ChoiceFormat 692
Class DateFormat 693
Class DecimalFormat 695
Class MessageFormat 696
Class NumberFormat 697
Class SimpleDateFormat 698

33 JAVA.UTIL 701

Interfaces 701
Classes 701
Exceptions 702
Interface and Class Details 702
Interface Collection 702
Interface Iterator 703
Interface List 703
Interface Map 704
Interface Observer 705
Interface Set 705
Class ArrayList 706
Class BitSet 707
Class Calendar 708
Class Collections 711
Class GregorianCalendar 712
Class HashMap 713
Class HashSet 714
Class Locale 715

Class Observable 717
Class Properties 717
Class PropertyPermission 719
Class ResourceBundle 720
Class StringTokenizer 720
Class Vector 721

34 JAVA.UTIL.JAR 725

Classes 726
Exceptions 726
Class Details 726
Class JarEntry 726
Class JarFile 727
Class JarInputStream 728
Class JarOutputStream 729
Class Manifest 730

INDEX 733

Dedication

To my wife Amanda, who gave me time to write this book and who proofread my work till all hours of the night, and to Matthew, Wesley, and Daniel, who waited anxiously for Dad to finish "the book."

Acknowledgments

I want to acknowledge the many people who have helped me with coding issues and technical details. They include my colleagues at Sun Educational Services, especially Simon Roberts and more than one JavaSoft engineer, without whose help this book would not have been possible. I would also like to mention the help I have gotten from numerous individuals on the RMI-Users mailing list run by Sun. Of course, I also want to acknowledge my editors at Sams, who have borne with my often slow progress and individual perspective.

I appreciate Macmillan for giving me the opportunity to improve my own Java knowledge and publish a book at the same time. Finally, this book would not have seen daylight without the help of my supportive wife, Amanda. She has been my proofreader, laughing with me through countless bizarre or amusing typos.

About the Author

Kenneth Litwak has worked for Sun Microsystems as a Java programming instructor since early 1998. Prior to that, he worked on Java projects including e-commerce, security, and distributed processing. Ken also has several years of experience as a COBOL programmer and as a database kernel engineer for IBM. Ken has a B.S. in Computer Information Systems from California Polytechnic University, Pomona, California, as well as a B.A. and an M.Div. in biblical studies. When not teaching Java or writing a Java book, Ken works on his doctoral dissertation in New Testament studies, rides his road bike, and is dad to three energetic boys.

Tell Us What You Think!

As the reader of this book, *you* are our most important critic and commentator. We value your opinion and want to know what we're doing right, what we could do better, what areas you'd like to see us publish in, and any other words of wisdom you're willing to pass our way.

As an executive editor for Sams Publishing, I welcome your comments. You can fax, email, or write me directly to let me know what you did or didn't like about this book—as well as what we can do to make our books stronger.

When you write, please be sure to include this book's title and author as well as your name and phone or fax number. I will carefully review your comments and share them with the author and editors who worked on the book.

> Fax: (317) 581-4770
> E-mail: java@mcp.com
> Mail: Tim Ryan
> Executive Editor
> Sams Publishing
> 201 W. 103rd Street
> Indianapolis, IN 46290 USA

To download the code in this book, visit our Web site at www.samspublishing.com/product_support, and then enter this book's ISBN: 0672316544.

Introduction

The latest version of Java, renamed from JDK 1.2 to Java 2 SDK Standard Edition Version 1.2, is a significant enhancement to the Java programming language. This version has many new features, such as Swing for coding cool-looking GUIs; a new `Collection` Framework, which adds support for dealing with collections of objects; and the Extension mechanism for adding your own classes to Java's SDK classes. Java now offers new JDBC features such as scrollable result sets, remote activation of RMI objects, and improved performance. There are many reasons to move from JDK 1.0 or 1.1 to Java 2. This book is designed to help you make this transition. If you are new to Java, you'll find here a rich API set to accomplish almost any programming task you need. This book is designed to help you put the features of Java 2 to optimal use.

The Audience for This Book

Pure Java 2 has two audiences. First, it is for developers who are relatively new to Java and who need to reinforce what they've learned.

This book is not a tutorial. Instead, it is written for developers, who are already familiar with at least basic elements of Java and who are aiming to improve their knowledge. So, although the first several chapters cover basic syntax, there are not many brief, simple programs to show how to use each basic piece of the language.

The second audience is made up of experienced Java programmers who need to look up how to do some specific task. The core of the book is Part II, which covers programming techniques and will be especially helpful to more experienced programmers. I have provided examples of how to accomplish tasks that are important or not well-understood. I have in many cases intentionally gone beyond what I've found in most other books on Java. For example, this book includes information on the following topics that are seldom covered in other books:

- How an external event-handling class can communicate back to the GUI that registered the listener object
- How RMI performs better, as a rule, if you pass remote object references rather than passing objects by value
- How you can use remote objects as parameters in an RMI remote method invocation
- How to get data from the dialog box back to the main GUI screen
- How to use resource bundles
- How to format data when displaying it

Among techniques that are important to know, I've provided examples for doing RMI remote activation and examples of using MediaTracker to monitor the downloading of multiple images for an applet. Along with these and other techniques, I've provided ample notes, tips, and cautions useful to all Java programmers who want to write better code and avoid common pitfalls.

For the most part, you'll be able to pick up this book, find the subject you want to write code for, and find an example of how to do it, along with any advice I think is important. You will also find many tips and suggestions relating to object-oriented design

2 Introduction

issues. I'm quite keen on designing classes and applications properly first, and only later optimizing them if appropriate. Therefore, many sections in this book address design questions. You will find that the better you get as a Java programmer, the more you'll be able to stop focusing on syntax and focus instead on design. You'll find several suggestions here to help you design better classes and applications. My belief is that the syntax is easy. Writing truly object-oriented code that will be relatively easy to maintain is more challenging, and that's why I've put this material in the book.

How This Book Is Organized

This book contains three parts, each with a specific function.

Part I, the Conceptual Reference, is an accelerated introduction that explains the features of the Java 2 SDK, as well as some of the fundamental programming techniques you will need to be aware of as you proceed through this book. Part I is an ideal starting point for developers who are fairly new to Java.

Part II, the Techniques Reference, is intended more for experienced Java programmers. It is the main focus of this book. This invaluable reference contains concise descriptions of many crucial aspects of the Java 2 SDK. It also features well-commented, commercial-quality code that you can use directly in your programs. This part of the book is also handy for developers who simply want to look at an example to get ideas or refresh their memory regarding how to implement a given technique. So if you need an example—such as how to do remote activation, how to use a linked list, or how to create a policy file to grant your applet more freedom—all those techniques are covered in Part II.

Part III is a Syntax Reference that helps you look up the most common or important classes and interfaces in Java 2. You'll find strategically placed advice and explanatory code snippets throughout.

Features of This Book

This book is not meant to be exhaustive. JDK 1.0 had about 220 classes. JDK 1.1 had about 500. Java 2 has over 1,600 classes and interfaces. Just listing all those classes and interfaces, with all their methods and data members, would take a whole book in itself. I had to be selective. I have chosen programming techniques that I think are either critical for a Java developer to know or are not well-understood but still helpful to know. When I was learning Java, I looked through lots of Java books that didn't tell me how to do what I thought should have been explained. I've covered those topics for you here.

Along the way, you'll find many places where I've offered tips, advice, or warnings. I learned a lot of my Java the hard way—by coding—and I've found many ways to make your programs better (not to mention ways to make your life as a developer harder). You will find the following here:

- Guidance and examples to help you write your code as cleanly, elegantly, and simply as possible.
- Object-oriented design suggestions to help you create better classes. Knowing syntax and writing good, maintainable code are two different things. This book helps you accomplish both.

- The use of design patterns. I think these strategies for solving design problems can be helpful in organizing a program.

> **NOTE**
>
> The source code for the examples given in this book can be found on the Macmillan Web site. To download the code, go to `http://www.mcp.com/product_support/`. Enter this book's ISBN—0672316544—in the Book Information and Downloads text field, and click Search.

- UML, the Unified Modeling Language, is used to show class hierarchies, especially in Part III. This notation, developed by the Three Amigos—Booch, Rumbuagh, and Jacobsen—at Rational has become a de facto standard for creating artifacts for object-oriented analysis and design.
- I wrote this book with real programmers in mind. I have had to write silly little "Hello, World" programs in more languages than I care to remember. Such programs are not very useful, and certainly no one would pay you to write such an application. Instead, my approach is to write real code that can easily be expanded into a meaningful application.
- With rare exceptions, I have used the same basic problem domain throughout the book: a graduate school library (where I spend much of my time working on my doctoral dissertation). The continuity of one problem domain should prove helpful. The examples focus on library cards, books, and book catalog searches, rather than on a myriad of different things, as some books do.

I hope you will find this book a valuable resource that you reach for regularly while you work. If you have questions about its contents, you can email me at `javajedi2@yahoo.com`, and I'll send you a reply in due time. May you always brew hot, robust Java.

Kenneth D. Litwak
Milpitas, California
September 1999

PART I

CONCEPTUAL REFERENCE

CHAPTER 1

What Is Java?

Java Overview

Java is three things in one:

- Java is a programming language.
  It is similar, in various ways, to many other programming languages, with heavy influence from C (basic syntax and operators) and Smalltalk (object-oriented features).
- Java is an environment.
  In the following sections, I will talk about the Java virtual machine (JVM). A key part of Java is a runtime environment that supports Java programs. There are many features, such as garbage collection, multithreading, and resource management, provided by the Java environment. It is this runtime environment, including the Java interpreter, class loader, bytecode verifier, and so forth, that shields your application or Applet code from the operating system. The environment schedules your threads, loads your code, manages memory for you, and makes calls to native OS routines as needed. If the JVM cannot accomplish its task without a native OS call, it will make such a call. Your code won't be aware of this call.
- Java is the equivalent of a huge class library.
  This library is similar to one you might buy for C++. There are classes for dealing with URLs, doing GUI programming, doing distributed object programming with RMI or CORBA, and so forth. Unlike many languages (C, for instance), Java comes with support for doing most of the things you need to do, already coded, from basics such as collection classes to complex distributed objects such as a Java wrapper object for a legacy COBOL program.

Java Is Platform-Neutral

This is where the "write once, run anywhere" motto for Java comes in. How does this work? First, you write a Java source file and compile it. When you compile Java source code, the result is a .class file that contains bytecode. The bytecode is the same no matter what platform you are on, provided that you are using a Sun-Compliant JVM. There is essentially nothing in the byte code values that is platform-specific.

When you execute the class file using a given JVM that is Sun-compliant, the JVM deals with platform dependencies. Therefore, you can take the same compiled .class file and run it on any system with a Sun-compliant JVM. So if I write a Java program on Solaris, I can run it on a Mac or Windows 98 or OS/2 without having to recompile.

There are a few small items that are not platform-neutral, such as the difference between / and \ in directory names, or the number of mouse buttons. You can plan for these differences depending upon what your application does.

This platform independence is a very important feature in Java. It means that you can develop on one system and run on another without doing very much porting of the code. It means that you can have diverse client systems, but only one version of the client code. You can have multiple systems in the middle-tier, but only one version of the Java middle-tier business logic code. Java can reduce desktop maintenance costs by allowing for only one version of the client regardless of the OS on the client. It also provides for scalability on the server-side because you can run the same middle-tier business logic on any number of systems.

Java, through the JVM and the use of interpreted bytecode, shields your program from any differences that appear on different platforms. As Chapter 8, "GUI Programming I: Applications," describes, your object's request to create a Java button or some other OS-dependent entity (for example, a thread) will be handled by a routine that is specific to the platform. Your Java code, however, has nothing in it specific to the platform. In cases where something specific to the platform is needed, Java provides various means for dealing with the dependency, such as system properties for file and path separators.

> **NOTE**
>
> *Bytecode* refers to specific opcodes generated by the Javac compiler (or by other means) as the JVM-specific equivalent of your source code. Opcodes represent the instruction set that Java supports at a low level, such as an `add two floats together` opcode or a `create new int array` opcode. The opcodes are published. You can write a program using only bytecode. No knowledge of bytecode is needed to program in Java, but it is an important concept to understand. You must know the difference between using the Java interpreter and a JIT (just-in-time compiler) or HotSpot.

Java Is Object-Oriented

Like Smalltalk, but unlike C++, Java was designed from the start to be an object-oriented language. So Java supports inheritance, encapsulation, and polymorphism, the three major OO constructs that distinguish a language as object-oriented. Java supports the object model. All true objects have

- Identity
  Objects can be referred to by some kind of identifier. In Java, you can use a human-readable name, like okButton. Java internally refers to objects by an object reference.
- State
  Java uses data members (also known as member variables) to define state. Generically, these are an object's attributes. This might include the background color of a Label object or the number of elements in a Vector object(which is part of its state, and not merely a calculated value).
- Behavior
  Object behavior is defined in Java by methods. They follow in large part the Smalltalk model in which a method call is similar to sending a message to an object.
  A well-designed object-oriented system or program consists of multiple, distinct, cooperating objects, working together to accomplish some task, such as processing an e-commerce order. To help support this concept, Java provides the framework for the three essentials of a proper object-oriented program. These three elements separate true object-oriented languages from procedural languages like C or a quasi-object languages such as Ada.
- Encapsulation
  Encapsulation represents the notion of attributes and behavior forcing one complete entity, in which the state and behavior are tightly integrated. There is no close connection semantically between a C struct and a C function, which uses fields in the struct. In Java, data members and methods go together into one class. That class defines what an object that has both certain attributes and behaviors is like. This is a powerful idiom that enables a developer to define a class for an object that creates itself, provides a means for other objects to act upon it or make requests of it, and internally takes care of its own state. This will be explained more thoroughly in Chapter 3, "Java Program Features."

NOTE

A Java program that reflects proper encapsulation is far superior to a program that merely has data and code in the same source file. In a typical procedural program, any code can do whatever it wants to the data, and there is nothing to semantically create a relationship between the data and the code. Many non-object-oriented programs allow code to put lots of invalid values into data. Nothing is responsible for safeguarding the state of the data.

- Inheritance
  Java supports the capability of one class to derive data members and methods from a pre-existing class by stating that the former class "extends" (inherits) from the latter. The power of this mechanism will be seen throughout Part II,

"Technique Reference." For example, all the GUI components inherit a huge number of methods and data members from the parent class, Component, as do user-defined GUI components, which generally subclass (inherit from) Component. Like Smalltalk, but unlike C++, Java only permits single inheritance in order to prevent bugs that can result from improper multiple inheritance. This will be covered more in Chapter 4, "Data Types."

- Polymorphism
Java provides the capability to call a given method defined in multiple classes. It enables the system to figure out which class's method should to be called. This is both a compile-time and runtime process. Let me illustrate this using the well-known Smalltalk example: You create an Animal class and two subclasses—Dog and Parrot. Each of these three classes has a talk() method. You then create an object of type Dog, and you call its talk() method as follows:

```
fido.talk();
```

Because the class Dog inherits a talk() method from Animal but overrides it, Java needs to determine the correct version of the talk() method to execute. It will call the method defined in the Dog class. Because of the superclass/subclass relationship, you can also use a superclass name and substitute a subclass instance for it. Here's a short example:

```
public wash(Animal a)
     {
       if(a instanceof Dog)
         a.washWithDogShampoo();
     }
```

This illustrates the idea of substitution; it enables me to call the wash() method and provide a parameter of type Dog. Java knows that a Dog is not an Animal per se, but it also knows that Dog is a subclass of Animal and so allows a Dog object for a parameter. Then, inside the method, the parameter can be tested to determine its actual type. Polymorphism is discussed more in Chapter 4.

Java Is Network-Ready

Java comes with many classes, especially those in the package java.net, to provide for easily using sockets, server sockets, reading URLs, encoding and decoding URLs, and so forth. Many of these functions can require a lot of code (in C, for example). Java masks a lot of the complexity by providing classes for you that already implement the hard parts, such as creating socket connections, reading the contents of a URL as a file, and translating back and forth between domain names and IP addresses.

Java Is Extensible

You can easily add classes and plug in new methods to classes, creating new classes through subclasses. This makes Java very easy to augment with your own classes or even to modify. Java 2, as I'll discuss later in the chapter, even supports a feature called *extensions* that enable you to create user-defined classes. The JVM treats these as core Java 2 classes.

Java Is a Better C

The Java designers set out to make a language that would be easy for C developers to learn. It would C syntax in general, but would avoid many problems associated with C:

- Java does not allow you to use pointers.
  The biggest difficulty in C programming has to do with memory allocation—that is, pointer errors. You run into these errors because C allows you to perform so many tricks with pointers. Java avoids these memory allocation problems by not allowing you to use any pointers. Java does have object references, but you are not allowed to modify the values in them. (An exception is getting a new reference to a new object, reusing the same object reference variable.)
- Java does not allow multiple inheritance.
  The designers of Java deemed multiple inheritance a feature that programmers either didn't understand very well or abused too often. The results were program errors and hard-to-maintain code.
- Java primitives are always represented in the same way, regardless of platform. This is another thing that makes Java safer to use than C. This is also one of the features that make it platform-neutral—primitives are always represented the same way, regardless of the OS the JVM is running on. So, for example, an int is always a 32-bit signed number in Java, and bits are always represented in big-endian format. There is never a problem with an int being two bytes on one system and four bytes on another. It doesn't matter what the OS does because an int is always the same on every JVM.
- Java doesn't allow you to pass parameters by reference.
  All parameters are passed by value. That means that you can't do sneaky things with a parameter in a method. Even object references are passed by value, so changing an object reference in a called method doesn't change the real object reference. You can use the value of the object reference in a called method to change its data members or call the object's methods, but you can't change which object the object reference points to. There's no spoofing the runtime system.

NOTE

Java has also been spared templates, which are part of C++. They are a fairly complex construct, and there's a lot to know before you can use templates correctly. It's easy to get them wrong. That is why Java does not provide them.

Java Is Secure

Security is a major feature of Java. You don't have to buy separate software to get security for Java, as you would for other programming and scripting languages.

Java provides security through

- Protection domains
  Java is designed from the ground up to be secure. That means, among other things, that an applet running in a browser can't merrily thrash your client

system as an ActiveX control might do. This is because the protection domain of downloaded applet code does not normally have permission to do nasty things to your system. Java provides for fine-grained, policy-based permissions for given codebases or code signers.
- Access control lists
An alternative facility exists in Java to define users and groups as having specific access privileges.
- Support for authentication and privacy
Although encryption and decryption are not part of Java 2 as such, Java does support them and provides for authentication through digitally signing code and documents; creating digital certificates; key pairs; and—as part of the Java 2 SDK—message digits for privacy, authentication, and verification of message contents.
- Bytecode verification for distrusted code
Java 2, unlike previous versions, only truly trusts code that is in the SDK. All distrusted code is checked to be sure the bytecode symbols are valid. In this way, the JVM can determine if a class file contains something that is illegal or meaningless in Java. A hacker cannot put a Trojan horse or virus in the middle of a class file. In the event of foul play, the bytecode verifier will see opcodes that don't match anything valid and refuse to load the class definition. This is done under the control of a classloader that understands protection domains. Java has a number of features built in to prevent distrusted code from doing bad things to your system. When your applet class is downloaded from a Web server, it cannot run in the browser until the bytecode verifier has inspected the class file. The verifier validates the applet's format and verifies that all the checksums are correct, that the class file starts with the magic number `cafebabe`, and that all the byte codes are valid. This means that you can't take any file, such as a virus program, rename it to a class file, and expect it to be run by the browser's JVM. If a class file does not start with the letters `cafebabe`, the bytecode verifier will refuse to load the class.

NOTE

A "magic number" is a special character or characters or set of bytes that appears at or near the beginning of a file to tell a program the file's type. For example, there is a magic number used in all Windows .exe files to indicate that they represent an executable program for a Microsoft Windows system. Java's magic number tells the bytecode verifier that the file being examined is supposed to be a class file and is not some virus or Trojan horse merely renamed to have the .class suffix.

These elements are elaborated in Chapter 16, "Java Security."

The Java 2 SDK provides a new policy-based security model, described in Chapter 2, "New Features in Java 2." In this model, you can specify at a fine-grained level that a given class can read directory `c:\temp` but not write to it, and that this same class can have read/write privileges on `C:\Accounts\ExpenseReports`.

Java Is Multithreaded

Being able to run multiple threads in the same application is a powerful feature. It's very rare that a computer's CPU is utilized 100% of the time. Multithreading enables your program to do multiple tasks concurrently, and thus get more processing done in less time than it could with just one thread. Java can use multiple threads.

In Java, using multithreading is natural because the JVM is already using multiple threads. This contrasts sharply with multithreading in C or C++, which can be quite complex. You might use multithreading, for example, if you have an applet that displays a user interface and, while the user is looking at the screen, runs a `MediaTracker` object on a separate thread to download images for animation.

The Java Virtual Machine

The core of Java, which makes it able to do its magic, is the Java Virtual machine, or JVM. I'm not going to cover the JVM in its entirety. There's a specification available at the JavaSoft Web site for anyone interested in all the details. Instead, I will just explain what the JVM does, and why it's so important to Java. The JVM runs as a process, started with the `java` command.

The JVM may be thought of as a mini-operating system and a CPU all in one. It provides many of the same features as an OS, such as memory management, task management, thread scheduling (in cooperation with the native OS), and so on. It has its own set of registers, a stack, a heap, and a global String buffer.

When you run a Java program, it runs as a thread within the JVM process. It is the JVM's responsibility to load your class files, interpret them, and execute them. When you issue a command like `java GreatGUI`, the JVM loads the class definition for GreatGUI and calls the `main` method of the GreatGUI class.

> **NOTE**
>
> If you're thinking to yourself that your applets don't have a `main` method, you're right. However, before your applet can start, the browser has to start Java. You are notified about this on the status line of the browser. After the browser has started Java and executed the `main` method of its own GUI class that has a `Frame` object (discussed in Chapter 8), your applet is essentially instantiated and added to the invisible frame that the browser, rather than your applet, owns. Almost all Java code requires a `main` method. (The exceptions will not be covered here.)

It is the JVM that makes it possible for the same class file to run on any platform. The JVM takes your platform-neutral byte code and interprets it to run platform-specific machine code. It can also compile it into native code with a JIT (a just-in-time compiler that compiles and caches your code, usually one method at a time). Thus, it is in the JVM where your code results, if needed, in native OS calls. In the JVM, your platform-neutral threading code gets turned into platform-specific threading code. In the JVM, your Java I/O methods result in platform-dependent I/O calls. This happens for you automatically.

Java allocates threads as needed for your application. The JVM manages the memory of your program. So, when I create a JTable object, or an AudioClip, or a plain old float, Java allocates memory for both objects and primitives. Java determines when these items are no longer referenced, and, therefore, can have their memories reclaimed. The JVM, without any prompting from the user, runs the Garbage Collector thread (when possible or required) to reclaim used, unreferenced memory.

Garbage Collector

For those with experience in C++, Java's constructors will seem pretty familiar, although there are some differences. You'll look in vain, for example, for a destructor in Java. The JVM not only frees you of the need to call destructors to release memory, you can't do so even if you want to. This is all under the control of the JVM. There is a separate thread in the JVM for garbage collection, similar to that in Smalltalk.

There are two important aspects of this garbage collection thread. First, you can request, but not force, garbage collection, by a call to System.gc(). Second, because the garbage collector thread is a low-priority thread, if there are other, higher priority threads hogging the CPU, the garbage collector thread might never get scheduled to run unless or until the JVM completely runs out of memory and calls the garbage collector to free up some memory.

The garbage collector performs an asynchronous task. That means that, basically, if it's running, nothing else in the JVM runs. As currently implemented, the garbage collector uses a "mark and sweep" algorithm for reclaiming memory. This is, however, implementation-dependent, and it's wholly possible that someone will implement a JVM that uses a different algorithm for garbage collection. If you really want to use a different approach to garbage collection, you can write your own JVM, a nontrivial task.

The Java 2 SDK

It is the Java 2 SDK, the Java Software Development Kit, that contains all the classes you need to develop Java programs, tools for compiling, running, debugging, and profiling your code. The Java Runtime Environment (JRE) runs your code in a JVM. The main differences between the JRE alone (which browsers have) and the Java 2 SDK are the tools and extra classes used for development. When you want to develop in Java, you need to obtain a Java 2 SDK. The simplest way to get it is to go to the JavaSoft Web site to the link for Products and APIs and chose the Java 2 SDK. It's a fairly large download, so it will take a while, unless you have a fast T1 line or the like. Let's look at the components of the Java 2 SDK.

Classes

The Java 2 SDK contains class files for all the classes defined in the Java API specification, plus some others. They are in class file format. Additionally, there is source code for many of the classes, but you can't just compile the source code to have a working Java system. To get all the source code necessary, you need to license the code. We'll look at the classes in-depth later.

Tools

There are several tools provided, most of which live in the `bin` subdirectory of the Java 2 SDK directory. For example, the `javac` command for compiling Java source files (ending in `.java`) to class files (ending in `.class`) resides in the `bin` directory. The `java` command for running classes in the JVM is also in the `bin` directory. The `jar` utility for creating jar files and working with them is also in the `bin` subdirectory.

JAR FILES

Because they will be referred to so many times, let's talk about what a jar file is. If you've used Microsoft Windows, you are probably familiar with zip files, developed by PKWare. Zip files, however, don't work correctly in Solaris. That is, there's no support in Solaris (or most versions of UNIX) for a .zip file. The UNIX `tar` command cannot work with a .zip file, and tools to unzip a .zip file, such as WinZip or the more basic pkunzip, do not run on UNIX. Jar files are a Java-specific, platform-neutral form of a zip file that can be read or written on any platform that has a Sun-compliant JRE.

This means that, because the jar utility can extract the contents of a jar file, the jar utility can also be used to unzip a zip file on Solaris or Windows, even if the zip file has nothing to do with Java.

Prior to Java 2, the class files for Java were put in a file called `classes.zip`. Now they are divided into multiple jar files, such as `rt.jar`.

CAUTION

It is critically important that you never unzip the 1.0 or 1.1 classes.zip files or unjar the jar files for the Java 2 SDK. If you do, your Java environment will be broken, and you'll have to delete everything and start installation of the Java 2 SDK from scratch.

Jar files are now pretty much the *de facto* way to package and deploy your code. JavaBeans go in jars. Extensions go in jars. Applets should be put in jars to improve download performance. Enterprise JavaBeans require a `.jar` file. The jar utility is very easy to use, so there's no reason not to use it.

Another important tool is the javadoc utility. You can use javadoc to produce documentation about your classes. The Java API documentation was produced using javadoc. It lists class, methods, and data members. You can use additional javadoc tags to specify author, date, and so forth. There's even a deprecated tag so you can mark code you wrote previously as deprecated. This means that when the code is compiled, you'll get a deprecation warning for your own code. You might do this, for example, if it's 1:00 a.m., and you code a hack just to get the product out the door the next morning. You might mark that hack as deprecated to remind yourself to go back and do it right when you have spare time.

There is a minimalist debugging tool called jdb, that I won't cover because it's being replaced and because it's so unintuitive and hard to use. If you need to debug code, you should use an IDE with an integrated debugger.

The javap utility can provide information about a class, such as its data members and methods.

Versions

There have been three main versions of the JDK: 1.0, 1.1 and Java 2. All the version numbers that have a more specific number, like JDK 1.02, represent bug fix versions. The latest 1.0 version is JDK 1.02. The last 1.1 version is JDK 1.1.7. What was called JDK 1.2, however, is now part of what is called the Java 2 SDK Standard Edition Version 1.2, or more simply, Java 2. You might see the latest Java version referred to by the longer official name, as Java 2 or as JDK 1.2 (including most Java software documentation as of August 1999).

The difference then between, say, JDK 1.1.4 and 1.1.7 is bug fixes, although there have been some significant changes between versions. JDK 1.02 has about 220 classes. JDK 1.1 has about 500 classes. The Java 2 SDK has over 1600 classes. Even with this book that is meant to help you with the most important or difficult methods in many of these classes, you'll still need to become familiar with the Java 2 SDK API documentation.

Because of the differences between versions, you need to be careful about your choice of version. For example, because all the major Web browsers support JDK 1.02, but don't all fully support JDK 1.1, if you want to write an Applet that runs without any special support on all major browsers, as of this writing (August 1999), you need to code it with JDK 1.02 APIs. There are ways to get around this situation, such as using the Java plug-in. Or, you can install your Applet with an appropriate JRE on the user's machine.

The latest version of Netscape provides JDK 1.1 support. Internet Explorer 5 supports some flavor of Java, although it is not, legally speaking, Sun-compliant. In fact, you can never expect to see Netscape or Microsoft provide support for Java 2. The only way this will be available, it appears, is with the Java plug-in, available as a separate download from Sun. With this plug-in installed, you will be able to run Java 2.

NOTE

Because of important changes in the security model of Java 2, signed applets that worked under JDK 1.1 will not be allowed out of the sandbox unless they also have a policy file that supports the added functions.

Apart from a solution like one of those just described, or unless you dictate the version of the browser that users can run with your Applet, you can't expect to use the Java 2 SDK features, such as Swing, in your applet.

CHAPTER 2

New Features in Java 2

There are several significant new features in Java 2. These include a new GUI framework (Swing), a new policy-based security model, remote object activation, weak references, package versioning, enhancements to reflection, new features (such as scrollable cursors) in JDBC 2.0, and more. This chapter is not intended to be a comprehensive treatment of these features; rather, it is an overview of the most significant new features in Java 2.

Swing/Java Foundation Classes

Although Swing has been available in several releases for almost two years, it has only become part of the SDK in Java 2. Swing is part of the Java Foundation Classes (the official name) or JFC for short.

The Java Foundation Classes are derived, more or less, from the Internet Foundation Classes from Netscape (IFC). JFC, however, has gone well beyond anything available in the IFC packages.

The Java Foundation Classes contain much more than Swing, but Swing is the most noteworthy part of the JFC. Swing and JFC are often used synonymously, and even if that is not technically proper, I will do the same. The package names for the JFC begin with javax.swing. This is a change from earlier names, such as com.sun.java.swing and java.swing. Unlike similarly named packages (such as javax.servlet), the JFC packages are considered core packages. This is true in spite of the naming convention that is normally reserved for a standard extension.

The Java Foundation Classes include the following features:

- Swing
- Pluggable Look and Feel (PLaF)
- Accessibility
- Java 2D classes
- MVC (Model-View-Controller)
- Drag and Drop

The topics in the list above are explored in the following sections. There will be additional coverage of these topics in Chapter 8, "GUI Programming I: Applications."

Swing

Swing is a GUI framework that adds significant new functionality to Java GUIs and is intended to be a complete replacement for the AWT. One of the most important innovations in Swing is support for numerous components that are not platform-dependent as the AWT components are.

Every AWT component has a native peer. That is, for every Java GUI object you instantiate, a native C function is called to create the corresponding native component on the specific operating system you are using. Such components in Java are called *heavyweight*.

Swing, on the other hand, except for a few heavyweight containers, makes all its components lightweight. A *lightweight* component does not have a native peer, but borrows its system resources from its heavyweight container.

Because Swing components do not depend upon native peers, they can look however they want to look. This means that Swing offers to developers a whole new set of components that are not available through the AWT. These include a tree control (JTree), a multicolumn list box (JTable), a tabbed Panel (JTabbedPane), slider bars, progress bars, ToolTips, toolbars, and several other components.

Pluggable Look and Feel

Swing has the capability to make your components look like those of the platform they are running on. So, your JButton will look like a Win32 button on Windows NT, but the JButton will look like a Motif button on Solaris. Or, you can decide that you want your application's user interface to look the same no matter what platform you are using. To accomplish this, you select one look and feel that will always be used. Swing comes with a default look and feel, called Metal. (The Metal look and feel is going to be renamed the Java look and feel at some point in the future.)

In addition, you might decide that you want a consistent look and feel across platforms (which I think is a great feature), but you do not wish to use Metal. If that is the case, you can use Swing to create your own look and feel. This is not, however, a task for the faint of heart. After you create your own look and feel, you'll probably use it in all your applications, just as you would use Metal.

> **NOTE**
>
> The first JFC class appeared in JDK 1.1. It is the `ScrollPane`, a really handy component that saves developers from all the nastiness involved in using scrollbars. It is an especially important component because scrollbars are buggy and do not work correctly in the Win32 versions of JDK 1.0 and, to a lesser extent, 1.1.

Accessibility

This feature provides APIs to enable a user to run an application without a mouse or even a keyboard. After a developer has added accessibility to an application, a user can hover the mouse over a component and hear, on a speech synthesizer, information like "Click this button to submit your order." Also, when you have added accessibility support to your application, a user can attach a microphone and a speech synthesizer and instead of having to type or use the mouse, he can say "File, Open."

> **TIP**
>
> It is a federal requirement that if two products offer comparable features, and only one of them has accessibility provided, the government must purchase the product that offers accessibility.
>
> There are many European countries with similar regulations. Because Javasoft does most of the work for you, and you can get accessibility into your application with very little work, there's little reason not to add it. Physically challenged individuals, especially, will be able to use your application more easily and appreciate your attention to their needs.

Java 2D Classes

The Java 2D APIs are designed to provide for advanced drawing techniques (including support for Affine transforms and other specialized drawing routines), graphics, and imaging. The classes cover text, images, and line art and are part of the `java.awt` and `java.awt.image` packages, rather than being in their own package. The APIs include a rendering model which covers composites, fills and strokes, coordinate systems, transforms, and so forth.

Although the old Graphics class provides for drawing some basic shapes, like rectangles and ovals, the new Java 2D Graphics APIs provide for drawing any shape. Geometric shapes are now implementations of the `Shape` interface. There are new fill and pen styles provided through the Paint and Stroke interfaces. The `AffineTransform` provides for linear transformations of 2D coordinates, such as scale, rotate, and shear. There are now multiple coordinate systems, divided into two groups: user space, which is device-independent; and device space, which is platform-dependent. Implementations of the Composite interface, such as `AlphaComposite`, provide for color composition. Fonts are defined by a series of `Glyphs`, which are a series of `Shapes`.

Incidentally, Java 2 provides new facilities for creating and installing fonts for Java to use, and the classes for dealing with fonts have changed significantly. The Java 2D APIs provide many features, but are fairly specialized. The reader will need to consult a book more specific to the 2D APIs to get more details, although the basic APIs are documented in Part II (Techniques Reference) of this book.

The Java 2D packages also include a new printing model that provides additional support for higher resolution printing and better manipulation of multipage documents. The new model also supports the concept of a "book." That is, you can ask to have multiple "pageable" (multi-page) objects joined together in the printed output with appropriate page numbering.

CAUTION

As of this writing there are still some problems with Java printing, even in the Java 2 SDK version. Because the new printing model seeks to be platform-independent, its current performance is quite slow on some platforms, and it produces very large PostScript files when trying to print very small amounts of text. The Java team is aware of these issues and hopes to improve printing in the near future.

Swing Design Philosophy: MVC

Swing components are implemented with the model-view-controller design pattern taken over from Smalltalk. This means that you can change the data model for a component without changing its appearance, and vice versa. For example, if your data model for a `JTable` contains a Boolean value, true/false or yes/no, you can change the view of this data so that the viewable column in the `JTable` has a `JCheckBox` that can be checked for yes and unchecked for no. You don't need to modify the data to change the view to a `JCheckBox`.

TIP

The model-view-controller pattern is quite powerful, and I recommend its use highly, especially for n-tier applications with a presentation layer and a data layer. The reader should consult a design pattern book to learn more, for example, *Design Patterns: Elements of Reusable Object-Oriented Software*, written by the "Gang of Four," or Mark Grand's *Patterns in Java*.

In general, every Swing component has two classes associated with it, a UI class that contains the view and controller code and a model class that contains the data model. For more detailed information on Swing, see *Pure JFC Swing* by Satyaraj Pantham (also published by Sams).

Drag and Drop

The drag-and-drop facility enables you to define drag sources and drop targets. Currently, this really only works on plain text, but it is slated to support other data types.

The Policy-Based Security Model

Prior to the Java 2 SDK, the primary means of providing security in Java was through the SecurityManager class. Anyone who has run an applet in a browser has seen the SecurityManager class at work. By default, the SecurityManager class allows no interaction with client system resources or connections with other systems except the server that the applet was downloaded from.

Its methods consist of check*xxx* methods where read, write, loadLibrary, and so on replace the *xxx*. If the method returns false, which is the default behavior, the operation is not allowed. In general, browsers take the default form of the SecurityManager class or modify the behavior just a little bit. That forces unsigned applets to run inside the sandbox. They are not allowed to read or write files on the local system, load libraries on the local system, modify thread groups, or access certain system properties. (System properties are represented by a Properties object and can be obtained by the System.getProperties() method.) In addition, unsigned applets cannot open socket connections to servers other than the one the applet was downloaded from. The use of a SecurityManager object is optional.

NOTE

For the Remote Method Invocation (RMI), the RMISecurityManager is still necessary, and it uses policy files to determine permissions.

The new policy-based security model of Java 2, the Java 2 SDK, provides for much finer-grained security. Now it is possible to create a policy file, using the policytool utility, which specifies in detail the rights of any class, user, or application to access system resources. So, you can specify that class AccountsReceivable has the right to read from the C:\Generalledger directory, but not to write to it.

One of the frustrations for applet writers prior to the Java 2 SDK has been that an applet could not directly access a local printer. Your applet had to send data to the Web server, and the Web server had to send email or a custom HTML page back to the client in order for the end user to print it. Now, you can use RuntimePermissions to let an applet print, but you can still restrict it in every other way. These policy files enable you to set much better control over specific classes. They are more restrictive where it's needed, and less restrictive where it's not. This applies to both applications and applets. The SecurityManager class is still present for backwards compatibility, so you can still use it if you wish; but the new policy-based security model will probably be more satisfactory.

RMI Enhancements

There have been important changes made to Remote Method Invocation, Java's mechanism for distributed object programming in an all-Java environment. Here are three new features worth talking about:

- RMI now has support for using IIOP, Internet Inter-ORB Protocol.
  IIOP is used by CORBA. Prior to the Java 2 SDK, RMI used only JRMP, Java Remote Method Protocol. With the capability to use IIOP, RMI applications can now talk with CORBA applications. As of February 1999, this support for RMI to use CORBA is only in beta form, but I expect it to be finalized soon. This does not mean that RMI is going to be replaced slowly by CORBA using `JavaIDL`. It does mean that Javasoft is providing the means for interoperability between RMI and CORBA applications.

> **NOTE**
>
> This interoperability will enable an architecture that uses a CORBA client to talk to an Enterprise JavaBean. It helps facilitate using a CORBA base on which to build an EJB server. Lots of new architectural possibilities open up through the use of IIOP with RMI. You no longer have to make an either/or choice between CORBA and RMI in a system architecture. Each can be used where most appropriate.

- RMI provides an activation framework.
  Prior to Java 2, an RMI client could only communicate with an existing remote object if that remote object already existed, instantiated by a server-side application. If you created the client first, the client failed to find the remote object and got an exception. Now that RMI provides you with an activation framework, you can create and use a remote object from the client system on-the-fly, before any program on the server has created it. This is a very helpful feature. To do this, you use a new kind of remote object called an `Activatable`.
- RMI enables you to use different kinds of sockets.
  Prior to Java 2, the only kind of socket you could use for RMI was a standard TCP socket. It is now possible to create a custom socket factory and use different kinds of sockets. For example, you might create your own sockets for encryption or perhaps compression. The code to create a custom socket factory to provide these custom sockets for you is fairly straightforward. The only hard part is defining the socket class itself.

JDBC 2.0 Enhancements

There are several enhancements to JDBC in Java 2, including the new JDBC version number 2.0. Perhaps the two most significant enhancements are scrollable cursors and updateable result sets. Before discussing them, let's briefly review JDBC. JDBC provides a database-neutral way to send requests to a database management system (DBMS). Usually, this is done with SQL, Structured Query Language, although other options such as OQL, Object Query Language, are technically possible. In order to provide for this flexibility, JDBC depends upon third parties to provide JDBC drivers. A driver implements the interfaces in the `java.sql` package, such as `Statement` and `Connection`. Java does not check the SQL statements you code for validity. It merely treats them as `String` objects. These `Strings` are passed to a JDBC driver for parsing and sending on to the relational database management system (RDBMS). One of the significant issues that arises from this architecture is that it is possible to code a SQL statement in the Java program that the database driver is not capable of processing. This might occur either because the driver doesn't support the requested SQL feature (such as a PreparedStatement—a lacuna in MS Access, for example), or, more likely, the RDBMS doesn't support it. For example, JDBC supports prepared statements. Some people learn to use JDBC by programming with MS Access, although this is not a viable solution for a commercial application. Although RDBMSs, such as Oracle, support prepared statements, Access does not. Therefore, trying to use a feature that the driver doesn't understand, or the database doesn't support will probably cause a SQLException to be thrown because what you are asking for "does not compute" for the driver.

Because drivers and database vendors on the whole did not support scrollable cursors, JDBC provided no support for them either. Due to many requests from developers, JDBC 2.0 now has support for scrollable cursors. What's a scrollable cursor? Before we answer that, let's look at what a cursor is. When you make a SQL call through JDBC, if you do a select (a query), you get back an object that implements the java.sql.ResultSet interface. This object contains zero or more rows of data from the relational database against which you did the query.

To process a specific row, JDBC requires you to point your code at that row. The mechanism for pointing is a called a cursor. It's the same idea as moving the cursor to a particular row in a spreadsheet or a particular line in a document within a word processing program. When you first get a ResultSet object back from a query, the cursor is pointing to a spot above or before the first row in the ResultSet. To get to the first row, you need to use code like this:

```
ResultSet rs = aStatementObject.executeQuery("select * from BookList");
(whilte(rs.next() == true)
    {
       // Process the columns in the row in here
    }
```

The ResultSet method next() causes the cursor to advance one row. When you first begin processing the ResultSet, the cursor is sitting above row one, so to get to the first row, row one, you need to call the next() method.

Prior to JDBC 2.0, you could only do one thing with a cursor: move forward through a ResultSet. This sometimes caused difficulties. For example, you might have needed to step through the rows to count them or examine them before actually processing them. In order to process the data, you had to repeat the query because you could not make the cursor back up, nor you could you process a row in the ResultSet unless the cursor was pointed at it. JDBC 2.0 addresses this problem by providing support for scrollable cursors. A scrollable cursor can not only move forward, but it can also move backwards. In fact, there are methods to move forward, backward, go to the first row, go to the last row, go to a specific row, and so forth. This way, you can step through your ResultSet to count the rows, and then go back to the start of the ResultSet and process each row.

Prior to Java 2, in order to modify a table within a database, you had to explicitly code a SQL statement and execute it with JDBC. This means essentially speaking or coding in two different languages, alternating between Java and SQL. JDBC 2.0 provides the capability to change a database table by changing the `ResultSet`, using Java methods. For example, you can insert a row into the `ResultSet`. This causes a row to be inserted in the underlying database table. You can also change a value in a row in the `ResultSet`. This will cause that value to be changed in the table in the database. Again, of course, you have to have a JDBC 2.0-compliant driver for this to work. This feature allows most of your database code, after you've gotten a `ResultSet`, to be all in Java rather than a mix of Java and SQL. Your code stays object oriented this way.

Package Versioning

Given that source code changes frequently, due to enhancements or bug fixes, it's possible for a situation to arise in which the client code depends upon a particular version of the sever-side code. In another case, an applet that needs several classes from multiple packages might have dependencies upon a particular version of the package. Anyone who has worked with multiple versions of Swing has probably run into this. Swing methods that worked with Swing 0.5 don't work with Swing 0.7. Code that compiled fine with Swing in the Java 2 SDK beta2 doesn't compile with Swing classes in the Java 2 SDK FCS. So how can you manage this problem of needing a specific version of code? Java 2 provides support for package versioning. That is, you are able to provide information as part of your package that tells its version number. Within certain parameters, the version number scheme is up to the developer. The version information is specified in a manifest file in the jar file in which the package is contained. There are a set of versioning APIs available so that a class can interrogate the version of a package and refuse to run if the version number is not acceptable.

Reference Objects

Prior to Java 2, the only time you might get to interact with the JVM when an object was about to be cleaned up by the garbage collector was during finalization. Java 2 provides a new approach to dealing with objects. These reference objects, as they are called, provide for "weak references," that is, they provide a way to keep a reference to another object that is, otherwise, no longer referenced by any meaningful object. This allows a reference object to do limited processing when the garbage collector determines that an object is eligible to have its memory reclaimed. This approach provides a mechanism for performing tasks relating to an object that was just cleaned up by the garbage collector. Reference objects permit an application to keep a reference to an object even though its memory allocation is reclaimed by the garbage collector. This can speed up processing.

Extensions

When dealing with packages and calls to methods in classes in various packages, the Java runtime system needs to be able to find the class or package. In general, this is done by specifying the class's or package's location with the CLASSPATH environment variable or with the -classpath command line option. Suppose, however, that you have a class or classes that many applications need to use, such as a logging class on a server machine. You now have another choice besides setting the CLASSPATH. You can make the class an extension. By making the class an extension, Java views it as part of the core Java 2 classes, and Java can always find it.

There are two ways to do an extension. Before you can use either approach, you have to put the class file(s) into a jar file. The first way to make an extension is to install the class as an extension. To do this, all you have to do is put the jar file in the jre/lib/ext (\jre\lib\ext on Win32 platforms) subdirectory under the directory for the JDK. If you put the jar file there, the classes are automatically treated as core JDK classes, and you don't have to set the CLASSPATH to point to these classes. The Java runtime knows where the JDK classes are. The second way is through a downloaded extension. To get a downloaded extension, you need to put a manifest file in the jar that wants to use the class(es) in the extension. The manifest file needs to refer to the jar file that contains the desired classes. Suppose, for example, you need classes that are in the Logging.jar file in an applet. The applet's jar file would contain a manifest file that includes the Class-Path header, which follows:

Class-Path: Logging.jar

In both cases, you do not need to set the location of the classes through the CLASSPATH. The use of extensions is, of course, completely optional, but you may find it useful. It enables you to install classes, especially third-party packages, and not have to worry about customizing the CLASSPATH variable anywhere.

Collections

Prior to Java 2, the support for collections has been minimal, and developers have frequently created their own or used a third party's collection classes, such as those of the KL Group. Previous versions of the JDK had arrays, vectors, and enumerations. These have been superseded by a whole new set of collection classes in Java 2, a collection framework that provides a unified way to deal with groups of objects. The collection framework is built around six interfaces, including Collection, Set, List, SortedSet, Map, and SortedMap. Collections can be modifiable or unmodifiable, mutable or immutable, and fixed-size or variable-size. Some collection implementations limit the kind of object they can contain and restrict objects in other ways, such as preventing duplicate elements. The Enumeration interface has been replaced with an iterator object that will be more familiar to developers who have used collections in other languages. There are implementations provided for the interfaces. For example, the Set interface is implemented by the HashSet and TreeSet classes. The List interface is implemented by ArrayList and LinkedList. The Map interface is implemented by HashMap and TreeMap. Like many of the Swing classes, the Collection framework provides several abstract classes that contain minimal implementations, such as AbstractSet and AbstractList. One key advantage of these new classes is that you no longer need to use a third party's class library to get Collection functionality, but can get it directly from the JDK core classes.

The new collection framework provides the basis for easily defining new collection data types. It expands the previously available set of collections significantly and provides for developing algorithms to work with multiple kinds of collections.

Sound

Prior to Java 2, playing a sound file in an applet was easy. You could just do a `getAudioClip()`, or even just use the `play()` method, pointing to a sound file. The file did, however, have to be of type `.au`. Occasionally, someone on the Internet would ask why the `.wav` file he had converted to an `.au` file did not work in his applet. Playing sound in a Java application, however, has been quite challenging, requiring a developer to use `sun.` packages rather than `Java.` packages, which were not guaranteed to stay the same from JDK version to JDK version. In other words, sound in applications was basically unsupported. The Java 2 SDK changes this with a new sound engine. This engine provides support for playing sound in applications because the engine supports additional file types.

In Java 2, you can now play `.AIFF`, `.AU`, and `.WAV` files. In addition, there is support for MIDI file formats, such as `MIDI TYPE 0`, `MIDI TYPE 1`, and `RMF`. The new Java Sound APIs support 9-bit and 16-bit mono and stereo sound. Through a new method, both applets and applications can play sound without requiring an `AppletContext` by calling

```
public static final AudioClip newAudioClip(URL url)
```

This new feature will assist developers who want to put sound in their applications, confident that it will be supported.

Other Enhancements

There have also been other enhancements. `JavaIDL` has been made part of the JDK, instead of being a separate set of APIs. Jar files have been enhanced, both in terms of command line options and in methods to read to and write from jar files. There have been enhancements to object serialization, internationalization, math, networking, reflection, and resources. Support has been added for a new JVM debugging API (in response, no doubt, to the complaints of developers about the almost nonexistent Java debugger that came with previous JDKs). There is also support for a new JVM profiler. Finally, much work has been done to enhance performance. Sun sees this version of Java as the one that is really ready for full enterprise computing deployment—ready for prime time.

CHAPTER 3

Java Program Features

This chapter provides a brief overview of the essential elements of a Java program. These include

- Layout
- Naming
- Punctuation
- Required methods

Basic Layout

Java code is placed in a file that must end in .java. There is a required structure for the file's contents, although some of the elements are optional. The list below shows the order of required and optional elements.

- <Comments may be placed anywhere in the file>
- <Package statement>
- <Import statement(s)>
- One or more class or interface definitions

At a minimum, a source file must contain one class or interface definition, as shown in the following code:

```
class LibraryCard
    {
    }
```

There is an important requirement for the file name. It must match the name of a class or interface defined in the .java file.

> **NOTE**
>
> Java, like UNIX, is strictly case sensitive. That means that a Date object called Today is totally different and unrelated to a Date object called today.

Class Definition

A class definition is bounded by curly braces ({}) and has no other punctuation (unlike C++). This class definition contains no methods or attributes.

In order for classes outside the current package (a specific directory path) to access the class or interface defined in a .java file, the class or interface is generally defined as `public`, as shown in the following code:

```
public LibraryCard
    {
    }
```

For any .java file, there may be only one public, non-`static`, outermost class. The keyword `static` is explained in Chapter 4, "Data Types," and Chapter 5, "Methods." An *outermost class* is simply a class that does not contain an inner class.

Package Statement

A package statement identifies the directory path for a given class. The following shows a typical .java file with a package statement.

```
package gradschool.library;
public class LibraryCard
    {
    }
```

A package statement, which ends with a semicolon (;), specifies a relative path to the class file. In this example, the compiler will look in the directory library, which is a subdirectory of `gradschool`, which is a directory relative to some starting point. This starting point might be either the current working directory or its parent directory, `gradschool`, which would normally be listed in the CLASSPATH environment variables or specified in a command line switch `-classpath`. It is not necessary to specify a package. If no package is specified, the class goes into a default package created by the compiler. All classes must be in packages. It is unnecessary for you to know that this package exists for compiling or running the code.

Import Statements

When compiling a class, Java might need to find other classes that are named (used) in the class definition. The compiler must know where to look for these classes that are named in the import statement. For example, if you have this code

```
Vector v = new Vector()
```

you need an import statement that points to java.util so that the compiler can find the class definition of `Vector`. This enables the compiler to validate that this is a real class and that the methods you call are defined for `Vector`. There are two ways to specify this. The most common way is to use import statements. An import statement specifies a package name and, potentially, a file specifier that tell the compiler where to find the class or interface file. Listing 3.1 shows import statements used in a .java file.

Listing 3.1   A Source File with Import Statements
```
import java.awt.*;      // Look through all the classes in the
                        // java.awt directory if necessary
                        // to find a class definition.
Import java.sql.*;
import javax.servlet.*;
import java.awt.event.*;   // Each directory level must be explicitly specified.
                           // The "*" refers only to files, not directories.
Public class LibraryCard
    {
       ResultSet rs;
       Panel pan1;
       AwtEvent ae;
       }
```

This class has multiple import statements. When the javac compiler hits the statement

`ResultSet rs;`

the compiler searches through the directories of the packages `java.awt`, `java.sql`, `javax.servlet`, and `java.awt.event` until it finds the `ResultSet.class` file or it runs out of directories to search.

It is also possible, although less common, to specify the package name as a prefix to a class name. This avoids ambiguity if a class definition contains two classes (from different packages) that have the same name. An example is shown in the following code:

```
public class LibraryCard
    {
       java.util.GregorianCalendar expirationDate;
       java.lan.String cardholderName;
       }
```

> **NOTE**
>
> Because the package `java.lang` holds essential core classes, such as `java.lang.Object`—the parent class of all other classes—, the compiler automatically provides an import statement for `java.lang.*;`.

> **NOTE**
>
> A Java import statement is not at all like a C header `include`. You can have as many import statements as you wish in a program, and these statements do not increase the size of the .class file. They merely provide a means for Java to find the classes at compile time. In the compiled .class file, all class names are prefixed with their package names. An import statement is only used at compile time. These statements provide a pointer to enable the compiler to find classes. They don't bring any code into your class definition.

Comments

Java supports three kinds of comments:

- `//`
  This is a single-line comment.
- `/* some comment */`
  This is a multi-line comment.
- `//* some comment */`

This is a javadoc comment. As in the preceding forms, this comment may be one or more lines long. A javadoc comment is a comment processed and turned into HTML text by the javadoc utility, which is used to generate the Java API doc from javadoc comments in the class source files of the Java 2 SDK.

Names

In addition to the requirement that a class name exactly match the name of the .java file, there are three things to bear in mind about naming classes, interfaces, variables, and methods.

- Avoid names that are the same as keywords. So, for example, do not use `default` as the name of anything, because `default` is a Java keyword.
- By convention, class and interface names begin with a capital letter. Variables that serve as constants are all capitals with underscores between words. A capital letter starts each word in the name of the class, interface, method, or variable. Everything else begins with a lowercase letter.
- A variable may start with a letter, an underscore, or a $.

Listing 3.2 shows examples of these rules and conventions.

Listing 3.2   Naming Examples

```
public class LibraryCard      // A class name starts with a capital letter
    {
    public static final int STUDENT_CARD = 1;  // Class Constants
    public static final int FACULTY_CARD = 2;
    public static fianl int ALUMNI_CARD = 3;
    String borrowerName;  // Variable starting with a lowercase letter
    String $borrowerID;   // variable starting with a $
    float _currentFines;  // Variable starting with an underscore
    public boolean computerCurrentFines()
                            // method name starting with lowercase letter
        {
        // Code to compute a fine goes here
        }
    }
```

NOTE

You can, of course, ignore the naming conventions (but not the rules). It will, however, make your code harder for others to understand.

Punctuation

Punctuation in Java is fairly simple:

- Statements, as shown above, end with a semicolon.
- Classes, interfaces, and methods use curly braces to enclose their definitions.
- Java ignores whitespace when compiling.

Required Methods

There are three kinds of Java programs: applications, Applets, and Servlets. Servlets are outside the scope of this book. Applets will be considered in Chapter 9, "GUI Programming II: Applets." Here, I will focus only on applications. Every Java application—but not class—must have a method that looks like the one in listing 3.3.

Listing 3.3   Source File with the main Method Defined
```
public class LibraryCard
    {
       String borrowerName;
        float fines;
         public static void main(String[] args)
             {
                System.exit(0);   // The proper (but optional) method
                                  // to exit a Java application
             }
        }
```

The only required method is main. It has several important parts to its signature:

- public—This part of its signature grants access to this method from anywhere. This is necessary for the JVM to call the method from outside of the application.
- static —This method is not associated with an instance of a class. If it were, the method could not be called until the class was instantiated, which cannot be done until the main method is entered. The main method must be static so it can be entered before there are any instances of this class.
- void — Every method must have a return type, which must immediately precede the method name. The return type void means that the method returns nothing. Unlike C, this cannot be changed to any other return type.
- main — The mandatory name of the method must be part of its signature. The main method has one parameter — args. The parameter name may be whatever you want to use, as long as it is defined as an array of Strings. Unlike C, there is only one parameter. You can use the length attribute to find the number of elements in the array. Also, unlike C, the number of elements in the array does not include the name of the program being run. So, if you type the command line

    ```
    java MyProgram Hot Java
    ```

    the result would be an args array that contains two elements, Hot and Java.

> **TIP**
>
> Although many books put lots of code in the `main` method, I suggest that you treat the `main` method, and the class that contains the `main` method, as driver code. That is, the `main` method should only tell other classes to do work, not do any work itself.

CHAPTER 4

Data Types

There are two basic data categories in Java: objects and primitives. All data members and local variables must have a data type that is either a primitive or some class type.

Primitives

There are eight kinds of primitives. There are two numeric groups, floating point and integer, plus `boolean`. These could have been created as classes (as in Smalltalk), but not doing so was an optimization made for better performance. Because primitives are used so often, making them objects would greatly degrade performance. The primitive data types are shown in Table 4.1.

Table 4.1   Java's Primitive Data Types

Primitive	Description
byte	One byte long, signed value.
short	Two-byte long, signed value.
int	Four-byte long, signed value. This is Java's main primitive for doing integral arithmetic.
long	Eight-byte long, signed value.
float	Four-byte long, signed floating point value.
double	Eight-byte long, signed floating point value.
char	Two-byte long, Unicode character.
boolean	Non-numeric value of true or false.

Here's a simple class definition that contains some declarations of primitives:

```
Class Primitives
    {
    byte b;
    int i = 5;
```

Chapter 4: Data Types

```
    float f = 1.41414F;
    double d = 34.5;
    char c = 'K';
    short s = 6;
    long l = 334L;
    boolean aBool = true;
    public boolean computeSomeStuff()
      {
         b = 5;         // Set a value for a previously-defined variable.
         int x = I * 5; // Create a local variable and
                        // give it a computed value
                        //    using an instance variable defined above.
         aBool = false; // Modify the value of an instance variable.
         return aBool;  // return a value from the method
                        //   matching the return type
      }
} // End class definition Primitives
```

boolean

Note that the word `boolean` begins with a lowercase b. The `boolean` primitive data type has two possible values: true and false. These are also both lowercase words. If statements and `while` loops require a testable condition that will resolve to a `boolean` value of true or false. A statement such as

`if(x) // WRONG.`

won't compile. So, if you're accustomed to writing C code that tests for a value, such as `0` equals `false` and `1` equals `true`, forget that here. Java doesn't make that translation for you. You must have a statement like this one:

`if(x == 7)`

The compiler can look at this statement and see that its result will be true or false.

> **CAUTION**
>
> Be sure not to use an uppercase letter at the start of a primitive type. Doing so will cause Java to think you want a wrapper class of that name. Thus, `Float` is a wrapper class, not a float primitive. Failure to observe this distinction will cause all sorts of grief for the compiler.

char

Java comes with support for internationalization built in. A big part of this support comes through the use of Unicode characters. The `char` data type is based on sixteen-bit Unicode characters. Unicode enables you to specify all the characters of most character sets for the world's languages. The trick here is to have a font that supports the characters you want to display. If your font doesn't support, for example, \u5567, that character will not display properly. Java always uses Unicode internally.

> **NOTE**
>
> Although Java can support the entire Unicode character set, a given computer system may not have a font that can support that character. For example, if your program is designed to display Russian or Hebrew, it is important to verify that a font is installed that supports the appropriate Unicode character ranges for those languages.

Unlike C, Java does not support signed characters. The Java designers felt that signed characters and unsigned numbers were sources for program bugs.

> **CAUTION**
>
> Although `shorts` and `chars` are the same size, and you could theoretically use a `char` for a numeric value, this should be avoided. Because a `char` is unsigned, the only way to get the compiler to accept the assignment of a `char` to a `short` is to cast it. Otherwise, the compiler will give an error. Again, the Java designers felt that unsigned numbers were a bad thing, so it is best to use `chars` only for characters, and not for numbers.

byte

The smallest of the integral data types is the `byte`. Note that this primitive type, like all the primitive types, starts with a lowercase letter. The uppercase version refers to a class, not a primitive. Because all numeric types are signed, a `byte` is signed. A `byte` is eight bits long. The numeric range of a `byte` is -2^{-7}–2^{7-1}. Java's basic numeric integral type is an `int`. The significance of that causes the following:

```
byte b1 = 1;
byte b2 = 2;
byte b3 = b1 * b2;   //WRONG.  THIS WON'T COMPILE.
```

What happens here is that Java converts b1 and b2 to ints before it multiplies them. Because you can't put an `int` (32 bits long) into a byte(eight bits long) without losing a lot of bits, Java won't do this unless you force it to do so by casting. *Casting* is a method for telling the system to treat one data type as if it is another data type. This is done in Java by placing the type you want in parentheses before the name of a variable of some other type. Java requires that the cast makes sense semantically. To do the above, you need to code either

```
byte b1 = 1;
byte b2 = 2;
byte b3 = (byte) (b1 * b2);
```

or

```
byte b1 = 1;
byte b2 = 2;
int i1 = b1 * b2;
```

Chapter 4: Data Types

If you use the equivalent in Java of a constant, such as

```
public static final byte b1 =5;
```

the compiler will automatically convert the value to the right size and type for computation.

short

A short is sixteen bits long. Because it is also a signed number, its numeric range is $-2^{-15}-2^{15-1}$. Because a short is signed, and a char is not signed, a char is numerically larger than a short, so you cannot assign a char to a short. You might run into a situation in which unsigned integers, written by a C program, must be read with Java. This is not a problem because Java can read unsigned bytes with an InputStream object into signed ints.

int

An int is a four-byte number—thirty-two bits. Its numeric value is $-2^{-31}-2^{31-1}$. Again, this is the main integral data type, to which Java promotes smaller numbers when it does computations. As I mentioned in Chapter 1, "What Is Java?," Java accomplishes being platform-neutral (in part) by always making an int 32 bits in every JVM, a short always 16 bits, a long always 64 bits, and so forth. This saves Java from the problems that C programmers encounter when porting code between platforms. For example, an int in a C program can be two bytes on one OS and four bytes on another.

long

A long is sixty-four bits long—eight bytes. Its numeric value range is $-2^{-63}-2^{63-1}$. This is the largest integral type. Because the default integral type is an int, if you want to indicate that a literal number, such as 456, is a long, you need to append an l or L to it in this way: 456l or 456L.

> **CAUTION**
>
> You should be cautious about using a long because most systems only support 32-bit numbers without using emulation. The amount of code required to emulate a long is considerable from a performance point of view. Using a long as a loop counter could cause significant performance degradation.

float

A float is the first of two floating point primitives. A float is four bytes or 32 bits long. It complies with the IEEE 754 specification for this data type. The default type of a floating point number is a double, like this:

```
double d = 15.6; // With no other indication,
                 // this is interpreted as a double value
```

Therefore, to set a float primitive to a literal value, you need to tell the compiler it is a float literal, not a double literal, by using f or F, in this way: 34.6f or 5566.2334F.

You can code

```
float f1 = 442.6f;
```

but to initialize a double you would use the following:

```
double d1 = 445.332;
```

double

A `double` is an eight-byte (or sixty-four bit) number that is also a floating point value. You can also use exponential notation with `float`s and `double`s. A `double` complies with the IEEE 754 specification for this data type. Because most systems can only do 64-bit emulation, don't use a `double` when a `float` would do. Generally, the performance hit for emulation is significant.

> **CAUTION**
>
> In compliance with IEEE 754, floating point arithmetic supports additional, special values, such as *NaN*, which means "not a number." This is the result of floating-point division by zero in Java. In integral arithmetic, Java would throw an exception for a program attempting to divide by zero. This means that, when using floating-point numbers, you must be more careful in checking operands or results.

That's it for primitives. Because all the numeric primitives are signed, the only way to move a value from a large primitive (like a `long`) to a smaller primitive (like an `int`) is to use casting. The compiler will not permit you to lose precision unless you tell the compiler, "Hey, I'm a programmer. Trust me."

Classes

Classes define what an object will be like, its state and behavior. If I create a primitive and initialize it as in

```
int x = 6;
```

there is a memory location set aside that contains the number 6 as an `int`. x refers directly to that memory location. If, however, I code

```
JFrame mainFrame = new Frame();
```

mainFrame is not the name of the `JFrame` object, but an object reference to the `JFrame` object. This has important ramifications. Consider this little class definition:

```
public class Book
    {
      boolean reservedStatus;
        int checkOutPeriod;
        String title;
    }
```

When another class does

```
Book b = new Book();
```

memory is allocated for the data members `reservedStatus` and `checkOutPeriod`. Furthermore, that memory is given default, initial values, such as `false` for a `boolean` and 0 for an `int`. The data member title, however, being an object reference, is treated differently.

No memory is allocated for the `String` title yet. An object reference named title is reserved. It gets the default initial value of `null`; I don't mean it gets a `String` spelled `"null"`; I mean it has no value. That's like a C pointer with a value of 0. It does not point to any object at all. There's no memory allocated for the title `String` object. This leads to perhaps the most common Java exception. It occurs when a developer declares an object reference such as `title`, but does not instantiate the object.

Instantiating the object allocates memory and returns an object reference value that is stored in the object reference `title`. Object references may be pointers, but they don't have to be. On Win32 systems, object references contain handles to the objects rather than pointers. Another (perhaps obvious) difference between objects and primitives is that objects can contain other objects and primitives.

> **NOTE**
>
> There might be times, such as when creating `Panel` objects for a GUI, when it is unimportant to specifically store the object reference. It is perfectly legal to create an object but not store its object reference. The object still exists. It simply cannot be referred to by your code.

Defining Classes

Use the `class` keyword to define a class, in this way:

```
class CheckOutDialog
```

There are keywords that you can use with the `class` keyword. These include an access level like `public`. It may also include other keywords like `abstract`. The class definition consists of the class signature, as shown previously, plus matching curly braces:

```
class CheckOutDialog
    {
    }
```

This is the minimal code required to define a class. Of course, this dialog isn't very useful, but it illustrates the point. Unlike C++, Java does not end definitions with a semicolon. In addition, unlike C++, Java does not allow you to define a class's methods outside the class definition. Everything that is part of a class definition must be inside those two curly braces. Remember that a class definition does not create an object. It is simply a blueprint for an object. You still need to create an object using the class definition.

Inheritance: Extends

The next option is to specify the relationship between your class and another class. There are two main types of relationships between objects: IsA and HasA. An IsA relationship is one in which one class is a subtype, or specialized form of the other class. For example, a Boeing 747 is a special kind of plane. A Boeing 747 is a plane. Note that this relationship is only unidirectional. That is, a Boeing 747 is a plane, but a plane is not necessarily a Boeing 747. A HasA relationship is a relationship in which one object contains or uses another object. For example, a plane has an engine, but a plane is not an engine. So a plane has a HasA relationship with an engine, but a plane does not have an IsA relationship with an engine.

In Java, the way to specify an IsA relationship is by using the extends keyword:

```
class Monograph extends Book
    {
    }
```

In Java, every object, regardless of its class, inherits, extends, or has an IsA relationship with the class Object. Object is the top class in the class hierarchy. Everything that is true of the class Object is true of every other class that you can define in Java, whether it's part of the Java 2 SDK or a user-defined class. Everything inherits from or subclasses Object.

Because a class inherits the methods and data members of its superclasses, and Object is the superclass of all classes, you get every method that Object has in every other class. Because Object has a toString() method to represent the object as a String, every other class inherits this toString() method. Let's look at another very important example. The Component class hierarchy is a good illustration of the benefits of inheritance. It is shown in Figure 4.1.

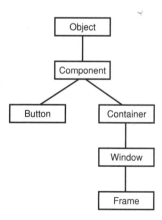

Figure 4.1

The Component class hierarchy.

40 Chapter 4: Data Types

In Figure 4.1, you can see that Component inherits from Object. What's more important is what inherits from Component. A Component has many methods and data members that it shares with all its subclasses. All AWT and JFC components subclass the Component class. Because a Button is a Component, it gets all Component's methods and data members for free, just because it extends Component:

```
public class Button extends Component
```

The Container class also extends Component, so that everything a Component is, a Container is also. Because a Component can be added to a Container, a Container, as a Component, can be added to another Container. That's how I can add a Panel to a Frame or another Panel. Everything that a Container is, a Window is.

A Window object, however, is not merely a rectangular-shaped object that can contain other Components. It is a visible Component that you can display on the screen. A Frame has an IsA relationship with a Window. You hardly ever, however, display a Window because it has no title bar, no maximize or minimize buttons, or anything else. It's just a visual rectangle to which you can add Component objects.

As a Window, a Frame has all this and more. A Frame also has a title bar, a title bar icon, and maximize, minimize, and close buttons. You can set the background and foreground color of a Frame on the screen, but the Frame gets these methods from the Component class. It is not a special feature of just Frame objects. Instead, it inherits the methods for setting the foreground and background and a Color property for the foreground and background color from the Component class.

From the Container class, the Frame class inherits the add method for adding a Component. From the Window class, Frame gets addWindowListener.

The Frame class gets all kinds of methods and data members for free by extending Window. The Window class gets all kinds of methods and data members by extending Container, which gets all kinds of methods and data members by extending Component, which extends Object. Inheritance through extending a superclass is a very important feature of Java.

Creating Instances of Classes: Constructors

The primary way to instantiate an instance of a class is to invoke a constructor for that class. A constructor must be called as part of the process of creating an object. Unlike C++, Java has no matching destructor because garbage collection is the JVM's job. Here's a class with a user-defined constructor:

```
class Book   // Simple Book class definition
    {
    String title;

    public Book(String bookName)
        {
        title = bookName;
        System.out.println("New book added to the collection:  " +
```

```
                                            title);
                            // Print a message to the command line
        }
} // End Book class definition
```

Here's the constructor's signature for this class:

```
public Book(String bookName)
```

Like a method signature, it has an access modifier, `public`. It has a method name, `Book`, which must match the name of the class. It has a parameter list, consisting of one parameter, an object of type `String` called `bookName`. There's one really important thing missing, however, compared to a normal method signature. There is no return type for the constructor. In fact, if you code a constructor with a return type

```
public Book Book(String bookName)
```

based on the theory that a `Book` constructor returns a `Book` object, or

```
public void Book(String bookName)
```

based on the theory that a constructor returns nothing, Java will look at your method signature and say, "This is a normal method, not a constructor." Don't give a constructor a return type. Otherwise, all the code you wrote to build an object in a constructor will be ignored when you try to call your constructor. If you call a constructor that has a return type, but also has a parameter list instead of empty parentheses, (), you'll get a compile error. Java won't be able to find a constructor with that parameter list.

Constructor Signature

You can code a constructor that takes one or more arguments, or no arguments at all. It's generally a good idea to code both. You also have to decide about the appropriate access modifier. If, as in most JDK classes, you want to be able to instantiate the class from anywhere, you should give the constructor a public access modifier.

If you want to be able to make an instance in any other class in the package, but not outside the package, use package default access. If you want to be able to create an instance from the package or from subclasses in other packages, use `protected`. Finally, you might want to make it impossible for any other class to instantiate your class directly. In that case, you should give it a `private` constructor. In order to call this constructor, you'll have to come up with a static method in the class that returns a reference to the object and optionally executes the private constructor. Some classes, such as JDBC drivers, call their own private constructor from a static initializer, and a developer cannot get an instance of the class directly at all. In part, that's how these classes get to be singletons. Because singletons must call their own constructors, they can check to see whether there is already an instance and reject any request to make another one.

Default Constructors

Generally, it is not necessary to code a constructor for your class. When you need a constructor, the compiler creates a constructor for you if you don't supply one. The constructor that the compiler creates for you is called the *default constructor*. Although the compiler supplies a constructor for you, the one it supplies doesn't do much. If I had not coded a constructor for the Book class, the compiler would have made one like this:

```
public Book()
{
}
```

There is no code in this constructor. It doesn't initialize anything. It will, however, call its parent's constructor by trying to call the parent's zero-argument constructor. In addition, during construction of the object, the JVM will perform default initialization, such as setting object references to null. So if Book subclasses Object directly, the default constructor in Book is the following:

```
class Book
    {
    String title
    public Book()
        {
          Object();
          // It calls Object's zero-argument constructor.  This is
          // not the actual constructor name, but it conveys
          // the correct idea.
        }
    }
```

Every constructor has to call its parent's constructor, explicitly or implicitly, or a constructor of the same class. Because Java does this, it is a good idea to provide your own zero-argument constructor. The compiler will insert a call for that form of the constructor into any other constructor that you code, if it doesn't explicitly call its parent's constructor. It does this because of how the JVM creates objects (which is discussed below). Here are points to remember:

- Java uses constructors in the process of creating an object instance.
- Every constructor (except Object's) explicitly or implicitly calls its parent class's constructor.
- The implicit constructor call will be to a zero-argument constructor.
- If you do not code a constructor for your class, Java will create a zero-argument, empty constructor for you.
- If you provide a constructor that takes at least one parameter, Java will not create a zero-argument constructor for you.

In general, it is a good idea to code a zero-argument constructor. By doing so, you make your class much easier to use when it is subclassed. If you provide a zero-argument constructor, or provide no constructor at all, a subclass of your class will compile perfectly when Java inserts a call to the zero-argument form of the constructor for your class. Most JDK classes provide a zero-argument constructor.

> **NOTE**
>
> Although most JDK classes provide a zero-argument constructor, one notable exception is the Dialog class. This class does not have a zero-argument constructor. It does, however, have multiple constructors that take one or more parameters. Therefore, when you try to subclass Dialog, you must explicitly call a Dialog constructor with one or more parameters. This can be a bit inconvenient until you get used to this requirement.

This is, however, only a convenience item for other developers who use your class. If your class is never subclassed, it doesn't matter whether you have a zero-argument constructor or not.

Overloading Constructors

It is possible to specify multiple constructors for one class. Here's an example:

```
class Book
    {
      String title;
      String author;
        public Book(String aTitle, String anAuthor)
            {
              title = aTitle;
              author = anAuthor;
            }
        public Book()
            {
              this("No subject", "nobody");
                              // Call the constructor for the Book class
                              //   that accepts two String parameters
                              //   and supply default values, since the
                              //   caller didn't provide any values
            }
        public Book(String anAuthor)
            {
              this("No subject", anAuthor);
                              // Call the Book constructor that takes
                              //   two parameters, supplying one
                              //   default value and one supplied by
                              //   the caller
            }
```

I'll talk more about this later, but for now, suffice it to say that coding

```
this(<zero or more parameters>);
```

calls the constructor for the class this, which is coded so that it has a matching parameter list. So, you might code a constructor that takes no arguments, and one or more constructors that take one or more arguments. The only real requirement when coding two or more constructors is that they cannot have the same parameter list.

Invoking Parent Constructors

I talked previously about calling a parent's or superclass's constructor. Just as

```
this(<zero or more parameters>)
```

calls a constructor from the same class as this, so you can call the constructor of the class that your class immediately extends by using

```
super(<zero or more arguments>)
```

You call this for your own class, and super for its parent's class. In case you are wondering, there is no way to skip classes and call the constructor two classes up. You must call the constructor of the immediate parent class. Let's see an example using the Dialog class, which has no zero-argument constructor:

```
public class BookCheckOutDialog extends Dialog
    {
       public BookCheckOutDialog(Frame a Frame, String title, boolean mode)
           {
             super(aFrame, title, mode);
           }
    }
```

The class definition says that BookCheckOutDialog extends, or subclasses, Dialog. That means that Dialog is the immediate superclass of BookCheckOutDialog. So the call to super(aFrame, title, mode) in the BookCheckOutDialog constructor calls the constructor of the parent class Dialog.

It is possible to explicitly call a zero-argument constructor of the parent class as well. For example, I could code

```
public class Journal extends Periodical
    {
      public Journal()
           {
              super(); // Call the Periodical class zero-argument constructor
                      // explicitly.
              Catalog.addJournalVolume();
                           // A static method in the
                           // Catalog class to
                           // add a journal to the library catalog
                           // system
           }
    }
```

If you don't explicitly call this constructor, the compiler will insert such a call for you. It is a requirement that if you code an explicit call to the superclass's constructor, this call to super() must be the very first line in your constructor. It may not go anywhere else.

How Objects Are Created by the JVM

Here are the steps performed by the JVM to make a new object:

1. Allocate memory to hold the object.
2. Walk up the class hierarchy to the top, via calling the constructor of the superclass from each higher-level class, for example, super() calls super() calls super(), all the way up to Object. Then start making an instance of each object going back down the inheritance hierarchy. So for a Frame object, this means
   A. Make an object of type Object.
   B. Make an object of type Component (although because Component is abstract this doesn't technically happen).
   C. Make object of type Container
   D. Make an object of type Window.
   E. Make an object of type Frame.

Here's an analogy that might help you understand this activity. In order for me to exist, my father and mother had to exist first. In order for my mother to exist, her mother and father had to exist. In order for her parents to exist, my great grandparents on my mother's side had to exist, and so forth.

In a similar way, for a Frame object to exist, its parent object, which is a Window, had to exist. For a Window object to exist, its parent class Container, had to be instantiated, and so forth. It might help if you think of a Frame object containing a Window object, plus the data and methods that are unique to a Frame above and beyond those of the Window. That Window object, however, contains a Container object, and the Window object contains both the Container object and the data members and methods that are unique to a Window above and beyond those provided by a Container, and so forth. Figure 4.2 might help you visualize this.

After all these constructors get called, Java performs default initialization of data members for your class. Next, Java performs explicit initialization and then executes the rest of your constructor. Finally, if appropriate, Java returns an object reference value to your program, in this way:

Frame f = new Frame();

This constructor called on the Frame class causes the previously mentioned steps to be executed, culminating in an object reference to a Frame object being assigned to the object reference variable f.

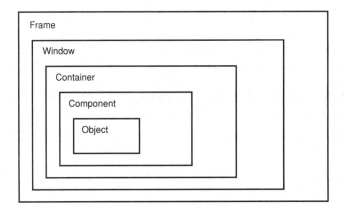

Figure 4.2

An Object with its superclass objects.

Initialization of Data Members

There are two kinds of initialization you can do for an object: default and explicit.

Here's an example of default initialization:

```
public class LibraryCard
    {
      String patronID;
       float outstandingFine;
         int booksCheckedOut = 0;
    }
```

This class has three data members. The first two, `patronID` and `outstandingFine`, have no values assigned to them. The third, `booksCheckedOut`, is set to zero. When an instance of the `LibraryCard` class is created, the value of `booksCheckedOut` starts off as zero. The other two data members are assigned values by the system. The value a data member gets depends on the data type of data member. That is, all data members are initialized to default values if they are not explicitly initialized. Here's a list of what you get for a given data type:

> `float` is set to `0.0f`
> `double` is set to `0.0`
> `long` is set to `0L`
> `int` is set to `0`
> `short` is set to `0`
> `byte` is set to `0`
> `boolean` is set to `false`
> `char` is set to `'\u0000'`
> All object references are set to `null`

Because all object references are set to null by default, it is critical that you instantiate the related objects before using them, or your program will fail. The good news here is that if this happens, Java will always throw a NullPointerException at a specific location, instead of simply attempting to use a null pointer. C or C++ would make the attempt, with the resultant unpredictable results.

You can also use explicit initialization. Explicit initialization sets data members to the values you specify. So, if you set a String to "Litwak", this is the value it will be given when the object is instantiated. There is, however, an issue of where to put the code for instantiating and explicitly initializing data members.

NOTE

Because there was a JDK 1.0 feature that potentially required it, I learned to declare data members outside of any method. However, I did instantiate them and give them a value inside the class's constructor, unless it was a primitive. In that case, I felt comfortable initializing outside of the constructor. This issue does exist in Java 2.

In some cases, you can only instantiate and initialize an object inside a method. Although objects of many classes can be instantiated outside any method, I suggest that you don't mix the two approaches. Because some things really need to be initialized inside a constructor or method, I suggest that you declare data members outside of any method or constructor (the minimum requirement for them to be data members and not local variables) and then instantiate them. Set their value in a constructor or method appropriately.

CAUTION

It is very important to note that if you declare a variable inside a method, which makes it a local variable, Java will do nothing to initialize it, not even give it a null value for an object. You must initialize local variables to some value before using them, even if that value is zero.

Abstract Classes

There are two kinds of classes in Java: concrete classes and abstract classes. A *concrete* class is a class that you can use to make an instance. An abstract class, on the other hand, cannot be instantiated. Syntactically, an abstract class is any class that contains at least one abstract method. Consider a class `Airplane`:

```
public class Airplane
    {
       int numberofWings;
       String engineType;
         public boolean startEngine()
             {
                // logic to start an engine goes here
             }
    }
```

This class specifies a generic airplane. Although it is syntactically correct, there are a couple of potential problems with this class definition that give rise to the need for abstract classes. First, there's no such thing as a generic airplane. There are Boeing 747s, there are F15s, there are Gypsy Moth biplanes, but there is no such thing as a generic airplane. Instead, `airplane` represents an abstract concept. Because it is only a concept and there is no such thing as a generic airplane, it would be inappropriate to instantiate it.

The second problem is that various airplanes do the same thing, but in very different ways. So, a jet airliner starts its engines in a different manner from a Sopwith Camel triplane. A jet fighter starts its engines in a different manner from a Cessna propeller-driven plane. That means that there's no code that can be put into the `startEngine()` method that will cover every kind of plane that might be subclassed from `Airplane`.

Still, every kind of motor-driven plane should have a method for starting its engine(s). To define a base class `Airplane` that deals with these two problems, two changes are necessary, both using the keyword `abstract`:

```
abstract class Airplane
    {
       int numberofWings;   // Declare two data members,
                            // one for the number of
                            //  wings the plane has
       String engineType;   // and one for the number of
                            // engines the plane has
                            // These should be properties common to
                            // all subclasses.  So you wouldn't necessarily want
                            // to specify the number of wheels as sea planes
                            // may not have any wheels
       public abstract boolean startEngine();
    }  // End class definition for Airplane
```

First, I've declared that the class is abstract. This means it is impossible to make an instance of the class `Airplane`. Second, I've turned `startEngine()` into an abstract method. Notice that besides the keyword `abstract`, the method ends with a semicolon and has no curly braces at all. All the methods in the book up until now have been concrete methods. They all were executable. An abstract method cannot be executed. In addition to the `abstract` keyword and semicolon, this method could have parameters. Like a C++ virtual function, this abstract method is meant to be overridden in a subclass. It has no code intentionally.

Technically speaking, an abstract class is any class that contains at least one abstract method. So adding an abstract method to a class makes that class abstract, and it cannot be instantiated. By itself, this method is not very useful. Its purpose can only be understood in the context of its use in an abstract base class with concrete subclasses. It's very important to understand that an abstract class can have many concrete methods, with lots of code in them; but if there is at least one abstract method, the class is an abstract class.

Abstract Classes

A good example of this kind of class is the `java.awt.Component` class. It contains several concrete methods and data members, but you cannot instantiate a `Component`. You cannot instantiate any class that is abstract. You can only instantiate subclasses of `Component`, like `Button` or `JFrame`.

Okay, so every type of plane should have a `startEngine()` method. If the class subclasses `Airplane`, I am guaranteed that all concrete subclasses of `Airplane` will have a `startEngine()` method. I can enforce this through the use of an abstract method, without having to inspect any code. If I create an abstract class, every class that subclasses my abstract class, like `F15` or `SopwithCamel`, must implement all the abstract methods in my abstract base class, `Airplane`, or the subclass itself is considered an abstract class by the compiler.

> **NOTE**
>
> You will get compiler errors if you don't implement all these methods, but don't mark your class as `abstract`. The compiler will complain that you have an abstract class, but didn't label it as `abstract`. You must implement the methods in the abstract base class so that your subclass is a concrete class.

So, I create an `F15` class and a `Boeing747` class that both subclass `Airplane`, and I know that `Airplane` has an abstract `startEngine()` method, I can be confident that both subclasses have each implemented a `startEngine()` method with code that makes sense for the specific class. So I might have this:

```
class F15 extends Airplane
                    // The concrete class inherits from the abstract class
    {
      public boolean startEngine()
                    // Remove the abstract keyword in the subclass'
                    // overridden version of the method.  Everything
                    // else in the method signature must match the
                    // abstract version exactly
          {
                    // Start the F15 jet engine and crank up the afterburner
              return true;
          }
    }  // End F15 class definition
class Boeing747 extends Airplane  // Another concrete
                    // class that inherits from an
                    // abstract class
    {
      public boolean startEngine()
            {
                    // Start the jet liner's multiple engines
            ¦
    }           // End Boeing747 class definition
```

You want to have a specific startEngine() method for each kind of aircraft. There's a specific design reason for using an abstract base class. The main reason for using an abstract base class is that you have a generic data type, such as Airplane, or Account, or Person, or Product, that you don't logically want an instance of.

Instead, you want to have lots of subclasses of the base class, and you want to make sure that every child class has an implementation of a specific method. That implementation must be logically unique to the child class. Therefore, you make the base class abstract and make the method that you want every subclass to implement abstract as well. Now the compiler will force every subclass to implement the method. In case you're thinking that plain inheritance of a method would be sufficient, it's not. If I declare a concrete method that every subclass inherits, the subclasses are not required to explicitly implement it. Therefore, subclasses are inheriting only a generic implementation. Jet liners, jet fighters, propeller-driven biplanes, and rocket planes (like the X-15) don't all start the same way. Each class, therefore, needs its own version of startEngine(), and an abstract method is exactly the tool to accomplish this. When you have a group of related classes, and you want to require them all to implement a given behavior, consider making them subclasses of an abstract base class that has an abstract version of that method. This design approach is to be contrasted with using an interface, which I'll discuss later. Also, let me note that abstract classes sometimes have a create sort of method and serve as object factories. That is, you don't want to make an instance of the abstract class, but you are using a concrete method in the abstract class to produce some other type of object. You'll need to consult a book on design patterns for further information.

Final Classes

Making a data member or method final means that the data member or method cannot be overridden in a subclass or modified in any way at runtime. The same holds true for classes. A class that is declared as final cannot be subclassed or overridden. This again serves as a security feature in Java. No one can modify my CreditCard or Login class. The class String was made final because of several nefarious hacker tricks that could be used if Strings were not final. It is more common to make data members final than it is to make classes final, but you can find uses for this in class declarations.

Some Important Common Classes

The following is a short list of classes that every Java developer needs to understand. More than one of these classes will be used in just about any commercial program.

String	Vector
Date	Properties
Object	Calendar
Class	Thread
System	Wrapper classes
Runtime	Arrays

You'll explore these classes in the following sections.

String

Just about the most common class used in Java programs, besides `Object` (which is always the base class of every other class, so it's used implicitly), is the `String` class. Unlike C, a `String` in Java is not merely a contiguous set of characters in memory, followed by a null terminator, `\0`. Instead, Java `Strings` are objects, with properties and behaviors. The JVM has a special place in which `Strings` commonly reside, called the `String` literal pool. The way to create a `String` that is placed in the `String` literal pool is like this:

```java
String author = "Josephus"; // Note the use of double quotes.
                            //   This is how String
                            //   literals are delimited in Java
```

This line of code, when it is executed, causes a `String` literal, `"Josephus"`, to be placed in the `String` literal pool.

The other way to create a `String` is to use an explicit constructor:

```java
String author = new String("Josephus");
```

This statement places a `String` object in memory on the heap, rather than merely putting the `String` literal `"Josephus"` in the `String` literal pool. Although it does not make much difference which of these two approaches you take, remember which one you used. It affects how you compare two `Strings` to each other. Here are two ways to compare two `Strings` to each other:

```java
public class Book
    {
      String author;
      String title;
        public Book(String anAuthor, String aTitle)
             {
                author = anAuthor;
                title = aTitle;
             }
        public compareBooks(String title1, String title2)
             {
               if(title1.equals(title2))
                   { // Use the equals() method to compare these two Strings
                     System.out.println("Book 1 equals() Book 2");
                   }
               if(title1 == title2)
                   { // Use the == operator to compare these two Strings
                     System.out.println("Book 1 == Book 2");
                   }
             } // End Book class definition
```

52 Chapter 4: Data Types

As a rule, the method `equals()` compares the contents of two objects, whereas generally the `==` operator compares object references only. So, if you create two `Button` objects

```
Button b1= new Button("OK");
Button b2 = new Button("OK");
```

and then try to compare them with the `==` operator

```
if(b1 == b2)
   {
     System.out.println("You can't ever get here");
   }
```

the comparison will fail. You are comparing object references, not the contents of the objects. In the case of `Strings`, however, the rules are different. If you use the code in the `Book` class shown earlier, you are creating two `Strings`:

```
String author = "the value of anAuthor";
```

This creates a `String` in the `String` literal pool. If you create a second `String` with the same value, such as

```
String author1 = "Josephus";
String author2 = "Josephus";
```

Java will put the first `String` literal, `"Josephus"`, in the `String` literal pool and puta reference to it in the `author1` object reference variable. When you try to create `author2`, the system will check the `String` literal pool, determine that the `String` literal `"Josephus"` already exists, and simply return a reference to the existing `String` literal. At the end of these two statements, you have

- One copy of the `String` literal `"Josephus"` in the `String` literal pool
- The `Object` reference in `author1` pointing to this literal `String` in the pool
- The object reference in `author2` pointing to the same physical `String` literal in the pool

The upshot of this is that, whether you compare the object references with the `==` operator, which compares object references, or with the `equals()` method, which compares the contents of each object, both tests will return true.

The case is quite different if one or both of the `Strings` was created as a separate object, as in this example:

```
String author1 = "Josephus";
String author2 = new String("Josephus");
```

If you run this code, `author2` does not have a literal value put in the `String` literal pool. Instead, the `String` `"Josephus"` is part of a separate `String` object. If you do it this way, or define both with the `String` constructor, signaled by the use of the word new, here's what happens when you compare them:

```
if(author1 == author2)
    {
       System.out.println("Won't happen.  The object references will" +
                                       " never be equal");
    }
if(author1.equals(author2))
    {
       System.out.println("This should return true, " +
                                       "since the contents of each" +
                                       " String are equal, even if the object " +
                                       " references are different.)"
    }
```

So remember that to compare two `Strings` and be sure that you are always testing for equal content, use the `equals()` method.

There is one other point about `Strings` that is worth mentioning. `Strings` are immutable, first-class objects. That means that when you create a `String` in memory, that `String` cannot be changed there. You can modify a `String` with the concatenation operator, +, like this:

```
String s = "Dead Sea";
s = s + "Scrolls";
```

This does not, however, change the original `String`. Instead, Java essentially acquires a brand new piece of memory that is big enough for the whole new `String`, copies the old one into this new one, and adds the new piece, `"Scrolls"`, to it. The old version of the `String` is then available for garbage collection. If your code has to do a lot of `String` manipulation, you can potentially use up lots of memory. You might consider using `StringBuffer` instead of `String`. Although it's a little more work to use `StringBuffer`, the `StringBuffer` class does enable you to append characters to the original memory area, rather than copying the old version to a new, larger location. This can result in a significant performance gain in some text manipulation-intensive programs such as word processing.

Date

In JDK 1.0, a `Date` object had to serve two roles: a moment in time and a date such as a calendar date. In JDK 1.1, these roles were split into two groups. Now, in Java 2, the `Date` class, as in JDK 1.1, represents a moment in time. The former methods in the `Date` class, which treated it as a calendar-type date, have been deprecated. You are encouraged to use the `Calendar` class and its subclasses instead.

NOTE

Because you should be using `Calendar` and its subclasses instead of using `Date`, I won't show any examples of using `Date` on its own. It is used with the `Calendar` classes and classes in `java.text`. It is important, but it does not stand on its own.

54 Chapter 4: Data Types

In JDK 1.1, JavaSoft introduced the Calendar class, built by Taligent. The Calendar class and its subclasses represent calendar-type dates. You should use these if you want to deal with dates in your program. In JDK 1.1, there were some suboptimal features in the Calendar class hierarchy. Java 2 improves on these to make the Calendar classes more useful.

There is, however, still a use for the Date class. I suggest using the Date class if you need to measure how long it takes for something to happen. You can create a Date object before performing some activity, do the work, and then create a second Date object. If you subtract the value of the first Date object in milliseconds from the value of the second Date object in milliseconds, you'll find out approximately how long it took to perform the work.

Object

Because the class Object is at the top of the class hierarchy for all classes, you should know what's in it. The Object class provides several methods that every other class inherits. Of special note is the clone method. If you can live with a shallow copy, you can use the clone method to actually copy an object of any kind. If not, you need to implement your own deep copy in your subclass. Object has the wait() and notify() methods that are used for thread synchronization. Because Object is the superclass for all other classes, you can use an instance of Object anywhere you want something else. That is, you can make generic methods, such as those used by the Vector class. Here's a sample method:

```
public String testObject(Object someObj)
    {
    String className = null;
    if (someObj instanceof Button)
        className = "Button";
    if (someObj instanceof Window)
        className = "Window";
    return className;
    }
```

This method accepts an object of type Object. Using the Vector class, you can pass any reference type at all to this method. Internally, you can test the type of object or operate on it in other ways. This means that you only need one method, not a method for every single object type.

Apart from this kind of code, it is unusual to use the Object class directly. It is much more common to use methods inherited from it, such as wait().

Class

The class Class has several handy methods that you can use for getting information about an object and for loading a class. You can use

```
Class.forName("class name");
```

to load a class, which is generally how you load a JDBC driver for database programming in Java. If you want to print the name of the class of an object, you can code

```
public boolean displayClassName(Object someObject)
   {
     System.out.println(someObject.getClass().getName());
   }
```

To get some basic information about a class, you can use methods in the `Class` class. To get more detailed information, you'll need to use reflection, covered in the Technical Reference section.

System

The `System` class has several important and handy methods in it. You use `System.in`, `System.out`, and `System.err` to address standard input, standard output, and standard error, respectively. The `System` class has methods to set a `SecurityManager` object, which is more relevant to JDK 1.0 or 1.1 than Java 2, but is still available for backwards compatibility. The `System` class also has methods for getting one or more `System` properties, such as the root directory and user name. The `System` class also has a method for copying one array to another array, `arraycopy()`. The `System` class is one of the classes in the JDK that is a singleton. That is, you can't instantiate it yourself. There's no way to call a `System` constructor. It's taken care of for you and you get exactly one in your JVM.

Here are some examples of methods you might call with an object of type `System` (of which there is never more than one):

```
public boolean snoopSystem()
    {
      Properties p = System.getProperties();
      long time = System.currentTimeMillis();
      System.setSecuritymanager(new CommerceSecurityManager());
                   // Install a new custom-made
                   // SecurityManager class.
      return true;
    }
```

Runtime

Like the `System` class, the `Runtime` class only has one instance at one time. In an earlier JDK, it was possible to instantiate additional `Runtime` objects. These additional objects were of no help to you, however, because only the current `Runtime` object, created for you by the JVM, had links to the objects you might need. The `Runtime` class has a method for executing other programs, `exec()`, and methods to get the amount of free and total memory in the JVM. This class can do some significant tasks, so be sure you understand the methods and their implications before you use them. Here are a few things you can do with the `Runtime` class:

56 Chapter 4: Data Types

```
public boolean checkStuff()
    {
    long freeMem = System.getRuntime().freeMemoery();
                    // Get the amount of free memory
                    // Note the use of the System
                    // class to access the Runtime
                    // object getRuntime() is also a
                    // method of the class Runtime
    System.getRuntime().gc(); // Please take out
                    // the memory garbage
    }
```

NOTE

If you want a Java program to run Acrobat or Notepad, use exec(). Be aware, however, that this usually makes your code platform-specific because you'll generally be executing a program with a platform-dependent path. For those on a Win32 system who want to execute an MS DOS program, don't try to code

getRuntime().exec("copy file1 file2"); // This is wrong. Don't do it.

This is wrong because copy is not a program. It's part of the command shell. Instead, ask for Command.com to execute, passing it the copy command as a parameter to Command.com.

Vector

Java has basically two kinds of objects for dealing with arrays of things: array and Vector. At least, this was true before the Java 2 Collection classes. What's important to note here is that arrays can contain only one kind of data type (or subtypes of that type), no matter how many elements there are, and arrays are fixed in size. Arrays can't grow. Vectors, on the other hand, can grow dynamically and can accept objects of varying types. Notice that I said that Vectors can accept varying kinds of objects. That means that a Vector cannot accept a primitive. All the methods for the Vector class accept parameters of type Object (and thus any subclass of Object, which is every other class). If you need to put primitives into a Vector, put them in a wrapper class like Boolean or Integer. Here's an example of using a Vector that would be suitable for e-commerce tier 1 to tier 2 communication:

```
private boolean sendParms()
    {
    Vector dataVector = new Vector(10,2);
                    // For performance reasons,
                    // always use the two-argument
                    // constructor
    dataVector.addElement(lastNameString);
    dataVector.addElement(firstNameString);
    dataVBector.addElement(qyIntegerWrapper);
```

```
        dataVector.addElement(todayGregCalendar);
        tier1ObjOutStr.writeObject(dataVector);
                        // Write all the data values
                        // out as one big object
                        // by using a Vector
        return true;
    }
```

You might also use a Vector for getting a list of components from a Container or saving the values of a column from a JDBC ResultSet (covered in Chapter 17, "JDBC: Java Database Programming").

Properties

The Properties class is a subclass of HashTable. A Properties object is a combination of name and value pairs. There are System properties, like root directory and username, mentioned above, as well as properties such as Java vendor URL, Java version, and several other values. You can also create your own Properties objects. You should consider doing this to make configuration files, similar to those you might find in an .ini file or the Windows registry. Unlike the Win32 registry, however, a Java Properties object stored in a file is platform-independent. This makes it a much better choice for storing configuration information. Here's a simple example of getting a System property:

```
public String buildConfigFilePath()
    {
      String sep = System.getProperty(file.separator);
      String path = "." + setp + "GreatClasses" + sep + "SuperGUI.class";
                        // Dynamically create a file path
                        // after getting the system-
                        // dependent file separator.
                        // This code is fully portable.
        return path;
    }
```

Calendar

I mentioned this class above. It is used for dealing with dates. The Calendar class itself is not what you want to instantiate. You want to use a subclass of Calendar, such as GregorianCalendar. If you need some other kind of calendar, such as a Jewish calendar, you should subclass Calendar to achieve this. The JDK only supplies the GregorianCalendar subclass. I mentioned above that there are some suboptimal features in the Calendar classes, and one of those protected methods in GregorianCalendar still exists.

Hopefully you won't need them. The Calendar class will let you set a day, month, year, and time, including time zone, and adjust that time for daylight savings time. You can inquire of this Calendar object all these values plus the day of the week, week of the

58 Chapter 4: Data Types

month, month of the year, and so forth. Here's a code snippet for making and using a GregorianCalendar:

```
public Calendar createDate()
    {
    GregorianCalendar today = new GregorianCalendar(adjTimeZone);
                        // Make a calendar object,
                        // It is set for a specific
                        // time zone and optionally
                        // adjust for daylight
                        // savings time.
    Date now = new Date();
    today.setTime(now);   // Set the actual date
    System.out.println("The month is: " + today.get(Calendar.MONTH));
                        // Print the month
    return today;
    }
```

Thread

As mentioned earlier in the book, Java supports and uses multithreading. You can create your own Thread objects. Threads execute a run() method. Any logic you want them to perform goes in the run() method. There are, basically, two ways to do this. One is to create a Thread subclass that has its own run() method. The other is to create a class that has a Thread object as a data member and a run() method in the class for the Thread to run. In the latter case, your class needs to implement the Runnable interface. The Runnable interface has one method, run. So your class needs to implement the run method.

```
class ImageGetter implements Runnable
    { // This is not sufficient to actually meaningfully use this Thread
    Thread getterThread;
    MediaTracker mt;
    public boolean getImages()
        {
        getterThread = new Thread(this);
                        // Create a Thread object and pass
                        // in a Runnable object, in this case the
                        // current ImageGetter object.
        getterThread.start();   // Tells the Thread to start running
        }
    public void run()
        {
        mt = new MediaTracker(this);
        }
    } // End of class ImageGetter
```

To execute this code, you code in another class:

```
Runnable r = new ImageGetter();
r.getImages();
```

You need a Runnable object for a Thread. I haven't shown you code here for making a Thread subclass. There's a reason for that. From a design point of view, I would argue that you almost never want to create Thread subclasses. Here's why: A Thread represents a unit of execution, or subprocess. The odds of your having a class that logically has an IsA relationship with an execution context is pretty slim. You should not, from a design point of view, define classes that extend other classes, but are not really specialized forms of that base class. You will almost never have a class in a design that is a specialized form of an execution context. Using the Runnable interface in a class instead enables you to have proper design in which you subclass a meaningful class and simply define your subclass to contain a Thread. Threads will be discussed in Chapter 11, "Multithreaded Programming in Java."

Wrapper Classes for Primitives

As mentioned above, you can't put a primitive into a Vector, and there might be other times that you want to pass a primitive as an object. You can do this in a number of ways, one of which is to put the primitive into a wrapper class instance. There is a wrapper class for each primitive (see Table 4.2).

Table 4.2 Mapping Between Primitives and Corresponding Wrapper Classes

Primitive	Wrapper Class
float	Float
int	Integer
boolean	Boolean
short	Short
byte	Byte
char	Character
long	Long
double	Double

You can use one of these in an insertElement call for a Vector object. These classes can come in handy, but remember that a Boolean is a totally different thing from a boolean; the two terms are not interchangeable in your code. You can't use an Integer wrapper class object where you need an int, or vice-versa. Trying to do so can lead to compiler type-mismatch errors.

Arrays of Objects

Because arrays are not classes as such, but are objects for which there is not a specific API section, I'll treat them here. An array is a multi-element object that can hold 0 to n instances of an object or any number of a given primitive. Note the implication here. You can only put one kind of thing in a given array. Unlike C, Java arrays are not merely contiguous memory areas. Instead, an array is an object, and implicitly extends Object. Although it is possible to define a class for an array, each array has an associated class automatically defined by the JVM, which can be accessed by the getClass() method of the class Object. First, let's look at how to declare an array:

```java
public class ArrayMaker
    {
       int[] intArray;          // The preferred way to declare a Java array
       String stringArray[];    // Another way to declare an array,
                                // a concession to C programmers
       public ArrayMaker()
          {
            intArray = new int[6];
                                  // Create an array that will accept six
                                  // int elements
            stringArray = {
                    "Plato, Aristotle", "Tacitus", "Jerome", "Augustine"};
                                  // Explicitly initialize an array with
                                  // five String elements
          }
       public boolean initializeArrays()
          {
            intArray[0] = 5;
            intArray[1] = 3;
            intArray [5] = 7;
            System.out.println(stringArray[stringArray.length - 1]);
          }
    }
```

This small class is meant to illustrate several things at once. First there are two basic ways to declare an array. To declare an array, you use one or more pairs of [] in the declaration. Java does this by beginning with the data type, followed by [], followed by the object reference to the array object.

It is also possible to compromise and code it the C way, in which the [] follow the object reference name. I recommend the Java way because I think it's easier to read. You can read it straight across: Type is int; it's an array; its name is intArray.

Using the second approach, you have to read it in this way: data type is String, the object reference is stringArray, and it is an array. Wait, I have to go back and see what kind of array it is. Oh, it's a String array. I think the Java way is more intuitive. It is a matter of style primarily, but most Java programmers declare arrays the Java way.

I instantiate the arrays in the class's constructor. In the first case, I state that the array of type int has six elements, but I don't immediately give them values. After this statement is executed, there will be an array in memory for holding six ints. Because I didn't initialize these elements, Java will give them a default value. Because they are ints, the default value will be zero. It is also possible to instantiate and initialize an array at the same time, whether it contains primitives or objects, as I have done in the case of the stringArray object. You could even code

```java
Panel[] panelArray = {new Panel(), new Panel(), new Panel()};
```

That is, you can instantiate any object within an array definition. When you use this style for initializing an array, Java counts how many elements you put inside the curly braces. That is how long the array will be. Until you instantiate an array, it has no length. After you instantiate it, it has a fixed length. You cannot add elements. Next, you can see in the `initialize()` method that I assign values to some of the elements of the `intArray` object. Note that the first element I give a value to is element 0, [0]. Like C, arrays start counting elements at zero, so the range of the number of the elements of `intArray` is 0[nd]5, rather than 1–6 (WRONG). Because arrays are objects, they have properties. One of those properties is a `length`. There's no `sizeof` operator in Java, and, in the case of arrays, all you need to know is how many elements there are. You can get that by using

```java
int x = someArray.length;
```

Note that this is not a method call. It is a data member that you don't have to define. Because the value of `length` is always going to be one greater than the number of the highest element in the array, to examine the highest element, you need to look at `length - 1`. In your case, there are six elements in the `intArray`, but the highest element is element 5, because the first element is `intArray[0]`. So if you subtract one from the length which is six, you get five. You can use this information to loop through an array in a for loop, for example. This is discussed further in Chapter 7, "Syntax."

There's another feature of arrays in Java that you need to know. Java provides for arrays of arrays, or ragged arrays. C supports multidimensional arrays of contiguous memory. Java doesn't work like that. Let's say I have this declaration:

```java
int[][] doubleIntArray = new int[6][5];
```

In C, there would be thirty contiguous elements together. In Java, however, the location in memory of the second dimension for any given element in the first dimension is unpredictable. That means the memory for `doubleIntArray[0][1]` might be nowhere near the location in memory of `doubleIntArray[3][6]`. Because Java works this way, you can do something like this:

```java
public class ArrayMakerNd
   {
     int[][] intArray;
     public ArrayMakerNd()
        {
          intArray = new int[6][];
             // Create an array that will accept six int arrays
        }
     public boolean initializeArrays()
         {
           intArray[0] = new int[10];
           intArray[1] = new int[4];
           intArray [5] = new int[97];
           return true;
         }
   }
```

So you can define different length second dimensions. It will help if you don't think of them as second dimensions, but as simply another array. Java may allocate memory for any of these arrays wherever it wishes. So, if you are wondering if Java can do three-dimensional arrays, the answer is that you can do any level of arrays of arrays you want, dynamically. You can have fifteen dimensions if you want. Notice, also, that it is illegal to do this:

```
int[][] intArray = new int[][6];  //WRONG. Can't specify second "dimension"
                                  // without the first.
```

CHAPTER 5

Methods

Much that needs to be said about defining methods has appeared in earlier chapters, but there are other important features of method definition.

Method Signatures

As shown in Chapter 3, "Java Program Features," a method signature's syntax looks like this:

```
<access modifier> <other modifiers> return-type
                method-name(<parameters>) <throws
                exception-class>
```

Again, the <> pairs mean this is optional. Unlike C, you do not need method prototypes. The compiler resolves method names which occur farther down in the class definition or in other classes without a problem, as long as the compiler can find the class and method. The same holds true for data members, which may be coded at the bottom of a class definition. The javac compiler doesn't care.

Parameter Names

Choose names carefully for clarity. Apart from names that don't communicate anything meaningful like doIt(), avoid the common technique of naming parameters the same as data members. Listing 5.1 shows poor parameter name choices.

Listing 5.1   Poor Parameter Name Choices
```
public class LibraryCard
    {
    String name;
      int value;
public boolean verify(String name, int value)
    {
      name = "Ted";   // Don't do this
```

continues

Listing 5.1 continued
```
                    // if you want to assign "Ted" to the
                    // data member name.
    }
}
```

When Java looks at a variable name in a method, it has to decide in each case whether you are referring to a data member, local variable, or parameter. By default, Java first assumes you meant a parameter. In the preceding code, that is not what was intended, because the string `"Ted"` is assigned not to the data member name but to the parameter name supplied in the method call. To avoid this confusion, you need a way to distinguish between the data member and the parameter.

this

This ambiguity in the code, which might result in unexpected results, is avoided by using the `this` object reference. The object reference that points to the current object whose code you are executing at the moment is `this`. You don't declare `this` yourself. It's supplied by the Java runtime system. So if I'm in the verify method, and I want to ask the current object to do something, I could code

```
this.someMethod();
```

Except for special uses we will see later, it is generally redundant to code `this`. In the preceding example, however, we need to use `this`. Listing 5.2 shows the class with a modification that removes the ambiguity and behaves as desired.

Listing 5.2 Using the this Object Reference to Disambiguate a Variable Name
```
public class LibraryCard
    {
      String name;
        int value;
public boolean verify(String name, int value)
      {
        this.name = "Ted";   //  Using "this" means
                             //  "apply this to the data member of this
                             //  instance."
        this.name = name;    //  You have to use "this" to assign the
                             //  parameter's value to the
                             //  data member if they have the same name.
      }
    }
```

> **NOTE**
>
> Using the name of a data member for a parameter is confusing. Also, writing extra code with `this` prefixed to it is really suboptimal. I recommend that you avoid having to do this, or having to remember, by always using a different parameter name than any data member name.

Modifiers

There are a numberof modifiers you can use concurrently or by themselves in the definition of a method. These modifiers, such as `final` and `static`, provide various functions in terms of how they make your methods behave. Each has design and execution considerations and consequences, so they should all be used with care. For example, the `final` modifier makes your method non-overrideable. That's good for security, but it might not be desirable if you are shipping classes that you expect others to subclass, because they will not be able to change a final method's definition. Static methods are methods that can be used independently of an instance. They can be handy for running mathematical formulas, but in general they make your code less flexible. A class with nothing but static methods isn't going to be meaningful to create instances of. Do you really want a singleton? If not, avoid static methods. Each modifier is explained in the following sections.

CAUTION

In a Java 2 environment, especially with Hotspot, you should not use `final` or `static` to get the compiler to inline the method. You do not want to tie the hands of the compiler or runtime system (Hotspot) that way, because your effort to make your code inlined may in fact result in suboptimal runtime execution. You should leave the compiler and the runtime environment, especially Hotspot, free to inline or not, as seems best to the JVM.

Final

A method that is marked `final` cannot be overridden. There are a couple of reasons to do this. One is for security purposes. If you want to be sure no one overrides your method and redirects a user ID and password—or the credit card number or other sensitive information—to an inappropriate destination, you should code your method as `final` so that no one can inherit the name and change its behavior in a subclass. Another reason might simply be that you really don't want anyone to change how the method works in a subclass. For example, it implements very specialized business logic that is very sensitive, and you don't want that logic modified at all. If the method is final, all subclasses get this sensitive logic for free, and if it needs to be changed, it needs to be changed only once, even though you also get the benefits of inheritance.

Static

Marking a method as `static` indicates that the method can be used with or without an object instance, because it is a *class method*. You might use this because you want to be able to use a method even if there is no instance of the class. The most important example is `main`, but you can easily do this with any class to do any sort of processing. From a practical perspective, you can think of a `static` method or variable as existing in memory only once. In other words, if five objects call a given static method, they are all calling the same copy. Static methods are associated with a class and are sometimes called *class methods*. You can invoke them without needing an object reference. Instead, you only need the name of the class and the name of the method. Here is a common example of this:

```
Properties p = System.getProperties();
```

The class `System` has several static methods, including one called `getProperties()`. To execute this method, it is not necessary (or, in this case, even possible) to obtain an object reference to the `System` class. Instead, you simply use the class name and append to it the name of the method. If you have a class that contains static methods, but you have one or more instances of it, you might use either the class name or the object reference name. For example, Listing 5.3 shows a class, `Catalog`, that has a static method and a public constructor.

Listing 5.3 A Class with a Static Method
```
public class Catalog
    {
    String catalogName;
    public Catalog(String name)  // Constructor
        {
          catalogName = name;
        }
    public static String getCatalogName()  // Accessor method
        {
          return catalogName;
        }
    }  // End Catalog class definition
```

Now, I can execute the `getCatalogName` static method two ways from another class:

```
public class Searcher
    {
    String name;   // Catalog name
    public Searcher()
        {
         name = Catalog.getCatalogName()
         // Use the class name
         Catalog myCat = new Catalog ("Aers and Letters");
         name = myCat.getCatalogName()
         // Create an instance and use the object reference name
        }
    }   // End Searcher class definition
```

CAUTION

Beware of making all your methods static. This might sound like an easy way to code, but it means that you never need a constructor. That's right. Since there are no instance methods, if all your data is defined as static, you never need to instantiate objects of this class. In fact, you can't instantiate objects of a class that has only static variables and static methods. You can have only one of whatever class you are defining in memory at once.

Also, you create problems for yourself if you want to serialize the object for this class. In the case of a static object, the one "object" essentially equals the in-memory copy of the class definition. Java provides only default values for static fields of serialized objects. Serialization is discussed fully in Chapter 12, "I/O in Java." This is a significant deficiency and should be avoided unless there are compelling reasons not to. The use of singletons also makes such classes difficult to subclass.

> **NOTE**
>
> An object that cannot be instantiated, for which there is always only one instance because all the data and methods are static, is called a *singleton* in design pattern parlance. Unless there is a clear rationale for having only one "instance," it is considered bad design to use only static methods and variables in an object.

The other main use of static methods is to simply execute a function, like computing a square root, in which you don't really need an object. Suppose you want to get a random number. You don't need any special objects. You only want a numeric value, so you use java.lang.Math's

```
public static double random()
```

method. This returns a "random" double number between equal to or greater than 0.0 and less than 1.0. Because that's all you wanted, there's no point in creating a Math object just to get this number. Thus, this method is a static method.

You might also use a static method when you need to run some code that does a task not specifically related to an object. An example is the

```
public static void gc()
```

method. This method requests that garbage collection take place. It is a static method in the System class. The java.lang.System class itself is a singleton that cannot be instantiated by any user-defined object. I don't specifically need an object after this method call; I just need a way to make the gc() call. You have to have some class own the method, because it's not legal to have a method outside a class. Therefore, an appropriate class was chosen for this method.

Access Modifiers

The purpose of access modifiers is to find which objects have access to your object's methods (or data members). In general, you want to provide public interfaces to your private data, while making most of your methods that do real work, as well as your data, private. There are times when other options might be desirable. For example, you might allow the classes in your package to have access to your methods. In this case, you might give them package-level access. Or, you might want all the classes of your package, and any subclasses in any other packages, to have access to your methods, an essential ingredient of inheritance by those subclasses. In that case, you might make your classes protected. For well-encapsulated classes, which minimize maintenance, I recommend that you keep your methods and data as inaccessible as possible while still providing for reasonable access by other objects to get work done. As stated in an earlier chapter, there are four access modifiers.

Public

Methods designated public can be called from any class in any package. Most of the methods in the JDK classes are public so you can call them from your own classes. Listing 5.4 shows the definition of public methods.

Listing 5.4 A Class with a Public Method
```
public class GUI extends Frame
    {
      public GUI()
          {
            setBackground(Color.blue);
            setSize(400,300);
            setVisible(true);
          }
      }  // End of GUI class definition
```

This class, GUI, extends Frame, and Frame inherits methods from Window, Container, and Component. Since those methods, like setVisible(), are public, I can call them from my GUI class.

Protected

If I used a methodthat was marked protected, I would only be able to call it, such as disableEvents(), from the java.awt package or from a subclass of Frame. I'd still be okay here because GUI subclasses and inherits from Frame. I changed my class definition so it does not subclass Frame, as shown in Listing 5.5.

Listing 5.5 A Class Illegally Using a Protected Method
```
public class GUI
    {
      Frame aFrame;
      public GUI()
          {
            aFrame = new Frame();
            aFrame.setBackground(Color.blue);
            aFrame.disableEvents();   // Error: Call to a protected
                                      // method from an ineligible
                                      // class
            aFrame.setSize(400,300);
            aFrame.setVisible(true);
          }
      }  // End of GUI class definition
```

Because disableEvents() was defined as protected rather than public, this class would not compile. This is because GUI would not be part of the same package, java.awt, and does not subclass Frame, so you would not have access to this method. It's okay to mark a method as protected. Just be sure you understand the implications of that access modifier. You restrict how your class can be used—at least, this method of your class.

Private

Private methods cannot be accessed by any object of another class, although they can be accessed from other methods defined by the same class. This is the appropriate access modifier for methods that do the real work in your class. They implement the actual logic that your object needs to carry out, such as validating data, and modifying private data members. In contrast to private methods, an object's public methods are for other objects to request that your object do something, and yet to not provide direct access to your object's data. A public method should then call a private method to get real work done. Listing 5.6 shows a class that declares both public and private methods accordingly.

Listing 5.6   A Class with Both Public and Private Methods

```
public class Book
    {
      private String borrower;
      public boolean checkOutBook(String borrowerID)
          {
            public boolean result;
            result = validateBorrower(borrowerID);
            result = checkOut(borrowerID);
            return result;
          }

      private boolean validateBorrower(String id)
          {
            result = false;
            // Check database for ID
            // if(id - CURRENT)
                 result = true;
            return result;
          }

      private boolean checkOut(String ID)
          {
            borrower = id;
          }
    }
```

In this code, checkOutBook() is marked public, so it can be called from anywhere. The method checkOut(), however, is marked private. This means that objects not of type Book cannot access this method.

TIP

Access level is an important design principle that will lower your program maintenance. If checkOut() were public, any object could call the method and set the borrower ID, even if the ID were totally bogus. Because the methods validateBorrower() and checkOut() are both private, the actual data member borrower is protected from any object that is not a Book, just putting whatever it wants to in this field when it publicly calls the checkOut() method. This means one kind of object cannot corrupt the data in an object of another class.

Making the methods that do actual work private, and having them called from public methods, also means that you can change your implementation all day long in validateBorrower(), such as switching from a flat file to an object database management system (ODBMS). No other class is affected by this change because no other class participates in how objects of your class get work done. This helps maximize encapsulation and cohesion and minimizes coupling between classes.

Package-Level Default

Package-level access limits access to methods of one class to only the same class or other classes in the same package. Package-level default access is more restrictive than protected but less restrictive than private access, in which objects can call the methods. There is no keyword for package-level access. This is the access level you get if you specify nothing. This permits classes in the same package to access methods of a class in the same package but doesn't allow subclasses outside of the package—or, indeed, any classes outside the package to use the method. You might find that for some classes that need to function solely inside a package, methods that you might otherwise mark as public should be package-level access, with the other methods of the class marked as private.

This could be reasonable if you had, say, a class that did bank transaction logging inside the Banking package but there was no reason for any class to subclass this application-specific class outside the package. Or, you might have a Catalog class in the gradschool.library package that should be accessible from classes that find books or add books to a Library object's collection, but there might not be a good reason to allow any class outside the gradschool.library package to access any methods of the Catalog class, while giving full access to the getter/setter methods of the Catalog class in other classes in the same package. Remember, you don't need to allow others to subclass your classes.

Other Modifiers

A number of other modifiers are useful in defining methods. You can specify that a method should synchronize its resources, or that the method is for a native code implementation. These options are discussed next.

Native

Declaring a method as native means that you are giving the signature for a method that will be actually coded in another language, such as C. You can then call this code from a Java method. This feature is called the Java Native Interface, or JNI. This is a big topic that whole books cover, so this section will just point you to the basics.

> **CAUTION**
> This topic has a lot of potential "gotchas," so I recommend it only for experienced Java programmers.

Native methods are used when you really need to accomplish something that you can't accomplish in the JVM. This might be special number crunching that you think might be better done in C, or it might be using C, for example, to call a proprietary API that Java can't call, like IMS DL/I to hook up Java to a legacy application. Since other languages such as C vary from platform to platform, calling a native method is by definition non-portable code. So if you decide to not write 100% pure Java applications, be aware that they will need even more testing because of the need to validate the non-Java code on multiple platforms.

Listing 5.7 shows a small sample class.

Listing 5.7   A Class That Declares a Native Method
```
public class IntenseMath
     {
       static
              {
                System.loadLibrary("intense");
              }

              public native long doIntenseCalculation(long numb);
     }
```

Notice that the `doIntenseCalculation()` method is marked as `native` but has no method body. A native method is implemented in another language, like C or C++. There are rules to observe about accessing Java data members, arrays, Strings and the like, and you'll need to check on them when you write JNI code.

After you've written the Java class(es) and the native methods in another language, you need to create a special JNI header, `.h`, file. You use the javah tool to do this. The header file must be named after the Java class that calls the native method. So in this example, the header file is called `IntenseMath.h`. The javah utility produces the header file for you, and you should not edit the file. You then need to use this header file in the native function. Once you've created the header file, and then created the native method, you need to compile them. As a last step, you need to create a shared library for the native code to reside in, which can then be loaded by Java when the static initializer method runs and loads the "intense" library. Because creating a shared library is a platform-specific activity, you need to check the specific syntax for your platform.

That's the minimal basics of doing this in Java. You can also call C++ functions, but you have to adhere to C naming conventions. In addition, JNI can allow your Java code to be called from C as well as making calls to C.

The keyword `native` signals to the compiler that the method implementation is done in another language elsewhere. Java uses native methods to call native peer code for AWT components all the time, so JNI, while not portable, is pretty common in the JDK, though Javasoft is working to reduce the amount of C code with each release. Finally, let me note that in Java 2, you can have control over the version of the shared library you load, and there is new support to avoid loading multiple copies of the same shared library or having namespace collisions.

Using JNI is a very complicated topic and is not "Pure Java," so it will not be covered further in this book.

Synchronized

You might mark a method as `synchronized`. What this does is cause Java to acquire a lock on the object whose synchronized method was invoked. This prevents other

72 Chapter 5: Methods

threads from invoking this or another synchronized method on the same object simultaneously. The general purpose of marking a method as synchronized is to protect resources from being corrupted. To illustrate this, think about a semaphore object—a flag that shows whether a particular resource is in use. Listing 5.8 shows a class with such a flag, used to track appointments at the library's reference desk.

Listing 5.8   A Class That Illustrates a Resource That Can Be Changed Incorrectly by Multiple Threads

```
class ApptBook
    {
      Vector appts;       // A Vector for storing Appointment objects
      boolean inUseFlag;  // A flag to show if the ApptBook object is
                          // in use
      ApptBook()
         {
           appts = new Vector(50,2);
                       // Instantiate the appts Vector, being careful
                       // to specify an initial number
                       // of elements and a reasonable
                       // amount by which to increase the capacity
              inUseFlag = false;
         }
      boolean addAnAppt(Appointment app)
             {
                       // You'd have to define an Appointment
                       // class for this to compile
                boolean result = false;
                if(inUseFlag == false)
                       // If the ApptBook object is not in use,
                       // do this:
                   {
                     InUseFlag = true;
                       // Set the flag to show this ApptBook
                       // object is in use
                      appts.addElement(app);
                      result = false;
                   }
                 inUseFlag = false;
                       // Show you are done with the ApptBook
                       // object
              return result;
             }
     } // End class definition for ApptBook
```

There's a potential problem. If multiple threads call the addAnAppt method at the same time, you could get corrupted data. Here's how:

1. ThreadA calls addAnAppt and sees that the inUseFlag equals false but stops running before the inUseFlag is set to true.
2. ThreadB calls addAnAppt and sees that the inUseFlag equals false.

3. ThreadB adds an element.
4. ThreadA adds an element, now in the wrong order.

Without making this more complicated, the simple issue is that, because you can't predict when a given thread will stop or start executing, especially when moving from platform to platform, you have no idea where in this code you might be when your thread stops or starts running again. This could lead to data inconsistency because one thread thinks that the inUseFlag is false when logically it should not be because the other thread has already tested it and should have exclusive control of the ApptBook object. We need a way to prevent ThreadB from entering the addAnAppt method at all until ThreadA has executed the entire method, no matter how long that takes. Listing 5.9 shows an improved version that does not have the potential for incorrect changes being made to the inUseFlag by multiple threads. The way to do this is with the synchronized keyword.

Listing 5.9 A Class Illustrating the Use of the synchronized Keyword
```
class ImprovedApptBook
    {
    Vector appts;       // A Vector for storing Appointment objects
    boolean inUseFlag;  // A flag to show if the ApptBook object is
                        // in use
    ImprovedApptBook()
        {
        appts - new Vector(50,2);
                    // Instantiate the appts Vector, being careful
                    // to specify an initial number of elements and
                    // a reasonable amount by which to increase the
                    // capacity
            inUseFlag = false;
        }
    synchronized boolean addAnAppt(Appointment app)
            {
                    // You'd have to define an Appointment
                    // class for this to compile
            boolean result = false;
            if(inUseFlag == false)
                    // If the ApptBook object is not in use,
                    // do this:
                {
                InUseFlag = true;
                    // Set the flag to show this ApptBook object is
                    // in use
                appts.addElement(app);
                result = false;
                }
            inUseFlag = false;
                    // Show you are done with the ApptBook object
            return result;
            }
    } // End class definition for ImprovedApptBook
```

> **NOTE**
>
> With the addition of the `synchronized` keyword, the `inUseFlag` is unnecessary. Since only one thread might call the method at a time, only one thread might act upon the object at runtime. I've left it in to illustrate that a synchronized method can be used to protect a resource.

I've added the keyword `synchronized` to the `addAnAppt` method. This simple change guarantees that only one caller can execute this code at one time. The way this works is that the objects in a synchronized method each have an object lock. That lock is acquired by the first caller of the method. You have to have the object lock to enter the synchronized method. In my office, there's a supply cabinet. To open the cabinet, you have to have the key. There is only one key. So if you get to the key when it's not in use, you can go open the supply cabinet. If the key is in use, you have to wait for whomever has the key to bring it back, and then it's your turn.

When a synchronized method is exited, the object lock is released by the holder and can be acquired by another caller. If that caller has been waiting to enter the synchronized method, it now acquires the object lock and may enter the code. It's possible to have many callers waiting for the object lock at one time. See Chapter 11, "Multithreaded Programming in Java," for more information on synchronized methods.

Overloading Methods

The basic idea of overloading a method is that it is easier to call a method called `println` with varying data types, like this:

```
System.out.println(some String)
System.out.println(some double)
System.out.println(some boolean)
```

than to have to call special methods for each of these (the following are fictitious methods that don't exist):

```
System.out.printlnString(some String)
System.out.printlnDouble(some double)
System.out.printlnBoolean(some boolean)
```

In the first set of methods, I, as the programmer, don't have to remember or look up 5, 10, or 20 versions of `println` in order to call it for multiple data types. The Java designers thought the first form was easier. As a result, Java provides the ability for you to define multiple versions of the same method which must differ only in the parameter list. This makes calling the `println` method much easier. As long as there's a form of `println` defined that accepts the data type you supply, the compiler will select the correct version of the method and at runtime you will call that specific version of the method. You may change other features of the method signature as well, such as the return type, but the key thing that you need to change is the type and/or number of parameters. Another example would be a `Painter` class with a `draw` method. You could call the `draw` method, passing in one of a set of given shapes, such as

```
public boolean draw(Rectangle r)
public boolean draw(Ellipse e)
public boolean draw(Point p)
```

All you really need to know is that to get a shape drawn, you need a `Painter` object instance and that the `Painter` object has a draw method. You call `draw()` and pass in a shape and the `Painter` takes care of the rest, because the compiler figures out which of the several `draw()` methods you need to have invoked. So if you define a class that needs to do a similar kind of thing to multiple kinds of primitives or objects, consider using overloaded methods.

Polymorphism: Overriding Methods

It's common, when you create subclasses from a base class, to need to change the way a specific method is implemented. If your subclass modifies the method signature or behavior of a method that it inherits from a superclass (within certain limits), we call that method in the subclass an "overridden method." Let's look at an example in Listing 5.10.

Listing 5.10   An Example of a Superclass and a Subclass That Overrides a Method of the Superclass

```
public class Book
    {
      public GregorianCalendar dueDate;
      public boolean checkOut()
          {
            dueDate = new
                       GregorianCalendar(new
                       ↪SimpleTimeZone(-8 * 60 * 60 * 1000,
                       ↪zoneID));
                       // This is insufficient code
                       // for making a proper GregorianCalendar
                       // object, but it will serve as an
                       // illustration. You'll have to add more
                       // to get a real GregorianCalendar object.
                       dueDate.set((Calendar.DAY_OF_YEAR)+28);
                       // Set the due date to be four weeks from now.
                       return true;
          }
    } // End definition of class Book
class ReservedBook extends Book
    {
      public boolean checkOut()
          {
             super.checkOut();   // First, optionally, call the parent's
                                 // version of the method.
             dueDate.set()Calendar.DAY_OF_YEAR)-27);
                                 // Reserved books may be checked
                                 // out for only one day, so reset
                                 // the due date by subtracting 27 days
```

continues

Listing 5.10 continued

```
                            // from it. Still, we need a dueDate
                            // data member, so call on the
                            // superclass's method by the same name
                            // to do its work, and then tweak that
                            // result or do any extra work you might
                            // need to do.
        return true;
    }
}   // End definition of class ReservedBook
```

What I've done here is created a `Book` class and defined a `checkOut()` method in it. In that method, I create a `GregorianCalendar` object to represent the due date for when the book must be returned to the library. I'm assuming here a four-week period that a patron can have a book checked out from the library. This is the `checkOut()` method for a normal `Book`. If a book is on reserve for some reason (such as when a professor wants it available readily to everyone in a class), the book can only be checked out for one day.

At the same time, there's no need to write the code to create a `GregorianCalendar` object twice, once in `Book` and once in `ReservedBook`. Instead, my `ReservedBook` class needs to modify the logic for setting the due date just a bit. Therefore, I'll modify the `checkedOut()` method in the `ReservedBook` class by overriding it, but I can still call the `checkedOut()` method of the parent class, `Book`. It's not at all a requirement for the subclass to call the superclass's overridden method. It was useful here, but might not be in other cases.

There are some rules about what you can do in an overridden method in the subclass:

- You cannot override a superclass's static method as an instance method. This would not change just the logic carried out by the method, but also the nature of the method, making it an instance method instead of a class method. It is permissible for a subclass to override a static method in a superclass, which effectively hides the static method in the superclass. It is also illegal for a static method in a subclass to override an instance method in a superclass. It is legal for a static variable to override an instance variable.
- An overridden method cannot throw more `Exception` types than the superclass's version. I'll cover exceptions in Chapter 10, "Exceptions." For right now, simply accept that in the definition of a method you can list exceptions that can be thrown by the method, as shown in Listing 5.11.

Listing 5.11   A Class with a Method Declaring That It Throws Exceptions
```
public class Networking
    {
        public boolean ping() throws IOException, MalformedURLException
            {
                // Ping the server
            }
    }   // End of class definition Networking
```

Polymorphism: Overriding Methods 77

In this class, the `ping()` method is declared as throwing two Exception subtypes: IOException and MalformedURLException. Don't worry about what these are. You'll learn about them later. What's important to note here is that the method signature says that it is possible, in case of error, for this method to throw one of these two Exception types. Now, if I code a subclass, I can declare fewer Exception types, but not more. Listing 5.12 illustrates this.

Listing 5.12   A Subclass That Overrides a Method and Declares That It Throws Fewer Exceptions than the Superclass's Version
```
public class NetProtocolA extends Networking
    {
    public boolean ping() throws IOException
            {
            // Do a ping with this network protocol,
            // but since this protocol doesn't deal
            // with URLs, it makes no sense to
            // declare that your method can throw
            // a MalformedURLException. That will
            // never happen, so don't make other
            // developers write code to catch
            // this when it can't happen.
            }
    } // End class definition for NetProtocolA
```

I've removed one of the Exception subtypes because this networking protocol doesn't deal with URLs. This is legal to do. On the other hand, the code in Listing 5.13 is definitely *not* legal.

Listing 5.13   A Subclass That Illegally Overrides a Method Based on the Declaration of Thrown Exceptions
```
public class NetProtocolB extends Networking
    {
    public boolean ping() throws IOException,
    ↪MalformedURLException, RemoteException
                    // DON'T DO THIS. IT'S ILLEGAL
            {
            // Do a ping with this network protocol.
            }
    } // End class definition for NetProtocolB
```

Here I've overridden the `ping()` method and declared that it can potentially throw one of three Exception subtypes. This is not legal and won't compile.
- A third requirement is that the overridden method must have the same return type. You cannot change return types or go from a void to a specific return type. So you can't write the code shown in Listing 5.14.

Listing 5.14 A Class That Illegally Overrides a Superclass's Method by Changing the Return Type
```
public class Book
    {
      public boolean checkOut()
           {
           //  Check out a book
           }
    }
class ReservedBook extends Book
    {
       public String checkOut() // ILLEGAL. Won't compile.
           {
              // Check out a reserved book
           }
    }
```

- You are not permitted to make the overridden method more private in access than the superclass's method. For example, if the method in the superclass is public, you cannot make the overridden method version protected. You can, however, make your method more public. This way, if the parent's method is protected, you can override the method and make it public. Listing 5.15 shows an example.

Listing 5.15 An Example of a Subclass That Overrides a Parent's Method by Making the Access Level Broader from Where It Permits Access
```
public class Book
    {
      boolean checkOut() // The access level is package-level default
           {
           //  Check out a book
           }
    }
class ReservedBook extends Book
    {
       public String checkOut() // The overridden method's access level
                                // is public, which means more objects
                                // can call this method than the
                                // parent's version.
           {
              // Check out a reserved book
           }
    }
```

Also note that you cannot override a private method in a superclass. You can't really see this method anyway, so that shouldn't be a problem. However, you might want to think about whether a superclass should have private methods.

CHAPTER 6

Interfaces

I said previously that everything in a Java program is done by objects interacting with other objects and that those objects must be defined by classes. Well, that's basically true, but there is one important exception. Java has a special entity called an *interface*. I don't mean the term in the generic sense that *interface* is often used in software parlance, as a way to access some code. This use of interface essentially refers a list of abstract methods that specifies the names of behaviors that classes can have. An interface, however, has no implementation of the methods in it. Abstract methods have no implementation, but must be implemented by a subclass of the abstract class that declares the abstract method(s). There is, however, another way to create abstract methods. They can be declared in an interface. The Java 2 SDK provides several excellent examples of what an interface can do.

> **TIP**
>
> An interface is a powerful mechanism for defining behavior among unrelated classes. I suggested earlier that an abstract class is a good tool for enforcing common behavior among related subclasses. An interface is an effective way to enforce behavior among potentially unrelated classes.

An Example from GUI Event-Handling Interfaces

Let me illustrate interfaces through GUI event handling. An event is basically an action such as clicking a button, selecting a Menu item, or clicking on an item in a List box. The type of event that is generated when you click a Java button object with the mouse is an `ActionEvent`.

Chapter 6: Interfaces

Think of all the Applets and applications written in Java that have an OK or Submit button or the like. No one class, even with hundreds of methods, could provide for all these buttons.

This problem is solved by using an interface for event handling. An interface declares the name of the method to call, but it leaves the implementation of OK-button logic completely open. It also provides for a common method name where this code can be placed. The mechanism created to do this is in the form of an interface, the `ActionListener` interface, which is defined in the following way:

```
public abstract interface ActionListener extends EventListener
```

Because this is an interface, it does not define a class. In fact, an interface can only contain `public`, `static`, `final` data members and `abstract` methods.

> **NOTE**
>
> Notice that the interface signature, which is similar to a class signature, contains the word `abstract`. Because an interface is abstract by definition, including the word `abstract` is not necessary, but there's no harm in doing so. You might keep the `abstract` keyword in your own interface definitions to remind people that they must implement the methods in it if they use the interface.

It is possible for one interface to inherit from, or extend, another interface. This is fairly common in the Java 2 SDK.

This interface has only one method defined in it:

```
public void actionPerformed(ActionEvent event);
```

Briefly, here's how GUI event handling works:

1. You create a GUI object.
2. You create an object that implements the `ActionListener` interface. That means the object implements all the methods in the `ActionListener` interface. There's only one method in this interface, so a class that implements it only has to implement that one method. For example,

    ```
    class OKButtonHandler implements ActionListener
        {
           public void actionPerformed(ActionEvent event)
               {
                   // Handle a click of the OK button in the window
               }
        }
    ```

3. Hook up this class to the OK button with code like this:

    ```
    okButton.addActionListener(new OKButtonHandler());
    ```

Now, here's how the use of the interface benefits a developer. The addActionListener method registers an instance of the OKButtonHandler class with the Java runtime. That registration tells the JVM that, when an ActionEvent is created for a click on the okButton GUI component, the object that ought to handle this ActionEvent is the instance of the OKButtonHandler class.

There's a special mechanism to tell Java which method to call in the OKButtonHandler class. Java doesn't really know anything much about the OKButtonHandler class. However, Java does know that this object is an ActionListener object. That means Java knows that you have promised that this object implements the ActionListener interface. Because this object implements this interface, you have set up a contract with the Java runtime that your object has an actionPerformed() method. Therefore, the object that keeps track of registered event-handler objects, AwtEventMulticaster, knows that it can simply call the appropriate method for any object that implements the ActionListener interface: actionPerformed. So, without knowing anything about your listener object and without having a clue about what your OK button needs to do in your application or Applet, the Java runtime can get a mouse click on the OK button, generate an ActionEvent instance, and call the actionPerformed() method of the OKButtonHandler object.

By saying your class implements an interface, you are making a contract with the system that you are going to implement all the methods of the interface your class is declared to implement. So, for example, if you have

```
public class CatalogSearcher implements Runnable
```

you've just made a promise to the system that your CatalogSearcher class implements all the methods in the Runnable interface. There happens to be only one such method:

```
public void run()
```

You use the Runnable interface for working with threads. So when you create and start a thread, the JVM knows that it can call the run() method of the CatalogSearcher class. In this way, a Java interface enables you to declare to the Java runtime that you are going to require your class to implement methods of an interface. You can use this to enforce common behavior, with different implementations, across numerous, disparate, unrelated classes.

You do not have to deal with events to use interfaces. You might have an interface that declares the methods to be used by the data model in a model-view-controller architecture. The controller component does not need to know anything about the data model. It only needs to know about the methods listed in the interface. The controller can then simply call those methods on any object that implements the interface. I strongly recommend this as a design approach. It helps separate the view from the data model. Other examples in the Java 2 SDK where an interface is used include Observer-Observable, the Runnable interface for multithreading, and the interfaces in java.sql which form the basis of how JDBC lets you communicate with databases in a database-neutral way. JDBC provides an excellent example of something else that interfaces are

82 Chapter 6: Interfaces

good for. Let's say that you want to create an object, and it's not so important to you from which class the object is instantiated. Rather, what's really important is that the object implements a given interface.

Everything you've studied for creating an object returns an object that is of a specific class type—for example,

```
Window w = new Window();
```

There is, however, a way to define a method that can return multiple kinds of objects. You can code the following:

```
Connection conn = DriverManager.getConnection(dataaseURL);
```

Without explaining at this moment what a database URL is or what a database connection is, I want you to notice that Connection is not a class name. It is the name of an interface found in the java.sql package. What this line of code says is, "Return to me any object whatsoever that implements the Connection interface." As you'll see later, that might mean a database connection to an Oracle database, a Sybase database, or a database connection to an InstantDB database. You don't know, and it does not matter as far as you're concerned. You just need an object that implements all the methods in the Connection interface. So, let me emphasize again: an interface is essentially a contract between the implementing class and other classes that all the methods in the interface are available in the class that implements the interface.

In the same way that a class is defined, an interface is defined in a .java file in this way:

```
public interface Logging
    {
      public boolean writeLog(byte[] logrec);
  // Write a log record with an arbitrary byte array
    }
```

This interface should be defined in a .java file, generally without any other classes or other interfaces. You put this in a file named Logging.java.

So far, I've talked mainly about methods. It is possible to define variables in an interface. You might want all classes that implement the interface to have these variables, defined as static final constants, available to them. So, you might decide that the file name you want an object to use when writing a log file is Logging.txt. You could provide for this by making that name a constant in the Logging interface:

```
public interface Logging
    {
      public static final String Logging_File_Name = "Logging.txt";
      public boolean writeLog(byte[] logrec);
  // Write a log record with an arbitrary byte array
    }
```

Interface Contents

All the variables in an interface need to be `public`, `final`, and `static`. That's reasonable because you are trying to assure that all classes using the interface have this same value. If you want a common variable, it is implemented by a base class.

Interface Contents

Here again are the elements that can go into an interface:

- `public`, `static`, `final` data members. This is about the closest you get in Java to a global constant. By default, even if you don't declare them as such, all the data members of an interface are `public`, `static`, and `final`. So you could code
  ```
  int MAIN_BRANCH_NUMBER = 01;
  ```
  or you could code
  ```
  public static final int MAIN_BRANCH_NUMBER = 01;
  ```
  The Java Language Specification says that it is strongly discouraged to redundantly specify these keywords. I happen to disagree and feel strongly that, for the sake of those who don't know the rules, you should specify the keywords. Doing so is useful for documentation purposes and certainly doesn't hurt anything. What's more, the keywords show that the developer understands what he or she is doing. You can, however, omit them without the compiler giving you any grief.

- abstract methods
  By definition, all the methods in an interface are `abstract` because they have no implementation. So it's legal to code
  ```
  public interface Logging
      {
        public abstract boolean writeLog(byte[] logRec);
      }
  ```

You are not allowed to put any code in the `writeLog()` method inside the interface definition. Like an `abstract` method inherited by a concrete subclass, a class that is declared as implementing an interface must implement every single method in the interface. So, in a class that implements the `Logging` interface, you must implement the `writeLog()` method, or the class definition will not compile. Here is a legal version of a class that implements logging:

```
public CardCatalog implements Logging
    {
      public boolean writeLog(byte{} logrec)
          {
              System.out.println(logrec);  // Write the log record to the
                                           // command line. You probably
                                           // wouldn't do this in real life
                                           // but it illustrates a way to
                                           // implement the interface's
                                           // writeLog method.
          }
    }   // End class definition for CardCatalog
```

Chapter 6: Interfaces

There might be times when an interface contains one or more methods that you have no interest in implementing. The requirement to implement all the methods can be met in a fairly minimal way. The following illustrates this idea.

```
public CardCatalog implements Logging
    {
      public boolean writeLog(byte[] logrec)
            {
                // A pair of curly braces and nothing more constitutes
                //"implementing" a method
            }
    }   // End class definition for CardCatalog
```

If you do not want to have the method do anything, you can simply code a pair of curly braces and leave it at that. This makes the compiler happy, and you don't have to write any code. In general, outside of GUI event handling, you probably won't do this. If, however, you don't want to implement a method, the preceding code shows you how to avoid it. Be aware, of course, that if you do this for certain methods and interfaces, you defeat the point of the interface. For example, you never want to do this:

```
public class CatalogSearcher implements Runnable
    {
      public void run()
            [
                // the run() method has no code in it
            }
    }
```

The preceding code ensures that, if someone tries to create a `Thread` and use your `run()` method, nothing happens. The `Thread` becomes dead essentially immediately. (Other users will know your class has the `run()` method because it implements the `Runnable` interface.) There's no point to making a class `Runnable` if you don't implement the `run()` method with actual code.

Finally, you have to make an interface available to classes just as though it were a class. You must compile the interface. If you used the `Logging` interface above, and put it in a file called `Logging.java`, you would compile it like this:

```
javac Logging.java
```

Compiling an interface creates a `.class` file, even if the contents do not represent a class as such.

CHAPTER 7

Syntax

Now that you've got the object-oriented foundation down, you can look at the basic syntax elements. Here Java will look very much like C, and that's by design. One of Java's design goals, as you may remember from Chapter 1, "What Is Java?," is to be easy for C programmers to learn. Therefore, a lot of the basic syntax is the same.

Punctuation

You've already seen the basics of Java punctuation. Statements are ended with a semicolon (;). You can also use the comma to separate identifiers, like this:

```
int x, y, z; // This declares three ints, called x, y and
z respectively
```

The other main punctuation you regularly use are curly braces. You use curly braces, followed by no punctuation, to delimit class definitions and method definitions, like this:

```
class Book
    {
    method checkOut()
         {
         } // End definition of method checkOut()
    } // End of class definition for Book
```

Class definitions are not followed by a semicolon as a C struct or C++ class definition is. Also, as noted earlier, all the methods of a given class must be defined inside the curly braces that delimit the class definition. Parentheses are used to enclose the parameters for a method call and are included in the method signature, even if there are no parameters. Finally, like C, extra white space is ignored by the Java compiler. So, whether you write elegant, highly readable code, like

```
public class Book
    {
      public String author = "none";
      public String title = "none";
      public String isbn;
      public String callnumber;
       public boolelan checkOut()
             {
               int checkOutPeriod = 28;
               // Do checkOut logic here
             }
    }
```

or relatively unreadable code (like the following) is up to you.

```
public class Book  {
      public String author = "none"; public String title = "none";
      public String isbn, callnumber;
       public boolean checkOut()  { int checkOutPeriod = 28;
              // Do checkOut logic here  }   }
```

I think the former is much more readable and easier to maintain, so I recommend its use. In particular, aligning curly braces vertically rather than using K & R-style, which buries curly braces in code, will make your code much more readable and will help resolve unmatched curly brace errors.

Keywords

Java has several keywords. You should avoid giving classes, methods, or variables the same names as these keywords. You've already seen several of them, but for completeness, here are several of the common keywords:

abstract	static	break
native	class	if
volatile	interface	else
public	for	do
private	default	while
protected	void	switch
synchronized	return	case
instanceof	package	continue
final	import	

> **NOTE**
>
> Java has the keyword goto, but it is merely reserved. It is not implemented, so you cannot use goto yourself for anything, nor can you, thankfully, use goto in your code.

Operators

There are several kinds of operators in Java, including relational, bitwise, and arithmetic.

Logical Operators

The two logical operators in Java are

AND: &&

OR: ||

These are primarily used in `if` and `while` tests. For example, you might have

```
if(x > 5 && y < 12)          // if both conditions are true,
                             // do the following
    System.out.println("x qualifies");
else                         // They are not both true
    if(a ==3 || b < 7)       // if one or both of these
                             // conditions is true do the
                             // following code
        System.out.println("a might qualify");
```

The AND condition says that both Boolean tests must resolve to `true` for the overall test to be `true`. Remember that an `if` test must resolve to a Boolean condition of `true` or `false`. The OR test says that either the first or subsequent Boolean tests must resolve to `true` for the overall statement to resolve to `true`.

> **NOTE**
>
> Java uses "short-circuit" processing of && and ||. That is, if the system can tell that the first condition makes the statement `true` or `false` and doesn't need to check the second condition, it omits the second test. For example, if I code
>
> if(a == 1 && b == 2)
>
> and a does not equal 1, the system won't bother performing the test of b because the outcome of that test won't affect whether the whole statement evaluates to `true`. The test of a == 1 already resolved to `false`, making the whole expression false.

Arithmetic Operators

First there are the basic operators for doing arithmetic:

+ Adds two numbers together.

- Subtracts one number from another.

Chapter 7: Syntax

* Multiplies two numbers together.
/ Divides one number by another.
% Modulo division of one number by another. This returns only the remainder from a division.

There are also postfix operators that provide shorthand notation for operations on two operands. So, instead of coding

```
int x = 7;
 x = x +5;
```

you can simply code

```
x+= 5;
```

There is likewise a complementary -= operator that behaves similarly, except that it performs subtraction. There are also similar operators for most operations, such as

&= which means op1 = op1 & op2

¦= which means op 1= op1 ¦ op2

<<= which means op1 = op1 << op2

>>=which means op1 = op1 >> op2

>>>= which means op1 = op1 >>> op2

^= which means op1 = op1 % op2

NOTE

These operators can be used within the scope of other expressions. So you might code
```
if((x ++ y) >10) // Add x to y and then compare to 10
```

Increment/Decrement Operators: ++ and --

Another useful pair of arithmetic operators are the increment and decrement operators. These two operators add or subtract one from the value of a variable—for example,

```
int x = 6;
x++;  // After this statement, x equals 7
x—;   // After this statement, x equals 6
It is legal, of course, to code
x = x -1;
```

and

```
x = x + 1;
```

The increment and decrement operators are merely shorthand ways of doing this, as are the prefix and postfix operators. Like the former, because you can use the increment and decrement operators in compound statements, you want to be careful when you decide whether to code

```
x++
```

or

```
++x
```

The former expression evaluates to the value of x and then adds one to it. The latter, ++x, adds one to x first and then evaluates x to determine the value of the expression. Java *always* evaluates expressions from left to right. Operators of equal precedence are also evaluated from left to right. Therefore, ++x is evaluated first, and then x is evaluated in a compound expression. So,

```
int y = 0;
y = (x++) - c;
```

has a different result from

```
int y =0;
y = (++x) -c;
```

In the first version, c is subtracted from x, the result is put in y, and then x is incremented by one. In the second, x is incremented by one, c is subtracted from it, and then the result is put into y. So the order of operation is important.

Relational Operators

These operators are used to compare two operands. They include

==	Is equal
!=	Is not equal
<	Is less than
>	Is greater than
<=	Is less than or equal to
>=	Is greater than or equal to
!	Not

These should be fairly self-explanatory. They are used in `if` and `while` tests, like this:

```
while(x <= 19)
    {
       // Do some logic here until x is greater than 19
    }
```

One of the really big improvements in basic syntax in Java or C relates to the == operator. In C, it is possible to code:

```
if(x = y)  // Legal in C, ILLEGAL in Java
```

Frequently, such code is written accidentally. It was meant to be

```
if(x == y)  // Legal in Java and C
```

The = assignment operator merely assigns one operator to another. In this case, x would be given the value in y. The == equality relational operator, on the other hand, just tests for equality. In the first case, the C compiler lets you assign y to x, and then tests to see if x is non-zero. If so, the statement is true. As noted previously, Java requires tests to resolve to true Boolean statements that equal true or false. Therefore, (x = y) is not that kind of statement because an assignment never resolves in Java to true or false; therefore, you must use the == operator to compare two values for equality. In this way, Java eliminates a common and hard-to-find bug that has caused unexpected results in more than one C program.

CAUTION

You might run into trouble if you code

```
if(aBooelan = aBoolean)
```

because this is one exception to what is required to make the statement resolve to a Boolean. Because one does not usually compare Boolean variables, this error is unlikely but possible.

The ?: Operator

Because the ?: operator also relates to testing for equality, it belongs with these relational operators. This operator is shorthand for an if statement. Here is its syntax:

```
<test condition> ? <return value for true> : <return value for false>
```

Here's an example:

```
int w = a < b ? 5 : 4;
```

This statement says, if a is less than b, set w to 5. Otherwise, set w to 4. Although this notation exists, it is not used very often, and it is recommended that you use more common if-else statements for readability, but it is certainly syntactically legal. This statement can be used for assignment, as in the preceding statement, but can also be used in other contexts in which you need to evaluate a value.

Bitwise Operators

Java provides several operators that let you work on data at the bit level. You might, for example, want to save space in memory by putting several flags into one byte, representing each by one bit. Applied to a character in a word processing program, the flags might mean highlighted or normal, fixed width font or proportional font, italic or normal, and so on, with each bit representing two possible states, based on the fact that a bit can only be zero (off) or one (on). Or, you might use a set of bits to show which rows in a page of a relational database table are locked, provided your RDBMS supports row-level locking. There are numerous applications, and bits are regularly used this way to describe the pixels on a computer screen.

The operators used for modifying bits in Java are identical to C, except for the >>> operator described following. Here's a brief overview of how the bitwise operators work. The scope of this book does not allow a tutorial on binary arithmetic, so if you are not familiar with this, you might wish to consult a book that discusses hexadecimal numbers and hex arithmetic in detail. For some applications, the bitwise operators are just the right tool for the job. It's possible, however, to go through your whole programming career and never use them, so if this is very foreign, don't stress over it. Here are the bitwise operators.

NOTE

Java likes to work at the `int` level, not at the byte level. That means that, for the bit shift operators in particular, even if what you try to use is a byte, Java will first promote it to an `int` before evaluating the expression. This can lead to unexpected results, such as compiler problems for mismatched types, if you try to work with values of different sizes or of too small a size. Always be sure to provide for getting an `int` result, or be sure to cast the result to something more appropriate for your application.

AND: &

The & operator is used to AND two sets of bits together. Here's how it works. Java compares the bits in the same bit position in each of the two operands. So, for example, bit 6 in operand1 is compared to bit 6 in operand2. You should count bits from the left to the right for this discussion, and the first position is bit 0.

```
byte b1 = 15;
byte b2 = 12;
b1 &= b2;
```

When Java does an AND operation, it looks at the corresponding bits in each operand and either changes the value in the result, or uses the current value from operand1. Here are the rules for what is done:

- If the bits in both operands equal 1, the bit in the result is set to 1.
- If the bit in one operand is 1 and the bit in the other operand is 0, the bit in the result is set to 0.
- If the bits in both operands are 0, the bit in the result is set to 0.

Figure 7.1 illustrates these rules.

Op1	Op2	Op1 & Op2
0	0	0
0	1	0
1	0	0
1	1	1

Figure 7.1

The result from an AND operation.

Now back to the code snippet. In binary, these are the representations of b1 and b2, and the results when you AND them together:

```
b1    00001111 &
b2    00001010
----------
b1    00001010
```

You can use the & operator to keep a bit on if it's on in another operand; otherwise, turn it off.

OR: |

The | operator is used to OR two sets of bits together. Here's how it works. Java compares the bits in the same bit position in each of the two operands. So, for example, bit 6 in operand1 is compared to bit 6 in operand2. You should count bits from the left to the right for this discussion, and the first position is bit 0.

```
byte b1 = 15;
byte b2 = 26;
b1 |= b2;
```

When Java does an OR operation, it looks at the corresponding bits in each operand and either changes the value for the result or leaves it as it is in operand1. Here are the rules for what is done:

- If the bits in both operands equal 1, the bit in the result is set to 1.
- If the bit in one operand is 1 and the bit in the other operand is 0, the bit in the result is set to 1.
- If the bits in both operands are 0, the bit in the result is set to 0.

Figure 7.2 illustrates these rules.

Op1	Op2	Op1 | Op2
0	0	0
0	1	1
1	0	1
1	1	1

Figure 7.2
The result from an OR operation.

Now back to the code snippet. Here, in binary, are the representations of b1 and b2, and what you get when you OR them together:

```
b1      00001111 |
b2      00011010
----------
b1      00011111
```

You can use the | operator to keep a bit on if it's on in either operand.

XOR: ^

The ^ operator is used to XOR, or exclusively OR, two sets of bits together. Here's how it works. Java compares the bits in the same bit position in each of the two operands. So, for example, bit 6 in operand1 is compared to bit 6 in operand2. You should count bits from the left to the right for this discussion, and the first position is bit 0.

```
byte b1 = 10;
byte b2 = 12;
b1 ^= b2;
```

When Java does an XOR operation, it looks at the corresponding bits in each operand and either changes the value for the result or leaves it as it is in operand1. Here are the rules for what is done:

- If the bits in both operands equal 1, the bit in the result is set to 0.
- If the bit in one operand is 1 and the bit in the other operand is 0, the bit in the result is set to 1.
- If the bits in both operands are 0, the bit in the result is set to 0.

Figure 7.3 illustrates these rules.

Op1	Op2	Op1 ^ Op2
0	0	0
0	1	1
1	0	1
1	1	0

Figure 7.3

The result from an exclusive OR operation.

Now back to the code snippet. Here, in binary, are the representations of b1 and b2 and what you get when you XOR them together:

```
b1    00001010 ^
b2    00001100
-----------
b1    00000110
```

So you can use the ^ operator to essentially flip bits on and off. Because the XOR can flip bits like this, it is often used in graphics operations. You can modify the screen and then do an XOR to restore the original state of pixels.

Left Shift: <<

The left and right shift operators essentially do binary arithmetic on the operand. They multiply (left shift) or divide (right shift) the operand by a power of 2. You should think of each bit position in a byte as a power of two. In a byte, the right-most bit is the bit position for 2^0. The left-most bit in a byte is the bit position for 2^7. It's important to remember that when doing this sort of operation, as in other mathematical operations, Java promotes bytes to ints. It is best to define operands that you want to do bit shifts on as ints or longs to start. Ints are better because longs require emulation, which can cause a performance problem. Here's an example of how the << operator works.

```
Byte b =3;   // The binary representation of b is 00000011
b = b << 2;  // Multiply b by 2²
```

The result of this operation is that b now equals 00001100. That is, all the bits were shifted left two positions. In the statement

```
b = b << 2;
```

the 2 indicates how many places to shift the bits to the left, or what power of two by which to multiply the byte b. Also, like all mathematical operations in Java, bit shift operations are signed. So numbers are kept positive or negative as a rule, except when you use the >>> operator.

> **NOTE**
>
> Due to hardware issues, Java will not perform a shift of 32. If you specify 32 for the number of bits to shift left or right, Java will do nothing. If you specify a number higher than 32, Java will shift it by the modulo of the number you specify and 32 (number of places to shift%32).

You can use the << operator to multiply, or shift, bits to the left, with zeros filling in the low-order bits. This does not apply to the sign bit, the left-most bit position. If the high-order bit was 0 to start, at the end of the shift, it is still 0. If the high-order bit is 1, which means the number is negative, the high-order bit is still one after the shift operation (except, possibly, in the case of an overflow). One of the consequences of this is that if you do a left or right shift operation on a byte, rather than an int, when Java promotes the byte to an int, you might get this:

```
byte b = -1;  // Binary form:  11111111;
```

If you do

```
b <<= 2;
```

the result is

```
11111111111111111111111111111100
```

That is, Java did the shift, but it turned the byte into an int, so Java propagates the sign bit over and over to get up to 32 bits.

Right Shift: >>

The right shift operator works in the opposite direction from the left shift operator. All the elements of the left shift operator, keeping the numeric sign bit the same, propagating the sign bit when you promote from a byte to an int, and so on, is the same. The only difference is that the bits are shifted to the right. This amounts to division by a power of 2. So, if you have

```
byte b = 10; // Binary form is 00001010
b >>= 3;
```

this says to shift the bits in b three positions to the right, or divide it by 2^3. The result hence would be 00000001, or in decimal, 1. The high-order bits are replaced by 0, and the three right-most bits simply fall off.

Unsigned Right Shift: >>>

Those familiar with C will have recognized all the operators until now. The unsigned right shift operator, however, is unique to Java. This operator instructs the system to perform a right shift, like the right shift operator previously, but not to maintain the numeric sign. If you do an unsigned right shift of a negative number, the high-order bits are replaced by zeros, and a negative number becomes a positive number, because the high-order bit is no longer 1 but 0. You might want to think of this as a "right shift and absolute value" operation. Here's an example:

```
byte b = -5; // Binary form: 11111011
int I  = b >>> 1; // Put the result in an int because of promotion
```

This tells the system to shift all the bits right one position, or divide by 2^1. The result is

01111111111111111111111111111101

Notice that the number is no longer negative (the high-order bit is not 1 anymore but 0). This doesn't mean that this number no longer has a sign. It simply means that it is now positive because an unsigned right shift will always set the high-order bit to 0, which equates to "positive."

Complement: ~

The complement operator is the last of the bitwise operators. It is the easiest to understand. It simply flips bits to the opposite value. If the bit is 1, it is turned to 0. If it is 0, it is turned to 1, like this:

```
byte b = 5;  // Binary form:  00000101
b = ~b;
```

The result is 11111010. There are not any special rules here. It simply reverses the bits.

Let me make one final note about bit manipulations. There is a class in java.util called BitSet. A BitSet is a vector of bits. Its methods include and, or, and xor, to perform operations similar to what I've been describing. It also has get and set methods so you can specifically modify a single bit, as well as other useful methods. So if you will be doing a lot of work with bits, and being able to deal with specific bits easily is important, you might want to use a BitSet rather than simply doing these operations on an int. If you don't have experience with hex arithmetic, a BitSet might be easier for you to use.

Control Flow

There are five basic statements or constructs that modify the control flow of a program:

```
if-else

do-while

while

for

switch
```

if-else

The if statement, with an optional else, is a simple construct for conditionally executing a block of code. Here is the basic format:

```
if(boolean statement)
        // some code
<else>
        <// some code>
```

Java evaluates the Boolean statement in the `if` clause. If the clause evaluates to `true`, the code following the `if` statement is done. If it is `false`, the code immediately after the `if` clause is skipped. You might also optionally supply an `else` clause. In this case, if the `if` clause evaluates to `true`, the code between `if` and `else` is performed. If the If clause resolves to `false`, the code immediately following the `else` keyword is executed. Both the `if` clause and the `else` clause can govern one or multiple statements. Here is an example.

```
If(x < 10)
     System.out.println("x is small");
else
      System.out.println("x is not so small");
```

Again, I don't have to code an `else` clause, but frequently you might want to do certain code if a condition is `true`, and other code if it is `false`. As noted earlier, it is a requirement that an `if` clause provide a test that resolves to a Boolean, using a relational operator (unless the operand is itself a Boolean). Therefore, you cannot code something like this:

```
if(doSomething())
      System.outprintln("We did stuff");
```

The compiler might not know ahead of time whether the statement will evaluate to `true` or `false`, but it has to be able to determine that it will. A method call, unless the method returns a Boolean, does not satisfy that requirement. You can, however, code

```
if(doSomething() == 0)
      System.out.println("doSomething() returned 0");
```

You might also use the `!` operator:

```
if(! (name.equals("Barney"))
      System.out.println("The name is not Barney, thank you.");
```

I can also have multiple lines of code like this:

```
if(bookStatus == OVERDUE)
    {
     sendOverdueNotice();
     libraryCardFine += .25;
    }
else
      {
        putBookOnHold(true);
        sendRecallNotice();
      }
```

To have multiple statements executed for the `if` or `else` clause, you need to put the statements inside a pair of curly braces. In fact, for readability, and to avoid accidentally introducing bugs, you should consider always putting your code for an `if-else` statement inside curly braces, even if there is only one line of code to be executed.

do-while

The do-while and while loops are similar because in both constructs, a Boolean condition in the while clause is tested to see if the loop should be executed. Here's the syntax for a do-while loop:

```
do
    {
    // Some code to do conditionally
    }
while(some boolean condition);
```

Just as in C, this is a way to execute a block of code multiple times based on a condition in the while loop. Unlike C, however, the while condition must resolve to a Boolean, just like a Java if clause. As long as the condition is true, the do loop will be done. When the while condition becomes false, the loop is no longer executed and you go to the next line of code after the while statement. This means that the do-while loop is always executed at least once because the loop is executed and then the while condition is tested. Here's an example:

```
do
    {
    assignBookDeweyDecimalNumber(); // give the book a number like
                                    // "BS 2595.3 BA 1990"
    addBookToCatalog();
    }
while(MORE_NEW_BOOKS == true);
```

Here, while there are more new books to add to the library's collection, this code will assign a call number to the book and add it to the library's electronic catalog database.

while

A while loop is similar in function to a do-while, with one important difference. A do-while loop is always executed at least once. A while loop can be executed zero or more times. Here's the syntax:

```
while(boolean condition)
    {
    // Do some code in a loop
    }
```

Because the while test is done at the start of the loop, if it is false the first time, the loop will not be executed at all. The code will immediately skip to the first statement after the while loop. If the while condition resolves to true, the loop will be executed until the while condition is false. Here's an example:

```
 while(MORE_NEW_BOOKS == true)
{
    assignBookDeweyDecimalNumber(); // give the book a number like
```

```
                              // "BS 2595.3 BA 1990"
    addBookToCatalog();
}
```

Here, I've rewritten the `do-while` loop into a `while` loop. This way, if there are no new books to add to the catalog at this time, the code won't be done at all. `while` and `do-while` loops work the same in Java as they do in C.

for

The `for` loop works the same way in Java as in C. Here's the basic syntax:

```
for(statement (usually initial value)>; <boolean test>;
➥ <statement expression>)
    // Some code
```

As for an `If` statement, I recommend that for readability, you put the code for the For loop inside curly braces. Here's an example:

```
for(int i = 0; i < patronArray.length; i++)
    {
      String mailingAddress = patronArray[i];
      sendLibraryNewsletter(mailingAddress);
    }
```

The For statement does four things:

- It creates and initializes an `int` to the value of 0. Just as a reminder, the first element in an array is element 0.
- Each time through the loop, the value of `i` is compared to the length of the array. The length, as noted in an earlier chapter, is the number of elements in the array. This is easily-maintained code. You can change the length of the array elsewhere, and this loop will still step through the whole array. The test is to compare the value of `i` to the length of the array. Because the first array element is element 0, you need to stop before the actual number that "length" is equal to, because otherwise, you'll get an `ArrayIndexOutOfBoundsException`.
- The `int` `i` is incremented by 1, using the increment operator, `++`.
- Inside the `for` loop is code that is performed the number of times the `for` statement is executed. Note that like C++, but unlike C, you can define the variable used for controlling the loop inside of it (`int i = 0`). You don't have to do this. You might define the variable that controls the loop outside of it, like this:

```
int i = 5;
for(;i < arrayLength; i++) // Keep initial semicolon!
    {
      // Do some code
    }
```

For a single statement to be done multiple times, curly braces are optional. To execute multiple statements, you must use curly braces. Unlike While and do-while loops, a For loop is generally used for a set number of times.

switch

The `switch` statement provides a mechanism to perform code conditionally based on whether a specific condition is true. It is like a set of `if` statements together. Here's the syntax:

```
switch (operand)
    {
       case case1:
              <code;>
              <break>
       case case2:
              <code;>
              <break>;
       <default:>
              <code;>
    }
```

You provide an operand and a number of case statements that provide alternative values for this operand. When a case statement is encountered that matches the actual value of the operand, the code following that case statement is executed until you either a) encounter a break statement, or b) you come to the end of the `switch` statement. That means that if you do code for a specific case, but do not follow that code with a break statement, you will fall through and do the code for all the succeeding case statements until the next break statement or the end of the `switch` statement. Using a break statement is very important unless you really want the code for all the succeeding cases executed.

The `switch` statement can be quite useful, but it is limited in the data types it can test. The `switch` statement can test integral types and `char`s. So I can code a `switch` statement that tests a `byte`, `short`, or `int`, but not a `long`, `float`, `double`, or any kind of object. You can also switch on a `char`. Listing 7.1 contains an example.

Listing 7.1 An Example of a Switch Statement

```
int request = getRequest();
switch (request)  // Call a method based on the value of request
    {
      case 1:  // Same as  "if(request == 1)
            {
              addBookToCatalog();
              break;
            }
        case 2:
            {
              putBookOnHold();
              break;
            }
        case 3:
            {
              putBookOnReserve();
```

```
            break;
        }
    default:
        {
            checkOutBook();
            break;
        }
}
```

In this `switch` statement, I state that I want to test the value of the request variable and perform logic based on its value. Then I provide three case statements. If the value of request is 1, the code for the case "1" is executed. The call to `addBookToCatalog()` is followed by a `break` statement. The `break` statement causes the program to exit the switch code block at that point and continue at the line following the switch block. If the value of request does not equal 1, it goes to the next case statement. It can be coded in any order, but putting the most common choices first is best for performance.

If the value of request is 2, the code for the case 2 case is executed. The method `putBookOnHold()` would be executed if request equals 2, and then there is a `break` statement. Again, if I didn't have the `break` statement, I would call the `putBookOnHold()` method, and then call the next method, `putBookOnReserve()`. That's not usually what you want, so be sure to use the `break` statement for each case code block. The final case is the "default" case—what you should use if request is not equal to 1, 2, or 3. What you do here is of course up to you. You might choose to do "error" code in the default case because the operand you are doing the switch on should have had a value that matched a case statement.

Modifying Control Flow: break and continue

It is possible to modify the flow of your code from within a loop like a `while` or `for` loop by using break or `continue`. You can use these two keywords with or without a label. You've already seen how to use break to get out of a `switch` statement, so the example here will show how to use labeled `break` and `continue` statements. The `break` keyword causes the loop to be exited completely. The `continue` statement causes the loop to be left and started again. That is, `break` means "exit completely," while `continue` means "do the next iteration through the loop." Listing 7.2 contains an example.

Listing 7.2   An Example of Using Break and Continue for Modifying Control Flow
```
BigLoop:  while(rs.next()!= null)
          // Go to the next row in the SQL ResultSet
    {
      String author = rs.getSring("Author");
          if(author != "Tacitus)
              {
                continue BigLoop;
                    // Do the while statement again
              }
          for(i=0, i < totalBookDetails.length; i++)
```

continues

Listing 7.2   continued

```
                        // for loop inside
                        // a while loop
            {
              if(publicationDate > 1950)
                        // Test the publication date
                 {
                   break;
                   // Leave the for loop but go ahead
                   // and do the while loop again.
                 }
              System.out.println(totalBookDetails[i]);
            }           // End for loop
        }               // End while loop
```

Using these loop control statements, you can break out of an inner loop, do another iteration of an inner loop, break out of an outer loop, or do another iteration of an outer loop, either with or without a label, depending upon what and where you put `break` or `continue`. The `break` statement serves the only really valid purpose of a `goto`, which is to get out of a loop. It does not violate the coding concept of having a single entry point and a single exit point from a method, a very important rule to follow.

> **NOTE**
>
> The `break` and `continue` statements can cause exceptions and therefore the execution of a `final` block.

PART II

TECHNIQUES REFERENCE

CHAPTER 8

GUI Programming I: Applications

There are two kinds of GUI code in Java: applications and applets. This chapter focuses on applications, whereas Chapter 9, "GUI Programming II: Applets," focuses on applets. Although Java GUI programs have many common elements, there is no specific class that a GUI *per se* has to be built upon. That is, applets must extend java.appletApplet. A stand-alone Java GUI program's classes do not have to extend any specific AWT class. This chapter covers

- Basic GUI coding in applications using the AWT
- Swing/JFC
- The Delegation event-handling model

Basic GUI Application Programming

Java provides a set of classes that forms a GUI framework called the Abstract Windowing Toolkit , or AWT for short. The purpose of the AWT is to enable developers to create one GUI program to run unchanged on multiple platforms. The AWT components all have *peers,* which are native GUI components. When you create a Java Button, you also create a native button, such as a Win32 button or a Motif button. The AWT is designed to fit the lowest common denominator. If a component doesn't exist on Windows, Motif, and Macs, it is not in the AWT. This is how the AWT provides for components that have an MS Windows look and feel on a Win32 platform, a Motif look and feel on Solaris, a Mac look and feel on a Mac, and so forth. Thus, your Java AWT components always have a native peer.

> **NOTE**
>
> It is possible to create a component that does not have a native peer. This is called a *lightweight component*. These components are much more flexible in appearance because they are not dependent on a platform-specific peer. This is the principle behind most Swing components that reduces memory requirements. More importantly, it means that Swing components are not constrained in appearance or behavior by what components a given platform natively provides because most Swing components do not use peers at all.

In a Java GUI, the main component, which all other components depend on, is a Frame. A Frame is the outermost "window" of your application. If you are using a word processing software package is written in Java, the outside border of the program, the rectangle that contains everything, is a Frame. Frame is a specific class in the java.awt package. All other GUI components—menus, scrollbars, buttons, and so forth—go inside of a Frame. Even other windows, such as dialog boxes, are dependent on the Frame in your application.

Figure 8.1 shows the class hierarchy for components.

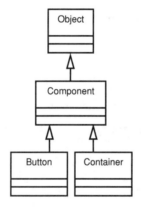

Figure 8.1

The AWT Component class hierarchy.

In this UML class diagram, you can see that Component subclasses Object. All Java GUI components (except for menu-related components) are a subclass of Component. Descending from Component are Button and Container. Many GUI components inherit directly from Component. Button was chosen as an example. In addition to providing many methods and data members that all other components inherit, Component provides the basic capability to display a component on the screen.

Java components such as Frame and Dialog are also subclasses of Component through Container. Because you place components into a Container, and because all Container classes subclass Component, you can put a Component into a Container, and that Container can be put into a Container just as though it were a Component. This is important for positioning components on the screen, our next topic. This inheritance hierarchy allows us to embed components in containers in components in containers in components!

Layout Managers

There are two ways to position a component inside a container. You can either specify the exact location, width, and height of the component in pixels. This is called *absolute positioning*. Alternatively, you can rely on a layout manager to determine the size and location of a component on the screen (although you have some control, which varies depending on the layout manager you choose).

Absolute Positioning

Although it is not a recommended technique, because many IDE tools use *absolute positioning*, this will be covered first. *Absolute positioning* is a means of specifying the exact size and location of every GUI component by pixels. You do this when you tell Java not to do anything about the sizing or positioning of components. You take on that responsibility completely.

Using Absolute Positioning (No LayoutManager): Code Example

You need to do two things to use absolute positioning. First, remove any LayoutManager implementation object from the GUI by setting its object reference to null. Second, define the position, width, and height in pixels of every component in the GUI (except for a MenuBar, which has a predefined location that cannot be changed without subclassing MenuBar). Listing 8.1 shows how to place a Button in a Frame using absolute positioning.

Listing 8.1   Absolute Positioning Using No LayoutManager Implementation (GUIDriver1.java)

```
import java.awt.*;
class GUI1 extends Frame
    {                   // Define a GUI class that subclasses Frame.
                        // This means that everything a Frame is,
                        // a GUI object is, and more.
    Button okButton;
                        // Declare components outside of any method
                        // so they will be visible to all methods.
    public GUI1()       // Constructor for class GUI.
                        // Do all the setup for the
                        // screen in the constructor -
                        // that is the best place.
        {
        setLayout(null);
                        // Set the value of the Layout Manager object
                        // reference to null, which means you are doing the
                        // layout yourself.
                        // By default, the LayoutManager object reference
                        // for a Frame object points to an instance of
```

continues

108 Chapter 8: GUI Programming I: Applications

Listing 8.1   continued

```
                            // the BorderLayout class.
                            // This tells Java you the developer
                            // are 100% responsible
                            // for the size and location of
                            // each and every Component in the Frame.
            okButton = new Button("OK");
                            // Instantiate the Button object, and give it the
                            // label of "OK".
            okButton.setBounds(new Rectangle(100,100,80,30));
                            // Define a rectangular
                            // area for the Component. All AWT components
                            // are rectangular.
                            //  The "100,100" gives the x,y coordinates
                            // for the component, relative to the top left
                            // corner of the Frame, which starts at 0,0.
                            // The width is 80 pixels.
                            // The height is 30 pixels.
            add(okButton);
                            // Add the Button to the Frame.
            setBackGround(Color.blue);
                            // Set the color of the Frame's background.
          setSize(400,300);
                            // Set the size of the Frame.
          setVisible(true);
                            // Make the GUI visible.
        }
    }                       // End class definition for GUI class.

public class GUIDriver1
    {
       public static void main(String[] args)
            {
              GUI1 gui = new GUI1();
                            // Create the gui and let the main thread exit.
            }
    }                       // End class definition GUIDriver1.
```

Figure 8.2 shows a user interface created using absolute positioning rather than a LayoutManager implementation class.

CAUTION

There are two mistakes that you as a novice Java programmer might make when using Frames. First, you might forget to call either setSize() or pack(). If you don't tell the system the dimensions of the Frame, it gets the default size of 0×0 pixels, no matter how many components you have placed in the Frame. Second, you might forget to call setVisible(true) . By default, Frames, and, hence, all their contents, are invisible.

Figure 8.2
An example of absolute positioning using setBounds().

I've defined two classes: GUI1 and GUIDriver1. Many (if not most) books on Java combine the contents of these two classes into one. I think this is a design problem because an object should be about one thing. So, a GUI object should logically be about GUIs (the user interface), not flow of control. The main method has nothing to do with the user interface, except for creating it. Therefore, it's best to think of main (and the class it is in) as a CEO or a general. It doesn't do anything itself. It orders other objects to do work. So I always separate main from any classes that actually do work or implement presentation or business logic. Logically, main doesn't belong in these classes. In a well-designed class, you should always be able to ask, "What is this object about?" If you put main in a GUI class, you can't give a single answer to that question because it depends on what method you are in.

TIP

All the code in this part of the book has a driver class. This approach has benefits for program maintenance. If the classes in an application are connected through a driver class, and main is in the driver class, you can more easily reuse the classes in other applications. You can, however, have a main method in every .java file as long as you don't call it, a technique used to provide for unit testing.

Next, notice that the class GUI1 extends Frame.

NOTE

While avoiding the debate about designing with inheritance versus containment, I think it's much easier to inherit from Frame than to instantiate a Frame object separately. If Javasoft ever changes the definition of Frame significantly, no approach to class design will avoid difficulties.

Because GUI1 extends Frame, all the methods and data members that a Frame has, a GUI1 object also has, along with all the data members and methods that a Window, a Container, and a Component have. These include a layout manager; a background color; size; a title bar with Minimize, Maximize, and Close buttons; and a visibility attribute.

In Listing 8.1, I set the object reference to the layout manager (which is otherwise set for you by the Container object you are using to a real object) to null. This tells the JVM that the GUI1 class is now totally responsible for specifying the x and y coordinates and the width and height of every single component that is added to the Frame.

> **CAUTION**
>
> Absolute positioning of components allows you to exercise total control over their size and location. This approach is easy and works well as long as you don't run your code on more than one platform. Although a Button that is 80×20 pixels looks good in Win32, it is unacceptable to the default font in Motif. This means you might be displaying totally illegible text on buttons and the like when your program runs on UNIX.
>
> So what might seem like an attractive solution is really an option that is not recommended. Layout managers never have these problems.

The next two lines create a Button object, called okButton, and specify its position in the Frame, as well as its width and height. The constructor specifies that the letters OK will appear on the Button when it is drawn on the screen. Buttons, like Label and Checkbox components in Java, allow you to specify text and justification for the text (left, right, or center), as well as a font. Unlike a Label, by default you can interact with a Button. It has two visual modes, Pressed and Unpressed. Also, as with a Label or Checkbox, you cannot put an icon on a Button. Only text is allowed.

Because all AWT components are rectangular in shape, I have to specify a rectangular area to contain the Button component. The first two numbers are the x and y coordinates, measured from the top-left corner of the Frame (or other container to which you are adding components), which is 0,0. You can use this approach for Panel and Dialog as well. The second pair of numbers specify width and height. Incidentally, Java won't tell you if there's a problem with two components overlapping, or if the MenuBar in the Frame overlaps and covers your components.

> **TIP**
>
> If you use absolute positioning instead of a layout manager, your GUI will appear better on every platform if you explicitly specify the font size and type to be used by the GUI components—for example: setFont("Serif", FONT.PLAIN, 14).

Leaving Positioning to Layout Managers

The best way to position and size components is to have a layout manager do it for you. The package java.awt contains the classes for performing the layout of GUI components on the screen and for creating, manipulating and interrogating the layout of those components. The java.awt package provides five layout managers: FlowLayout, BorderLayout, GridLayout, CardLayout, and GridBagLayout.

> **NOTE**
>
> Unlike most AWT classes, the layout manager classes inherit directly from `Object` rather than from `java.awt.Component`.

The following sections show examples of how to use each layout manager.

FlowLayout Code Example

The strategy used by the `FlowLayout` layout manager is to place components from left to right, top to bottom, as they will fit across the target container. The size of each component is based on the smallest size possible. That is, a `Button` with the text `OK` takes up less space than a `Button` with the text `Cancel`. Listing 8.2 shows an example of using `FlowLayout` to arrange and size components.

Listing 8.2 Using FlowLayout to Size and Position Components (GUIDriver2.java)

```
import java.awt.*;   // Needed to find java.awt classes
class GUI2 extends Frame
    {
    Button shortButton;
    Button mediumButton;
    Button veryLongButton;
    TextField nameTF;     // A TextField is a single-line
                          // text input field.
    TextField passwordTF;

    public GUI2()         // Construct a GUI2 object.
        {
        setLayout(new FlowLayout( FlowLayout.LEFT));
                          // Create a new layout manager object
                          // and replace the current layout
                          // manager object with the new one.
                          // Again, the JVM instantiated a layout
                          // manager object for you of type
                          // BorderLayout.

                          // FlowLayout allows for alignment
                          // requests of LEFT, CENTER and RIGHT.
                          // The default is FlowLayout.CENTER.

        setBackground(Color.blue);
                          // There are sixteen basic Java colors.
                          // Use the default blue color for a
                          // background.

        setSize(150,200); // Size the outer container.
        shortButton = new Button("Short");
        mediumButton = new Button("mid-Sized");
```

continues

Listing 8.2 continued

```
                            // Add three buttons with different labels.
        veryLongButton = new Button("Really BIG Button");
        nameTF = new TextField();
                            // This will be a short TextField
                            // because the FlowLayout layout
                            // only makes the component as big as
                            // it thinks it needs and nothing
                            // here gives it reason to make this
                            // TextField big.

        passwordTF = new TextField("*********");
                            // Give this TextField some length by
                            // giving it an initial value.
                            // This is essential for FlowLayout.
        add(shortButton);   // Add components to the GUI.
        add(mediumButton);
        add(veryLongButton);
        add(nameTF);

        add(passwordTF);

        setVisible(true);
      }
   }  // End class definition of GUI2.

public class GUIDriver2
    {
     public static void main(String[] args)
         {
          GUI2 gui = new GUI2();
          // Create the gui and let the main thread exit.
         }
     }  // End class definition GUIDriver2.
```

Figure 8.3 shows an example of a `Container` laid out using `FlowLayout`.

Figure 8.3

An example of Using FlowLayout to position components top to bottom, left to right as space allows.

In this program, I display a simple GUI with three Java Buttons and two TextFields. What's most important to notice is that the three buttons differ in size considerably, and that they are arranged to fit the available space, left to right, top to bottom. Each is big enough to fit the text label defined in its constructor, but nothing more. This is followed by two TextFields. One is very short—too short for most data entry items, except perhaps single-letter values like Y/N or M/F. The FlowLayout object didn't see a need for a field that was any larger. The second TextField is larger because it is initialized with a value. Although it was not done here, it is also possible to specify a width for a TextField in terms of columns, even though no value is specified:

```
TextField tf1 = new TextField("", 25);   // Make a TextField 25 columns wide.
```

> **CAUTION**
>
> Depending on the LayoutManager class, such a request for a specific width might not be honored. The GridLayout, for example, disregards such requests.

Because of this behavior of the FlowLayout class, this layout manager is not suitable for most GUI tasks. If you use FlowLayout, you might get a screen that looks the way you want—until the user attempts to resize the Frame. At that point, the positioning of components might change radically. To prevent this, you must make your container unresizable by coding this:

```
setResizable(false);  // Prevent the user from resizing the Frame.
```

Also, FlowLayout is practical only for very simple GUIs. Therefore, although the FlowLayout layout manager is simple to use, it generally leads to suboptimal GUIs. FlowLayout is the default layout manager for a Panel. Table 8.1 lists the default layout managers for the major Container classes you will generally use.

Table 8.1   The Default Layout Managers for Major Containers

Component	Default Layout Manager
Frame	BorderLayout
Panel	FlowLayout
Dialog	BorderLayout

BorderLayout Code Example

A second layout manager included in Java is BorderLayout. This layout manager works by dividing its container into five regions: North, South, West, East, and Center. You can place components in one or more of these five regions. Figure 8.4 shows what this looks like conceptually.

114 Chapter 8: GUI Programming I: Applications

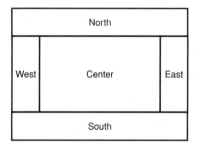

Figure 8.4
Conceptual picture of a container using a BorderLayout.

You do not need to put a component in every region. Any regions without components in them, except for Center, will be taken over by the area in the Center, even if there is no component in the Center region. Unlike FlowLayout, when a container with a BorderLayout is resized, the components in each region continue to have the same relative size and the same positions in the container. The West and East regions might get taller, but not wider. The North and South regions might get wider, but not taller. The Center region will expand to take unused space.

TIP

Because containers are components, you can place containers, such as a panel, into any of these five regions and place components into the panel. This is actually true for the other layout managers and is recommended because it provides both flexibility and the capability to create complex layouts. You must use a panel, for example, in order to place more than one component in a region of a BorderLayout-managed Frame. Nesting of containers within containers is a good technique for building complex layouts, without having to resort to GridBagLayout.

There are three ways to specify the location:
- Specify the location using the pre-defined public static final strings in the BorderLayout class, such as BorderLayout.SOUTH.
- Specify the location with a string, such as "East". These strings must be spelled exactly like this: "North", "South", "East", "West", and "Center". If they are not spelled as shown here, the code will compile, and it throws an exception at runtime.
- Use the public static final values predefined in BorderLayout, such as
    AFTER_LAST_LINE (South)
    AFTER_LINE_ENDS (East)
    BEFORE_FIRST_LINE (North)
    BEFORE_LINE_BEGINS (West)
These four values should not be combined with other specifiers for the constraint.

Listing 8.3 shows an example of using `BorderLayout`.

Listing 8.3 A BorderLayout Example
```
import java.awt.*;
class GUI3 extends Frame
    {
    Panel p1;
    Panel p2;
    Button okButton;
    Button cancelButton;
    Label northLabel;   // Labels for the Frame.
    Label centerLabel;
    Label westLabel;
    Label eastLabel;
    Label panelNorthLabel; // Labels for the Panel in the center of the Frame.
    Label panelSouthLabel;
    Label panelEastLabel;
    Label panelWestLabel;
    Label panelCenterLabel;


    public GUI3()      // constructor
        {
        setBackground(Color.lightGray);
                    // Use normal application color.
                    // Use the default layout for a
                    // Frame, which is BorderLayout.
        p1 = new Panel(new BorderLayout());
                    //  Override the layout for this Panel.
                    // A Panel is a borderless Container.
                    // Panel and set it to BorderLayout.
        p1.setBackground(Color.yellow);
                    // Make Panel's edges readily visible.
        p2 = new Panel();
                    // Use default layout: FlowLayout.
        p2.setBackground(Color.cyan);
                    // Make this Panel's edges readily visible.
        okButton = new Button("OK");
        cancelButton = new Button("Cancel");
        northLabel = new Label("North");
        westLabel = new Label("West");
        eastLabel = new Label("East");
        panelNorthLabel = new Label("p1 North");
        panelSouthLabel = new Label("p1 South");
        panelEastLabel = new Label("p1 East");
        panelWestLabel = new Label("p1 West");
        panelCenterLabel = new Label ("p1 Center");
        // Add Components to the Panels.
        p1.add(panelNorthLabel, BorderLayout.NORTH);
```

continues

Listing 8.3   continued

```
                    // Use constants for regions.
        p1.add(panelSouthLabel, BorderLayout.SOUTH);
        p1.add(panelEastLabel, BorderLayout.EAST);
        p1.add(panelWestLabel, BorderLayout.WEST);
        p1.add(panelCenterLabel, BorderLayout.CENTER);
                    // Then, add the Panel to the Center
                    // region of the Frame.
        add(p1,"Center");
                    // Use Strings for regions.
        p2.add(okButton);
                    // A form of add for other layouts
                    // since p2 is using FlowLayout.

        p2.add(cancelButton);
        add(p2, "South");
                    // Put this Panel in the South region
                    // of the Frame.
                    // Add Components to the Frame.
        add(northLabel, "North");
        add(eastLabel, "East");
        add(westLabel, "West");
        setTitle("BorderLayout Example");
                    // Set the Frame's title.
                    // This method is unrelated to the
                    // LayoutManager used.
        setSize(300,300);
                    // Size the Frame.
        setVisible(true);
                    // Make the Frame Visible
        }
    }  // End of GUIDriver3 class definition.

public class GUIDriver3
    {
       public static void main(String[] args)
            {
              GUI3 gui = new GUI3();
            }
    }
```

Figure 8.5 shows an example of a container laid out using BorderLayout.

Figure 8.5

An example of using BorderLayout in all five regions.

CardLayout Code Example

The CardLayout layout manager provides a Rolodex metaphor. That is, you create one container, such as a panel, and then create several "cards" to put into the first panel. No matter how many cards you create (usually this is done with panels that contain components), only one of these cards can be visible at one time, just as the cards in a Rolodex or a card catalog at the library are. The CardLayout does not control the size or position of any components. It controls the display of cards. So, for every card, you can choose a different layout—one card with FlowLayout, another with BorderLayout, and so forth. Listing 8.4 shows an example of how to use CardLayout.

> **TIP**
>
> You can use CardLayout to create the visual effect of a tabbed dialog, not available in the AWT. To do this, you put a CardLayout-based container on the GUI. Above it, use a row of buttons or labels. When you click on a button or label, you switch to the appropriate "card." Of course, the Swing JTabbedPane is easier to use and looks better, but using CardLayout and buttons is about the only way to do this using only AWT components.

Listing 8.4 Using CardLayout to Display Components (GUIDriver4.java)

```java
import java.awt.*;   // Needed to find java.awt classes.

class GUI4 extends Frame
    {
    Panel card1;
    Panel card2;
    Panel card3;
    Panel card4;
    Label cardLabel1;
    Label cardLabel2;
    Label cardLabel3;
    Label cardLabel4;
    CardLayout cl;
```

continues

Listing 8.4 continued

```java
    public GUI4()           // Construct a GUI4 object.
    {
      cl = new CardLayout();
      setLayout(cl);
                            // Create a new layout manager object
                            // and replace the current layout
                            // manager object with the new one.
                            // Again the JVM instantiated a layout
                            // manager object for you of type
                            // BorderLayout.
                            // You have to create and add the cards yourself.

      setBackground(Color.lightGray);
      setSize(200,200); // Size the outer container.
      card1 = new Panel();
      card2 = new Panel();
      card3 = new Panel();
      card4 = new Panel();
      cardLabel1 = new Label("This is card one");
      cardLabel2 = new Label("This is card two");;
      cardLabel3 = new Label("This is card three");;
      cardLabel4 = new Label("This is card four");
      card1.add(cardLabel1);
      card2.add(cardLabel2);
      card3.add(cardLabel3);
      card4.add(cardLabel4);
                 // Create "card" Panels and add Labels to them.
      add(card1, "one");
                 // The add method for a Container that uses CardLayout
                 // takes a "card" name and an optional String name
                 // for the card.
                 // The optional name is a logical name, not a Component
                 // name or object reference.
      add(card2, "two");
      add(card3, "three");
      add(card4, "four");
                 // Now there are four cards in the "deck," but only
                 // one card can be shown at once.
      cl.show(this, "one");
                 // Show the first card.
                 // This show() method is specifically
                 // for CardLayout, not the JDK 1.0
                 // method to display a GUI.
      setVisible(true);
                 // Make the GUI visible.
    }

    public boolean displayCards()
        {
```

Leaving Positioning to Layout Managers

```
                    // Cycle through the cards using Threads.
                    // This technique as it is shown here should NOT be used
                    // normally in a GUI because it causes the GUI to hang.
            try
                {
                  Thread.currentThread().sleep(5000);
                   cl.next(this);
                      // Show the next card.
                   Thread.currentThread().sleep(5000);
                   cl.next(this);
                   Thread.currentThread().sleep(5000);
                    cl.last(this);
                      // Show the last card.
                    Thread.currentThread().sleep(5000);
                  }
                catch(InterruptedException ie)
                      {}

              return true;
            }
    } // End class definition of GUI4.

public class GUIDriver4
    {
      public static void main(String[] args)
          {
            GUI4 gui = new GUI4();
            boolean result = gui.displayCards();
          }
    } // End class definition GUIDriver4.
```

Figure 8.6 shows an example of a container laid out using `CardLayout`.

Figure 8.6

An example of Using CardLayout.

This program uses a few basic methods of the `CardLayout` class. You can display a specific card using the `show()` method. You can show the `previous()`, `next()`, `last()`, or `first()` cards with method calls as well.

120 Chapter 8: GUI Programming I: Applications

> **NOTE**
>
> Do not confuse this `show()` method of the `CardLayout` class with the deprecated `show()` method that you can use to display a `Frame` object.

You can put anything you want to on a given card. A card can be any AWT component you want to use, generally a Container subclass. Again, using a `CardLayout` layout manager does not affect how components are organized on a given card. It only controls their display. As this code shows, in fact, you ask the `CardLayout` object to show the card, not the container it governs.

GridLayout Code Example

The `GridLayout` layout manager is easy to use. Unlike the `FlowLayout` class, `GridLayout` does not vary the size of components. That is, all components are the same size in a grid. The `GridLayout` layout manager divides the container it governs into a specified number of rows and columns as dictated by the constructor. You add components to the container, and they are placed in the grid left to right and top to bottom, one cell at a time. Each cell, as specified by the number of rows and columns, is equal in size, and every component is given the same size. This makes a `GridLayout` good for things like calculators, phone pads, and calendars, but bad for most data entry screens. You could also use it for thumbnail images.

As just stated, components are placed in cells in the order they are added to the container, and there is no way to specify explicitly that a given component should go in a given cell. You need to plan your grid according to what you are trying to accomplish.

> **NOTE**
>
> The "grid" created by the `GridLayout` layout manager only applies to layout. It is not a spreadsheet, nor does it provide any extra features beyond sizing and positioning components.

Listing 8.5 shows an example of using `GridLayout` to display a phone pad.

Listing 8.5   Using GridLayout to Lay Out a Set of Cells for a Phone Dialer (GUIDriver5.java)

```
import java.awt.*;

class GUI5 extends Frame
    {
    Panel gridPanel;
    Label label1;
    Label label2;
    Label label3;
    Label label4;
    Label label5;
    Label label6;
    Label label7;
    Label label8;
    Label label9;
    Label label0;
```

```java
    Label labelPound;
    Label labelStar;


    public GUI5()
       {
         setLayout(new GridLayout(4,3));
                        // Create a grid with four rows and three columns.

          setBackground(Color.lightGray);
          setSize(200,300); // Size the outer container.
          gridPanel = new Panel();
                  // Create the Labels for the phone pad.
           label1 = new Label("1");
           label2 = new Label("2");
           label3 = new Label("3");
           label4 = new Label("4");
           label5 = new Label("5");
           label6 = new Label("6");
           label7 = new Label("7");
           label8 = new Label("8");
           label9 = new Label("9");
           label0 = new Label("0");
           labelPound = new Label("#");
           labelStar= new Label("*");
                   // Add the Labels to the cells.
           add(label1);
           add(label2);
           add(label3);
           add(label4);
           add(label5);
           add(label6);
           add(label7);
           add(label8);
           add(label9);
           add(labelStar);
           add(label0);
           add(labelPound);
           setVisible(true);
         }

    } // End class definition of GUI5.

public class GUIDriver5
      {
        public static void main(String[] args)
          {
            GUI5 gui = new GUI5();
          }
      } // End class definition GUIDriver5.
```

Figure 8.7 shows an example of a container laid out using GridLayout.

Figure 8.7
An example of Using GridLayout to arrange components.

It is also possible to specify a space between (but not around) cells by using the hgap and vgap values in the constructor to specify the horizontal and vertical gap between cells.

CAUTION

If you specify too few or too many cells compared to the number of components you add to the container, the GridLayout layout manager decides for you what the number of rows and columns ought to be. In the latter case, even an empty cell has the same size as the others.

GridBagLayout Code Example

The fifth AWT LayoutManager class is the GridBagLayout layout manager. This is by far the most flexible and the most complex layout manager. Like the GridLayout class, GridBagLayout organizes components by cells. Unlike GridLayout, GridBagLayout allows components to span cells, allows you to place a component at a specific location, allows you to decide how much of a cell a component ought to take, and performs other tasks. These settings are done on a component-by-component basis, using a GridBagConstraints object. Because the focus here is on techniques, you will need to consult the API specification for details on what each parameter in the GridBagConstraints constructor means. Some of the more important parameters, however, are defined as follows:

- gridX—The cell column that the left edge of the component should start in.
- gridY—The row that the top of the component should start in.
- gridWidth—The number of cells wide that the component should be.
- gridHeight—The number of cells high that the component should be.
- GridBagConstraints.REMAINDER—Size the component so that it spans the number of cells remaining to the right or bottom of the container, depending on whether you used this for the gridWidth or gridHeight parameter.
- GridBagConstraints.RELATIVE—Place the component next in the row or column. This is an alternative to specifying a gridX or gridY.

Leaving Positioning to Layout Managers   123

> **NOTE**
>
> This class was designed by someone outside of Javasoft, and the documentation has never been optimal. Thus, you will need to experiment to see what various settings do.

GridBagLayout requires a fair amount of getting used to before you can predict just what a GUI using it will look like. You might need to tweak several parameters, one at a time, to get the desired effect. Listing 8.6 shows a basic example of using GridBagLayout to lay out a simple data entry screen.

> **TIP**
>
> You must have an idea of how your screen will look before you start specifying constraints, so it's best to draw it on paper first (preferably on graph paper) so that you can see the proportions of one component relative to another.

Listing 8.6   Using GridBagLayout for a Simple Data Entry Screen (GUIDriver6.java)

```java
import java.awt.*;

class GUI6 extends Frame
    {
    Panel centerPanel;
    Label nameLabel;
    Label emailLabel;
    TextField nameTF;
    TextField emailTF;
     GridBagConstraints c;
     Button okButton;
     Button cancelButton;

    public GUI6()
        {
        centerPanel = new Panel();
        GridBagLayout gridbag = new GridBagLayout();
        c = new GridBagConstraints();
                // Create a GridBagLayout layout manager,
                // then create a GridBagConstraints object to
                // use to size and position components.
        centerPanel.setLayout(gridbag);
                // Set the layout to GridBagLayout.
        c.fill = GridBagConstraints.BOTH;
                // Fill the cell with the component.
        c.weightx = 20;
        c.weighty = 100;
                // Weight cannot exceed 100 because it is a percentage.

        setBackground(Color.lightGray);
```

continues

Listing 8.6   continued

```java
        setSize(300,140);
                    // Size the outer container.
        Toolkit tk = Toolkit.getDefaultToolkit();
        Dimension d = tk.getScreenSize();
        setLocation((d.width-300)/2, (d.height-175)/2);
                    // Get the default Toolkit. The
                    // Toolkit is the AWT's "Swiss Army Knife."
                    // It helps provide lots of useful system
                    // resources and information.
                    // Here, it is used to get the platform's screen
                    // dimensions and set the size
                    // of the Frame dynamically.
        nameLabel = new Label("Name");
        nameTF = new TextField();
        c.fill = GridBagConstraints.NONE;
        add(nameLabel,c,0,0,1,1);
        c.fill = GridBagConstraints.HORIZONTAL;
        add(nameTF,c,1,GridBagConstraints.RELATIVE,3,1);
        emailLabel = new Label("Email address");
        c.fill = GridBagConstraints.NONE;
        c.weightx = 70;
        add(emailLabel, c,0,1,1,1);
        emailTF = new TextField();
        c.fill = GridBagConstraints.HORIZONTAL;
        add(emailTF,c,1,GridBagConstraints.RELATIVE,3,1);
        add(centerPanel, "Center");
        c.anchor = GridBagConstraints.SOUTH;
        c.weighty = 0;
        c.fill = GridBagConstraints.NONE;
                    // Only fill the space in the cell needed for a Button.
                    // Otherwise, you get enormous buttons.
        okButton = new Button("OK");
        add(okButton,c,0,2,1,1);
        cancelButton = new Button("Cancel");
        add(cancelButton,c,1,2,1,1);
        setVisible(true);
    }

    public void add(Component c, GridBagConstraints gbc,
                            int x,  int y, int w, int h)
    {
      gbc.gridx = x;
      gbc.gridy = y;
      gbc.gridwidth = w;
      gbc.gridheight = h;
      centerPanel.add(c, gbc);
    }
```

```
    }   // End class definition of GUI6.

public class GUIDriver6
    {
      public static void main(String[] args)
        {
          GUI6 gui = new GUI6();
        }
    }   // End class definition GUIDriver6.
```

Figure 8.8 shows an example of a container laid out using `GridBagLayout`.

Figure 8.8
An example of using GridBagLayout.

This code does not show how to use each parameter in the `GridBagConstraints` object. Instead, it shows that you need to change the value of a given field several times to get the desired effect. As you can see from Figure 8.8, the `GridBagLayout` layout manager has its own interesting features, and you might want to compensate for them to get the desired effect. Generally, you will have to experiment with the values of several fields to get the exact appearance you want. The payoff is a very flexible way to size and position components that works across all platforms without your having to do any platform-specific work.

> **NOTE**
>
> Many Java developers consider `GridBagLayout` too complicated to be worth the trouble. Instead, they opt for combining several panels, each with a specific layout manager implementation, to achieve the desired effect.

So far, the examples have used GUI components to illustrate how to use a layout manager to size and position components. There are other GUI components that have not been used yet. They will be shown later when event handling is discussed.

Java Foundation Classes

Because there is a companion volume on the Java Foundation classes, *Pure JFC Swing*, this section presents a brief treatment of how to code a Swing application. It will also present techniques for adding accessibility and drag-and-drop features to your programs.

The most notable feature of the Java Foundation class, hereafter JFC, is Swing. Swing is a replacement GUI framework, intended to be used instead of the AWT.

> **CAUTION**
>
> Unless you are using something similar to the Java Plugin for Java 2, using Swing in applets is not practical because it requires about a 1MB download of classes.

The main difference between the AWT and Swing is that all Swing classes are lightweight components, which means they can be drawn any way a developer wants, except for the heavyweight containers JFrame, JApplet, JWindow, and JDialog. That is, they do not require native peers. Because no C code on the native platform has to be called to make a platform-dependent component peer, Swing components may look and act however you want them to look and act.

> **NOTE**
>
> Even when using the AWT, you can code your own lightweight component by directly subclassing java.awt.Component, but that is beyond the scope of this book.

The practical result is that Swing provides several components not available through the AWT. For example, you no longer need to use a CardLayout and Buttons to simulate a tabbed dialog. Instead, you can use the JTabbedPane component, which functions like a tabbed dialog and is very easy to use. Swing is JavaSoft's direction for GUI development. There are a few important things to keep in mind in moving from AWT to Swing:

- Except for Canvas and Choice, Swing provides an equivalent to all the AWT GUI components. Generally you can find the Swing component's name by adding a J to the front of the AWT component. For example, Button becomes JButton, and Panel becomes JPanel.
- Although Swing still uses the same event handling model as the AWT, which is covered later in this chapter, its classes reside in the package javax.swing and in its subpackages. Unlike other javax package names, this package is a core package.
- You should avoid mixing Swing and AWT components. If you must do this, see Amy Fowler's article at the Swing Connection (http://java.sun.com/products/jfc/tsc/) on mixing heavyweight and lightweight components.
- Unlike the java.awt.Frame class, javax.swing.JFrame is built with multiple panes. There is a glass pane, root pane, drag-and-drop pane, and so forth (see the Swing Connection article on the various panes for more information). You do not add components directly to a JFrame; instead, you add the components to the JFrame's ContentPane. You can access this by doing either a setContentPane() or a getContentPane(). A default ContentPane (of type.java.awt.Container) is available, or you can replace the default with your own. You are allowed to add components to other panes, but you would do this only under special circumstances. You are not allowed to add components to the JFrame itself. In general, this is the only pane you need to be concerned with, although several more panes are present in a JFrame.

Although Swing is often used interchangeably with JFC, technically Swing is only one component of the JFC. Accessibility and other features are really separate (but require Swing).

Basic Swing Code Example

Writing a GUI using Swing is similar to writing a GUI using the AWT, except that the component names (and sometimes behavior) are changed, and you need to deal with the `ContentPane`. Listing 8.7 shows an example of a Swing GUI that illustrates some features of Swing—but definitely not all.

Listing 8.7   Basic Swing Coding Example Using JFrame, JList, and Other Swing Components (GUIDriver7.java)

```
import javax.swing.*;
import java.awt.*;

class GUI7 extends JFrame
    {    // Extend JFrame, just like Frame.
    JButton okButton;
    JButton cancelButton;
    JList subjectList;
    JScrollPane scrollPane;
    JCheckBox englishChkbox;
    JCheckBox frenchChkbox;
    JCheckBox germanChkbox;
    JRadioButton allLibRB;
    JRadioButton thisLibRB;
    ButtonGroup libSelectBG;
    JMenuBar menubar;   // Most Swing components have the same
    JMenu fileMenu;     // name as their AWT counterpart with a "J" prefix.
    JMenu helpMenu;
    JMenuItem newSearchMI;
    JMenuItem printResultsMI;
    JMenuItem exitMI;
    JMenuItem aboutAppMI;
    JMenuItem helpIndexMI;
    Container theContentPane;  // Add components to this pane.
    String[] catalogSubjects = {"Archaeology", "Biblical Studies",
                   "Dead Sea Scrolls", "Graeco-Roman History",
                   "Linguistics"} ;

    public GUI7()
        {
            // JFrame uses a BorderLayout, just like a Frame object.
            // No need to change that.
         setSize(600,440);
         setBackground(Color.blue);
            // Set the size and background of the JFrame.
         theContentPane = getContentPane();
```

continues

Listing 8.7   continued

```java
                // Get a reference to the existing ContentPane
                // so components may be added to it.
    okButton = new JButton("OK");;
    cancelButton= new JButton("Cancel");;
    JPanel buttonPanel = new JPanel(new GridLayout(7,1));
                // Create a JPanel and add the JButtons plus
                // empty JPanels in order to get the grid cells
                // and the JButtons to be an acceptable size.
    buttonPanel.add(new JPanel());
    buttonPanel.add(okButton);
    buttonPanel.add(new JPanel());
    buttonPanel.add(cancelButton);
    buttonPanel.add(new JPanel());
    buttonPanel.add(new JPanel());
    theContentPane.add(buttonPanel, "East");
                // Unlike java.awt.List, a JList cannot scroll on its own.
                // So create a JList and a JScrollPane for it.
    subjectList = new JList(catalogSubjects);;
    scrollPane = new JScrollPane();
    scrollPane.getViewport().setView(subjectList);
                // A JScrollPane provides for scrolling without any messy
                // code for scroll bars. You put a Component, even an image,
                // into a JScrollPane, and it lets the user scroll
                // with no programmatic intervention.
    JPanel listPanel = new JPanel(new BorderLayout());
    JLabel listLabel = new JLabel("Catalog Subject List");
                // Create a JList and a JLabel for it.
    listPanel.add(listLabel, "North");
    listPanel.add(scrollPane, "Center");
    theContentPane.add(listPanel, "West");
                // Create a JPanel to hold the JList and a descriptive
                // JLabel for it.
    JPanel choicePanel = new JPanel(new GridLayout(3,2));
    JPanel containingPanel = new JPanel(new BorderLayout());
    JLabel choiceLabel = new JLabel("Limit Results",
                                        SwingConstants.CENTER);
                // Create a JLabel and align the text to the center of
                // the JLabel's area.
    containingPanel.add(choiceLabel, "North");
    libSelectBG = new ButtonGroup();
                // Like a java.awt.CheckboxGroup, this is a non-visual
                // component that provides for mutually exclusive
                // JRadioButton selection.
    allLibRB = new JRadioButton("Graduate Library", true);
                // Provide two JRadioButtons.  Put them in a ButtonGroup
                // Use the constructor that takes a boolean to specify that
                //   this JRadioButton should be selected
                //   by default when the GUI appears.
    thisLibRB = new JRadioButton("All campus Libraries");
```

Java Foundation Classes

```java
        libSelectBG.add(allLibRB);
        libSelectBG.add(thisLibRB);
            // Create JRadioButtons and add them to a ButtonGroup to
            // get radio button, i.e., exclusive selection, behavior.
        englishChkbox = new JCheckBox("Works in English", true);
        frenchChkbox = new JCheckBox("Works in French");
        germanChkbox = new JCheckBox("Works in German");
            // Note that, unlike the java.awt.Checkbox class, the B in
            // JCheckBox is capitalized, as it should be.
         choicePanel.add(englishChkbox);
         choicePanel.add(thisLibRB);
         choicePanel.add(frenchChkbox);
         choicePanel.add(allLibRB);
         choicePanel.add(germanChkbox);
            // Remember that Components are added to grid cells
            // left to right, top to bottom.
        containingPanel.add(choicePanel, "Center");
        theContentPane.add(containingPanel, "Center");
            // The basic JMenuBar and JMenu methods are the same as for
            // the AWT counterparts, so this shows the
            // basics of an AWT menu.
        menubar= new JMenuBar();;
        fileMenu= new JMenu("File");
        helpMenu = new JMenu("Help");
        newSearchMI = new JMenuItem("New Search");
        printResultsMI = new JMenuItem("Print Results");
        exitMI= new JMenuItem("Exit");
        fileMenu.add(newSearchMI);
            // Create components for a program menu and then
            // build the menus.
         fileMenu.add(printResultsMI);
         fileMenu.add(exitMI);
         aboutAppMI = new JMenuItem("About Library application");
         helpIndexMI = new JMenuItem("Help Index");
         helpMenu.add(aboutAppMI);
         helpMenu. add(helpIndexMI);
         menubar.add(fileMenu);
         // menubar.setHelpMenu(helpMenu);
                // You can't make the above call as of Sept. 1999.
                // The setHelpMenu method puts the "Help" menu
                // on the far right.
                // However, while this works for a Menu object,
                // the setHelpMenu()method is not yet
                // implemented for JMenuBar, so use
           menubar.add(helpMenu);
                // of the JMenuBar class.
        setJMenuBar(menubar);
        setVisible(true);
    }
```

continues

130 Chapter 8: GUI Programming I: Applications

Listing 8.7 continued

```
   }   // End of class definition for GUI7.

public class GUIDriver7
    {
      public static void main(String[] args)
            {
              GUI7 gui = new GUI7();
            }
    }
```

Figure 8.9 shows an example of a Basic Swing GUI.

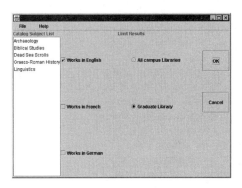

Figure 8.9
The basic Swing GUI with JButtons, JLabels, JList, JRadioButtons, and JScrollpane.

Much of how this GUI works, using Swing, should be familiar to you already. It uses the familiar layout managers: `BorderLayout`, `GridLayout`, and `FlowLayout`. It adds components to containers. The big difference in this regard is that the constructor for GUI7 gets the `ContentPane` of the `JFrame`.

This program also shows how to use menus. The methods used are almost identical to those for AWT menu creation. The two notable exceptions are that you use a `setJMenuBar()` in Swing rather than `java.awt.Frame`'s `setMenuBar()`. Also, `java.awt.MenuBar` supports a `setHelpMenu()` method that places the menu you designate on the far right of all the `Menu` objects on the `MenuBar`. The `JMenuBar` version of `setHelpMenu()`, as of July 1999, has not been implemented yet. The code compiles basically, but the program won't run if you try to use `setHelpMenu()`. Hopefully, JavaSoft will fix this soon.

In the AWT, the `Checkbox` class must do double-duty, functioning as a check box when not in a `CheckboxGroup` and functioning as a radio button when created with a `CheckboxGroup`. In Swing, `JRadioButton` is a separate class from `JCheckBox`.

> **CAUTION**
>
> Remember to put JRadioButtons in a ButtonGroup. If you do not do this, JRadioButtons function identically to JCheckBox components. That is, the choice of a specific JRadioButton will exclude other JRadioButtons from being selected.

In most other respects, this application is pretty similar to a basic AWT GUI.

> **NOTE**
>
> Swing is intended as a complete replacement for the AWT. Therefore, most of the other JFC features, such as Accessibility, depend on Swing. In addition, the Delegation event handling model, discussed later in this chapter, applies equally to Swing. Because Swing is what Javasoft wants developers to use, further examples will use Swing rather than the AWT counterparts. Where there are similar components, it should be easy to figure out how to code the AWT version.

Using Accessibility in a Java GUI Application

As mentioned in Chapter 2, "New Features in Java 2," the Accessibility feature of the JFC is intended to make Swing-based applications easier to use for the physically challenged. There are many things that you can do with the Accessibility APIs. This section shows a simple example of how to do some of them. Because almost all the work to make an application accessible has been done by the Swing team, there is little reason not to add this feature to your application.

The Accessibility APIs allow Java programs to use assistive technologies, such as Braille terminals. It is not necessary, however, for the program to run on a machine that features assistive technology. Rather, Accessibility APIs can work on any Java-enabled system, with or without assistive technologies.

There are two basic things that you can easily do with the Accessibility APIs. First, you can add AccesssibleText to a component. This is text that pops up like a ToolTip when the mouse pointer hovers over it. This feature lets you tell a user what the component is used for—for example, "Click this button to submit your order."

The second accessible feature you can add to a component is a mnemonic for a component or a keyboard accelerator for a menu. In fact, you need to add a keyboard accelerator to at least one JMenu component in a menu bar in order to make all the menus and menu items accessible components.

> **NOTE**
>
> In September 1999, Sun released a beta version of a bridge from Java's Accessibility APIs and assistive devices running under Microsoft Windows.

> **TIP**
>
> If you have an ImageIcon in a Component, you should do a setDescription() call for the ImageIcon to help blind users.

Listing 8.8 shows the preceding program with the addition of basic Accessibility features.

Listing 8.8   Accessibility Example Using JButtons, JMenus, and JMenuItems (GUIDriver8.java)

```java
import javax.swing.*;
import java.awt.*;
import javax.accessibility.*;
import java.awt.event.KeyEvent;

class GUI8 extends JFrame
     {      // Extend JFrame, just like Frame.
       JButton okButton;
       JButton cancelButton;
       JList subjectList;
       JScrollPane scrollPane;
       JCheckBox englishChkbox;
       JCheckBox frenchChkbox;
       JCheckBox germanChkbox;
       JRadioButton allLibRB;
       JRadioButton thisLibRB;
       ButtonGroup libSelectBG;
       JMenuBar menubar;
       JMenu fileMenu;
       JMenu helpMenu;
       JMenuItem newSearchMI;
       JMenuItem printResultsMI;
       JMenuItem exitMI;
       JMenuItem aboutAppMI;
       JMenuItem helpIndexMI;
       Container theContentPane;
       String[] catalogSubjects = {"Archaeology", "Biblical Studies",
                    "Dead Sea Scrolls", "Graeco-Roman History",
                    "Linguistics"} ;

     public GUI8()
          {
                // JFrame uses a BorderLayout, just like a Frame object
                // No need to change that.
            setSize(600,440);
            setBackground(Color.blue);
            theContentPane = getContentPane();
                // Set the JFrame's size and background color.
                // Then get the ContentPane reference from the JFrame.
            okButton = new JButton("OK");;
            cancelButton= new JButton("Cancel");
                // First, add mnemonics to the JButtons.
            okButton.setMnemonic('o');
            cancelButton.setMnemonic('c');
                // Second, add ToolTip text for accessibility.
```

```
okButton.setToolTipText("Press OK to search for books");
cancelButton.setToolTipText
                    ("Press Cancel to cancel the
                        subject search");
    // Third, set AccessibleName for the JButtons.
okButton.getAccessibleContext().setAccessibleName("okButton");
cancelButton.getAccessibleContext().
                    setAccessibleName("cancelButton");
        // The AccessibleName is part of the AccessibleContext
        // of a Component, which is the minimal amount of
        // information
        // an Accessible Component returns.
        // This is done using the getAccessibilityContext()
        // method.
JPanel buttonPanel = new JPanel(new GridLayout(9,1));
        // Create a JPanel and add the JButtons plus
        // empty JPanels in order to get the grid cells
        // and the JButtons to be an acceptable size.
 buttonPanel.add(new JPanel());
 buttonPanel.add(okButton);
 buttonPanel.add(new JPanel());
 buttonPanel.add(cancelButton);
 buttonPanel.add(new JPanel());
 buttonPanel.add(new JPanel());
 buttonPanel.add(new JPanel());
 buttonPanel.add(new JPanel());
        // Create JPanels to put into the JFrame.
 theContentPane.add(buttonPanel, "East");
        // Unlike java.awt.List, a JList cannot scroll on its own,
        // so create a JList and a JScrollPane for it.
 subjectList = new JList(catalogSubjects);;
 scrollPane = new JScrollPane();
 scrollPane.getViewport().setView(subjectList);
        // A JScrollPane provides for scrolling  without
        // any messy code for scrollbars.
        // You put a Component, even an image, into a JScrollPane
        //  and it lets the user scroll
        // with no programmatic intervention.
  JPanel listPanel = new JPanel(new BorderLayout());
  JLabel listLabel = new JLabel("Catalog Subject List");
  listPanel.add(listLabel, "North");
  listPanel.add(scrollPane, "Center");
        // Create a JList and JScrollPane for it
        // so it can be scrolled.
    theContentPane.add(listPanel, "West");
        // Create a JPanel to hold the JList and a descriptive
        // JLabel for it.
   JPanel choicePanel = new JPanel(new GridLayout(3,2));
   JPanel containingPanel = new JPanel(new BorderLayout());
```

continues

Listing 8.8 *continued*

```
JLabel choiceLabel = new JLabel("Limit Results",
                                SwingConstants.CENTER);
    // Create a JLabel and align the text to the center of
    // the JLabel's area.
containingPanel.add(choiceLabel, "North");
libSelectBG = new ButtonGroup();
    // Like a java.awt.CheckboxGroup, this is a non-visual
    // component that provides for mutually exclusive
    // JRadioButton selection.
allLibRB = new JRadioButton("Graduate Library", true);
    // Provide two JRadioButtons.  Put them in a ButtonGroup.
    // Use the constructor that takes a boolean
    // to specify that this JRadioButton should
    // be selected by default when the GUI appears.
allLibRB.setMnemonic('a');
thisLibRB = new JRadioButton("All campus Libraries");
thisLibRB.setMnemonic('t');
libSelectBG.add(allLibRB);
libSelectBG.add(thisLibRB);
englishChkbox = new JCheckBox("Works in English", true);
frenchChkbox = new JCheckBox("Works in French");
germanChkbox = new JCheckBox("Works in German");
englishChkbox.setMnemonic('e');
frenchChkbox.setMnemonic('r');
germanChkbox.setMnemonic('g');
    // Note that, unlike the java.awt.Checkbox class, the B in
    // JCheckBox is capitalized, as it should be.
 choicePanel.add(englishChkbox);
 choicePanel.add(thisLibRB);
    // Add the JRadioButtons to their JPanel.
 choicePanel.add(frenchChkbox);
 choicePanel.add(allLibRB);
 choicePanel.add(germanChkbox);
    // Remember that Components are added to grid cells
    // Left to Right, Top to Bottom.
containingPanel.add(choicePanel, "Center");
theContentPane.add(containingPanel, "Center");
    // The basic JMenuBar and JMenu methods are the same as for
    // the AWT counterparts, so this shows the
    // basics of an AWT menu.
menubar= new JMenuBar();;
fileMenu= new JMenu("File");
helpMenu = new JMenu("Help");
fileMenu.setMnemonic('f');
helpMenu.setMnemonic('h');
newSearchMI = new JMenuItem("New Search");
printResultsMI = new JMenuItem("Print Results");
exitMI= new JMenuItem("Exit");
newSearchMI.setMnemonic('n');
```

```
                    printResultsMI.setMnemonic('p');
                    exitMI.setAccelerator(KeyStroke.getKeyStroke(KeyEvent.VK_X,
                                    KeyEvent.SHIFT_MASK));
                        // Set keyboard accelerator to make all the menu objects
                        // accessible.
                    fileMenu.add(newSearchMI);
                        // Create components for a program menu and then
                        // build the menus.
                    fileMenu.add(printResultsMI);
                    fileMenu.add(exitMI);
                    aboutAppMI = new JMenuItem("About Library application");
                    helpIndexMI = new JMenuItem("Help Index");
                    helpMenu.add(aboutAppMI);
                    helpMenu.add(helpIndexMI);
                    menubar.add(fileMenu);
                        // Put JMenuItems in JMenus and JMenu objects in the
                        // JMenuBar.
                        // menubar.setHelpMenu(helpMenu);
                        // You cannot use this method at this time.
                        // The setHelpMenu method puts the "Help" menu on the far
                        // right. However, while this works for a Menu object the
                        // setHelpMenu() is not yet implemented for JMenuBar, so use
                    menubar.add(helpMenu);
                        // of the JMenuBar class.
                    setJMenuBar(menubar);
                    setVisible(true);
            }
     } // End of class definition for GUI8.

public class GUIDriver8
        {
          public static void main(String[] args)
                {
                  GUI8 gui = new GUI8();
                }
        }
```

Figure 8.10 shows an example of a GUI with Accessibility, although you will have to execute the program to really see the accessible features properly. You will probably need to look at the actual screen, as opposed to the figure, to see the keyboard accelerator indicators.

This application adds to the previous one (GUIDriver8.java) calls to the setMnemonics method (GUIDriver8.java). This provides a shortcut key to interact with a GUI component, including JMenu and JMenuItem components. In addition, the code calls setToolTipText() to set up the text that is displayed when the mouse pointer hovers over a component. When you set ToolTip text on a component, set a mnemonic, and then put the mouse pointer over the associated component, you get ToolTip-style text that contains both the ToolTip text and the mnemonic. As this code shows, adding Accessibility to code is quite simple.

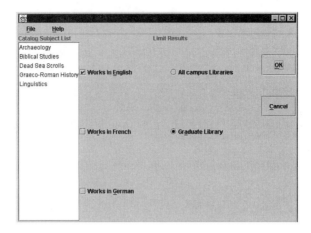

Figure 8.10

An example of using Accessibility through AccessibleText in a GUI.

Using Delegation Event Handling

Java 2 uses the Delegation event-handling mechanism introduced in JDK 1.1. This mechanism uses three main participants in user interactions with a Java GUI:

- Event sources—Components such as Button, JList, and JMenuItem, as well as Containers.
- Events—Defined by classes in java.awt.event. The class names have the form *xxx*Event, where *xxx* represents an event type, such as Action or Item. The main event types you will normally deal with are ActionEvents, ItemEvents, FocusEvents, MouseEvents, and WindowEvents. Other useful event classes include TextEvent and MouseMotionEvent.
- Event Listeners—Defined in java.awt.event. Class names have the form *xxx*Listener, where *xxx* is an event type, such as ActionListener, TextListener, and WindowListener. The event listeners are all Java interfaces. This means that to use them, you need to implement the interface in a user-defined event listener class.

An application defines a GUI. Then it instantiates event-listener objects. Next, the program registers a listener for a given GUI component. When the user interacts with that component (for example, by clicking a JButton), the action causes an ActionEvent to be generated.

NOTE

All GUI Components generate events. Some components generate multiple events of different types. Each component, however, has a *main* or preferred type of event that you should listen for, rather than listening for every event type that it produces. Although you might be able to detect a MouseEvent for a JButton, you should listen only for ActionEvents.

Adapter Classes 137

To register a listener on a component, you call an add*xxx*Listener() method, where *xxx* represents an event type, such as addActionListener() or addWindowListener(). Every such add*xxx*Listener() method takes as a parameter a reference to an object that implements the related interface. So addActionListener() takes as a required parameter an instance of a class that implements the ActionListener interface. There are four ways to implement the Listener class:

- A separate event-listening class
- An inner class that implements the event-listener interface
- An anonymous inner class that implements the event-listener interface
- The GUI class that contains the source component, which implements the interface itself

I recommend that, based on good object-oriented design principles, you use only the first option, a separate class that implements the event-listener interface. If you use any of the other three approaches, you end up creating a GUI class that is actually two classes in one: a user interface class and an event-handling class. This is a design problem. Also, you reduce any potential reuse of your GUI code. Any other approach also makes your GUI code more complicated, and in the case of anonymous inner classes, the code might be highly unreadable.

It should be noted that this may require creating multiple small event-handling classes that, unless packaged in a jar file, may take longer to download one by one.

Adapter Classes

As explained in Chapter 6, "Interfaces," a class that is declared as implementing an interface must implement all the methods declared by that interface. For an ActionListener, this is pretty simple, because the ActionListener interface defines only one method:

```
public void actionPerformed(ActionEvent e)
```

For other interfaces, however, that's not the case. For example, every GUI application should have a WindowListener. The WindowListener interface has several methods declared in it, most of which are not necessary for most programs. In order to implement this interface, you might have to create an event-listener class that has several empty methods, like the one shown here:

```
public void windowClosed(WindowEvente)
    { }
```

In order to save developers from having to write empty methods for conditions that programs do not need to deal with, Java provides Adapter classes. These are convenience classes that implement the various methods with empty curly braces, {}. By subclassing an Adapter class, you can override just the method(s) of interest to you, inheriting the empty methods from the Adapter class:

```
class WindowHandler extends WindowAdapter
    {
    // Only implement the WindowListener method you want to use.
    public void windowClosing(WindowEvent e)
```

```
            {
            System.exit(0);
            }
      }
```

The use of both approaches to event handling (creating a separate event-listening class and using an Adapter class) is illustrated in Listing 8.9. The code is arranged by class in logical order, so the program flow should be easy to follow in spite of the program's length.

Listing 8.9   Delegation Event Handling with Separate Event Listener Classes and Adapter Classes (GUIDriver9.java)

```
import javax.swing.*;
import java.awt.*;
import java.awt.event.*;
            // This import is needed for Event objects and Event listeners.

class GUI9 extends JFrame
      {     // Extend JFrame, just like Frame.
      JButton okButton;
      JButton cancelButton;
      JList subjectList;
      JScrollPane scrollPane;
      public JCheckBox englishChkbox;
      public JCheckBox frenchChkbox;
      public JCheckBox germanChkbox;
            // The three JCheckBox objects are declared as having
            // public access so that they can be seen from another class.
      JRadioButton allLibRB;
      JRadioButton thisLibRB;
      ButtonGroup libSelectBG;
      JMenuBar menubar;
      JMenu fileMenu;
      JMenu helpMenu;
      public JMenuItem titleSearchMI;
      public JMenuItem printResultsMI;
      public JMenuItem exitMI;
      JMenuItem aboutAppMI;
      JMenuItem helpIndexMI;
      JTextField titleTF;
      Container theContentPane;
      String[] catalogSubjects = {"Archaeology", "Biblical Studies",
                  "Dead Sea Scrolls", "Graeco-Roman History", "Linguistics"} ;

      public GUI9()
            {
                  // JFrame uses a BorderLayout, just like a Frame object.
                  // No need to change that.
            setSize(600,440);
            setBackground(Color.blue);
            theContentPane = getContentPane();
```

Adapter Classes 139

```java
        // Set the size and background color and get the
        // ContentPane reference.
titleTF = new JTextField();
JLabel titlelabel = new JLabel("Title Searched for:  ");
JPanel titlePanel = new JPanel(new GridLayout(2,1));
titlePanel.add(titlelabel);
titlePanel.add(titleTF);
theContentPane.add(titlePanel, "South");
        // This JTextField will be updated by a method called from a
        // JDialog to illustrate how to get input from a Dialog/JDialog
        // to another object easily, short of making remote method
        // calls
        // with RMI or CORBA.
okButton = new JButton("OK");
cancelButton= new JButton("Cancel");
JPanel buttonPanel = new JPanel(new GridLayout(9,1));
        // Create a JPanel and add the JButtons plus
        // empty JPanels in order to get the grid cells
        // and the JButtons to be an acceptable size.
 buttonPanel.add(new JPanel());
 buttonPanel.add(okButton);
 buttonPanel.add(new JPanel());
 buttonPanel.add(cancelButton);
 buttonPanel.add(new JPanel());
 buttonPanel.add(new JPanel());
 buttonPanel.add(new JPanel());
 buttonPanel.add(new JPanel());
            // In the above lines, I'm using a trick to get the JButtons
            // sized and positioned the way I want them. I do this by
            // creating a JPanel with a GridLayout arrangement.
            // Then I add empty JPanels and put them in the cells.
            // This creates more cells and thus makes each cell
            // shorter top to bottom. This technique also guarantees
            // that each JButton is aligned vertically and that all are
            // the same width, regardless of the text label for each.
            // Now, set up to listen for button clicks.
ButtonListener buttonListener = new ButtonListener(this);
        // Create an ActionListener object to listen for button
        // clicks.
        // In order for the buttonListener object to read/write
        // a Component on the screen, the listener object has
        // to have a reference to the GUI object.  Do this by
        // passing "this" (object reference of current GUI9
        // object) to the ButtonListener constructor.
   okButton.addActionListener(buttonListener);
   cancelButton.addActionListener(buttonListener);
        //  JButtons, Buttons and JMenuItems generate
        // ActionEvent objects.   This code "delegates"
        // responsibility for handling these ActionEvents from
```

continues

Listing 8.9 *continued*

```
            // the two JButtons to the buttonListener object.

    theContentPane.add(buttonPanel, "East");
            // Unlike java.awt.List, a JList cannot scroll on its own.
            // So create a JList and a JScrollPane for it.
    subjectList = new JList(catalogSubjects);;
    scrollPane = new JScrollPane();
    scrollPane.getViewport().setView(subjectList);
            // A JScrollPane provides for scrolling without any messy
            // code for scroll bars. You put a Component, even an image,
            // into a JScrollPane, and it lets the user scroll
            // with no programmatic intervention.
    JPanel listPanel = new JPanel(new BorderLayout());
    JLabel listLabel = new JLabel("Catalog Subject List");
    listPanel.add(listLabel, "North");
    listPanel.add(scrollPane, "Center");
    theContentPane.add(listPanel, "West");
            // Create a JPanel to hold the JList and
            // a descriptive JLabel for the JList.
    JPanel choicePanel = new JPanel(new GridLayout(3,2));
    JPanel containingPanel = new JPanel(new BorderLayout());
    JLabel choiceLabel = new JLabel
                        ("Limit Results", SwingConstants.CENTER);
            // Create a JLabel and align the text
            // to the center of the JLabel's area.
    containingPanel.add(choiceLabel, "North");
    libSelectBG = new ButtonGroup();
            // Like a java.awt.CheckboxGroup, this is a non-visual
            // component that provides for mutually exclusive
            // JRadioButton selection.
    allLibRB = new JRadioButton("Graduate Library", true);
            // Provide two JRadioButtons.  Put them in a ButtonGroup
            // Use the constructor that takes a boolean
            // to specify that this JRadioButton
            // should be selected by default when the GUI appears.
    thisLibRB = new JRadioButton("All campus Libraries");
    libSelectBG.add(allLibRB);
    libSelectBG.add(thisLibRB);
            // Create JRadioButtons and add them to a ButtonGroup
            // so they behave like radio buttons.
    englishChkbox = new JCheckBox("Works in English", true);
    frenchChkbox = new JCheckBox("Works in French");
    germanChkbox = new JCheckBox("Works in German");
            // Note that, unlike the java.awt.Checkbox class, the B in
            // JCheckBox is capitalized, as it should be
     choicePanel.add(englishChkbox);
     choicePanel.add(thisLibRB);
     choicePanel.add(frenchChkbox);
     choicePanel.add(allLibRB);
```

Adapter Classes 141

```java
choicePanel.add(germanChkbox);
    // Remember that Components are added to grid cells
    // Left to Right, Top to Bottom.
ChkBoxListener cbListener = new ChkBoxListener(this);
    // Create a Listener object for ItemEvent notification.
    // Pass it a reference to the current GUI object.
englishChkbox.addItemListener(cbListener);
frenchChkbox.addItemListener(cbListener);
germanChkbox.addItemListener(cbListener);
    // JCheckBoxes produce both Item and ActionEvent objects
    // when they are selected or deselected.  It is not
    // necessary to listen for any event unless you wish to
    // respond immediately to the JCheckBox changing state.
    // Otherwise, you could simply wait for something like the
    // OK button being clicked and then interrogate the state
    // of the JCheckBox (or java.awt.Checkbox).
    // If you do listen for events on the JCheckBox
    // you should listen for an ItemEvent.

containingPanel.add(choicePanel, "Center");
theContentPane.add(containingPanel, "Center");
    // The basic JMenuBar and JMenu methods are the same as for
    // the AWT counterparts, so this shows the basics of
    // an AWT menu.
menubar= new JMenuBar();;
fileMenu= new JMenu("File");
helpMenu = new JMenu("Help");
titleSearchMI = new JMenuItem("Search by title");
printResultsMI = new JMenuItem("Print Results");
exitMI= new JMenuItem("Exit");
    // Add ActionListeners to some JMenuItems
    // This allows you to detect the fact that a JMenuItem
    // was selected.
MenuProcessor menuProcessor = new MenuProcessor(this);
titleSearchMI.addActionListener(menuProcessor);
printResultsMI.addActionListener(menuProcessor);
exitMI.addActionListener(menuProcessor);
        // MenuItems and JMenuItems produce ActionEvents
        // when they are clicked.

fileMenu.add(titleSearchMI);
    // Create components for a program menu and then
    // build the menus.
 fileMenu.add(printResultsMI);
 fileMenu.add(exitMI);
 aboutAppMI = new JMenuItem("About Library application");
 helpIndexMI = new JMenuItem("Help Index");
 helpMenu.add(aboutAppMI);
 helpMenu.add(helpIndexMI);
```

continues

Listing 8.9 continued

```
              menubar.add(fileMenu);
              // menubar.setHelpMenu(helpMenu);\
              // Do not use this method as of Sept. 1999.
              // The setHelpMenu method puts the "Help" menu on the
              // far right.  However, while this works for a Menu object
              // the setHelpMenu() is not yet implemented for JMenuBar,
              // so use
                menubar.add(helpMenu);
              // of the JMenuBar class.
              setJMenuBar(menubar);
                  // Enable the Close button on the title bar of the JFrame
                  // so that it does something useful.  The default behavior
                  // is probably not what you want.
              addWindowListener(new Terminator());
              setVisible(true);
        }

                  // The following method exists so that another object,
                  //  here a JDIalog, can update the field by calling
                  // this method.
      public boolean setTitleText(String title)
            {
             titleTF.setText(title);
             titleTF.revalidate();
             return true;
            }

    }  // End of class definition for GUI9.

public class GUIDriver9
      {
       public static void main(String[] args)
              {
               GUI9 gui = new GUI9();
              }
      }


class ButtonListener implements ActionListener
                  // You must implement the Event listener interface
                  // for the Event type you are interested in processing.
      {
       GUI9 source;

       public ButtonListener(GUI9 g)
              {
               source = g;
                  // Save object reference to GUI9 object.
              }
```

Adapter Classes

```
          public void actionPerformed(ActionEvent e)
                // This is the only method in the ActionListener interface.
             {
              String command = e.getActionCommand();
                 // the getActionCommand method is a special method usable
                 // only with ActionEvents (so it is not a generic
                 // event handling method) that provides the "label"
                 // on the button.  If you are using a JButton
                 // which only has an ImageIcon and no text, you will need
                 // a more generic approach like e.getSource().
              if(command.equalsIgnoreCase("OK") )
                  JOptionPane.showMessageDialog
                (null, "OK Button Clicked", "Subject Search",
                        JOptionPane.INFORMATION_MESSAGE);
                 // This creates a JOptionPane, a pop-up message box
                 // that is informational. You could also create such a
                 // pop-up with options like yes/no, OK/Cancel and the like.
              if(command.equalsIgnoreCase("Cancel") )
                  JOptionPane.showMessageDialog
                    (null, "Cancel Button Clicked", "Subject Search",
                        JOptionPane.INFORMATION_MESSAGE);


             }
        } // End class definition for ButtonListener.

class ChkBoxListener implements ItemListener
        {
          GUI9 delegator;

          public ChkBoxListener(GUI9 g)
                {
                 delegator = g;
                }

          public void itemStateChanged(ItemEvent e)
                {
                  Object source = e.getItemSelectable();
                     // Returns a reference to an object of type Object
                     // that is an object reference for the Component
                     // object the user selected or deselected.
                  if(source == delegator.englishChkbox)
                      JOptionPane.showMessageDialog(
                          null, "englishChkbox selected/deselected",
                             "Subject Search",
JOptionPane.INFORMATION_MESSAGE);
                  if(source == delegator.frenchChkbox)
                      JOptionPane.showMessageDialog
                          (null, "frenchChkbox selected/deselected",
```

continues

Listing 8.9 continued

```
                            "Subject Search",
JOptionPane.INFORMATION_MESSAGE);
            if(source == delegator.germanChkbox)
                JOptionPane.showMessageDialog
                    (null, "germanChkbox selected/deselected",
                    "Subject Search",
JOptionPane.INFORMATION_MESSAGE);
            }
    } // End class definition for ChkboxListener.

class MenuProcessor implements ActionListener
    {
        GUI9 delegator;

        public MenuProcessor(GUI9 g)
            {
              delegator = g;
            }

        public void actionPerformed (ActionEvent e)
            {
              Object source = e.getSource();
                        if(source == delegator.titleSearchMI)
                    {
                      // If the user clicked the "Title Search"
                      // menu choice,
                      TitleSearchDialog tsDialog = new
                        TitleSearchDialog(delegator,
                                                    "Title Search Dialog",
                                                    true);
                      tsDialog.setSize(400,200);
                      tsDialog.setVisible(true);
                    }
              if(delegator.printResultsMI == source)
                    {
                      JOptionPane.showMessageDialog
                          (null, "Printing Results", "Print Status",
                            JOptionPane.INFORMATION_MESSAGE);
                    }
                if(source ==  delegator.exitMI)
                    System.exit(0);
            }

    } // End class definition for MenuProcessor.

class TitleSearchDialog extends JDialog
    {
      public GUI9 creator;
      public JTextField titleTextField;
```

```java
        public JButton okButton;
        public JButton cancelButton;

        public TitleSearchDialog(GUI9 g, String title, boolean modal)
                {
                    super(g,title, modal);
                        // Call the parent constructor for JDialog (or Dialog).  There
                        // is no default constructor, so you need to explicitly
                        // call the JDialog constructor with parameters.
                        // The three parameters are:
                        // A reference to a JFrame object (Frame object for a Dialog).
                        // A title String that appears on the title bar of the dialog.
                        // A boolean flag that states whether the dialog should be
                        // modal (true) or modeless (false).
                    creator = g;
                        // Save GUI9 object reference.
                    JPanel titlePanel = new JPanel();
                    JPanel buttonPanel = new JPanel();
                    titleTextField = new JTextField("", 50);
                    JLabel titleLabel = new JLabel("Enter a title to search for");
                    titlePanel.add(titleTextField);
                    getContentPane().add(titleLabel, "North");
                        // JDialogs, like JFrames use BorderLayout.
                    okButton = new JButton("    OK    ");
                        // Pad the text with blanks to make the JButton wider.
                    cancelButton = new JButton("Cancel");
                    TitleDialogButtonHandler tdbHandler =
                                new TitleDialogButtonHandler(this);
                        // Create a listener object with a reference to the
                        // current TitleSearchDialog object.

                    okButton.addActionListener(tdbHandler);
                    cancelButton.addActionListener(tdbHandler);
                    buttonPanel.add(okButton);
                    buttonPanel.add(cancelButton);
                    getContentPane().add(titlePanel, "Center");
                    getContentPane().add(buttonPanel, "South");
                }
    }

class TitleDialogButtonHandler implements ActionListener
    {
        TitleSearchDialog delegator;

        public TitleDialogButtonHandler(TitleSearchDialog tsd)
                {
                    delegator = tsd;
                        // Save a reference to the dialog object
                        // so the event handler can query the dialog's components.
```

continues

Listing 8.9 continued

```
            }

        public void actionPerformed(ActionEvent e)
                {
                 Object source = e.getSource();
                     // The getSource() method is a generic way to find out the
                     // Component that is the source of the event, and always
                     // works, whereas getActionCommand will not work if
                     // a JButton has only an ImageIcon and setActionCommand()
                     // was not executed for the JButton.
                 if(source == delegator.okButton)
                        {
                         boolean result = delegator. creator.setTitleText
                             (delegator.titleTextField.getText());
                         // Get the text from the titleTextField, and then
                         // use that String value to call the setTitleText() method
                         // in the GUI9 class.  This is an easy way to communicate
                         // back to the GUI object no matter how
                         // far it is removed from this event handler
                         // because the reference kept getting passed on.
                           delegator.dispose();
                         // Shut down the dialog.
                         // Do NOT just call setVisible(false) because this dialog is
                         // modal and your code will still be blocked
                         // until the dialog is dismissed.
                         }
                 if(source == delegator.cancelButton)
                         delegator.dispose();
                 }
       }

class Terminator extends WindowAdapter
      {
        // Inherit all the empty WindowListener methods from
        // the WindowAdapter convenience class, then override
        // the method of interest to you.  you need to be concerned with
        // the WindowListener methods, especially windowClosing()
        // in a GUI application (but NOT an Applet):
        // windowClosing().  The method windowClosed() is
        // not what you want for the Close
        // button on the JFrame's or (Frame's) title bar.
       public void windowClosing(WindowEvent e)
              {
                // You won't be back.
                System.exit(0);
              }
       } // End class definition of Terminator.
```

Figure 8.11 shows an example of using Delegation event handling. Just as with

Accessibility, you will have to execute the program to see it in action.

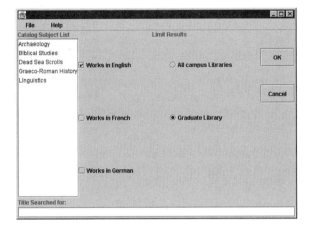

Figure 8.11

An example of using Delegation event handling (GUIDriver9.java).

This program illustrates several important points. First, it uses separate classes to handle events. This maximizes the potential for reusability and creates ease of maintenance while supporting good object-oriented design philosophy.

The two most common kinds of events you will "listen" for in most business-oriented application GUIs are ActionEvents and WindowEvents. The program also listens for ItemEvents, just to show you how to do it.

TIP

As noted in the program, you only need to listen for ItemEvents on Lists, JLists, JComboBoxes, JCheckBoxes, and so forth, if you intend to do some operation at the moment someone selects or deselects one of these. If all you want to do is check the status of the affected component when the user clicks the OK button or the like, you can ignore ItemEvents and simply query the state of the component. This simplifies your code.

You should listen for the main kind of event produced by the component. In the case of JMenuItems and JButtons (such as Button and MenuItem), this is an ActionEvent. To deal with button clicks or menu selections in this program, it creates a component such as a JButton and instantiates an instance of a class that implements the ActionListener interface. Then the GUI9 object registers the fact that it is delegating the responsibility for handling ActionEvents generated by the JButton to the ButtonHandler instance.

The `ButtonHandler` class shows an important technique for being able to track back to the delegating GUI. When the `ButtonHandler` object is instantiated, a reference to the GUI class is passed to the `ButtonHandler` object and saved. That reference can then be used later to interrogate or update components in the GUI or to execute methods of the GUI class. It is also valuable because if the `listener` object needs to display a dialog in response to a user request, an instance of `Frame` or `JFrame` is needed for the dialog's constructor, and the best way to do that is to provide the GUI's object reference.

Also important for an application (as opposed to an Applet) is using a `WindowListener`. There are several `WindowListener` methods, but the only one that you usually need to be concerned about is `windowClosing(WindowEvent e)`. This is the event created when a user clicks the Close button on the title bar of the Frame or JFrame window.

All the new classes in this example are simply event listeners, except for a `JDialog` subclass that illustrates two things. It shows how to handle events in another window from the main GUI (the same way as in the main GUI) and how to call back to methods in the main GUI class using an object reference from it. This program shows the general approach to event handling in a Java program. Except for the `WindowListener`, all the event listeners can be used equally in an Applet.

NOTE

Although listening for events using an observer-observable combination can be done anywhere, the event listeners and events defined in `java.awt.event` are used specifically for GUI programming.

Using Drag and Drop in Java

One of the new features in the Java 2 area of GUI programming is drag and drop. This feature is probably familiar to users of most common windowing systems. For example, in Solaris, you can "drag" a file from one directory to another using multiple File Manager windows. Java 2 provides a similar capability. You can click on a component, and while holding down the mouse, drag it to another application and release the mouse button. You "drop" the component on the application.

Drag and drop is new to Java, and it is limited in terms of what it will support. In fact, the default implementation in Java 2 only supports text. You can write your own code to do more if you wish. The interfaces and classes for the Java 2 drag and drop feature are found in `java.awt.dnd`. There are three important pieces in a drag-and-drop scenario:

- The `DragSource`—This is a component. Although the example here uses Swing components, you can use any subclass of `java.awt.Component`.
- `DropTarget`—This can be either a Java or non-Java target. For simplicity, the example here uses a Java `DropTarget`.
- `DataFlavor`—The `DataFlavor` is the type of thing being dragged and dropped. Currently there is only explicit Java 2 support for the text `DataFlavor`, although you can write code to drag and drop your own `DataFlavor`. For a drag-and-drop operation within the same JVM, the component being dragged is a `Transferable`. When the drag and drop is between two JVMs or between Java and a native program, the `DataFlavor` is usually provided with a `java.io.InputStream`.

Using Drag and Drop in Java 149

> **CAUTION**
>
> The `java.awt.dnd` package contains lots of classes with lots of methods with very similar names. When you select a class or method name to use, be careful to get the right one and spell it correctly.

A GUI component that is dragable must use

- `java.awt.dnd.DragSource`
- `java.awt.dnd.DragGestureRecognizer`
- `java.awt.dnd.DragGestureListener`
- `java.awt.datatransfer.Transferable`
- `java.awt.dnd.DragSourceListener`

> **NOTE**
>
> To provide a `DragSource` object for your application, you can either obtain one `DragSource` per JVM through `DragSource.getDefaultDragSource` or implement your own `DragSource` object to provide for every instance of `Component` objects that you want to drag and drop.

The `DragGestureRecognizer` shields you from platform dependencies caused by differences in mouse button usage for drag and drop. The actions related to dragging and dropping are called `DragGestures`, which are processed by a `DragGestureRecognizer`. There are several types of drag actions:

- ACTION_NONE—No action is taken.
- ACTION_COPY—The `DragSource` copies only the `DragSource`.
- ACTION_MOVE—The `DragSource` deletes the data when the drop operation completes successfully.
- ACTION_COPY or ACTION_MOVE—The `DragSource` performs either a Copy or Move, depending on the action requested by the `DropTarget`.
- ACTION_LINK or ACTION_REFERENCE—A data change to either the `DragSource` or `DropTarget` causes the same change to the other side of the drag-and-drop operation.

Listing 8.10 shows an example of a drag-and-drop program. It processes drag and drop by moving the contents of the drag area to the drop area. To implement this, the program does the following:

- Subclasses `JTextArea` to make a `DragSource`
- Subclasses `JTextArea` to make a `DropTarget`
- Creates a `DragGestureRecognizer` and a `DragSourceListener`
- Creates a `DropTargetListener`

To use the sample program, you type into the drag area on the top half of the screen. Then place your mouse pointer on the text you typed. Drag the mouse into the drop area on the bottom half of the screen. When you do the drag, the `DragGestureRecognizer` examines your action, such as ACTION_COPY, and determines if it is a valid action. If so, you can

150 Chapter 8: GUI Programming I: Applications

proceed with the drag. The `DragSourceListener` observes the drag to see if it is valid. When you get to the `DropTarget` area, the `DropTargetListener` implementation tracks the drop, including highlighting the drop area for you (when you do a valid drag and drop). The text in the drag source will disappear and reappear in the drop target area. This is shown in Listing 8.10.

Listing 8.10   Using Drag and Drop with Text (GUIDriver10.java)

```java
import javax.swing.*;
import java.awt.*;
import java.awt.dnd.*;
import java.awt.datatransfer.*;
import java.util.*;
import java.io.*;
import javax.swing.event.*;
import java.awt.event.*;


class GUI10 extends JFrame
    {
    DragTextArea dragArea;
    DropTextArea dropArea;
    JLabel dragLabel;
    JLabel dropLabel;
    JPanel dragPanel;
    JPanel dropPanel;

    Container theContentPane;

    public GUI10()
        {
        setSize(600,440);
        setBackground(Color.blue);
        theContentPane = getContentPane();
        theContentPane.setLayout(new GridLayout(2,1));
        // Set the size, background, and layout of the GUI. Also get
        // a reference to the ContentPane.
        dragLabel = new JLabel("Drag Source", SwingConstants.CENTER);
        dropLabel = new JLabel("Drop Target", SwingConstants.CENTER);
        dragArea = new DragTextArea(10,60);
        dropArea = new DropTextArea(10,60);
        // Currently, drag and drop works best with text. So, create two
        // JTextAreas, one for the source of the drag, and another for
        // the target of the drop operation.
        dragArea.setLineWrap(true);
        dropArea.setLineWrap(true);
        dragPanel = new JPanel(new BorderLayout());
        dropPanel = new JPanel(new BorderLayout());
        dragPanel.add(dragLabel, "North");
        dragPanel.add(dragArea, "Center");
        dropPanel.add(dropLabel, "North");
```

```java
                    dropPanel.add(dropArea, "Center");
                        // Create two JTextArea components to drag and drop between.
                    theContentPane.add(dragPanel);
                    theContentPane.add(dropPanel);
                    // Finish setting up the GUI and make it visible.
                    setVisible(true);
                }
    }   // End of class definition for GUI10.

public class GUIDriver10
        {
          public static void main(String[] args)
                {
                  GUI10 gui = new GUI10();
                }
        }

// Special JTexArea subclasses are defined here to
// user for drag source and drop target text areas.
class DragTextArea extends JTextArea
        {
            // This class provides a DragSource. You can type text into this
            // JTextArea and then drag the text to a DropTarget.
            DragSource dragSource;
            DragGestListener dragGestListener;
            DragSrcListener dragSrcListener;
            // You need a listener: one for the drag gesture with the mouse
            // and the second for drag actions from a specific source.
            public int dragAction = DnDConstants.ACTION_COPY_OR_MOVE;

            public DragTextArea(int r, int h)
                    {
                      super(r,h);
                      // Call the JTextArea constructor, passing rows and columns.
                      setOpaque(true);
                      dragSource = DragSource.getDefaultDragSource();
                      // Get a drag source object reference.
                      dragGestListener = new DragGestListener(this);
                            // Instantiate DragGestureListener.
                      dragSrcListener = new DragSrcListener(this);
                            // Listen for dragging actions.
                      dragSource.createDefaultDragGestureRecognizer(
                                                    this,
                                                    this.dragAction,
                                                    this.dragGestListener);
                            // Create a DragGestureRecognizer. This object determines
                            // that the mouse is in fact doing a drag, not some other
                            // action.
                    }
```

continues

Listing 8.10 continued

```java
    }   // End class definition for DragTextArea.


class DragGestListener implements DragGestureListener
        {
        // This class starts the drag operation if the action is
        // available.
        // It uses java.awt.datatransfer.StringSelection to transfer
        // the data from one JTextArea to another.

    DragTextArea textarea;

    public DragGestListener(DragTextArea dta)
           {
           textarea = dta;
           // Create a drag gesture listener for the drag
           // source text area.
           }

    public void dragGestureRecognized(DragGestureEvent e)
            {
            // This is similar to an actionPerformed method for
            // an ActionEvent.
            if((e.getDragAction() & textarea.dragAction) == 0)
                {
                System.out.println("Invalid drag action" +
                                      textarea.dragAction);
                return;
                }
            // Get the DragTextArea's text and put it inside
            // a Transferable object.
            Transferable transferable = new TransferableString
                 (textarea.getText() );
              // You need an object that implements Transferable
              // to drag it.
              try
                 {
                 e.startDrag(DragSource.DefaultCopyNoDrop,
                                transferable,
                                textarea.dragSrcListener);
            // Begin the drag, specifying the initial cursor,
            // the Transferable object, and
            // the drag source listener.
                 }
              catch( InvalidDnDOperationException idoe )
                    {
                    // If the drag failed, show the reason.
                    System.err.println( idoe.getMessage() );
```

Using Drag and Drop in Java

```java
                    }
              }
      }

class DragSrcListener implements DragSourceListener
       {
             // A listener to track the DND operation.

          DragTextArea textarea;

          public DragSrcListener(DragTextArea dta)
                {
                  textarea = dta;
                  // Save a reference to the drag source
                  // text area.
                }

         public void dragDropEnd(DragSourceDropEvent e)
              {
                // This is called when the drag gesture is completed.
                if( e.getDropSuccess() == false )
                     {
                       // If the drag and drop failed, print an error message
                       // to the console.
                       System.out.println( "Drop failed");
                       return;
                     }
                // Check the action selected by the drop target.
                  if(e.getDropAction() == DnDConstants.ACTION_MOVE)
                  // As of July 1999, Move, but not Copy, seemed to be the only
                  // workable choice. The Drag and Drop APIs have a ways to go
                  // to work well and be complete.
                   textarea.setText("");
                    // Clear the text area.
                }

            public void dragEnter(DragSourceDragEvent e)
                 {
                   // This is called when the drag starts.  The class and
                   // DragSourceEvent object are somewhat analogous to classes
                   // that implement MouseListener and MouseMotionListener.
                   DragSourceContext context = e.getDragSourceContext();
                   int dropAction = e.getDropAction();
                   if( (dropAction & textarea.dragAction) != 0)
                         {
                           context.setCursor
                               (DragSource.DefaultCopyDrop);
                           // When a drag starts, change the pointer shape.
                         }
```

continues

Listing 8.10   continued

```
                else
                    {
                       context.setCursor(DragSource.DefaultCopyNoDrop);
                       }
                }

    public void dragOver(DragSourceDragEvent e)
         {
         // This is called when you drag a Transferable over
         // something else .
         DragSourceContext context = e.getDragSourceContext();
         int userAction = e.getUserAction();
         System.out.println("dragOver user actions " + userAction);
         }

      public void dragExit(DragSourceEvent e)
          { }


      public void dropActionChanged (DragSourceDragEvent e)
            {
             DragSourceContext context = e.getDragSourceContext();
             context.setCursor(DragSource.DefaultCopyNoDrop);
            }
    }

class DropTextArea extends JTextArea
    {
    // This class subclasses JTextArea and is the target
    // for the drop operation.
    DropTgtListener dropTgtListener;
    int acceptableActions;
    public Color borderColor;
    DropTarget dropTarget;

    public DropTextArea(int r, int c)
         {
         super(r,c);
         borderColor=Color.green;
         // After calling the JTextArea's constructor, set the border
         // color of an object being dropped on this drop target for
         // a visual cue for dropping.
         dropTgtListener = new DropTgtListener(this);
              // Create a DropTargetListener.
          acceptableActions = DnDConstants.ACTION_COPY_OR_MOVE;
          dropTarget = new DropTarget(this,
                                       acceptableActions,
                                       dropTgtListener,
                                       true);
```

Using Drag and Drop in Java 155

```
                // Specify the component that is the DropTarget,
                // the acceptableActions, the DropTargetListener instance
                // and a boolean value to show if the DropTarget is
                // accepting drops.
        }

    private void showBorder(boolean borderFlag)
            {
              if(borderFlag)
                  {
                    setBorder( BorderFactory.createLineBorder
                        (this.borderColor, 10) );
                    // Display the border on the Transferable
                    // being dropped.
                  }
              else
                  {
                    setBorder( BorderFactory.createEmptyBorder() );
                  }
              getParent().validate();
              repaint();
            }

    }   // End of class definition for DropTextArea.

class DropTgtListener implements DropTargetListener
        {
        private Color borderColor;
        DropTextArea textArea;

        public DropTgtListener(DropTextArea dta)
              {
                textArea = dta;
                // Save a reference to the drop target text area.
              }

        private boolean isDragFlavorSupported(DropTargetDragEvent e)
              {
                // Determine if drag DataFlavor is acceptable.
                // The flavor refers to the type of data.
                // For example, a text flavor is supported while
                // a CORBA object or StarOffice spreadsheet might not be.
                // You can create your own flavor and write code to support it.
                boolean ok=false;
                if (e.isDataFlavorSupported(TransferableString.plainTextFlavor))
                      {
                    ok=true;
                      }
                else
```

continues

Listing 8.10 continued

```java
                if (e.isDataFlavorSupported(
                   TransferableString.localStringFlavor))
                        {
                          ok=true;
                        }
                   else
                        if
(e.isDataFlavorSupported(DataFlavor.stringFlavor))
                                {
                                  ok=true;
                                }
                          else
                                if (e.isDataFlavorSupported
                                   (DataFlavor.plainTextFlavor))
                                        {
                                          ok=true;
                                        }
        return ok;
      }

    private DataFlavor chooseDropFlavor(DropTargetDropEvent e)
         {
         // This method sets the flavor.
         if (e.isLocalTransfer() == true &&
         e.isDataFlavorSupported(TransferableString.localStringFlavor))
                {
                  return TransferableString.localStringFlavor;
                }
         DataFlavor theFlavor = null;
         if (e.isDataFlavorSupported(TransferableString.plainTextFlavor))
                 {
                   theFlavor = TransferableString.plainTextFlavor;
                 }
         else
                if (e.isDataFlavorSupported(
                   TransferableString.localStringFlavor))
                         {
                           theFlavor = TransferableString.localStringFlavor;
                           // Local String flavor is supported.
                         }
                   else
                         if (e.isDataFlavorSupported(DataFlavor.stringFlavor))
                                  {
                                    theFlavor = DataFlavor.stringFlavor;
                                  }
                            else
                                  if (e.isDataFlavorSupported
                                       (DataFlavor.plainTextFlavor))
                                    // If plain text flavor is valid.
```

```java
                            {
                            theFlavor = DataFlavor.plainTextFlavor;
                            }
            return theFlavor;
          }


    private boolean isDragOk(DropTargetDragEvent e)
        {
            // This method is used by dragEnter() and dragOver().
          if(isDragFlavorSupported(e) == false)
                {
                // If the flavor is invalid, the drop fails.
            System.out.println( " Problem in isDragOk:  no flavors chosen" );
            return false;
                }

            // The API doc on DropTargetDragEvent rejectDrag says that
            // the dropAction should be examined.
          int dropAction = e.getDropAction();
          System.out.print("dt drop action " + dropAction);
          boolean result = true;
          if ((dropAction & textArea.acceptableActions) == 0)
            result = false;
              // Test to see if the Drop action is acceptable.
              // Not all components can accept a drop.
          return result;
        }

    public void dragEnter(DropTargetDragEvent e)
        {
          // Feedback from acceptDrop or rejectDrop.
          if(isDragOk(e) == false)
                {
          System.out.println( "No entering to drop allowed");
          textArea.borderColor=Color.red;
          showBorder(true);
          e.rejectDrag();
          return;
                }
          textArea.borderColor=Color.green;
          showBorder(true);
          e.acceptDrag(e.getDropAction());
        }

    private void showBorder(boolean borderFlag)
            {
              // This method shows a border on a Transferable
              // inside the drop target.
```

continues

Listing 8.10 continued

```
            if(borderFlag)
                {
                  textArea.setBorder( BorderFactory.createLineBorder
                     (this.borderColor, 10) );
                }
            else
                {
                  textArea.setBorder( BorderFactory.createEmptyBorder() );
                }
            textArea.getParent().validate();
            textArea.repaint();
        }

    public void dragOver(DropTargetDragEvent e)
        {
          // This method is invoked when you drag over the drop target.
           // Provide feedback from dragOK() for dragOver().
          if(isDragOk(e) == false)
                {
                System.out.println( "DropTarget dragOver is not ok" );
                textArea.borderColor=Color.red;
                // Provide a visual cue that the drop is not acceptable.
                showBorder(true);
                e.rejectDrag();
                return;
                }
          e.acceptDrag(e.getDropAction());
        }

    public void dropActionChanged(DropTargetDragEvent e)
        {
          if(isDragOk(e) == false)
                {
                System.out.println
                    ( "DropTgtListener dropActionChanged is not allowed" );
                e.rejectDrag();
                }
          else
                 e.acceptDrag(e.getDropAction());
        }

    public void dragExit(DropTargetEvent e)
        {
          textArea.borderColor=Color.green;
          showBorder(false);
        }

    public void drop(DropTargetDropEvent e)
        {
```

```java
      // This method handles the drop action.
  Object content =null;
      // Perform the action from the getSourceAction() method on
      // the Transferable.
      // Call acceptDrop or rejectDrop
      // For the same JVM as the DragSource,
      // use TransferableString.localStringFlavor.
      // When you find a match for the flavor,
      // validate the operation on the DropTarget.
      // Get the Transferable object's data according to the
      // chosen flavor.
      // Transfer the data.

DataFlavor theFlavor = chooseDropFlavor(e);
// Validate the data flavor.
if (theFlavor == null)
     {
   System.err.println( "No valid DataFlavor found" );
   e.rejectDrop();
        showBorder(false);
   return;
     }

try
      {
        // Validate the drop action.
        e.acceptDrop(textArea.acceptableActions);
        // Accept drop Action.  COPY_OR_MOVE results in MOVE.
        content = e.getTransferable().getTransferData(theFlavor);
        if (content == null)
          throw new NullPointerException();
        // Throw an exception if the Transferable is empty.
      }
  catch (Exception ex )
      {
    System.err.println( "No transfer data obtained:" +
                       ex.getMessage());
    ex.printStackTrace();
    e.dropComplete(false);
    showBorder(false);
    return;
      }

if (content instanceof String )
    {
     // If the Transferable is a String, use it to update the
     // drop target text area. As this indicates, much about
     // drag and drop has to be done by the developer.
  String s = (String) content;
```

continues

Listing 8.10 continued

```java
            textArea.setText(s);
            }
        else
            {
            // If not a local String, use an InputStream to transfer data.
            if (content instanceof InputStream)
                {
             InputStream is = (InputStream)content;
             InputStreamReader isr = null;
            try
                    {
                    isr=new InputStreamReader(is,"Unicode");
                    }
                catch(UnsupportedEncodingException uee)
                    {
                  isr=new InputStreamReader(is);
                    }

            StringBuffer str = new StringBuffer();
            int i = -1;
            try
                    {
                while((i = isr.read()) >= 0 )
                        {
                    if (i != 0)
                            str.append((char)i);
                        }

                    textArea.setText(str.toString());
                }
                catch(IOException ioe)
                    {
                // As of July 1999, there is a bug when attempting to
                // drag to or from MS Word 97 so this won't work for that.
                    System.err.println( "cannot read" + ioe);
                    e.dropComplete(false);
                   showBorder(false);
                   JOptionPane.showMessageDialog(textArea,
                        ioe.getMessage(),
                        "Error",
                        JOptionPane.ERROR_MESSAGE);
                   return;
                  } // End of catch block.
                } // End of if block.
            else
                {
               e.dropComplete(false);
               showBorder(false);
               return;
```

```
            } // End of else block.
          e.dropComplete(true);
          showBorder(false);
            // There was a problem trying to transfer the data.
        } // End of drop() method.
    } // End of class definition for DropTgtListener.
```

The `TransferableString` class used in this example is shown in Listing 8.11.

Listing 8.11   The TransferableString Class Used for a Transferable in Drag and Drop from Listing 8.10 (TransferableString.java)

```
import javax.swing.*;
import java.awt.*;
import java.awt.datatransfer.*;
import java.io.*;
import java.util.*;
import java.util.List;

public class TransferableString implements Transferable, ClipboardOwner
      {
          // Implement the Transferable interface
          // to move dragged data.
       public static final DataFlavor plainTextFlavor =
                                   DataFlavor.plainTextFlavor;
       public static final DataFlavor localStringFlavor =
                                   DataFlavor.stringFlavor;
       public static final DataFlavor[] flavorArray = {
            TransferableString.plainTextFlavor,
            TransferableString.localStringFlavor};
       private String content;
       private static final List flavorList = Arrays.asList( flavorArray );

       public TransferableString(String s)
            {
             content = s;
            }

       public synchronized DataFlavor[] getTransferDataFlavors()
            {
             return flavorArray;
            }

        public boolean isDataFlavorSupported( DataFlavor flavor )
            {
             return ( flavorList.contains( flavor ) );
            }

        public synchronized Object getTransferData(DataFlavor flavor)
            throws UnsupportedFlavorException, IOException
```

continues

Listing 8.11   continued

```
            {
              if (flavor.equals(TransferableString.plainTextFlavor))
                 {
                    return new ByteArrayInputStream(content.getBytes
                       ("Unicode"));
                 }
              else
                    if (TransferableString.localStringFlavor.equals(flavor))
                       {
                          return content;
                       }
                    else
                       {
                          throw new UnsupportedFlavorException (flavor);
                       }
        }

    public void lostOwnership(Clipboard clipboard, Transferable contents)
        {
           System.out.println ("TransferableString lost ownership of " +
              clipboard.getName());
           System.out.println ("Text: " + contents);
        }
   } // End class definition for TransferableString
```

As you can see, simply copying a String from a JTextArea to another JTextArea is not a trivial task. There is code in this example for reading the dragged data through an InputStream. This is used in the case of a drag from a non-Java source. This functionality still had some bugs as of July 1999. When everything is working correctly, you will be able to drag and drop to and from Java and non-Java applications.

Figure 8.12 shows the screen before a drag-and-drop operation, and Figure 8.13 shows the screen after a drag-and-drop operation.

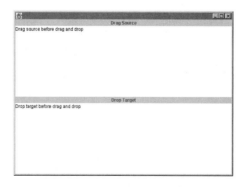

Figure 8.12

A screen before drag and drop.

Using Drag and Drop in Java 163

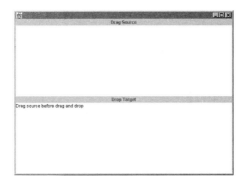

Figure 8.13
A screen after drag and drop.

CHAPTER 9

GUI Programming II: Applets

An Applet Overview

An applet is a special type of Java GUI program that is intended to be run inside a Web browser. Unlike the programs shown in Chapter 8, "GUI Programming I: Applications," an applet cannot run by itself but must be hosted by another program.

> **NOTE**
>
> You can code an applet class that can run in a standalone fashion as an application and as an applet hosted by a browser. This is unusual but can easily be accomplished. To do this, you code all the applet methods that are appropriate. Then you code a main method that one way or another instantiates a Frame, instantiates the applet subclass, adds the applet object to the Frame, and then calls the applet methods as appropriate. Because the applet is running as a standalone application, it must have a WindowListener object that deals with the windowClosing() method and also has a call to System.exit().

The essential reason for this is that an applet is a subclass of the Panel class. As explained in the last chapter, a standalone Java GUI application must use a Frame as the outermost window. Because you put a Panel in a Frame, and normally not vice versa, an applet does not have a Frame.

166 Chapter 9: GUI Programming II: Applets

> **NOTE**
>
> Technically speaking, an applet does have a `Frame`. When the Web browser detects an applet tag, it starts a Java program in the browser that instantiates a `Frame`. Then the applet class, after being downloaded, is instantiated and added to the `Frame` just as any AWT component would be. It is this Java program, which the browser runs, that has the `main` method and the `Frame`. Although it is possible to get to the `Frame` object through successive calls to `getParent()`, in general this approach of using the invisible `Frame` is a hack and is not recommended. The `Frame` object created by the browser is essentially invisible.

Because applets do not have their own `Frame`, there are some limitations to what an applet can do. First, it is generally difficult to add menus to applets. In an application, you can add menus to a `Menubar`, which is added to a `Frame`. `Menubars` cannot be added to `Panels`, so they cannot be added to applets easily.

> **CAUTION**
>
> It is possible to put a menu in an applet. Although is difficult to do, it is not nearly as difficult as returning user interaction with the menu to the applet. In general, you should avoid using a menu and find some other method for getting user choices.

Also, because of the lack of an immediate `Frame` object, applets do not normally have Dialogs. Dialogs, as shown in the preceding chapter, require an instance of a `Frame` for a constructor parameter. There are, again, ways to work around this, but none of them are very elegant. You can, for example, do this:

```
MyDialog md = new MyDialog(new Frame(), "Dialog in an Applet", true);
```

This statement creates a new `Frame` object on-the-fly to be used as the basis of the Dialog. Again, getting event notification back to the applet is a bit tricky, so this is usually avoided.

Applet Security Considerations

Generally speaking, applets are severely restricted as to what they are allowed to do on a user's system. They run, by default, in what is called the *sandbox*. The sandbox, which is implemented by the `java.lang.SecurityManager` class or a subclass of it, restricts applets from the following activities. Applets cannot

- Read from or write to the client machine's file system.
- Modify thread groups.
- Connect to any host besides the host they were downloaded from.
- Access any system properties related to the local machine's file system.

Because of these restrictions, an applet cannot execute code installed on a local machine, and therefore, an applet cannot print from the machine it is running on.

> **TIP**
>
> In Java 2, this particular problem (and, indeed, any given set of applet restrictions) can be overcome through the use of a policy file. In order to allow an applet to print, the client machine needs a policy file which specifies that the applet has the `RuntimePermission` for `PrintJob`.

Prior to Java 2, you could get around these limitations of the sandbox by signing your applet with a digital signature. In JDK 1.1, if a browser such as Netscape accepted signed applets, these signed applets could do whatever they wanted if the user let them execute. A signed applet in a JDK 1.1–compatible browser has carte blanche to do anything an application program can do. All a signature did was tell the user the probable source of the applet. The user had to decide whether to trust the applet source not do anything malicious. In Java 2, this has all changed. Now, signing an applet is not sufficient. It is now also necessary to have a policy file to specifically grant signed code permission for the activities you want an applet to perform. Note that you can grant all applets certain permissions with a policy file even if they are not signed, but you would probably not want to do this.

Main Applet Methods

Although an applet can have many methods, here are five main methods that you need to be aware of:

- init()
- start()
- paint()
- stop()
- destroy()

The init() method is the place to put code that sets up the applet screen, such as adding Buttons or text fields or creating Image objects within limits. It is also the place to start the downloading of images through a separate thread using the MediaTracker class discussed later. Think of init() as analogous to a constructor. Applets do not have explicit constructors.

The start() method is where you initiate what must happen when a user goes to your applet's Web page. Here is a sample scenario. Five Web pages are up, one of which has your applet on it. At first, the user is looking at another Web page. When he moves to your applet's Web page, the JVM calls the start() method of your applet. Now you begin animation or start playing sound—any task that should happen only while your applet is being looked at by the user.

The paint() method is used to paint the applet on the screen. Just as all Component subclasses have a paint() method, an applet has a paint() method. This method draws text, shapes, or images on the applet's surface. In fact, if your applet includes an image, the paint() method is called by the JVM whenever there are more pixels to add to the image as it is being downloaded. These cause the image to go from nonexistent to a clear picture.

Your applet must override and implement at least one of these three methods: init(), start(), or paint(). It must have at least one of these, but it can have all three. If it does not, you will not be able to put anything on the applet's screen or have it perform any work.

The stop() method is called by the JVM when the user switches from the Web page with the applet to another Web page. It is important to use the stop() method to halt activity that should not go on while the applet is not visible. This includes animation or the playing of sound files—anything that uses the CPU or that would interfere with the user.

The destroy() method is called when the applet's Web page is closed. It is used to free resources held by the applet. Because applets usually do not hold large resources or the kind of resources that must be closed (such as a file), there's generally no need to code this method.

Running Applets

Applets run in Web browsers and are loaded through HTML applet tags. The most important tags are covered here. Listing 9.1 shows sample HTML for running an applet.

Listing 9.1   Sample HTML to Run an Applet (MyApplet.html)

```
<HTML>
<Title>
This is a sample Applet HTML file
</Title>
<BODY>
<APPLET code=MyApplet   archive=Myjar.jar
width=400 height=300
codebase=http://www.gradschoollibrary.edu/Applets
alternatetxt="Get a Java-enabled browser"
vgap =5 hgap=5
<param name=imagefile >
value=http://www.gradschoollibrary/Applets/images/libraryentrace.gif>
</APPLET>
</BODY>
</HTML>
```

This book does not cover HTML, so the non-applet tags will not be discussed. In the order in which they appear, here is what each tag does.

The <APPLET> tag tells the browser that what follows is an applet that the browser must get from some disk, either locally or, more probably, remotely from a Web server.

The code keyword specifies the name of the class to load first for the applet. This is generally the name of the applet class you want to use, but it can be any class, as long as that class causes the applet subclass to be loaded.

The archive keyword tells the browser which (if any) .jar file(s) to download to find the classes and other resources needed by the applet.

> **TIP**
>
> Although using a `.jar` file is not necessary, it is highly recommended. A `.jar` file, by default, uses compression. It reduces the size of the downloaded code transmitted over the network, making downloading faster. In addition, `.jar` files reduce the overhead needed to make network connections for every individual file. If an applet has 10 classes, and there is no `.jar` file for the applet, the browser must make 10 separate connections (including a handshake) with the Web server's system. It must then request the download and then disconnect. There are multiple network trips required to do just the handshake. By using a `.jar` file, these trips are cut down to only one connect-download-disconnect cycle.

> **NOTE**
>
> Generally speaking, a browser must be at least JDK 1.1–compatible in order to use `.jar` files.

It is also possible to list multiple comma-delimited `.jar` files.

The `height` and `width` specify the size in pixels of the applet. Unlike a GUI application, an applet generally cannot specify its size internally through a `setSize()` call. Instead, this must be set in the HTML tags. You can specify either a precise pixel size or a percentage of the screen real estate. The `Applet` class does have a `resize()` method, but it is not supported on most browsers.

> **CAUTION**
>
> Be very careful when sizing an applet. Because it cannot dynamically be resized, as an application can, you have to live with the size you choose. Do not assume that all users have the high screen resolutions that you might have on a 21-inch monitor for a Sparc system. It is more likely that end users on the Internet have 15-inch monitors with maybe 800×600 resolution. If you specify a width of 900, you might end up with an OK button off the right side of the screen that a user has no way to reach.

The `codebase` refers to the directory (usually on a Web server) where the applet code resides. It is generally in a directory or a subdirectory of the directory that contains the source of the Web page, which is called the `Documentbase`.

The `alternatetext` keyword is used to specify text that will appear on the screen if the applet can't run for any reason. Failure might occur because the browser doesn't support Java or for some other reason, excluding an exception. You might put a message here such as "If you had a Java-enabled browser, you'd see a great applet here." Or, you might provide a link to a Web site where you can download a Java-enabled browser. It's up to you what to say with this tag. Remember that it shows up only if your applet cannot run because the browser won't support it.

You can specify how many pixels should separate the applet from what is around it by using the `hgap` and `vgap` options. The `hgap` value specifies horizontal separation, whereas `vgap` specifies the vertical gap between other Web page content and the applet.

170 Chapter 9: GUI Programming II: Applets

The final important option is to specify a parameter. The applet uses the `getParameter()` method to obtain the value specified in the parameter name. In the sample HTML, the applet uses a `getParameter("imagefile")` in order to get the name of the image file needed to display an image. Although the parameter name, imagefile, is not case-sensitive in your Java code, the value is case-sensitive. So you can code

`getParameter("iMaGeFile");`

and it would work. On the other hand, correctly specifying a case-sensitive value is critical for a filename. Systems like UNIX, which are case-sensitive, will not find the URL otherwise.

Using the AppletViewer

Java 2 provides a simple tool for testing your `Applet`, called AppletViewer. The AppletViewer tool can be quite handy for testing, especially because it has menu options to call, on request, each main applet method, such as `init`, `start`, or `stop`. At the same time, remember that the AppletViewer is not a browser. It cannot be used for viewing Web pages. It only executes the applet on a Web page and does not reflect browser-specific implementation choices that might affect your code. It is just a quick unit-testing tool that is no substitute for doing full testing. To invoke the AppletViewer, you need an HTML file that includes necessary applet tags. You call it in this way:

`Appletviewer <-debug> MyApplet.html`

The Java Plug-In

It's no secret that there are many incompatibilities among browsers, and different versions of the same browsers, such as Netscape, support different versions of Java. Other browsers, such as Internet Explorer, don't fully support Sun's definition of Java, omitting important core packages, such as `java.rmi`. To address these potential incompatibilities and to respond to the apparent slowness of vendors in making their browsers JVM–compliant with the latest Java version, Sun has introduced the Java plug-in. In essence, this plug-in replaces the JVM of the browser. This allows you to code a Java 2–based applet and run it on any client machine that has the Java plug-in for Java 2 installed, regardless of the browser version on the client machine. As of this writing (July 1999), it appears that Netscape will never support Java 2 in its browser's JVM, and Internet Explorer 5.0 supports only a partial version of JDK 1.1. Therefore, the only way to use Java 2–specific features in an applet is to use the Java plug-in for Java 2.

To use the Java plug-in, you need to change your applet tags. These tags tell the browser whether to use its own JVM or the plug-in's JVM. You are not required to use the plug-in at all times. You use it only when you go to a Web page that has the proper tags. The Java plug-in has a utility included with it that can change your applet tags appropriately. This is a simple way to get Java 2 features in your applet right now, instead of waiting and hoping that browser vendors, at some time in the future, will make their browsers Java 2–compliant.

> **NOTE**
>
> One of the best things about using the Java plug-in is that it provides Swing in the Java 2 version. It is not practical to use Swing in an applet, unless it is already resident on the client machine. Swing classes are more than 1MB in size, which would be a prohibitively large applet download.

Applet Programming

Applets, as `Panels`, conform to what was discussed about GUI programming in Chapter 8. This means you can add components to an applet, set the layout manager, add event listeners, and process user interaction. Yet, there are some things that applets are particularly good at, such as displaying images. The remainder of the chapter is devoted to showing how to code applets.

A Simple Applet: Code Example

Listing 9.2 illustrates code to show a minimal applet with some GUI components on it. Figure 9.1 shows the applet running in AppletViewer.

Listing 9.2   A Basic Applet Coding Example (BookSearch.html)
```
<HTML>
<TITLE>
Basic Applet Example for Pure Java
</TITLE>
<BODY>
<Applet code=BookSearchApplet.class height=100 width=200>
</Applet>
</BODY>
</HTML>
```

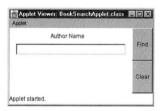

Figure 9.1

A simple applet running in the AppletViewer.

Listing 9.3 shows the code for this basic applet.

Listing 9.3   A Simple Applet Using the Applet Class (BookSearchApplet.java)
```
import java.Applet.*; // You need to import the Applet package for an Applet.
import java.awt.*;    // Use the AWT component classes.
public class BookSearchApplet extends Applet
```

continues

Listing 9.3 continued

```
                            // All Applets must subclass the
                            // java.Applet.Applet class.
{
  // Declare instance variables.
  Button findButton;
  Button clearButton;
  Label authorLabel;
  TextField authorNameTF;

  public void init()
          { // Override the init method to instantiate the GUI elements.
            // init() is the first method you can code for an applet that is
            // called by the browser.
            findButton = new Button("Find");;
            clearButton = new Button("Clear");
            authorLabel = new Label("Author Name");
            authorNameTF = new TextField("", 30);
            // Instantiate GUI components, including a Button, Label,
            // and TextField. Applets use the same GUI components
            // you would put into any Java GUI.
            setLayout(new BorderLayout());
                        // Override the default layout manager of the
                        // Applet, which is FlowLayout,
                        // just like a Panel.
            Panel tempP1 = new Panel();
                        // An applet is a Container and can hold
                        // other Containers, as well as components.
            Panel tempP2 = new Panel (new GridLayout(2,1));
                        // Create two Panels that will be used just for
                        // layout and do not need to be referenced
                        // elsewhere.

            tempP1.add(authorLabel);
            tempP1.add(authorNameTF);
            tempP2.add(findButton);
            tempP2.add(clearButton);
            add(tempP1, "Center");
            add(tempP2, "East");
                        // Add components to the Panels.
          }
} // End class definition BookSearchApplet.
```

This applet can be executed with either a browser or the AppletViewer. Because it uses no Java 2–specific features, it can run in most browser versions, such as the Icesoft browser, or Hotjava. This simple applet has only an `init()` method because there's nothing for a `paint` or `start` method to do, nor anything to stop, nor any resources to release in the `destroy()` method. Again, the `init()` method is used, inthis case, like a constructor.

Parameters in an Applet: Code Example

Listing 9.4 shows some sample HTML for an applet that uses parameters. The applet in Listing 9.5 illustrates how to read an applet parameter from the applet tag.

> **CAUTION**
>
> Applet parameters are always read as Java `Strings`. Therefore, to give a number to an applet, you need to convert it to a number, using a method such as `Integer.parseInt()`.

You can put anything you want into a parameter. The main advantage of using a parameter through the PARAM option is to specify information to the applet. This eliminates the need to recompile the applet and create a new .jar file for a small change, such as a new image of the week. It's much easier to modify the HTML source than to modify, recompile, and put the new applet version in a new .jar file. Figure 9.2 shows an applet that uses parameters running in the AppletViewer.

Listing 9.4 Sample HTML for an Applet That Uses Parameters (newBook.htm)
```
<HTML>
<TITLE>
Basic Applet with Parameters Example for Pure Java
</TITLE>
<BODY>
<Applet code=NewBookApplet.class height=200 width=350>
<PARAM NAME=Title Value="Dead Sea Scrolls in Recent Research">
</Applet>
</BODY>
</HTML>
```

Listing 9.5 An Applet That Uses Parameters (NewBookApplet.java)
```
import java.Applet.*; // You need to import the Applet package for an Applet.
import java.awt.*;
public class NewBookApplet extends Applet
                    // All Applets must subclass the
                    // java.Applet.Applet class.
   {
     Button nextButton;
     Label newTitleLabel;
     String newTitleString;

     public void init()
            // init() is the first user-defined method called in the applet.
         {  // Override the init method to instantiate the GUI elements.
            nextButton = new Button("Next");;
            newTitleLabel = new Label("The most recent book added to the " +
                                     "Library collection is");
            // Instantiate GUI components
            setLayout(new BorderLayout());
```

continues

Listing 9.5 continued

```
                    // Override the default layout manager of the Applet
                    // which is FlowLayout, just like a Panel.
        Panel tempP1 = new Panel(new GridLayout(1,5));
                    // Here's a trick. To make the nextButton appear
                    // smaller than a whole region on the BorderLayout,
                    // surround it with empty Panels. This will make
                    // the GridLayout create multiple, equal-sized
                    // cells.
                    // Add as many as needed to get the desired effect.
        tempP1.add(new Panel());
        tempP1.add(new Panel());
        tempP1.add(nextButton);
        tempP1.add(new Panel());
        tempP1.add(new Panel());
                    // The above code sets up a set of Buttons sized and spaced
                    // based on adding empty Panel objects to the same container.
        add(tempP1, "South");
                    // Put the nextButton in the bottom of the Applet.
        add(newTitleLabel, "North");
        newTitleString = getParameter("Title");
                    // Get the Parameter String and store it.
                    // All applet parameters are Strings.
        repaint();  // Make sure the Applet is repainted
                    // before it is displayed.
                    // Always call repaint(), never paint().
    }

    public void paint(Graphics g)
        {           // All drawing is done in the paint()
                    // method of a Component.
        g.drawString(newTitleString, 50,100);
                    // The drawString method of the java.awt.Graphics
                    // class draws the named String at the given
                    // x and y coordinates every time the paint()
                    // method is called.
        }
    } // End class definition NewBookApplet
```

This applet reads a parameter, saves its value, and then displays the parameter's value by painting it on the screen using the `drawString()` method. The `java.awt.Graphics` class has several methods for drawing `String`s and shapes, such as `drawRect()`. It also has methods for changing the color for drawing. Every time the applet is repainted, the `String` is drawn on its surface again. To paint on a specific component within the applet requires overriding `paint` specifically for that component.

Figure 9.2
An applet that uses parameters to set values.

TIP

It is very important to call repaint() and not paint(). There are two reasons. The first is that you want the JVM to give you a Graphics object for the paint() method. The second (and much more important) reason is that the JVM can coalesce multiple repaint() calls into one paint() call. It cannot do this with direct calls to paint(). Therefore, calling repaint() will probably make your program perform much better than calling paint() explicitly.

Sound in an Applet: Code Example

It is also possible, and really quite easy, to play sound files in a Java program.

NOTE

Prior to Java 2, it was easy to play sound in an applet, but problematic to do so in an application. Java 2 supports a new Sound API to enable easily playing sound in an application. That is beyond the scope of this book, however.

Java applets support only one file format for playing sound, apart from the new Sound API. This format is an .au file. To play sound in an applet, you create, either explicitly or implicitly, an AudioClip object, such as this one:

```
AudioClip ac = new AudioClip(getDocumentBase(), "space.au");
```

There are two ways to play a sound. You can either

- Play it once.
- Play it repeatedly in a continuous loop.

To play it once, you simply write

```
ac.play();
```

Listing 9.6 shows the HTML for an applet that plays sound, and Listing 9.7 shows the applet code itself for how to play a sound repeatedly in a loop. It illustrates the use of the start() and stop() methods to ensure that the sound file is played only while the

Web page that contains the applet is being viewed. Figure 9.3 shows the applet displayed in the AppletViewer, but of course you'll have to run it to hear the applet play sound (for which you need speakers or headphones).

Listing 9.6   Applet Playing Sound Example
```
<HTML>
<TITLE>
Example of an Applet that plays sound in a loop for Pure Java
</TITLE>
<BODY>
<Applet code=SoundApplet.class height=200 width=300>
</Applet>
</BODY>
</HTML>
```

Listing 9.7   An Applet That Plays a Sound File (SoundApplet.java)
```
import java.Applet.*; // You need to import the Applet package for an Applet.
import java.awt.*;
public class SoundApplet extends Applet
    // All applets must extend java.applet.Applet.
    {
    String soundFilename = "spacemusic.au";
    AudioClip ac;

    public void init()
        // init() is the first user-defined method called in an applet.
        {
        ac = getAudioClip(getCodeBase(), soundFilename);
                    // getAudioClip(URL, String) is an Applet method
                    // for retrieving a sound file.
                    // This is for applets only. To play sound
                    // in a Java application, you should use the new
                    // Java 2 Sound APIs.
                    // getCodeBase() returns the URL of the Applet code.
                    // Use this for .au files specific
                    // to the Applet, and store the sound file
                    // in the codebase directory.
                    // Remember that codebase can be specified in
                    // the HTML tags.
                    // Using a String variable for the filename
                    // allows you to dynamically change it through
                    // a getParameter() call.

        }


    public void start()
        // start() is called when you go to the Web page.
        {
```

```
            repaint();     // Call repaint() to update the applet's display.
                           // Never call paint().
            ac.loop();     // Start playing the sound file continuously
                           // in the start method.
                           // To just play the sound, call ac.play().
        }

        public void paint(Graphics g)
            // Dynamically draw the text with whatever the
            // sound filename is whenever paint() is called,
            // which is called by your code (through repaint())
            // and the JVM.
        {
            g.drawString("Now playing " + soundFilename, 40,50);
            // Draw the specified String at the given coordinates relative
            // to the upper-left corner of the applet, which is 0,0.
        }

        public void stop()
            // The browser calls stop() when you change to a
            // different Web page.
        {
            ac.stop();     // Be sure to stop playing the sound file when
                           // the user leaves this Web page.
        }

}   // End class definition SoundApplet
```

Figure 9.3

An applet that plays sound displayed in the AppletViewer (Sound.html).

Using Images in an Applet

Applets provide facilities for displaying images. These images can be either GIF or JPEG images.

178 Chapter 9: GUI Programming II: Applets

> **NOTE**
>
> Java actually provides fairly complex image manipulation APIs, such as `ImageProducer` and `ImageConsumer`, but these are beyond the scope of this book.

The two main scenarios for displaying an image are

- Displaying a single image
- Displaying multiple images, such as for animation

A Single Image in an Applet: Code Example

Displaying an image in an applet (or application) is fairly simple. You must

1. Get the image.
2. Draw it on the applet's surface.

Figure 9.4 shows an applet that displays a single image.

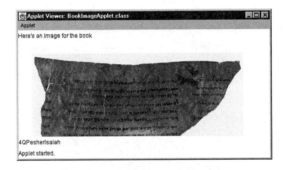

Figure 9.4

An applet that displays a single image.

Listings 9.8 and 9.9 show the HTML and the applet code for this applet, which displays a single image.

Listing 9.8   An Example of HTML for an Applet That Displays a Single Image (BookImage.html)

```
<HTML>
<TITLE>
Example of an Applet that displays an image for Pure Java
</TITLE>
<BODY>
<Applet code=BookImageApplet.class height=400 width=450>
</Applet>
</BODY>
</HTML>
```

Listing 9.9 An Example of an Applet That Displays a Single Image (BookImageApplet.java)
```java
import java.Applet.*; // You need to import the Applet package for an Applet.
import java.awt.*;
public class BookImageApplet extends Applet
    // All applets must subclass java.applet.Applet
    {
     Label bookLabel;
     Image bookImage;      // Need an Image object for images.
     Label titleLabel;
     // Declare instance variables.

     public void init()
         // init(), like a constructor, is the first user-defined
         // method normally called in an applet by the browser.
         {
         bookLabel = new Label("Here's an Image for the book");
         bookImage = getImage(getDocumentBase(), "4QpesherIsaiah_e.jpg");
                         // To get an image,
                         // you use the getImage method.
                         // getImage() requires a directory
                         // name and a filename.
                         // getDocumentBase() retrieves the
                         // URL for where the Web page
                         // came from.
         if(bookImage == null)
             System.out.println("getImage failed");
                         // If the getImage failed, report it
                         // on the command line.
         titleLabel = new Label("4QPesherIsaiah");
         setLayout(new BorderLayout());
                         // Override the default layout manager of the
                         // Applet, which is FlowLayout, just like a Panel.
         add(bookLabel, "North");
         add(titleLabel, "South");
         repaint();      // Force the screen to be updated.
                         // Always call repaint(), never paint().
                         // Extra repaint() calls need not hurt performance.
         }

    public void paint(Graphics g)
        // Do all drawing on the applet's surface, including the drawing of
        // images, in paint().
        {
         g.drawImage(bookImage, 30,50, this);
                         // drawImage draws an Image on the
                         // Component's surface, in this case
                         // an instance of the BookImageApplet.
                         // drawImage requires an Image object reference,
```
continues

Listing 9.9 continued

```
                        // x and y coordinates, and an
                        // ImageObserver instance.
                        // The Applet itself is an ImageObserver.
                        // The ImageObserver is the object to notify
                        // when pixels of the image are available
                        // to draw on the component.
    }
}   // End class definition BookImageApplet.
```

The most important thing to learn from this listing is the drawImage method. There are several forms of this method in the java.awt.Graphics class, including versions that take a specific image size in pixels. In this simple form, you provide the Image object reference, the x and y coordinates for the upper-left corner of the image relative to the whole applet (regardless of the layout manager used), and an ImageObserver. Generally, the value of the ImageObserver object reference will be this (the object reference to the current object—in this case, the applet itself).

Because the Component class implements the ImageObserver interface, most components can serve as an ImageObserver. It is the object that is notified of repaint() requirements. Notice that, because this applet does nothing to prevent it starting before the Image is fully downloaded, the ImageObserver in the drawImage method might conceivably be called several times—as more and more pixels are downloaded. In the case of a local system, the multiple calls are not as critical. However, they make a difference in a commercial applet downloaded from a Web server. Later we'll see a way to determine that the images are fully downloaded before they are displayed.

ImageObserver is an interface in the java.awt.image package. This interface is implemented only by the java.awt.Component class. The interface specifies several public static final values that each represent a possible state of the object, such as ALLBITS, which shows that all the bits of the image are now present. The interface has only one method, imageUpdate(). This method accepts as parameters an Image object reference, one or more flags as defined in the interface, and the x and y coordinates of where the image should be drawn, as well as the image's width and height.

Multiple Images in an Applet: Code Example

There are multiple ways to display multiple images. You might choose to use animation, in which case you need to display images at different places on the applet's surface. Or, you might want to create something such as a screen saver, changing the images after a given period of time. In either case, you need to decide how long a given image stays on the screen. Listing 9.10 shows another alternative. In this applet, the user can change the image being displayed using a Next or Previous button, similar to a slide show. This applet demonstrates the use of several MediaTracker methods, which are run through a separate thread. These methods deal with downloading multiple images while not tying up the user interface. This is very important.

> **TIP**
>
> The example in this section shows how to use the `MediaTracker` to track the downloading of `Images`. If you use the Swing `ImageIcon` class, you automatically get a `MediaTracker` to monitor the downloading so that it will be easier to code.

You might need to download several images before you can use them, but you also might want the user to be able to interact with the applet before the download is complete. The approach shown by this applet can be used to allow a user to interact with your applet through the AWT thread, while the applet uses a separate thread to download the images. In this particular case, there isn't anything else to do while waiting, but this can vary depending on the applet's purpose and UI. Figure 9.5 shows the applet displaying one of several images in the AppletViewer. Listing 9.10 shows the HTML file for this applet, and Listing 9.11 shows the applet code for displaying multiple images using `MediaTracker`.

Figure 9.5

An applet that uses MediaTracker to download multiple images in a separate thread.

Listing 9.10   An Example of the HTML for an Applet Displaying Multiple Images and Using MediaTracker (SlideShow.html)

```
<HTML>
<TITLE>
Example of an Applet that uses MediaTracker to load
multiple Images for Pure Java
</TITLE>
<BODY>
<Applet code=SlideShowApplet.class height=600 width=600>
```

continues

Listing 9.10 continued
```
</Applet>
</BODY>
</HTML>
```

Listing 9.11 An Applet That Uses MediaTracker to Download Multiple Images in a Separate Thread (SlideShowApplet.java)
```
// This Applet downloads multiple images and waits for the download to be
// complete before it displays them using a subclass of Canvas called
// ImageCanvas with its own paint() method. The way the Applet knows the images
// have all been downloaded successfully is with the MediaTracker class.
// It checks on the status of the downloading and can wait for it to
// complete on one or more Image objects. So if you have a problem downloading
// multiple images for an Applet, and no one else can help, maybe you can hire
// the MediaTracker.

import java.Applet.*;
import java.awt.*;
import java.awt.image.*; // Need this package to support Images here.
import java.awt.event.*;

public class SlideShowApplet extends Applet implements Runnable, ActionListener
    {
    // This applet, of course, extends Applet. It also implements Runnable,
    // the interface to use if you want to do
    //  multithreading in an applet since you cannot subclass Thread
    // (which is not recommended anyway), as well as
    // Applet. While unusual in this book, for simplicity this applet class
    // also serves as its own ActionEvent listener, implementing the
    // ActionListener interface by implementing actionPerformed().
            // The MediaTracker should always run with a separate
            // Thread to prevent your UI being frozen. To do this,
            // your Applet should implement the Runnable interface,
            // providing a run() method for the Thread to execute.
    Image[] images; // Declare an array of images to hold multiple
                    // Image objects.
    MediaTracker tracker;
            // Declare a MediaTracker.
    ImageCanvas icv;   // This is a custom component to use for displaying the
                       // images. Like any custom component, it has its own
                       // paint() method, which you have to call manually since
                       // the JVM doesn't know when it should repaint the
                       // component.

    Button btnNext;
    Button btnPrevious;
    int curImage = 0;
    final int DONE = (MediaTracker.ABORTED | MediaTracker.ERRORED
```

```
                    | MediaTracker.COMPLETE);



public void init()
    {
    setLayout(new BorderLayout());
            // Override Applet default LayoutManager.
    icv = new ImageCanvas();
    // Instantiate the custom component to display images.
    btnNext = new Button("Next");
    btnPrevious = new Button("Previous");
            // This Applet allows the user to step through the images
            // using buttons.
    images = new Image[7];  // Instantiate the Image array
    tracker = new MediaTracker(this);
            // The MediaTracker instance will track image loading for
            // this ImageObserver, the Applet instance.

            // Get specific images and add them
            // to the MediaTracker's list
            // of images to track.
    images[0] = getImage(getCodeBase(), "Paula3.jpg");
            // getCodeBase returns the URL of the applet's class file,
            // usually a directory on the Web server.
    tracker.addImage(images[0], 0);
            // After you instantiate an image, tell the MediaTracker
            // about the image. MediaTracker only tracks the download
            // progress of images it knows about.
    images[1] = getImage(getCodeBase(), "Atomium.jpg");
    tracker.addImage(images[1], 1);
    images[2] = getImage(getCodeBase(), "Peleton2.gif");
    tracker.addImage(images[2], 2);
    images[3] = getImage(getCodeBase(), "Carr13.jpg");
    tracker.addImage(images[3], 3);
    images[4] = getImage(getCodeBase(), "Stage15.gif");
    tracker.addImage(images[4], 4);
    images[5] = getImage(getCodeBase(), "Ph004.jpg");
    tracker.addImage(images[5], 5);
    images[6] = getImage(getCodeBase(), "jurgen3.jpg");
    tracker.addImage(images[6], 6);

    // First image is progressively rendered.
    if (images.length > 0)
       {
        icv.setImage(images[0]);
       }
            // The setImage method in the ImageCanvas class
            // sets the first image loaded as the first
```

continues

Listing 9.11   continued

```
            // one to appear.  Note that setImage()
            // is a user-defined method, not an SDK
            // method.
    add(icv, BorderLayout.CENTER);
    add(btnPrevious, BorderLayout.NORTH);
    add(btnNext, BorderLayout.SOUTH);
    btnPrevious.addActionListener(this);
    btnNext.addActionListener(this);
            // Add the ImageCanvas component
            // to the Applet. Then add the two
            // Buttons and register listeners on them.
    (new Thread(this)).start();
            // This is a compact way to start a Thread.
            // The constructor for Thread requires an object
            // that implements Runnable, as this Applet does.
            // The Thread instance is then made eligible to
            // execute using the start() method.

            // Print overall status information.
            // This is diagnostic info that will show up on the console.
            // Do not include it in a production Applet.
    try
        {
          while (!tracker.checkAll())
          // checkAll() checks the download status of all the images
          // the MediaTracker object is tracking. If it returns
          // false, the images are not fully downloaded yet.
              {
                Thread.sleep(1000);
                // Pause this thread for one second before the MediaTracker
                // checks the download status again.
              }
        }
            // If all the images haven't loaded yet,
            // sleep some more and hope they finish soon.

    catch (Exception e)
        {
          e.printStackTrace();
        }
    if (tracker.isErrorAny())
            // This method returns true if anything went wrong
            // while loading the images.
        {
          System.out.println("Not all images have been successfully " +
                         "loaded.");
          Object[] list = tracker.getErrorsAny();
          for (int i=0; i<list.length; i++)
              {
```

```java
                System.out.println(list[i]);
            }
    }
    else
        {
         System.out.println("All images have been successfully loaded");
        }
    for (int i=0; i<images.length; i++)
        {
         int s = tracker.statusID(i, false);
         // Look at each image and display its download status
         if ((s & MediaTracker.ABORTED) != 0)
             System.out.print("ABORTED ");
         if ((s & MediaTracker.COMPLETE) != 0)
             System.out.print("COMPLETE ");
         if ((s & MediaTracker.ERRORED) != 0)
             System.out.print("ERRORED ");
         if ((s & MediaTracker.LOADING) != 0)
             System.out.print("LOADING ");
          System.out.println();
        }
}


public void run()
            // The thread executes this code.
    {
      for (int i=0; i<images.length; i++)
         {
          try
              {
               tracker.waitForID(i);
              }
              // Wait for each image to complete loading.
           catch (Exception e)
              {
               e.printStackTrace();
              }
          repaint();
          // Repaint the screen once you've got the image.
         }
    }

public void actionPerformed(ActionEvent evt)
            // Process user clicks of the Next
            // and Previous buttons.
    {
      String arg = evt.getActionCommand();
      if ("Next".equals(arg))
```

continues

Listing 9.11 continued

```java
            {
              // If the user clicks the next button, move to the next image
              // and repaint the applet to update the image.
              if (curImage < images.length-1)
                 {
                   ++curImage;
                   repaint();
                 }
               else;
             }
         else
             if ("Previous".equals(arg))
                 {
                   // If the user clicks the Previous button,
                   // move back one image and repaint the applet.
                   // You could just as easily show the images in a loop
                   // with no user intervention. In that case, you would
                   // want to override the update() method to not erase the
                   // background and also use double buffering to quickly
                   // refresh the applet's display.
                   if (curImage > 0)
                       {
                         --curImage;
                         repaint();
                       }
                    else;
                 }
                // Change the current image based on the button click
                // and repaint, which will cause the ImageCanvas to
                // paint a different image.
        }

     public void paint(Graphics g)
         {
           if (tracker.isErrorID(curImage))
               {
                 icv.setImage(null);
               }
           else
               {
                 icv.setImage(images[curImage]);
               }
                     // In case of error, do nothing.
                     // Otherwise, change the Image.
           btnNext.setEnabled((tracker.statusID(curImage+1, false)&DONE) != 0);
           btnPrevious.setEnabled(
                (tracker.statusID(curImage-1, false)&DONE) != 0);
                     // Determine if a button should be disabled or not.
         } // End definition of paint method.
```

```java
    }

class ImageCanvas extends Canvas
    {
    Image image;
    boolean clear;

    public void setImage(Image image)
        {
          this.image = image;
          clear = true;
          repaint();
        }

    public void update(Graphics g)
        {
          paint(g);
        }

    public void paint(Graphics g)
        {
          if (image == null)
              {
                g.setColor(Color.red);
                g.fillRect(0, 0, getSize().width, getSize().height);
                // Set the background color of the ImageCanvas.
              }
          else
              {
                if (clear)
                    {
                      g.clearRect(0, 0, getSize().width, getSize().height);
                      clear = false;
                    }
                  // Clear the ImageCanvas drawing area.
                int w = image.getWidth(this);
                int h = image.getHeight(this);
                if (w >= 0 && h >= 0)
                    {
                      g.drawImage(image, (getSize().width-w)/2,
                          (getSize().height-h)/2, this);
                      // Draw the image on the applet based on the image's
                      // actual size.
                    }
                  // Get the size of the Image and draw it that size.
              }
        }
    }
} // End ImageCanvas definition.
```

188 Chapter 9: GUI Programming II: Applets

In this applet, I create a custom component, called an `ImageCanvas`. I use that to display the images. This component is told which image to use by the applet. When the applet starts, it loads seven images, all related to cycling or triathlon. Then, the applet creates a `MediaTracker` object to monitor the status of the downloading of the images.

> **NOTE**
>
> The `getImage()` call is asynchronous. That is, your program returns immediately after calling it, no matter how long it takes to actually complete downloading the image. That's why the actual image downloading can be monitored after the `getImage()` call.

The `MediaTracker` has each image of interest registered with it through the `addImage()` method. Then, the thread doing the loading just waits via the `MediaTracker` for all the images to load. When downloading is complete, it calls the `repaint` method, which calls the `paint` method independently of the `ImageCanvas` class. Remember, every component that needs its own custom painting needs its own `paint()` method.

This applet shows nothing but two buttons and some images. If you had a GUI that needed to show images, but you wanted to let the user interact with a more complex GUI while the images were being downloaded, you would need to modify the code so that the AWT thread could be notified that the download was complete, perhaps by setting a flag in the applet's data members or by inserting a synthetic event (a user-defined event) into the event queue and listening for that event in the applet.

> **TIP**
>
> All the applets in this chapter could also be run as applications. All that is needed to do that is to add a `main` method to them. This method calls `init()`, `start()`, and `paint()`, and optionally `stop()` or `destroy()`. Also, this `main` method instantiates the applet and creates a `Frame` to which to add the applet and a `WindowListener` so that the `Frame` can be closed. In this way, any applet can easily also run as an application, if that's desired. Note, however, that `getCodeBase()` and `getDocumentBase()` work only if the applet is run as an applet.

CHAPTER 10

Exceptions

Java provides a standard mechanism for dealing with errors: exception handling. This is a means to deal with unusual conditions that can arise during execution and provides for dealing it these conditions in a consistent way.

The Throwable Class

Java has a class called Throwable, from which two major classes, Error and Exception, inherit. Figure 10.1 shows the class hierarchy.

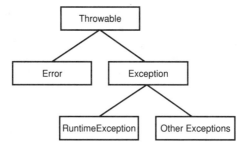

Figure 10.1

Class hierarchy for Error and Exception.

A Java developer normally doesn't do anything with Throwable, so I'll not consider this class. You have to have a class that is a subclass of Throwable, however, to throw an error or exception. All Throwable objects contain information on the execution stack for the executing Thread at the time the error or exception object was created. You also won't write any code to deal with Error or any subclasses of it. An Error stems from events like device failures or out-of-memory conditions.

Of the subclasses of `Exception`, of which there are many, there are two main groups. There are `RuntimeException` and other exceptions. `RuntimeExceptions` are normally not dealt with in your code. Such an `Exception` probably represents a program bug. For example, if your code tries to access an array element that does not exist, such as `myArrayElements[7]`, when there are only six elements in the `myArrayElements` object, this would cause an `ArrayIndexOutOfBoundsException`. Or, you might generate a `RuntimeException` trying to use an object before the object is instantiated, such as adding a button to a panel before executing a button constructor on the Button. This will cause a `NullPointerException`.

> **NOTE**
>
> Because these sorts of exceptions really represent problems in your code, you should not try to catch them or deal with them, but only to resolve them before you distribute your code. So don't apply exception-handling code to any runtime exceptions, which represent exceptions in the Java runtime.

The other major group of `Exceptions` that Java can throw is a non-`RuntimeException`. That is, there are lots of Exception subclasses that do not represent `RuntimeExceptions`, but are generated by other conditions in your program. You must deal with these sorts of `Exceptions`. Often these are `Exceptions` that a developer decided his or her code needed to throw under given circumstances. Java requires that you deal with these `Exceptions`.

Such an exception might not represent a bug or logic problem, as such. Rather, it might merely represent an anomalous condition that you might want to try to deal with in your code. Even if you do not wish to deal with the condition, the Java compiler won't let you not do something about a thrown `Exception`. Java has a rule. It's the "Handle or declare rule." At compile time, the compiler verifies that all checked exceptions are handled or declared in your code. At runtime, the JVM puts your choice to work.

This means that you either need to deal with a potential `Exception`, or tell Java to pass the `Exception` on up the call stack to your method's caller. Java will continue up the call stack, looking for some method that will deal with the exception. If it runs out of methods, the `Exception` is handled by the Java runtime by interrupting execution and displaying the exception on `System.err`.

Handling Exceptions: try-catch-finally

The mechanism that Java hasdefined for dealing with `Exceptions` is `try-catch-finally`. Here is the basic syntax:

```
try
    {
        // Put your code that might throw
        // an Exception inside a try block
    }
catch(<SomeExceptionClass>  excpObjRef)
        // Name a specific exception class
        // and an accompanying object reference.
    {
```

```
        // Put code here to deal with the Exception
        // type if it is thrown.
    }
finally
        // A finally block is optional
        // If present, it is always executed unless
        // a "return" statement is executed
         // before the finally block can be executed.
    {
        // Do something that you want to do in this method NO MATTER WHAT
    }
```

In the try block, you choose a method to call that may throw an Exception or a subclass of Exception.

> **CAUTION**
>
> If you fail to put code that may throw a checked exception inside a try block, and do not declare that the method throws an exception, the compiler will not compile your code.

The best way to know if a method can throw an exception is to check the API documentation. If the method or constructor might throw an Exception, it will say

```
someMethod (<parameters>) throws SomeExceptionClass
```

For example, the signature for the constructor for a FileInputStream is

```
public FileInputStream(String aFileName) throws FileNotFoundException
```

If the signature of the method or the constructor says throws someException, this method falls under the "handle or declare rule." After you put code in a try block, you then have to decide what to do about the Exception. You have two options. First, you can catch the Exception using a catch block. Or, second, you can declare that your method throws an Exception (discussed later). In the latter case, the code need not be in a try block.

Additionally, you might have a finally clause, in which you perform code that you want done all the time, whether you get an exception or not. For one try block, you might have essentially any number of catch blocks. Java processes catch blocks by examining the type of the Exception class listed in the catch block parameter list. The catch block whose Exception type matches the type of Exception thrown from the try block is executed.

try-catch Code Example

Listing 10.1   Basic try-catch Block Example (TryCatch.java)
```
import java.io.*;
import java.util.*;

class FileAccessor
```

continues

Listing 10.1 continued

```java
    {
       public boolean readAReadMe()
          {
            boolean result = false;

            try // Put code that could throw an Exception in a try block
               {
                 File f = new File("Readme.txt");
                 // Create a File object
                 FileInputStream fis = new FileInputStream(f);
                 // Create a FileInputStream object
                 result = true;
                 // Show success
               }
            catch(FileNotFoundException fnf)
               {
                 // Do something about the missing file
                   System.out.println ("The file was not found");
               }
            catch(IOException ioe)
               {
                 // Do something more general about an IOException
                   System.out.println ("Some IOException occurred");
                   ioe.printStackTrace();
               }
            catch(Exception excp)
               {
                  // Process another kind of Exception
                  System.out.println
                  [ccc]("Some non-IO kind of Exception occurred:   " +
                  excp.getMessage()); // Print the reason
                                      // for the exception
                  excp.printStackTrace();
                  // Show the call stack before this point
               }
            return result;
          }

    } // End of class definition for FileAccessor


public class ExceptionDriver
       {
          public static void main(String[] args)
               {
                  FileAccessor fa = new FileAccessor();
                      // Create a FileAcceessor object
                  fa.readAReadMe();
                      // Call a method on this FileAccessor object
```

```
            System.exit(0);
                // Exit the program
        }
}
```

In the try block, you put code that might throw an Exception. The constructor for a FileInputStream might throw an Exception. If the file does not exist, you will get a FileNotFoundException thrown by the JVM.

This exception object will be passed to the first catch block that has a compatible Exception subclass listed as the parameter type. In this case, there will be an exact match between the exception type and the class FileNotFoundException. If some other type of I/O exception occurs, this catch block will be skipped. If the file can be found but is unreadable, the second catch block will be called.

> **NOTE**
>
> One possible reason that Java might fail to find a file and, therefore, throw an IOException object occurs when you need to open a file on a diskette for writing. If the Write Protect tab is set to read-only, you will get an IOException that complains of an unreadable file.

You might get an IOException by trying to read from a file on a UNIX system for which you lack permission, like /etc/passwd. This condition will throw an exception object which instantiates a subclass of IOException other than FileNotFoundException. You haven't specifically planned on this condition, so just catch it with an IOException.

If you don't have either of these two catch blocks, or if the type of Exception subclass is other than FileNotFoundException or IOException, the catch block that takes an object of type Exception will be called, with the specific exception object passed as a parameter. More generally, the exception object is passed as a parameter to the first catch block that has a parameter of the same class or a superclass.

You might wish to think of these catch blocks as similar to overloaded methods. When a method is called in a try block that throws an Exception, the JVM looks for a catch block that has a compatible Exception subclass specified. If it finds none, and it does find a catch block with the base class Exception as the parameter type, it calls this catch block.

The class Exception and all its subclasses inherit several methods from Throwable. Two of them are particularly useful in debugging exceptions: getMessage() and printStackTrace(). The method getMessage returns a String that tells what caused the exception. The method printStackTrace() prints the stack trace.

> **NOTE**
>
> Frequently a stack trace can be several screens' worth of data. Fortunately, to debug the exception, you only have to look at the location listed in the first line or two of the stack trace. It will generally give the name of the .java file and a line number within that file where the specific exception was thrown, so you can go to that point in your code and figure out what happened.

So to summarize, Java will search through the catch blocks that follow your try block and will use the first catch block that has a parameter type that is compatible with the type of the exception object which was thrown. As implied previously, this can and often will be a superclass of the specific exception object's type. Because Exception is the superclass of all other Exception classes, it can be used in place of any of the other Exception subclasses. When Java calls a catch block, any catch blocks for the same try statement will be skipped.

NOTE

It is important to code your catch blocks from the most specific to the most general. This approach will offer the best chance to provide the user with specific, helpful information about what went wrong, or properly handle the exception yourself.

Handling Specific Exceptions

Assume that your application needs to have a configuration file to provide information about the environment the program should use, like where to store files. If you try to read this file and you get a FileNotFoundException, but you don't specifically catch a FileNotFoundException, you won't have any intelligent way to deal with it. If you do catch this type of exception, however, you can write code in the catch block to do something useful about it.

TIP

It might be useful to nest a try-catch combination in the catch block for a FileNotFoundException. You can nest try-catch constructs in a catch block. Suppose you need a configuration file for your program, and the program creates this configuration file for the client system the first time it runs. If the file doesn't exist, it might be the first time the program had been run on this system, because the file is built by the program as part of initialization. It would be quite unhelpful for the program to crash because it hadn't provided for a condition that is not unlikely to happen. To provide for this possible condition, you could put in a catch block to handle it, and the user will never know the difference.

If you don't think you can fix the problem the exception represents, you can at least provide an intelligent response. So, for example, if you got a custom-made exception, like a PrinterNotRespondingException object, you could display a pop-up dialog, like a JOptionPane, to tell the user to check the printer to see if it has a problem. If you do not catch specific exceptions, but only catch objects of type Exception, your program will not be able to readily resolve the problem on its own. You end up giving the user some unhelpful message like "Program error." It's almost always better to gracefully deal with exceptional conditions and, if possible, keep the program running. That will help your users resolve the problem.

finally Clause Code Example

There is an additional mechanism for dealing with an exception—namely, the finally clause. If you put a finally block in the same method with the try block, subsequent to the try block, you can put code in the finally block to deal with exceptions. Listing 10.2 shows how to use the finally clause.

Listing 10.2   Using finally with a try Block (ExceptionDriver2.java)

```java
import java.io.*;
import java.util.*;

class FileAccessor2
    {
      public boolean getConfigFile(String configFileName)
              {
                FileInputStream fis = null;  // Never declare something like
                                             // this in a try block.
                                             // It won't be visible anywhere
                                             // but in the try block.
                boolean result = false;
                try
                    {
                      fis = new FileInputStream(configFileName);
                      // This could throw an exception object.
                      // Do something with the config file.
                      Properties sysProps = new
Properties(System.getProperties());
                      sysProps.load(fis);
                      System.setProperties(sysProps); // Add application
                                                      properties
                                             // to system properties.
                      System.getProperties().list(System.out);  // List
                                                                properties.
                      result = true;   // Set the result to true.
                    }
                catch(FileNotFoundException fnfe)
                    {
                      System.out.println("File Not Found:  " + configFileName);
                    }
                catch(IOException ioe)
                    {
                      System.out.println("IOException loading " +
                                    configFileName);
                    }
                finally // This method is executed NO MATTER WHAT happened
                       // in the try block.
                    {
                      try
                          {
                            if(fis != null)
```

continues

Listing 10.2   continued

```
                    fis.close();
                    // Attempt to close the FileInputStream object.
                    // This flushes any buffers and does an actual
                    // write to disk of any cached data.
                }
                catch(IOException ioe)
                    { // close() may also throw an exception,
                     // so it needs to be placed within a try block
                     // accompanied by a catch block.
                    System.out.println(
                        "Couldn't close FIS: " + ioe.getMessage());
                    }
                System.out.println("In the finally clause");
                }
            return result;
            }  // End of getConfigFile method.
    }  // End of FileAccessor2 class definition.

public class ExceptionDriver2
    {
        public static void main(String[] args)
            {
                FileAccessor2 fa2 = new FileAccessor2();
                boolean result = fa2.getConfigFile("ConfigProps.dat");
                System.exit(0);
            }
    }
```

CAUTION

You should never declare any variables inside a `try` block if those variables need to be visible outside of it. In fact, if you do this, and attempt to access them outside the `try` block, the compiler will give you an error.

Any methods that might throw an exception, like a `FileInputStream` constructor, must be put inside a `try` block. You can also include statements inside a `try` block that don't throw an exception. The compiler doesn't care. The `finally` block is *always* called, in spite of any abrupt termination of a `try` or `catch` block (including a return statement). That means that whatever you put there should be something you always want done, no matter what, because it will take place whether the code in the `try` block succeeds or not.

So the `finally` block is useful for things like closing streams, writing log records, setting status flags, and other types of processing that should happen at the end of a method no matter what happened before that point. It is legal to code a `try` block, one or more `catch` blocks, and one `finally` block in the same method. That is, `catch` and `finally` blocks can coexist. You must not embed a `catch` block inside its related `try` block. You can, however, nest `try-catch` pairs in a `catch` block. You might also need to put a try-catch combination inside a finally clause if you call a method in a finally clause that might catch an exception. Because the close() method of a FileInputStream can throw an IOException, the close() method call must be in a try block, with an accompanying catch block. This means that it is possible for the code in finally, even though it is supposed to happen on success or failure of the try block, to throw its own exceptions.

Declaring a Method That Throws Exceptions: Code Example

Java requires that you handle an exception or declare in your method's signature that it throws one or more Exception types. You would typically do the latter if your method is not the appropriate place to handle the exception. If you take this approach, Java searches up the call stack to find some block of code that will handle the exception. If your code does not ever handle it, it will be printed on System.err. Listing 10.3 shows a method declared to throw an exception.

Listing 10.3 Declaring a Method that Throws an Exception (ExceptionDriver3.java)

```
import java.io.*;
import java.util.*;

class FileAccessor3
    {
     FileInputStream fis = null;

     public boolean readAReadMe() throws IOException, Exception
         {                   // This method may throw two
                             // kinds of Exceptions
                             // or one of their subclasses.
            boolean result = false;

            try // Put code that could throw
                // an Exception in a try block.
                {
                  File f = new File("Readme.txt");
        // Create a File object.
                  fis = new FileInputStream(f);
                                    // Create a FileInputStream object.
                  result = true;  // Show success.
                }
            // Because the method is declared as throwing
            // exceptions, no catch blocks are needed.
            finally
                {
                  // If you have no catch blocks, you have to
                  // have a finally block.
                  if(fis != null) // File actually opened.
                      fis.close();
```

continues

Listing 10.3 continued
```
                // No try needed because the method
                // throws exceptions.
            }
        return result;
        }

    } // End of class definition for FileAccessor3.


public class ExceptionDriver3
    {
        public static void main(String[] args)
                        throws IOException, Exception
            {
                FileAccessor3 fa3 = new FileAccessor3();
                fa3.readAReadMe();
                System.exit(0);
            }
    }
```

In a method that is declared as throwing an exception, you list all the exception classes that your method might throw at the end of the method signature. Or, you can list superclasses of those exceptions. I could have listed only Exception, but I also listed IOException to illustrate that you can list multiple, comma-delimited exceptions. When you code this in a method declaration, you are requiring a caller to handle the exception. It does not mean that the exception will be ignored. It only relieves your method of responsibility for handling the exception.

You can code a try block without any catch blocks. If you have no catch blocks, however, you must have a finally clause. Because the readAReadMe method is declared as throwing an IOException, the close() method does not need to be in a try block. In fact, this method didn't need any try blocks, but I used one to illustrate that you can have a try block without any catch blocks, which then requires a finally clause.

Creating Your Own Exception Classes: Code Example

You can also create your own exception subclass. First, you create a subclass of Exception. I'm going to create a PrinterNotRespondingException. A user-defined Exception class is shown in Listing 10.4.

Listing 10.4 User-Defined Exception (PrinterNotRespondingException.java)
```
public class PrinterNotRespondingException extends Exception
                        // Subclass Exception
    {
      String message;   // Define a place to
                        // put the reason for the exception.

        public PrinterNotRespondingException(String reason)
                        // Define a constructor.
```

```
        {
           message = reason;
                   // Store the reason for the exception in the
                   // exception object.
        }
   public String getMessage()
                       // Override getMessage and code
                       // your own version.
       {
          return message;
       }
   } // End definition of PrinterNotRespondingException.
```

This is the only time in which it is really proper to name a class by the name of a state instead of an entity, a role usually reserved for data members, not classes. An exception class generally subclasses (extends) Exception or a subclass of Exception, such as RuntimeException. Less commonly, you could subclass Throwable, but I recommend that you do that only if you have a specific reason not to subclass Exception, lest you confuse others about whether this is an exception or error. As a rule, the subclasses are defined in the package most appropriate to the exceptional condition. For example, SqlException is defined in the package java.sql.

Exception subclasses need to provide some common elements. There needs to be a String to store the reason for the exception. Also, there needs to be a constructor for the exception, which accepts a String to put into the reason data member. You may optionally code a getMessage method as well to return the reason for the exception along with other information if you wish, or simply use the inherited version of getMessage().

Now that I've defined the class for the Exception subclass, I need a method that can throw this exception. Listing 10.5 illustrates this.

Listing 10.5   Using a User-Defined Exception (ExceptionDriver4.java)
```
class PrintMaker
    {
      // This method attempts to test the printer
      // to verify that it's ready.
      public boolean testPrinterStatus(String printerName)
                           throws PrinterNotRespondingException
                               // A method that can throw an
                               // Exception needs to
                               // declare this.  The caller is
                               // expected to handle the Exception.
            {
              boolean result = checkThePrinter(printerName);
                       // This is a pretend method.
              if(result == false)
                  throw new PrinterNotRespondingException{printerName +
                               "not responding in testPrinterStatus()");
```

continues

Listing 10.5 *continued*

```
            //  Instantiate a new PrinterNotRespondingException object
            //  and "throw" it.  This passes it to the
            //  caller of testPrinterStatus().
                return result;
            }   // End testPrinterStatus method definition.

        public boolean checkThePrinter(String printerName)
                // This is a pretend
                // method to illustrate
                // exception throwing.
                {
                  return false;
                }
    }   // End of class definition for PrintMaker.

public class ExceptionDriver4
    {
      public static void main(String[] args)
            {
              PrintMaker pm = new PrintMaker();
              try // Call a method that might throw an exception.
                {
                  boolean result =
                      pm.testPrinterStatus("Shakespeare1");
                }
              catch(PrinterNotRespondingException pnre)
                {
                  System.out.println("Failed on printer status" +
                                     pnre.getMessage());
                }
            }
    }
```

> **NOTE**
>
> A method is declared to throw an exception with the `throws` keyword. The exception is actually thrown with the `throw` keyword.

A method is declared to throw a `PrinterNotRespondingException`. Because this method ought to fail if the printer doesn't respond properly, I certainly don't want to catch a `PrinterNotRespondingException`. Instead, I want to send to the caller a `PrinterNotRespondingException` and force them to handle it or declare it. To pass an exception to a caller, you must first create an `Exception` object using the constructor for the `Exception` subclass. Then you use the `throw` keyword to pass the exception object from this method to the JVM, which passes it to the caller to deal with.

To provide for this, your method's signature must state that it throws an exception of the type the method throws or a superclass of the type that your method throws. So you could declare that your method "throws Exception" instead, but this would be less helpful to other developers using your code or trying to understand it.

> **CAUTION**
>
> Never instantiate the exception object before the time it is actually needed. If you create the exception object when your application starts, when you print the stack trace, the trace will likely contain misleading information. This is because the stack information will be from the stack at the time the object was created, not from the stack at the time the exception was being thrown.

Handle or Declare?

How do you decide whether to use `try-catch` (handle the exception) or declare that your method throws an exception (declare)? Usually, it is best to use `try-catch` because your method is in the best position to know what is really wrong and do something intelligent about it. On the other hand, you might be in a low-level method and feel that any exceptions you get should be passed up to your caller. This is a decision left to the reader. If I were writing a class library of low-level routines, I might declare that my methods threw exceptions. Otherwise, I would recommend that you use `try-catch` blocks in your code.

CHAPTER 11

Multithreaded Programming in Java

One of Java's design goals was to be multithreaded. Whenever you run a Java program, there are multiple threads executing. Java provides the capability for you to easily add additional threads to your program. Adding threads is much simpler in Java than in languages like C or C++. This chapter will show you how to create and use threads to your advantage.

In Java, as in other languages, a thread is an execution context or subprocess. The Thread class is provided to run multiple threads in your program. You can use multiple threads for many tasks, such as printing a long document while the user continues to use the GUI. To assist you in using threads, this chapter covers

- Thread states
- Creating Threads
- Primary Thread methods
- Using the synchronized keyword
- Avoiding deadlocks with wait() and notify()

Thread States

A Java Thread object has four states:

- Initialized—Entered by calling a constructor from the Thread class
- Runnable—Entered by calling the Thread class's start() method
- Nonrunnable—Entered by calling any number of methods, such as wait(), yield(), join(), or suspend() on the Thread object
- Dead—Entered by completing the run() method for the Thread object or by calling stop()

NOTE

A Thread can move from nonrunnable to runnable easily. A Thread that is dead (and eligible for garbage collection if all the references are gone) cannot return to a runnable state.

Creating Threads

There are two ways to create a Thread object. Listing 11.1 shows the approach you should use most often (from an object-oriented design perspective).

Creating Threads with Runnable Objects: Code Example

You can create a Thread in two ways. You may create a Thread using an instance of a class that implements the Runnable interface. This is the best choice generally from an object-oriented design perspective. Or, you can subclass the Thread class to make an object that inherits from Thread. The former, generally superior approach is shown in Listing 11.1.

Listing 11.1 Creating a Thread with a Runnable Object (ThreadDriver1.java)

```
class BookFinder implements Runnable
       // Threads need a Runnable object for their constructor.
       // That is, they need an object that implements the
       // Runnable interface. The Runnable interface
       // has one method: public void run().
 {
   Thread t;
   String bookTitle;

   public BookFinder(String title)
           // Make a Runnable instance.
       {
         bookTitle = title;
         t = new Thread(this);
            // The constructor for Thread takes an instance of a Runnable,
            // and at this point, there is an instance, the current
            // BookFinder instance. This form of the constructor tells the
            // Thread object where to find the run() method,
            // which is THE method that runnable Threads execute.
         t.start();
            // Make the Thread Runnable - eligible to execute.
       }

   public void run()
       {
         System.out.println("Now searching the book database for" +
                       bookTitle);
         try
             {
               Thread.currentThread().sleep(1000);
               // Use the static Thread method currentThread()
               // to get a reference to the currently executing Thread
```

```
                    // and tell that Thread to sleep, or pause, for 1000
                    // milliseconds. It may sleep longer but should sleep
                    // at least that long. This is because this Thread
                    // might be pre-empted while sleeping, so it might
                    // take over one second to get back to it.
                }
                    // Catch possible Thread exception.
                catch(InterruptedException e)
                    {
                        // Nothing meaningful to do for this case,
                        // so do nothing.
                    }
                System.out.println("Found " + bookTitle);
            }
    } // End class definition of BookFinder.

public class ThreadDriver1
    {
        public static void main(String[] args)
            {
                BookFinder bf = new BookFinder("Pensees by Pascal");
                    // Create an instance of the BookFinder class that will
                    // start a separate Thread to look for the book in
                    // the library collection (simulated).
            }
    }
```

In this example, a class called BookFinder implements the Runnable interface. This signals to the system that the BookFinder class has agreed to the contract to implement the run() method. Next, a thread is constructed, and the constructor is passed a Runnable instance. The code for a Thread object to execute must be defined inside a run() method definition. The run() method in a given class can call other methods, but there is no way to tell a thread to execute some other method instead of run(). You can put any object in the constructor call, as long as it implements the Runnable interface. To help make this clear, look at this code snippet:

```
Runnable runner = new BookFinder("An Unscientific Postscript by Kierkegaard"));
Thread t = new Thread(runner);
```

The constructor call here could return an object of any class that you wanted to put there, as long as it implemented the Runnable interface.

NOTE

The capability to code a generic method that can return an instance of any class that implements the interface listed as the return type is very powerful. It enables, for example, the java.sql.DriverManager getConnection method to return any object of any kind that implements the Connection interface. This makes for very flexible code.

The Thread object is made executable by the start() method. When the thread is scheduled to run, the Thread object executes the run() method code. I've put code in the middle of this method to get the currently executing Thread and make it sleep at least 1000 milliseconds. The sleep() method expects a parameter in milliseconds. When the Thread object completes the run() method, it becomes dead, having finished its task. The method call sleep() might throw an exception, InterruptedException. If your thread is interrupted, there's nothing you can do, so there's usually little point in putting any code in the catch block. To make anything meaningful happen, you have to be able to tell the CPU to reschedule your thread immediately. Because you can't do that, there's really nothing to do in this method, except perhaps call sleep() again.

NOTE

There is a relationship between a Java Thread object and a thread, whether it is a green thread in the JVM or a kernel thread. The exact relationship, however, depends on multiple factors, including the JVM implementation and the OS. In general, you can think of the relationship between a Thread and a thread as being similar to that between an AWT component and its native peer. This means that your call to sleep() or wait() really affects a thread, whether it is a kernel thread (most likely) or green or something else. Because the exact relationship is implementation-dependent, I will use the term Thread even when it is most likely a thread of some kind that is affected.

Creating a Thread Subclass: Code Example

There is another way to create a Thread that involves subclassing the Thread class itself. This is not a recommended technique, because it generally violates good OO design principles. The reason is that you almost never define classes that have a true IsA relationship with an "execution context." You should not, as Rumbuagh warns, inherit just to get behavior. If you do want to subclass Thread, Listing 11.2 shows an example.

Listing 11.2   An Example of Subclassing java.lang.Thread (ThreadDriver2.java)

```
class BookFinder extends Thread
    // Extend the Thread class and code a run() method.
{
  String bookTitle;

  public BookFinder(String title)
      {
        bookTitle = title;
      }

  public void run()
      {
        System.out.println("Now searching the book database for" +
                        bookTitle);
        try
          {
            sleep(1000);
```

```
                // Use the static Thread method currentThread()
                // to get a reference to the currently executing Thread
                // and tell that Thread to sleep, or pause, for 1000
                // milliseconds. It may sleep longer but should sleep
                // at least that long. This is because this Thread
                // might be pre-empted while sleeping, so it might
                // take over one second to get back to it.
            }
                // Catch possible Thread exception.
            catch(InterruptedException e)
                {
                // Nothing meaningful to do for this case,
                // so do nothing.
                }
            System.out.println("Found " + bookTitle);
        }
    } // End class definition of BookFinder.

public class ThreadDriver2
    {
      public static void main(String[] args)
          {
            BookFinder bf = new BookFinder("Pensees by Pascal");
            bf.start();
                // Start the Thread executing.
                // This will cause the BookFinder run() method to execute
                // eventually, now that start()has made the Thread
                // runnable.
          }
    }
```

Here, the `run()` method is put inside a subclass of the `Thread` class. Instead of implementing the `Runnable` interface, this class extends the thread and provides its own `run()` method, instead of another class providing it. In general, this approach is less desirable from an object-oriented design perspective. The odds are very low that you are going to define many classes that have an IsA relationship with an execution context. This is an example of incorrect inheritance—inheriting just to get out of writing some code, even though there is no logical relationship between the superclass and subclass. Therefore, it's usually much better to use the method shown in Listing 11.1.

Since you generally already have to create a subclass of something anyway when working with multithreading, there's no point to subclassing `Thread` as well. You might just as well implement `Runnable` in the other subclasses you need to define.

Primary Thread Methods

There are a number of important `Thread` methods, some of which you've already seen:

- `start()`—Moves a thread from the initialized state to the runnable state. This does not make the thread execute. It makes the thread eligible for execution whenever it is scheduled.

> **CAUTION**
>
> Operating systems differ in the way they schedule threads. Solaris 7, for example, uses pre-emptive multitasking, whereas Windows 95 uses round-robin time slicing. Because Java is platform-neutral, it can run on any number of systems, any of which can have a different scheme for scheduling threads. You can't predict how long a given thread will execute for before it is interrupted or pre-empted, even on a specific system. You cannot write code that can handle all cases. Therefore, your code should always be written with the assumption that your thread may stop executing temporarily at any moment.

Being runnable means that the Thread is now in the pool of runnable `Threads`, waiting to execute. It might be some time before it actually gets to run, depending upon a number of factors, such as what else is running on the system.

> **NOTE**
>
> Unlike some earlier JVMs, Java 2 uses native threads, if possible, rather than green threads by default. This means that in a system with multiple CPUs, various threads in your program may be scheduled on separate CPUs.

- `sleep()`—This causes the `Thread` to become nonrunnable for at least the length of the `sleep()` method's parameter, which specifies a time in milliseconds for the thread to pause, as long as the `sleep()` isn't interrupted. The `sleep()` method yields control of the CPU to any thread (of any priority) that the JVM wishes to schedule.
- `yield()`—This method conditionally relinquishes control of the CPU. The condition is that there is a thread of equal or greater priority waiting to execute (that is, a `Thread` that is runnable, as opposed to a `Thread` in the wait state). So although a call to `sleep()` will make the thread cease executing at least temporarily, `yield()` might not cause the thread to pause its execution (if there are no qualified threads available).
- `join()`—This method is used if you want some code to execute only after another thread has finished execution. This is not a very common method. You would use it this way:

```
Runnable r1 = new BookFinder("Against Apion by Josephus"
Thread t1 = new Thread(r1);
t1.start
t1.join();
long timeGap = System.getCurrentTimeMillis();
```

The call to `getCurrentTimeMillis()` won't execute until t1 has completed executing `BookFinder`'s `run()` method. You can optionally specify a time interval in the `join()` method call. This time gap, specified in milliseconds and, optionally in nanoseconds, tells how long to wait for the joined Thread to complete its work. If it is still not done after that interval, the caller of the `join()` method is allowed to resume execution.

> **NOTE**
>
> Most operating systems cannot slice time finely enough to wait an interval of a nanosecond meaningfully. Therefore, the nanoseconds parameter is generally not very useful. In addition, it is difficult to guess, even for one specific system, how much work could get done in 15 nanoseconds, let alone what would be an appropriate interval for all systems. Therefore, you should probably just skip this optional parameter.

- `suspend()` and `resume()`—This pair of methods lets you stop a thread from executing (and make it nonrunnable) immediately and then make it runnable again at a later time. This pair of methods is *deprecated* in Java 2. The reason is that the `suspend()` method can cause a deadlock.
  For example, a `Thread` `t1` is using a resource and has an object lock (described later) on that resource. If `t1` is suspended, it can neither execute nor give up the object lock. Another `Thread` that needs the same resource, and the object lock will never get it. `t1` holds the lock and can't execute because it is suspended. To prevent this kind of deadlock, these two methods have been deprecated in Java 2. Do not use them. Instead, use better multithreaded programming algorithms.
- `stop()`—The `stop()` method causes a thread to immediately halt in its tracks and die. Unlike `suspend()`, the thread will release the resources it has locks on, but it will not clean up the state of objects it is working with.
  For example, if the `Thread` is using a database connection from a connection pool, it will not be able to give the connection back or notify any other object of its death. It is immediately terminated. This could leave output streams unflushed and unclosed. In view of its dangers, this method has also been *deprecated* in Java 2. If you want a thread to be able to terminate before it reaches the end of its `run()` method, you should provide a flag such as the following:
  `boolean stopRunning= false;`
  and use this flag inside the run() method, perhaps like this:
  ```
  public void run()
     {
       while(stopRunning == false)
           {
             // Do important stuff.
           }
       // Clean up resources.
     }
  ```
  This way, the thread can shut itself down cleanly.

Using Synchronization

When there are multiple `Threads`running in a JVM, it is possible that multiple `Threads` will want to modify the same resource (object) at the same time. The simplest way to illustrate this is with the classic producer-consumer model. Imagine an array of float primitives:

`float[] fltArray = new float[6];`

This creates an array for holding six float primitives. In the producer-consumer model, a Thread, t1, tries to add floats to this array as fast as it can. Another Thread, t2, the consumer, tries to read and remove those floats as fast as it can. Typically, some kind of counter would be used to track which slot in the array last had a float put in it or taken from it. Listing 11.3 shows an unsynchronized (dangerous) way to implement this.

Listing 11.3   Unsynchronized Producer-Consumer Example (ThreadDriver3.java)

```
import java.util.*;   // import for java.util.Date.

class Producer implements Runnable
     {
      Thread t1;
      DateHolder dates;

      public Producer(DateHolder d)
          {
           dates = d;
               // Get object reference to the Date Array.
           t1 = new Thread(this);
               // Create a new Thread using a Runnable object instance.
           t1.start();
               // Make the Thread runnable, and eligible for execution.
          }

      public void run()
          {
           for(int i = 0; i < 100; i++)
               {
                // Add 100 elements to the DateHolder array.
                 while(dates.counter < (dates.dateArray.length -1) )
                // Test to be sure there is space in the DateHolder array.
                     {
                      dates.counter++;
                      int j = dates.counter;
                      dates.dateArray[j] = new Date();
                // Put a Date object in the DateHolder array.
                     }
                   try
                       {
                        Thread.currentThread().sleep(100);
                       }
                   catch(InterruptedException e)
                       {}
                // Give another thread a chance to run
                // by causing the current Thread to sleep briefly.
                // Must catch the possible InterrruptedException.
               }
          }
     }
```

```
class Consumer implements Runnable
    {
    // This class is for reading Date objects from a Date array
    // as fast as possible.
    Thread t2;
    DateHolder dates;

    public Consumer(DateHolder d)
        {
         dates = d;
            // Get object reference to the Date Array.
         t2 = new Thread(this);
            // Create a new Thread using a Runnable object instance.
         t2.start();
            // Make the Thread runnable, and eligible for execution.
        }

    public void run()
        {
         for(int i =0; i < 100; i++)
            {
            // Remove 100 elements to the DateHolder array.
             while(dates.counter > 0)
            // Test to be sure there are elements in the DateHolder array.
                {
                  int j = dates. counter;
                  Date d = dates.dateArray[j];
                  dates.counter--;
                  System.out.println("Last date extracted was " + d);
                // Get a Date object out of the DateHolder array.
                }
              try
                {
                  Thread.currentThread().sleep(100);
                // Make current Thread sleep briefly.
                }
              catch(InterruptedException e)
                {}
            // Give another thread a chance to run.
            }
        }
    }

class DateHolder
    {
```

continues

Listing 11.3 continued
```
    // This class is an array for Date objects.
    // It is a resource that is shared
    // among multiple Thread objects.
    Date[] dateArray;
    int counter = 0;

    public DateHolder()
        {
          dateArray = new Date[100];
        }
} // End class definition for DateHolder.

public class ThreadDriver3
    {

    public static void main(String[] args)
        {
          DateHolder dueDates = new DateHolder();
              // Simulate getting book due dates.
          Producer pro = new Producer(dueDates);
              // Start an object putting dates into the
              // DateHolder dateArray.
          Consumer con = new Consumer(dueDates);
              // Start an object removing dates from the
              // DateHolder dateArray.
        }
} // End class definition of ThreadDriver3
```

This program shows a basic producer-consumer scenario. The problem is that there's a huge logic bug here. Both the Producer thread and the Consumer thread are updating the dateArray object and the counter. That's okay, in principle, unless a scenario such as the following occurs:

1. Thread t1 increments the counter.
2. Thread t1 becomes nonrunnable (perhaps it is pre-empted).
3. Thread t2 goes to the dateArray and removes the Date object at the position indicated by the counter. Because t1 might never have put anything there, this slot in the dateArray is null.
4. Thread t2 decrements the counter by 1.
5. Thread t1 puts a new Date object in the dateArray based on the current value of the counter. This is the wrong place to put it.

This sort of scenario is completely plausible. You cannot determine when a thread will stop executing, either because it is pre-empted, uses up its time slice, or for any number of other reasons. The result is that t2 prints bogus data for a Date object (a null value). Thread t1 overwrites a valid Date object with a new value that Thread t2 might never see because the counter is now messed up.

Java provides a means to deal with this. It's called synchronizing. Essentially, this means that no two threads can access the same object, if they both synchronize on it. To do this, you use the `synchronized` keyword. When you synchronize on a piece of code, or a method, you are given an object lock for the object in the code. As long as your thread owns that object or monitor lock, no other thread can access that object or primitive.

As an analogy, picture a supply cabinet at work that has a lock with only one key. If I have the key, you can't access the cabinet. You have to wait until I return the key. Object locks work the same way. To enter a synchronized code block, a thread has to obtain the object lock. If another thread has the lock, that `Thread` does not give up the lock until it exits the synchronized code block. This is done automatically for you by the JVM. All you need to do is something like the following:

```
public synchronized push(Date d)
   {
      dateArray[counter] = d;
   }
```

or

```
public boolean push(Date d)
      {
         synchronized(this)
            {
               dateArray[counter] = d;
               }
      }
```

You can either make a whole method synchronized, or synchronize just a block of code inside a method.

NOTE

Synchronizing just one block of code can give you greater concurrency, because you hold the object lock no longer than absolutely necessary. At the same time, the performance of your program will be worse because extra system method calls are made for you when you synchronize on just a block of code, rather than on a whole method.

Synchronization Code Example

Listing 11.4 shows an improved, and more OO, version of the program.

Listing 11.4 Using Synchronization with Threads (ThreadDriver4.java)
```
import java.util.*;  // import for java.util.Date.

class Producer implements Runnable
      {
        Thread t1;
        DateHolder dates;
```

continues

Listing 11.4 continued

```java
    public Producer(DateHolder d)
        {
          dates = d;
             // Get object reference to the Date Array.
          t1 = new Thread(this);
             // Create a new Thread using a Runnable object instance.
          t1.start();
             // Make the Thread runnable, and eligible for execution.
        }

    public void run()
        {
          for(int i = 0; i < 100; i++)
              {
                dates.push(new Date() );
                // Add 100 elements to the DateHolder array.
                  try
                      {
                        Thread.currentThread().sleep(100);
                      }
                    catch(InterruptedException e)
                        {}
                    // Give another Thread a chance to run.
              }
        }
    } // End class definition for Producer.



class Consumer implements Runnable
    {
      Thread t2;
      DateHolder dates;

    public Consumer(DateHolder d)
        {
          dates = d;
             // Get object reference to the Date Array.
          t2 = new Thread(this);
             // Create a new Thread using a Runnable object instance.
          t2.start();
             // Make the Thread runnable, and eligible for execution.
        }

    public void run()
        {
          for(int i =0; i < 100; i++)
              {
                // Remove 100 elements to the DateHolder array.
```

```
                    Date d = dates.pop();

                     try
                         {
                          Thread.currentThread().sleep(100);
                         }
                      catch(InterruptedException e)
                         {}
                     // Give another thread a chance to run.
                    }
                }
    } // End Class definition for Consumer.


class DateHolder
    {
      Date[] dateArray;
      int counter = 0;

      public DateHolder()
          {
            dateArray = new Date[100];
          }

      public synchronized boolean push(Date d)
          {
            while(counter < (dateArray.length -1) )
                 // Test to be sure there is space in the DateHolder array.
                       {
                        counter++;
                        int j = counter;
                        dateArray[j] = d;
                   // Put a Date object in the DateHolder array.
                   break;
                    // Leave while loop.
                    }
             return true;
         }

      public synchronized Date pop()
           {
             Date d = null;
             while(counter > 0)
                 // Test to be sure there are elements in the DateHolder array.
                {
                 int j = counter;
                 d = dateArray[j];
                 counter--;
                 System.out.println("Last date extracted was " + d);
```

continues

Listing 11.4 continued

```
            // Get a Date object out of the DateHolder array.
          break;
        }
      return d;
    }

} // End class definition for DateHolder.

public class ThreadDriver4
  {

  public static void main(String[] args)
      {
      DateHolder dueDates = new DateHolder();
          // Simulate getting book due dates.
      Producer pro = new Producer(dueDates);
          // Start an object putting dates into the
          // DateHolder dateArray.
      Consumer con = new Consumer(dueDates);
          // Start an object removing dates from the
          // DateHolder dateArray.
      }
  } // End class definition of ThreadDriver4.
```

I've added two methods to the `DateHolder` class: `push()` and `pop()`. The `push()` method adds `Date` objects to the `dateArray` object, and the `pop()` method removes `Date` objects from the `dateArray` object. The `push()` method is called by thread `t1` and the `pop()` method is called by thread `t2`. This is an improvement over the last version of the program. However, because `push()` and `pop()` are both synchronized, there is no way for the `push()` method to access the `dateArray` object or the counter until the `pop()` method has completed and returned the object lock to the JVM, and vice versa. There's no way for data to be corrupted or missed in this version. Using the synchronized keyword helps insure data integrity.

> **NOTE**
>
> To get the benefit of synchronization, all the methods that access the shared resources must be synchronized. If `push()` is synchronized and `pop()` is not, synchronization does not guarantee anything. The `pop()` method can freely modify the counter, for example, because it doesn't need the object lock to do so.

You cannot enter synchronized code without the object lock, so if the `pop()` method is being executed, and thread `t1` calls the `push()` method, it will have to wait until it receives the object lock before it actually can execute the `push()` method.

Avoiding Deadlocks with wait() and notify()

So now we've seen how threads can prevent corrupting shared data. There's now a new problem that, unfortunately, we've introduced. That problem is the potential for deadlock, or the "deadly embrace." Here's how it works.

Consider two threads, t1 and t2. Both threads need to work with two resources, obj1 and obj2, in order to complete their work. Now, here's the problem scenario.

1. t1 gets an object lock for obj1.
2. t2 gets an object lock for obj2.
3. t1 can't proceed without the object lock for obj2, but t1 can't get that lock because t2 owns it.
4. t2 cannot proceed without obj1, but it cannot get that object lock because t1 owns it.

The result of this scenario is a deadlock. Because neither thread can complete its work without a resource it cannot have, and neither Thread will release its object lock until its work is complete, neither thread can go any further. They both simply freeze.

CAUTION

Java provides no means to end a deadlock, nor does it provide much info about deadlock. When a deadlock occurs, you will not see an exception or stack trace. The console will not show that anything is wrong. Your program will simply stop executing (at least the relevant threads). Diagnosing such a condition usually requires a lot of research, though the amount of research can be reduced through the use of various third-party tools such as JProbe or OptimizeIt!. Therefore, it is very important to design multithreaded programs very carefully and use all the resources you can find that help you with the design.

To avoid the deadly embrace, you need a way for a Thread to voluntarily release its object lock, at least temporarily, so that another thread can acquire a shared resource and complete its work. Java provides a mechanism for doing this—using wait() and notify(). These two methods are inherited from the class java.lang.Object so any object can call wait() or notify(). Here's what these two methods do:

- wait()—Gives up the object lock(s) acquired for the current synchronized code block or method and becomes nonrunnable.
- notify()—Tell a wait()ing thread that it can wake up and prepare to get the object lock back. This does not give the object lock to the wait()ing thread. It merely tells the wait()ing thread that it can wake up and prepare to get the lock. That process is done for you by the JVM. You don't write code to "wake up and prepare to get the object lock."
- It's important to note that you are only allowed to call wait() or notify() from synchronized code. Because these methods apply specifically to object locks, that makes perfect sense. If you are not in synchronized code, you don't have an object lock, so calling wait() would not give up an object lock. There is another method, notifyAll() that does the same thing as notify, except that it wakes up all threads that are wait()ing.

wait() and notify() Code Example

Listing 11.5 shows a new version of our producer-consumer program that uses `wait()` and `notify()`.

> **NOTE**
>
> As you'll see in Listing 11.5, it's crucial that you put code into your synchronized method to verify that, when you wake up from the `wait()` call and get the object lock, you proceed to do work. The `notifyAll()` method might wake up your thread when that is not appropriate. You don't want to go ahead and run if that doesn't make sense.

Listing 11.5 Example of Using wait() and notify() (ThreadDriver5.java)

```java
import java.util.*;   // import for java.util.Date

class Producer implements Runnable
     {
     Thread t1;
     DateHolder dates;

     public Producer(DateHolder d)
          {
          dates = d;
             // Get object reference to the Date Array.
          t1 = new Thread(this);
             // Create a new Thread using a Runnable object instance.
          t1.start();
             // Make the Thread runnable, and eligible for execution.
          }

     public void run()
          {
          for(int i = 0; i < 100; i++)
               {
               dates.push(new Date() );
               // Add 100 elements to the DateHolder array.
                 try
                      {
                      Thread.currentThread().sleep(100);
                      }
                    catch(InterruptedException e)
                         {}
                    // Give another Thread a chance to run.
               }
          }
     } // End class definition for Producer.
```

```java
class Consumer implements Runnable
    {
      Thread t2;
      DateHolder dates;

      public Consumer(DateHolder d)
          {
            dates = d;
              // Get object reference to the Date Array.
            t2 = new Thread(this);
              // Create a new Thread using a Runnable object instance.
            t2.start();
              // Make the Thread runnable, and eligible for execution.
          }

      public void run()
          {
            for(int i =0; i < 100; i++)
                {
                // Remove 100 elements to the DateHolder array.
                  Date d = dates.pop();

                   try
                       {
                        Thread.currentThread().sleep(100);
                       }
                     catch(InterruptedException e)
                       {}
                  // Give another thread a chance to run.
                }
          }
    } // End Class definition for Consumer.


class DateHolder
    {
      Date[] dateArray;
      int counter = 0;

      public DateHolder()
          {
            dateArray = new Date[1];
          }

      public synchronized boolean push(Date d)
          {
            while(counter >= (dateArray.length -1) )
                {
                  try
```

continues

Listing 11.5 continued

```java
                    {
                      wait();
                    }
                catch(InterruptedException ie)
                    { }
                // There is no room in the dateArray, so
                // so give up the object lock.
                // Put this Thread into a wait (non-runnable) state
                // and wait for some space in the dateArray.
            } // This test needs to be done in a while loop.

        counter++;
        dateArray[counter] = d;
                // Put a Date object in the DateHolder array.
        notify();
                // Tell the other Thread that is popping
                // to wake up and get ready to go.  This Thread is about to
                // release the object lock.
        return true;
        }

    public synchronized Date pop()
        {
        Date d = null;
        while(counter < 0)
                // Test to be sure there are elements in the DateHolder array.
            {
              try
                    {
                      wait();
                    }
                catch(InterruptedException ie)
                    { }
                // There are no elements in the dateArray,
                // so give up the object lock.
                // Put this Thread into a wait (non-runnable) state
                // and wait for some elements in the dateArray.
            } // This test needs to be done in a while loop.
        d = dateArray[counter];
        counter--;
        System.out.println("Last date extracted was " + d);
                // Get a Date object out of the DateHolder array.
        notify();
                // Tell the push() Thread to wake up.
        return d;
        }

    } // End class definition for DateHolder.
```

```
public class ThreadDriver5
   {
    public static void main(String[] args)
       {
        DateHolder dueDates = new DateHolder();
            // Simulate getting book due dates.
        Producer pro = new Producer(dueDates);
            // Start an object putting dates into the
            // DateHolder dateArray.
        Consumer con = new Consumer(dueDates);
            // Start an object removing dates from the
            // DateHolder dateArray.
       }
   } // End class definition of ThreadDriver5.
```

Both the push() and pop() methods have had a call to wait() and notify() added to them. Notice that the call to wait(), in each case, is inside a while loop. It could be inside an if statement, but that would be a problem. If the pop method checks in an if statement to see if there are any elements in the dateArray and finds there are none, it calls wait(). Then, it wakes up from the push method's notify() call when the Thread for pop() gets an object lock. The Thread executing pop() proceeds, because now it has the object lock. There's no way of knowing at this point, however, if there are any elements in the dateArray object. This thread might have been notify()ed by some other thread doing a notify() or notifyAll(). That would cause the pop() method to try to take an element from an invalid position in the dateArray object. The wait() call must be done inside a while loop. That way, if there's no element to retrieve in the pop() method or no space left in the push() method, wait() will be called again and again until conditions are right to execute the rest of the method.

The notify() method is the next to last statement in each method. The notify() call could be put almost anywhere in the method after the while loop. The notify() method does not cause the wait()ing thread to start executing. It merely moves it to a different queue where it can await the object lock, which will not be available until the method that calls notify() actually completes. So here's a potential scenario:

1. Enter the push() method with the object lock.
2. Test to see if it is valid to add an element to the dateArray object.
3. Potentially go into a wait state, becoming nonrunnable.
4. Potentially be awakened and given the object lock by another method that does a notify() or notifyAll() and then gives up the object lock.
5. Test again, to see if the Thread called wait(). If not, work can proceed.
6. When work can proceed, add an element to the dateArray object.
7. Call notify().
8. Return true.
9. Exit the push() method and give up the object lock.
10. Let the system give the object lock to the thread running the pop() method.

CAUTION

This small sample program has one more potential problem that you should avoid in your code. It is possible in this scenario for the thread calling `push()` to `wait()` and the thread calling `pop()` to `wait()`. This would leave both threads `wait()`ing with no mechanism to wake up either thread. Although that is unlikely here, it is possible and unpredictable. One of the worst things about this kind of problem is that it might happen on system A, but not system B. To avoid this, you need to add extra code to your program to make sure that multiple methods, which synchronize on the same data, cannot all put their calling Threads into a `wait()` state at the same time. This problem will probably not happen here because the code uses an array. Other types of collections or data structures might create such a problem more readily.

CHAPTER 12

I/O in Java

This chapter introduces you to the techniques for performing input and output and dealing with files in Java. The classes to support I/O in Java are primarily in the package java.io. This package contains a lot of stream classes—some that are fairly common, and some that are used relatively rarely. This chapter focuses on the most common or important I/O classes and techniques.

Before proceeding, let me make a clarification of terminology in this chapter. When I say InputStream or OutputStream, I am referring to those two specific classes. When I say "input stream" or "output stream," I am referring to any class that is a subclass of InputStream or OutputStream. Likewise, there are the Reader and Writer classes, and Readers and Writers, which are subclasses of these two classes.

A Quick Overview of Stream

The concept of a *stream* is just that—a continuous stream of bytes, traveling between a program and a file, between two threads, or between two programs. Some I/O classes require the use of sockets. Sockets will be dealt with in Chapter 14, "Java Network Programming." The stream classes in Java, such as FileInputStream, are byte-oriented. They read and write data one byte at a time or in groups of bytes. These are the only kind of classes for I/O in JDK 1.0.

JDK 1.1 introduced Reader and Writer, which are character-based. Internally, Java uses Unicode, 16-bit characters. To write out to a file using, for example, a FileOutputStream, Java formerly had to translate characters from Unicode characters to smaller ASCII characters. Then, when the file was read back into a Java program, Java again had to do conversion, this time from 8-bit ASCII characters to 16-bit Unicode characters. Using Reader and Writer eliminates this conversion. In general, it is much better to use Readers and Writers than to use the older stream classes. In fact, many of the methods and even some classes that support byte streams are now deprecated and have been replaced by a corresponding Reader or Writer class. Generally, Reader and Writer subclasses are best suited for handling text, while stream classes are better suited for other applications, such as processing Java primitives and entire objects.

An Overview of the Main Stream, Reader, and Writer Classes

The parent class of all input streams is the abstract class InputStream.

InputStream provides a limited number of methods, such as read(), read(byte[] b), mark(), and reset(). There are a number of InputStream subclasses. These include

- FileInputStream—Used for reading files at the byte level
- SequenceInputStream—Used for combining multiple files into one input stream
- PipedInputStream—Used for reading a stream through a pipe from another Thread or the like
- DataInputStream—Used for reading Java primitives, such as float, char, int, and boolean, as well as for reading in UTF strings
- ObjectInputStream—Used for reading in both primitives and serialized objects
- PushbackInputStream—Used for reading one or more bytes and then returning those bytes to the input stream, potentially to read them again
- LineNumberInputStream—Used for reading a file one line at a time and getting the number of the line read, suitable for a program editor, for example
- StreamTokenizer—Used for reading in a stream in tokens
- BufferedInputStream—Used for reading in large amounts of data, or buffering input for efficiency
- ByteArrayInputStream—Used for reading in data from an array of bytes

The base class of all output streams is OutputStream, which is abstract. OutputStream has a few basic methods, such as write(), write(byte[] b), flush(), and close(). Some of the main OutputStream classes are

- FileOutputStream—Used for writing out files at the byte level
- PrintStream—Used for writing out lines of output, often to the console
- PipedOutputStream—Used for writing data to a pipe between Threads and the like
- BufferedOutputStream—Used for writing out data in large blocks, using buffers for efficiency
- ObjectOutputStream—Used for writing out primitives and serialized objects to a stream
- ByteArrayOutputStream—Used for writing data out to a byte array

> **NOTE**
>
> The type of standard input (`System.in` in Java) is an `InputStream`. The type of standard output (`System.out` in Java) is `PrintStream`.

The base class for Reader classes is `Reader`, an abstract class with a small number of basic methods, such as `read()`, `read(char[] c)`, `reset()`, `mark()`, and `close()`. Some important `Reader` subclasses include

- `FileReader`—Used for reading files at the Unicode character level
- `BufferedReader`—Used for reading large block of data, as characters, through a buffer
- `CharArrayReader`—Used for reading a char array
- `InputStreamReader`—Used for converting an `InputStream` to a `Reader`. This allows you to read whole characters from `System.in`, for example.
- `LineNumberReader`—Used for reading whole lines with line numbers returned
- `PipedReader`—Used for reading input through a pipe, between two `Threads`, for example

The `Writer` class is the abstract base class for all Writers. It has a small number of basic methods, such as `write()`, `write(char[] c)`, `flush()`, and `close()`. The `Writer` subclasses include

- `FileWriter`—Used for writing files on a character-oriented level
- `BufferedWriter`—Used for writing out large blocks of data as Unicode characters using buffers
- `CharArrayWriter`—Used for writing out char arrays
- `PipedWriter`—Used for writing data to a pipe as chars, such as between two Threads
- `PrintWriter`—Used for writing output as lines of chars

As you can see from this list, there are `Reader` and `Writer` classes to match most stream classes. Also, for most input stream or `Reader` classes, there is an output stream or `Writer` counterpart.

> **TIP**
>
> In general, you should use `Reader` and `Writer` classes rather than stream classes for character-based I/O. However, the `Reader` and `Writer` classes by default can be up to three times slower than the stream classes. To avoid this performance penalty, be sure to set the `Reader` or `Writer` class you use so that it will use buffering. This will offset the disadvantage of using `Reader` and `Writer` classes.

Using Files in Java

To really use streams, you need to use files. So this chapter will cover files first. Java supports two kinds of files:

- `File`—Can only be written to sequentially
- `RandomAccessFile`—Can be read from or written to at any point in the file

To be able to use a file in Java, you create a `File` or `RandomAccessFile` object.

> **WARNING**
>
> It is critical to remember that creating a `File` object such as
> `File myFile = new File("/export", config.dat");`
> does not have anything to do with whether or not this file exists. You can execute this constructor for a nonexistent file. Java does not throw an exception for a nonexistent file until you actually try to create a stream that uses the file.

File: Code Example

The `File` class has three constructors and a number of useful methods. Here are the three constructors:

```
File("file name")
File("Directory name")
File("directory name", "Filename")
```

You can, of course, define the `String` objects used for the directory name and filename elsewhere. In general, you probably would do so for flexibility in your code. You can find out a fair amount of information about a file. Listing 12.1 shows some of the methods in action.

Listing 12.1   An Example of Using the File Class (FileDriver1.java)

```java
import java.io.*; // Import the java.io package.
import java.util.*;

class FileExplorer
    {
      File dirName;
      File theFile;
      byte[] data;

      public FileExplorer()
            {
              String temp = " Input to the file:  100-10-2234";
              data = temp.getBytes();
                      // Convert the String into a byte array.
              dirName = new File("C:\\PureJava\\source\\chap12");
                      // Create a directory File object.
              theFile = new File(dirName, "tempdata.dat");
                      // Create a File object, specifying both
                      // the directory for the file
                      // and the filename.
                      // Note the use of double backslashes in the path
                      // name "\\".
                      // This is, of course, only needed in Win32
                      // environments.
              try
                    {
```

Using Files in Java 227

```java
            FileOutputStream fos = new FileOutputStream(theFile);
                // The FileOutputStream takes a File in
                // one of its constructors.
            fos.write(data);
                // Write out a byte array of data.length
                // number of bytes.
            fos.flush();
                // Be sure all data goes to disk from cache.
            fos.close();
                // Close the stream.
        }
    catch(IOException e)
        {
          System.out.println("IOException " + e.getMessage());
        }
    }

public boolean printFileInfo()
    {
      try
        {
          FileInputStream fis = new FileInputStream(theFile);
                    // Create a FileInputStream to read the file.
          fis.read(data);
          fis.close();
          System.out.println(data);
                    // Print the file contents.
          System.out.println("The file can be read: " +
                theFile.canRead());
                    // Is the file readable?
          System.out.println("The file can be written to: " +
                 theFile.canWrite());
                    // Is the file writeable?
          System.out.println("The file exists: " +
                  theFile.exists());
                    // Does the file exist?
          System.out.println("The absolute path of the file is: " +
                  theFile.getAbsolutePath());
                    // What is the file's absolute path?
          System.out.println("The canonical file path is: " +
                   theFile.getCanonicalPath());
                    // What is the canonical path?
          System.out.println("The path is: " +
                  theFile.getPath());
                    // What is the path of the file?
          System.out.println("The file name is: " +
                   theFile.getName());
                    // What is the name of the file?
          System.out.println("Is the File object the absolute path: " +
```

continues

Listing 12.1 continued

```java
                                theFile.isAbsolute());
                            // Does the File object represent the
                            // absolute path?
                System.out.println("The File object represents a file: " +
                                theFile.isFile());
                            // Does the File object represent a file?
                System.out.println("The File object represents a directory: "
                                + theFile.isDirectory());
                            // Does the File object represent a directory?
                System.out.println("The file is hidden: " +
                                theFile.isHidden());
                            // Is the file hidden?
                Date modDate = new Date(theFile.lastModified());
                System.out.println("The file was last modified: " +
                                modDate.toString());
                            // When was the file last modified?
                System.out.println("The file is: " +
                        theFile.length() + " bytes long");
                        // How long is the file?
                theFile.delete();
                        // You can delete a physical file
                        // as well as call mkdir() on a file object
                        // or renameTo() a new filename.

                        // Finally, list the contents of this directory.
                String[] fileList = dirName.list();
                for(int i = 0; i < fileList.length; i++)
                    System.out.println(fileList[i]);
                }
            catch(IOException e)
                {
                  System.out.println("IOException " + e.getMessage());
                }

        return true;
        }

    } // End class definition for FileExplorer.

public class FileDriver1
    {
      public static void main(String[] args)
            {
              FileExplorer fe = new FileExplorer();
              fe.printFileInfo();
              System.exit(0);
            }
    }
```

This program illustrates a number of points. It shows how to create a basic byte-oriented stream, FileOutputStream, and also FileInputStream. It shows how to create a byte array from a string with the getBytes() method. It shows how to read to and write from a stream and, implicitly, from a file. It also shows several of the methods in the File class that provide information about the file.

> **TIP**
>
> The File method list() could be used with the method isDirectory() to recursively step through an entire file system and print out its contents.

Although calling delete() is not normally recommended, this program also shows the use of the delete() method. Note that if this call to delete() is removed, you can call the program over and over, and it will still end up with the same contents. It will not append or add any data beyond the original 32 bytes.

RandomAccessFile Code Example

Java also has a RandomAccessFile class, which is an important feature for file I/O. You might, for example, create a File object today and write through it to a physical file. In a Java program, if you use that file again tomorrow by writing to it, its original contents are thrown away. You essentially start from scratch. A RandomAccessFile does not work that way. You can write to it, close it, and write to it again, without losing any data. This is shown in Listing 12.2. In order to modify or append to a RandomAccessFile object's underlying physical file, you need to seek() to a specific location. Doing so positions the file pointer just before that location.

> **NOTE**
>
> There is no open() method or create() method for a file, as might be present in some system calls or other programming languages, such as C. Java creates and opens file for you in whatever manner the platform you are using requires, and your code does not have to know anything about it.

Listing 12.2 Using a RandomAccessFile (FileDriver2.java)
```
// RandomAccessFile example
import java.io.*;

class RandomProcessor
   {
   RandomAccessFile raf;
   String fileName = "NewTitles.txt";
   int i = 0;    // Better performance as an instance variable.
   String[] titles = {"New Titles in the Library",
                      "Truth is Stranger than It Used to Be",
                      "How Shall We Then Live?",
                      "The Pilgrim\'s Regress"};
            // Define a String array.
```

continues

Listing 12.2 continued

```java
    public RandomProcessor()
        {
        try
            {
            raf =new RandomAccessFile(fileName, "rw");
                    // Instantiate a RandomAccessFile object
                    // for read and write.
                    // Specifying only "r" instead of "rw" means
                    // read-only in this application.

                    // Note the need to put the constructor in a try
                    // block.
            }
        catch(FileNotFoundException fnfe)
            {
            System.out.println("File " + fileName +
                            "not found" + fnfe.getMessage());
            }
        }

    public boolean readSomeStrings()
        {
        try
            {
            raf.seek(0);
            for(i = 0; i < titles.length; i++)
                {
                // Read until end of file.
                String s = raf.readUTF();
                System.out.println(s);
                }
            System.out.println (raf.readUTF());
            }
        catch(Exception e)
            {
            System.out.println("Error reading file:
                            " + e.getMessage());
            }

        return true;
        }

    public boolean writeSomeStrings()
        {
        try
            {
            for(i = 0; i < titles.length; i++)
                {
                raf.writeUTF(titles[i]);
```

```
                            // Write some modified UTF-8 Strings to the file.
                        }
                            // Now, write data to a specific location
                            // in the file: the end.
                    raf.seek(raf.length());
                            // seek() goes to a specific byte location
                            // in the file. The length() method, not to be
                            // confused with the length data member of arrays,
                            // returns the number of bytes in the file.
                            // This particular combination writes at the end
                            // of file.
                        raf.writeUTF(titles[1]);
                    }
                catch(IOException ioe)
                    {
                        System.out.println("Error writing file:  " +
                                            ioe.getMessage());
                    }

                return true;
            }
    } // End class definition RandomProcessor.

public class FileDriver2
    {
        public static void main(String[] args)
            {
                RandomProcessor rp = new RandomProcessor();
                rp.writeSomeStrings();
                rp.readSomeStrings();
                System.exit(0);
            }
    }
```

UTF strings, used in the preceding listing, will be explained later.

Performing I/O in Java

This section shows how to perform several important tasks in Java using streams and `Readers` and `Writers`, including

- Byte-oriented I/O
- I/O with Java Primitives
- Write and read lines of text
- Write and read entire objects

Performing I/O Using FileInputStream and FileOutputStream: Code Example

`FileInputStream` and `FileOutputStream` are the basic, concrete classes for doing I/O. Despite their names, you do not need to use them for writing to or reading from files as such. You should select the stream, `Reader`, or `Writer` that you want to use based on the granularity or level of abstraction you want to work at. You choose `FileInputStream` and `FileOutputStream` to work at the byte level. Listing 12.3 shows a simple example of using these two streams to write and read bytes.

Listing 12.3   Using FileInputStream and FileOutputStream (FileDriver3.java)

```java
// Byte-oriented I/O with FileInputStream and FileOutputStream example
import java.io.*;

class ByteProcessor
    {
    FileInputStream fis;
    FileOutputStream fos;

    String fileName = "BookInfo.txt";
    String book = "Pascal, Blaise, Pensees, PN 1901 P43 T64";
    byte[] dataIn;
    byte[] dataOut;

    public ByteProcessor()
        {
        try
            {
            fos = new FileOutputStream(fileName);
            // Instantiate a FileOutputStream for writing.
            // If a SecurityManager were instantiated, this
            // constructor call would cause a checkWrite() method
            // to verify that this class has permission for this.
            // Note the need to put the constructor in a try
            // block.
            }
        catch(IOException ioe)
            {
            System.out.println("File " + fileName +
                                        "error" + ioe.getMessage());
            }
        }

    public boolean writeBookCatalogInfo()
        {
        try
            {
            dataOut = book.getBytes();
            // Create a byte array
            fos.write(dataOut);
            // Write a byte array to the FileOutputStream.
            // This will cause the file, if it does not exist, to be
            // created before it is written to.
            fos.flush();
            fos.close();
```

```java
                    fos = null;
                    // Flush the stream to force the data to disk.
                    // Close the FileOutputStream so the file can be read.
                    // Then set the object reference to null to
                    // encourage garbage collection.
                    }
                catch(IOException e)
                    {
                      System.out.println("Error writing file:   " +
                                       e.getMessage());
                    }

                return true;
                }

        public boolean readBookCatalogInfo()
                {
                  try
                    {
                      fis = new FileInputStream(fileName);
                    // Create a FileInputStream object on the file.
                    // The physical file needs to exist when you do this.
                      dataIn = new byte[dataOut.length];
                      fis.read(dataIn, 0, dataIn.length);
                    // Read from the file from offset 0 for a given length.
                      String temp = new String(dataIn);
                    // Convert to a real String.
                      System.out.println(temp);

                    }
                catch(IOException ioe)
                    {
                      System.out.println("Error reading file:   " +
                                       ioe.getMessage());
                    }
                  return true;
                }
        } // End class definition PrimitiveProcessor.

public class FileDriver3
    {
      public static void main(String[] args)
            {
              ByteProcessor bp = new ByteProcessor();
              bp.writeBookCatalogInfo();
              bp.readBookCatalogInfo();
              System.exit(0);
            }
    }
```

Usually, you use FileInputStream and FileOutputStream as the basis of other stream classes when you wrap classes.

> **TIP**
>
> As you'll see throughout this chapter, it is common to *wrap* one stream or Reader or Writer class inside another. The idea here is that you start with the basic level of abstraction, such as bytes, using FileOutputStream and FileInputStream, and then you encapsulate this inside another I/O class that has a higher level of abstraction such as an ObjectOutputStream or ObjectInputStream.

Although the example shows the use of byte arrays for I/O, you can write individual bytes to a FileOutputStream one at a time and read them back in with a FileInputStream one at a time. That might be particularly useful if reading data created by another programming language, such as C.

Performing I/O on Java Primitives Using DataInputStream and DataOutputStream: Code Example

These classes are used if you want to work with Java primitive data types, such as float, int, and so forth. Instead of having to write four bytes to implicitly make an int in a file, you can simply do a writeInt() call. These two streams also support UTF strings. DataInputStream has a method called readUTF(), and DataOutputStream has a method called writeUTF(). Unfortunately, not all languages can be represented through Unicode. For example, the Korean alphabet and other pictographic languages cannot be expressed completely with only two-byte Unicode characters.

To circumvent this limitation, Java can work with UTF strings. *UTF* stands for *UCS Transformation Format*. *UCS* stands for *Universal Character Set*. Unlike Unicode, which uses two bytes for every character, a UTF character is variable in length. The character begins with the number of bits required to uniquely represent the character, followed by the bit pattern for the character. This might be three bytes, or four bytes, or more. Java enables you to write such characters to or from a stream. You can also use readUTF() and writeUTF() to deal with plain English strings. If you code

```
writeUTF("Death to gotos");
```

under the covers, Java does the UTF translation necessary. As a rule, you use this approach for strings that can be expressed in Unicode, but this is also the method you use to write a String object if you were using a DataOutputStream or DataInputStream for other reasons. Listing 12.4 illustrates using a DataOutputStream and DataInputStream to write Java primitives and read them from a file.

Listing 12.4   Using DataInputStream and DataOutputStream (FileDriver4.java)

```
// Java Primitive-oriented I/O with DataInputStream and DataOutputStream
import java.io.*;

class PrimitiveProcessor
```

```java
{
 DataInputStream dis;
 DataOutputStream dos;

    // Data for output.
 int outDay1 = 5;
 float outTemp1 = 75.5F;
 String cityName1 = "Milpitas";
 float outTemp2 = 120.2F;
 String cityname2 = "Chicago";

    // Data for input.
  int inDayNum = 0;
  float inTemp1 = 0.0f;
  float inTemp2 = 0.0f;
  String inCity1 = null;
  String inCity2 = null;
  String fileName = "Primitives.txt";
  FileOutputStream fos;

  public PrimitiveProcessor()
        {
         try
              {
                fos = new FileOutputStream(fileName);
                dos = new DataOutputStream(fos);
              // You need an OutputStream for the constructor, so
              // wrap a FileOutputStream in a DataOutputStream.
               }
         catch(IOException ioe)
                 {
                   System.out.println("File " + fileName +
                                               "error" + ioe.getMessage());
                 }
          }

   public boolean writeTemperatureInfo()
         {
           try
               {
                 dos.writeInt(outDay1);
                 dos.writeFloat(outTemp1);
                 dos.writeUTF(cityName1);
                 dos.writeFloat(outTemp2);
                 dos.writeUTF(cityname2);
                // There are specific write methods for every
                // Java primitive data type.
                 dos.flush();
                 dos.close();
```

continues

Listing 12.4 continued

```java
                dos = null;
            // Flush the stream to force the data to disk.
            // Close the DataOutputStream so the file can be read.
            // Then set the object reference to null to
            // encourage garbage collection.
            }
        catch(IOException e)
            {
              // Deal with any I/O-related errors
              // Almost all the methods of classes in java.io throw
              // exceptions
              System.out.println("Error writing file:  " +
              e.getMessage());
            }

        return true;
    }

    public boolean readTemperatureInfo()
        {
          try
            {
              FileInputStream fis = new FileInputStream(fileName);
              dis = new DataInputStream(fis);
              // "Wrap" the FileInputStream in a DataInputStream to
              // process data at a higher level of abstraction.
              // The DataInputStream constructor requires this.
              // Create a DataInputStream object on the file.
              // The physical file needs to exist when you do this.
              inDayNum = dis.readInt();
              inTemp1 = dis.readFloat();
              inCity1 = dis.readUTF();
              inTemp2 = dis.readFloat();
              inCity2 = dis.readUTF();
              // Instead of having to read a certain
              // number of bytes manually to assume
              // int or float, you can simply read a whole
              // primitive, and Java will
              // extract the correct number of bytes from the file.
              // Note that you must extract or read the data types
              // in the same order you wrote them. If you write
              // a float and a char,
              // in that order, you must not do readChar() followed by
              // readInt() if you want
              // correct results.
              System.out.println("On day " + inDayNum + ", while it was");
              System.out.println("a pleasant " + inTemp1 +
                                 " in " + inCity1);
              System.out.println("it was a nasty hot and muggy " +
```

```
                            inTemp2);
                System.out.println("in " + inCity2);
              }
            catch(IOException ioe)
                {
                  System.out.println("Error reading file:  " +
                                        ioe.getMessage());
                }
            return true;
          }
    } // End class definition PrimitiveProcessor

public class FileDriver4
    {
      public static void main(String[] args)
          {
            PrimitiveProcessor pProcessor = new PrimitiveProcessor();
            pProcessor.writeTemperatureInfo();
            pProcessor.readTemperatureInfo();
            System.exit(0);
          }
    }
```

As this program illustrates, it is very common, and often required, that you wrap one kind of stream in another, because a DataOutputStream, for example, requires an InputStream object, or an object that is a subclass of InputStream, as input. As you can tell from the code, the DataInputStream and DataOutputStream classes are oriented towards writing Java primitives, plus methods for reading and writing strings. There are also methods for reading or writing the entire file at once, including all the primitives using a byte array. It might be useful to write primitives without writing whole objects, such as when you send a discrete value from a client to a server over a socket. You can use a DataOutputStream for that purpose.

Reading and Writing Lines of Text: Code Example

There are multiple techniques for writing and reading lines of text. This next example, Listing 12.5, shows a way to write out and then read in lines of text from a file. Although you can use stream classes for this, these are generally deprecated. You should use Reader and Writer classes instead, because they work at the Unicode character level, instead of the byte level, as discussed earlier.

Listing 12.5   Reading and Writing Lines of Text with BufferedReader and PrintWriter (FileDriver5.java)
```
import java.io.*;

class TextProcessor
    {
      private FileWriter fw;
      private PrintWriter pw;
```

continues

Listing 12.5 continued

```java
    private File textFile;
    private FileReader fr;
    private BufferedReader br;
    private String[] books = { "Rhetorica by Aristotle",
                    "Against Apion by Josephus",
                    "4QMMT author unknown",
                    "Peloponesian War by Thucydides"};
    // Declare a String array of book titles from antiquity

    public TextProcessor()
        {
          //Do file initialization in the constructor
          try
            {
              textFile = new File("AncientTexts.txt");
              // Define a new file
              fw = new FileWriter(textFile);
              // Connect the file to a FileWriter object for output
              pw = new PrintWriter(fw);
              // Wrap the FileWriter in a PrintWriter so you can write output
              // by lines, not characters
            }
          catch(IOException e)
              {
                // There are many reasons this might fail, like the
                // write-protect tab on a diskette being set to
                // write-protect the disktte.
                System.out.println("Cannot create file because of " +
                                                    e.toString());
              }
        }

    public void writeOutput()
      {
        for (int i=0; i< books.length; i++)
            {
              // Step through the array, and write each
              // element to the file a s "line".
              pw.println(books[i]);
            }
        pw.flush();
        // Force everything from the buffer to the physical file.
        pw.close();
        // Close the writer.
      }

    public void readInput()
```

```
    {
    try
        {
        // Read the file into memory, one "line" at a time.
        // For this to work, the data in the file must be
        // organized as "lines" with carriage returns.
         fr = new FileReader(textFile);
         br = new BufferedReader(fr);
         // Open the file with a FileReader and wrap the
         // character-oriented reader in a line-oriented reader.
         for(int i =0; i < books.length; i++)
            {
            String line = br.readLine();
            // Read a line and print it.
            System.out.println(line);
            }
        }
    catch(IOException e)
        {
        System.out.println("Read failed because of " + e.toString());
        }
    }

} // End class definition TextProcessor.

public class FileDriver5
   {

   public static void main(String args[])
      {
      TextProcessor textP = new TextProcessor();
      textP.writeOutput();
      textP.readInput();
      System.exit(0);
      }
   }
```

This program uses two main Reader and Writer classes: BufferedReader and PrintWriter. BufferedReader can read lines of text. The PrintWriter class is like the PrintStream class, except that PrintWriter works at the Unicode character level, rather than the byte level, as does the PrintStream class.

NOTE

For those with a C/C++ background who are looking for a way to produce formatted output with some method such as println(), Java does not support this task the way C does. There is no equivalent for the C function printf().

240 Chapter 12: I/O in Java

> **TIP**
>
> You can use the `BufferedWriter` to make it easier to read a `String` from the command line as well. You wrap `System.in` in an `InputStreamReader`, which converts from bytes to chars, and then wrap the `InputStreamReader` in a `BufferedReader` object. Then you can read the whole command line at once by using the `readLine()` method of the `BufferedReader` class.

Reading and Writing Objects

Java provides the capability to write an entire object, not just its pieces, to a stream so that you can send a whole object across the network.

> **TIP**
>
> Because `Vectors` allow you to insert any number of disparate objects, `Vectors` are often used to send data across a network. Usually, the client and server programs have agreed on the format of the `Vector` in terms of which slot holds which element, but that decision is up to you. This procedure is often used in e-commerce applications to send customer information in one object.

Object Serialization

The mechanism that Java uses to send an entire object is called *object serialization*. This is a key technology in Java, and it shows up in other places, such as RMI. It can also be used to make an object persistent. When you serialize an object, Java creates a special version of your object, a copy of it, which includes information on each field. If you write an object to disk, and then view the file, you will see things like "`java.lang.String`" followed by the value of a `String` that is in your object. Java not only copies your object, but any dependent objects that your object contains as well.

> **CAUTION**
>
> Object serialization is a handy feature, but it should be used carefully. Serializing huge objects with lots of dependent objects can have a serious negative impact on network throughput.

Using object serialization, you can write an object to a stream and have another object read the serialized object in as an object, not just a set of primitives or unrelated fields. Java ships the data members, but not the method code of your object. The receiving system must be able to locate the class definition.

> **CAUTION**
>
> Because a serialized object is a copy, changes you make to an object you read from a stream are not propagated to the original object without additional coding on your part.

In order to be allowed to serialize an object, you must implement the Serializable interface. The good news is that this interface contains no methods. All you actually have to do is put this interface in the class signature:

```
public class Book implements Serializable
```

Most classes in the Java distribution are serializable. A few classes, such as Thread, are not (because it would make no sense to have them serializable). In addition, you can decide if a specific field in your class should not be serialized. There are at least two reasons not to serialize:

- If it makes no sense to serialize it (for example, a temporary String whose value need not be saved).
- If it is sensitive data you do not want exposed publicly. Serialization makes no distinction between public and private data members, so you might not want to serialize the credit card numbers of your customers.

To make a specific field within your object unserializable, you mark it as *transient*.

```
class Customer implements Serializable
    {
      private transient String creditCardNumber;
      private String CustName;
    }
```

In this small class, when you serialize an object of type Customer, Java will send a copy of the current value of the custName String, but will only provide a place marker for the value of creditCardNumber, because the latter is marked as transient. Incidentally, static data members are not copied, but given default values when they are turned back into an object by the object reading the object stream.

ObjectOutputStream and ObjectInputStream: Code Example

There are two classes specifically designed for dealing with objects, ObjectOutputStream and ObjectInputStream. These streams can deal with objects and primitives. If all you need to do is deal with primitives, however, you should use DataInputStream and DataOutputStream because of the extra overhead incurred with an object stream. Listing 12.6 shows how to write an object to a stream and how to read an object from a stream.

Listing 12.6 Writing and Reading Objects Using ObjectOutputStream and ObjectInputStream (FileDriver6.java)

```
// Reading and Writing Objects in Java.
import java.io.*;

class ObjectProcessor
    {
    FileInputStream fis;
    FileOutputStream fos;
```

continues

Listing 12.6 continued

```java
    ObjectInputStream ois;
    ObjectOutputStream oos;
    Book theBook;  //Serializable object
    String fileName = "Objects.txt"; // File for making serialized
                                     // object persistent.

  public ObjectProcessor()
      {
      try
            {
             fos = new FileOutputStream(fileName);
             oos = new ObjectOutputStream(fos);
            // You need an OutputStream for the constructor, so
            // wrap a FileOutputStream in an ObjectOutputStream.
             }
      catch(IOException ioe)
              {
                System.out.println("File " + fileName +
                                            "error" + ioe.getMessage());
              }
           theBook = new Book("Lewis", "C.S.", "The Chronicles of Narnia",
                              "PR6023.E926 C5", 5);
              // Create a Book object. This is serializable.
      }

  public boolean writeBookToStream()
       {
       try
            {
             oos.writeObject(theBook);
             // To write the object to a stream
             // just call writeObject with a reference
             // to a serializable object - pretty easy!
             oos.flush();
             oos.close();
             // Flush the stream to force the data to disk.
             // Close the DataOutputStream so the file can be read.
             }
         catch(IOException e)
               {
                 // The object might not be serializable, or there might
                 // be any number of file problems.
                 System.out.println("Error writing object:   " +
                 e.getMessage());
               }
           return true;
       }

    public boolean readBookFromStream()
```

```java
          {
           try
               {
                FileInputStream fis = new FileInputStream(fileName);
                ois = new ObjectInputStream(fis);
                Book someBook = (Book)ois.readObject();
                // Create an ObjectInputStream, wrapping a
                // FileInputStream.
                // Then do a readObject() call.  This returns an object.
                // In order to get it into the proper format for a Book
                // object, you must cast it to the data type Book.
                System.out.println(someBook.toString());
                // Call the overridden version of toString for this
                // class.
                // Most, if not all, user-defined classes really ought
                // to have a toString() method defined.
                ois.close();
               }
            catch(IOException ioe)
                {
                 System.out.println("Error reading object:   " +
                                    ioe.getMessage());
                }
            catch(ClassNotFoundException cnfe)
                // This exception is thrown if the object that reads in
                // the serialized object can't load the class
                // definition via a class loader.
                {
                 System.out.println("Error loading Book class:   " +
                                    cnfe.getMessage());
                }
           // The recipient object's JVM must be able to locate the class
           // of the object you are trying to read.
            return true;
           }
    } // End class definition ObjectProcessor.

public class FileDriver6
    {
       public static void main(String[] args)
          {
            ObjectProcessor op = new ObjectProcessor();
            op.writeBookToStream();
            op.readBookFromStream();
            System.exit(0);
          }
    }

class Book implements Serializable
```

continues

Listing 12.6 continued

```
    {
        // This class is marked as implementing the Serializable
        // interface, which has no methods. This is a flag to show the
        // objects instances of this class can be serialized.
        private String lastName;
        private String firstName;
        private String title;
        private String callNumber;
        private int numberOfCopies;

        public Book( String l, String f, String t,  String c, int n)
            {
                // Perform explicit initialization in the constructor.
                lastName = l;
                firstName = f;
                title = t;
                callNumber = c;
                numberOfCopies = n;
            }

    public String toString()
            {
            // This is a custom toString() method. It lets you
            // print the Book object in a meaningful form.
            String temp = "Author last name: " + lastName +"\n\r" +
                    "Author First name:  " + firstName + "\n\r" +
                    "Title:   " + title + "\n\r" +
                    "CallNumber:  " + callNumber + "\n\r" +
                    "Copies:   " + numberOfCopies;
            return temp;
            }
    }  // End of class definition for Book.
```

This program has three classes, a driver class, `FileDriver6`, a serializable class, `Book`, and a class that writes `Book` objects to a stream and reads them back from the file through an `ObjectInputStream`. Note the use of the overridden `toString()` in the `Book` class. Although this approach has not been used in the book, it is usually a good idea for a class to provide its own `toString()` method because the implementation from `Object` is probably not what you want to print for the String representation of an object. For more on this, see the discussion on *canonical objects* at http://www.artima.com/designtechniques/canonical.html.

You can use `ObjectInputStream` and `ObjectOutputStream` to write any variety of objects, because the stream does not care about what kind of object is passed over it. You can serialize a `Customer` object, an `Account` object, or a `Payment` object. You can then mix them with primitives, if that is appropriate, for example, with an `int` to tell how many instancesof a given class to expect.

CHAPTER 13

Reflection

The Reflection mechanism, new in JDK 1.1, is a means to allow one object to interrogate another object and discover its data members, methods, and supported interfaces at runtime. In GUI programming in Java, you might commonly use a method such as getSource() or getClass() to identify the component that generated an event. The Reflection mechanism, however, is more generalized than this usage and can be used by any object at any time to learn about an unknown object at runtime. For those with CORBA background, this process is similar to dynamic interface invocation—that is, learning about an object from the Interface repository and then creating and using that object. Because Reflection is not very complicated, this chapter is relatively short. The classes for Reflection are in the package java.lang.reflect.

> **NOTE**
>
> Most Java programs don't need to perform Reflection. Reflection is primarily useful for situations in which you want to learn about an object, but all you have to work with is an object reference. Your programs operate more efficiently when you know what you are going to be working with up front (as you usually do). Reflection is most suited to development tools like class browsers, GUI builders, and debuggers.

This chapter covers the following parts of the Reflection API:

- Learning about a class's name and data members
- Learning about a class's methods
- Learning about an Interface
- Working with data and methods unknown to your code until runtime

246 Chapter 13: Reflection

Reflection is fairly straightforward to use; there is not much in the way of theory needed to use the Reflection APIs to discover information about an object.

For every class in your application, the JRE provides an immutable Class object, which provides information about the class. You use the Reflection APIs with the Class object to obtain Constructor, Method, and Field (data member) objects. These objects can be used to retrieve information about the corresponding constructors, methods, and fields. A Class object might also be used to retrieve information about a Java interface, such as its methods and public, final, static data members.

Discovering the Name and Attributes of a Class

The first step to find out anything about a class or interface is to retrieve its Class object. There are three main ways to obtain a Class object:

- Use the getClass() method on an instance of an unknown class—for example, Class class = someInstance.getClass();
- Use the .class suffix on a known class—for example, Class class = java.awt.TextEvent.class;
- Use the Class.forName method with a String that contains the name of the class—for example, Class class = Class.forName(stringNameOfClass);

The best approach to use depends upon whether the class is known at compile time (use the .class suffix), is known only at runtime (use Class.forName()), or is a mystery object reference (getClass()).

Using Reflection to Retrieve Class Information: Code Example

Listing 13.1 shows a program that retrieves basic information about a class, including its name, superclass, modifiers, and data members. In this specific case, I am going to use reflection on the java.awt.Frame class, but any class, including user-defined classes, can be used.

Listing 13.1 Displaying Class Name and Attributes Using Reflection APIs (Reflector1.java).
```
import java.lang.reflect.*;
import java.awt.*;

class ClassBrowser1
      {
      Frame fr;
      public ClassBrowser1()
            {
            // Instantiate a Frame object.
            fr = new Frame("Reflecting Frame");
            }

      public boolean browse()
            {
            // While I didn't do it here, you could just as easily
```

Discovering the Name and Attributes of a Class 247

```
// code this method as "browse(Object someObject)"
// and use Reflection to discover the class of
// "someObject."

// Get the class object using an object instance.
Class theClass = fr.getClass();

// Get the superclass Class object.
Class superClass = theClass.getSuperclass();

// Print the Name of the class and its superclass.
System.out.println("Class name is " + theClass.getName());
System.out.println("Superclass name:  " + superClass.getName());

// Get class modifiers.
// The class java.lang.reflect.Modifier has methods to test for
// several class modifiers and to list them all together.
int mods = theClass.getModifiers();
if(Modifier.isPublic(mods))
      System.out.println("Class is public");
if(Modifier.isProtected(mods))
     System.out.println("Class is protected");
 if(Modifier.isPrivate(mods))
        System.out.println("Class is private");

// Another example.
Class compClass = java.awt.Component.class;
int compMods = compClass.getModifiers();
System.out.println(Modifier.toString(compMods)) ;

// Get the interfaces for a given class.
// Since java.awt.Frame does not implement multiple
// interfaces, here's a class that does.
Class serverClass = java.rmi.server.RemoteObject.class;
Class [] remoteInterfaces = serverClass.getInterfaces();
// Now that you have the class' interfaces, print them.
System.out.println("Class " + serverClass.getName() +
                                    "has these interfaces: ");
for(int i = 0; i < remoteInterfaces.length; i++)
     System.out.println(remoteInterfaces[i].getName());

// Now show the fields of an object.
Field[] classFields = theClass.getFields();
for(int j = 0; j < classFields.length; j++)
     {
      System.out.println("Field Name: " +
                           classFields[j].getName());
      System.out.println("Field data type: " +
                 classFields[j].getType().getName());
```

continues

Listing 13.1 continued

```
                    // use getType() to get a field's data type
                    // and make in human-friendly with getName().
                    int fieldMods = classFields[j].getModifiers();
                    // Get the modifiers for fields, like
                    // final or static.
                    System.out.println("Field modifiers:  " +
                        Modifier.toString(fieldMods));
                }
                // getFields() returns the fields or data members of a class.
                // getType() returns their data type or class.
                // getModifiers() return info about them.
                return true;
            }
    }

public class Reflector1
    {
      public static void main(String[] args)
            {
              ClassBrowser1 cb = new ClassBrowser1();
              cb.browse();
              System.exit(0);
            }
    }
```

Before you run this program, be aware that it produces more than one screen of output, so you might want to redirect the output to a file or pipe it to "more."

In this example, there are a number of different reflection methods used. The most important is getClass(). This returns a Class object. To get the name of the class for which the Class object exists, you need to call the getName() method on the Class object. You can get the superclass by calling getSuperclass().

TIP

By using the combination of getSuperclass() and getName(), you can walk your way up the class hierarchy for any class and list the names of the superclasses.

You can use getModifiers to get an int value that contains flags for the modifiers of the source Class object. You can use this to determine if a class is final, abstract, and so forth. You can use the getFields() method to get the data members or fields of a Class. The getType() method returns the data type of the data member, whereas getModifiers, when used with a field, returns an int value that describes the modifiers for the field. In the case of both a class and a field, you interrogate the results of getModifiers() with static final values in the java.lang.reflect.Modifier class.

Getting Constructor and Method Information with Reflection

Just as you can get information on class attributes and data members, you can use the Reflection APIs to get information on the methods of a class. The getConstructors() method returns a group of Constructor objects for each constructor in the class. The getMethods() method returns an array of Method objects, one for each method in the class.

Reflection of Constructor and Method Information: Code Example

Listing 13.2 shows how to get the methods and constructors for a class. As with fields, you can obtain the modifiers for a constructor or method, and the parameters as well. You could then use this information to create an instance of the class or call a method on an instance of the class.

Listing 13.2 Getting the Constructors and Methods of a Class Using the Reflection APIs (Reflector2.java)

```java
import java.lang.reflect.*;
import java.awt.*;

class ClassBrowser2
    {
      Frame fr;
      public ClassBrowser2()
            {
              fr =  new Frame("Reflecting Frame");
            }

      public boolean browse()
            {
            // Get the class object using an object instance.
            Class theClass = fr.getClass();
            // Get the constructor(s) of the class.
            Constructor[] theConstructors = theClass.getConstructors();

            // Print the Name of the class and its constructor(s).
            System.out.println("Class name is " + theClass.getName());
            String className = theClass.getName();
            for(int i = 0; i < theConstructors.length; i++)
                {
                  System.out.print(className + "(");
                  Class[] theParmTypes =
                      theConstructors[i].getParameterTypes();
                  for(int j = 0; j < theParmTypes.length; j++)
                      {
                        String parm = theParmTypes[j].getName();
                        System.out.print(parm);
```

continues

Listing 13.2   continued

```
                    if(theParmTypes.length > 1
                      && theParmTypes.length > j+1)
                        System.out.print(", ");
        // Print the Constructor signature with good formatting.
                    }
          System.out.println(")");
          System.out.println(" ");
        } // End of for loop for number of Constructor objects.
    // Now print the methods.
    System.out.println("Methods");
    Method[] theMethods = theClass.getMethods();
    for(int i = 0; i < theMethods.length; i++)
            {
              int mods = theMethods[i]. getModifiers();
              System.out.print(Modifier.toString(mods));
    // First print the method's modifiers.
              System.out.print(" " +
                  theMethods[i].getReturnType().getName());
    // Next print the return type.
              System.out.print(" " + theMethods[i].getName() + "( ");
    // Print the method name.
              Class[] theParmTypes = theMethods[i].getParameterTypes();
    // Get an array of the parameters, if any,
    // for a given method.
                if(theParmTypes.length == 0)
                    System.out.println(")");
                else
                    {
                      for(int j = 0; j < theParmTypes.length; j++)
                          {
                            // Walk through the array of
                            // parameters. Get the parm's
                            // data type, and print the type.
                            // Provide for the situation that there
                            // might be multiple parameters
                            // so that the print-out is formatted
                            // nicely.
                            String parm = theParmTypes[j].getName();
                            System.out.print(parm);
                            if(theParmTypes.length > 1
                              && theParmTypes.length > j+1)
                                System.out.print(", ");
                          }
                      System.out.println(")");
                    } // End else block.

            } // End outer for loop.
        return true;
    }
```

```
        }

public class Reflector2
    {
      public static void main(String[] args)
         {
           ClassBrowser2 cb = new ClassBrowser2();
           cb.browse();
           System.exit(0);
         }
    }
```

This program shows the use of the `getConstructors()` method to retrieve a class's constructors and the `getMethods()` method to retrieve the methods of a class. It shows the use of `getParameterTypes()` to see the parameters of the constructors and methods, `getReturnType()` to retrieve the return type of a method, and `getModifiers()` to get the modifiers for a method. This particular example uses `Frame`. If you want a shorter output, you can use another class, such as `Panel`.

Discovering Interface Information

Just as you can retrieve information on a class, you can use the Reflection APIs to interrogate an interface. You can find out what interfaces it extends, what methods it declares, and the data members it defines.

Interface Reflection: Code Example

Because there are so many important interfaces, and because your object, like the `RemoteObject` in Listing 13.1, may implement one or more interfaces, it is important to be able to use reflection on interfaces. Listing 13.3 shows a program to interrogate an interface. This code is similar to the two previous examples.

Listing 13.3 Using Reflection APIs to Interrogate an Interface (Reflector3.java)
```
import java.lang.reflect.*;

class ClassBrowser3
    {
      public boolean browse()
         {
           // Get the class object for an interface.
           Class theClass = java.sql.Connection.class;
           // Get the interface's name.
           System.out.println("Class name is " + theClass.getName());
           String className = theClass.getName();
            // Print the interface's modifiers.
            int mods = theClass.getModifiers();
            System.out.println(Modifier.toString(mods));

             // Get the interface's fields, if any.
             Field[] theFields = theClass.getFields();
```

continues

Listing 13.3 *continued*

```java
            for(int j = 0; j < theFields.length; j++)
                {
                    System.out.println("Field Name: " +
                                    theFields[j].getName());
            // Use getFields() to obtain an array of the fields,
            // if any, in the interface. You can then get the modifiers.
            // Of course, if you know the rules for a Java interface, you
            // know that the fields can only be public static final,
            // regardless of their data type.
                    System.out.println("Field data type: " +
                            theFields[j].getType().getName());
            // Get all the modifiers for each field
                    int fieldMods = theFields[j].getModifiers();
                    System.out.println("Field modifiers:  " +
                        Modifier.toString(fieldMods));
                }
            // getFields() returns the fields or data members of a class.
            // getType() returns their data type or class.
            // getModifiers() return info about them.

            System.out.println("The interface has the following methods");
            // Now print the methods.
            Method[] theMethods = theClass.getMethods();
            // As with a class, getMethods() returns the methods of
            // the interface.
            for(int i = 0; i < theMethods.length; i++)
                {
                    int theMods = theMethods[i].getModifiers();
             // Get the modifiers of each method
                    System.out.print(Modifier.toString(theMods));
             // First print the method's modifiers.
                    System.out.print(" " +
                        theMethods[i].getReturnType().getName());
            // Next print the return type.
                    System.out.print(" " + theMethods[i].getName() + "( ");
            // Print the method name.
                    Class[] theParmTypes = theMethods[i].getParameterTypes();
            // Get the parameter types of each method
                    if(theParmTypes.length == 0)
                        System.out.println(")");
                    else
                        {
                          for(int j = 0; j < theParmTypes.length; j++)
                            {
                                String parm = theParmTypes[j].getName();
                                System.out.print(parm);
                                if(theParmTypes.length > 1
                                   && theParmTypes.length > j+1)
                                    System.out.print(", ");
```

```
                        }
                        System.out.println(")");
                    } // End else block.

                } // End outer for loop.
            return true;
            }
        }
    }
public class Reflector3
    {
        public static void main(String[] args)
            {
              ClassBrowser3 cb = new ClassBrowser3();
              cb.browse();
              System.exit(0);
            }
    }
```

Modifying Data Members and Calling Methods

The three examples so far have shown interrogating classes and interfaces from their class definitions. The methods used so far, such as getFields(), provide static information about what a class looks like. This is useful if you want to get information about what a class or interface contains. If you want to find out about an object and then use it, or find out what fields and methods a class contains so that you can make an instance of that class and modify its values or call its methods, you can use the methods provided by the Reflection APIs. First, you can create an object using a constructor, and then you can set or get attribute values or call methods. You can create an object in Java by calling the following:

- A zero-argument constructor—Use the newInstance() method, catching the NoSuchMethodException (in case there is no zero-argument for the class).
- A constructor that takes arguments—Create a Constructor object and then call the newInstance() method on the Constructor object.

Class Manipulation: Code Example

Once you've got all the information on a class, you can use it to manipulate an instance of the class. Listing 13.4 shows how to construct an object, using our old friend java.awt.Frame, and then modify field values and calling methods.

Listing 13.4 Using the Reflection APIs to Create and Manipulate Objects (Reflector4.java)

```
import java.lang.reflect.*;
import java.awt.Color;

class ClassBrowser4
    {
        Class theClass ;
        Object object;
```

continues

Listing 13.4 continued

```java
    public boolean manipulateObject(String className)
        {
        // Get the class object using Class.forName().
        try
            {
              theClass = Class.forName(className);
              // Print the Name of the class.
              System.out.println("Class name is " + theClass.getName());
              object = theClass.newInstance();
            }
        catch(InstantiationException ine)
            {
              // This means you failed to create an instance.
              // This might be due to security constraints,
              // memory constraints, or other causes.
              System.out.println("Instantiation error for " +
                        className + ":  " +ine.getMessage());
            }
        catch(IllegalAccessException iae)
        // You might not have the permissions to access
        // the class or a member or method of it. This
        // might depend on the reflection permission.
            {
              System.out.println("Illegal Access error for " +
                  className + ":  " +iae.getMessage());
            }
         catch(ClassNotFoundException cnfe)
          // The class loader could not find your class definition.
            {
              System.out.println("Class not found  " +
                  className + ":  " +cnfe.getMessage());
            }

          // Now get and set field values.
          // This requires the use of the get() and set() methods
          // of the java.lang.reflect.Field class.  These are not
          // methods of the target object, in this case, a Frame.
          Field xValue;
          int xInt = 50;
          try
              {
               xValue = theClass.getField("x");
               System.out.println("The value of the field is:  " +
                   xValue.getInt(object));
               xValue.setInt(object, xInt);
               System.out.println("The value of the field is:  " +
                   xValue.getInt(object));
               // Get the specific field you are interested in.
               // Print its value.
```

Modifying Data Members and Calling Methods 255

```java
            // Set it to a new value.
            }
    catch(NoSuchFieldException nsfe)
    // The field doesn't exist. Remember, this
    // is runtime discovery, so the compiler
    // doesn't know if the field is spelled right,
    // and so forth.
            {
              System.out.println
                  ("No such field:  x " +
                  nsfe.getMessage());
            }
    catch(IllegalAccessException Ille)
            {
              System.out.println("Illegal access:  x " +
                  Ille.getMessage());
            }

// Change to another class.
java.awt.Frame fr = new java.awt.Frame();
theClass = fr.getClass();
// Get a class object for the Frame object.
Class[] parmTypes = new Class[] {String.class};
// Set up a list of parms. setTitle() takes one String.
Object[] args = new Object[] {"New Frame"};
try
      {
       Method setTitleMethod =
           theClass.getMethod("setTitle", parmTypes);
       // Create a callable method statement.
       setTitleMethod.invoke(fr, args);
       // Call the setTitle() method on the
       // Frame object.
      }
catch(Exception excp)
          {
           System.out.println("Failed in method call:  " +
               excp.getMessage());
          }
fr.setSize(200,100);
fr.setBackground(Color.blue);
fr.setVisible(true);
// Directly call some methods on the same
// Frame object, setting its size, background
// and visibility.
try
      {
       Thread.currentThread().sleep(4000);
      }
```

continues

Listing 13.4 continued

```
            catch(InterruptedException inte)
            // Keep the Frame visible briefly so you can see the new title.
                {}
            return true;
            }
    }

public class Reflector4
    {
      public static void main(String[] args)
          {
            ClassBrowser4 cb = new ClassBrowser4();
            cb.manipulateObject("java.awt.Point");
            System.exit(0);
          }
    }
```

This program shows how to do two things: get/set field values and call methods. Although the program has some knowledge of what variables and methods are available, you could, without much work, modify it to be completely blind to the available methods and data members. That would make it suitable for a GUI builder or debugger that does not know at compile time what kind of objects it will encounter in your code. The program starts off getting and setting a data member, x, in an object of type java.awt.Point. Then the program changes to work with java.awt.Frame. The reason for the change is that, although a Point object contains easy-to-access data members, Frame does not. On the other hand, it's easier to show the result of a method call on a Frame than on a Point, and the logic used here might be needed in a GUI builder tool when the user wants to change the title on the Frame.

The major differences in this program from earlier examples in the chapter is the use of get and set methods on an object. The java.lang.reflect.Field class provides several get and set methods. They cover getting and setting primitive values, such as getBoolean() and get(), for getting and setting values that require objects, such as a Button or a Date.

NOTE

One data type not covered here is an Object that is an array. The procedures for dealing with arrays are not much different from those shown previously in this chapter, with the addition of a getComponent() method for getting the value of a given array element.

CHAPTER 14

Java Network Programming

As noted in Chapter 1, "What Is Java?," in the list of basic Java features, Java is network-savvy or network-ready. It's easy to do low-level network programming in Java. It is much easier to program using sockets in Java than it is in C or C++. There are two important aspects to Java's network support. First, Java covers up much of the complexity and platform-specific code required, for example, to use sockets. The second property of Java networking is that Java comes with classes to support the Internet and the World Wide Web (WWW). Java's networking support focuses primarily on TCP/IP and HTTP.

> **NOTE**
>
> Networking requires connecting between systems, even between two threads of a program on the same physical system. The systems in a networked environment need host names and IP addresses. Therefore, you will need to run the programs in this chapter (and do your own Java network programming) on a system with an IP address. Frequently, laptop computers, and other computers with no permanent IP connection, do not have permanent IP addresses, so these examples might not work on a laptop system.

Java, by default, uses TCP/IP for its networking protocol. Although networking across heterogeneous network protocols is beyond the scope of this book, be aware that you might need to find ways to communicate from a Java program using TCP/IP to another network protocol, such as LU 6.2, a common IBM mainframe protocol. Actually, Java supports two kinds of socket communication: TCP (Transport Control Protocol) sockets and UDP (User Datagram Protocol) sockets. This chapter covers the following:

- Core networking concepts
- Getting information on IP addresses and host names

- Creating a simple TCP/IP client and server application
- Creating a simple UDP client and server application
- Working with URLs to access data on the Web

Core Networking Concepts

Java uses the protocol of the Internet, TCP/IP. In order to communicate using TCP and UDP, you must be able to identify the system you want to communicate with from your program. This system—indeed, any system in a network—is called a *host*, which can be either a *client* or *server* in a given application.

NOTE

Client and server are relative terms. A "client" for our purposes is a program or its related host calling another program (the server), which may or may not be on a different host (the server host) than the "client."

A host generally has a name. For example, I once had a system called *Dagobah*. Every host, however, must have an address. This address is an IP (Internet Protocol) address, consisting of four period-delimited numbers, such as 234.255.255.255. (This is a randomly chosen number and is not intended to correspond to any real system.) IP addresses are used to uniquely identify a given host on a network, including the Internet network.

NOTE

In practice, large companies have only one number for outsiders to connect to and that will internally route messages to a specific internal IP address. This is desirable because the number of available IP addresses would otherwise quickly be exhausted.

A common mechanism for mapping between the host name and the host's IP address is domain name service (DNS). The next section will show this mapping in Java. You might think of an IP address as analogous to your company's phone number. If someone calls me at Sun through the main switchboard number, he won't reach me. He needs my phone extension, one way or another. My extension is analogous to a port number.

Programs run on hosts at a given port number. A port is not a physical entity, like a place into which you plug cables. A port is a logical software construct. In fact, unlike my phone extension, which is assigned by the phone company (I assume), a port number is a random number chosen out of the air. As a rule, the lower numbers (up to about 1024) are reserved for well-known services. For example, SMTP, the email server, usually runs on port 25. HTTP, the protocol used by Web servers, generally runs on port 80. To be sure you are not in conflict with a system service, it is generally a good idea to pick a number greater than 2000. Other than that, the only real requirement is that all the parties in a network application agree on the same port number. For example, if the server program is running on *Sisera* at port 3456, all the clients trying to access the program using that port number must connect to the server program using the host name *Sisera* (or its equivalent IP address) and the port number 3456.

Using another port will not work. It would be like trying to reach me at a nonexistent phone extension.

To work with a port, you create a socket. A socket, like a port, is a logical software construct. Again, you can make TCP or UDP sockets. This chapter has examples of doing both. Before you see them, here is a basic guideline to use in deciding, if you have a choice, which type of socket and which type of communication to use.

- If your application requires reliable host-to-host communication with failure notification if an error occurs, use TCP sockets.
- If your application can work with less than complete reliability, without error notification, use UDP sockets.

CAUTION

Because many firewalls refuse to allow UDP packets through, UDP sockets are an inappropriate choice for an Internet-based application.

For example, in an e-commerce application, you want to be sure that messages go each way reliably and that you get notified of any network error. Therefore, you use TCP sockets for e-commerce, if you use sockets directly. If you are writing an application that sends the latest sport scores to client systems, it is probably not too serious an error if one message from the server does not arrive. If the next message is sent five minutes later, that is probably good enough. In this case, there's probably no reason to bear the much higher overhead of using TCP sockets. UDP sockets can be used. This is not to say that UDP sockets are unreliable, but they do not guarantee delivery of data in the same way a TCP socket does. They are not as reliable as TCP sockets only in terms of error notification.

NOTE

Many applications use sockets without even knowing it. For example, JDBC drivers (discussed in Chapter 17, "JDBC: Java Database Programming") often use sockets. ORBs often use sockets to ORB initialization. RMI (discussed in Chapter 15, "RMI") uses sockets to connect to the RMIregistry (typically port number 1099) and to connect to remote objects (the socket number varies). Object buses typically use them as well. So you often use sockets, even when you did not explicitly create them. In fact, any network communication in Java uses sockets in some way, whether it is visible to you or not.

The main classes that support networking are in the package `java.net`, although you often need classes for socket I/O from `java.io`.

Working with Host Names and IP Addresses

The class `java.net.InetAddress` provides support for getting host names with IP addresses or getting IP addresses using host names. Listing 14.1 shows a program that uses several of these methods.

Host Information Using INetAddress: Code Example

The INetAddress class exists to allow a program to find out IP addresses based on host names and host names based on IP addresses. The INetAddress class also provides a mechanism to identify the current host on which the program is running, which can be quite helpful in many situations that call for an IP address or INetAddress object.

Listing 14.1   Getting Host IP Information Using the INetAddress Class (NetDriver1.java)

```java
import java.io.*;
import java.net.*;

class Addressor
     {
       InetAddress theHost;

       public boolean displayInetData()
             {
              try
                  {
                     theHost = InetAddress.getLocalHost();
                     System.out.println("Local host: " + theHost);
                  }
              catch(UnknownHostException uhe)
                     { }
              // This returns information on your system.  If Java cannot
              // find the local host, your host lacks an IP address currently.
              // When you try to access information on a host you may
              // get an UnknownHostException if it is not found.
              // To make this code work more places, it will only deal with
              // the Local host, i.e., your system running the code.
              String hostName = theHost.getHostName();
              String hostAddress = theHost.getHostAddress();
              // Obtain a host name and address.  Since you can make
              // an InetAddress object from any host you can connect to,
              // You could get one of these values for any host to
              // which you can connect, as long as you have either
              // the name or the IP address.
              System.out.println("Host Name: " + hostName);
              System.out.println("Host Address:  " + hostAddress);
              try
                  {
                     System.out.println("Host address by host name:  " +
                                    InetAddress.getByName(hostName));
              // The getByName() method returns an InetAddress object
              // which you could use to get the IP address with
              // or getAddress() or getHostAddress().
                     System.out.println("Host address as String:  " +
                                    hostAddress.toString());
                  }
```

```
            catch(UnknownHostException unhe)
                {
                    System.out.println("The local host is invalid.");
                }
            return true;
        }
    }
public class NetDriver1
    {
      public static void main(String[] args)
            {
              Addressor addr = new Addressor();
              addr.displayInetData();
            }
    }
```

This program shows you how to easily manipulate IP addresses. If you want to use the logical name of a given system, but only have the IP address, you can use getByName(), and then getHostName() to retrieve the logical name.

Creating a TCP Client and Server Application

Creating TCP sockets is easy in Java. The client program creates a java.net.Socket. The server program does that as well, but more important, the server creates a java.net.ServerSocket.

TIP

You can use a ServerSocket in your program to your advantage, even if you are not doing networking. Because a ServerSocket is connected to a given port number, and only one program can use that port number, you can prevent a user from running multiple copies of your program by instantiating a ServerSocket on a specific port. If the user then tries to run another copy of your program, the program will throw an exception. This occurs because it is illegal to have two ServerSockets set to the same port on a given host. This is provided that your host has an RXP/IP stack.

First, run the server program. The server program does the following:

1. Creates a ServerSocket
2. Calls the accept() method on that ServerSocket
3. Gets a connection from a client
4. Grabs a reference to the Socket object returned from the accept() call
5. Opens an InputStream and/or OutputStream on that socket
6. Communicates with the client

The accept() call blocks until some program connects to the port number that is related to the ServerSocket.

> **TIP**
>
> Because the `accept()` method blocks, you might wish to put code into your server program that accepts some kind of input from an administrative client program. That program can tell the server program to shut down gracefully, instead of just terminating. For example, if a client sends the String `"Bye"`, the server program exits.

When a client runs, it does the following:

1. Creates a socket, using the server name/IP address and port number. This automatically causes the client to connect to the server, provided the server is listening for a connection with the `accept()` method.
2. The client opens an `InputStream` and/or `OutputStream` on the `Socket` object.
3. The client communicates with the server.

Socket connections automatically generate an `InputStream` and `OutputStream`. You simply obtain a reference to this stream, which already exists.

TCP Socket with Socket and ServerSocket: Code Example

The nature of the communication between the client and the server is totally defined by the programmer. You have to decide what kind of data should go from the client to the server and back again. Many Java applications, such as e-commerce programs that use sockets, send `Vectors` back and forth. Because a `Vector` can accept virtually any type of data (except for primitives, unless they are wrapped in a wrapper class), you might create a `Vector` that has the customer name in element zero, the customer address in element one, the phone number in element two, and the variable number of items that the customer wishes to purchase in the next several elements. Java makes no requirements about the content of the communication, as long as you use data types that are valid for the type of stream you wrap around the `InputStream` or `OutputStream`.

Listings 14.2 through 14.4 show a sample TCP server and client combination. The client and server are going to send each other objects using an `ObjectInputStream` and an `ObjectOutputStream`. In the programs, note the order of getting the `InputStream` and `OutputStream` from the socket.

> **CAUTION**
>
> The order between client and server is *critically important*. If you ignore this and, for example, have both the client and server perform a `getInputStream()` first, your program will simply hang forever on both sides. Both the server and any clients should call `getOutputStream()` before calling `getInputStream()`.

The server program is set up to handle any number of clients because each client gets a new server-side thread assigned to it. Listing 14.2 shows the Server, Listing 14.3 shows the client, and Listing 14.4 shows the `BookQuery` class.

Listing 14.2 TCP Server Program Using Sockets and ServerSockets (NetDriver2a.java)

```java
import java.io.*;
import java.net.*;

class TCPServer
      {
        InetAddress theServer;
        int port = 5555;
        ServerSocket srvSock;

        public TCPServer()
              {
                try
                      {
                        srvSock = new ServerSocket(port);
              // Create a ServerSocket.
                      }
                catch(IOException ioe)
                      {
                        System.out.println
                            ("Error creating ServerSocket:  " +
                            ioe.getMessage());
                      }
              }

        public boolean processConnections()
              {
                boolean exit = false;
                while(exit == false)
                  try
                      {
                        Socket sock = srvSock.accept();
              // Call accept() in a loop in order to
              // easily handle client connections on separate Threads.
                        new SocketHandler(sock);
                      }

                catch(IOException ioe)
                      {
                        System.out.println
                            ("Error creating Socket:  " + ioe.getMessage());
                      }

                return true;
              }
      }
class SocketHandler implements Runnable
      {
```

continues

Listing 14.2 *continued*

```java
    Socket theSocket;

    public SocketHandler(Socket s)
          {
            theSocket = s;
            Thread thr = new Thread(this);
            thr.start();
            // Run this client session through a separate Thread.
          }

    public void run()
          {
            try
                {
                  ObjectOutputStream oos = new ObjectOutputStream(
                         theSocket.getOutputStream() );
                  ObjectInputStream ois = new ObjectInputStream(
                         theSocket.getInputStream() );
                  System.out.println("Opened object streams");
                // Get the built-in InputStream and OutputStream
                // from the Socket.
                      BookQuery bq = (BookQuery)ois.readObject();
                // Read a BookQuery from the client's socket stream.
                      System.out.println("Book query:   " + bq.toString());
                // Display the BookQuery object.
                      String result = "Seven books found";
                      oos.writeObject(result);
                      ois.close();
                      oos.close();
                      theSocket.close();
                      // Close the Socket.
                      // This does not affect the ServerSocket.
                }
            catch(IOException ioex)
                {
                  System.out.println
                      ("Error reading from client socket: " +
                        ioex.getMessage());
                }
            catch(ClassNotFoundException cnfe)
                {
                  System.out.println
                      ("Error findingobject stream class: " +
                         cnfe.getMessage());
                }
            }
    }

public class NetDriver2a
```

```
        {
    public static void main(String[] args)
          {
           TCPServer svr = new TCPServer();
           svr.processConnections();
          }
   }
```

Listing 14.3   TCP Client Program Using Sockets (NetDriver2b.java)
```
import java.net.*;

class TCPClient
     {
       InetAddress theHost;
       Socket aSocket;

       public TCPClient()
             {
              // Get the host name to use in connecting to the Server.
               try
                  {
                    theHost = InetAddress.getLocalHost();
                    // Get the INetAddress of the host.
                    String hostName = theHost.getHostName();
                    // Get the name of the host.
                    aSocket = new Socket(hostName, 5555);
                    // Open a Socket using the host name and
                    // the pre-decided port number.
                  }
             catch(UnknownHostException uhe)
                 {
                   System.out.println("Could not connect to server");
                 }
             catch(IOException ioe)
                    {
                      System.out.println("Error creating Socket " +
                             ioe.getMessage());
                    }
             }


       public boolean sendBookQuery()
             {
              try
                    {
                      ObjectOutputStream oos = new ObjectOutputStream(
                             aSocket.getOutputStream());
                      // Obtain a reference to the Socket's
                      // OutputStream.
```

continues

Listing 14.3 continued

```
                // Then wrap the stream in an
                // ObjectOutputStream so you can
                // write objects across the network.
                ObjectInputStream ois = new ObjectInputStream(
                        aSocket.getInputStream());
                // Obtain a reference to the InputStream
                // of the Socket and then
                // wrap the InputStream in an
                // ObjectInputStream so you can read
                // objects and not just primitives
                // from the Socket.
                BookQuery query = new BookQuery(
                        BookQuery.AUTHOR_SEARCH,
                        "Lewis, C.S.");
                oos.writeObject(query);
                // Write this BookQueryObject to the network.
                String response = (String)ois.readObject();
                System.out.println("Search results:  " + response);
                oos.close();
                ois.close();
                aSocket.close();
                // First close the ObjectOutputStream and
                // ObjectInputStream, and then close the Socket.
                // This is cleaner than the client merely terminating.
            }
            catch(IOException ioe)
                {
                    System.out.println("Error getting Socket streams.");
                }
            catch(ClassNotFoundException cnfe)
                // readObject can fail if the class definition
                // for what you want to read in cannot be found.
                {
                  System.out.println("Error accessing a class "
                      + cnfe.getMessage());
                }
            return true;
        }
    }

public class NetDriver2b
        {
          public static void main(String[] args)
            {
              TCPClient client = new TCPClient();
              // Make an instance of the client
              // and call its bookQuery method to simulate
              // searching a library catalog.
              client. sendBookQuery();
```

            }
    }

Listing 14.4   BookQuery Class Used by the Client and Server (BookQuery.java)
// This class is used to submit a book query to the library server.

```
import java.io.*;

public class BookQuery implements Serializable
    {
      public static final int AUTHOR_SEARCH = 10;
      public static final int TITLE_SEARCH = 20;
      public static final int KEYWORD_SEARCH = 30;
      // It is common to use public static int fields to test
      // against, especially in switch statements,
      // which use integral types. This allows the
      // compiler to check what you are comparing to,
      // and guarantees consistency for
      // setting or comparing values.
      int searchType = 10;
      String author;
      String title;
      String keyword;

      public BookQuery(int sType, String sValue)
          // This is the constructor for the BookQuery class.
          {
            switch(sType)
            // This is applicatoin code to implement the catalog search.
                {
                  case AUTHOR_SEARCH :
                        {
                          searchType = sType;
                          author = sValue;
                          break;
                        }
                  case TITLE_SEARCH :
                        {
                          searchType = sType;
                          title = sValue;
                          break;
                        }
                  case KEYWORD_SEARCH :
                        {
                          searchType = sType;
                          keyword = sValue;
                          break;
                        }
                } // End switch statement.
```

continues

Listing 14.4 continued

```java
    }

    public String >toString()
        {
          String temp = "Search type: ";
          String type = null;
          switch( searchType)
               {
                  case AUTHOR_SEARCH :
                  // Simulate an author search of a card catalog.
                        {
                          type = "Author search";
                          break;
                        }
                  case TITLE_SEARCH :
                  // Simulate a title search of a library catalog.
                        {
                          type = "Title search";
                          break;
                        }
                  case KEYWORD_SEARCH :
                  // Simulate searching a library catalog by keyword.
                        {
                           type = "Keyword search";
                           break;
                        }
               } // End switch statement.
                 // Concatenate a hypothetical result
                 // of a card catalog search in a String.
          temp += " " + type + "  Author:   " + author +
                 "  Title: " + title +
                 "  Keyword: " +keyword;
          return temp;
          // Return the String, whatever its contents.
        }
}
```

To run this application, start the server first. The server creates a `ServerSocket` on port 5555 on the current server host, which, of course, can (and probably will) be different from the client system. The server then enters a loop in which it does an `accept()` call. Whenever a client connects to the server program (by creating a socket for the servers host at port 5555), the server program creates a separate object which runs on its own thread to handle the client request. There is no code in the server to shut down in response to a specific client request or server-side administrative GUI event, but (as noted earlier) you should put one in your server code.

Whenever a client starts up, it creates a socket on the appropriate host and a port (the system the client wants to reach, which is probably not the client's host). The client then gets an `OutputStream` and an `InputStream` on the socket. In both the server and client, you can wrap the streams from the socket in any kind of stream and, optionally, the Reader or Writer class you wish to use. So the InputStream can be wrapped in an InputStreamReader and then a BufferedReader to read input one line at a time. You can send anything you wish over a socket connection, from raw bytes to complex objects.

> **CAUTION**
>
> If possible, avoid sending very large objects and quite complex objects. As noted in the discussion of serialization in Chapter 12, "I/O in Java," passing large or complex objects can cause performance problems.

Using Datagram Packets and UDP Sockets

The other approach to coding with sockets is to use UDP sockets. Unlike TCP sockets, UDP sockets do not create a connection between client and server, but rather they take a "fire and forget" approach. That is, your client or server sends a Datagram packet to the other system and then goes on with other work. Sometime later, the other system should receive the packet, but, in general, there is no way for the sender to be sure that the packet arrived successfully. UDP sockets allow you to write programs that use asynchronous communication, programs in which objectA sends data out on the network and then goes on with its work, while objectB waits on its socket to receive input. This is an appropriate structure for several kinds of applications, such as stock tickers, clock systems, and news reporting, to name a few. Listings 14.5 and 14.6 show a simple Datagram server and client that pass strings back and forth.

UDP Using DataGramPacket and DatagramSocket: Code Example

When an application needs to operate in an asynchronous mode, or in a manner in which the server and client are only loosely coupled at best, UDP communication is the natural choice, as long as high reliability is not a requirement of the application. In Listings 14.5 and 14.6, there is a sample server and sample client for UDP communication in Java. Here's the server:

Listing 14.5   Using Datagram Sockets and Packets (NetDriver3a.java)

```
// Simple Datagram/UDP Server.
import java.io.*;
import java.net.*;

class UDPServer
   {
      DatagramSocket socket = null;
      DatagramPacket sendPacket;
        DatagramPacket recvPacket;
        byte[] outBuffer;
        byte[] inBuffer;
        InetAddress clientAddress;
        int clientPort;
```

continues

Listing 14.5 continued

```java
    public UDPServer()
    {
      try
      {
       socket = new DatagramSocket(5555);
       // Create a new Datagram socket on the server.
       inBuffer = new byte[20];
          // Create a buffer to get client input.
       outBuffer = new byte[500];
       System.out.println(
                "Library server started on port 5555");
      }
      catch(SocketException se)
      {
       System.out.println("Error creating server datagram socket: " +
           se.getMessage());
      }
        }

    public boolean getClientRequests()
      {
       boolean loop = true;
       while(loop == true)
       {
        try
            {
             recvPacket = new DatagramPacket(inBuffer, inBuffer.length);
       // Create a DatagramPacket to receive client requests.
               socket.receive(recvPacket);
       // Wait for a client request.  This code
       // blocks until it gets input.
               clientAddress = recvPacket.getAddress();
               clientPort = recvPacket.getPort();
               // Extract from the DatagramPackt where it came from.
               String text = new String(recvPacket.getData(),
                                0,
                             recvPacket.getLength());
       // Extract the contents of the DatagramPacket.
               if(text.equals("bye"))
               {
                loop = false;
                break;
               }
       // Provide a way for clients to stop
       // the server gracefully.
                String msg = "The book named _Till We Have Faces_" +
                              "is overdue by five days";
                outBuffer = msg.getBytes();
       // Put the bytes in a byte array.
```

Using Datagram Packets and UDP Sockets 271

```
                    sendPacket = new DatagramPacket(outBuffer,
                                               outBuffer.length,
                                               clientAddress,
                                               clientPort);
        // Create a DatagramPacket to send
        // back to the client, using the address and port
        // of the client, which was extracted
        // from the DatagramPacket the client sent.
                    socket.send(sendPacket);
        // Send the DatagramPacket to the
        // client and start again.
                }
            catch(IOException ioe)
                {
                  System.out.println("Error with Packets: " +
                            ioe.getMessage());
                }
             }
            // Since any kind of socket does I/O, it can
            // get an I/O exception.
            socket.close();
            return true;
            }
    } // End class definition for UDPServer.

public class NetDriver3a
    {
     public static void main(String[] args)
        {
         UDPServer server = new UDPServer();
         boolean result = server.getClientRequests();
         // Create a UDPServer object and have it wait on
         // client requests.
         if(result == true)
            System.out.println("Library server failed");
         System.exit(0);
         }
     }
```

Here's the client:

Listing 14.6   Using Datagram Sockets and Packets in a UDP Client (NetDriver3b.java)
```
// Simple Datagram/UDP Client.
import java.io.*;
importf java.net.*;

class UDPClient
    {
```

continues

Listing 14.6   continued

```java
    DatagramSocket socket = null;
    DatagramPacket sendPacket;
    DatagramPacket recvPacket;
    byte[] outBuffer;
    byte[] inBuffer;
    InetAddress serverAddress;
    int serverPort = 5555;

    public UDPClient()
    {
     try
        {
         socket = new DatagramSocket();
           // Create a new Datagram socket.
           // The client does not need to use a specific
           // port number since this socket is on
           // the client machine.
         inBuffer = new byte[500];
           // Create a buffer to get server input.
         outBuffer = new byte[20];
        }
     catch(SocketException se)
        {
            System.out.println("Error creating server datagram socket: " +
                se.getMessage());
        }
    }

    public boolean getBookStatus()
    {
     try
        {
            String msg = "23456";
         outBuffer = msg.getBytes();
    // Put the bytes in a byte array.
            serverAddress = InetAddress.getLocalHost();
            sendPacket = new DatagramPacket(outBuffer,
                                            outBuffer.length,
                                            serverAddress,
                            serverPort);
    // Create a DatagramPacket to send
    // to the server, using the LocalHost address
    // and the port number of the server.
            socket.send(sendPacket);
    // Send the library card number to the server.

            recvPacket = new DatagramPacket(inBuffer,
                                            inBuffer.length);
    // Create a DatagramPacket to receive
```

```
        // the server's response.
            socket.receive(recvPacket);
        // Wait for a response from the server.
        // The client blocks until it gets input from the server.
          String text = new String(recvPacket.getData(),
                                    0,
                    recvPacket.getLength());
        // Extract the contents of the DatagramPacket.
            System.out.println("Response from Server:   " + text);
            socket.close();
            }
        catch(IOException ioe)
            {
            System.out.println("Eror with Packets: " +
                ioe.getMessage());
            }

    return true;
    }
    } // End class definition for UDPServer.

public class NetDriver3b
    {
      public static void main(String[] args)
          {
      UDPClient client = new UDPClient();
      boolean result = client.getBookStatus();
      if(result == false)
          System. out.println("Library server failed");
      System.exit(0);
      }
      }
```

Working with URLs in Java

So far, this chapter has covered fairly low-level programming for programs that use networking. Although you can send any kind of data across a socket, sockets are not the best way to access a URL (Uniform Resource Locator) on the World Wide Web. This section shows how to use URLs in your Java program. You can read from a URL or check a URL for validity even if you are not running a program on the Web. A URL provides a unique domain name or address to access a remote system, using a Web browser or other program that can access the Web. The classes to support accessing URLs are in java.net, as are the other networking classes shown so far. The class java.net.URL provides a class that represents a URL on the Web. This is a much easier way to handle network communication than the lower-level TCP and UDP socket classes. In this book, a URL represents an Internet address, whereas an instance of the URL class will be called a URL object. A URL consists of two parts:

- A protocol, such as HTTP, ftp, or RMI
- A unique address for some resource or resources

For example, the URL http://www.javasoft.com specifies the HTTP protocol and www.javasoft.com specifies resource address. The latter resource address should be unique among URL addresses. A URL object in Java always represents an absolute URL address, even if it is made using a relative URL address. A URL object provides methods to extract the host name, the directory, and so forth. If you want to use the URL for more than just reading data, you can call the URL class's openConnection() method. It is simple to make a URL object:

```
URL suned = new URL("http://suned.sun.com");
```

This creates the URL object suned. This is an absolute URL. That is, it contains enough information to get to the resource without any other information. It is also possible to create a URL object with a relative URL. For example:

```
URL suned = new URL ("http://suned.sun.com");
URL sunedUSA = new URL(suned, "/usa/centers.html");
```

The sunedUSA URL object is formed by adding a relative URL "/USA/centers.html" to an absolute URL "http://suned.sun.com". In the constructor, suned specifies a URL object that represents the base, absolute URL. The second field represents the additional directory and filename information being added to the absolute path. You can also specify a port number or a reference value. If you do not have the complete URL as a string, but have parts of it (such as the protocol, host name, and port number), there are two other constructors that take either parts of a URL or the individual pieces (that is, protocol, host name, port, directory, and filename).

NOTE

These are "write once, read many times" objects. After you have created them, you can get values of specific parts of a URL object, but you cannot modify them.

All the constructors for a URL object can throw a MalformedURLException. This means that the protocol for the URL is null or unknown; for example, htpt would cause a MalformedURLException.

As you will see in the sample code below, there are several methods for accessing the components of a URL object, such as getHost() and getPort().

You can read from or write to a URL. You can read either by just getting an InputStream from the URL object or by creating a URLConnection object, which will let you write to the URL as well. In the sample program here, the code uses a cgi-bin script, set up by Sun, to let you test your ability to write to a URL. You can read back the contents of the URL to get your input, which is reversed by the cgi-bin script, called backwards. This illustrates the capability of your code to do a POST operation, for example, to a CGI script, or, much better, to a servlet, directly using the HTTP protocol. A URLConnection object provides four main ways to access a URL:

- getContent
- getHeaderField
- getInputStream
- getOutputStream

There are several commonly used methods for obtaining header information:

- getContentEncoding
- getContentLength
- getContentType
- getDate
- getExpiration
- getLastModifed

Listing 14.7 shows a sample program that demonstrates how to create a URL object, interrogate it, read directly from a URL with the URL object, and read from and write to a URL with a URLConnection object.

Listing 14.7   Accessing URLs with the URL, URLConnection, and URLConnection Classes (NetDriver4.java)

```
// Simple URL handling program.
import java.net.*;
import java.io.*;

class URLHandler
    {
      URL url;

      public URLHandler()
            {
              try
                    {
                      url = new URL("http://suned.sun.com/usa/centers.html");
                    }
                catch(MalformedURLException mal)
                  // This exception occurs for invalid
                  // or syntactically wrong URLs.
                    {
                      System.out.println("Bad Protocol:   " + mal);
                    }
            }

      public boolean displayURLInfo()
            {
              try
                    {
                      System.out.println("Protocol:    " + url.getProtocol());
                      System.out.println("Host name:   " + url.getHost());
                      System.out.println("Port Number: " + url.getPort());
                      System.out.println("File name:   " + url.getFile());
                      System.out.println("Reference:   " + url.getRef());
                // Print the contents of the URL.
                      BufferedReader br = new BufferedReader(
                                              new InputStreamReader(
```

continues

Listing 14.7 continued

```
                                           url.openStream())));
        // Open an InputStream on the URL location.
            String urlContent = null;
            while ((urlContent = br.readLine()) != null)
                System.out.println(urlContent);
            br.close();

        // Here's an alternative, HTTP-specific way to
        // work with a URL:  URLConnection.
            URLConnection urlConn = url.openConnection();
        // You could also use an HttpURLConnection.
            BufferedReader bufferedReader = new BufferedReader(
                                        new InputStreamReader(
                                        urlConn.getInputStream()));
            while ((urlContent = bufferedReader.readLine()) != null)
                System.out.println(urlContent);
            bufferedReader.close();

        // Now, create a URLConnection and write to the URL
        // You would use this technique to do a POST, for
        // example, to send data to a CGI script or, much
        // better, a Servlet.
        // This code uses a pre-made CGI script at the
        // Javasoft website so that every reader can execute
        //  the code.
            String backwardsString = URLEncoder.encode
                                ("Library card number:  12345");

            URL cgiURL = new URL
                        ("http://java.sun.com/cgi-bin/backwards");
            URLConnection conn = cgiURL.openConnection();
        // Create a URL object for the cgi script URL.
        // Then connect to the URL with a URLConnection.
            conn.setDoOutput(true);
            PrintWriter pw = new PrintWriter(conn.getOutputStream());
            pw.println("string=" + backwardsString);
            pw.close();
        // This wrote a String to the URL.
            BufferedReader buff = new BufferedReader(
                                    new InputStreamReader(
                                    conn.getInputStream()));

            while ((urlContent = buff.readLine()) != null)
            System.out.println(urlContent);
            buff.close();
            }
        catch(IOException ioe)
            {
```

```
                    System.out.println("Error reading URL:  " +
                                                 ioe.getMessage());
                }

            return true;
            }
    }

public class NetDriver4
    {
      public static void main (String[] args)
            {
            URLHandler handler = new URLHandler();
            boolean result = handler.displayURLInfo();
            System.exit(0);
            }
    }
```

This program uses both absolute and relative URLs to create URL objects. It also uses URLConnection objects to read from and write to a URL. There are several classes in java.net for doing further manipulation of URL content, headers, and so forth. If, for example, you need to work with a special content type, you might subclass ContentHandler. To do more advanced work with URLs, check the java.net API documentation.

CHAPTER 15

RMI

Remote Method Invocation, RMI, is Java's built-in facility for developing distributed object applications. Chapter 14, "Java Network Programming," showed techniques for low-level, socket-based communication. Sockets are built around sending bytes. RMI provides a way to call methods on objects on other systems. It operates at a higher level of abstraction than socket-based programming, even though RMI does use sockets under the covers. This chapter focuses on basic RMI programming techniques. Four topics are covered in this chapter:

- A brief overview of RMI architecture
- How to call a remote object's methods
- How to call a remote method using a client-side remote object
- How to perform remote activation

RMI Architecture Overview

RMI's architecture is similar to CORBA's. Before getting into this, let me stress that the use of the words *client* and *server* are relative. Any object on any tier of an application can be a client or a server. Even an object on tier 1 can act as a server. To deal with this terminology problem, I am going to call a program that normally resides on a server system on tier 2-n a *remote factory*.

> **NOTE**
>
> The examples in this chapter do not actually implement the factory pattern as generally understood. I acknowledge this, but I think it is worse to call a class that merely instantiates another a *server*. Servers do more than just make a single object. At the same time, it is fairly trivial to turn a remote factory, as defined in this chapter, into a real object factory. This is done by making the `server` class create a remote object with a `getInstance()` method for a second remote object.

In RMI, a basic method call to a remote object follows this path:

1. The client calls a method of a remote object.
2. This call is intercepted by a *stub*, which is a client-side proxy for the remote object, which is generally on another physical host. Think of it as a remote reference to the remote object.
3. The stub passes the remote method call to the client-side Remote Reference Layer, RRL, which starts the process of preparing the parameters for passing to the remote object. The RRL calls the Transport Layer, which works with the RRL to *marshal* (convert arguments, method calls, references, and return values into a special stream needed by the wire protocol to send to another object) the method call with its parameters into a marshalling stream.
4. The Transport Layer sends the serialized parameters in the marshalling stream over the network using Java Remote Method Protocol, JRMP.
5. The Transport Layer on the server side receives the marshalling stream and begins the process of unmarshalling the marshalling stream. The Transport Layer calls upon the server-side Remote Reference Layer to unmarshall and deserialize the remote method parameters as necessary.
6. The server-side RRL passes the method call and its parameters to the *skeleton*, which is a server-side proxy for the remote object.
7. The skeleton forwards the method call with its parameters to the remote object.
8. The remote object executes its method and, optionally, sends back a result (as the return type from the method) to the client, back through the skeleton, to the RRL. The result goes on to the Transport Layer, across the network using JRMP, to the client-side Transport Layer, to the RRL, to the stub, and finally back to the client object that called the remote method back in step 1. RMI depends heavily upon object serialization, covered in Chapter 12, "I/O in Java." If you are unfamiliar with object serialization, you should read that section before proceeding with this chapter.

Parameters for Remote Methods

As just stated, RMI serializes parameters in remote method calls. Actually, RMI passes two different types of entities in method calls:

- Serialized objects—These are serialized copies of the local value the client uses as a parameter to the remote method.
- Remote references—If the parameter of a remote method is a *remote object*, defined and instantiated on the client side, RMI sends a remote reference (stub) as a marshalled parameter—not a copy of the object.

This distinction is very critical to the performance of your RMI applications. If you send small values, such as a string that represents a birth date or telephone number, it will not result in a very significant data transfer of marshalled data.

If, on the other hand, you send a very large, complex object, such as a jet airliner or nuclear attack submarine, the marshalled parameter might involve hundreds of thousands of bytes of marshalled data. Serialization copies every object and every dependent object.

In the case of the jet airliner, for example, the plane body, every engine, every wheel, every window, every seat, every seat belt, every tray table—everything—must be sent by value. The result is quite a large object. Therefore, using local objects for parameters is probably acceptable for a simple e-commerce application but probably is not acceptable for a complex CAD drawing object.

> **TIP**
>
> Some developers find RMI too slow. Often, however, it is not RMI *per se* that is slow, but the application that is sending very large objects as local parameters. These are copied across the network by value, which is a very inefficient method. If you must deal with big objects, use remote objects instead of local objects for parameters. This will cut down the network traffic significantly.

If, on the other hand, an *object* is defined as a remote object in RMI terms, only the remote reference, or stu, will be passed over the network, greatly reducing the amount of data sent and improving the speed of execution.

> **TIP**
>
> RMI uses URLs to locate remote objects. When RMI is run on Windows clients, it can take noticeably longer than on Solaris clients. This is because Windows spends a great deal of time doing DNS name resolution. Name resolution is done much more quickly on Solaris. For this reason, if you plan to use RMI between server-side objects, I recommend that you do not use a Windows-based server if performance is a concern.

Finding Remote Objects

The benefit of using Remote Method Invocation is that your object can call a method of another object in another JVM, usually on another physical host system. In order to do this, however, you need to find the object and get a reference to it, just as you would for a local object in the same JVM. The primary mechanism for locating remote objects in RMI is called the `RMIRegistry`.

The `RMIRegistry` is a fairly simple program that contains remote references to remote objects, along with a logical name to use for finding the object. For example, you might have a remote object that represents a shopping cart for an e-commerce application. In your program, the name of the reference to the object might be `scRemote1`. In the `RMIRegistry`, you can assign it the logical name `ShoppingCart`. This gives client programs a meaningful name to use when searching for the object. The programs are not required to know the name of the remote object reference that occurs in the code of the remote factory class.

In order to run an RMI application, you must start the `RMIRegistry` before you run any of your own code, whether you are running the remote factory, the remote object (even with remote activation), or the remote factory program.

> **NOTE**
>
> Generally speaking, the `RMIRegistry` must execute on the same system that the remote object (discussed in the following section) runs on. In the preceding example, if the `shopping cart` objects run on a server called cyrus, the `RMIRegistry` must also run on cyrus. If you have a remote object for logging these e-commerce transactions, and you want that object to run on a server called golden, you also have to run an `RMIRegistry` on golden. You must know the server that the remote object (and hence, the `RMIRegistry`) is on. The server name has to be hard-coded some place the caller of the remote object can find. This might be in a file, a URL hidden in a Web page, or in the caller's code.
>
> You can circumvent this requirement by using the Java Naming and Directory Interface (JNDI). Sun has provided what is called a *service provider interface* (SPI) to connect various `RMIRegistry`s to JNDI. Your program can just ask JNDI for the location of a shopping cart by using a logical name. The location of the remote object and the matching `RMIRegistry` are returned. See the Javasoft Web site for more information on JNDI.

> **TIP**
>
> You can avoid using the `RMIRegistry` if you use the `exportObject()` method of `UnicastRemoteObject` (discussed in the following section).

This, in brief, is how RMI works. More information on the details of the Remote Method Invocation architecture may be found at http://www.javasoft.com/products/jdk/1.2/docs/guide/rmi/spec/rmiTOC.doc.html.

Calling a Remote Object's Methods

This section steps through a basic RMI application. First, you will go through the steps required to build and execute a simple RMI application.

Create a Remote Interface: Code Example

First, you need to create a remote interface, with this basic format:

```
public interface someInterface extends Remote
```

This interface must extend the `java.rmi.Remote` interface, which contains no methods but marks your interface as appropriate for RMI. In this interface, you define all the methods you want your remote object to have that will be visible to a remote client. Because you are going across address spaces, it is not sufficient to make the methods public. You need to do this additional work so that RMI can provide the mechanism for your remote client to find your remote object.

The methods defined in a remote interface are all the methods you want callers to access. A remote object is like any other object in that it can have any number of private methods about which callers know nothing. The methods that go in a remote interface are the *business logic* methods a caller needs your remote object to perform.

For example, the remote interface for a library catalog might look like the code in Listing 15.1. I will discuss each piece of this application separately because each piece has its own important aspects.

Listing 15.1   A Sample Remote Interface (Borrowable.java)
```
// Remote interface definition for a library book.
import java.rmi.*;
import java.util.*;
interface Borrowable extends Remote
    {
    // A remote interface must extend jva.rmi.Remote.
    public boolean isCheckedOut() throws RemoteException;
    // All the methods in a remote interface MUST
    // be declared as throwing RemoteException.
    public boolean checkOut(String cardNumber, Date d)
                                        throws RemoteException;
    public boolean checkIn(String cardNumber, Date d)
                                        throws RemoteException;

    }
```

The `Borrowable` interface I designed has three methods that can be called by other objects. Any implementing classes can have as many other methods as necessary; they simply cannot have other methods that RMI will let clients call on the implementing object. Observe that each remote method is declared as calling a `RemoteException`. Doing this is required.

Implement a Remote Object Class Definition: Code Example

The remote object you want to access, whether it is a shopping cart, or a bank account, or an airline reservation system, must have a class definition that follows these rules:

- It must implement the related remote interface, which must extend the `Remote` interface.
- The class must extend `java.rmi.server.UnicastRemoteObject`.
- The class must have a coded constructor that is defined to throw a `RemoteException` (in case anything goes wrong while trying to instantiate it remotely). You cannot merely accept the default constructor the compiler would generate if no constructor was defined for the class.

NOTE

Technically, you do not have to subclass `UnicastRemoteObject`. However, this class provides several helpful methods that you need. If for some reason you need to subclass some other class, you can still define a class to be a remote object. You need to define your own remote versions of `hashCode()`, `equals()`, and `toString()`.

This class implements the business logic your remote object provides to callers (see Listing 15.2). Just as the methods in the interface are declared to throw a `RemoteException`, the methods in this class are declared to throw `RemoteExceptions`.

> **TIP**
>
> If, in fact, you know that your method can't throw a `RemoteException`, you can implement the method but omit the `throws` clause. Java does not allow you to throw more exception types than you have declared in a method's signature in an interface. However, it does not forbid throwing fewer.

Listing 15.2 The Class Definition for a Remote Class (Book.java)
```
// Remote object for a Book class.
// This class allows for checking the status of a book,
// checking out the book, and checking in the book.
// It requires a library card number and a Date object.
import java.util.*;
import java.rmi.*;
import java.rmi.server.*;

public class Book extends UnicastRemoteObject
                              implements Borrowable
    {
    // All RMI remote object classes need to implement
    // the related remote interface that defines their remotely
    // callable methods, and such classes should extend
    // from UnicastRemoteObject.
    private Date borrowDate;
    private Date returnDate;
    private String borrowerID; // Library card number.
    private String title;
    private boolean checkedOut = false;

    public Book(String bookName) throws RemoteException
          {
          // The constructor of a remote object must be defined
          // as throwing a remote exception.
          title = bookName;
          }

    // Implement the methods in the remote interface.
    public boolean isCheckedOut()
                      throws RemoteException
          {
           return checkedOut;
          }

    public boolean checkOut(String cardNumber, Date d)
                                    throws RemoteException
          {
```

```
              borrowerID  = cardNumber;
              borrowDate = d;
              return true;
            }

    public boolean checkIn(String cardNumber, Date d)
                                    throws RemoteException
            {
              borrowerID  = cardNumber;
              returnDate = d;
              return true;
            }

    } // End class definition for Book.
```

As you can see, there is not much involved in creating a class definition for a remote object. You add the necessary imports and subclass `UnicastRemoteObject`. The class must also implement your remote interface (which declares the business logic methods you wish to call). The class definition is complete except for adding any private methods you need in addition to the remotely callable methods. The `Book` class has none, although in real life it probably would have several.

Create a Remote Factory on a Server: Code Example

Now that the class for the remote object is defined, it is necessary to define a class that can instantiate the remote object. Actually, this class has two jobs: instantiate the remote object and register the remote object with the `RMIRegistry`. The first task is just like instantiating any local object. Generally, this program runs on the same host as the remote object.

The second task is accomplished through the use of either the `bind()` or `rebind()` method. (You can remove an object, or unregister it from the registry with the `unbind()` method.) Choosing between the `bind()` and `rebind()` method is easy. The `bind()` method binds an object to the `RMIRegistry`. If you call `bind()` a second time for an object that is already bound to the `RMIRegistry`, you get an exception.

Alternatively, you can use `rebind()` to bind the remote object (actually, you put a stub in the RMIRegistry). Even the first time, it binds the object to the `RMIRegistry` and allows you to replace the existing object. You need to bind an object to the `RMIRegistry` any time you modify it. If you have done proper object-oriented design, that should not happen frequently, but it will happen—especially during unit testing.

Here are all the methods for naming classes:

- `bind(String, Remote)`—Binds the name to the specified remote object
- `list(String)`—Returns an array of strings of the URLs in the registry
- `lookup(String)`—Returns the remote object for the URL
- `rebind(String, Remote)`—Rebinds the name to a new object and replaces any existing binding
- `unbind(String)`—Unbinds the name

TIP

You can use the `list()` method in a manner similar to Java Reflection (see Chapter 14) and the CORBA dynamic invocation to discover objects in the `RMIRegistry` of another host.

The `RMIRegistry` stores a URL for the remote object to enable your client to find the remote object. The URL has the format

`rmi://hostname:portNumber/logicalName`

The parts of this URL are explained in the following list:

- `hostname` is the name of the physical host the object runs on.
- `portNumber` is the port number the object runs on (is bound to).
- `logicalName` is the logical name you gave in the `bind()`/`rebind()` call. The hostname defaults to the host the `RMIRegistry` is running on, and the default port number is the port number of the `RMIRegistry` (port 1099).

CAUTION

The HotJava browser from Sun contains an `RMIRegistry` built in. If you have HotJava running on the same system as the remote object, you will potentially bind to HotJava's `RMIRegistry`, and not to the `RMIRegistry` you started separately. This can cause a conflict between the two `RMIRegistrys` for the 1099 port. What's more, the `RMIRegistry` in HotJava is transient—not persistent as is the normal `RMIRegistry` you start at the command line. Therefore, it is best to shut down HotJava, if it is running on the remote object host, before you run the remote factory code or start the `RMIRegistry` separately.

CAUTION

Be aware that the default Java policy restricts port access for ports above 1024. Since the RMIRegistry's default port is 1099, this is a problem for your program, because it won't be able to access the registry. Be sure that your remote object uses a higher port number than the reserved port numbers. An even better idea is to create a custom RMI policy file that overrides this restriction. See Chapter 16, "Java Security," to learn how to create a policy file.

One other important issue is security. RMI is very particular about allowing a client to execute a method on a remote object. If you attempt to do this without a `SecurityManager` object in place, RMI will restrict you to only loading classes in the local classpath. This means that your RMI code works fine if it is on the same host but breaks if the remote object is on a host other than the one your client is on. So, instead of pretending this restriction does not exist, the remote factory class will instantiate an `RMISecurityManager` class instance that will permit some basic class loading. You will need to do this for a remote object running on another system so that there's no unit test-type example that won't work anywhere else.

Calling a Remote Object's Methods 287

Listing 15.3 shows a simple remote factory for creating a `Book` remote object and binding it to the `RMIRegistry`.

Listing 15.3 Creating and Registering a Remote Object Using rebind()
(RemoteDriver1.java)

```java
import java.rmi.*;
import java.rmi.server.*;
// You need the java.rmi package to get the Naming service methods
// and for the RMISecurityManager.
// You need java.rmi.server for the support classes for the Book class,
// which uses several java.rmi.server classes, especially UnicastRemoteObject.
import java.net.*;
// This class is used to instantiate and register a Book object.
// Once that is done, this object is done with its work.

class RemoteFactory1
    {
       public RemoteFactory1()
            {
              System.setSecurityManager(
                     new RMISecurityManager());
              // Instantiate an RMISecurityManager to
              // allow proper RMI execution.
            }

       public void createRemoteBook()
            {
              try
              // You must do this in a try block because the
              // method class can throw Remote exceptions.
                   {
                     Book remoteBook =
                            new Book("How Shall We Then Live?");
              // Instantiate the remote object.  To the factory
              // object, this is just another local object.
                        Naming.rebind("RemoteBook", remoteBook);
              // Bind (or rebind) the remote object instance to
              // the RMIRegistry.
              // The rebind() method takes two parameters:
              // 1. A logical name to identify the object by.
              // 2. The object reference.
              // It is best to make the logical name clearly
              // relate to the object reference.
              // It is not, however, necessary.  The logical name
              // for this object could be "SillyPenguin", but that
              // would not help anyone understand your code or
              // use your remote objects.
                   }
              catch(RemoteException re)
```

continues

Listing 15.3   continued

```
                  {
                    System.out.println(re.getMessage());
                  }
                catch(MalformedURLException mue)
                  {
                    System.out.println(mue.getMessage());
                  }
                System.out.println("Remote Book object ready to go");
                // Unlike a CORBA application, nothing is
                // needed to keep the remote factory class
                // from exiting.
              }
      }
public class RemoteDriver1
      {
        // This class launches the remote "factory" object.
        // It is, of course, not a true object factory.
        public static void main(String[] args)
              {
                RemoteFactory1 rf = new RemoteFactory1();
                rf.createRemoteBook();
              }

      }
```

If you have CORBA experience, you might be thinking that this looks an awful lot like CORBA, in which you also run a "factory" program to bind/rebind a newly created remote object. Also, like CORBA, RMI uses a client-side stub and a "server"-side skeleton. In general, you will find that RMI is simpler to use than CORBA and also has a lighter-weight framework. As you can see in the sample code, you do not need to do the narrowing of naming contexts and object references that is needed in CORBA. This is possible because RMI deals only with Java objects.

Implement a Client Program: Code Example

Now that you have a class defined for your remote object and a remote factory class to create the remote object and register it with the RMIRegistry, you need to create a client to request the services of the remote object. The mechanism for this is very important. You do not simply instantiate a remote object by calling its constructor:

```
Book aBook = new Book(
                "Pilgrim's Progress");  // WRONG; ILLEGAL
                                        // Don't do this!!!
```

Instead, you access a remote object solely through its remote interface. In this case, you ask for an object of type Borrowable. This means that you are asking the JVM to give you an object, any object of any class, that implements the Borrowable interface. It might sound odd, but doing this provides you a very important benefit. This mechanism means that the developer who implements the remote object's class can change that class at will, modifying its logic, private data members, and methods significantly. As long as the interface definition does not change, the client code does not have to be modified one bit. Using an interface this way leads to very loosely coupled client-remote object relationships, which ease maintenance and reduce complexity in applications.

> **NOTE**
>
> This same pattern is used by Java elsewhere, such as in JDBC. In it, a driver is an interface implementation, and callers need know nothing about the database driver class itself. This pattern is also used in Enterprise Java Beans, where a caller of an EJB knows nothing about the class of the bean, but knows its home and remote interfaces. This pattern is a very powerful mechanism for decoupling objects. Consider it for use in your own applications to add flexibility and reduce maintenance headaches.

As noted earlier, the RMIRegistry stores the RMI URL for a remote object. The client needs that URL to find the remote object. The remote factory used the Naming class to bind a remote object to the RMIRegistry. The client uses the Naming class to look up a remote object in the RMIRegistry using the Naming.lookup() method. This method takes an RMI URL as a parameter. In Listing 15.4, the URL looks like this:

```
rmi://localhost/Borrowable
```

Note that you do not specify the name of the class, but the logical name given to the object by the remote factory. After you have an object that implements the interface, you can call remote methods just as though the remote object is local. The work of sending marshalled data over the network is done for you under the covers.

Listing 15.4 Basic RMI Client Using Naming.lookup() (ClientDriver1.java)

```
// RMI Client
// This example assumes there is only one remote object
// of interest. In many situations, you would need to provide
// some identifier to get a specific instance.

import java.rmi.*;   // Package for java.rmi.Naming.
import java.util.*;
class RMIClient1
      // This client can and likely will be a second-tier program.
      {
       String server = "localhost";
       String rmiUrl = "rmi://";
       String remoteClass = "RemoteBook";
       // These are the pieces to use to find the Remote object.
       String libraryCardNumber = "1234";

      public RMIClient1()
            {
             if (System.getSecurityManager() == null)
                System.setSecurityManager(new RMISecurityManager());
```

continues

Listing 15.4 continued

```java
            // Set up a Securitymanager for RMI.
        }
    public boolean useLibrary()
            {
              boolean result = true;
              // Initialize the return value.
              try
                  {
                    rmiUrl = rmiUrl + server +
                            "/" + remoteClass;
                    // Create a URL with rmi as the protocol.
                    Borrowable remoteBook = (Borrowable)
                        Naming.lookup(rmiUrl);
                // Request a remote object, any remote object,
                // which implements the Borrowable interface
                // registered in the RMIRegistry.
                // Now call some remote methods on the
                // remote object.
                    System.out.println("The book is  checked out: " +
                            remoteBook.isCheckedOut());
                    boolean outResult =
                            remoteBook.checkOut(libraryCardNumber,
                                                    new Date());
                    if(outResult == true)
                       System.out.println("Book checked out successfully");
                    else
                            result = false;
                    boolean inResult =
                            remoteBook.checkIn(libraryCardNumber, new Date());
                    if(inResult == true)
                            System.out.println("Book checked in");
                    else
                            result = false;
                  }
              catch(Exception e)
                    {
                      System.out.println("RMI error: " +
                                e.getMessage());
                      // The try block could produce a RemoteException
                      // or a MalformedURLException.
                      result = false;
                    }
              return result;
            }
    }


public class ClientDriver1
    {
```

```
public static void main(String[] args)
    {
     RMIClient1 rc = new RMIClient1();
     boolean result = rc.useLibrary();
     if(result == false)
          System.out.println("Error using the Library");
    }
}
```

The client program does a lookup on the remote object through the `Naming.lookup(*)` method. This method asks the `RMIRegistry`, which resides on the host named in the RMI URL, for a reference to a remote object that matches the logical name `RemoteBook`. The reference returned is a reference to some object that implements the `Borrowable` interface. The reference must be cast to the interface type `Borrowable`. That's all the coding that is required for a basic RMI application. There are a few more steps, however, before you are finished.

Generate a Stub and Skeleton

RMI uses *stubs* and *skeletons,* which are proxies to the remote object. The stub is used on the client side, and the skeleton is used on the remote object's side. The stub and skeleton are generated for you by the `rmic` program. To run it, call `rmic` and give it a command line parameter that equals the name of the class for the remote object, in this case `Book`:

```
rmic Book
```

This runs against the class file, not the source file. The output is two files: `Book_Stub.class` and `Book_skel.class`. If the remote object is running on a separate host from the client code (which is usually the case), the stub must be on the client's system, and the skeleton must be on the remote object's system. Because all the Java source files need the interface definition, the remote interface source file, `Borrowable.java`, needs to be available on both the client system and the remote object's system. Now that you know about the pieces of the RMI architecture, Figure 15.1 shows the entire architecture.

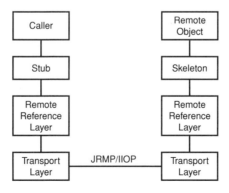

Figure 15.1

RMI architecture.

Start the RMIRegistry

On Solaris type: `rmiregistry` (or `rmiregistry &` to run it in the background).

On Windows type: `rmiregistry` (`start rmiregistry` to run it in the background).

You should start the `RMIRegistry` in the directory where the server-side code is located or in a directory that the `RMIRegistry` can find through the classpath set in your environment.

Start the Remote Factory Program Using a Policy File

If you just try to run the program, you will get an `AccessControlException` because you lack `SocketPermission` for port 1099. I will discuss policy files in depth in Chapter 16. For now, suffice it to say that you need a policy file.

> **CAUTION**
>
> The sample programs include a policy file, `RMI.jp`. This policy file essentially grants everything to everyone. Normally, you do want to use such a liberal policy file, so make sure you use this file only to run the sample programs. Do not use it in a production environment. There, it defeats the whole point of Java's security mechanism in Java 2.

To run the remote factory program, type

```
java -Djava.security.policy=RMI.jp RemoteDriver1
```

Run the Client

The client is equally restricted by the `RMISecurityManager` object, which grants very little authority to code, so the policy file is needed here as well. To run the client, type

```
java -Djava.security.policy=RMI.jp ClientDriver1
```

If all goes well, you should see some messages including

```
"Book checked out successfully"
```

> **NOTE**
>
> RMI is very particular about where the `RMIRegistry` is started, where the stub and skeleton are, and security permissions. Any number of exceptions might be encountered. If something goes wrong and you get an exception, verify that everything was started with the right arguments in the right directories. Also be sure that the RMI URL is correct.

That's all there is to creating and running a basic RMI application.

Calling a Remote Object with a Remote Object Parameter: Code Examples

The code so far has used local parameters. RMI made a copy of the `libraryCardNumber` string and serialized it in a marshalling stream. For such a small piece of data, that is fine. A

Calling a Remote Object with a Remote Object Parameter 293

very large object might create a performance problem. In the following steps, I will show you how to use a remote object for a parameter so that only the remote reference (and not the whole object) is passed when a remote method call is made by the client. Most of the code and the steps are the same as those for a basic RMI program that passes local objects for parameters, except that you need a remote object for the `libraryCardNumber`. Therefore, the code will be changed to accept a `LibraryCard` object that is defined as a remote object.

Here are the steps to call a remote method with a remote object as a parameter:

1. Define a remote interface for the remote object that will have its remote reference passed as a parameter. Instead of just a library card number, there is now a class for library cards. The class implements the `Issueable` remote interface, shown in Listing 15.5.

Listing 15.5 The Issueable Remote Interface (Issueable.java)
```
// Remote Interface for Cards
// Use as a remote object on the client side of an RMI
// conversation (in this example).

import java.rmi.*;
import java.util.*;
public interface Issueable extends Remote
    // A remote interface should extend Remote.
    {
    // Provide some class constants for a library card.
     public static final int UNLIMITED_BOOKS = 1;
     public static final int ONE_YEAR_CHECKOUT = 2;

    // Declare remote business methods.
    public boolean setExpiration(GregorianCalendar gc)
            throws RemoteException;
    public boolean setPrivilges(int privilege)
            throws RemoteException;
    public String getCardNumber()
                    throws RemoteException;
    // All the remote methods are declared as
    // throwing a remote exception.

      public void setFines(float newFine)
                    throws RemoteException;

      public float getFines()
                    throws RemoteException;
    }
```

The reason for this interface definition, again, is solely to provide for treating the class that implements it as a definition for making remote objects. To accomplish this, the class must implement the `Remote` interface. The class that implements the `Issueable` interface in your application is called `LibraryCard`.

2. Now you need to create a class that implements the remote interface shown in step 1. This class definition is needed on the client side, while the stub you generate must be accessible in some fashion to the caller on the server. The code for this class is shown in Listing 15.6.

Listing 15.6 Class Definition for LibraryCard, a Remote Object Class (LibraryCard.java)

```
// Client-side remote object
// LibraryCard class.
import java.rmi.*;
import java.rmi.server.*;
import java.util.*;

class LibraryCard extends UnicastRemoteObject
        implements Issueable
    {
      // Extend UnicastRemoteObject and implement
      // remote interface.
      String cardNumber;
      GregorianCalendar expirationDate;
      int[]  privileges;
      float fines;

      // Note that, like all remote class definitions,
      // the constructor for a remote object must
      // be declared to throw a RemoteException.
      public LibraryCard(String cardNumb)
                    throws RemoteException
          {
            cardNumber = cardNumb;
            privileges = new int[4];
          }

      // Now code business methods.
      // These methods also are declared as throwing
      // remote exceptions, which are sent in this case
      // to the server-side remote object.
      public boolean setExpiration(GregorianCalendar gc)
                                throws RemoteException
          {
            expirationDate = gc;
            return true;
          }

    public boolean setPrivilges(int privilege)
          throws RemoteException
       {
         privileges[0] = privilege;
         // Allow for one privilege at this time.
         return true;
```

```
        }

    public String getCardNumber() throws RemoteException
          {
            return cardNumber;
          }

    public void setFines(float newFine) throws RemoteException
          {
            fines = fines + newFine;
          }

    public float getFines() throws RemoteException
          {
            return fines;
          }
  }
```

3. Modify the server-side remote object to use the client-side remote object. This is fairly straightforward and involves the following steps:
   - Change the `Borrowable` interface method declarations to accept parameters of type `LibraryCard` rather than a string.
   - Change the `Book` class to implement the new methods, extracting data from a `LibraryCard` by calling its remote methods rather than working with a copy of the data sent by the client.
   - Modify the `RemoteDriver` to use the new version of the `Book` class.

   These small changes can be seen in `Borrowable2.java`, `Book2.java`, and `RemoteDriver2.java`.
4. Modify the client-side program to use the new `LibraryCard` remote object. This is a small change. First, instantiate an object of type `LibraryCard`. Because this class extends `UnicastRemoteObject`, it is automatically exported for you by RMI when you call a remote method. Next, you change the method calls to use the object reference. (In this case, as far as RMI is concerned, it really points to a stub.) The new client is shown in Listing 15.7.

Listing 15.7   RMI Client That Passes a Remote Object Parameter (ClientDriver2.java)
```
// RMI Client
// This example assumes there is only one remote object
// of interest. In many situations, you would need to provide
// some identifier to get a specific instance.

import java.rmi.*;   // Package for java.rmi.Naming.
import java.util.*;
class RMIClient2
      {
        String server = "localhost";
```

continues

Listing 15.7 continued
```
    String rmiUrl = "rmi://";
    String remoteClass = "RemoteBook2";
    // These are the pieces to use to find the Remote object
    // on the "server."
    LibraryCard libCard;

public RMIClient2()
        {
          if (System.getSecurityManager() == null)
                  System.setSecurityManager(
                          new RMISecurityManager());
          // Set up a SecurityManager for RMI.
          // Otherwise, you will get a SecurityException
          // when you attempt to access a server-side
          // remote method.
          try
          // Wrap the remote calls in a try block,
          // because they may throw a RemoteException.
                {
                  libCard = new LibraryCard("1234");
                }
          catch(RemoteException re)
                {
                  re.printStackTrace();
                  System.out.println(re.getMessage());
                }
          // Instantiate a "remote object" here to be used
          // as a parameter in a remote method call.
        }

    public boolean useLibrary()
        {
         boolean result = true;
         try
                {
                  rmiUrl = rmiUrl + server +
                          "/" + remoteClass;
                  Borrowable2 remoteBook2 =  (Borrowable2)
                          Naming.lookup(rmiUrl);
            // Request a remote object, any remote object,
            // which implements the Borrowable interface.

                  // Now call some remote methods on the
                  // remote object.
                     System.out.println("The books is checked out: " +
                             remoteBook2.isCheckedOut());
                     boolean outResult =
                             remoteBook2.checkOut(libCard,
```

```java
                                                    new Date());
                // This time, pass a remote object reference
                // as a method parameter. This should not
                // marshal a copy of the LibraryCard object
                // but just send its stub.
                    if(outResult == true)
                       System.out.println
                           ("Book checked out successfully");
                    else
                            result = false;
                    boolean inResult =
                            remoteBook2.checkIn(libCard, new Date());
                     if(inResult == true)
                            System.out.println("Book checked in");
                    else
                            result = false;
                }
            catch(Exception e)
                   {
                     System.out.println("RMI error: " +
                              e.getMessage());
                    // The try block could
                    // produce a RemoteException
                    // or a MalformedURLException.
                    result = false;
                    }
              return result;
            }
    }


public class ClientDriver2
    {
     public static void main(String[] args)
            {
              RMIClient2 rc = new RMIClient2();
              boolean result = rc.useLibrary();
              if(result == false)
                  System.out.println("Error using the Library");
             }
    }
```

5. Create stubs and skeletons for everything. Run rmic to create stubs and skeletons for both the Book and LibraryCard remote classes. At runtime, the Book2 class must be able to find the stub for the LibraryCard class, just as the ClientDriver2 class must be able to find the stub for the Book2 remote class.
6. Start the RMIRegistry. Start the RMIRegistry in the chap15 directory or set your classpath to be able to find the chap15 directory. Next, start the RMIRegistry. It must be able to find the stubs and skeletons for both Book2 and LibraryCard.

7. Run the remote factory `RemoteDriver2`:
   `java -Djava.security.policy=RMI.jp RemoteDriver2`

8. Run the client `ClientDriver2`. If all goes well, you should see this on the client's command line:
   ```
   java -Djava.security.policy=RMI.jp RemoteDriver2
   Remote Book object ready to go
   ```

   In the window for the server side and in the client side window, you will see this:
   ```
   java -Djava.security.policy=RMI.jp ClientDriver2
   The book is checked out: false
   Book checked out successfully
   Book checked in
   ```

   As you can see from this code, it is possible to define a remote object on the client side of an application and send it to the server side by reference. The RMI does not have to send a marshalled copy. In the previous example, using this technique probably did not improve performance noticeably. If, however, I replace the `LibraryCard` class with a complex CAD drawing or a complex object (such as a 747 airplane, a nuclear submarine, or a hotel), this procedure becomes an important way to speed up performance.

Creating a Remote Object from a Client: Remote Activation Code Examples

The techniques shown so far use remote objects that already exist.

NOTE

> The creation of remote objects on a sever by a factory or other program running on the sever machine, without a client, is a key feature that distinguishes RMI and CORBA from DCOM. DCOM does not automatically support the use of existing remote objects. Instead, it requires that objects be created. This requirement makes it harder to share a remote object across clients. RMI has no trouble doing this.

There are times, however, when you don't want to depend on a "server-side" program to take care of setting up a remote object for you. You might want to do this to save memory, for example, or to decouple the client application from the server application. The means to do this is the new Java 2 feature called *activation*.

Remote activation provides the framework to create a remote object on-the-fly from the client. To support remote activation, you use `rmid`, the RMI daemon, to control remotely activating an object. As in previous procedures, the RMIRegistry must be running. The RMIRegistry runs at the same time as `rmid`.

The steps required for activation are similar to normal RMI programming with the addition of a `setup` class. The `setup` class "sets up" the activation environment for you, and then the client can make calls to create remote objects. These are intercepted by `rmid`, which then uses the setup info to instantiate the remote object.

Here are the steps to perform object activation in RMI. Any steps that are the same as steps discussed earlier in this chapter are not explained again. For information on them, see the previous sections of this chapter.

1. Create a remote interface.
2. Implement the remote interface. Three changes must be made to the remote object's class definition—in this case, Book:
   - Change
     ```
     import java.rmi.server.*;
     ```
     to
     ```
     import java.rmi.activation.*;
     ```
   - Extend Activatable instead of UnicastRemoteObject:
     ```
     public class Book extends Activatable implements Borrowable
     ```
   - Change the implementation class's constructor to support activation:
     ```
     public Book(String bookName,
                 ActivationID actID, MarshalledObject mo)
                     throws RemoteException
     {
         // Register the object with the activation
         // system and export it on an anonymous port
         // by calling the superclass constructor.
         // The MarshalledObject would be a serialized
         // object passed to the Book class.
         super(actID, 0);
         // No MarshalledObject passed, so use 0.
         // Do other constructor-related stuff.
     }
     ```

Listing 15.8 shows the activatable version of Book.

Listing 15.8   An Activatable Remote Object (ActivatableBook.java)
```
// Remote object for a Book class.
// This class allows for checking the status of a book,
// checking out the book and checking in the book.
// It requires a library card number and a Date object.

import java.util.*;
import java.rmi.*;
import java.rmi.activation.*;
    // Instead of importing java.rmi.server.*, to get things like
    // UnicastRemoteObject, you import java.rmi.activatin.*;
import java.io.*;
public class ActivatableBook extends Activatable
                             implements Borrowable
    {
    // All RMI remote object classes need to implement
    // the related remote interface that defines their remotely
    // callable methods. Activatable classes should inherit
```

continues

Listing 15.8 *continued*

```java
    // from Activatable, not UnicastRemoteObject.
    private Date borrowDate;
    private Date returnDate;
    private String borrowerID; // Library card number.
    private String title;
    private boolean checkedOut = false;

    public ActivatableBook(ActivationID actID,
                        MarshalledObject mo)
                                    throws RemoteException
        // Look at this constructor. It does not just take
        // initialization data. In fact, the data to
        // initialize the activatable object is hidden
        // inside the MarshalledObject mo.
        {
        // Register the object with the activation
        // system and export it on an anonymous port
        // by calling the superclass constructor.
        // The MarshalledObject would be a serialized
        // object passed to the Book class.
        super(actID, 0);
        // No MarshalledObject passed, so use 0.
        try
            {
              title = (String)mo.get();
            }
        catch(ClassNotFoundException moge)
            // This exception is thrown if the
            // RMIClassLoader can't find your class
            // definition at runtime.
                {
                  System.out.println("MarshalledObject get failed:  " +
                            moge.getMessage());
                }
            catch(IOException ioe)
                {
                  System.out.println("MarshalledObject creation failed:
                            " + ioe.getMessage());
                }
        }

    // Implement the methods in the remote interface.
    public boolean isCheckedOut()
                    throws RemoteException
        {
         return checkedOut;
         }

    public boolean checkOut(String cardNumber, Date d)
```

```
                              throws RemoteException
        {
         borrowerID  = cardNumber;
         borrowDate = d;
         return true;
        }

    public boolean checkIn(String cardNumber, Date d)
                              throws RemoteException
        {
         borrowerID  = cardNumber;
         returnDate = d;
         return true;
        }

} // End class definition for ActivatableBook.
```

3. Create a setup class. The setup class, which is what the Javasoft documentation calls this class, creates the information needed by the activatable class. The setup class passes the information about the activatable class to rmid, the activation daemon, registers a remote reference (an instance of the activatable class's stub class) and a moniker (chosen by the developer) with the RMIRegistry, The setup class exists to create the activation information. It does not need to create the actual remote object nor does it need to stay in memory.

   Here are the steps to create a setup class:
   1. Make the appropriate imports.
   2. Install a SecurityManager.
   3. Create an ActivationGroup instance.
   4. Create an ActivationDesc instance.
   5. Declare an instance of your remote interface and register with rmid.
   6. Bind the stub to a name in the RMIRegistry.

   Listing 15.9 shows a setup class for the Book remote object class.

Listing 15.9   Activation setup Class for a Remote Object (RemoteDriver3.java)
```
// This is a setup class for remote activation of an RMI object.
// It does not as such make the remote object.
// Rather, it creates the framework for the client
// to make the remote object on-the-fly.
import java.rmi.*;
import java.rmi.activation.*;
import java.security.CodeSource;
import java.util.Properties;
import java.net.*;
import java.io.*;
class RemoteSetup
      {

        String location = "http://localhost:8080/";
```

continues

Listing 15.9 *continued*

```
        // Note the trailing /. This is essentially
        // a directory name and must end with this character.
    MarshalledObject mo = null;
    Properties sysProps;

    public RemoteSetup()
        {
          System.setSecurityManager(
                  new RMISecurityManager());
          // Instantiate an RMISecurityManager to
          // allow proper RMI execution.
          // Even if you did not otherwise need it,
          // Activation requires a SecurityManager to be
          // installed in the JVM at runtime.
        }

    public void prepareRemoteBookActivation()
        {
          try
              {
                // First, get a copy of the system properties.
                // Since a java.security.policy parameter was
                // supplied on the command line to run this
                // program, that property is included.
                // Activation needs to know where the policy file
                // resides. This means, since policy files
                // are only used in Java 2 that Activation can
                // only be used in Java 2.
                sysProps = (Properties)System.getProperties().clone();
                // Clone the system properties so that your code
                // doesn't trash the existing system properties.

                // Now, make an ActivationGroupDesc,
                // an ActivationGroupID,
                // and an ActivationGroup.
                ActivationGroupDesc.CommandEnvironment actCmdEnv = null;
                ActivationGroupDesc bookGroup =
                            new ActivationGroupDesc(sysProps,
                                                actCmdEnv);
                System.out.println("Made an ActivationGroupDesc");
                // Create an ActivationGroupDesc (activation
                // descriptor) which contains the security
                // policy info.

                // Now register the ActivationGroupDesc
                // with the Activation system and get an ID
                // for it.
                ActivationGroupID actGrID =
                        ActivationGroup.getSystem().registerGroup(
```

Creating a Remote Object from a Client: 303

```
                    bookGroup);
        System.out.println("Made an ActGrpID");
        // Next, explicitly create an ActivationGroup.
        ActivationGroup.createGroup(actGrID, bookGroup, 0);
        // This method takes three parms:
        //     ActivationGroupID id
        //     ActivationGroupDesc desc
        //     long incarnation
        System.out.println("Made a group");
        // Next, create an ActivationDesc object.
        mo = new MarshalledObject("How Shall  We Then Live?");
        System.out.println("Made a marshalledobject");
        // Create a MarshalledObject to pass parameters
        // to the Book constructor.
        ActivationDesc desc = new ActivationDesc
                    (actGrID, "ActivatableBook",
                      location, mo);
        System.out.println("made an act desc");
        // Give rmid enough info to instantiate
        // the activatable object.

        Borrowable activatableBook =
            (Borrowable)Activatable.register(desc);
        System.out.println(
            "Ready to activate a Book");
        System.out.println("Activatable contents:   " +
            activatableBook.toString());

          Naming.rebind ("ActivatableBook", activatableBook);
// Bind (or rebind) the remote object instance to
// the RMIRegistry.
// The rebind() method takes two parms:
// 1. A logical name to identify the object by
// 2. The object reference
// It is best to make the logical name clearly
// relate to the object reference.
// It is not, however, necessary. The logical name
// for this object could be "SillyPenguin", but that
// would not help anyone understand your code or
// use your remote objects.
        }
catch(RemoteException re)
        {
        System.out.println(re.getMessage());
        }
 catch(ActivationException acte)
        {
        System.out.println(" Activation failed:   " +
                acte.getMessage());
```

continues

Listing 15.9 continued

```
                                acte.printStackTrace();
                }
                catch(IOException ioe)
                {
                    System.out.println("MarshalledObject creation failed:  "
                            + ioe.getMessage());
                    ioe.printStackTrace();
                }
                System.out.println ("Remote Book object ready to go");
                System.exit(0);
                // Exit the setup program.
            }
    }

public class RemoteDriver3
        {
            public static void main(String[] args)
                {
                    RemoteSetup setup = new RemoteSetup();
                    setup.prepareRemoteBookActivation();
                }
        }
```

In this code, the activation group descriptor, `ActivationGroupDesc` object, provides the RMI daemon, `rmid`, with all the information necessary to contact the appropriate JVM to create the object (either the currently running JVM or a new one started by `rmid`). After you have an `ActivationGroupDesc` object, you can register it with the activation system and get an ID for it. You can use the `ActivationGroupDesc` object and the ID to create an `ActivationGroup`. After creating an `ActivationGroup` object, the program creates an `ActivationDesc` (Activation descriptor) object to provide `rmid` with the necessary information to instantiate the `activatable` object. There are several constructors that the code might use. This form uses the activation group ID, the name of the `activatable` class, the location of the `activatable` class, the `MarshalledObject` data and whether the `activatable` object can be restarted.

4. Create a client to activate the `activatable` object. There is very little a client actually has to do differently when using activation as opposed to the mechanics of using an existing remote object on another host. In fact, all that is different about the client in Listing 15.10 is the name of the remote class to `lookup()`.

Listing 15.10 Client for RMI Activation (ClientDriver3.java)

```
// RMI Client
// This example assumes there is only one remote object
// of interest. In many situations, you would need to provide
// some identifier to get a specific instance.

import java.rmi.*;   // Package for java.rmi.Naming.
```

Creating a Remote Object from a Client: 305

```java
import java.util.*;
class RMIClient3
      {
       String server = "localhost";
       String rmiUrl = "rmi://";
       String remoteClass = "ActivatableBook";
       // These are the pieces to use to find the Remote object.
       String libraryCardNumber = "1234";

      public RMIClient3()
            {
             if (System.getSecurityManager() == null)
               System.setSecurityManager(new RMISecurityManager());
             // Set up a Securitymanager for RMI.
            }

      public boolean useLibrary()
            {
             boolean result = true;
             try
                  {
                   rmiUrl = rmiUrl + server +
                            "/" + remoteClass;
                   Borrowable remoteBook =  (Borrowable)
                        Naming.lookup(rmiUrl);
                // Request a remote object, any remote object,
                // that implements the Borrowable interface.

                // Now call some remote methods on the remote object.
                   System.out.println("The book is checked out: " +
                            remoteBook.isCheckedOut());
                   boolean outResult =
                        remoteBook.checkOut(libraryCardNumber,
                                                        new Date());
                   if(outResult == true)
                      System.out.println("Book checked out successfully");
                   else
                        result = false;
                   boolean inResult =
                            remoteBook.checkIn(libraryCardNumber, new Date());
                    if(inResult == true)
                            System.out.println("Book checked in");
                    else
                            result = false;
                  }
             catch(Exception e)
                  {
                   System. out.println("RMI error: " +
                        e.getMessage());
```

continues

Listing 15.10 continued

```
                    // The try block could produce a RemoteException
                    // or a MalformedURLException.
                    result = false;
                }
            return result;
            }
    }


public class ClientDriver3
    {
      public static void main(String[] args)
            {
              RMIClient3 rc = new RMIClient3();
              boolean result = rc.useLibrary();
              if(result == false)
                  System.out.println("Error using the Library");
            }
    }
```

5. Run rmic on the activatable class:
   rmic ActivatableBook

6. Run the RMIRegistry:
   rmiregistry

7. Run rmid in another window:
   rmid

8. Run the setup program:
   java -Djava.security.policy=RMI.jp RemoteDriver3

9. Run the client:
   java -Djava.security.policy=RMI.jp ClientDriver3

This technique allows you to write RMI programs that can dynamically create a remote object on another system to do work for you on another host.

In each of these sample programs, I have run all the code from one directory. This will not be the usual situation. As you have seen, both the client and server need to know about the interface to the remote object. It is possible, however, to dynamically download the remote stub from one system to another.

Before you decide to do this, be aware that it is a bit tricky. It is not hard, but it does require several steps that must be done exactly. If you run into trouble attempting remote downloading of stubs, see

http://www.javasoft.com/products/jdk/1.2/docs/guide/rmi/codebase.html

This is more of a configuration issue than a coding issue, so I am not going to step through an example. Briefly, though, here's what you will need to do to remotely download a stub on demand:

Creating a Remote Object from a Client: 307

1. Do all the normal compilation and run `rmic` on the remote object class(es).
2. On the client machine, make absolutely certain that the stubs cannot be found in any place that the classpath points. If you overlook this, you will get the stubs from the classpath and not the ones you want to download.
3. Start the `RMIRegistry` in a directory that will not let the `RMIRegistry` find the stubs through the classpath.
4. Put the stubs in a place the client can reach, often a directory on a Web server for which the client has or can easily get the URL.
5. Start the server with the `java.rmi.server.codebase` property to point to the exact location of the code. In the case of a Web server-based applet, the codebase property must point to the codebase of the applet.
6. Start the client. If the server knows the correct location of the stubs, you've specified everything correctly, and the `RMIRegistry` was started in the correct location (`/temp` or `c:\temp` is a good choice), everything should work. If it does not, consult the preceding URL for troubleshooting. This is a handy technique. Be warned, however, that the RMI-USERS mailing list (run by Sun) probably has more posts about problems encountered while doing this procedure than about any other topic.

TIP

You can find lots of helpful information on using RMI on the RMI-USERS mailing list. You can subscribe by sending the message `subscribe RMI-USERS` *your name* to `listsever@java.sun.com`.

CHAPTER 16

Java Security

One of Java's design features is that the language is secure. There are several features of Java that support security, such as message digests and access control lists, not to mention the support provided by the Java Cryptography Extension, or JCE. The focus of this chapter is the new support for security in Java 2: policy-based permissions. This topic focuses not so much on code but on tools that support security. In this chapter, security relates primarily to control of assets, or what a program is allowed to do on a given system. This chapter covers the following topics:

- Using policy-based permissions
- Creating a policy file
- Signing code
- Creating a digital certificate

Using Policy-Based Security

In JDK 1.0 and 1.1, security in terms of use of system resources was governed by the java.lang.SecurityManager class. Fundamental to the SecurityManager class and policy-based permissions as well is the principle that if a right is not expressly granted, your code does not have it. The SecurityManager class consists of several methods, mostly check*xxx*, where *xxx* is the name of some operation that could adversely affect a host's data, such as checkRead() and checkWrite(). When you tried an operation that might be a security violation, Java called the appropriate SecurityManager method to see if it was okay to allow you to perform the operation. For example, this constructor call in an applet running in a Web browser:

```
FileInputStream fis = new
FileInputStream("AddressBook.dat");
```

would cause `checkRead()` to be called, and by default the read operation would be disallowed. You would get a `SecurityException`. By default, the `SecurityManager` class prohibits most everything. For example, the `SecurityManager` class in most Web browsers prohibits an applet from reading files, writing files, loading native libraries, modifying thread groups, or connecting to a host other than the host from which the applet was downloaded.

The `SecurityManager` class was limited in that it usually granted or withheld privileges from all code. There was no easy way to dynamically grant permission to one applet to read from a host's file system while denying another applet this privilege. The browser vendor would have had to know ahead of time which classes to grant privileges to and which classes to withhold privileges from. That is clearly impractical. So if the `SecurityManager` granted permission for some operation, it generally granted it for all classes.

The `SecurityManager` class is generally used only in Web browsers. It can be used by applications to limit their own actions, but this is less common. To have a `SecurityManager` present, you must explicitly instantiate it, with code like this:

```
System.setSecurityManager(new SecurityManager());
```

Browsers typically call code like this when the JVM is started. Once a `SecurityManager` object (or an instance of a subclass of `SecurityManager`) has been instantiated in a JVM, it cannot be removed or replaced, for obvious reasons. If you could replace it on-the-fly, the `SecurityManager` class would not provide much security.

This security framework causes code to run in what is called the *sandbox*. You can do whatever you want in the sandbox, but you cannot get outside of it. Generally all the restrictions just mentioned apply to code in the sandbox. This could be a major issue if a user wanted to print from an applet or if an applet wanted to write a configuration file on the user's system. Even if the end user wanted this, the applet was unable to do so because it was a security violation and the `SecurityManager` object would not allow it.

To mitigate this, JDK 1.1 introduced the concept of a *signed* class. Signing code had the effect of granting your applet more privileges. For example, if I write an applet and digitally sign it (to be described later), and you download it, you are given the option to let it execute. If you allow a signed applet to run in a pre-Java 2 environment, the applet could do anything it wanted to do. However, if you allowed signed code that was from a malicious source to run, it could prove harmful to your system.

Java 2 introduces a new middle ground: fine-grained, policy-based permissions. A permission is a specific category of resource or operation that you wish to allow. For example, you would use `SocketPermission` to allow a program to access more sockets than it can by default or to access sockets in ways not permitted by default. `SocketPermission` needs to be expanded for RMI to work in Java 2, as you can see in Chapter 15, "RMI."

Many permission classes have subpermissions. For example, `java.lang.RuntimePermission` has a number of permissions that are granted through it, arranged hierarchically. For example, `RuntimePermission` allows you to grant `queuePrintJob`, by which you give permission to print to a program running on your system. Or, you might grant `readFileDescriptor` so that a program can read a file on your system.

The Java 2 security model is based on *protection domains*. A protection domain correlates roughly to a running program. At runtime, the permissions granted through all the relevant policy files for a protection domain are placed into one large policy object. This policy object exists solely for the JVM to consult it for permissions.

To be very explicit about the role of a policy file, a policy file resides on a "client's" system. If a `SecurityManager` object is instantiated, methods that make security checks invoke methods of the `SecurityManager` object. The `SecurityManager` in Java 2 does not simply call `checkRead()` or `loadLibrary()` and return a boolean result, as in JDK 1.0 or 1.1. Instead, the Java 2 `SecurityManager` checks the list of permissions that have been granted through any relevant policy file.

> **NOTE**
>
> Permissions are cumulative. If there are three policy files accessed for a given client-side program, all the permissions will add together into a comprehensive set of permissions. There is no such thing as taking away a permission. If one policy file grants a permission that the other policy files do not grant, the permission is granted. There is no "anti-permission" syntax.

Before looking at how to create a policy file, you need to know where to find a policy file. If you go to the directory in which the SDK or JRE resides (JAVA_HOME in the example), you should be able to navigate to the appropriate directory:

```
JAVA_HOME/jre/lib/security (UNIX)
JAVA_HOME\jre\lib\security (Windows)
```

In this directory are two very important files. The first is `java.security`, which specifies where to find policy files, like this:

```
policy.url.1=file:${java.home}/lib/security/java.policy
policy.url.2=file:${user.home}/.java.policy
```

These two lines point to the location of the policy files the system expects by default. The first points to `java.home/jre/lib/security/java.policy`. This is the default Java policy file, and it grants precious little. The second policy file, called `.java.policy`, lives in the `user.home` directory. On UNIX, that is the `$HOME` directory. On Windows, this is generally `C:\`, the root directory. This latter policy file would be defined by the developer and given to the end user to put in the `user.home` directory. It is also possible to create your own policy file elsewhere, on an application-specific basis, for example. That would be a good choice if you want just your application to have a given set of permissions. For an application as opposed to an applet, you could make this policy file part of the distributed code, installed with a product such as InstallAnywhere. To tell Java to use this custom policy file, you would type this at the command line:

```
java -Djava.security.policy=myPolicyfile.jp MyCode
```

This will run your code using this policy file. I did this consistently in the RMI examples in Chapter 15. So there are three places for a policy file: jre/lib/security (pretty limited), user.home (there is no default version), and a custom policy file in a directory of your choice.

Let me emphasize again that you can code a policy file that works just fine with your applet or application. That's not enough. You must get that file installed on the client's machine in the right place. This means that for a Java 2 applet, you must do the following:

1. Code a policy file for the applet.
2. Get the applet on a Web page that causes the Java 2 plug-in to run. (This is the only way I know to run Java 2 in Netscape or Internet Explorer, as of September 1999.) This means the proper applet tags are used to trigger the use of the plug-in.
3. Have the user install the policy file in an appropriate place. For an applet, the most likely place is user.home. Be sure to warn the user of the significance of this. That policy, because of its location, will apply to every applet or application that runs on the client's system.
4. Have the user bring up the applet on a browser that is configured to use the Java 2 plug-in.

One final important point about permissions is that they can be granted to one of three groups:

- All code
- Code signed by one or more individuals
- Code from a specific code domain, such as java.sun.com or www.ibm.com

You can grant permissions to any code signed by Ken Litwak, or to any code from java.sun.com.

For more information on policy files, refer to the following URL:

http://java.sun.com/products/jdk/1.2/docs/guide/security/PolicyFiles.html

Creating a Policy File

Java 2 provides a tool to make it easy to create a policy file. It is called the policy tool. To run the policy tool, go to the command line and type

policytool

On most systems, this will bring up the policy tool, along with an error message, such as Could not find Policy file: C:\Windows\.java.policy. Just click OK. It's not really a problem. Figure 16.1 shows the policy tool when you first start it.

Creating a Policy File 313

Figure 16.1
The main Policy Tool screen.

To make this practical, I will step through making a policy file.

1. Click Add Policy Entry. This brings up a dialog box in which you can select permissions, as shown in Figure 16.2.

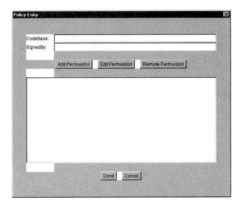

Figure 16.2
Adding a permission to a policy file.

2. You have a choice now. You have to decide whether to grant the permission to code signed by someone or code from a specific domain, or grant the permission to all code. In order to grant permission to all code to use these permissions (probably not the usual approach), type nothing in either text field and click Add Permission.
3. Choose permissions to grant. Click Permission, and then select `FilePermission`. You can either choose Target Name and type a specific filename in the field to the right or choose All Files. Click All Files.

314 Chapter 16: Java Security

> **NOTE**
>
> Although it's less common than using SDK-defined permissions such as `ReflectPermission`, it is possible to create your own `Permission` object by subclassing `java.security.Permission` and coding your own `implies()` method.

4. Permissions often (but not always) have actions associated with them. `FilePermission` has several actions. Click the Actions list box, as shown in Figure 16.3, and select the last choice, read, write, delete, execute. Then click OK.

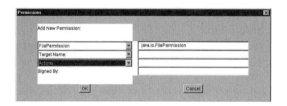

Figure 16.3

The Add New Permission dialog box.

5. Repeat this cycle to grant a `Runtimepermission` to `queuePrintJob`.
6. Click Done.
7. Ignore the error that the signer does not have keys yet.
8. Save the file in a directory. I am putting it in `C:\Purejava\source\chap16\custom.jp`. You will not be prompted to save the file. You need to explicitly select the File menu and then choose Save.
   The suffix `jp` is not required, but I think it is helpful to identify this as a Java policy file.
9. Exit the policy file.

Now that we have the policy file, we need to sign some code.

Sample Code for Digital Signing

First you need code to sign. Listing 16.1 shows a short program that I am going to sign with a digital signature.

Listing 16.1 Basic Application to Sign Digitally (PrivilegeDriver.java)
```
// This program has little in the way of security-related code.
// The program's purpose is to provide code that will need more permissions
// than the default java.policy file grants so that you can't run this
// program successfully without granting it additional permissions.
import java.io.*;

class PrivilegedFileAccessor
    {
    private FileWriter fw;
```

```
private PrintWriter pw;
private File textFile;
private FileReader fr;
private BufferedReader br;
private String[] books = { "Rhetorica by Aristotle",
                "Against Apion by Josephus",
                "4QMMT author unknown",
                "Peloponesian War by Thucydides"};


public PrivilegedFileAccessor()
    {
      try
         {
           // Attempt some normally restricted actions.
           // Without proper permissions, these
           // constructors will throw security exceptions.
           // You should NOT catch SecurityException.
           textFile = new File("AncientTexts.txt");
           fw = new FileWriter(textFile);
           pw = new PrintWriter(fw);
           // This code attempts to create
           // a File object, a FileWriter object,
           // and a PrintWriter object.
           // Under the default permissions,
           // this will not be allowed.
         }
      catch(IOException e)
           // Catch any IOExceptions that occur.
           // Never catch Security-related exceptions.
           {
            System.out.println("Cannot create file because of " +
                          e.toString());
           }
    }

  public void writeOutput()
    {
      for (int i=0; i< books.length; i++)
         {
          pw.println(books[i]);
          // Write out the books to a file
          // using a PrintWriter.
         }
      pw.flush();
      pw.close();
      // Flush the buffer to force everything to disk
      // and close the writer.
    }
```

continues

Listing 16.1 continued

```java
    public void readInput()
        {
        try
            {
            fr = new FileReader(textFile);
            // Attempt to open a reader on the file.
            br = new BufferedReader(fr);
            // Wrap the FileReader in a BufferedReader
            // for much easier and more efficient I/O.
            for(int i =0; i < books.length; i++)
                {
                String line = br.readLine();
                System.out.println(line);
                // Read a line from the file and
                // print it on standard out.
                }
            }
        catch(IOException e)
            {
            System.out.println("Read failed because of " + e.toString());
            }
        }

    } // End class definition PrivilegedFileAccessor.

public class PrivilegeDriver
    {

    public static void main(String args[])
        {
        System.setSecurityManager(new SecurityManager());
        // Install a SecurityManager object.
        // Java 2 will require a policy file or
        // you will not be permitted to run this
        // but will instead get a security exception.
        PrivilegedFileAccessor pfa = new PrivilegedFileAccessor();
        pfa.writeOutput();
        pfa.readInput();
        System.exit(0);
        }
    }
```

This same program with different class names appears in Chapter 12, "I/O in Java." The real difference between the two versions is the single line of code I added to `main`:

```java
System.setSecurityManager(new SecurityManager());
```

This installs a `SecurityManager` object in the JVM running this program. Because the default policy file does not grant permission to do reads or writes to files, this code will fail. Here's the output from simply executing like this:

```
java PrivilegeDriver
Exception in thread "main" java.security.AccessControlException: access denied
java.io.FilePermission AncientTexts.txt write)
        at java.security.AccessControlContext.checkPermission(AccessControlC
        xt.java:195)
        at java.security.AccessController.checkPermission(AccessController.j
        403)
        at java.lang.SecurityManager.checkPermission(SecurityManager.java:54)
        at java.lang.SecurityManager.checkWrite(SecurityManager.java:958)
        at java.io.FileOutputStream.<init>(FileOutputStream.java:96)
        at java.io.FileOutputStream.<init>(FileOutputStream.java:62)
        at java.io.FileOutputStream.<init>(FileOutputStream.java:132)
        at java.io.FileWriter.<init>(FileWriter.java:43)
        at PrivilegedFileAccessor.<init>(PrivilegeDriver.java:26)
        at PrivilegeDriver.main(PrivilegeDriver.java:75)
```

This is unacceptable, because we want this program to be able to read and write files, even if it still restricted in other ways. So we will use the policy file created earlier to run the code:

```
java -Djava.security.policy=custom.jp PrivilegeDriver
```

This time the correct output is printed on the console:

```
Rhetorica by Aristotle
Against Apion by Josephus
4QMMT author unknown
Peloponesian War by Thucydides
```

In case you have trouble making this work, here is a list of the contents of `custom.jp` that does work:

```
/* AUTOMATICALLY GENERATED ON Mon Sep 06 20:48:07 PDT 1999*/
/* DO NOT EDIT */

grant {
  permission java.io.FilePermission "<<ALL FILES>>", "read, write, delete,
  ↪execute";
  permission java.lang.RuntimePermission "queuePrintJob";
};
```

> **TIP**
>
> If you want to check for a given permission, you can call
>
> `AccessController.checkPermission(some permission object);`
>
> The method accepts a `java.security.Permission` object that you construct on-the-fly. You might do this if you wanted to know what was allowed by the JVM before attempting it and getting an exception. You might then inform the user that a permission is lacking, which prevents you from doing what your program is supposed to do.

Procedure for Digitally Signing Code

A digital signature is intended to provide some measure of confidence for the end user that code will not do bad things, based on the user's trust in the code signer. For example, if you get an applet signed by me and you trust me, you will be more likely to let that code run with extra permissions than you would unsigned code from an anonymous source. Of course, my electronic signature, which is produced with my private encryption key, could be forged. That is, someone else could sign some code and claim that it is from me. To deal with this, digital certificates are used to validate that a given signature is from the alleged source. You can generate your own certificates, which makes sense in an intranet situation, but you may prefer to go through a certificate authority for an Internet-wide application.

A third party who verifies signatures and issues certificates to authenticate those signatures is called a *certificate authority*, or CA. You go to the CA and ask for a certificate, providing your digital signature. The CA, in exchange for payment, issues you a digital certificate that includes your signature and public key. The certificate is signed by the CA. Netscape includes a certificate for Verisign, the most well-known CA (http://www.verisign.com). This certificate is used to verify the CA's signature.

The certificates generated by a CA are of differing values. It is possible to get a certificate for a fairly small amount, such as $10, using your email address as the validation to prove to the CA that your signature actually belongs to you. That's not worth much on the Internet because you can supply any email address you want. On the other hand, you can get a very expensive and very valuable digital certificate. In that case, the CA might send someone to your office to go through financial records and interview other people to verify that you are who you say you are.

This section is concerned with the Java 2 tools for signing code:

- jarsigner—For signing jar files
- keytool—For managing keys and certificates

You can actually verify a digital signature in Java in three ways. You can use

- jarsigner
- APIs in your code
- Permissions in a policy file that are granted to a specific signer or set of signers

The certificate that provides verification of a digital signature can be stored in the `keystore` database on a host. You can retrieve a certificate from the `keystore` using

`keytool -export`

You can also add a certificate from someone else to your `keystore` using

`keytool -import`

A `keystore` database may contain both trusted certificates and key/certificate pairs, which consist of the private key and the public key certificate. A *key* is essentially a random bit-pattern used for hashing or encrypting data. Keys should be totally random, but in practice they are pseudo-random. Many algorithms exist to make them more random, but that is beyond the scope of this book.

The `keytool` can generate private keys and matching public key certificates, import certificates to the `keystore`, export certificates from the `keystore`, and manage your `keystore`. `keystore` is password-protected.

A key is essentially a binary value used to encrypt or decrypt data. The exact method that is used with the key to encrypt or decrypt data depends on the encryption algorithm used. There are several algorithms, such as Blowfish, in use. The best algorithms are published so that encryption experts can look for holes in the algorithms that wold allow a hacker to break the key's code easily. It is essential that keys be kept secret. If you obtain my keys, you can decrypt confidential data I've encrypted or encrypt data, pretending to be me.

Keys come in two flavors: symmetric and asymmetric. Asymmetric keys require much more processing but are much more secure. Typically, data encrypted with tools such as SSL uses symmetric keys. Keys can be public or private. I use my private key to encrypt data for you. You use my public key to decrypt it. You can use my public key to encrypt data, and that encrypted data can only be decrypted using my private key.

Several steps are required in the code-signing process—some by a developer, and some by a user of the developer's code. Here are the steps:

1. Put the class file(s) for your application or applet into a jar file. A jar file, discussed more in Chapter 19, "Utility Classes," is similar to a zip file but is platform-neutral. Java provides support to put files into a jar file and then extract them again. To create a jar file containing our `PrivilegeDriver.java` file, type the following on the command line:
   `jar cf Driver.jar *.class`

   You can put any kind of resource that is intelligible to Java in a jar file. Here we are putting only `.class` files into the jar file.
2. Assuming that you do not already have a private key, you use `keytool` to generate a private key to use in signing code and a public key for others to use in verifying your signature.

Type the following on the command line (you would change the values for your own application in real life):

```
keytool -genkey -alias JavaMaster -keypass javam123
 -keystore purejava -storepass purej123
```

This is all typed as one command on one line. After you press Enter at the end of this command, you will be asked several questions. These values are placed inside the certificate generated by this command. The more unique and unpredictable your answers, the harder your private key will be for an attacker to compute. This command has several parts:

- `genkey`—What you want to do—namely, generate a key pair.
- `alias`—A name, usually for a role in your organization. This is the name used in the policy file for a code signer.
- `keypass`—A password for the private key you are creating. This password must be used when accessing the `keystore` for this private key.
- `keystore`—The name of the `keystore` database you want to use.
- `storepass`—The password for the `keystore` database you are creating.

TIP

For greater security when generating keys, do not use the `keypass` or `storepass` option. Instead, allow the keytool to prompt you for a password when you access `keystore`.

When the command completes successfully, it generates a public/private key pair for you and a self-signed certificate that contains the public key and the data values you entered.

3. Now that you have a key pair and a certificate, you can sign your jar file by typing this:

```
jarsigner -keystore purejava -signedjar signedDriver.jar Driver.jar
 JavaMaster
```

Press Enter. You will be prompted for the key and `keystore` passwords.

CAUTION

When you do this, the passwords you are prompted for show up as clear text on the screen. So be sure that you do not type this in easy view of others and that you do not leave it on a screen others can readily see if you step away momentarily. Otherwise, your passwords may be compromised, and with them the whole point of signing code.

4. Now you export the self-signed certificate. To allow someone else to use your signed code, the other person needs a copy of your certificate. To get a certificate to send to that individual, type this at the command line:

```
keytool -export -keystore purejava -alias JavaMaster -file JavaMaster.cer
```

You will be prompted for the `keystore` password. Once again, when you type it, the password will appear in plain text on the screen.

All of these actions are performed by the developer. The next few steps need to be performed by the user who wants to execute your program.

5. Import the certificate as a trusted certificate into the user's keystore. So far, there is only a keystore for the developer. In this step I will create a second keystore in the same directory to show you how this is done. If you import to a keystore that does exist, the keytool will create a keystore by that name for you and import the certificate as a trusted certificate into the new keystore. Type this command:

```
keytool -import -alias User -file JavaMaster.cer -keystore userstore
```

In this version of the command, no password is supplied, so you will be prompted for one. I will use user123. The keytool tool will print out the certificate information and ask you to verify that this should be a trusted certificate. Type yes. Here's what appears on my screen:

```
C:\Purejava\Source\chap16>keytool -import -alias User -file
➥JavaMaster.cer -key
store Userstore
Enter keystore password:  user123
Owner: CN=Ken Litwak, OU=Sun, O=SunEd, L=Milpitas, ST=CA, C=US
Issuer: CN=Ken Litwak, OU=Sun, O=SunEd, L=Milpitas, ST=CA, C=US
Serial number: 37d4a303
Valid from: Mon Sep 06 22:30:43 PDT 1999 until: Sun Dec 05 21:30:43 PST
➥1999
Certificate fingerprints:
        MD5:  5D:59:57:10:7B:BC:0F:E5:D7:F7:52:21:28:09:14:C9
        SHA1: A4:FF:6F:2B:EE:D4:26:2D:26:88:BC:98:87:A7:FB:7E:D3:2F:
            ➥1B:42
Trust this certificate? [no]:  yes
Certificate was added to keystore
```

In a real application, you would likely compare the "fingerprints" in the certificate to the fingerprints supplied from some other trusted source. If they match, the certificate has not been altered. If the fingerprints do not match, you should not trust this certificate. If the JavaMaster needs to obtain the fingerprints so that they can be compared with those on the certificate the user got, the JavaMaster could type

```
keytool -printcert -file JavaMaster.cer
```

6. The next step is to set up a policy file based on the code signer's signature and certificate. Acting as the recipient of signed code and the certificate, you need to create a policy file that specifies the code signer and the keystore.

CAUTION

The default expiration period for a certificate is 90 days. Unless the person who generated the certificate modified this, you may need to get a new certificate to use signed code periodically.

322 Chapter 16: Java Security

Once again, start the policy tool program by typing
`policytool`

On the initial screen, you can see the familiar text fields for the policy file and `keystore`. This time, fill in the `keystore` with the name `Userstore`. Be sure you start the policy tool in the directory that contains this `keystore` database. To do this, choose Change Keystore from the main Edit menu. In the text field for the `keystore`, type the URL for the `keystore`, like so:
`file:/C:/purejava/source/chap16/Userstore`

This will likely be different on your system. The `keystore` type is the same as the default, so leave this text field blank. Figure 16.4 shows the policy tool screen for entering the keystore.

Figure 16.4

Creating a policy file that uses a keystore for signed code.

CAUTION

The `keystore` location is specified with a URL, so make sure you use forward slashes (/) even if you are working in Windows, where you would expect to use \ to specify a path.

Now click OK to accept this `keystore`.
Now click Add Policy Entry. Here you will specify that you are granting permission to code signed by JavaMaster. That is, you are granting permissions to code that resides in a jar file signed by JavaMaster.

Figure 16.5 shows the dialog to add the `FilePermission` to the policy file. Now, as you did before, choose `FilePermission` and grant the right to read, write, delete, and execute on all files, as shown in Figure 16.6.

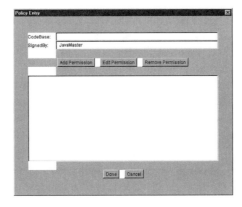

Figure 16.5

Adding a code signer to a policy entry.

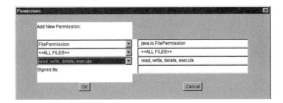

Figure 16.6

Granting FilePermissions.

Click Done and then OK. Choose Save As from the File menu and type the name `Userpolicy.jp`.

7. Now execute the program with the new policy file:
   ```
   java -Djava.security.policy=Userpolicy.jp -cp signedDriver.jar
   ➥PrivilegeDriver
   ```
   This executes the `PrivilegeDriver` class's main method from the `PrivilegeDriver.class` file in the `signedDriver.jar` file. You use the `cp` option to specify the classpath of the class file, which in this case is the jar file `signedDriver.jar`.

   If you have typed everything correctly, the program should run, just as in the first version earlier in this chapter. If not, you should go through the steps again and verify that you typed everything exactly as shown here, except that you may need to change paths.

Creating Custom Permissions

You have seen how to create a policy file that uses predefined permissions. It may be the case, however, that your application needs to define its own permissions. This is easy to do in Java.

User-Defined Permission Code Example

You can check to see if a specific permission has been granted to your code by creating a Permission object of that type, such as a FilePermission object. Then you can check for that permission using the checkPermission() method of the AccessController class. This method does not return a value. If you have the permission, the method simply completes. If you do not have the permission, or if the values specified in the permission object that is the parameter to the checkPermission method are incorrect or invalid, you will get an AccessControlException.

In order to create a permission, you need to define a class for the permission that subclasses java.security.Permission or java.security.BasicPermission. The difference between these two is that BasicPermission is for simple permissions that require only a name, whereas Permission requires a constructor that accepts both a name and an action. You also must override the implies() method of the Permission class in your subclass, but this is often unnecessary if you subclass BasicPermission. To use this permission class, you need to grant the permission in a policy file. Listing 16.2 uses the policy file Book.jp.

Listing 16.2 shows how to check for a given permission and how to create and use your own permission.

Listing 16.2   User-Defined Permissions (PermissionDriver.java, Book.jp)

```
import java.io.*;
import java.security.*;

class PermMaker
	{
	public boolean checkPermissions()
		{
		FilePermission filePerm = new java.io.FilePermission
			("<<ALL FILES>>", "execute");
		// Create a FilePermission object that represents execute
		// permission on all files. You can have lots of other
		// possibilities here. Any file or path is acceptable, as
		// well as other actions like "write", "read", and "delete".
		AccessController.checkPermission(filePerm);
		// This will simply return if your program has the permission
		// or throws an AccessControlException if you do not have the
		// permission or if the permission values are incorrect or
		// invalid.
		ReservePermission rp = new ReservePermission("Professor");
		// This same permission must be in a policy file on the user's
		// system.
		// For example, if the program requires a ReservePermission for
		// a professor in order to reserve a book,  then the protection
		// domain will be checked by this method call at runtime to
		// verify that such a permission exists.
		// To test this, run the program both with and without the
		// policy file Book.jp or another policy file which contains
		// the ReservePermission with the name "Professor".
```

Creating Custom Permissions

```java
            return true;  // You won't get here unless you have the
                          // permission.
          }

     public boolean reserveBook(String title)
            {
             // Do logic to reserve a book.
             System.out.println(title +
                                " has been put on three-month reserve");
             return true;
            }
     }  // End class definition for PermMaker.

public class PermissionDriver
     {
      public static void main(String[] args)
            {
             PermMaker pm = new PermMaker();
             boolean result = pm.checkPermissions();
             if(result == true)
                  pm.reserveBook("Paradise Lost");
             System.exit(0);
            }
     }  // End PermissionDriver class.

// Create a Permission subclass that subclasses BasicPermission
// since ReservePermission is a simple permission.
// It is possible to subclass java.security.Permission as
// well if you need actions as well as names in your permission.
class ReservePermission extends java.security.BasicPermission
     {
      String name;
      String action;

      // Although actions are not used by this
      // permission class, you still need to code
      // two constructors, one that accepts actions.

      public ReservePermission(String name)
            {
             super(name);
             // Call the BasicPermission constructor with one parm.
            }

      public ReservePermission(String name, String actions)
            {
             super(name, actions); // Call the parent constructor with
                                   // two parameters.
            }
     }
```

To execute this program and see what happens without the policy file, type

```
java PermissionDriver
```

This will throw an `AccessControlException`. To bypass this exception, type the following on the command line:

```
java -Djava.security.policy=Book.jp
```

Here is the policy file `Book.jp`:

```
/* AUTOMATICALLY GENERATED ON Sun Nov 07 23:15:00 PST 1999*/
/* DO NOT EDIT */

grant {
  permission java.io.FilePermission "<<ALL FILES>>", "execute";
  permission java.io.FilePermission "<<ALL FILES>>", "write";
  permission ReservePermission "Professor";
};
```

I recommend that you experiment with this program and policy file (or a backup copy of them!). See what happens if you remove the `checkPermission` call for `FilePermission` and you run the program without the policy file. This mechanism means that you can write a program that requires your own permissions. If the user does not have those permissions, he or she cannot run your program properly. In this way, you protect assets from improper access by unauthorized users. Here's the output that I get on my system:

```
java -Djava.security.policy=Book.jp PermissionDriver
Paradise Lost has been put on three-month reserve
```

Message Digests

So far, this chapter has been concerned with permissions. The last topic to be covered is totally unrelated to permissions. A *message digest,* which is not unique to Java, is a hash value for a message. More specifically, a message digest is the following:

- A unique binary hash value for a specific message. No two messages will produce the same message digest value.
- A value computed using a message digest algorithm (not covered here)
- A hash value that cannot be used to determine the original message. Actually, it is possible to get the original message from the message digest, but statistically speaking, the sun will burn out before then, so for all practical purposes, it is impossible.

Because a specific message digest will be computed only for a specific message, you can use a message digest to verify that a message sent to you has not been changed.

Be aware, however, that in and of itself, a message digest proves nothing for the text of a message. Consider the following scenario:

1. You create a message and a message digest for it and send it to the head librarian over the Internet, asking the library to buy a certain book.

2. I intercept your message. I change the message to ask the librarian to have the library subscribe to a comic book series. I compute a new message digest value and send the message and digest value to the librarian.
3. The librarian gets the message and the digest. The library's software computes the message digest for the message I sent, and the computed digest matches the digest I sent.
4. The librarian, not having read this chapter, assumes the message is valid because the message digest is valid, and sends you a note, rejecting your goofy request.

The point is that, to make a message digest valid, the sender must keep a copy of the digest that the sender can compare to the digest that the recipient of a message got. This is the only way in which a message digest will be useful.

MessageDigest Code Example

Listing 16.3 shows how to create a `MessageDigest` object and compute a message digest. You'll then need to figure out how you want to send it to the recipient so that the recipient of your message and message digest can compare the digest she got to the one you supplied separately. If they match, you and she know that the message was not tampered with along the way.

Listing 16.3   Creating a MessageDigest (DigestDriver.java)

```
import java.io.*;
import java.security.*;

class DigestMaker
     {
        public boolean buildDigest()
                                throws
java.security.NoSuchAlgorithmException
              {
               MessageDigest md5Digest = MessageDigest.getInstance
➥("MD5");
               // Get an initialized MessageDigest object. Note the use of
               // a factory-type method, getInstance(). Once you have
               // a MessageDigest object, you can use it to compute a digest
               // value.
               // MD5 is a specific message digest algorithm.
               try
                    {
                     File ancientTextFile = new File("AncientTexts.txt");
                     // Get a file on which you can compute a digest.
                     FileInputStream fis =
                     ➥new FileInputStream(ancientTextFile);
                     byte[] message = new byte[ (int)
                     ➥(ancientTextFile.length())];
                     // Create a byte array the size of the message you want
```

continues

Listing 16.3 continued

```
                    // to make a message digest for.
                    fis.read(message);
                    // Read the whole file into the byte array
                    // called message.
                    md5Digest.update(message);
                    // The update method updates the
                    // MessageDigest object with the specified
                    // byte array (the message contents).
                    byte[] theMsgDigest = md5Digest.digest();
                    // Perform the final hash computation and related
                    // operations such as padding.
                    System.out.println("The computed message digest is: " +
                                theMsgDigest);
                    System.out.println("The algorithm used to create the " +
                                            "message digest is ");
                    System.out.println(md5Digest.getAlgorithm());
                     // Display the MessageDigest algorithm
                     // You can make your own MessageDigest with a
                     // different algorithm.
                     // This exception is thrown if the algorithm
                     // in the MessageDigest.getInstance() method
                     // is unknown to the system. You can write your
                     // own algorithms.
                }
                catch(IOException ioe)
                    {
                    // There's a problem with the file.
                    System.out.println(ioe.getMessage());
                     ioe.printStackTrace();
                    }

            return true;
            }

        } // End class definition for DigestDriver.

public class DigestDriver
        {
        public static void main(String[] args)
                    throws java.security.NoSuchAlgorithmException
                // It is rare to put a throws clause in the definition of
                // main, but main is calling a method that could throw
                // this exception. This could also be in a try-catch
                // structure but is done this way to show that it can be done.
            {
              DigestMaker dm = new DigestMaker();
              boolean result = dm.buildDigest();
```

```
            System.exit(0);
        }
   }  // End DigestDriver class.
```

Here is the output on my system:

```
java DigestDriver
The computed message digest is: [B@726f3341
The algorithm used to create the message digest is
MD5
```

After running this, you would send the `AncientTexts.txt` file along with your message digest to someone else, and the recipient could compare his or her message digest value to the version you saved of it. If they match, you know the file was not tampered with in transit.

CHAPTER 17

JDBC: Java Database Programming

Just as Java provides for platform independence, Java provides a mechanism for dealing with databases in a vendor-transparent way. The mechanism for this is Java Database Connectivity (JDBC).

Conceptually, JDBC is loosely based on ODBC, a standard in relational database connectivity published by Microsoft (though originally developed jointly by Microsoft and Sybase). The reason for this similarity is to make JDBC easier to learn. Other than that, there is no connection between JDBC and ODBC.

The support for database programming in Java is found primarily in the java.sql package. If you are unfamiliar with this package, take a quick look at Chapter 31, "java.sql." You will notice something very different about this package from any that we have looked at in earlier chapters. Almost everything defined for this package is a Java interface rather than a class. There are a few classes, but most of the JDBC functionality we are concerned with comes through vendor-implemented classes for the many interfaces in this package.

Chapter 15, "RMI," emphasized the value of using an interface to access the methods of a class that you cannot access directly. Using an interface eases maintenance by making the client completely decoupled and unaware of the class that implements the remote object. In the same way, the use of interfaces in JDBC means that your program is independent of the classes a vendor uses to provide database connectivity and functionality. When you change vendors for your database driver or your database, your code can remain largely unchanged.

> **NOTE**
>
> JDBC will allow you to write very vendor-specific code, such as using Oracle's PL-SQL. In some cases, this might be appropriate because companies, on the whole, do not change database vendors very often (although I know of exceptions). Be aware, however, that being vendor-specific limits the flexibility of your code. JDBC lets you write generic SQL that is not tied to any specific vendor, and I recommend that you strive to do so, unless performance considerations dictate otherwise.

Essentially, a vendor is required to implement all the interfaces in `java.sql`, and your method calls request objects that implement those interfaces.

Creating a Database Connection

You need a database connection to talk to a database system. There are two key elements in a database connection:

- `java.sql.DriverManager`
- A JDBC Driver

It is the responsibility of the `DriverManager` class to maintain a list of instances of JDBC drivers available to a given JVM at runtime. Essentially, this list provides information about the object reference of a driver and the subprotocol, or database type, that it supports. When a program requests a database connection, the `DriverManager` goes through the list, asking each driver if it can process the `getConnection()` request. The search is based on the database URL supplied in the `getConnection()` call, which is discussed later in this chapter. The `DriverManager` tells the first driver that satisfies the caller's request to provide the caller with a connection to the database. The `DriverManager` really doesn't understand the database URL at all. It just gives it to a driver and asks if the driver can deal with the URL properly or not.

A JDBC driver gets itself added to the list maintained by the `DriverManager` using the `registerDriver()` method. Generally, but not always, this method is called inside a driver's static initializer block, which often calls a private constructor and then calls `registerDriver()`. A static initializer, as you may recall from Chapter 4, "Data Types," provides code outside the scope of a method. This code is called as soon as the class definition is loaded by the `classLoader`. A Java program does not generally expressly call the constructor of a JDBC driver. After the driver is registered, it is ready to use.

> **CAUTION**
>
> DriverManager calls the first suitable driver in its list to provide a connection. Therefore, if you have multiple drivers loaded, any of which can satisfy a given connection request, be sure that they are in preferential order. You can do this either by loading the driver classes in the order you want to use them or by using the jdbc.drivers system property on the command line:
> `java -Djdbc.drivers=driver1, driver2, driver3`

Here are the steps to create a database connection:

1. Load the database driver.

Creating a Database Connection

2. Request a connection using an appropriate database URL.

For example, you might code this:

```
Class.forName("MyDriver.class");
Connection conn = DriverManager.getConnection(dbURL);
```

The `forName()` method of the class `Class` causes the named class to be loaded, whether it is a database driver or something else. For a JDBC driver, this call results in the driver's class being loaded. The driver's class also instantiates and registers itself with the `DriverManager` class.

The `DriverManager.getConnection()` method shows the power of Java interfaces. This method's return type is `Connection`. A `Connection`, however, is not a class but an interface. This means that the code is asking for an object, any object whatsoever, as long as it implements the `Connection` interface. This method frees your code from having to know anything about how the vendor implements the class that implements the `Connection` interface. You don't care. All you care about is getting a database connection object back. An interface can free you from being tightly coupled to a given class. In this code, I can change the driver class or the implementation of the `Connection` interface, and the caller never knows the difference. No changes are needed to the client code.

If the `classLoader` cannot find the driver class, you will get a `ClassNotFoundException`. In this case, check your import statements to be sure that you are pointing to the correct package for the driver. If the `getConnection()` method fails, you will get a `SQLException`.

After you have a connection, you can go on to get `Statement` objects, run queries, update tables, and the like. The key to getting the right connection is the database URL. Here is a string that specifies this:

protocol:subprotocol:other parameters

For example, you might have

`jdbc:sybase:U=Me,P=newpass,S=Doghouse`

The protocol should be `jdbc`. The subprotocol identifies the database type. This could be `oracle`, `sybase`, `msql`, `jdbc:odbc`, and so forth. The parameters following the second colon are optional and depend on the specific driver's requirements. They often consist of user ID, password, and host name.

> **TIP**
>
> Database connections are fairly expensive to create, so many enterprise-level applications create *connection pools* in which many connection objects live for use by clients. If a connection requires a user ID and password, it is customary to have the DBA set up roles rather than specific users in the database system. Then, a real user ID is matched in the second tier to a role, and a connection for that type of role is given to the client to use.

NOTE

Many relational database systems might be used here. To enable the greatest number of readers to access the same system, the examples use *InstantDB*, a 100% pure Java RDBMS, available from www.instantdb.co.uk. The code, however, except for the driver, is generic and should work with any RDBMS.

When you run the code with a different RDBMS and driver, a problem might occur, because InstantDB does not like a semicolon at the end of statements. Although many JDBC programs commonly use the semicolon, it is not mandated by the SQL standard or the JDBC standard. If your system complains about how statements end, try putting a semicolon at the end of the SQL statement itself (not the Java statement).

TIP

Java does not parse SQL code when it compiles it. All that Java does is check that you have a valid string. If you want to have the SQL parsed before you try executing it, use SQLJ, standardized by Oracle. SQLJ first parses and validates your SQL and then wraps it in JDBC code that you can put in any program.

Listing 17.1 shows a simple JDBC program that illustrates the basic steps you need to take in your program:

1. Create a database URL.
2. Load the driver. (Any decent driver instantiates and registers itself with DriverManager).
3. Get a database connection.
4. Create a `Statement/PreparedStatement/CallableStatement`.
5. Use the statement to execute SQL (or other kinds of statements the database driver and database understand).

TIP

Many legacy systems have IMS databases. An IMS database, developed by IBM, is hierarchical and does not understand SQL. There is now, however, a JDBC driver that works with IMS. It lets you call IMS directly from a JDBC statement, just as you would do from a C or COBOL program.

Database Connection and Table Creation: Code Example

In order to access a database system, you must connect to it. In order for you to work on data, it must be in a table. Hence, Listing 17.1 shows you how to get a connection to an RDBMS and then shows you how to use DDL in JDBC to create a table. The program then shows you how to use the SQL Insert statement through JDBC to insert data into a table.

Listing 17.1   Database Connection Example Using JDBC (DBDriver1.java)

```java
import java.sql.*;  //Import all the JDBC classes.
// The following imports are just for InstantDB.
import jdbc.idbDriver;
import jdbc.*;
import java.net.URL;
import java.io.*;
import java.util.*;

class TableMaker
    {
       Connection con=null;
       Statement stmt;

          public boolean createCatalog()
              {
              boolean result = true;
              String dbURL =
                 "jdbc:idb:c:\\purejava\\source\\chap17\\purejava.prp";
              // The format of this URL is dictated in part
              // by Java and in part by InstantDB.
              // Protocol:  jdbc
              // Sub-protcol:  idb
              // Driver-specific part:  location of properties file
              // used by InstantDB.
              // The dbURL generally tells Java
              // the database the driver is for, the user id
              // and password, the database and the host the
              // database resides on.
              try
                  {
                    // Enable DriverManager logging.
                   DriverManager.setLogStream(System.out);
                     // Print DriverManager info to the console.
                     // This is deprecated but useful.
                     Class.forName("jdbc.idbDriver");
                     // Load the JDBC driver class into
                     // memory. The driver instantiates itself
                     // and registers itself with DriverManager.
                     con = DriverManager.getConnection (dbURL);
                     // Get a database connection from the
                     // appropriate driver.
                  }
              catch (Exception e)
                  {
                   System.out.println("Failed to
                       load jdbc.idbDriver driver.");
                   result = false;
                  }
```

continues

Listing 17.1 continued

```
            // Catch all Exceptions.  You could optionally
            // catch specific Exceptions including SQLException.
            try
                 {
                   stmt = con.createStatement();
                   // Now that you have a Connection, create
                   // a Statement object so you can send
                   // SQL calls to the JDBC driver.
                 }
            catch (SQLException e)
                 {
                   System.err.println("problems connecting to "
                       + dbURL);
                   result = false;
                 }

              try
                 {
                   // Execute SQL commands to create table,
                   // and insert data.
                   // The Statement method execute() is used
                   // for DDL and CallableStatements.
                   // The method executeUpdate() is for
                   // insert, update, and delete.
                   stmt.execute("DROP TABLE BookCatalog");
                   stmt.execute("CREATE TABLE BookCatalog ("+
                        "CallNumber char(4) PRIMARY KEY NOT NULL," +
                     // Not a realistic call number.
                        "Author char (30),"+
                        "Title varchar(60),"+
                        "Notes varchar(60)," +
                        "Copies int)");
                   stmt.executeUpdate(
                        "INSERT INTO BookCatalog " +
                             "values ('Lew1', 'Lewis, C.S.'," +
                             "'Till We Have Faces','Fiction', 3)");
                   stmt.executeUpdate(
                      "INSERT INTO BookCatalog " +
                           "values ('Col1', 'Colson, Charles',"
                           "'How Now Shall We Live?'," +
                           "'Non-Fiction. Contemporary Issues', 4)");
                    stmt.executeUpdate(
                        "INSERT INTO BookCatalog " +
                             "values ('Mid1', 'Middleton, J. Richard',"+
                             "'Truth is Stranger than It Used to Be'," +
                             "'Non-Fiction. Postmodernism', 4)");
```

Creating a Database Connection 337

```
                    stmt.executeUpdate(
                        "INSERT INTO BookCatalog " +
                            "values ('Lew2', 'Lewis, C.S.'," +
                            "'Out of the Silent Planet', null, 2)");

              con.close();
            }
      catch (Exception e)
            {
              System.err.println("problems with SQL sent to "+ dbURL+
                    ": "+e.getMessage());
              result = false;
            }
          return result;
        }

   } // End class definition for TableMaker.

public class DBDriver1
    {
      public static void main(String[] args)
            {
              TableMaker tm = new TableMaker();
              tm.createCatalog();
              System. exit(0);
            }
    }
```

> **CAUTION**
>
> You must be sure, if you decide to use InstantDB, to set up the properties file correctly. See the following setup notes for more information.

The properties file provided with the examples is called PureJava.PRP. The main part you might have to change, depending on your system, includes these lines:

```
!relativeToProperties=1
tablePath=c:\\instantdb\\tables
tmpPath=c:\\instantdb\\tmp
systemPath=c:\\instantdb\\system
indexPath=c:\\instantdb\\index
```

These statements need to be changed to reflect your directory structure if it is not as shown. I created an instantdb directory on my C: drive under Win98. Whether you put it there, or under /export/software/instantdb, is not important. What is important is that the properties file has the correct paths in it.

Your classpath must also include

```
c:\instantDB\Classes\idb.jar;c:\instantDB\Classes\idbf.jar;c:\
instantDB\Classes\idbexmpl.jar
```

In addition, you will probably need to change this line in the program

```
String dbURL ="jdbc:idb:c:\\purejava\\source\\chap17\\purejava.prp";
```

to match your directory structure. Since this is the structure I used for testing, and the directory structure will doubtless be different for the site you download the code from, you will most certainly need to change this.

> **NOTE**
>
> If you encounter trouble, check the documentation that comes with InstantDB, especially the `install.htm` file. If you continue to have difficulties, you may want to contact the makers of InstantDB (http://www.instantdb.co.uk/).
>
> I got this to work on my system in about 30 minutes. If you already have another RDBMS, you might want to use that instead.

> **CAUTION**
>
> If you have something like Microsoft Access, you should not use that for the examples here. Access is far too feature-poor to be useful for learning most JDBC features. For example, Access can't do prepared statements. The same can be said of MiniSql.

This program drops the `BookCatalog` table (if it exists). Depending on your RDBMS, this might be a problem if the table doesn't exist yet. In this case, you should remove the statement and then recompile the program before running it again. The program then creates a table to hold book information and inserts four rows into the table.

> **NOTE**
>
> This chapter assumes that you understand the basics of RDBMSs and SQL. If you do not know SQL, there are many books on the subject, such as the *Practical SQL Handbook*.

The most common SQL statement you might see in a program is `Select`, which is used to retrieve one or more rows from a table in an RDBMS. A *row* is a record that consists of one or more columns, or discrete values. When you execute a select statement, you get back a `ResultSet` object. Like `Driver`, `Connection`, and `Statement`, `ResultSet` is an interface. Your code knows nothing about the class that implements the `ResultSet`.

> **NOTE**
>
> You cannot pass a `ResultSet` object from, for example, the tier-two program that owns the connection to a tier-one client. The problem is that the `ResultSet` is valid only in the context in which it is created. What's more, the tier-one program receiving the `ResultSet` doesn't know the class of the `ResultSet` implementation. That means it can't actually map the object. If you need to pass a `ResultSet`,

you must define a class that maps to the columns of the `ResultSet`, filling in objects of that class with information from successive rows of the `ResultSet`. You then store these objects in another object. This is frequently done using a `Vector`, an array built from a `Vector`, or some other `Collection` object, such as a `TreeMap`. You pass this collection to the tier-one client.

A `ResultSet` represents rows and columns. You step through the rows of the `ResultSet` with the `next()` method. You obtain the values of each column with a `getxxx()` method, where *xxx* refers to a specific Java datatype, like `int`, `float`, `String` or `Object`. The `java.sql.ResultSet` definition lists several `getxxx()` methods to choose from. You pick the one that maps the SQL data type correctly to the Java datatype. Don't try to use `getFloat()` and put its value in an `int`.

Suppose that you want to examine the contents of a `ResultSet` but do not know the schema of the table it came from. You can do this successfully using `ResultSetMetadata`, another interface in `java.sql`. After you have obtained a `ResultSet`, you can get `ResultSetMetaData` by coding

```
ResultSet rs = stmt.executeQuery("select * from Employee");
ResultSetMetadata rsmd = rs.getMetadata();
```

After you've got the `ResultSetMetaData`, you can create a report that prints out the contents of the table. The `ResultSetMetadata` object can tell you how many columns there are, what the names of the columns are, the data type of each column, the size of each column name, and so forth. You can then use this information to access each column of each row to get its data. The `getxxx()` methods allow you to specify either a column number or column name to access a given column.

You can access the columns in any order, but it is best to access them in a left-to-right fashion. I recommend that you only use the column name to access a column in a `getxxx()` method. The reason is that some RDBMSs allow you to drop a column. That can mean, for example, that what was column 4 becomes column 3. If you use column numbers to access data, you might end up printing a report based on hardcoded column numbers that displays job title where gender used to be. When you use column names, if a column is dropped, you get a `SQLException`. The exception is inconvenient, but it prevents you from using incorrect data.

Prior to JDBC 2.0, which is part of Java 2, you could only go forward in a `ResultSet`. That is, you called `next()` to get to the first row, and then `next()` to get to each successive row until you reached the end of the `ResultSet`. When you got to the end of the `ResultSet`, that was it. You could not go backwards. Also, if you used the same `ResultSet` object reference again, the first `ResultSet`, as you might imagine, was destroyed. A small but growing number of JDBC drivers support JDBC 2.0. I'll say more about this later, but for right now, the examples assume the JDBC 1.0 type of `ResultSet`.

> **NOTE**
>
> Most of the new JDBC 2.0 features are in interfaces specified in `javax.sql`. They are considered standard extensions that a JVM vendor can choose to implement or not implement. Therefore, it's safer, as of September 1999, to use the approach that is sure to work with any JDBC driver. This includes treating `ResultSets` as a read-once set of rows.

JDBC supports three types of SQL statements (although your driver might not support all three):

- Dynamic statements
- Prepared statements
- Callable statements

Before I explain each of these and show you how to use them in a Java program, let's look at how a SQL statement is treated. The Java program passes the SQL statement as a string to the JDBC driver. The JDBC driver, after some processing (which varies with the driver and the driver type), sends the SQL statement on to the database engine. At the database engine, the statement is parsed, compiled, and optimized. The output of this process is a *query plan,* which describes how the database engine will actually go about getting the requested data.

Several factors go into the contents of the query plan, such as whether useful indexes exist for the table, the database engine's own capabilities (such as DB2/MVS's sequential pre-fetch capability), and other factors. This query plan is then cached, either in the database engine or the driver instance. This is all invisible to the Java program, except that the process takes time that affects the performance of the Java program.

The premise of a `PreparedStatement` in Java, just as for a prepared statement in SQL, is that, if you need to execute the same statement over and over—changing only parameter values, you shouldn't be required to go through the parse-compile-optimize cycle over and over. Instead, a `PreparedStatement` is parsed, compiled, optimized and has a query plan generated for it just once.

Here's an example. In a Customer table, you have a list of customer names whose data needs to be changed to show that these customers get a discount on shipping. You use the customer name to find the customer's row, and then you update the shipping charges percentage column. You might issue 10,000 update statements, each one being parsed, compiled, and optimized. With a `PreparedStatement`, however, you only need to *prepare* the statement once. That action parses, compiles, and optimizes the statement, and it also generates the statement's query plan.

Now, each time you want to use the `PreparedStatement` that contains the SQL update statement, you use only the `setxxx()` methods to change the value of the customer name and submit the statement. In general, you should find the performance of `PreparedStatements` superior to dynamic statements, which must be complied every single time.

> **CAUTION**
>
> Not all databases systems support `PreparedStatements`. Some lightweight databases, such as Microsoft Access, do not understand `PreparedStatements`. MiniSql also does not understand a `PreparedStatement`. If your RDBMS does not know how to use a `PreparedStatement`, I advise you to get a real database engine. Always verify that both your RDBMS and your JDBC driver can handle `PreparedStatements`. If you attempt to use a `PreparedStatement` on a driver or RDBMS that does not understand a `PreparedStatement`, a `SQLException` will be thrown.

A `CallableStatement` is Java's mechanism for handling a stored procedure. A stored procedure is generally one or more SQL statements stored as one function in a compiled form inside a database engine. You simply call the stored procedure as you call a method. As in a `PreparedStatement`, you use question marks (?) to specify the position of parameters are replacing. Because stored procedures vary in how a vendor implements them or how you call them, they will be the least-portable kind of statement across RDBMSs.

> **NOTE**
>
> Although the SQL 1992 standard permits stored procedures to take parameters of types `in`, `out`, and `inout`, Java only allows types `in` and `out`. You must call a special method, `registerOutParameter()` to use a parameter of type `out`, because it is contrary to the way Java normally passes parameters or processes parameters.

ResultSet and ResultSetMetadata: Code Example

JDBC provides interfaces for both the `ResultSet`, that contains the rows you retrieved from the database, and for `ResultSetMetadata`, which describes the `ResultSet`. The metadata can be used to find out several pieces of information about the rows you got back, such as how many columns there are, the data type of each column, and the name of each column. In fact, you could use this data to query a table you knew nothing about and create a report showing column names and displaying the contents of the rows without ever having seen the table schema (the definition for the table).

Listing 17.2 shows how to obtain and process a `ResultSet` including `ResultSetMetadata`.

Listing 17.2 Example of Processing a ResultSet with next() and get Methods (DBDriver2.java)

```
import java.sql.*;   //Import all the JDBC classes.
// The following imports are just for InstantDB.
import jdbc.idbDriver;
import jdbc.*;
import java.net.URL;
import java.io.*;
import java.util.*;

class TableReader
```

continues

Listing 17.2   continued

```java
{
    Connection con=null;
    Statement stmt;

    public boolean readTable()
        {
        boolean result = true;
        String dbURL =
        ➥"jdbc:idb:c:\\purejava\\source\\chap17\\purejava.prp";
        // The format of this URL is dictated in part by
        // Java and in part by InstantDB.
        // Protocol:  jdbc
        // Subprotcol:  idb
        // Driver-specific part: location of properties file
        // used by InstantDB.
        try
            {

            // Print DriverManager info to the console
            // This is deprecated but useful.
            Class.forName("jdbc.idbDriver");
            // Load the JDBC driver class into
            // memory. The driver instantiates itself
            // and registers itself with DriverManager.
            con = DriverManager.getConnection (dbURL);
            // Get a database connection from the
            // appropriate driver.
            }
        catch (Exception e)
            {
            // ClassNotFoundException if the
            // classloader can't find your driver class.
            // SQLException if you simply couldn't
            // connect. In the first case,
            // check your classpath.
            // In the second case, validate
            // the contents of the database URL
            // (and for InstantDB the properties file too).
            System.out.println
            ➥("Failed to load jdbc.idbDriver driver.");
            result = false;
            }
        try
            {
            stmt = con.createStatement();
            // Now that you have a Connection, create
            // a Statement object so you can send
            // SQL calls to the JDBC driver.
```

```
            }
    catch (SQLException e)
        {
         System.err.println("problems connecting to "
             + dbURL);
         result = false;
        }

     try
        {
         // Retrieve all the rows from the table with
         // a ResultSet and print the contents of
         // the ResultSet.
         ResultSet rs = stmt.executeQuery(
              "SELECT * from BookCatalog");
         // Get the metadata.
         // You must have a ResultSet object
         // to get a ResultSet.
         ResultSetMetaData rsmd = rs.getMetaData();
         System.out.println("Column Number" +
                 "\tColumn Name" +
                 "\t\t Column Type");
         for(int i = 1; i <= rsmd. getColumnCount(); i++)
             {
              System.out.println(i +"\t\t" +
                          rsmd.getColumnName(i) +
                          "\t\t\t" +
                          rsmd.getColumnTypeName(i));
             }
         // getColumnCount() returns the number of columns.
         // getColumnName() returns the name of the column.
         // getColumnTypeName() returns the SQL column.
         // type by name
         System.out.println("Call #" + "\tAuthor" +
              "\t\tTitle" +
              "\tNotes" + "\tCopies");
         while(rs.next() == true)
             {
              System.out.print(rs.getString("CallNumber"));
              System.out.print("\t" + rs.getString("Author"));
              System.out.print("\t" + rs.getString("Title"));
              System.out.print("\t" + rs.getString("Notes"));
              System.out.println("\t" +
              ⇒rs.getString ("Copies"));
             }
```

continues

Listing 17.2 continued

```
                con.close();
            }
        catch (Exception e)
            {
                System.err.println("problems with SQL sent to "+ dbURL+
                    ": "+e.getMessage());
                result = false;
            }
        return result;
        }

}    // End class definition for TableMaker.

public class DBDriver2
    {
        public static void main(String[] args)
            {
                TableReader tr = new TableReader();
                tr.readTable();
                System.exit(0);
            }
    }
```

As this example shows, you use a `ResultSet` object, meaning an object that implements the `ResultSet` interface, to get the rows back from the SQL query that uses Select. Before the program interrogates the `ResultSet` contents, it creates a `ResultSetMetaData` object and prints some basic information from a `ResultSet`. This code gets the count of columns, the names of the columns, and the names of the SQL data types for each column. You can use this to create a report. If you look at the various get*xxx*() methods, you can see that the code uses `getString()` to return the value from both char- and varchar-type columns. On the other hand, to retrieve an int, you use `getInt()`. It is important to map the column data type to an appropriate Java data type. In some cases, one Java data type will map to multiple SQL types. You do not have to get every column. I could have gotten just the Title column.

> **NOTE**
>
> If you decide to use column numbers rather than column names, be aware that column numbers, unlike numbers in an array, start at 1, not 0.

It is possible to retrieve data from a column as an unknown type by using `getObject()`.

These select statements are dynamic statements. Each is separately parsed, compiled, and optimized to generate a query plan, and then executed. As stated earlier, a `PreparedStatement` will generally be more efficient. So Listing 17.3 shows how to create and use a `PreparedStatement`. When you create a `PreparedStatement`, you need to supply parameters, as mentioned earlier. You set the values of those parameters with set*xxx*() methods, which correspond to the get*xxx*() methods described earlier.

To set an arbitrary data value you can use setObject(). Here is the basic way to create a PreparedStatement:

```
PreparedStatement updateCopies = con.prepareStatement(
    "UPDATE BookCatalog SET Copies = Copies+1 WHERE Author = ?");
```

To set the parameter values, you use a set*xxx*() statement like this:

```
updateCopies.setString(1, "Lewis, C.S.");
```

The 1 in the setString() call refers to the parameter number in the PreparedStatement. It has nothing to do with the column number of the value. The second value, in this case a String, is the value that should be substituted for the ? before the SQL statement is executed.

PreparedStatement: Code Example

Although the next sample program shows the PreparedStatement being done only three times, typically it is probably not worth the overhead for just a few executions. The exact break-even point for doing dynamic statements rather than PreparedStatements depends on the specific JDBC driver, but I'd guess you need to do the PreparedStatement at least 10 times to make it worth the trouble. To execute the PreparedStatement, you would code this:

```
int rowsUpdated = updateCopies.executeUpdate();
```

If you use a SQL insert, update, or delete, you should get an int back that tells you how many rows are affected. You should *always* test this value. If it is less than 1, the SQL statement did nothing, which probably indicates an error.

Listing 17.3 Using a PreparedStatement Object in JDBC (DBDriver3.java)

```
import java.sql.*;   //Import all the JDBC classes.
// The following imports are just for InstantDB.
import jdbc.idbDriver;
import jdbc.*;
import java.net.URL;
import java.io.*;
import java.util.*;

class PreparedWorker
    {
       Connection con=null;
       PreparedStatement updateCopies;
        Statement stmt;

         public boolean updateTable()
             {
              boolean result = true;
              String dbURL =
              "jdbc:idb:c:\\purejava\\source\\chap17\\purejava.prp";
              // The format of this URL is dictated in part by
```

continues

Listing 17.3 *continued*

```java
            // Java and in part by InstantDB.
            // Protocol:  jdbc
            // Sub-protcol:  idb
            // Driver-specific part: location of properties file
            // used by InstantDB.
            try
                {

                // Print DriverManager info to the console.
                // This is deprecated but useful.
                Class.forName("jdbc.idbDriver");
                // Load the JDBC driver class into
                // memory. The driver instantiates itself
                // and registers itself with DriverManager.
                con = DriverManager.getConnection (dbURL);
                // Get a database connection from the
                // appropriate driver.
                }
            catch (Exception e)
                {
                System.out.println
                ➥("Failed to load jdbc.idbDriver driver.");
                result = false;
                }
            try
                {
                // First, display data before changing it.
                // This uses the same code as in DBDriver2.java.
                stmt = con.createStatement();
                ResultSet rs = stmt.executeQuery(
                        "SELECT * from BookCatalog");
                System.out.println("Call #" + "\tAuthor" +
                        "\t\tTitle" +
                        "\tNotes" + "\tCopies");
                  while(rs.next() == true)
                        {
                        System.out.print(rs.getString("CallNumber"));
                        System.out.print("\t" + rs.getString("Author"));
                        System.out.print("\t" + rs.getString("Title"));
                        System.out.print("\t" + rs.getString("Notes"));
                        System.out.println("\t" +
                        ➥rs.getString("Copies"));
                        }
                // Now that you have a Connection, create
                // a PreparedStatement to save statement
```

Creating a Database Connection 347

```
            // execution time.
            updateCopies = con.prepareStatement(
                             "UPDATE BookCatalog SET " +
                             "Copies = Copies+1 WHERE Author = ?");
            // Note that you write the SQL statement before you
            // try to execute it.
        }
    catch (SQLException e)
        {
          System.err.println("problems connecting to "
               + dbURL);
          result = false;
        }

      try
        {
         // A PreparedStatement provides execute(),
         // executeUpdate() and executeQuery(). Since we are
         // using an insert statement, use executeUpdate().
         updateCopies.setString(1, "Lewis, C.S.");
         int rowsUpdated = updateCopies.executeUpdate();
         if(rowsUpdated < 1)
               System.out.println("Failed to update
                      ➥BookCatalog " +
                      "table for number of copies");
         updateCopies.setString(1, "Colson, Charles");
          rowsUpdated = updateCopies.executeUpdate();
            if(rowsUpdated < 1)
               System.out.println("Failed to update
                      ➥BookCatalog " +
                      "table for number of copies");
         updateCopies.setString(1, "Middleton, J. Richard");
          rowsUpdated = updateCopies.executeUpdate();
            if(rowsUpdated < 1)
               System.out.println("Failed to update
                      ➥BookCatalog " +
                      "table for number of copies");
         // Now do a select to show that the change
         // took place.
         ResultSet rs = stmt.executeQuery(
              "SELECT * from BookCatalog");
          // We are not using a scrollable ResultSet,
          // so we need to get a new ResultSet.
          System.out.println("Call #" + "\tAuthor" +
                "\t\tTitle" +
                "\tNotes" + "\tCopies");
           while(rs.next() == true)
                {
```

continues

Listing 17.3 continued

```
                        System.out.print(rs.getString ("CallNumber"));
                        System.out.print("\t" + rs.getString ("Author"));
                        System.out.print("\t" + rs.getString ("Title"));
                        System.out.print("\t" + rs.getString ("Notes"));
                        System.out.println("\t" +
                        ➥rs.getString("Copies"));
                        }
                    con.close();
                }
        catch (Exception e)
            {
              System.err.println("problems with SQL sent to "+ dbURL+
                  ": "+e.getMessage());
              result = false;
            }
          return result;
        }

  } // End class definition for TableMaker.

public class DBDriver3
    {
      public static void main(String[] args)
            {
              PreparedWorker pw = new PreparedWorker();
              pw.updateTable();
              System.exit(0);
            }
    }
```

When you run this code, you see the contents of the `BookCatalog` table, followed by updates (via a `PreparedStatement`) to the `BookCatalog` table, followed by a query to show the newly updated contents of the `BookCatalog` table. As noted before, you use a set*xxx*() method to put a parameter value into the `PreparedStatement`. You would probably want to use a `PreparedStatement` in a loop. You then retrieve, from a file or some other source, the changing parameter values for each loop.

Using Callable Statements

The third kind of statement that Java supports is a `CallableStatement`, which supports stored procedures. Because InstantDB does not (as of September 1999) support stored procedures, I will show you a code snippet that you can modify to work with stored procedures in your code. The format for stored procedures varies from vendor to vendor, so you should check your DBMS vendor's documentation to see how to use a stored procedure from Java. As noted earlier, a stored procedure is a set of SQL statements stored in the database itself.

> **NOTE**
>
> Some vendors, notably Oracle, are adding support for coding stored procedures in Java, but this is not supported widely yet. In Oracle's case, there is a JVM embedded in the database engine. Be aware that if several copies of a stored procedure run at one time, and they all run in separate JVM instances on the database server machine, this could pose a scalability issue. This depends entirely on how a vendor implements this feature.

Suppose that a stored procedure is written called SHOW_NEW_BOOKS, which shows new books by category and date range. Your Java program is going to call this stored procedure. JDBC uses a `CallableStatement` to call the stored procedure. A `CallableStatement` includes the name of the stored procedure and, optionally, parameter names. Like a `PreparedStatement`, the parameters are indicated by ? in the `CallableStatement`. Assume that the SHOW_NEW_BOOKS stored procedure takes two parameters: the subject category ID and the date from which to begin displaying titles. The date is in the form of a `java.sql.Date`, a subclass of `java.util.Date`. Here's how the `CallableStatement` might look:

```
java.sql.Date beginDate = java.sql.Date.valueOf("1999-01-01");

// Since you need the java.sql.Date, not the java.util.Date, make
// that explicit, in case your program also imports java.util.
// Otherwise, the compiler might not know which one you mean, and you
// could get a compile error.
CallableStatement cs = con.prepareCall("{call SHOW_NEW_BOOKS(? ,?)}");
cs.setString(1,"Contemporary Issues"); // Set subject parameter.
cs.setDate(2,beginDate); // Set date to start search from.
ResultSet rs = cs.execute();
```

A stored procedure can return a `ResultSet` or a specific result and modify the parameters you submit. These parameters must be registered with

`registerOutParameter(int parameterIndex, int sqlType)`

This is necessary *only* if you want to have the stored procedure modify this value. If the stored procedure returns a `ResultSet`, you use the familiar get*xxx*() methods to retrieve values from the rows in the `ResultSet`.

A stored procedure can be quite handy if multiple applications call the same SQL statements to accomplish the same purpose. Your organization can have your group's best SQL programmer put together a well-tuned stored procedure.

JDBC 2.0 Techniques

This section gives a brief overview of the most important JDBC 2.0 enhancements to the JDBC core APIs. Although they are very interesting, the standard extensions, such as support for reading rows of any tabular data source (such as a spreadsheet) and allowing an Enterprise JavaBean to work with connection pools, are not covered. Here are the main new features of the JDBC 2.0 core APIs:

- Scrollable `ResultSets`—You can move both forward and backward in a `ResultSet`.
- Programmatic updates to a `ResultSet`—You can modify the contents of a `ResultSet` using Java method calls. This automatically updates the underlying relational table.
- Batch updates—You can submit multiple DML statements, like insert or update, at once.
- User-defined data types—You can define your own data types and map them to Java classes.
- SQL3 data types—You can use new SQL3 data types, such as blobs (Binary Large Objects) and clobs (Character Large Objects).

Scrollable ResultSet

JDBC 2.0 provides support for a scrollable `ResultSet`. Using this, you can do the following:

- Skip down to a row.
- Skip up to a row.
- Go to the top of the `ResultSet`.
- Go to the bottom of the `ResultSet`.

You can move around to arbitrary locations in the `ResultSet` without having to query again. This feature was not in JDBC 1.0 because not enough vendors supported it at that time.

TIP

You can use scrollable `ResultSets` to determine how many rows are in your `ResultSet` before processing it. All you do is call `last()` on the `ResultSet` to get to the last row. Next, get the row number. That will tell you how many rows are in your `ResultSet`.

Scrollable ResultSet: Code Example

No treatment of JDBC 2.0 would be complete without an example of how to use this important feature. This feature means that you no longer have to do a query twice—once to count the rows and a second time to process them. To use a scrollable `ResultSet`, you have to require that a `Statement` object support scrolling, doing something similar to the following:

```
Statement stmt =
  con.createStatement(ResultSet.TYPE_SCROLL_SENSITIVE,
                      ResultSet.CONCUR_READ_ONLY);
```

The `createStatement()` call is similar to the one you've already seen, except that it adds two new arguments. The first argument specifies the scrolling for the `ResultSet` and is a `public static final int` defined in the `ResultSet` class. Here are the possibilities:

- `TYPE_FORWARD_ONLY` — Can only scroll the `ResultSet` forward, which is the default.
- `TYPE_SCROLL_INSENSITIVE` — Can scroll in any direction, but the `ResultSet` is generally not modified if others modify the underlying table.
- `TYPE_SCROLL` — Can be scrolled in any direction. The `ResultSet` is generally modified if others modify the underlying table.

The second parameter specifies whether the `ResultSet` can be updated. Here are the two possible values:

- `CONCUR_READ_ONLY` — The `ResultSet` cannot be modified.
- `CONCUR_UPDATABLE` — The `ResultSet` can be modified.

After this, you can get a `ResultSet` as usual and can move around with methods like `absolute()` to go to a specific row, `relative()` to go to a row relative to the current one, `previous()` to go backwards one row, and the like. Listing 17.4 shows an example of how to create and use a scrollable `ResultSet`.

Listing 17.4 JDBC 2.0-Only Scrollable ResultSet Example (DBDriver4.java)

```
// Create and use a scrollable ResultSet.
import java.sql.*;   //Import all the JDBC classes.
// The following imports are just for InstantDB.
import jdbc.idbDriver;
import java.net.URL;
import java.io.*;
import java.util.*;

class ScrollingReader
      {
         Connection con=null;
         Statement stmt;

         public boolean readTable()
               {
               boolean result = true;
               String dbURL =
         ➥"jdbc:idb:c:\\purejava\\cdrom\\chap17\\purejava.prp";
               // The format of this URL is dictated
               // in part by Java and in part by InstantDB.
               // Protocol:  jdbc
               // Subprotcol:  idb
               // Driver-specific part:  location of properties file
               // used by Instantdb.
               try
                     {
                     // Print DriverManager info to the console.
                     // This is deprecated but useful.
                     Class.forName("jdbc.idbDriver");
```

continues

Listing 17.4 continued

```java
            // Load the JDBC driver class into
            // memory. The driver instantiates itself
            // and registers itself with DriverManager.
            con = DriverManager.getConnection (dbURL);
            // Get a database connection from the
            // appropriate driver.
        }
    catch (Exception e)
        {
        System.out.println
        ➥("Failed to load jdbc.idbDriver driver.");
        result = false;
        }
    try
        {
        stmt = con.createStatement
                    (ResultSet.TYPE_SCROLL_SENSITIVE,
                     ResultSet.CONCUR_READ_ONLY);
        // Now that you have a Connection, create
        // a Statement object so you can send
        // SQL calls to the JDBC driver.
        // This Statement will create a ResultSet that is:
        // 1. Scrollable and sensitive to modifications to
        // the underlying table. This could also be
        // TYPE_SCROLL_INSENSITIVE in this particular case.
        // 2. Read-only ResultSet.
        }
    catch (SQLException e)
        {
        // Either the program failed to get
        // a connection, which is probably a
        // database URL or database setup problem, or
        // the creation of the Statement
        // object failed (possibly because the
        // database engine or driver does not support
        // scrollable ResultSets).
        System.err.println("problems connecting to "
            + dbURL);
        result = false;
        }

    try
        {
        // Retrieve all the rows from the table with
        // a ResultSet and print the contents of
        // the ResultSet.
        ResultSet rs = stmt.executeQuery(
            "SELECT * from BookCatalog");
        // Now scroll around the ResultSet.
```

```
rs.absolute(3); // Go to a specific row.
int rowNumb = 0;
rowNumb = rs.getRow();
// Get the row number, which should be 3.
System.out.println
➥("The row number, which should be 3 is:   " +
                                rowNumb);
System.out.println("Title:   " +
                rs.getString("Title"));
// Print the title to show
// that the row has actually changed.
rs.relative(-2);  // Go backwards two rows.
rowNumb = rs.getRow();
// Get the row number which should be 1.
System.out.println
➥("The row number, which should be 1 is:   " +
                                rowNumb);
System.out.println("Title:   " +
                rs.getString("Title"));
rs.next(); // Move forward to row 3.
rs.next();
rs.previous();  // Move backward to row 2.
 rowNumb = rs.getRow();
// Get the row number, which should be 2.
System.out.println
➥("The row number, which should be 2 is:   " +
                                rowNumb);
System.out.println("Title:   " +
                rs.getString("Title"));
// Print the title to show
// that the row has actually changed.

// Now test to see if we are still
// in the ResultSet bounds.
rs.next();   // Move forward one row.
rs.last();   // Go to the last row.
rowNumb = rs.getRow();
// Find out how many rows are in the ResultSet.
System.out.println("There are " + rowNumb +
                "rows in the ResultSet");
if (!rs.isAfterLast())
    {
        // Have we walked off the
        // bottom of the ResultSet?
        // If not, show a row.
        System.out.print(rs.getString ("CallNumber"));
        System.out.print("\t" + rs.getString ("Author"));
```

continues

Listing 17.4 continued

```
                             System.out.print("\t" + rs.getString ("Title"));
                             System.out.print("\t" + rs.getString ("Notes"));
                             System.out.println("\t" +
                             ➥rs.getString("Copies"));
                     }
                 // Now go past the end of the ResultSet and work
                 // backwards, printing each row.
                 System.out.println
                 ➥("Here are the rows in reverse order");
                 rs.afterLast();
                 while(rs.previous() == true)
                         {
                         System.out.print(rs.getString ("CallNumber"));
                         System.out.print("\t" + rs.getString ("Author"));
                         System.out.print("\t" + rs.getString ("Title"));
                         System.out.print("\t" + rs.getString ("Notes"));
                         System.out.println("\t" +
                         ➥rs.getString("Copies"));
                         }
             con.close();
             // Closing the Connection also destroys the ResultSet and
             // Statement objects, at least as usable entities.
             }
        catch (SQLException e)
                 {
                 // First, show SQLState.
                 System.err.println("SQLState:   " + e.getSQLState());
                 System.err.println("problems with SQL sent to "+ dbURL+
                     ": "+e.getMessage());
                 result = false;
                 }

         return result;
         }

    } // End class definition for ScrollingReader.

public class DBDriver4
    {
      public static void main(String[] args)
            {
            ScrollingReader scrRdr = new ScrollingReader();
            scrRdr.readTable();
```

```
            System.exit(0);
        }
    }
```

Here's the output as it appears on my system:

```
InstantDB - Version 3.11 beta 1
Copyright (c) 1997-1999 Instant Computer Solutions Ltd.
main SELECT * from BookCatalog
The row number, which should be 3 is:   3
Title:  Truth is Stranger than It Used to Be
The row number, which should be 1 is:   1
Title:  Till We Have Faces
The row number, which should be 2 is:   2
Title:  How Now Shall We Live?
There are 4rows in the ResultSet
Lew2    Lewis, C.S.     Out of the Silent Planet        null    2
Here are the rows in reverse order
Lew2    Lewis, C.S.     Out of the Silent Planet        null    2
Mid1    MIddleton, J. Richard   Truth is Stranger than It Used to Be
Non-Fiction. PostModernism      4
Col1    Colson, Charles How Now Shall We Live?  Non-Fiction.
Contemporary Issues     4
Lew1    Lewis, C.S. Till We Have Faces          Fiction 3
```

Batch Updates

JDBC 2.0 allows for batch updates. In the code in DBDriver1.java, I called insert five separate times. Using a batch update, I could have made just one call that passed all the insert statements to the JDBC driver and on to the database engine. Making fewer calls improves your program's performance.

Modifiable ResultSets

JDBC 2.0 allows you to modify a ResultSet directly and have the changes reflected in the underlying table automatically. You can insert a row into a ResultSet, delete a row from a ResultSet, or change a value in a column in a ResultSet, and Java automatically changes the underlying table for you. This allows you to work with the data in a Java-centric way, after you've obtained the ResultSet. You are not required to make SQL calls for each thing.

NOTE

As of September 1999, InstantDB allows you to use updatable ResultSets. Although the changes to the ResultSet do affect the underlying table, the ResultSet itself will not show the changes until you repeat the query. So you will have to do a query to verify that your changes actually took effect.

Updatable ResultSet: Code Example

Unlike the example in Listing 17.4, the `ResultSet` must be instantiated with `CONCUR_UPDATABLE` to allow the `ResultSet` to be updated. The `createStatement()` call in Listing 17.5 creates a `Statement` object that generates an updatable `ResultSet`. The `ResultSet` is also scrollable. This is not required for an updatable `ResultSet`, but if you are changing the `ResultSet`, you will probably find it helpful to be able to scroll around the `ResultSet`.

As well as updating a table, you can insert rows into it or delete rows from it. You insert a row into an updatable `ResultSet` using `insertRow()`. You may think of this as a separate buffer for a row; it is not a part of the `ResultSet` returned from the query as such. To insert a row, you move to the insert row by calling `moveToInsertRow()`, use `updatexxx()` methods to set the column values, and then use `insertRow()` to insert the row into the `ResultSet`. The driver will insert the row into the underlying table.

Listing 17.5 gives an example of how to modify a `ResultSet`.

CAUTION

Simply asking for an updatable `ResultSet` does not guarantee that you will get one. The JDBC driver might not support this feature and might return a read-only `ResultSet` to you. You can help ensure that your `ResultSet` will be updatable by specifying a SQL query that includes the primary key column in the columns selected and does a select from only one table. You can test to see if you received an updatable `ResultSet` by coding the following:

```
int concurType = rs.getConcurrency();
```

If `concurType` equals `1007`, the `ResultSet` is read-only. If it equals `1008`, the `ResultSet` is updatable.

To change a given row, you must move to it. If you decide after updating an existing row that you want to cancel the updates, call `cancelRowUpdates()` before you call `updateRow()`, which must be called normally in order to permanently modify the row.

Listing 17.5   JDBC 2.0-Only Updatable ResultSet Example (DBDriver5.java)

```
// Create and use a scrollable ResultSet.
import java.sql.*;   //Import all the JDBC classes.
// The following imports are just for InstantDB.
import jdbc.idbDriver;
import java.net.URL;
import java.io.*;
import java.util.*;

class Updater
    {
        Connection con=null;
        Statement stmt;
```

```java
public boolean modifyResultSet()
    {
    boolean result = true;
    String dbURL =
➥"jdbc:idb:c:\\purejava\\cdrom\\chap17\\purejava.prp";
    // The format of this URL is dictated in part by
    // Java and in part by InstantDB.
    // Protocol:  jdbc
    // Sub-protcol:  idb
    // Driver-specific part:  location of properties file
    // used by Instantdb.
    try
        {
        // Print DriverManager info to the console.
        // This is deprecated but useful.
        Class.forName("jdbc.idbDriver");
        // Load the JDBC driver class into
        // memory. The driver instantiates itself
        // and registers itself with DriverManager.
        con = DriverManager.getConnection (dbURL);
        // Get a database connection from the
        // appropriate driver.
        }
    catch (Exception e)
        {
        System.out.println
➥("Failed to load jdbc.idbDriver driver.");
        result = false;
        }
    try
        {
        con.setAutoCommit(false);
        // Prevent auto-commit of work. Instead, do your
        // own transaction management of the resource
        // manager - in this case, the database.
        stmt = con.createStatement
                    (ResultSet.TYPE_SCROLL_SENSITIVE,
                    ResultSet.CONCUR_UPDATABLE);
        // Now that you have a Connection, create
        // a Statement object so you can send
        // SQL calls to the JDBC driver.
        // This Statement will create a ResultSet that is:
        // 1. Scrollable and sensitive to modifications to
        // the underlying table. This could also be
        // TYPE_SCROLL_INSENSITIVE in this particular case.
        // 2. Updatable ResultSet.
        }
    catch (SQLException e)
```

continues

Listing 17.5 continued

```
         {
           // Either the program failed to get a connection,
           // which is probably a database URL or database
           // setup problem, or the creation
           // of the Statement object failed (possibly
           // because the database engine or driver does not
           // support scrollable ResultSets).
           System.err.println("problems connecting to "
               + dbURL);
           result = false;
         }

       try
         {
           // Retrieve all the rows from the table with
           // a ResultSet and print the contents of
           // the ResultSet.
           ResultSet rs = stmt.executeQuery(
               "SELECT * from BookCatalog");
            // Show the contents of the ResultSet.
           while(rs.next() == true)
               {
                 System.out.print(rs.getString ("CallNumber"));
                 System.out.print("\t" + rs.getString ("Author"));
                 System.out.print("\t" + rs.getString ("Title"));
                 System.out.print("\t" + rs.getString ("Notes"));
                 System.out.println("\t" +
                 ➥rs.getString("Copies"));
               }

           // Now update a specific row.
           rs.absolute(3); // Go to a specific row.
           // Change the number of copies.
           rs.updateInt("Copies", 8);  // Update the
                                       // ResultSet.
           // The updatexxx methods on a ResultSet
           // generally take two parameters:
           // a column name or number, and a value.
           // updateInt() is used here to change
           // the int value in the Copies column.
           rs.updateRow();
           // You MUST call updateRow() before moving
           // the cursor for this row to be updated.
           // If you fail to call this, the updated
           // values will be lost, and the row will
           // return to its previous state.
```

```java
// If you decide that you don't want to keep the
// changes to a row, you can call
// cancelRowUpdates(), to cancel all your updates
// to the row, as long as you have NOT called
// updateRow() yet.

// Now insert a row into the ResultSet.
rs.moveToInsertRow();
// Move to the inset row.
rs.updateString("CallNumber", "Pasc");
rs.updateString("Author","Pascal, Blaise" );
rs.updateString("Title", "Pensees");
rs.updateString("Notes", "Philosophy");
rs.updateInt("Copies", 2);
rs.insertRow();
// Use an updatexxx method for every column.
// Then call insertRow() to insert the row into
// the ResultSet. The underlying table is not
// changed until insertRow() is called.

// The ResultSet keeps track of the row you were
// on before calling moveToInsertRow(). While you
// are on the insert row, you can call
// moveToCurrentRow() to return to the current
// row.
rs.moveToCurrentRow();
System.out.println("The current row number is:  " +
                                rs.getRow());
// Display the current row number.
// Move back to the current row after the insert.
// You could also move to a different row using
// any of the methods for a scrollable ResultSet,
// like first().
rs.first();
// Move to the first row.
rs.deleteRow();
// Delete a row from a ResultSet.
// The visibility of changes you make depends on
// the database driver and, to an extent, the
// isolation level set.
// In order to see the changes for sure, close the
// ResultSet and repeat the query.
con.commit();
// Commit your work.
rs.close();
// Close the ResultSet and do a new query.
// In general, you don't have to do this, because
// doing a new query destroys the old ResultSet,
```

continues

Listing 17.5 continued

```
                    // but this is cleaner.
                    rs = stmt.executeQuery(
                        "SELECT * from BookCatalog");
                    // Show the contents of the ResultSet.
                    while(rs.next() == true)
                        {
                         System.out.print(rs.getString ("CallNumber"));
                         System.out.print("\t" + rs.getString ("Author"));
                         System.out.print("\t" + rs.getString ("Title"));
                         System.out.print("\t" + rs.getString ("Notes"));
                         System.out.println("\t" +
                        ➥rs.getString("Copies"));
                        }
                con.close();
                // Closing the Connection also destroys the ResultSet and
                // Statement objects, at least as usable entities.
                }
        catch (SQLException e)
                {
                // First show SQLState.
                System.err.println("SQLState:   " + e.getSQLState());
                System.err.println("problems with SQL sent to "+ dbURL+
                    ": "+e.getMessage());
                result = false;
                }

        return result;
        }

   } // End class definition for Updater.

public class DBDriver5
    {
      public static void main(String[] args)
            {
               Updater updtr = new Updater();
               updtr.modifyResultSet();
               System.exit(0);
            }
    }
```

Here is the output on my system:

```
InstantDB - Version 3.11 beta 1
Copyright (c) 1997-1999 Instant Computer Solutions Ltd.
```

```
main SELECT * from BookCatalog
Lew1    Lewis, C.S.       Till We Have Faces       Fiction 3
Col1    Colson, Charles How Now Shall We Live?  Non-Fiction.
Contemporary Issues     4
Mid1    MIddleton, J. Richard    Truth is Stranger than It Used to Be
Non-Fiction. PostModernism      4
Lew2    Lewis, C.S.       Out of the Silent Planet         null    2
The current row number is:   3
main SELECT * from BookCatalog
Col1    Colson, Charles How Now Shall We Live?  Non-Fiction.
Contemporary Issues     4
Lew2    Lewis, C.S.       Out of the Silent Planet         null    2
Mid1    Middleton, J. Richard    Truth is Stranger than It Used to Be
Non-Fiction. PostModernism      8
Pasc    Pascal, Blaise  Pensees Philosophy       2
```

You can see that the number of copies of *Truth is Stranger than It Used to Be* has been changed to 8, that the book *Till We Have Faces* is gone, and that Pascal's *Pensees* has been added. We have updated the table by updating the `ResultSet` using Java methods rather than SQL calls.

> **NOTE**
>
> The order of rows in a `ResultSet` has nothing to do with the order of rows in the underlying table. The driver keeps track of which rows were selected and updates the rows in the underlying table. Because of this, if you insert a row into a `ResultSet`, there is no way to know where in the table the row will be inserted. The order of rows in the underlying table is indeterminate.

Other Important Points to Remember

There are some other points not specific to a particular technique that you should know and incorporate into your programs. These include limiting `ResultSet` size and doing your own transaction management.

Limit ResultSet Size

I said earlier that JDBC 2.0 allows you to get the number of rows in a `ResultSet`. You should use this information to limit the amount of data you send to a client. Let's say that your middle-tier database access code (tier two is where this code belongs) makes a call and returns 10,000 rows. Realistically (even if your user's system can hold that much data, and you don't mind the download time required to copy it to the client system), the user is not going to read 10,000 rows worth of data.

In order to be more practical and prevent huge network loads, many companies limit the size of a `ResultSet`. In other words, if the `ResultSet` contains 10,000 rows, the middle-tier program will send rows to the client in 50-row chunks (often in an array or `Vector`). It sends more only when the user asks for more. Sometimes, a company will send a message that tells the user to limit his search because the `ResultSet` is too large. I recommend doing this for the sake of performance and optimum network usage by your program.

Turn Off Auto-Commit

Java, by default, *commits* (flushes to disk) your work after each SQL call. This sounds fine, unless you are trying to do a transaction, which is a logical unit of work. You should think of a transaction as a series of steps that must all complete successfully. If they do not, none should complete at all. Here's a simplified example. Let's say I pay for auto insurance from my checking account. Each month, a SQL `Update` call is made to subtract, say, $100.00 from my checking account.

Using the default `autoCommit` setting, which has `autoCommit` turned on, this statement will be committed—that is, made permanent in the database. Then a SQL update call is made to add $100.00 to my auto insurance company's account. This statement fails for some reason. Now I have a data integrity problem, and I'm short $100.00. The deduction from my checking account was already committed. The addition to my insurer's account makes no difference to my account. This is a transaction. Either both SQL update calls should succeed, or both should fail.

To accomplish this, you should create your own transaction. First, call `setAutoCommit(false)` to turn off `autoCommit`. Second, do each SQL call through an `executeUpdate()` method. As each call returns, verify that it succeeded. If all the SQL calls are successful, call `commit()`. If any of the calls fails, call `rollback()`, which undoes every change made since the last `commit()` call. This will help ensure data integrity. What you gain is a lot more important than the tiny bit of coding you save by using `autoCommit`.

Set the Isolation Level

You should always set the isolation level of your program's connection to the database by calling

```
myConnection.setTransactionIsolation(isolation level);
```

A transaction isolation level refers to how exclusive the control of the data needs to be. Five isolation levels are available in JDBC, although a given RDBMS may not support them all:

- `TRANSACTION_NONE` — No transaction support.
- `TRANSACTION_READ_COMMITTED` — No dirty reads are allowed, but phantom rows and nonrepeatable reads are permitted. A *dirty read* refers not to something salacious, but to reading data that is in an inconsistent state. For example, a bank might want to know the total of all funds in all accounts, even if the number is approximate because it is constantly changing. If a result that is pretty close to accurate is good enough, you can increase concurrency by permitting dirty reads.
  A *phantom row* means that a row has been deleted from the rows that represent your `ResultSet`. This means you are looking at a no-longer-existent row. A *repeatable read* means the same rows are read over and over without changes to the data between reads. This reduces concurrency. You need to strike the

appropriate balance in your application between concurrency and exclusive control of the data. Of course, this is also influenced by how small a unit of a table your RDBMS can lock, ranging from a row to the whole table.

- `TRANSACTION_READ_UNCOMMITTED` — Dirty reads, nonrepeatable reads, and phantom rows are permitted.
- `TRANSACTION_REPEATABLE_READ` — No nonrepeatable reads or dirty reads are allowed, but phantom rows are allowed.
- `TRANSACTION_SERIALIZABLE` — No dirty reads, phantom rows, or nonrepeatable reads are allowed.

CHAPTER 18

Text

The java.text package contains classes and interfaces to assist you in formatting text, dates, and numbers in a manner independent of natural languages. What this really means for you is that java.text provides mechanisms for reformatting data based on a given locale, so that you can easily internationalize your applications. You can format text independently of language or locale as well. These classes can also be used simply to improve your output. For example, you can convert a Date object, which is similar to a long primitive in content, into an actual date in the form *month, day number, year number*. The classes here are similar to those in the java.util package, the subject of Chapter 19, "Utility Classes." There are no significant new concepts to learn, just techniques to apply the available methods.

The classes in java.text provide three main functions:

- Iterating over text
- Formatting and parsing data
- String collation

These classes can step through text based on characters, words, sentences, or line breaks. This package is primarily designed for providing internationalization in your application. Specifically, you can write your application in a language- and locale-independent way, dynamically formatting data for a specific locale on-the-fly.

> **NOTE**
>
> This chapter does not examine other issues in internationalization, such as using foreign fonts, for which Swing provides support.

This chapter focuses on two topics:

- Simple program internationalization
- Formatting text dates and numbers

Basic Internationalization in a Java Application

Internationalization is usually referred to as *i18n*, because there are eighteen letters between the initial *i* and the final *n*. Here is a simple example of the type of code that might benefit from being internationalized:

```
public GUI()
    {
       Label nameLabel = new Label("Name");
       TextField greeting = new TextField("Hello");
       ...
    }
```

The user interface this type of code generates works fine in the U.S., but it might not work well in other countries where English is either not the primary language, such as Japan or France, or in a country where English has different idioms than in the U.S. It is important to be able to modify this English text to a more appropriate language for a given locale.

> **NOTE**
>
> To support internationalization, you need to use `ResourceBundle`. Although this class is not in `java.text`, doing locale-specific translation is what much of `java.text` is for, so it seems reasonable to discuss it here. Just remember that you need `java.util` for a `ResourceBundle`.

To be able to provide for internationalization, you want translations of the words in your GUI into other languages you want to support.

The mechanism to do this is a *properties file*. A properties file, one for each language you wish to support, provides language-specific equivalents for key names that remain the same. For the word `"Hello"` (used in the previous sample code):

The English version would say `greeting="Good Day"`;

The French version would say `greeting="Bon Jour"`;

The German version would say `greeting="Guten Tag"`;

When your program runs, it loads the correct properties file based on the locale, and then Java automatically uses the correct language-specific version. Say, for example, that you have a screen with an OK button. You don't want to use OK in every locale; you would rather use an appropriate equivalent. So you define locale-specific equivalents in every properties file for the application. To access the locale-specific value, you call the `getString()` method:

```
getString("OK")
```

Basic Internationalization in a Java Application

The correct version of "OK" to get depends upon the locale. You create a `Locale` object that specifies the language and country, and then you pass this `Locale` object to methods of other objects that use the locale information. In this first example, the most important locale-sensitive object is a `ResourceBundle`, which contains the language-specific values for a given locale.

Locale and ResourceBundle Classes: Code Example

You obtain a `ResourceBundle` with a `getBundle()` call that accepts two parameters, the name of the properties file minus the specific language and country, and a `Locale` object that specifies the language and country. These are concatenated together by the JVM to construct the actual properties filename to be used. Listing 18.1 provides a simple example of internationalizing an application with `ResourceBundle`.

Listing 18.1 Internationalizing an Application with ResourceBundle and Properties Files (TextDriver1.java)

```
// Simple Internationalized Program.
import java.util.*;

class Bundler
     {
       Locale theLocale;
       String theCountry;
       String theLanguage;
       ResourceBundle theBundle;

       public Bundler(String c, String l)
            {
              theCountry = c;
              theLanguage = l;
              theLocale = new Locale(theLanguage, theCountry);
              // Set the locale to the user's input values.
              // In an applet you would have to derive the
              // locale through the system properties.
              theBundle = ResourceBundle.getBundle(
                    "MessagesBundle", theLocale);
              // Create a ResourceBundle for the chosen
              // locale. The ResourceBundle contains
              // the locale-specific values. You could create
              // several ResourceBundles when your
              // program starts, but generally, you only
              // create them one at a time.
            }

      public boolean displayLocaleText()
           {
             // Now that you have the right ResourceBundle
             // for the specified locale, print out the values
             // from the ResourceBundle for a partially
```

continues

Listing 18.1 continued

```
            // locale-specific message.
            System.out.println("You can search for a " +
                    theBundle.getString("book"));
            System.out.println("by specifying either the "+
                     theBundle.getString("author"));
            System.out.println("or by " + theBundle.getString("title"));
            System.out.println("The catalog system will reply " +
                    "with a " + theBundle.getString("message"));
            System.out.println("to tell you if the " +
                    theBundle.getString("book") + " was found");
            return true;
        }

    } // End class definition for Bundler.

public class TextDriver1
    {
    // To execute, type:
    // TextDriver1 EN us
    // or
    // TextDriver1 DE de.
    public static void main(String[] args)
            {
            Bundler bundler = new Bundler(args[0], args[1]);
            bundler.displayLocaleText();
            }
    }
```

Listings 18.2 and 18.3 show the `Properties` files used for the `ResourceBundle`.

Listing 18.2   MessageBundle_de_DE.properties
```
book = das Buch
title = der Titel
author = der Schopfer
message = das Botschaft
```

Listing 18.3   MessageBundle_en_US.properties
```
book = Book
title = Title:
author = Author:
message = Message
```

This program accepts console input, the language, and the country. These are used to create a `Locale` object. The language is a pair of lowercase letters that conform to the choices specified in ISO-639. You can find a complete list of the ISO-639 codes at http://www.ics.uci.edu/pub/ietf/http/related/iso639.txt. The country code consists of two uppercase letters and conforms to ISO-3166. A copy of ISO-3166 can be found at http://www.chemie.fuberlin.de/diverse/doc/ISO_3166.html.

You can also specify a third parameter that specifies an arbitrary value specific to your program. This could be used to request a font that is specific to UNIX or Windows, for example. The `Locale` class also provides constants for some locale parameters, such as JAPANESE or JAPAN. That `Locale` object is used to select the correct properties file to build a `ResourceBundle`. The program then uses the `ResourceBundle` to display locale-specific text using the `getString()` method.

> **CAUTION**
>
> If the specified `Properties` file is not found, a default `Properties` file is used instead.

> **TIP**
>
> You should be sure to provide a default `.properties` file for your application so that the user doesn't have to specify a locale and so that the program works even if the user doesn't specify a locale. The default `Properties` file alleviates the need to have a `Properties` file for every possible locale.

This approach of using `Locales` and `ResourceBundle` objects allows your program to easily adapt to new locales. There is much more to `ResourceBundle`, such as `ListResourceBundle`, for which you should consult the Java documentation.

Formatting Text

Besides the wording of elements, such as error messages, GUI component labels, log messages, and the like, there are many items in data that must be formatted for a specific locale. These include currency, dates, time, measurements, titles (like Mr. or Mrs.), numbers, phone numbers, and postal addresses.

> **TIP**
>
> Avoid long, multielement messages that require translation of several items. Because numerous languages have a distinctive word order, it can be difficult to translate these messages.

You can also check to see which locales are supported to a locale-sensitive class. You can do this with the following code:

```
Locale localeList[] = DateFormat.getAvailableLocales();
for (int i = 0; i < localeList.length; i++)
    {
       System.out.println(localeList[i].toString())
    }
```

This code will display a list of language and country codes, which will not be very user-friendly. If you want to produce output that is user-friendly, replace the `toString()` method in this preceding code snippet with the `Locale.getDisplayName` method, in this way:

```
Locale localeList[] = DateFormat.getAvailableLocales();
for (int i = 0; i < localeList.length; i++)
```

```
    {
    System.out.println(localeList[i].getDisplayName())
    }
```

You can also find the default locale by calling the `getDefault()` method.

Formatting Numeric Data

This section describes how to format numbers and currency. When formatting numeric data, you can use two approaches:

- Use the predefined formats available through the `NumberFormat` class.
- Use a pattern for formatting data, such as a String pattern with `DecimalFormat`. This allows you to format values in a locale-independent way, such as replacing commas with decimal points. You use a pattern `String` to accomplish this.

Numeric Formatting: Code Example

There are two main ways to customize numeric values: `NumberFormat` and `DecimalFormat`. The former is for simple, straightforward formatting, and the latter is for custom formatting. Listing 18.4 shows how to use `NumberFormat` for predefined formats and `DecimalFormat` for customized formatting with patterns.

Listing 18.4   Formatting Values with NumberFormat, DecimalFormat, and DecimalFormatSymbols (TextDriver2.java)

```
// Program to format data with help from java.text.
import java.text.*;
import java.util.*;

class Formatter
    {
    Locale usLocale;
    Locale deLocale;
    NumberFormat usNumberFormatter;
    NumberFormat deNumberFormatter;
    String formattedValue;

    public Formatter()
        {
          usLocale = new Locale("EN", "us");
          deLocale = new Locale("DE", "de");
          // Create two Locale objects to use in formatting
          // for specific locales.
        }

    public boolean formatForLocale()
        {
          // Use predefined formatting from the
          // java.text.NumberFormat class, which
          // requries a Locale object.
          System.out.println("Number formatting:");
          Float amount = new Float(1253200.55);
```

```java
usNumberFormatter =
   NumberFormat.getNumberInstance(usLocale);
deNumberFormatter =
   NumberFormat.getNumberInstance(deLocale);
// Create two Locale objects to use in formatting
// for specific locales.
formattedValue = usNumberFormatter.format(amount);
System.out.println(formattedValue + " " +
                                 usLocale.toString());
// Print the value according to US format.
formattedValue = deNumberFormatter.format(amount);
System.out.println(formattedValue + " " +
                                 deLocale.toString());
// Print the value according to the German format.
System.out.println("Currency Formatting:");
Float price = new Float(265500.34);
usNumberFormatter =
   NumberFormat.getCurrencyInstance(usLocale);
deNumberFormatter =
    NumberFormat.getCurrencyInstance(deLocale);
// Call getCurrencyInstance() instead of
// getNumberInstance().
formattedValue = usNumberFormatter.format(price);
System.out.println(formattedValue + " " +
                                 usLocale.toString());
// Print the value according to US format.
formattedValue = deNumberFormatter.format(price);
System.out.println(formattedValue + " " +
                                 deLocale.toString());
// Print the value according to the German format.
// Note: NumberFormat knows how to format
// numbers, but knows nothing about currency
// exchange rates. You will have to add additional
// logic somewhere for that in a real application.
System.out.println("Percentage Formatting:");
// Convert a decimal to a percentage.
Float fraction = new Float(0.83);
usNumberFormatter =
    NumberFormat.getPercentInstance(usLocale);
deNumberFormatter =
    NumberFormat.getPercentInstance(deLocale);
// Call getPercentInstance() instead of
// getNumberInstance().
formattedValue = usNumberFormatter.format(fraction);
System.out.println(formattedValue + " " +
                                 usLocale.toString());
// Print the value according to US format.
formattedValue = deNumberFormatter. format(fraction);
System.out.println(formattedValue + " " +
```

continues

Listing 18.4   continued

```
                                        deLocale.toString());
            // Print the value according to German format.
            // Use custom formatting.
            // First, do locale-independent formatting.
            String dollarString = "$###,###.##";
            double amt = 5234425.773;
            DecimalFormat dollarFormatter =
                new DecimalFormat(dollarString);
            String output = dollarFormatter.format(amt);
            System.out.println(amt + " is formated to " + output);
            // Note in the output that only two numbers follow the
            // decimal point in the formatted version.
            DecimalFormatSymbols dfSymbols =
                    new DecimalFormatSymbols(usLocale);
            dfSymbols.setDecimalSeparator('*');
            dfSymbols.setGroupingSeparator('-');

            String formatString = "###,###.0##";
            DecimalFormat dfFormatter =
                    new DecimalFormat(formatString, dfSymbols);
            dfFormatter.setGroupingSize(3);
            double dbl = 7334455.6678;
            System.out.println("Before custom formatting" +
                            " the number is:   " +
                    dbl);
            System.out.println("With custom formatting" +
                            " the number is: " +
                dfFormatter.format(dbl));

            return true;
            }
    }

public class TextDriver2
    {
      public static void main (String[] args)
            {
              Formatter form = new Formatter();
              form.formatForLocale();
            }
    }
```

This program shows how to use the `NumberFormat` and `DecimalFormat` classes to format numbers and currency. Calling a method such as `getCurrencyInstance()` returns an object you can use to produce a locale-sensitive currency amount. Using methods from `DecimalFormatSymbols`, on the other hand, allows you to specify the separator character and the decimal point character to use when you format a number.

> **CAUTION**
>
> When you use a pattern, such as "##,###.##", you might cause truncation of the value to the right of the decimal point. That might be acceptable. If it is not, you either specify more fields or round the value appropriately *before* you try to format it.

For formatting numbers and currency, see the `DecimalFormat` class in the Java API doc. The options for constructing a pattern are listed in Table 18.1. (This table comes from the Java API documentation from Sun for this class.)

Table 18.1 Pattern and Format Options for DecimalFormat

Symbol	Meaning
0	A digit.
#	A digit; zero shows as absent.
.	Placeholder for decimal separator.
,	Placeholder for grouping separator.
E	Separates mantissa and exponent for exponential formats.
;	Separates formats.
-	Default negative prefix.
%	Multiply by 100 and show as percentage.
?	Multiply by 1000 and show as per mille.
¤	Currency sign. Replaced by currency symbol. If doubled, replaced by international currency symbol. If present in a pattern, the monetary decimal separator is used instead of the decimal separator.
X	Any other characters can be used in the prefix or suffix.
'	Used to quote special characters in a prefix or suffix.

Formatting Dates and Times

Just as it is possible to format numbers and currency, it is possible with classes from `java.text` to format dates and times.

Date and Time Using DateFormat: Code Example

The principles are essentially the same as formatting numbers, so I'll get right to the code. Listing 18.5 shows how to format dates and times using both predefined, locale-sensitive formats, and creating custom formats for locale-independent formats.

Listing 18.5   Using DateFormat and SimpleDateFormat (TextDriver3.java)
```
// Program to format data with help from java.text
import java.text.*;
import java.util.*;

class DateShaper
   {
   {
    Locale usLocale;
    Locale deLocale;
```

continues

Listing 18.5 continued

```java
    DateFormat usDateFormatter;
    DateFormat deDateFormatter;
    String formattedDate;
    Date theDate;

    public DateShaper()
        {
          usLocale = new Locale("EN", "us");
          deLocale = new Locale("DE", "de");
          // Create two Locale objects to use in formatting
          // for specific locales.
          theDate = new Date();
          // The java.text classes use Date
          // objects for showing dates, even though
          // most methods of the Date class are
          // deprecated.
        }

    public boolean formatDates()
        {
          // Use getDateInstance to use predefined
          // date formats.
          usDateFormatter = DateFormat.getDateInstance(
                                          DateFormat.DEFAULT,
                                          usLocale);
          formattedDate = usDateFormatter.format(theDate);
          System.out.println(formattedDate + " " +
                  usLocale.toString());
           deDateFormatter = DateFormat.getDateInstance(
                                          DateFormat.DEFAULT, deLocale);
          formattedDate = deDateFormatter.format(theDate);
          System.out.println(formattedDate + " " +
                  deLocale.toString());
           // DateFormat.DEFAULT is one of five
           // choices. Here are the others:
          usDateFormatter = DateFormat. getDateInstance(
                                              DateFormat.SHORT,
                                              usLocale);
          formattedDate = usDateFormatter.format(theDate);
          System.out.println("Short form:  " + formattedDate + " " +
                  usLocale.toString());
           deDateFormatter = DateFormat.getDateInstance(
                                              DateFormat.SHORT,
                                                           deLocale);
          formattedDate = deDateFormatter.format(theDate);
          System.out.println("Short form:  " + formattedDate + " " +
                  deLocale.toString());
           // Medium date:
          usDateFormatter = DateFormat.getDateInstance(
```

```
                                    DateFormat.MEDIUM,
                                    usLocale);
 formattedDate = usDateFormatter.format(theDate);
 System.out.println("Medium form:   " + formattedDate + " " +
         usLocale.toString());
  deDateFormatter = DateFormat.getDateInstance(
                                    DateFormat.MEDIUM,
                                                deLocale);
  formattedDate = deDateFormatter.format(theDate);
  System.out.println("Medium form:   " + formattedDate + " " +
         deLocale.toString());
  // Long form:
  usDateFormatter = DateFormat.getDateInstance(
                                    DateFormat.LONG,
                                    usLocale);
  formattedDate = usDateFormatter.format(theDate);
  System.out.println("Long form:     " + formattedDate + " " +
         usLocale.toString());
  deDateFormatter = DateFormat.getDateInstance(
                                    DateFormat.LONG,
                                                deLocale);
  formattedDate = deDateFormatter.format(theDate);
  System.out.println("Long form:     " + formattedDate + " " +
         deLocale.toString());
  // Full form:
  usDateFormatter = DateFormat.getDateInstance(
                                    DateFormat.FULL,
                                    usLocale);
  formattedDate = usDateFormatter.format(theDate);
  System.out.println("Full form:     " + formattedDate + " " +
         usLocale.toString());
  deDateFormatter = DateFormat.getDateInstance(
                                    DateFormat.FULL,
                                                deLocale);
  formattedDate = deDateFormatter.format(theDate);
  System.out.println("Full form:     " + formattedDate + " " +
         deLocale.toString());
  // You can also get just the Time,
  // getTimeInstance(), in these
  // locale-specific formats or both the date
  // and time. Here is an example of the
  // API for both date and time.
  usDateFormatter = DateFormat.getDateTimeInstance(
                                    DateFormat.FULL,
                                    DateFormat.FULL,
                                    usLocale);
  formattedDate = usDateFormatter.format(theDate);
  System.out.println("Full form:     " + formattedDate + " " +
         usLocale.toString());
```

continues

Listing 18.5 continued

```
            deDateFormatter = DateFormat.getDateTimeInstance(
                                            DateFormat.FULL,
                                            DateFormat.FULL,
                                                            deLocale);
   formattedDate = deDateFormatter.format(theDate);
   System.out.println("Full form:  " + formattedDate + " " +
           deLocale.toString());
// Perform custom formatting of dates and time.
String datePattern = "yyyy.MM.dd G 'at' hh:mm:ss z";
SimpleDateFormat sdf =
            new SimpleDateFormat(datePattern,
                                                            usLocale);
   String formattedDate = sdf.format(theDate);
   System.out.println(datePattern + "    " +
                                    formattedDate);
   datePattern = "EEE, MMM d, ''yy";
   sdf = new SimpleDateFormat(datePattern,
                                                            usLocale);
   formattedDate = sdf.format(theDate);
   System.out.println(datePattern + "    " +
                                    formattedDate);
   // Show the date and time with two custom
   // formats.
   // You can also use DateFormatSymbols
   // to modify how dates and times are formatted.
   DateFormatSymbols dfSymbols;
   String[] defaultWeek;
   String[] modifiedWeek;

   dfSymbols =
          new DateFormatSymbols(usLocale);
   defaultWeek = dfSymbols.getShortWeekdays();
   System.out.println("Default short weekday names:");
   for (int i = 0; i < defaultWeek.length; i++)
            {
              System.out.println(defaultWeek[i]);
            }
    System.out.println("Modified weekday names:");
    String[] shortDayNames = {
          "", "Su", "Mo", "Tu", "We", "Th", "Fr", "Sa"};
     dfSymbols.setShortWeekdays(shortDayNames);

     modifiedWeek = dfSymbols.getShortWeekdays();
     for (int i = 0; i < modifiedWeek.length; i++)
            {
              System.out.println(modifiedWeek[i]);
            }

       sdf = new SimpleDateFormat("E", dfSymbols);
```

```
                String theDay = sdf.format(theDate);
                System.out.println(theDay);

            return true;
            }
    }
public class TextDriver3
    {
      public static void main (String[] args)
            {
              DateShaper ds9 = new DateShaper();
              ds9.formatDates();
            }
    }
```

As you can see from this program, you can use predefined data and time formats using the `DateFormat` class and calling

- getDateInstance()
- getTimeInstance()
- getDateTimeInstance()

For customizing date and time values, you can use `SimpleDateFormat` instead. There are lots of different ways to combine formatting options, such as

```
EEE, MMM d, ''yy
```

which produces, on today's date, the value

```
Sat, Aug 21, '99
```

The `SimpleDateFormat` class provides the information in Table 18.2 on formatting. (This table is taken from the Java API documentation for `SimpleDateFormat` from Sun Microsystems, Inc.)

Table 18.2 Information Provided by SimpleDateFormat.

Symbol	Meaning	Presentation	Example
G	Era designator	(Text)	AD
y	Year	(Number)	1996
M	Month in year	(Text & Number)	July & 07
d	Day in month	(Number)	10
h	Hour in am/pm (1~12)	(Number)	12
H	Hour in day (0~23)	(Number)	0
m	Minute in hour	(Number)	30
s	Second in minute	(Number)	55
S	Millisecond	(Number)	978
E	Day in week	(Text)	Tuesday
D	Day in year	(Number)	189

continues

Table 18.2   continued

Symbol	Meaning	Presentation	Example
F	Day of week in month	(Number)	2 (2nd Wednesday in July)
w	Week in year	(Number)	27
W	Week in month	(Number)	2
a	am/pm marker	(Text)	PM
k	Hour in day (1~24)	(Number)	24
K	Hour in am/pm (0~11)	(Number)	0
z	Time zone	(Text)	Pacific Standard Time
'	Escape for text	(Delimiter)	
' '	Single quote	(Literal)	'

> **NOTE**
>
> If you do not specify a locale when you instantiate a `DateFormat` object, the default locale will be used.

The `DecimalFormatSymbols` class provides for changing separator and decimal point characters, among other things. Similarly, the `DateFormatSymbols` class provides for creating custom date formats. For example, the `setWeekdays()` method allows you to define your own names for the days of the week. You have freedom to set the various properties any way you want.

> **TIP**
>
> Although the example programs show simple, single items, you can also use these formatting techniques with multivalue, complex messages. To do this, you create a "template" with parameters that accept the formatted value. Support for complex message formatting is provided with the `MessageFormat` class.
>
> Multivalue message formatting is needed when using languages besides English because of variation in word order. English puts the verb after the subject, but German puts it at the end of the sentence. Hebrew, on the other hand, can put the verb first in the sentence. Since word order may vary widely, you cannot simply put the values in the same place in a message across languages.

Although they are not covered here, there are also classes for supporting testing characters, parsing text, and comparing `Strings`. See the `java.text` package for examples, such as the `Character` or `Collator` classes in the Java API doc.

CHAPTER 19

Utility Classes

The package java.util contains many classes that do not logically belong elsewhere. Several of these classes are very important, such as Date, Vector, EventObject, GregorianCalendar, and Properties. Most of these classes have been around since JDK 1.0, or at least JDK 1.1. This chapter focuses primarily on what is new in Java 2: the Collection Framework. There is also coverage of two classes that are quite important in Java programs: GregorianCalendar and Properties. While EventObject is an important class, you generally encounter it only through a subclass, such as java.awt.event.ActionEvent.

The Collection Framework

The Collection Framework is intended as a major enhancement over prior support for collections, which was fairly minimal. Previously Java had only Vector, Hashtable, and Enumeration, as well as arrays, for collections. This was not sufficient for many programs, and developers needed to either purchase third-party classes or write their own. The Java Collection Framework addresses the lack of a robust set of collection classes. Support has been added for multiple types of bags and sets. Java's Enumeration mechanism has been superseded by an Iterator.

The Collection Framework consists of two parts: interfaces and implementations. The purpose of this distinction is that a set, for example, may be implemented in different ways. Therefore, Set should be an interface, not a class.

Simply put, a collection is an object that contains multiple elements. It can be treated as one object, or the individual elements may be treated separately. A collection can contain many different types of data—sometimes of the same data type, such as addresses in an address file, or of disparate types of customer information for an e-commerce transaction, such as name, address, phone number, and email address. The real

380 Chapter 19: Utility Classes

core of the Collection Framework consists of the interfaces, for which algorithms can be written that apply to any class that implements the given interface. The Collection classes in java.util are simply implementations of the interfaces for the convenience of developers.

Collection Interfaces

The interfaces provided in the Collection Framework allow you to access and manipulate elements in a collection in a manner that is independent of the implementation of the collection. There are two groups of interfaces in the Collection Framework, one that begins with the Collection interface and a second that begins with the Map interface. These are shown in Figures 19.1 and 19.2, respectively.

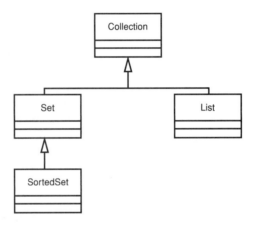

Figure 19.1
Inheritance hierarchy for the Collection interface.

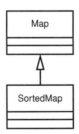

Figure 19.2
Inheritance hierarchy for the Map interface.

The reason there are two inheritance hierarchies is that while SortedSet is a special kind of Set, and Set is a special kind of Collection, the Map interface represents a different way of viewing data, even though a Map does represent a collection of items. Based on the interface definitions, a Map does not have an IsA relationship with a Collection.

Collection Interfaces

> **NOTE**
>
> In order to provide for interfaces that cover many different implementations, several methods declared in these interfaces are optional, in the sense that a given implementation does not need to support this operation if it is inappropriate. If a method that is not supported is called on an object of a class that does not support that operation, an `UnsupportedOperationException` is thrown.
>
> The Collection Framework was designed to provide a complete set of powerful and flexible ways to implement collections. In order to allow for simple implementations, however, there are several optional methods. You can skip those in our implementation if you wish.

There are four main interfaces:

- `Collection` — A `Collection` is a group of objects that are elements of the `Collection`. No subclasses directly implement the `Collection` interface, but most classes that implement sub-interfaces accept a `Collection` object in their constructors. A `Collection` may represent a group of objects that contains duplicates or a group of elements that are unique in the `Collection`.
- `Set` — The `Set` interface provides methods for a `Collection`, which allows no duplicate elements. In the library example I've been using, a `Set` might be used to represent library patrons or card catalog entries.
- `List` — A `List` provides methods for a `Collection` that contains an ordered sequence of elements. A `List` may contain duplicate elements. Vectors implement the `List` interface.
- `Map` — A `Map` represents an object that contains key/value pairs, in which the pairs are unique. A hashtable illustrates this.

> **NOTE**
>
> You can view a `Map` implementation as a `Collection` by using one of the `Collection` views, `keySet`, `values`, or `entrySet`.

Two other interfaces, `Comparable` and `Comparator`, can be used to compare the elements of one or more collections. `Comparable` provides methods for automatic sorting of elements in a natural order. The `Comparator` interface provides methods for you to have complete control over the ordering of elements in a `Collection`, in particular implementations of `SortedSet` and `SortedMap`. Both of these maintain elements in ascending order. These two interfaces provide the ability to sort generic objects as long as they implement the `Comparable` interface or as long as a suitable `Comparator` object is provided. Several core Java classes, such as `String` and the primitive wrapper classes like `Integer`, implement the `Comparable` interface, allowing them to be easily sorted. You do not have to write your own sorting mechanism from scratch.

Here are the basic methods implemented by all `Collection` implementation classes:

```
int size();
boolean isEmpty();
boolean contains(Object element);
```

```
boolean add(Object element);    // Optional
boolean remove(Object element); // Optional
Iterator iterator();
```

There are optional methods as well (optional in the sense that an implementation class does not have to give them a meaningful implementation):

```
boolean addAll(Collection c);
boolean removeAll(Collection c);
```

There are also two methods to create arrays from the Collection implementation:

```
Object[] toArray();
Object[] toArray(Object a[]);
```

These methods are fairly self-explanatory, especially if you've ever used a Vector. These are generalized methods. This means that the add() method does not require that an element cannot be a duplicated. That is an implementation detail of a specific class.

As mentioned, the Iterator class, an instance of which is returned by the iterator() method, is similar to an Enumeration but improves upon the Enumeration class by providing a way to remove elements of the collection through which the program is iterating. An Iterator can be used on any type of Collection. That is, its methods, like hasNext() or remove(), work on any kind of Collection, whether an unsorted Set with no duplicates or a SortedList with duplicates.

Methods such as addAll() and removeAll() are "bulk methods"; that is, they work on an entire Collection at one time, allowing you to do mass adds, mass deletes, mass comparison tests, and so forth.

TIP

You can turn a Collection, coll, into a Set containing no duplicates by doing this:
Collection uniqueElements = new HashSet(coll);

For a complete list of the methods in each Collection Framework interface, see Chapter 33, "java.util." There is more that could be said about the Collection interfaces, but it is time to move on to techniques for using their implementation classes.

Collection Implementations

This section covers techniques for using some of the implementation classes. It is not exhaustive, but it is illustrative.

NOTE

It is possible to create your own implementations of the interfaces using the abstract implementations, such as AbstractList. In fact, the abstract classes provide implementation for some of the methods. You just need to provide the implementations for some of the basic methods.

The class names for implementation classes are made of two parts: the implementation name and the interface name, such as HashMap, a Map implementation based on hashing. Table 19.1 shows the main implementation classes by interface.

Table 19.1 Implementation Classes for Each Main Collection Interface

Interface	Implementing Classes
Set	HashSet
	TreeSet (implements SortedSet)
List	ArrayList
	LinkedList
Map	HashMap
	TreeMap (implements SortedMap)

Here are some important features of all these Collection Framework implementation classes:

- Consistent names—All are built on the implemented interface.
- Consistent behavior—All these classes implement the optional methods in the interfaces. Every one of these classes permits null elements, keys, and values.
- All these classes use unsynchronized methods.
- All have fail-fast Iterators, which fail quickly if they detect concurrent modification.
- All are serializable.
- All these classes implement the clone() method.

The combination of methods that do not use synchronization and fast-fail Iterators is critically important. A Vector's methods are potentially slower than a HashMap's methods because a Vector uses synchronized methods. This prevents two Threads from modifying a Vector element in an unpredictable manner. A HashMap's methods do not use synchronization. This means that a HashMap is vulnerable to undesirable modification. To deal with this, the Iterator for a Collection object will fail quickly in a safe manner if it detects some other object is updating the HashMap concurrently. If you have coded your application to use a HashMap, while avoiding incorrect concurrent updates to a HashMap, your program will run faster than an equivalent program that uses a Vector instead of a HashMap.

CAUTION

The fast-fail mechanism comes into play only when the underlying collection is changed such that the Iterator is no longer valid. This means that you could do concurrent updates that do not corrupt the state of the data as far as the Iterator is concerned, but still have inconsistent updates.

Vector continues to use synchronized methods in Java 2. The rationale for using unsynchronized methods is that synchronization is often of no benefit because only one

Thread is using the Collection object, and therefore there is no danger of concurrent updates putting the data into an incorrect or inconsistent state. Thus, synchronization helps the minority of applications while penalizing the majority needlessly.

TIP

If you need to use a synchronized version of a Collection object's methods, you can wrap the object with a synchronization wrapper. The synchronization wrappers allow any Collection implementation to use synchronization.

Sun suggests that when dealing with a Collection implementation you assign its instance to an interface type, so that you can deal with the object in an implementation-independent way, with the specific implementation choice based on performance requirements. In keeping with this suggestion, the following code examples are built around the interface, not the specific class. So there are examples for using a Set, a List, and a Map.

Set Implementations

In this section I will show how to use a Set implementation. Sets allow for a Collection that contains only unique values.

NOTE

Attempting to add a duplicate element does not produce an Exception of any kind. The operation is simply not successful, and there is nothing you need to do about the JVM's action.

There are two implementation classes for the Set interface in java.util: HashSet and TreeSet. A HashSet uses a hashtable to store its elements. A TreeSet stores its elements in a balanced binary tree called a *red-black tree*. According to an article at the Java Developer's Connection (http://developer.javasoft.com), a HashSet performs better than a TreeSet. All the Collection classes support the Collection method iterator(). An Iterator provides a means for stepping through a Collection of any kind. It will be implemented differently for a Set than for a Map or List, but a developer does not have to be concerned with how an Iterator works for a given Collection implementation class. To use an Iterator, you call its hasNext() method, which returns true if there are more elements to traverse and false if there are no more elements in the Collection to traverse.

HashSet Code Example

Sets are easy to create, and the HashSet is a simple yet handy implementation of the Set interface. Listing 19.1 shows how to create and use a HashSet.

Listing 19.1   Using a HashSet (SetDriver.java)
```
import java.util.*;

class SetMaker
   {
```

```
        Set bookSet;

        public SetMaker()
              {
              // Make a HashSet to hold the names of
              // Graeco-Roman Historiographers.
              bookSet = new HashSet();
              bookSet.add("Seutonius");
              bookSet.add("Thucydides");
              bookSet.add("Tacitus");
              bookSet.add("Josephus");
              bookSet.add("Xenophon");
              bookSet.add("Luke");
              // Here a HashSet is created and its object
              // reference is assigned to an object of type Set,
              // i.e., an object that implements the Set interface.

              // Next use the Collection method add() to add
              // elements to this HashSet.  This approach lets
              // the developer call the same Collection methods
              // regardless of how a given implementation class
              // like HashSet, actually adds an element to the
              // underlying set object.
              }
public boolean traverseSet()
          {
          Iterator iterator = bookSet.iterator();
          // Create an Iterator object, again using
          // a generic Collection method, not a specific
          // HashSet method.
          while (iterator.hasNext())
          // hasNext() returns true if there is another
          // element in the Collection to which to move.
                {
                System.out.println ("Graeco-Roman Historiographer:   " +
                        iterator.next());
                // next() steps to the next element in the Collection.
                }
             System.out.println("The maximum value in the HashSet is "
                  + Collections.max(bookSet));
             // This uses a static method of the Collections class
             // Find the maximum value in the Set.
              bookSet.add("Luke");
              // Attempt to add a duplicate element.  This should have no effect.
              System.out.println("HashSet after attempting to add" +
                                                 " a duplicate value ");
              // A new Iterator is needed to iterate again.
              Iterator anotherIterator = bookSet.iterator();
```

continues

Listing 19.1   continued

```
            while (anotherIterator.hasNext())
                {
                    System.out.println("Graeco-Roman Historiographer:   " +
                        anotherIterator.next());
                }
            return true;
        }

    } // End class definition for MapMaker.

public class SetDriver
    {

      public static void main(String args[])
          {
            SetMaker sm = new SetMaker();
            boolean result = sm.traverseSet();
            System.exit(0);
          }

    }
```

In keeping with the library theme, this program stores the names of important Graeco-Roman history writers in a `HashSet`. Then it prints them. Here is the output:

```
C:\Purejava\Source\Chap19>java SetDriver
Graeco-Roman Historiographer:   Xenophon
Graeco-Roman Historiographer:   Seutonius
Graeco-Roman Historiographer:   Tacitus
Graeco-Roman Historiographer:   Josephus
Graeco-Roman Historiographer:   Thucydides
Graeco-Roman Historiographer:   Luke
The maximum value in the HashSet is Xenophon
HashSet after attempting to add a duplicate value
Graeco-Roman Historiographer:   Xenophon
Graeco-Roman Historiographer:   Seutonius
Graeco-Roman Historiographer:   Tacitus
Graeco-Roman Historiographer:   Josephus
Graeco-Roman Historiographer:   Thucydides
Graeco-Roman Historiographer:   Luke
```

What you should notice about this list is that it is not sorted at all. You should also notice that the elements were printed out from the `HashSet` in the order they appear in it, which is different from the order in which you added them to the `HashSet`. This is a function of the value of each element's hash code. You can also find the minimum and maximum values of any `Collection`. It is illustrated here by looking for the element with the maximum value. In this case, that might not be meaningful, but it would be in many applications. To show that attempting to add a duplicate element has no effect on the `HashSet`, the program also attempts to add a duplicate entry.

List Implementations

This section shows how to use a List implementation. Lists permit duplicate values to be added. They also provide ordering. By default this is natural ordering, or ordering by ascending value. There are several methods that apply more readily to Lists than to Sets, as will be shown in the sample code. A List adds to the methods provided by a Collection the ability to retrieve a specific element based on an index, such as element 5 in the collection.

One of the differences between an array and a Collection is that an array is fixed in size once instantiated, while a Collection can grow dynamically. An ArrayList is essentially an array that can be enlarged. An ArrayList allows any kind of value, including null, and implements all the optional Collection methods. It uses an array internally but can grow. It is roughly equivalent to a Vector, except that an ArrayList's methods are unsynchronized. As the following code snippet shows, an ArrayList can be created much like a Set:

```
List subjectList = new ArrayList();
 subjectList.add("History");
subjectList.add("Philosophy");
subjectList.add("Religion");
subjectList.add("Literature");
Iterator iterator = subjectList.iterator();
while (iterator.hasNext())
     {
        System.out.println(iterator.next());
    }
```

Not only can you easily make a List, but you can change between Set and List in your code with minimal effort, as your needs change.

List Code Example

Lists are easy to create. Because the various Collection subinterfaces all provide many of the same methods, this code is practically identical to the code for using a HashSet—except that it uses an ArrayList instead.

Lists can use several algorithms (methods for performing useful tasks, such as sorting a List) with the Collections.sort() method, which is most relevant to a List. Here are some other examples:

- Collections.shuffle() —Mixes up the order of elements.
- Collections.binarySearch() —Performs a binary search for an element.
- Collections.reverse() —Reverses the order of the elements in the List.

CAUTION

Be careful not to confuse the Collection interface with the Collections class, which ends with an *s*. The latter provides implemented methods that can be defined and used independently of the Collection implementation.

TIP

You can convert a simple array into a `List` using the method `Arrays.asList()`, like this:

```
String holdings[] = {"Books", "Journals", "Manuscripts"};
List holdingsList = Arrays.asList(holdings);
```

There is also a `LinkedList` class, which implements a `List` as a linked structure. Although it provides all the expected operations for a stack, a queue, or a double-ended linked list (deque), a developer does not have to go through the usual pain of maintaining previous and next references, as would be necessary when implementing a linked list in C. This is all done for you by the `LinkedList` class. The `LinkedList` class has specific methods for manipulating the first and last elements of the list.

NOTE

Since there is a separate `Stack` class, the need to use the `LinkedList` class is reduced, and in general it is preferable to use `ArrayList`.

While the preferred `List` implementation is `ArrayList`, the sample program in Listing 19.2 shows how to create and use a `LinkedList`, including the constructor that takes a `Collection`—in this case, an `ArrayList`.

Listing 19.2   Using a LinkedList (ListDriver.java)

```java
import java.util.*;

class ListMaker
    {
    ArrayList bookList;
    LinkedList authorList;

    public ListMaker()
        {
        // Make an ArrayList to hold the names of
        // Graeco-Roman Historiographers.
        bookList = new ArrayList();
        bookList.add("Seutonius");
        bookList.add("Thucydides");
        bookList.add("Tacitus");
        bookList.add("Josephus");
        bookList.add("Xenophon");
        bookList.add("Luke");
        // Here an ArrayList is created. Then
        // this ArrayList is used in the constructor of a LinkedList.
        // This must be a LinkedList in order to access
        // LinkedList-specific methods.
        authorList = new LinkedList(bookList);
        }

public boolean traverseList()
```

```
        {
         Iterator iterator = authorList.iterator();
         // Get an Iterator for the LinkedList
         // then step through the LinkedList.
          while (iterator.hasNext())
         // hasNext() returns true if there is another
         // element in the Collection to which to move.
                {
                   System.out.println("Graeco-Roman Historiographer:   " +
                           iterator.next());
                   // next() steps to the next element in the Collection.
                }
         // Now use the sort algorithm to produce a sorted list.
         Collections.sort(authorList);
         Iterator anotherIterator = authorList.iterator();
         // Create an Iterator object, again using
         // a generic Collection method, not a specific LinkedList method.
         System.out.println(" ");
         System.out.println("LinkedList presented in" +
                                       " sorted order ");
          while (anotherIterator.hasNext())
                {
                   System.out.println("Graeco-Roman Historiographer:   " +
                           anotherIterator.next());
                }
           // Now add an element to the front of the LinkedList.
           authorList.addFirst("Lucian");
           // Now add an element to a specific location.
           authorList.add(4, "Polybius");
           // Now show that a duplicate can be added to a list.
           authorList.add("Luke");
           // Now iterate a final time through the LinkedList to see
           // the results of the additions.
           Iterator thirdIterator = authorList.iterator();
           System.out.println(" ");
            System.out.println("LinkedList after" +
                                       " adding more elements ");
           while (thirdIterator.hasNext())
                {
                   System.out.println("Graeco-Roman Historiographer:   " +
                           thirdIterator.next());
                }
           return true;
         }

    } // End class definition for MapMaker.

public class ListDriver
    {
```

continues

Listing 19.2   continued

```
    public static void main(String args[])
       {
         ListMaker lm = new ListMaker();
         boolean result = lm.traverseList();
         System.exit(0);
       }
  }
```

This code departs from the statement made earlier that it is best to use the interfaces and their methods rather than coding something like

```
ArrayList al = new ArrayList();
```

The reason this code is different is that since the `List` interface does not support all the methods available to a `LinkedList`, it was necessary to work specifically with an object of type `LinkedList` and an object reference of type `LinkedList`. This code also illustrates that, unlike with a `Set`, you can add a duplicate to a `List`. Notice also, as in the earlier example, that you need to get a new `Iterator` object if you want to traverse a `Collection` multiple times using `next()`. Here is the output from the program:

```
java ListDriver
Graeco-Roman Historiographer:   Seutonius
Graeco-Roman Historiographer:   Thucydides
Graeco-Roman Historiographer:   Tacitus
Graeco-Roman Historiographer:   Josephus
Graeco-Roman Historiographer:   Xenophon
Graeco-Roman Historiographer:   Luke
LinkedList presented in sorted order
Graeco-Roman Historiographer:   Josephus
Graeco-Roman Historiographer:   Luke
Graeco-Roman Historiographer:   Seutonius
Graeco-Roman Historiographer:   Tacitus
Graeco-Roman Historiographer:   Thucydides
Graeco-Roman Historiographer:   Xenophon

LinkedList after adding more elements
Graeco-Roman Historiographer:   Lucian
Graeco-Roman Historiographer:   Josephus
Graeco-Roman Historiographer:   Luke
Graeco-Roman Historiographer:   Seutonius
Graeco-Roman Historiographer:   Polybius
Graeco-Roman Historiographer:   Tacitus
Graeco-Roman Historiographer:   Thucydides
Graeco-Roman Historiographer:   Xenophon
Graeco-Roman Historiographer:   Luke
```

First, the contents of `LinkedList` are printed using an `Iterator`. Then the `Collections.sort()` method is used to sort the contents. This does not merely display the elements in sorted order but modifies the order of the elements as they exist in the linked structure. Then, to show additional `LinkedList` features, an element is added to the start of the `List` with `addFirst()`, an element is added to a specific location (element 4, with elements beginning at element 0), and then a duplicate element is added to the end of the list.

> **NOTE**
>
> An `Iterator` does not support adding elements while iterating through a `List`. If you attempt this, a `ConcurrentModificationException` is thrown, followed by a fast-fail. There is a subinterface, called `ListIterator`, that permits `add`, `set`, and `remove` while iterating through a `List`. It's instantiated like this:
>
> `ListIterator iterator = bookList.listIterator(bookList.size());`

Map Implementations

As noted, a `Map` contains name/value pairs. Each entry in the `Map` contains two values: one for the key and the other for the value. A `Map` cannot contain any duplicates, and no ordering is mandated. There are two general purpose `Map` implementations: `HashMap` and `TreeMap`. You would use `TreeMap` if the order of items in the `Map` was important. Otherwise, you would simply use a `HashMap`.

Map Code Example

A `Map`'s methods are not synchronized. If multiple `Thread`s attempt to update the `Map` at once, an exception may be thrown, and the data will likely end up in an unpredictable state. If you want to allow concurrent updates but also want `Thread`-safety, you can wrap the `Map` (or any other type of `Collection`) in a synchronized wrapper. In this case, I am using `Collections.synchronizedMap`. This provides synchronization without a developer having to create a special subclass of `Map` just to get synchronization, or use the older, less desirable `Hashtable`. Listing 19.3 shows an example of using a `TreeMap`.

Listing 19.3   Using a TreeMap to Provide an Ordered Map Object (MapDriver.java)
```
import java.util.*;

class MapMaker
    {
    Map bookMap;

    public MapMaker()
        {
        bookMap = Collections.synchronizedMap(new TreeMap());
        // Make a TreeMap and wrap it with a synchronizedMap
        // wrapper to make the TreeMap methods synchronized
        // which they are not by default.
        bookMap.put("Lewis, C.S.", "The Lion, the Witch and the Wardrobe");
        bookMap.put("Schaeffer, Francis", "How Shall We then Live?");
        bookMap.put("Pascal, Blaise", "Pensees");
        bookMap.put("Authors unknown", "Septuagint");
        bookMap.put("Philo", "Life of Moses");
```

continues

Listing 19.3 *continued*

```
        // Use put() to add name-value pairs into a TreeMap.
        }

    public boolean traverseMap()
        {
          Iterator iterator = bookMap.entrySet().iterator();
          // Obtain an Iterator based on the Collection view "entrySet".
          while (iterator.hasNext())
                {
                  Map.Entry e = (Map.Entry)iterator.next();
                  System.out.println(e.getKey() + ", "
                                  + e.getValue());
                  // The entrySet view contains both keys and values.
                }

            // Search the TreeMap for a particular value.
            System.out.println("");
            if(bookMap.containsKey("Lewis, C.S."))
                  System.out.println("Author C.S. Lewis found");
            else
                    System.out.println("Author not found");

            // Next, return just the keys.
            Iterator keyIterator = bookMap.keySet().iterator();
            // Obtain an Iterator based on the Collection view "keySet".
            System.out.println("");
            System.out.println("Print just the keys " +
                                            "for the TreeMap");
            while (keyIterator.hasNext())
                  {
                    System.out.println(keyIterator.next());
                    // The keySet view contains only keys.
                  }
          return true;
        }
    } // End class definition for MapMaker.

public class MapDriver
    {

    public static void main(String args[])
        {
          MapMaker mm = new MapMaker();
          mm.traverseMap();
          System.exit(0);
        }



    }
```

Notice that the input was ordered in the TreeMap based on the natural order of the key. That is, the Map was created in ascending order based on the key, in this case author names.

You can use Collection views to iterate through a Map's contents. In fact, using Collection views is the only way to iterate through a Map's contents. You can print the keys, the values, or both from a Map. Here's the basic code to iterate a Map's keys:

```
for (Iterator iterator = theMap.keySet().iterator();  iterator.hasNext(); )
        {
          System.out.println(iterator.next());
        }
```

To iterate through the values in a Map, you could do this:

```
for (Iterator iterator= theMap.entrySet().iterator(); iterator.hasNext();)
        {
          Map.Entry e = (Map.Entry) iterator.next();
          System.out.println(e.getKey() + ": " + e.getValue());
        }
```

Here's the output from the program:

```
C:\Purejava\Source\Chap19>java MapDriver
Authors unknown, Septuagint
Lewis, C.S., The Lion, the Witch and the Wardrobe
Pascal, Blaise, Pensees
Philo, Life of Moses
Schaeffer, Francis, How Shall We then Live?

Author C.S. Lewis found

Print just the keys for the TreeMap
Authors unknown
Lewis, C.S.
Pascal, Blaise
Philo
Schaeffer, Francis
```

You can also search a Map for a specific key with containsKey() or a specific value with containsValue(). You can also change the value of a given value for a specific key during iteration over the Map using setValue() or remove an element using remove(), provided the specific Map implementation supports these methods.

There is one other handy thing you can use a Map for: a multimap. There is no class or interface for a multimap because it is not used very often. To make a multimap, you can create a Map that uses a Set or a List for a value. In this way, you might create a foreign language dictionary, in which an English word serves as the key and a Set containing another language's potential equivalents is listed. Or, you might use a List to provide a multielement description foran inventory item named in the key.

GregorianCalendar

In JDK 1.0, the Date class, which is a measure of the number of milliseconds that have passed since the start of the current era, was used for calendar-type dates. You would create a Date object and set its day, month, year, and time as needed. The Date class, however, lacked several important properties, such as support for daylight savings time and time zones. In response to these gaps, Javasoft introduced the Calendar and GregorianCalendar classes in JDK 1.1. Beginning with JDK 1.1 and now in Java 2, the java.util.Date class is intended to be used for a "moment in time." That is, if you need to compare two time values or subtract an earlier time from a later time, to find out how long something took to happen, the Date class is one appropriate way to do this. The Calendar class and its subclasses support internationalization as well. These classes also provide for making a time stamp independent of a particular calendar.

TIP

> A preferable method for getting moments in time in milliseconds, which you can then compare and manipulate, is through calling
>
> System.currentTimeInMillis()
>
> Since this does not require objects to be instantiated by you, it will likely perform better than creating and manipulating two Date objects. As noted elsewhere in this book, object allocation and deallocation are the most expensive activities you can perform in Java.

The "current era" is from UNIX and equals midnight on January 1, 1970. So a Date object represents the number of milliseconds that have passed since then or, in the case of a date value prior to the start of the era, the milliseconds from the start of the era back to the date. In JDK 1.0, the Date class supported this function as well as serving as the class to use for calendar-type dates. As of JDK 1.1, all the methods that relate to calendar-type dates have been deprecated. You should not use this class for calendar-type dates.

The Calendar and GregorianCalendar classes were added to JDK 1.1 to use for calendar-type dates. The Calendar class is the base class, but the only concrete subclass in Java 2 is GregorianCalendar, which allows you to manipulate Gregorian and Julian dates.

NOTE

> To create a class for a calendar system other than Gregorian or Julian, I recommend that you subclass Calendar if possible, in order to get some of the functions such as time zones. You should make your own separate class that does not subclass Calendar only if you need to support a calendar system that is totally foreign to the month, day, and year system of Calendar. This might be the case for, say, a Chinese or Jewish calendar. The Calendar class does not lend itself well to lunar-oriented calendars, so using the Calendar as a base class for a calendar that needs to track the 14th of Nisan would be rather awkward.

You should use the GregorianCalendar class to create and manipulate calendar-type dates. This class includes support for year, month, day, day of the week, week of the month, daylight saving time, and time zones.

> **NOTE**
>
> The GregorianCalendar class, developed by Taligent, has some quirks. In particular, there are methods that should probably be public that are protected. This makes them much more difficult to use, because you have to subclass Calendar to use them. There is also no handy way to format and print a GregorianCalendar object. You have to convert it to a Date object first and then use SimpleDateFormat's methods! Still, the Calendar and GregorianCalendar classes are a big improvement over Date for tracking calendar-type dates.

GregorianCalendar Code Example

Besides telling you that you should use GregorianCalendar instead of Date, there is nothing else conceptually to know. Listing 19.4 shows how to create, interrogate, and modify a GregorianCalendar object. There are a number of ways to create a GregorianCalendar object, ranging from accepting a default time zone and the current time in the default locale to specifying the time zone and the precise year, month, day, and time you want.

Listing 19.4 Using the GregorianCalendar Class (CalendarDriver.java)

```
// Basic GregorianCalendar Program.
import java.util.*;
import java.text.*;

class DateInfo
    {
      SimpleTimeZone pdt;
      // A GregorianCalendar needs a time zone.

      public boolean displayCalenderInfo()
          {
            // Get time zone ids.
            String[] tzIds = TimeZone.getAvailableIDs(-8 * 60 * 60 * 1000);
            // If no ids were returned, something is wrong, so quit.
            if (tzIds.length == 0)
                return false;
            else;

            // Create a Pacific Standard Time zone.
            pdt = new SimpleTimeZone(-8 * 60 * 60 * 1000, tzIds[0]);
            // Set up rules for daylight savings time
            pdt.setStartRule
                  (Calendar.APRIL, 1, Calendar.SUNDAY, 2 * 60 * 60 * 1000);
            pdt.setEndRule
```

continues

Listing 19.4 *continued*

```
                (Calendar.OCTOBER, -1, Calendar.SUNDAY, 2 * 60 * 60 *
                1000);
        // Create a GregorianCalendar with the Pacific Daylight time zone
        // and the current date and time.
        // NOTE: You can set a superclass equal to a subclass instance.
        Calendar calendar = new GregorianCalendar(pdt);
        // Create a GregorianCalendar object using
        // Pacific Daylight Time, accounting
        // for Daylight savings time. This does not
        // actually set the date in this object.
        // That is done, oddly enough, with a Date
        // object and the setTime() method as shown below.
        Date trialTime = new Date();
        // Gets the current moment.
        calendar.setTime(trialTime);
        // Set the GregorianCalendar object's date and time
        // to the current moment.
        // Print a bunch of interesting things.
        System.out.println("Calendar data members and methods");
        System.out.println("ERA: " + calendar.get(Calendar.ERA));
        System.out.println("YEAR: " + calendar.get(Calendar.YEAR));
        // Print the era and year. This era is BC or AD.
        // Note: Months begin with 0.
        System.out.println("MONTH: " + calendar.get(Calendar.MONTH));
        System.out.println("WEEK_OF_YEAR: " +
                            calendar.get(Calendar.WEEK_OF_YEAR));
        System.out.println("WEEK_OF_MONTH: " +
        calendar.get(Calendar.WEEK_OF_MONTH));
        // Print month and week information.
        // These values are all numeric. You would need to convert them
        // to make them user-friendly. The Calendar class has static
        // final values to match all the possibilities, so you could
        // test the value in a switch statement to come up
        // with the correct String to display or print.
        // Caldendar.Date = day of month
        System.out.println("DATE: " + calendar.get(Calendar.DATE));
        System.out.println("DAY_OF_MONTH: " +
            calendar.get(Calendar.DAY_OF_MONTH));
        System.out.println("DAY_OF_YEAR: " +
            calendar.get(Calendar.DAY_OF_YEAR));
        System.out.println("DAY_OF_WEEK: " +
            calendar.get(Calendar.DAY_OF_WEEK));
        System.out.println("DAY_OF_WEEK_IN_MONTH: "
                + calendar.get(Calendar.DAY_OF_WEEK_IN_MONTH));
        // Prints information about the time of day next.
        // AM =0, PM =1
        System.out.println("AM_PM: " + calendar.get(Calendar.AM_PM));
        System.out.println("HOUR: " + calendar.get(Calendar.HOUR));
        System.out.println("HOUR_OF_DAY: " +
```

```
                              calendar.get(Calendar.HOUR_OF_DAY));
System.out.println("MINUTE: " + calendar.get(Calendar.MINUTE));
System.out.println("SECOND: " + calendar.get(Calendar.SECOND));
System.out.println("MILLISECOND: " +
                              calendar.get(Calendar.MILLISECOND));
System.out.println("ZONE_OFFSET: "
         + (calendar.get(Calendar.ZONE_OFFSET)/(60*60*1000)));
// Print the time.
System.out.println("DST_OFFSET: "
         + (calendar.get(Calendar.DST_OFFSET)/(60*60*1000)));
// Now print a nicely formatted date.
System.out.println(DateFormat.getDateInstance().format
         (calendar.getTime()));

System.out.println("Current Time, with hour reset to 3");
// Now change the date and display the data again.
calendar.clear(Calendar.HOUR_OF_DAY);
calendar.clear(Calendar.MONTH);
// Clear the values you want to change.
calendar.set(Calendar.HOUR, 3);
calendar.set(Calendar.MONTH, 11);
System.out.println("ERA: " + calendar.get(Calendar.ERA));
System.out.println("YEAR: " + calendar.get(Calendar.YEAR));
System.out.println("MONTH: " + calendar.get(Calendar.MONTH));
System.out.println("WEEK_OF_YEAR: " +
                              calendar.get(Calendar.WEEK_OF_YEAR));
System.out.println("WEEK_OF_MONTH: " + calendar.get
                                   (Calendar.WEEK_OF_MONTH));
System.out.println("DATE: " + calendar.get(Calendar.DATE));
System.out.println("DAY_OF_MONTH: " +
                              calendar.get(Calendar.DAY_OF_MONTH));
System.out.println("DAY_OF_YEAR: " +
                              calendar.get(Calendar.DAY_OF_YEAR));
System.out.println("DAY_OF_WEEK: " +
                              calendar.get(Calendar.DAY_OF_WEEK));
System.out.println("DAY_OF_WEEK_IN_MONTH: "
         + calendar.get(Calendar.DAY_OF_WEEK_IN_MONTH));
System.out.println("AM_PM: " + calendar.get(Calendar.AM_PM));
System.out.println("HOUR: " + calendar.get(Calendar.HOUR));
System.out.println("HOUR_OF_DAY: " +
                              calendar.get(Calendar.HOUR_OF_DAY));
System.out.println("MINUTE: " + calendar.get(Calendar.MINUTE));
System.out.println("SECOND: " + calendar.get(Calendar.SECOND));
System.out.println("MILLISECOND: " +
                              calendar.get(Calendar.MILLISECOND));
System.out.println("ZONE_OFFSET: "
         + (calendar.get(Calendar.ZONE_OFFSET)/(60*60*1000)));
// Time zone offset in hours.
 System.out.println("DST_OFFSET: "
```

continues

398 Chapter 19: Utility Classes

Listing 19.4 continued

```
                        + (calendar.get(Calendar.DST_OFFSET)/(60*60*1000)));
            // in hours
            // Now print a nicely formatted date.
            System.out.println(DateFormat.getDateInstance().format
                    (calendar.getTime())); 

            return true;
          }
    }

public class CalendarDriver
      {
         public static void main (String[] args)
           {
             DateInfo di = new DateInfo();
             boolean result = di.displayCalenderInfo();
             if (result == true)
                 System.exit(0);
             else
                 System.exit(-1);
          }
      }
```

Here is the output from running the program on September 27, 1999:

```
Calendar data members and methods
ERA: 1
YEAR: 1999
MONTH: 8
WEEK_OF_YEAR: 40
WEEK_OF_MONTH: 5
DATE: 27
DAY_OF_MONTH: 27
DAY_OF_YEAR: 270
DAY_OF_WEEK: 2
DAY_OF_WEEK_IN_MONTH: 4
AM_PM: 0
HOUR: 11
HOUR_OF_DAY: 11
MINUTE: 54
SECOND: 57
MILLISECOND: 680
ZONE_OFFSET: -8
DST_OFFSET: 1
Sep 27, 1999
Current Time, with hour reset to 3
and month reset to December
ERA: 1
YEAR: 1999
MONTH: 11
```

```
WEEK_OF_YEAR: 1
WEEK_OF_MONTH: 5
DATE: 27
DAY_OF_MONTH: 27
DAY_OF_YEAR: 361
DAY_OF_WEEK: 2
DAY_OF_WEEK_IN_MONTH: 4
AM_PM: 0
HOUR: 3
HOUR_OF_DAY: 3
MINUTE: 54
SECOND: 57
MILLISECOND: 680
ZONE_OFFSET: -8
DST_OFFSET: 0
Dec 27, 1999
```

You can see here that, except for providing a formatted date (which you can modify), all the values are numeric. You would need to convert these to String representations after you get them. There is not much conceptually to master here. It is simply a matter of constructing a GregorianCalendar object, setting its values, and then getting them back out.

Note that when you want to modify a value in a GregorianCalendar object, you should call the clear() method of the Calendar class with the specific data member you want to change, such as DAY_OF_WEEK or MONTH. Then you set the new value in the data member. Also, notice that you should use DateFormat or SimpleDateFormat class from the java.text package to print a nicely formatted date. For more on formatting dates, see Chapter 18, "Text." Without formatting, the data values from a GregorianCalendar object can be easily manipulated, but they are not very user friendly.

Using Properties

Anyone who has worked with Microsoft Windows for very long has encountered .ini files or the Registry. Both .ini files and the Registry contain configuration information. Similar information is often placed in a .login or .cshrc file in UNIX. Java also has a facility for storing application-specific information: a Properties object, which can be stored in a file if necessary. Many programs need configuration information, such as the appropriate directory to look in for a specific file, or the name of a host to use to find a database or the port to use for starting the JavaIDL orb. The Java way to deal with the need for such configuration values is to create a file using a Properties object, which consists of name/value pairs.

When you run a Java program, be it an application, an applet, or a servlet, there are system properties available to interrogate. You can examine a specific property, such as the file separator for a system, like / or \, by calling the getProperty() method of the System class like this:

```
String fileSep = System.getProperty("file.separator");
```

Chapter 19: Utility Classes

This returns the platform-dependent value of the file separator on a given system. You could use this to dynamically build a platform-specific file path from platform-independent Java code. You could get all the available system properties at once by coding

```
Properties props = System.getProperties();
```

You can also change the value of a property by using the put() method.

> **CAUTION**
>
> Be cautious when modifying a system property as opposed to a user-defined property. The setting affects all subsequent work within the JVM.

You can also create your own properties, like rmi.host, to specify the hostname for an RMI remote object and the host that the corresponding RMIRegistry is running on. Or, you might want to keep a running total or base value, such as lastAccountNumber. You can store anything you want, as long as it can be stored as a String. Both the property name and the property value must be Strings.

You have already seen several system properties being used or described, such as java.security.policy and jdbc.drivers. Using Properties greatly enhances the flexibility of your program. You can change a property without having to change your code. You can get Properties from the command line, from applet parameter tags, or from a flat file, among other choices. It is a lot less bug-prone an approach than actually going into your code and hard-coding a value that may end up making your code platform-dependent.

Properties Code Example

To use a Properties object, you work with key-value pairs, either getting a value using a key or setting a value for a key. Listing 19.5 shows how to create a Properties object; get the system properties; add a new, user-defined property; and then save the new property by writing the Properties object to a file.

Listing 19.5   Using the Properties Class (PropDriver.java)

```java
// Create and Modify a Properties object.

import java.io.*;
import java.util.*;

class SystemInfo
    {
      private Properties userProperties;
      private FileInputStream fis;
      private File userPropFile;
      private String userFileName;
      private String userName;

      public SystemInfo(String userID)
          {
```

```
            userFileName = userID + "Props" + ".txt";
            userName = userID;
        }

    public void getSystemInfo()
        {
            Properties sysProps = new Properties(System.getProperties());
            // Get the system properties.
            sysProps.list(System.out);
            // List the system properties to standard out.
            String userDir = System.getProperty("user.dir");
            System.out.println("User working directory is " + userDir);
            String separator = System.getProperty("file.separator");
            setUserInfo(userDir, separator);
        }

    private void setUserInfo(String dir, String fs)
        {
            FileOutputStream fos = null;
            String wholeFileName = dir + fs +  userFileName;
            userProperties = new Properties();
            // Create a new file using the File(String) constructor.
            userPropFile = new File (wholeFileName);

            if(userPropFile.exists() == false)
                {
                  // Property file doesn't exist, so create it.
                  try
                      {
                       userPropFile = new File(wholeFileName);
                       fos = new FileOutputStream(userPropFile);
                      }
                  catch(IOException e)
                      {
                       System.out.println("Error creating user Properties file");
                      }
                  // It may be that the first time you need to use a
                  // configuration file made with a Properties object that
                  // the file  doesn't exist, so be prepared for that.
                  // This would most likely happen the first time the program
                  // runs on a given system.
                  // "Put" some new property values in.
                  try
                      {
                       userProperties.put("USER", userName);
                       userProperties.put("WORKING.DIR",  dir);
                       userProperties.store(fos, "User Properties");
                       fos.flush();
                       fos.close();
```

continues

Listing 19.5   continued

```
            }
        catch(IOException e)
            {
              System.out.println
                  ("Error creating user Properties file because " +
                  e.toString());
            }
        } // End if block
    else;
    try
        {
          fis = new FileInputStream(userPropFile);
          userProperties.load(fis);
        }
    catch(IOException e)
        {
          System.out.println("Error opening user Properties file" +
                            e.toString());
        }
     try
        {
          fis.close();
        }
     catch(IOException e)
        {
          System.out.println ("Error closing user Properties file " +
                            e.toString());
        }
    // Now we've saved our own custom Properties file to use later
    // and read the file back in using load() to put the file's
    // contents into a Properties object. Now display the file's
    // contents.
    System.out.println("Here is the retrieved contents " +
                      "of the user properties file");
    userProperties.list(System.out);
    // Now, modify the system properties.
    Properties sysProps = System.getProperties();
    // Get all the system properties.
    System.out.println("Current System Properties");
    sysProps.list(System.out);
    // The list() method returns all the properties in the
    // Properties object.
    sysProps.setProperty("great.java.book", "Pure Java 2");
    // Use setProperty() to add or change a property.
    System.out.println("Modified system properties");
    sysProps.list(System.out);
    }

  } // End class definition for SystemInfo.
```

```
public class PropDriver
    {
      public static void main(String[] args)
         {
           SystemInfo info = new SystemInfo("Buzz");
           info.getSystemInfo();
           System.exit(0);
         }
    }
```

This program does several things. First, it lists the current system properties using the `list()` method against the `Properties` object returned from `System.getProperties()`, which contains all the current system properties. Next, the program creates a new `Properties` object, adds two properties to it, including `user.name` and `user.dir`, and then stores it.

> **NOTE**
>
> The old way to save a `Properties` object to a file was to use the `save()` method. This method was deprecated in Java 2, because `save()` does not throw an `IOException` if there is an IO error. In Java 2, you should use the `store()` method, which does throw an `IOException` if an IO error occurs. So `store()` is safer to use, because you are notified if a problem occurs.

Then the program reinitializes the contents of the `userProperties Properties` object from the file using the `load()` method. Finally, the program gets the system properties and then adds to those properties an additional system property, `great.java.book`. It then lists the modified system properties. Notice that when you added the new property, it did not necessarily show up at the end of the list of properties. This is because a `Properties` object is not merely a list of properties, but is a subclass of `Hashtable`. So the value of the key for the new property was hashed, and that hash was used to determine where the new property would go.

You can use `getProperty()` to get a specific property, `setProperty` to add or modify a property, and `load()` and `store()` to read a `Properties` object from and write a `Properties` object to a file. Observe that all properties are strings, and the key for a property is generally a period-delimited name. Properties allow your program to save or read its own configuration values, making your code much more flexible.

You often simply need to know a given system property. All the system properties are properties in a `Properties` object created at runtime, which describes the runtime environment, including platform-dependent information.

PART III

SYNTAX REFERENCE

CHAPTER 20

java.applet

This chapter is the first of several that provides abbreviated API documentation for core packages, classes, and interfaces. UML class diagrams are provided for the classes. Because there is already a *Pure JFC Swing* book that details the JFC classes and because there are over 1,600 classes in Java 2, not every class will be covered in this chapter. Those that are most commonly used or are important in other respects are listed here.

> **NOTE**
>
> In each chapter of Part III, you will find a brief description of a main package and its uses. There might also be several subpackages in a given chapter. So, for example, java.awt.event is covered in Chapter 21, "java.awt." For each package or subpackage, the interfaces are listed first, followed by the classes. A class definition includes a class hierarchy diagram using UML, data members, inner classes, and methods.

Package Name: java.applet

This package provides the basic framework for creating applets.

> **NOTE:**
>
> Remember that an applet is simply one GUI component that uses other GUI components, performs AWT event handling, and potentially uses classes in many other packages.

Interfaces

AppletContext
AppletStub
AudioClip

Class

Appet

Interface and Class Details

Interface AppletContext

public abstract interface **AppletContext**

The AppletContext interface provides methods to obtain information about an applet's enclosing Web page, other applets, and the applet's environment. As shown here, your applet can obtain an AppletContext and then get information:

```
AppletContext ap = getAppletContext();
Sring appletName = ap.getApplet();
// Get the name of the current applet.
ap.showDocument("http://www.GradLibraray.edu/index.html");
// Replace the current web page with the one at this URL.
ap.setStatus("Check out complete");
// Update the text in the browser's status window.
```

Alternatively, you can use similar methods that are implemented in the java.applet.Applet class itself for some of these methods.

Methods

public Applet	**getApplet**(String appletName)
public Enumeration	**getApplets**()
public AudioClip	**getAudioClip**(URL aUrl)
public Image	**getImage**(URL imageUrl)
public void	**showDocument**(URL aUrl)
public void	**showDocument**(URL aUrl, String targetString)
public void	**showStatus**(String aStatus)

Interface AppletStub

public abstract interface **AppletStub**

The AppletStub interface declares the methods used by an AppletStub, which is attached to an applet at runtime. This stub provides an interface between the applet and the program running it, such as a browser. It is not normally used by an applet developer.

Methods

public boolean	**isActive**()
public URL	**getDocumentBase**()
public URL	**getCodeBase**()
public String	**getParameter**(String aName)
public AppletContext	**getAppletContext**()
public void	**appletResize**(int theWidth, int theHeight)

Interface AudioClip

public abstract interface **AudioClip**

The public abstract interface AudioClip provides methods that can be implemented to allow the playing of sound clip objects by an applet. Here is an example of part of an applet that can play sound continuously while the applet's web page is displayed:

```
public class SoundApplet extends Applet
   {
    public void init()
        // Called when the applet is instantiated.
        {
         AudioClip ac = getAudioClip
             ("http://www.soundlib.com/JazzSampler.au");
        }
    public void start()
        // Called when you go to the web page.
        {
         ac.loop();
        }

    public void stop()
        // Called when you leave the web page.
        {
         ac.stop();
        }
   }  // End SoundApplet class definition.
```

> **TIP**
>
> To be a good web citizen, always be sure that you stop() an applet playing sound in the applet's stop() method. Otherwise, even when you go to a totally different web page at a different web site, the music will still be playing. Imagine how annoying it would be to hear the same song repeatedly. Even if you liked it when it first played, you'd hate it after 20 minutes, and you would probably have to shut down the browser to stop it.

public void	**play()**
public void	**loop()**
public void	**stop()**

Class Applet

public class **Applet**
              extends Panel

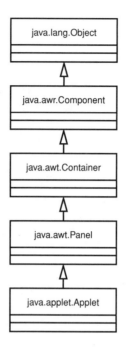

The Applet class is the class that all applets must extend. It contains methods for obtaining applet resources, such as getAudioClip() for AudioClips and getImage() for Images.

Your code never calls the constructor for an Applet. It is called by a Java program running inside the browser, outside of your control. The applet instance is instantiated by this program, which then calls the applet's init() method. Your applet GUI component is then added to an invisible Frame created by this application. You can tell the application is starting because the browser's status line says that it is starting Java. This application is required to run your applet, and the application is hosted by the browser. Thus, your applet is not a stand-alone program. The browser's JVM starts the whole process by calling the main method of the application.

Constructor

```
public     Applet()
```

Methods

```
public final void           setStub(AppletStub aStub)
public boolean              isActive()
public URL                  getDocumentBase()
public URL                  getCodeBase()
public String               getParameter(String aName)
public AppletContext        getAppletContext()
public void                 resize(int theWidth, int theHeight)
public void                 resize(Dimension dim)
```

public void	**showStatus**(String message)
public Image	**getImage**(URL aUrl, String aName)
public static final AudioClip	**newAudioClip**(URL url)
public AudioClip	**getAudioClip**(URL aUrl)
public AudioClip	**getAudioClip**(URL aUrl, String aName)
public String	**getAppletInfo**()
public Locale	**getLocale**()
public String[][]	**getParameterInfo**()
public void	**play**(URL aUrl)
public void	**play**(URL url, String name)
public void	**init**()
public void	**start**()
public void	**stop**()
public void	**destroy**()

CHAPTER 21

java.awt

The number of AWT classes is quite large. Although many of them are listed here, some of the less-common classes have been omitted. For those, consult the *Pure JFC Swing* book in this series or the Java API documentation.

The following provides a quick view of the interfaces and classes in the AWT packages.

Package Name: java.awt

This package provides Java GUI components, event handling, and related classes.

Interfaces
```
ActiveEvent
Adjustable
Composite
CompositeContext
ItemSelectable
LayoutManager
LayoutManager2
MenuContainer
Paint
PaintContext
PrintGraphics
Shape
Stroke
Transparency
```

Classes
```
AlphaComposite
AWTEvent
AWTEventMulticaster
AWTPermission
BasicStroke
BorderLayout
Button
```

Canvas
CardLayout
Checkbox
CheckboxGroup
CheckboxMenuItem
Choice
Color
Component
ComponentOrientation
Container
Cursor
Dialog
Dimension
Event
EventQueue
FileDialog
FlowLayout
Font
FontMetrics
Frame
GradientPaint
Graphics
Graphics2D
GraphicsConfigTemplate
GraphicsConfiguration
GraphicsDevice
GraphicsEnvironment
GridBagConstraints
GridBagLayout
GridLayout
Image
Insets
Label
List
MediaTracker
Menu
MenuBar
MenuComponent
MenuItem
MenuShortcut
Panel
Point
Polygon
PopupMenu
PrintJob
Rectangle
RenderingHints
RenderingHints.Key
Scrollbar
ScrollPane

SystemColor
TextArea
TextComponent
TextField
TexturePaint
Toolkit
Window

Exceptions

AWTException
IllegalComponentStateException

Errors

AWTError

Package Name: java.awt.datatransfer

This package provides facilities for transferring data between applications through copy, cut, and paste operations.

Interfaces

ClipboardOwner
FlavorMap
Transferable

Classes

Clipboard
DataFlavor
StringSelection
SystemFlavorMap

Exceptions

UnsupportedFlavorException

Package Name: java.awt.dnd

This package provides support for drag-and-drop operations.

Interfaces

Autoscroll
DragGestureListener
DragSourceListener
DropTargetListener

Classes

DnDConstants
DragGestureEvent
DragGestureRecognizer

Chapter 21: java.awt

DragSource
DragSourceContext
DragSourceDragEvent
DragSourceDropEvent
DragSourceEvent
DropTarget
DropTarget.DropTargetAutoScroller
DropTargetContext
DropTargetDragEvent
DropTargetDropEvent
DropTargetEvent
MouseDragGestureRecognizer

Exceptions
InvalidDnDOperationException

Package Name: java.awt.event

This package provides classes and interfaces to support GUI event handling in both the AWT and Swing classes.

Interfaces
ActionListener
AdjustmentListener
AWTEventListener
ComponentListener
ContainerListener
FocusListener
InputMethodListener
ItemListener
KeyListener
MouseListener
MouseMotionListener
TextListener
WindowListener

Classes
ActionEvent
AdjustmentEvent
ComponentAdapter
ComponentEvent
ContainerAdapter
ContainerEvent
FocusAdapter
FocusEvent
InputEvent
InputMethodEvent
InvocationEvent
ItemEvent
KeyAdapter

```
KeyEvent
MouseAdapter
MouseEvent
MouseMotionAdapter
PaintEvent
TextEvent
WindowAdapter
WindowEvent
```

Package Name: java.awt.font

This package provides classes and interfaces to support manipulating and interrogating fonts.

Interfaces
```
MultipleMaster
OpenType
```

Classes
```
FontRenderContext
GlyphJustificationInfo
GlyphMetrics
GlyphVector
GraphicAttribute
ImageGraphicAttribute
LineBreakMeasurer
LineMetrics
ShapeGraphicAttribute
TextAttribute
TextHitInfo
TextLayout
TextLayout.CaretPolicy
TextLine.TextLineMetrics
TransformAttribute
```

Package Name: java.awt.geom

This package provides classes and interfaces for 2D geometric objects.

Interfaces
```
PathIterator
```

Classes
```
AffineTransform
Arc2D
Arc2D.Double
Arc2D.Float
Area
CubicCurve2D
```

CubicCurve2D.Double
CubicCurve2D.Float
Dimension2D
Ellipse2D
Ellipse2D.Double
Ellipse2D.Float
FlatteningPathIterator
GeneralPath
Line2D
Line2D.Double
Line2D.Float
Point2D
Point2D.Double
Point2D.Float
QuadCurve2D
QuadCurve2D.Double
QuadCurve2D.Float
Rectangle2D
Rectangle2D.Double
Rectangle2D.Float
RectangularShape
RoundRectangle2D
RoundRectangle2D.Double
RoundRectangle2D.Float

Exceptions

IllegalPathStateException
NoninvertibleTransformException

Package Name: java.awt.print

This package provides classes and interfaces to support printing.

Interfaces

Pageable
Printable
PrinterGraphics

Classes

Book
PageFormat
Paper
PrinterJob

Exceptions

PrinterAbortException
PrinterException
PrinterIOException

java.awt Interface and Class Details

Interface ActiveEvent
public abstract interface **ActiveEvent**

This interface provides the API for an event to dispatch itself.

Methods
public void   **dispatch**()

Interface Adjustable
public abstract interface **Adjustable**

This interface specifies fields and methods for an item that contains an adjustable numeric value within a set range of values. It is used by the Scrollbar and JScrollBar classes.

Fields
public static final int   **HORIZONTAL**
public static final int   **VERTICAL**

Methods
```
public int      getOrientation()
public void     setMinimum(int minumum)
public int      getMinimum()
public void     setMaximum(int max)
public int      getMaximum()
public void     setUnitIncrement(int unit)
public int      getUnitIncrement()
public void     setBlockIncrement(int block)
public int      getBlockIncrement()
public void     setVisibleAmount(int visibleAmt)
public int      getVisibleAmount()
public void     setValue(int v)
public int      getValue()
public void     addAdjustmentListener(AdjustmentListener l)
public void     removeAdjustmentListener (AdjustmentListener l)
```

Interface Composite
public abstract interface **Composite**

This interface provides methods for drawing a graphics primitive in a graphics context and combining the primitive with colors for rendering.

Methods
```
public CompositeContext      createContext(ColorModel inColorModel,
                                 ColorModel outColorModel,
                                 RenderingHints someHints)
```

Interface CompositeContext
public abstract interface **CompositeContext**

This interface declares the methods used for a `CompositeContext` to describe the environment for operations on `Composite` objects.

Methods
```
public void      dispose()
public void      compose(Raster source, Raster target,
                         WritableRaster writableTarget)
```

Interface ItemSelectable
public abstract interface **ItemSelectable**

This interface declares methods for objects that contain items of which zero or more can be selected.

Methods
```
public Object[]  getSelectedObjects()
public void      addItemListener(ItemListener listener)
public void      removeItemListener(ItemListener listener)
```

Interface LayoutManager
This interface declares the methods for implementing a `LayoutManager` object, such as an instance of `FlowLayout`.

public abstract interface **LayoutManager**

Methods
```
public void       addLayoutComponent(String componentName,
                         Component component)
public void       removeLayoutComponent(Component component)
public Dimension  preferredLayoutSize(Container parentContainer)
public Dimension  minimumLayoutSize(Container parentContainer)
public void       layoutContainer(Container parentContainer)
```

Interface LayoutManager2
public abstract interface **LayoutManager2**
                         extends LayoutManager

This interface is an extension to the `LayoutManager` interface to provide for constraint-based layouts, primarily from tool providers.

Methods
```
public void       addLayoutComponent(Component component,
                         Object constraintObject)
public Dimension  maximumLayoutSize(Container targetContainer)
public float      getLayoutAlignmentX(Container targetContainer)
```

```
public float        getLayoutAlignmentY(Container targetContainer)
public void         invalidateLayout(Container targetContainer)
```

Interface MenuContainer

```
public abstract interface MenuContainer
```

This interface declares methods for a MenuContainer class.

Methods

```
public Font         getFont()
public void         remove(MenuComponent comp)
public boolean      postEvent(Event evt)
```

Interface Paint

```
public abstract interface Paint
                      extends Transparency
```

This interface provides methods for generating color patterns by Graphics2D-related objects.

Methods

```
public PaintContext    createContext(ColorModel colorModel,
                          Rectangle devBounds,
                          Rectangle2D rectBounds, AffineTransform xForm,
                          RenderingHints renderHints)
```

Interface PaintContext

```
public abstract interface PaintContext
```

This interface declares methods for defining an environment in which color patterns are generated.

Methods

```
public void         dispose()
public ColorModel   getColorModel()
public Raster       getRaster(int x, int y, int w, int h)
```

Interface PrintGraphics

```
public abstract interface PrintGraphics
```

This interface declares methods for a print graphics object for a page.

Method

```
public PrintJob     getPrintJob()
```

Interface Shape

```
public abstract interface Shape
```

This interface declares methods for defining geometric shapes.

Methods

```
public Rectangle      getBounds()
public Rectangle2D    getBounds2D()
public boolean        contains(double x, double y)
public boolean        contains(Point2D pt2D)
public boolean        intersects(double x, double y, double width,
                          double height)
public boolean        intersects(Rectangle2D rect2D)
public boolean        contains(double x, double y, double width,
                          double height)
public boolean        contains(Rectangle2D rect2D)
public PathIterator   getPathIterator(AffineTransform affTran)
public PathIterator   getPathIterator(AffineTransform affTran,
                          double flat)
```

Interface Transparency

public abstract interface **Transparency**

This interface provides fields and methods for common transparency modes.

Fields

```
public static final int OPAQUE
public static final int TRANSLUCENT
```

Methods

```
public int getTransparency()
```

Class AWTEvent

public abstract class **AWTEvent**
                        extends EventObject

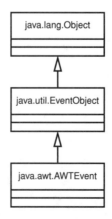

AWTEvent is the base class for all AWT event classes, such as ActionEvent.

Fields

protected int	**id**
protected boolean	**consumed**
public static final long	**COMPONENT_EVENT_MASK**
public static final long	**CONTAINER_EVENT_MASK**
public static final long	**FOCUS_EVENT_MASK**
public static final long	**KEY_EVENT_MASK**
public static final long	**MOUSE_EVENT_MASK**
public static final long	**MOUSE_MOTION_EVENT_MASK**
public static final long	**WINDOW_EVENT_MASK**
public static final long	**ACTION_EVENT_MASK**
public static final long	**ADJUSTMENT_EVENT_MASK**
public static final long	**ITEM_EVENT_MASK**
public static final long	**TEXT_EVENT_MASK**
public static final long	**INPUT_METHOD_EVENT_MASK**
public static final int	**RESERVED_ID_MAX**

Constructors

public	**AWTEvent**(Event event)
public	**AWTEvent**(Object source, int id)

Methods

public int	**etID**()
public String	**toString**()
public String	**paramString**()
protected void	**consume**()
protected boolean	**sConsumed**()
protected void	**finalize**() throws Throwable

Class AWTEventMulticaster

public class **AWTEventMulticaster**
    extends Object
    implements ComponentListener, ContainerListener,
    FocusListener, KeyListener, MouseListener,
    MouseMotionListener, WindowListener, ActionListener,
    ItemListener, AdjustmentListener, TextListener,
    InputMethodListener

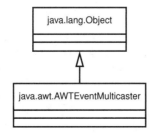

This class handles multicast event dispatching, serving as the glue coupling a Component, events produced by it, and listeners that process those events. Rather than letting the JVM do its event propagation, it is implemented by an application to do its own event handling. Here is code showing the basics of using this class:

```
public ToggleSwitch extends Component
    {
    ActionListener listener = null;
    // In addition to methods to define the ToggleSwitch's
    // appearance and other properties, you use
    // AWTEventMulticaster to handle events on the
    // component.
    public void addActionListener(ActionListener l)
        {
          listener =
              AWTEventMulticaster.add(listener, l);
        }

     public void removeActionListener(ActionListener l)
        {
          listener =
                AWTEventMulticaster.remove(listener, l);
        }

    public void processEvent(AWTEvent e)
        {
        // An event which generates an "action" event.
        if(listener != null)
           {
            listener.actionPerformed(new ActionEvent());
           }
        }
    }
```

Fields

protected final **EventListener**   a
protected final **EventListener**   b

Constructors

protected   **AWTEventMulticaster**(EventListener a, EventListener b)

Methods

Protected eventListener	**remove**(EventListener listener)
public void	**componentResized**(ComponentEvent compEvt)
public void	**componentMoved**(ComponentEvent compEvt)
public void	**componentShown**(ComponentEvent compEvt)
public void	**componentHidden**(ComponentEvent compEvt)
public void	**componentAdded**(ContainerEvent compEvt)
public void	**componentRemoved**(ContainerEvent contEvt)

public void	**focusGained**(FocusEvent focusEvt)
public void	**focusLost**(FocusEvent focusEvt)
public void	**keyTyped**(KeyEvent keyEvt)
public void	**keyPressed**(KeyEvent keyEvt)
public void	**keyReleased**(KeyEvent keyEvt)
public void	**mouseClicked**(MouseEvent mouseEvt)
public void	**mousePressed**(MouseEvent mouseEvt)
public void	**mouseEntered**(MouseEvent mouseEvt)
public void	**mouseExited**(MouseEvent mouseEvt)
public void	**mouseDragged**(MouseEvent mouseEvt)
public void	**mouseMoved**(MouseEvent mouseEvt)
public void	**windowOpened**(WindowEvent windowEvt)
public void	**windowClosing**(WindowEvent windowEvt)
public void	**windowClosed**(WindowEvent windowEvt)
public void	**windowIconified**(WindowEvent windowEvt)
public void	**windowDeiconified**(WindowEvent windowEvt)
public void	**windowActivated**(WindowEvent windowEvt)
public void	**windowDeactivated**(WindowEvent windowEvt)
public void	**actionPerformed**(ActionEvent actionEvt)
public void	**itemStateChanged**(ItemEvent itemEvt)
public void	**adjustmentValueChanged**(AdjustmentEvent adjEvt)
public void	**textValueChanged**(TextEvent textEvt)
public void	**inputMethodTextChanged**(InputMethodEvent imEvt)
public void	**caretPositionChanged**(InputMethodEvent imEvt)
public static	**add**(ComponentListenerComponentListenerlistenerA, ComponentListener listenerB)
public static	**add**(ContainerListener ContainerListenerlistenerA, ContainerListener listenerB)
public static	**add**(FocusListener listenerA, FocusListener listenerB)
public static	**add**(KeyListenerA, KeyListener, KeyListener listenerB)
public static	**add**(MouseListener listenerA, MouseListener listenerB)
public static	**add**(MouseMotionListener listenerA, MouseMotionListener listener)
public static	**add**(WindowListener listenerA, WindowListener listenerB)
public static	**add**(ActionListener listenerA, ActionListener listenerB)
public static	**add**(ItemListener listenerA, ItemListener listenerB)
public static	**add**(AdjustmentListener AdjustmentListener listenerA, AdjustmentListener listenerB)
public static	**add**(TextListener listenerA, TextListener listenerB)
public static	**add**(InputMethodListener listenerA, InputMethodListener listenerB)

public static	**remove**(ComponentListener listenerA, ComponentListener listenerB)
public static	**remove**(ContainerListener listenerA, ContainerListener listenerB)
public static	**remove**(FocusListener listenerA, FocusListener listenerB)
public static	**remove**(KeyListener listenerA, KeyListener listenerB)
public static	**remove**(MouseListener listenerA, MouseListener listenerB)
public static	**remove**(MouseMotionListener listenerA, MouseMotionListener listenerB)
public static	**remove**(WindowListener listenerA, WindowListener listenerB)
public static	**remove**(ActionListener listenerA, ActionListener listenerB)
public static	**remove**(ItemListener listenerA, ItemListener listenerB)
public static	**remove**(AdjustmentListener listenerA, AdjustmentListener listenerB)
public static	**remove**(TextListener listenerA, TextListener listenerB)
public static	**remove**(InputMethodListener listenerA, InputMethodListener listenerB)
protected static	**addInternal**(EventListener listenerA, EventListener listenerB)
protected static	**removeInternal**(EventListener listenerA, EventListener listenerB)
protected void	**saveInternal**(ObjectOutputStream stream, String internalString) throws IOException
protected static	**save**(ObjectOutputStream stream, String aString, EventListener listener) throws IOException

Class BorderLayout

```
public class BorderLayout
            extends Object
            implements LayoutManager2, Serializable
```

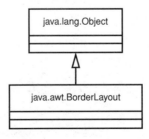

This class defines a layout manager for arranging and sizing components in a container. It divides the container into five regions: North, South, East, West, and Center. By default, the Center is the largest area. This is the default layout manager for Frames and Dialogs. Here's a code snippet that shows the use of this layout manager:

```
Frame fr = new Frame("Welcome to the Grad Library");
// A Frame has a BorderLayout by default.
Button searchButton = new Button("Search");
TextField searchValue = new TextField("          ");
Label searchlabel = new Label("Enter search Value below");
fr.add("North", searchLabel);
fr.add("Center", searchValue);
fr.add("South", searchButton);
```

Fields

```
public static final String    NORTH
public static final String    SOUTH
public static final String    EAST
public static final String    WEST
public static final String    CENTER
public static final String    BEFORE_FIRST_LINE
public static final String    AFTER_LAST_LINE
public static final String    BEFORE_LINE_BEGINS
public static final String    AFTER_LINE_ENDS
```

Constructors

```
public      BorderLayout()
public      BorderLayout(int hGap, int vGap)
```

Methods

```
public int          getHgap()
public int          getVgap()
public void         setVgap(int vGap)
public void         addLayoutComponent(Component c, Object constraintsObj)
public void         addLayoutComponent(String compName, Component c)
public void         removeLayoutComponent(Component c)
public Dimension    minimumLayoutSize(Container cont)
public Dimension    preferredLayoutSize(Container cont)
public Dimension    maximumLayoutSize(Container cont)
public float        getLayoutAlignmentX(Container cont)
public float        getLayoutAlignmentY(Container cont)
public void         invalidateLayout(Container cont)
public void         layoutContainer(Container cont)
public String       toString()
```

Class Button

```
public class Button
            extends Component
```

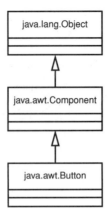

This class implements a *clickable* button GUI component. It has two appearances: pressed and nonpressed.

```
Panel buttonPanel = new Panel();
buttonPanel.setLayout(new GridLayout(3,1);
Button searchButton = new Button("Search");
Button clearButton = new Button("Clear");
Button helpButton("Help");
buttonPanel.add(searchButton);
buttonPanel.add(clearButton);
buttonPanel.add(helpButton);
// This creates three Buttons and puts them into one Panel.
// By using the GridLayout, the Buttons are aligned
// vertically and are all the same size.
```

Constructors

```
public    Button()
public    Button(String aLabel)
```

Methods

```
public void       addNotify()
public String     getLabel()
public void       setLabel(String aLabel)
public void       setActionCommand(String aCommand)
public void       addActionListener(ActionListener listener)
public void       removeActionListener(ActionListener listener)
protected void    processEvent(AWTEvent evt)
protected void    processActionEvent(ActionEvent evt)
protected String  paramString()
```

Class Canvas

```
public class Canvas
            extends Component
```

java.awt Interface and Class Details

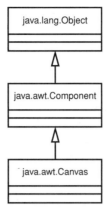

A Canvas represents a blank rectangular area that normally does not generate events, but on which an application can draw or receive user input. This can be done only after the Canvas receives explicit focus from the application.

Constructors

```
public      Canvas()
public      Canvas(GraphicsConfiguration configuration)
```

Methods

```
public void    addNotify()
public void    paint(Graphics gr)
```

Class CardLayout

```
public class CardLayout
             extends Object
             implements LayoutManager2, Serializable
```

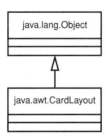

CardLayout is a layout manager for a container that provides a means to implement a GUI that supports a Rolodex-like appearance. When you add components or containers to the CardLayout, it logically treats them as cards, only one of which can be displayed at one time.

Constructors

```
public      CardLayout()
public      CardLayout(int hGap, int vGap)
```

Methods

```
public int          getHgap()
public void         setHgap(int hGap)
public int          getVgap()
public void         setVgap(int vGap)
public void         addLayoutComponent(Component c, Object constraintsObj)
public void         addLayoutComponent(String compName, Component com)
public void         removeLayoutComponent(Component com)
public Dimension    minimumLayoutSize(Container aContainer)
public Dimension    maximumLayoutSize(Container aContainer)
public float        getLayoutAlignmentX(Container aContainer)
public float        getLayoutAlignmentY(Container aContainer)
public void         invalidateLayout(Container aContainer)
public void         layoutContainer(Container aContainer)
public void         first(Container aContainer)
public void         next(Container aContainer)
public void         previous(Container aContainer)
public void         last(Container aContainer)
public void         show(Container aContainer, String card)
public String       toString()
```

Class Checkbox

```
public class Checkbox
                extends Component
                implements ItemSelectable
```

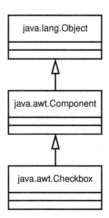

A Checkbox component is a GUI element that can be set to an on or off state by clicking on it. The appearance of a Checkbox is determined in part by whether it is functioning as a standalone check box or as a radio button (by being added to a CheckboxGroup).

Here is a code snippet showing how to instantiate Checkboxes and give them radio button behavior:

```
CheckboxGroup cbg = new CheckboxGroup();
Checkbox cb1 = new Checkbox("English", true, cbg);
    // Create a Checkbox that is checked when the
    // application first starts. Make the Checkbox
    // behave like a radio button by putting it in a
    // CheckboxGroup (a non-visual object).
Checkbox ch2 = new Checkbox("French", cbg, false);
Checkbox cb3 = new Checkbox("German", false, cbg);
```

> **NOTE**
> Be aware that Checkbox is spelled with a lowercase b, but the Swing counterpart, JCheckBox, uses an uppercase B—as it should, following conventional Java naming practices.

Constructors

public	**Checkbox**()
public	**Checkbox**(String label)
public	**Checkbox**(String label, boolean state)
public	**Checkbox**(String label, boolean state, CheckboxGroup group)
public	**Checkbox**(String label, CheckboxGroup group, boolean state)

Methods

public void	**addNotify**()
public String	**getLabel**()
public void	**setLabel**(String label)
public boolean	**getState**()
public void	**setState**(boolean state)
public Object[]	**getSelectedObjects**()
public CheckboxGroup	**getCheckboxGroup**()
public void	**setCheckboxGroup**(CheckboxGroup g)
public void	**addItemListener**(ItemListener l)
public void	**removeItemListener**(ItemListener l)
protected void	**processEvent**(AWTEvent e)
protected void	**processItemEvent**(ItemEvent e)
protected String	**paramString**()

Class CheckboxGroup

```
public class CheckboxGroup
            extends Object
            implements Serializable
```

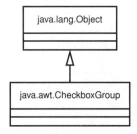

A CheckboxGroup is a non-visual object whose sole purpose is to make the on/off state of multiple Checkbox objects mutually exclusive. That is, if three Checkbox items are added to a CheckboxGroup, only one can be on at one time. CheckboxGroup is neither a visual component nor an AWT component.

Constructors

```
public      CheckboxGroup()
```

Methods

```
public Checkbox     getSelectedCheckbox()
public Checkbox     getCurrent()
public void         setSelectedCheckbox(Checkbox box)
public void         setCurrent(Checkbox box)
public String       toString()
```

Class Choice

```
public class Choice
              extends Component
              implements ItemSelectable
```

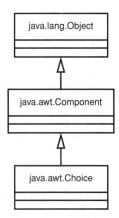

A Choice component provides a noneditable, nonscrollable, drop-down list of selectable items. You can select only one item at a time. The following snippet shows how to create and populate a Choice component:

```
Choice searchChoice = new Choice();
searchChoice.add("Author");
searchChoice.add("Title");
searchChoice.add("Subject");
```

Constructors

```
public      Choice()
```

Methods

```
public void         addNotify()
public int          getItemCount()
public int          countItems()
public String       getItem(int index)
public void         add(String item)
public void         addItem(String item)
public void         insert(String item, int index)
public void         remove(String item)
public void         remove(int position)
public void         removeAll()
public String       getSelectedItem()
public Object[]     getSelectedObjects()
public int          getSelectedIndex()
public void         select(int pos)
public void         select(String str)
public void         addItemListener(ItemListener l)
public void         removeItemListener(ItemListener l)
protected void      processEvent(AWTEvent e)
protected void      processItemEvent(ItemEvent e)
protected String    paramString()
```

Class Color

```
public class Color
               extends Object
               implements Paint, Serializable
```

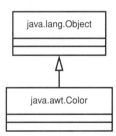

The class Color provides fields and methods for setting colors in components, including 16 default colors. Generally, you simply use a color as a parameter to a method, such as setBackground():

```
theFrame.setBackground(Color.blue);
theFrame.setForeground(Color.yellow);
```

> **TIP**
>
> You can also use a `Color` object you have constructed by providing values for red, green, and blue. All the colors you see on a television, for example, are made up of only red, green, and blue pixels. If the color you want is not provided, you can use these three colors to create any color needed in an application.

Fields

```
public static final Color    white
public static final Color    lightGray
public static final Color    gray
public static final Color    darkGray
public static final Color    black
public static final Color    red
public static final Color    pink
public static final Color    orange
public static final Color    yellow
public static final Color    green
public static final Color    magenta
public static final Color    cyan
public static final Color    blue
```

Constructors

```
public      Color(int red, int green, int blue)
public      Color(int red, int green, int blue, int Alpha)
public      Color(int rgbValue)
public      Color(int rgbaValue, boolean hasAnAlpha)
public      Color(float red, float green , float blue)
public      Color(float red, float green, float blue, float alpha)
public      Color(ColorSpace colorSpace, float[] componentArray,
                  float theAlpha)
```

Methods

```
public int           getRed()
public int           getGreen()
public int           getBlue()
public int           getAlpha()
public int           getRGB()
public Color         brighter()
public Color         darker()
public int           hashCode()
public boolean       equals(Object obj)
public String        toString()
public static Color  decode(String name) throws NumberFormatException
public static Color  getColor(String name)
public static Color  getColor(String name, Color value)
```

```
public static Color      getColor(String prop, Int val)
public static int        HSBtoRGB(float aHue, float sat, float brightVal)
public static float[]    RGBtoHSB(int red, int green, Int blue,
                                  float[] hsbvalues)
public static Color      getHSBColor(float hue, float sat, float brightVal)
public float[]           getRGBComponents(float[] compArray)
public float[]           getRGBColorComponents(float[] compArray)
public float[]           getComponents(float[] compArray)
public float[]           getColorComponents(float[] compArray)
public float[]           getComponents(ColorSpace cspace, float[] comps)
public float[]           getColorComponents(ColorSpace colorSpace,
                                  float[] comps)
public PaintContext      createContext(ColorModel colorModel, Rectangle rect,
                                  Rectangle2D rect2d,
                                  AffineTransform affineTxform,
                                  RenderingHints rendHints)
public int               getTransparency()
```

Class Component

```
public abstract class Component
                      extends Object
                      implements ImageObserver, MenuContainer,
                      Serializable
```

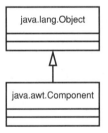

The Component class is the superclass of all nonmenu-related AWT GUI component classes. Extending it directly results in a lightweight class with no native peer. Along with several abstract methods, the Component class provides several useful concrete methods. An application generally does not use this class directly.

Fields

```
public static final float    TOP_ALIGNMENT
public static final float    LEFT_ALIGNMENT
```

Constructors

```
protected     Component()
```

Methods

```
public String             getName()
public void               setName(String name)
```

Chapter 21: java.awt

public Container	getParent()
public java.awt.peer.ComponentPeer	getPeer()
public void	setDropTarget(DropTarget target)
public DropTarget	getDropTarget()
public final Object	getTreeLock()
public Toolkit	getToolkit()
public boolean	isValid()
public boolean	isDisplayable()
public boolean	isVisible()
public boolean	isShowing()
public boolean	isEnabled()
public void	setEnabled(boolean b)
public void	enable()
public void	enable(boolean b)
public void	disable()
public boolean	isDoubleBuffered()
public void	enableInputMethods(boolean enableFlag)
public void	setVisible(boolean flag)
public void	show()
public void	show(boolean b)
public void	hide()
public Color	getForeground()
public void	setForeground(Color c)
public Color	getBackground()
public void	setBackground(Color c)
public Font	getFont()
public void	setFont(Font font)
public Locale	getLocale()
public void	setLocale(Locale locale)
public ColorModel	getColorModel()
public Point	getLocation()
public Point	getLocationOnScreen()
public Point	location()
public void	setLocation(int x, int y)
public void	move(int x, int y)
public void	setLocation(Point pt)
public Dimension	getSize()
public Dimension	size()
public void	setSize(int w, int h)
public void	resize(int w, int h)
public void	setSize(Dimension dim)
public void	resize(Dimension dim)
public Rectangle	getBounds()
public Rectangle	bounds()
public void	setBounds(int x, int y, int w, int h)
public void	reshape(int x, int y, int w, int h)
public void	setBounds(Rectangle rect)
public int	getX()
public int	getY()
public int	getWidth()

public int	getHeight()
public Rectangle	getBounds(Rectangle rv)
public Dimension	getSize(Dimension dim)
public Point	getLocation(Point pt)
public boolean	isOpaque()
public boolean	isLightweight()
public Dimension	getPreferredSize()
public Dimension	preferredSize()
public Dimension	getMinimumSize()
public Dimension	minimumSize()
public Dimension	getMaximumSize()
public float	getAlignmentX()
public float	getAlignmentY()
public void	doLayout()
public void	layout()
public void	validate()
public void	invalidate()
public Graphics	getGraphics()
public FontMetrics	getFontMetrics(Font font)
public void	setCursor(Cursor cur)
public Cursor	getCursor()
public void	paint(Graphics gr)
public void	update(Graphics gr)
public void	paintAll(Graphics gr)
public void	repaint()
public void	repaint(long t)
public void	repaint(int x, int y, int w, int h)
public void	repaint(long t, int x, int y, int w, int h)
public void	print(Graphics gr)
public void	printAll(Graphics gr)
public boolean	imageUpdate (Image image, int flags, int x, int y, int w, int h)
public Image	createImage(int w, int h)
public boolean	prepareImage(Image theImage, ImageObserver obsrvr)
public boolean	prepareImage(Image theImage, Int w, int h, ImageObserver obsrvr)
public int	checkImage(Image theImage, ImageObserver obsrvr)
public int	checkImage(Image theImage, int w, int h, ImageObserver observr)
public boolean	contains(int x, int y)
public boolean	inside(int x, int y)
public boolean	contains(Point pt)
public Component	getComponentAt(int x, int y)
public Component	locate(int x, int y)
public Component	getComponentAt(Point pt)
public void	deliverEvent(Event event)
public final void	dispatchEvent(AWTEvent event)

Chapter 21: java.awt

```
public boolean              postEvent(Event event)
public void                 addComponentListener
                                (ComponentListener listener)
public void                 removeComponentListener
                                (ComponentListener listener)
public void                 addFocusListener(FocusListener
                                listener)
public void                 removeFocusListener(FocusListener
                                listener)
public void                 addKeyListener(KeyListener listener)
public void                 removeKeyListener(KeyListener listener)
public void                 addMouseListener(MouseListener
                                listener)
public void                 removeMouseListener(MouseListener
                                listener)
public void                 addMouseMotionListener
                                (MouseMotionListener listener)
public void                 removeMouseMotionListener
                                (MouseMotionListener listener)
public void                 addInputMethodListener
                                (InputMethodListener listener)
public void                 removeInputMethodListener
                                (InputMethodListener listener)
public InputMethodRequests  getInputMethodRequests()
public InputContext         getInputContext()
protected final void        enableEvents(long events)
protected final void        disableEvents(long events)
protected AWTEvent          coalesceEvents(AWTEvent existingEvent,
                                AWTEvent nextEvent)
protected void              processEvent(AWTEvent event)
protected void              processComponentEvent(ComponentEvent
                                event)
protected void              processFocusEvent(FocusEvent event)
protected void              processKeyEvent(KeyEvent event)
protected void              processMouseEvent(MouseEvent event)
protected void              processMouseMotionEvent(MouseEvent
                                event)
protected void              processInputMethodEvent
                                (InputMethodEvent event)
public boolean              handleEvent(Event event)
public boolean              mouseDown(Event event, int x, int y)
public boolean              mouseDrag(Event event, int x, int y)
public boolean              mouseUp(Event event, int x, int y)
public boolean              mouseMove(Event event, int x, int y)
public boolean              mouseEnter(Event event, int x, int y)
public boolean              mouseExit(Event event, int x, int y)
public boolean              keyDown(Event event, Int theKey)
public boolean              keyUp(Event event, int theKey)
public boolean              action(Event event, Object whichObject)
```

public void	addNotify()
public void	removeNotify()
public boolean	gotFocus(Event event, Object whichObject)
public boolean	lostFocus(Event event, Object whichObject)
public boolean	isFocusTraversable()
public void	requestFocus()
public void	transferFocus()
public void	nextFocus()
public boolean	hasFocus()
public void	add(PopupMenu popup)
public void	remove(MenuComponent popup)
protected String	paramString()
public String	toString()
public void	list()
public void	list(PrintStream output)
public void	list(PrintStream output, int indentation)
public void	list(PrintWriter output)
public void	list(PrintWriter output, int indentation)
public void	addPropertyChangeListener (PropertyChangeListener listener)
public void	removePropertyChangeListener (PropertyChangeListener listener)
public void addPropertyChange	Listener(String propertyName, PropertyChangeListener listener)
public void removePropertyChange	Listener(String propertyName, PropertyChangeListener listener)
protected void	firePropertyChange(String propertyName, Object oldValue, Object newValue)
public void	setComponentOrientation (ComponentOrientation o)
public ComponentOrientation	getComponentOrientation()

Class Container

public class **Container**
       extends Component

The Container class is the superclass for all containers, such as Window, Frame, Dialog, Panel, and all Swing components. Generally, an application does not use this class directly, unless it is an IDE that builds GUIs.

Constructors

public   **Container**()

440 Chapter 21: java.awt

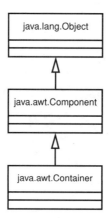

Methods

public int	**getComponentCount**()
public int	**countComponents**()
public Component	**getComponent**(int n)
public Component[]	**getComponents**()
public Insets	**getInsets**()
public Insets	**insets**()
public Component	**add**(Component comp)
public Component	**add**(String name, Component comp)
public Component	**add**(Component comp, int index)
public void	**add**(Component comp, Object constraints)
public void	**add**(Component comp, Object constraints, int index)
protected void	**addImpl**(Component comp, Object constraints, int index)
public void	**remove**(int index)
public void	**remove**(Component comp)
public void	**removeAll**()
public LayoutManager	**getLayout**()
public void	**setLayout**(LayoutManager mgr)
public void	**doLayout**()
public void	**layout**()
public void	**invalidate**()
public void	**validate**()
protected void	**validateTree**()
public void	**setFont**(Font f)
public Dimension	**getPreferredSize**()
public Dimension	**preferredSize**()
public Dimension	**getMinimumSize**()
public Dimension	**minimumSize**()
public Dimension	**getMaximumSize**()
public float	**getAlignmentX**()
public float	**getAlignmentY**()
public void	**paint**(Graphics g)
public void	**update**(Graphics g)
public void	**print**(Graphics g)

```
public void         paintComponents(Graphics g)
public void         printComponents(Graphics g)
public void         addContainerListener(ContainerListener l)
public void         removeContainerListener(ContainerListener l)
protected void      processEvent(AWTEvent e)
protected void      processContainerEvent(ContainerEvent e)
public void         deliverEvent(Event e)
public Component    getComponentAt(int x, int y)
public Component    locate(int x, int y)
public Component    getComponentAt(Point p)
public Component    findComponentAt(int x, int y)
public Component    findComponentAt(Point p)
public void         addNotify()
public void         removeNotify()
public boolean      isAncestorOf(Component c)
protected String    paramString()
public void         list(PrintStream out, int indent)
public void         list(PrintWriter out, int indent)
```

Class Cursor

```
public class Cursor
            extends Object implements Serializable
```

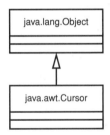

This class provides for the bitmapped representation of the mouse cursor. Note that you can control the shape of the cursor within the borders of your Java application, but not the shape of the cursor elsewhere on the desktop or in other programs.

Fields

```
public static final int     DEFAULT_CURSOR
public static final int     CROSSHAIR_CURSOR
public static final int     TEXT_CURSOR
public static final int     WAIT_CURSOR
public static final int     SW_RESIZE_CURSOR
public static final int     SE_RESIZE_CURSOR
public static final int     NW_RESIZE_CURSOR
public static final int     NE_RESIZE_CURSOR
public static final int     N_RESIZE_CURSOR
public static final int     S_RESIZE_CURSOR
public static final int     W_RESIZE_CURSOR
```

```
public static final int      E_RESIZE_CURSOR
public static final int      HAND_CURSOR
public static final int      MOVE_CURSOR
protected static Cursor[]    predefined
public static final int      CUSTOM_CURSOR
protected String             name
```

Constructors

```
public          Cursor(int type)
protected       Cursor(String name)
```

Methods

```
public static Cursor    getPredefinedCursor(int type)
public static Cursor    getSystemCustomCursor
(String name) throws    AWTException
public static Cursor    getDefaultCursor()
public int              getType()
public String           getName()
public String           toString()
```

Class Dialog

```
public class Dialog
            extends Window
```

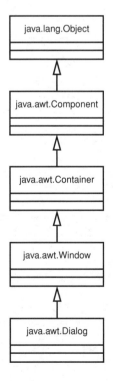

A `Dialog` is a subclass of `Window` that has a title and a border. It is generally used for user input and has two states: modal and modeless. A modal `Dialog` blocks until it is dismissed. A modeless `Dialog` does not lock the application. A `Dialog` must always be owned by a `Frame` or `Dialog` instance.

> **TIP**
>
> For the sake of good class design and reusability, you should always subclass the `Dialog` class when defining a dialog. Otherwise, you must repeatedly write code for things such as login dialogs and pop-up message box dialogs.

Here's a code snippet that shows calling and constructing a `Dialog` object.

In the GUI program:

```
Dialog loginDialog = new LoginDialog(theFrame,
                                     "Login Screen",
                                     true);
loginDialog.setSize(500,400);
loginDialog.setVisible(true);
```

In the `LoginDialog` class:

```
public class LoginDialog extends Dialog
    {
    Frame frameRef;
    public LoginDialog(Frame fr, String title,
                       boolean modal)
        {
        super(fr, title, modal);
        frameRef = fr; // Save for later use to
                       // do callbacks to GUI.
        // finish constructing the dialog.
        }
    }
```

Call `dispose()` to destroy the dialog.

> **NOTE**
>
> This class does not have a zero-argument constructor. You must call the `Dialog` constructor with parameters, and you need to call `super()` with at least a reference to a `Frame`. Because you need a `Frame`, and because accessing and using the `Frame` in which an applet exists is difficult at best, it is generally not practical to use a dialog in an applet. Generally, you will need to use some other mechanism to change screens, such as using a `CardLayout` with Buttons or `Labels` along one side to simulate a tabbed dialog—unless, of course, you use Swing. Then, you can use the much better `JTabbedPane`.

Constructors

```
public      Dialog(Frame owner)
public      Dialog(Frame owner, boolean modal)
public      Dialog(Frame owner, String title)
public      Dialog(Frame owner, String title, boolean modal)
public      Dialog(Dialog owner)
public      Dialog(Dialog owner, String title)
public      Dialog(Dialog owner, String title, boolean modal)
```

Methods

```
public void        addNotify()
public boolean     isModal()
public void        setModal(boolean b)
public String      getTitle()
public void        setTitle(String title)
public void        show()
public boolean     isResizable()
public void        setResizable(boolean resizable)
protected String   paramString()
```

Class FileDialog

```
public class FileDialog
             extends Dialog
```

The `FileDialog` class represents a predefined dialog that matches the look and feel of the platform that the dialog is running on. You can use a `FileDialog` to get the directory and filename to use in opening or saving a file. By default, the dialog displays as an Open dialog, although you can specify that it should display as a Save As dialog. You do not have control over its appearance, although you do need to call `setVisible(true)` on it.

> **CAUTION**
>
> It is critically important to remember that a `FileDialog` only gets directory and filenames for you. It does not actually access any files, nor does it actually save a file to persistent storage.

Fields

```
public static final int    LOAD
public static final int    SAVE
```

Constructors

```
public      FileDialog(Frame parent)
public      FileDialog(Frame parent, String title)
public      FileDialog(Frame parent, String title, int mode)
```

java.awt Interface and Class Details 445

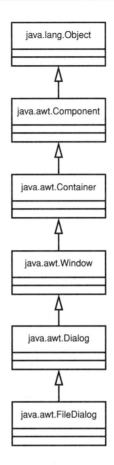

Methods

```
public void         addNotify()
public int          getMode()
public void         setMode(int mode)
public String       getDirectory()
public void         setDirectory(String dir)
public String       getFile()
public void         setFile(String file)
public FilenameFilter getFilenameFilter()
public void         setFilenameFilter(FilenameFilter filter)
protected String    paramString()
```

Class FlowLayout

```
public class FlowLayout
              extends Object
              implements LayoutManager, Serializable
```

Chapter 21: java.awt

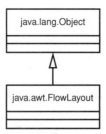

The `FlowLayout` layout manager uses two basic principles to lay out and size the components in a `Container`. It arranges components from left to right, top to bottom. Also, it sizes a component according to the minimum size required to display it properly. This means that when you use `FlowLayout` to position and size two buttons, the two buttons will be of different widths if their text labels are of different lengths. For this reason, and because of its simple layout strategy, this layout manager is not used much compared to the other choices.

Fields

```
public static final int    LEFT
public static final int    CENTER
public static final int    RIGHT
public static final int    LEADING
public static final int    TRAILING
```

Constructors

```
public     FlowLayout()
public     FlowLayout(int align)
public     FlowLayout(int align, int hgap, int vgap)
```

Methods

```
public int         getAlignment()
public void        setAlignment(int align)
public int         getHgap()
public void        setHgap(int hgap)
public int         getVgap()
public void        setVgap(int vgap)
public void        addLayoutComponent(String name, Component comp)
public void        removeLayoutComponent(Component comp)
public Dimension   preferredLayoutSize(Container target)
public Dimension   minimumLayoutSize(Container target)
public void        layoutContainer(Container target)
public String      toString()
```

Class Font

```
public class Font
            extends Object
            implements Serializable
```

java.awt Interface and Class Details

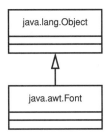

The Font class represents the font for drawing text on a component. You can specify the style, type, and size of a font like this:

```
Font aFont = new Font("Serif", Font.BOLD, 14);
TheFrame.setFont(aFont);
```

You can make the appearance of your GUI more consistent between platforms if you always specify the font by doing a setFont() on the container.

Fields

public static final int	**PLAIN**
public static final int	**BOLD**
public static final int	**ITALIC**
public static final int	**ROMAN_BASELINE**
public static final int	**CENTER_BASELINE**
public static final int	**HANGING_BASELINE**
protected String	**name**
protected int	**style**
protected int	**size**
protected float	**pointSize**

Constructors

public	**Font**(String name, int style, int size)
public	**Font**(Map attributes)

Methods

public java.awt.peer.FontPeer	get**Peer**()
public static Font	get**Font**(Map attributes)
public AffineTransform	get**Transform**()
public String	get**Family**()
public String	get**Family**(Locale l)
public String	get**PSName**()
public String	get**Name**()
public String	get**FontName**()
public String	get**FontName**(Locale l)
public int	get**Style**()
public int	get**Size**()
public float	get**Size2D**()
public boolean	is**Plain**()
public boolean	is**Bold**()

```
public boolean                                          isItalic()
public static Font                                      getFont(String nm)
public static Font                                      decode(String str)
public static Font                                      getFont(String nm,
                                                            Font font)
public int                                              hashCode()
public boolean                                          equals(Object obj)
public String                                           toString()
public int                                              getNumGlyphs()
public int                                              getMissingGlyphCode()
public byte                                             getBaselineFor(char c)
public Map                                              getAttributes()
public AttributedCharacterIterator.Attribute[]          getAvailableAttributes()
public Font                                             deriveFont(int style,
                                                            float size)
public Font                                             deriveFont(int style,
                                                            AffineTransform
                                                            trans)
public Font                                             deriveFont(float size)
public Font                                             deriveFont
                                                            (AffineTransform
                                                            trans)
public Font                                             deriveFont(int style)
public Font                                             deriveFont(Map
                                                            attributes)
public boolean                                          canDisplay(char c)
public int                                              canDisplayUpTo(String
                                                            str)
public int                                              canDisplayUpTo(char[]
                                                            text, Int start,
                                                            int limit)
public int                                              canDisplayUpTo
                                                            (CharacterIterator
                                                            iter, int start,
                                                            int limit)
public float                                            getItalicAngle()
public boolean                                          hasUniformLineMetrics()
public LineMetrics                                      getLineMetrics(String
                                                            str,
                                                            FontRenderContext
                                                            frc)
public LineMetrics                                      getLineMetrics(char[]
                                                            chars,
                                                            int beginIndex,
                                                            int limit,
                                                            FontRenderContext
                                                            frc)
public LineMetrics                                      getLineMetrics
                                                            (CharacterIterator
                                                            ci, int beginIndex,
```

	int limit, FontRenderContext frc)
public Rectangle2D	**getStringBounds**(String str, FontRenderContext frc)
public Rectangle2D	**getStringBounds**(String str, Int beginIndex, int limit, FontRenderContext frc)
public Rectangle2D	**getStringBounds**(char[] chars, int beginIndex, Int limit, FontRenderContext frc)
public Rectangle2D	**getStringBounds** (CharacterIterator ci, int beginIndex, int limit, FontRenderContext frc)
public Rectangle2D	**getMaxCharBounds** (FontRenderContext frc)
public GlyphVector	**createGlyphVector** (FontRenderContext frc, String str)
public GlyphVector	**createGlyphVector** (FontRenderContext frc, char[] chars)
public GlyphVector	**createGlyphVector** (FontRenderContext frc, CharacterIterator ci)
public GlyphVector	**createGlyphVector** (FontRenderContext frc, int[] glyphCodes)
protected void	**finalize**() throws Throwable

Class Frame

```
public class Frame
            extends Window
            implements MenuContainer
```

450 Chapter 21: java.awt

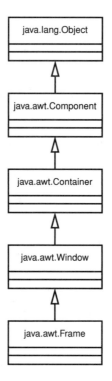

A `Frame` is a top-level container that has a title and a border and serves as the `main` window for a standalone Java GUI application. The following code snippet shows typical things to do with a `Frame`. In this case, the class subclasses `Frame` and serves as the main GUI class. This is a lot more convenient than creating a separate, cumbersome `Frame` object. The arguments for containing a `Frame` rather than extending it are inadequate because, if the definition of `Frame` changes significantly, your code is broken.

```
Public class LibraryGUI extends Frame
   {
    public LibraryGUI()
       {
        setBackground(Color.blue);
        setForeground(Color.yellow);
        setFont("Serif", Font.PLAIN, 15);
        setSize(500,400);
        setVisible(true);
       )
   }
```

CAUTION

It is critical that you call both `setSize()` and `setVisible(true)`. Otherwise, your GUI will either have dimensions of `0,0` or will not be visible.

Fields

```
public static final int    DEFAULT_CURSOR
public static final int    CROSSHAIR_CURSOR
public static final int    TEXT_CURSOR
public static final int    WAIT_CURSOR
public static final int    SW_RESIZE_CURSOR
public static final int    SE_RESIZE_CURSOR
public static final int    NW_RESIZE_CURSOR
public static final int    NE_RESIZE_CURSOR
public static final int    N_RESIZE_CURSOR
public static final int    S_RESIZE_CURSOR
public static final int    W_RESIZE_CURSOR
public static final int    E_RESIZE_CURSOR
public static final int    HAND_CURSOR
public static final int    MOVE_CURSOR
public static final int    NORMAL
public static final int    ICONIFIED
```

Constructors

```
public     Frame()
public     Frame(String title)
```

Methods

```
protected void          finalize()
                            throws Throwable
public void             addNotify()
public String           getTitle()
public void             setTitle(String title)
public Image            getIconImage()
public void             setIconImage(Image image)
public MenuBar          getMenuBar()
public void             setMenuBar(MenuBar mb)
public boolean          isResizable()
public void             setResizable(boolean resizable)
public void             setState(int state)
public int              getState()
public void             remove(MenuComponent m)
public void             removeNotify()
protected String        paramString()
public void             setCursor(int cursorType)
public int              getCursorType()
public static Frame[]   getFrames()
```

Class Graphics

```
public abstract class Graphics
                    extends Object
```

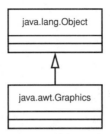

The Graphics class is an abstract class that provides methods for drawing onto components or containers on various devices. It is used for all drawing operations, including painting the screen, drawing an image off-screen, and drawing the screen to the printer, which is a graphics-related operation.

Constructors
protected   **Graphics**()

Methods

public abstract Graphics	**create**()
public Graphics	**create**(int x, int y, int width, int height)
public abstract void	**translate**(int x, int y)
public abstract Color	**getColor**()
public abstract void	**setColor**(Color c)
public abstract void	**setPaintMode**()
public abstract void	**setXORMode**(Color c1)
public abstract Font	**getFont**()
public abstract void	**setFont**(Font font)
public FontMetrics	**getFontMetrics**()
public abstract FontMetrics	**getFontMetrics**(Font f)
public abstract Rectangle	**getClipBounds**()
public abstract void	**clipRect**(int x, int y, int width, int height)
public abstract void	**setClip**(int x, int y, Int width, int height)
public abstract Shape	**getClip**()
public abstract void	**setClip**(Shape clip)
public abstract void	**copyArea**(int x, int y, int width, int height, int dx, int dy)
public abstract void	**drawLine**(int x1, Int y1, int x2, int y2)
public abstract void	**fillRect**(int x, int y, int width, int height)
public void	**drawRect**(int x, int y, int width, int height)
public abstract void	**clearRect**(int x, int y, int width, int height)
public abstract void	**drawRoundRect**(int x, int y, int width, int height, int arcWidth, int arcHeight)
public abstract void	**fillRoundRect**(int x, int y, int width, int height, int arcWidth, int arcHeight)
public void	**draw3DRect**(int x, int y, int width, int height, boolean raised)
public void	**fill3DRect**(int x, int y, int width, int height, boolean raised)
public abstract void	**drawOval**(int x, int y, int width, int height)

```
public abstract void     fillOval(int x, int y, int width, int height)
public abstract void     drawArc(int x, int y, int width, int height,
                             int startAngle, int arcAngle)
public abstract void     fillArc(int x, int y, int width, int height,
                             int startAngle, int arcAngle)
public abstract void     drawPolyline(int[] xPoints, int[] yPoints,
                             int nPoints)
public abstract void     drawPolygon(int[] xPoints, Int[] yPoints,
                             int nPoints)
public void              drawPolygon(Polygon p)
public abstract void     fillPolygon(int[] xPoints, int[] yPoints,
                             int nPoints)
public void              fillPolygon(Polygon p)
public abstract void     drawString(String str, int x, int y)
public abstract void     drawString(AttributedCharacterIterator
                             iterator, int x, int y)
public void              drawChars(char[] data, int offset, int length,
                             int x, int y)
public void              drawBytes(byte[] data, int offset, int length,
                             int x, int y)
public abstract boolean  drawImage(Image img, int x, int y,
                             ImageObserver observer)
public abstract boolean  drawImage(Image img, int x, int y, int width,
                             int height, ImageObserver observer)
public abstract boolean  drawImage(Image img, int x, int y,
                             Color bgcolor, ImageObserver observer)
public abstract boolean  drawImage(Image img, int x, int y, int width,
                             int height, Color bgcolor,
                             ImageObserver observer)
public abstract boolean  drawImage(Image img, int dx1, int dy1,
                             int dx2, int dy2, int sx1, int sy1,
                             int sx2, int sy2, ImageObserver observer)
public abstract boolean  drawImage(Image img, Int dx1, int dy1,
                             int dx2, int dy2, int sx1, int sy1,
                             int sx2, int sy2, Color bgcolor,
                             ImageObserver observer)
public abstract void     dispose()
public void              finalize()
public String            toString()
public Rectangle         getClipRect()
public boolean           hitClip(int x, int y, int width, int height)
public Rectangle         getClipBounds(Rectangle r)
```

Class Graphics2D
```
public abstract class Graphics2D
                extends Graphics
```

Chapter 21: java.awt

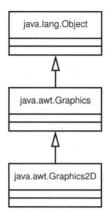

The `Graphics2D` class, a subclass of `Graphics`, provides more sophisticated support for drawing, including 2D drawing facilities.

Constructors

protected 1   **Graphics2D**()

Methods

public void	**draw3DRect**(int x, int y, int width, int height, boolean raised)
public void	**fill3DRect**(int x, int y, int width, int height, boolean raised)
public abstract void	**draw**(Shape s)
public abstract boolean	**drawImage**(Image img, AffineTransform xform, ImageObserver obs)
public abstract void	**drawImage**(BufferedImage img, BufferedImageOp op, int x, int y)
public abstract void	**drawRenderedImage**(RenderedImage img, AffineTransform xform)
public abstract void	**drawRenderableImage** (RenderableImage img, AffineTransform xform)
public abstract void	**drawString**(String str, int x, int y)
public abstract void	**drawString**(String s, float x, float y)
public abstract void	**drawString** (AttributedCharacterIterator iterator, int x, int y)
public abstract void	**drawString** (AttributedCharacterIterator iterator, float x, float y)

java.awt Interface and Class Details

```
public abstract void            drawGlyphVector(GlyphVector g,
                                    float x, float y)
public abstract void            fill(Shape s)
public abstract boolean         hit(Rectangle rect, Shape s,
                                    boolean onStroke)
public abstract GraphicsConfiguration   getDeviceConfiguration()
public abstract void            setComposite(Composite comp)
public abstract void            setPaint(Paint paint)
public abstract void            setStroke(Stroke s)
public abstract void            setRenderingHint
                                    (RenderingHints.Key
                                    hintKey, Object hintValue)
public abstract Object          getRenderingHint
                                    (RenderingHints.Key hintKey)
public abstract void            setRenderingHints(Map hints)
public abstract void            addRenderingHints(Map hints)
public abstract RenderingHints  getRenderingHints()
public abstract void            translate(int x, int y)
public abstract void            translate(double tx, double ty)
public abstract void            rotate(double theta)
public abstract void            rotate(double theta, double x,
                                    double y)
public abstract void            scale(double sx, double sy)
public abstract void            shear(double shx, double shy)
public abstract void            transform(AffineTransform Tx)
public abstract void            setTransform(AffineTransform Tx)
public abstract AffineTransform getTransform()
public abstract Paint           getPaint()
public abstract Composite       getComposite()
public abstract void            setBackground(Color color)
public abstract Color           getBackground()
public abstract Stroke          getStroke()
public abstract void            clip(Shape s)
public abstract FontRenderContext   getFontRenderContext()
```

Class GridBagConstraints

```
public class GridBagConstraints
            extends Object
            implements Cloneable, Serializable
```

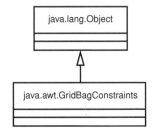

The `GridBagConstraints` class defines constraints that are used for sizing and positioning components with a container that has a `GridBagLayout` layout manager. The following code snippet shows an example of setting up the constraints for a component:

```
Panel bookPanel = new Panel();
BookPanel.setLayout(new GridBagLayout());
GridBagConstraints gbc = new GridBagConstraints();
Button checkOutButton = new Button("Check out");
gbc.gridx = 3;
gbc.gridy = 1;
gbc.gridwidth = 1;
gbc.gridheight = 1;
gbc.fill = GridBagConstraints.HORIZONTAL;
bookPanel.add(checkOutButton, gbc);
```

Fields

public static final int	**RELATIVE**
public static final int	**REMAINDER**
public static final int	**NONE**
public static final int	**BOTH**
public static final int	**HORIZONTAL**
public static final int	**VERTICAL**
public static final int	**CENTER**
public static final int	**NORTH**
public static final int	**NORTHEAST**
public static final int	**EAST**
public static final int	**SOUTHEAST**
public static final int	**SOUTH**
public static final int	**SOUTHWEST**
public static final int	**WEST**
public static final int	**NORTHWEST**
public int	**gridx**
public int	**gridy**
public int	**gridwidth**
public int	**gridheight**
public double	**weightx**
public double	**weighty**
public int	**anchor**
public int	**fill**
public Insets	**insets**
public int	**ipadx**
public int	**ipady**

Constructors

public	**GridBagConstraints**()
public	**GridBagConstraints**(int gridx, int gridy, int gridwidth, int gridheight, double weightx, double weighty, int anchor, int fill, Insets insets, int ipadx, int ipady)

Methods
public Object   **clone**()

Class GridBagLayout
public class **GridBagLayout**
        extends Object
        implements LayoutManager2, Serializable

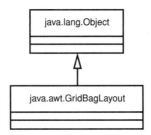

Fields
protected static final int	**MAXGRIDSIZE**
protected static final int	**MINSIZE**
protected static final int	**PREFERREDSIZE**
protected Hashtable	**comptable**
protected GridBagConstraints	**defaultConstraints**
protected java.awt.GridBagLayoutInfo	**layoutInfo**
public int[]	**columnWidths**
public int[]	**rowHeights**
public double[]	**columnWeights**
public double[]	**rowWeights**

Constructors
public   **GridBagLayout**()

Methods
public void	**setConstraints**(Component comp, GridBagConstraints constraints)
public GridBagConstraints	**getConstraints**(Component comp)
protected lookupConstraints	**GridBagConstraints**(Component comp)
public Point	**getLayoutOrigin**()
public int[][]	**getLayoutDimensions**()
public double[][]	**getLayoutWeights**()
public Point	**location**(int x, int y)
public void	**addLayoutComponent**(String name, Component comp)
public void	**addLayoutComponent**(Component comp, Object constraints)
public void	**removeLayoutComponent**(Component comp)

public Dimension	**preferredLayoutSize**(Container parent)
public Dimension	**minimumLayoutSize**(Container parent)
public Dimension	**maximumLayoutSize**(Container target)
public float	**getLayoutAlignmentX**(Container parent)
public float	**getLayoutAlignmentY**(Container parent)
public void	**InvalidateLayout**(Container target)
public void	**layoutContainer**(Container parent)
public String	**toString**()
protected java.awtGridBagLayoutInfo	**GetLayoutInfo**(Container parent, int sizeflag)
protected void	**AdjustForGravity**(GridBagConstraints constraints, Rectangle r)
protected Dimension	**GetMinSize**(Container parent, java.awt.GridBagLayoutInfo info)
protected void	**ArrangeGrid**(Container parent)

Class GridLayout

```
public class GridLayout
            extends Object
            implements LayoutManager, Serializable
```

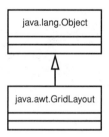

The GridLayout layout manager sizes and positions components in a grid consisting of rows and columns. Each grid cell, and hence every component, is equal in size, unlike components in a GridBagLayout, which may differ in size.

> **TIP**
>
> You can use a GridLayout in a Panel to get Buttons or Labels aligned vertically or horizontally and to make each component the same size. This contrasts with how FlowLayout sizes components. You do something like this:
>
> ```
> Panel buttonPanel = new Panel(new GridLayout(5,1));
> Button searchBtn = new Button("Search");
> Button resetBtn = new Button("Reset");
> Button helpBtn = new Button("Help");
> buttonPanel.add(searchBtn);
> ```

```
buttonPanel.add(new Panel());
buttonPanel.add(resetBtn);
buttonPanel.add(new Panel());
buttonPanel.add(helpBtn);
```

This code also shows another trick. By adding empty `Panel`s, you make the `Button`s shorter and/or space them as you wish.

Constructors

```
public      GridLayout()
public      GridLayout(int rows, int cols)
public      GridLayout(int rows, int cols, int hgap, int vgap)
```

Methods

```
public int        getRows()
public void       setRows(int rows)
public int        getColumns()
public void       setColumns(int cols)
public int        getHgap()
public void       setHgap(int hgap)
public int        getVgap()
public void       setVgap(int vgap)
public void       addLayoutComponent(String name, Component comp)
public void       removeLayoutComponent(Component comp)
public Dimension  preferredLayoutSize(Container parent)
public Dimension  minimumLayoutSize(Container parent)
public void       layoutContainer(Container parent)
public String     toString()
```

Class Image

```
public abstract class Image
                     extends Object
```

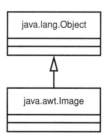

This class lets you create an image from a `.gif` or `.jpeg` file or from an image created in memory.

Fields

```
public static final Object    UndefinedProperty
public static final int       SCALE_DEFAULT
```

```
public static final int      SCALE_FAST
public static final int      SCALE_SMOOTH
public static final int      SCALE_REPLICATE
public static final int      SCALE_AREA_AVERAGING
```

Constructors
```
public     Image()
```

Methods
```
public abstract int              getWidth(ImageObserver observer)
public abstract int              getHeight(ImageObserver observer)
public abstract ImageProducer    getSource()
public abstract Graphics         getGraphics()
public abstract Object           getProperty(String name,
                                     ImageObserver observer)
public Image                     getScaledInstance(int width, int height,
                                     int hints)
public abstract void             flush()
```

Class Insets
```
public class Insets
            extends Object
            implements Cloneable, Serializable
```

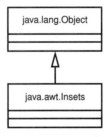

Insets represent the width of the border on each side of a container. The position within a container is relative to the insets.

Fields
```
public int      top
public int      left
public int      bottom
public int      right
```

Constructors
```
public     Insets(int top, int left, int bottom, int right)
```

Methods

```
public boolean    equals(Object obj)
public String     toString()
public Object     clone()
```

Class Label

public class **Label**
                extends Component

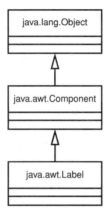

A Label is a GUI component for displaying read-only text. Normally Labels do not accept user interaction nor generate events. Labels can only display text, with left, right, or centered alignment. A Label is one of the few components that provides for alignment. Here's an example of making an aligned Label:

```
Label titleLabel = new Label("Title", Label.LEFT);
```

Fields

```
public static final int    LEFT
public static final int    CENTER
public static final int    RIGHT
```

Constructors

```
public    Label()
public    Label(String text)
public    Label(String text, int alignment)
```

Methods

```
public void       addNotify()
public int        getAlignment()
public void       setAlignment(int alignment)
public String     getText()
public void       setText(String text)
protected String  paramString()
```

Class List

public class **List**
                extends Component
                implements ItemSelectable

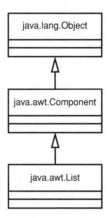

A List is a GUI component that contains a scrollable list of items. A List can support multiple or single selection modes. If there are more items than can be seen without scrolling, a vertical scrollbar is automatically provided. The items in the List are text-only items. The following code snippet shows how to create and populate a List:

```
Panel listPanel = new Panel(new BroderLayout());
List authorList = new List(4, true);   // Make a List that
                   // shows four rows to begin with and allows
                   // multiple selection.
authorList.add("Thucidedes");
authorList.add("Luke");
authorList.add("Seutonius");
authorList.add("Tacitus");
authorList.add("Josephus"):
authorList.add("Xenophon");
authorList.select(3);   // Select an item in the List
System.out.println("The item is:  " +
    AuthorList.getSelectedItem());
ListPanel.add("Center", authorList);
```

> **NOTE**
>
> A List component has its own scrollbars. This is unlike a Jlist, which must be placed in a JScrollPane in order to have scrollbars.

Constructors

```
public      List()
public      List(int rows)
public      List(int rows, boolean multipleMode)
```

Methods

public void	**addNotify**()
public void	**removeNotify**()
public int	**getItemCount**()
public int	**countItems**()
public String	**getItem**(int index)
public String[]	**getItems**()
public void	**add**(String item)
public void	**addItem**(String item)
public void	**add**(String item, int index)
public void	**addItem**(String item, int index)
public void	**replaceItem**(String newValue, int index)
public void	**removeAll**()
public void	**clear**()
public void	**remove**(String item)
public void	**remove**(int position)
public void	**delItem**(int position)
public int	**getSelectedIndex**()
public int[]	**getSelectedIndexes**()
public String	**getSelectedItem**()
public String[]	**getSelectedItems**()
public Object[]	**getSelectedObjects**()
public void	**select**(int index)
public void	**deselect**(int index)
public boolean	**isIndexSelected**(int index)
public boolean	**isSelected**(int index)
public int	**getRows**()
public boolean	**isMultipleMode**()
public boolean	**allowsMultipleSelections**()
public void	**setMultipleMode**(boolean b)
public void	**setMultipleSelections**(boolean b)
public int	**getVisibleIndex**()
public void	**makeVisible**(int index)
public Dimension	**getPreferredSize**(int rows)
public Dimension	**preferredSize**(int rows)
public Dimension	**getPreferredSize**()
public Dimension	**preferredSize**()
public Dimension	**getMinimumSize**(int rows)
public Dimension	**minimumSize**(int rows)
public Dimension	**getMinimumSize**()
public Dimension	**minimumSize**()
public void	**addItemListener**(ItemListener l)
public void	**removeItemListener**(ItemListener l)
public void	**addActionListener**(ActionListener l)
public void	**removeActionListener**(ActionListener l)
protected void	**processEvent**(AWTEvent e)
protected void	**processItemEvent**(ItemEvent e)
protected void	**processActionEvent**(ActionEvent e)
protected String	**paramString**()
public void	**delItems**(int start, int end)

Class MediaTracker

public class **MediaTracker**
            extends Object
            implements Serializable

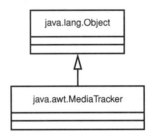

The MediaTracker class defines an object that can be used to track the loading/downloading of images to an application or applet. It can check on the status of the image(s) being loaded or wait for the loading to complete and then continue executing other code. It is customarily run in a separate thread dedicated to loading images.

> **NOTE**
>
> The use of this class can improve performance of an application or applet significantly. It allows the GUI to execute on the AWT thread, even though the images are still loading. It can also tell the main GUI or execute some GUI method when the images are completely downloaded. This lets your GUI be available much faster than it would be if you had to wait for all the images to load. It is also much more satisfying for the user, who does not have to look at an hourglass cursor for a long period of time.

Fields

```
public static final int    LOADING
public static final int    ABORTED
public static final int    ERRORED
public static final int    COMPLETE
```

Constructors

```
public     MediaTracker(Component comp)
```

Methods

```
public void        addImage(Image image, int id)
public void        addImage(Image image, int id, int w, int h)
public boolean     checkAll()
public boolean     checkAll(boolean load)
public boolean     isErrorAny()
public Object[]    getErrorsAny()
public void        waitForAll()
                       throws InterruptedException
public boolean     waitForAll(long ms)
```

```
                    throws InterruptedException
public int          statusAll(boolean load)
public boolean      checkID(int id)
public boolean      checkID(int id, boolean load)
public boolean      isErrorID(int id)
public Object[]     getErrorsID(int id)
public void         waitForID(int id) throws InterruptedException
public boolean      waitForID(int id, long ms) throws InterruptedException
public int          statusID(int id, boolean load)
public void         removeImage(Image image)
public void         removeImage(Image image, int id)
public void         removeImage(Image image, int id, int width,
                        int height)
```

Class Menu

```
public class Menu
            extends MenuItem
```

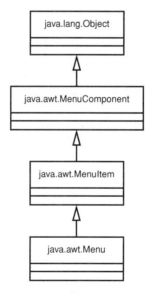

A Menu object placed on a MenuBar is a pull-down menu. Examples might be File, Edit, and Help. Here is a code snippet to illustrate the creation of a small Menu for an application:

```
MenuItem newMI = new MenuItem("New");
MenuItem openMI = new MenuItem("Open");
MenuItem copyMI = new MenuItem("Copy");
MenuItem pasteMI = new MenuItem("Paste");
Menu fileMenu = new Menu("File");
Menu editMenu = new Menu("Edit");
fileMenu.add(newMI);
fileMenu.add(openMI);
```

```
editMenu.add(copyMI);
editMenu.add(pasteMI);
MenuItem aboutMI = new MenuItem("About");
Menu helpMenu = new Menu("Help");
HelpMenu.add(aboutMI);
MenuBar mb = new MenuBar();
mb.add(fileMenu);
mb.add(editMenu);
mb.setHelpMenu(helpMenu);
theFrame.setMenuBar(mb);
```

TIP

To get cascading menus, in which selecting one menu choice displays multiple menu choices to the right, you add a Menu m1 to a Menu m2 and then add MenuItems to m1.

CAUTION

You cannot readily add a MenuBar to any container but a Frame. Therefore, it is extremely difficult to add a menu to an applet. The easiest alternative is to use a CardLayout that displays multiple Panels (cards) in the applet. To select a specific card, you put a row of Buttons above the Panels and click the Button of the desired screen. This simulates a tabbed dialog.

Constructors

public	**Menu**()
public	**Menu**(String label)
public	**Menu**(String label, boolean tearOff)

Methods

public void	**addNotify**()
public void	**removeNotify**()
public boolean	**isTearOff**()
public int	**getItemCount**()
public int	**countItems**()
public MenuItem	**getItem**(int index)
public MenuItem	**add**(MenuItem mi)
public void	**add**(String label)
public void	**insert**(MenuItem menuitem, int index)
public void	**insert**(String label, int index)
public void	**addSeparator**()
public void	**insertSeparator**(int index)
public void	**remove**(int index)
public void	**remove**(MenuComponent item)
public void	**removeAll**()
public String	**paramString**()

Class MenuBar

public class **MenuBar**
          extends MenuComponent
          implements MenuContainer

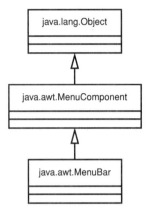

A MenuBar component provides a menu bar for the outermost window of an application, a Frame. Unlike most components, it is not added to the Frame, but placed in the Frame with the setMenuBar method. A MenuBar cannot be placed in any other container. You cannot directly add a MenuBar to an applet. See the description of java.awt.Menu for an example of using a MenuBar. You can only put a MenuBar in a Frame, but this restriction does not apply to a JmenuBar. This makes building menus in Swing easier and much more flexible.

Constructors
public   **MenuBar**()

Methods

public void	**addNotify**()
public void	**removeNotify**()
public Menu	**getHelpMenu**()
public void	**setHelpMenu**(Menu m)
public Menu	**add**(Menu m)
public void	**remove**(int index)
public void	**remove**(MenuComponent m)
public int	**getMenuCount**()
public int	**countMenus**()
public Menu	**getMenu**(int i)
public Enumeration	**shortcuts**()
public MenuItem	**getShortcutMenuItem**(MenuShortcut s)
public void	**deleteShortcut**(MenuShortcut s)

Class MenuItem

public class **MenuItem**
           extends MenuComponent

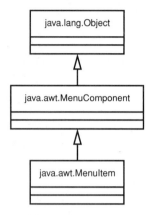

A MenuItem object represents one menu item in a menu, such as Open on a File menu. MenuItems must be placed in a menu. They cannot stand by themselves. See the description of java.awt.Menu for an example of using MenuItems.

Constructors

```
public      MenuItem()
public      MenuItem(String label)
public      MenuItem(String label, MenuShortcut s)
```

Methods

```
public void             addNotify()
public String           getLabel()
public void             setLabel(String label)
public boolean          isEnabled()
public void             setEnabled(boolean b)
public void             enable()
public void             enable(boolean b)
public void             disable()
public MenuShortcut     getShortcut()
public void             setShortcut(MenuShortcut s)
public void             deleteShortcut()
protected final void    enableEvents(long eventsToEnable)
protected final void    disableEvents(long eventsToDisable)
public void             setActionCommand(String command)
public String           getActionCommand()
public void             addActionListener(ActionListener l)
public void             removeActionListener(ActionListener l)
protected void          processEvent(AWTEvent e)
protected void          processActionEvent(ActionEvent e)
public String           paramString()
```

Class MenuShortcut

public class **MenuShortcut**
            extends Object
            implements Serializable

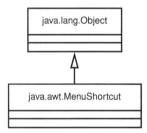

A MenuShortcut represents a keyboard shortcut to perform a specific MenuItem choice. Just as when you click on a MenuItem, the shortcut generates an ActionEvent for the MenuItem. Here's a code snippet showing how to create a shortcut:

```
Menu fileMenu = new Menu("File");
MenuItem openMI =
        new MenuItem("Open",
                     new MenuShortcut(KeyEvent.VK_N));
openMI.setActionCommand("Open");
 // Required for shortcut
fileMenu.add(openMI);
```

Constructors

public	**MenuShortcut**(int key)
public	**MenuShortcut**(int key, boolean useShiftModifier)

Methods

public int	**getKey**()
public boolean	**usesShiftModifier**()
public boolean	**equals**(MenuShortcut s)
public boolean	**equals**(Object obj)
public int	**hashCode**()
public String	**toString**()
protected String	**paramString**()

Class Panel

public class **Panel**
            extends Container

A Panel is a basic container. It has no border or title bar. It is best to put Components into Panels and then put Panels into Frames in order to increase the flexibility of a GUI. Doing this is also essential for creating complex screens using the AWT. You cannot do much with a Panel by itself. It is only a rectangle with no borders. In fact, the Panel class is often subclassed in order to create a bordered panel. Here is simple code for creating a Panel:

```
Panel pan = new Panel();
Pan.setLayout(new GridLayout());
pan.setBackground(Color.blue);
theFrame.add(pan, "West");
```

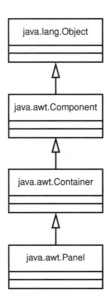

Constructors

```
public    Panel()
public    Panel(LayoutManager layout)
```

Methods

```
public void    addNotify()
```

Class Point

```
public class Point
              extends Point2D
              implements Serializable
```

A Point represents a visual point based on x and y coordinates in the coordinate space.

Fields

```
public int    x
public int    y
```

java.awt Interface and Class Details

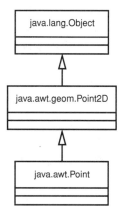

Constructors

```
public    Point()
public    Point(Point p)
public    Point(int x, int y)
```

Methods

```
public double    getX()
public double    getY()
public Point     getLocation()
public void      setLocation(Point p)
public void      setLocation(int x, int y)
public void      setLocation(double x, double y)
public void      move(int x, int y)
public void      translate(int x, int y)
public boolean   equals(Object obj)
public String    toString()
```

Class PopupMenu

```
public class PopupMenu
            extends Menu
```

The `PopupMenu` class provides for a pop-up menu that appears at given coordinates within a `Component`. Because some platforms do not support a right mouse button, the `PopupMenu` class does not directly support activation through the right mouse button.

Constructors

```
public    PopupMenu()
public    PopupMenu(String label)
```

Methods

```
public void    addNotify()
public void    show(Component origin, int x, nt y)
```

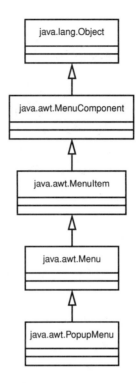

Class PrintJob
```
public abstract class PrintJob
                    extends Object
```

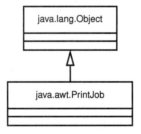

A `PrintJob` object provides for printing a `Graphics` object to a printing device. You request a `PrintJob` object from the system and return it when done. It provides for the print dialog automatically. The `PrintJob` object has been superseded by the `PrinterJob` class in Java 2.

Constructors
```
public    PrintJob()
```

Methods

```
public abstract Graphics    getGraphics()
public abstract Dimension   getPageDimension()
public abstract int         getPageResolution()
public abstract boolean     lastPageFirst()
public abstract void        end()
public void                 finalize()
```

Class Rectangle

```
public class Rectangle
              extends Rectangle2D
              implements Shape, Serializable
```

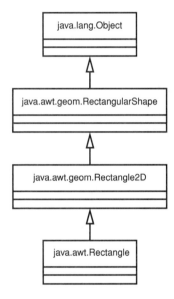

The Rectangle class represents a rectangular area on the screen. Because all JDK AWT components are rectangular in shape, a Rectangle object can be used to specify the bounds of another component. Making a Rectangle is fairly simple. You can use it in a number of ways. One way is to define the rectangular area that a component, sized with absolute positioning, should fill. Here's a code snippet to illustrate this:

```
Panel pan = new Panel();
pan.setLayout(null);
Label bookLabel = new Label("Book Info");
bookLabel.setBounds(new Rectangle(50,50,120,20));
// Using absolute positioning is not recommended because this
// component will only look good on one platform.
pan.add(bookLabel);
```

Fields
```
public int      x
public int      y
public int      width
public int      height
```

Constructors
```
public    Rectangle()
public    Rectangle(Rectangle r)
public    Rectangle(int x, int y, int width, int height)
public    Rectangle(int width, int height)
public    Rectangle(Point p, Dimension d)
public    Rectangle(Point p)
public    Rectangle(Dimension d)
```

Methods
```
public double         getX()
public double         getY()
public double         getWidth()
public double         getHeight()
public Rectangle      getBounds()
public Rectangle2D    getBounds2D()
public void           setBounds(Rectangle r)
public void           setBounds(int x, int y, int width, int height)
public void           setRect(double x, double y, double width,
                              double height)
public void           reshape(int x, int y, int width, Int height)
public Point          getLocation()
public void           setLocation(Point p)
public void           setLocation(int x, int y)
public void           move(int x, int y)
public void           translate(int x, int y)
public Dimension      getSize()
public void           setSize(Dimension d)
public void           setSize(int width, int height)
public void           resize(int width, int height)
public boolean        contains(Point p)
public boolean        contains(int x, int y)
public boolean        contains(Rectangle r)
public boolean        contains(int X, int Y, int W, int H)
public boolean        inside(int x, int y)
public boolean        intersects(Rectangle r)
public Rectangle      intersection(Rectangle r)
public Rectangle      union(Rectangle r)
public void           add(int newx, int newy)
public void           add(Point pt)
public void           add(Rectangle r)
public void           grow(int h, int v)
public boolean        isEmpty()
```

```
public int            outcode(double x, double y)
public Rectangle2D    createIntersection(Rectangle2D r)
public Rectangle2D    createUnion(Rectangle2D r)
public boolean        equals(Object obj)
public String         toString()
```

Class ScrollPane

```
public class ScrollPane
               extends Container
```

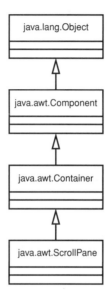

A ScrollPane is a special container that provides horizontal and vertical scrollbars and manages user scrolling automatically. It is far superior to the Scrollbar class and provides great flexibility in scrollbar usage. Here's an example of how to make one:

```
ScrollPane sp = new ScrollPane(SCROLLBARS_ALWAYS);
// Create a ScrollPane that always shows scrollbars.
Panel pan = new Panel();
// ScrollPanes must be put in a container.
pan.add(sp);
sp.add(bigImage);
```

Fields

```
public static final int    SCROLLBARS_AS_NEEDED
public static final int    SCROLLBARS_ALWAYS
public static final int    SCROLLBARS_NEVER
```

Constructors

```
public    ScrollPane()
public    ScrollPane(int scrollbarDisplayPolicy)
```

Methods

```
protected final void   addImpl(Component comp, Object constraints,
                               int index)
public int             getScrollbarDisplayPolicy()
public Dimension       getViewportSize()
public int             getHScrollbarHeight()
public int             getVScrollbarWidth()
public Adjustable      getVAdjustable()
public Adjustable      getHAdjustable()
public void            setScrollPosition(int x, int y)
public void            setScrollPosition(Point p)
public Point           getScrollPosition()
public final void      setLayout(LayoutManager mgr)
public void            doLayout()
public void            layout()
public void            printComponents(Graphics g)
public void            addNotify()
public String          paramString()
```

Class TextArea

```
public class TextArea
            extends TextComponent
```

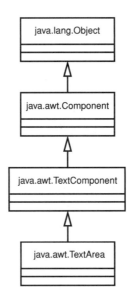

A TextArea provides an area for typing or viewing multiple lines of text, although the entire contents are accessed programmatically as one String object. A TextArea provides its own scrollbars. By setting scrolling to SCROLLBARS_VERTICAL_ONLY, the TextArea object will do automatic word-wrap. Other than this feature, a TextArea is a fairly simple text editing area, in contrast to a JEditorpane, for example.

Fields

```
public static final int    SCROLLBARS_BOTH
public static final int    SCROLLBARS_VERTICAL_ONLY
public static final int    SCROLLBARS_HORIZONTAL_ONLY
public static final int    SCROLLBARS_NONE
```

Constructors

```
public    TextArea()
public    TextArea(String text)
public    TextArea(int rows, int columns)
public    TextArea(String text, int rows, int columns)
public    TextArea(String text, int rows, int columns, int scrollbars)
```

Methods

```
public void         addNotify()
public void         insert(String str, int pos)
public void         insertText(String str, int pos)
public void         append(String str)
public void         appendText(String str)
public void         replaceRange(String str, int start, int end)
public void         replaceText(String str, int start, Int end)
public int          getRows()
public void         setRows(int rows)
public int          getColumns()
public void         setColumns(int columns)
public int          getScrollbarVisibility()
public Dimension    getPreferredSize(int rows, int columns)
public Dimension    preferredSize(int rows, int columns)
public Dimension    getPreferredSize()
public Dimension    preferredSize()
public Dimension    getMinimumSize(int rows, int columns)
public Dimension    minimumSize(int rows, int columns)
public Dimension    getMinimumSize()
public Dimension    minimumSize()
protected String    paramString()
```

Class TextComponent

```
public class TextComponent
            extends Component
```

The TextComponent class is the superclass of TextField and TextArea. Normally, a TextComponent is not instantiated directly, but because TextComponent has many methods that are useful for both TextField and TextArea, familiarity with TextComponent is quite helpful.

Fields

```
protected transient TextListener     textListener
```

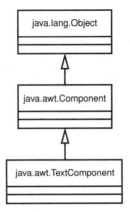

Methods

public void	removeNotify()
public void	setText(String t)
public String	getText()
public String	getSelectedText()
public boolean	isEditable()
public void	setEditable(boolean b)
public int	getSelectionStart()
public void	setSelectionStart(int selectionStart)
public int	getSelectionEnd()
public void	setSelectionEnd(int selectionEnd)
public void	select(int selectionStart, int selectionEnd)
public void	selectAll()
public void	setCaretPosition(int position)
public int	getCaretPosition()
public void	addTextListener(TextListener l)
public void	removeTextListener(TextListener l)
protected void	processEvent(AWTEvent e)
protected void	processTextEvent(TextEvent e)
protected String	paramString()

Class TextField

public class **TextField**
           extends TextComponent

A `TextField` is a GUI component that allows the entering of a single line of text.

Constructors

public	TextField()
public	TextField(String text)
public	TextField(int columns)
public	TextField(String text, int columns)

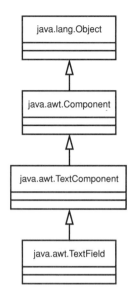

Methods

```
public void        addNotify()
public char        getEchoChar()
public void        setEchoChar(char c)
public void        setEchoCharacter(char c)
public void        setText(String t)
public boolean     echoCharIsSet()
public int         getColumns()
public void        setColumns(int columns)
public Dimension   getPreferredSize(int columns)
public Dimension   preferredSize(int columns)
public Dimension   getPreferredSize()
public Dimension   preferredSize()
public Dimension   getMinimumSize(int columns)
public Dimension   minimumSize(int columns)
public Dimension   getMinimumSize()
public Dimension   minimumSize()
public void        addActionListener(ActionListener l)
public void        removeActionListener(ActionListener l)
protected void     processEvent(AWTEvent e)
protected void     processActionEvent(ActionEvent e)
protected String   paramString()
```

Class Toolkit

```
public abstract class Toolkit
                    extends Object
```

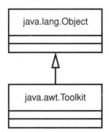

This is the abstract superclass of all `Toolkit` implementations and has several useful methods, such as `getImage()`. The `Toolkit` subclasses bind components to their native peer implementations. Here's one of the many handy things you can do with a `Toolkit` object:

```
// Get Screen size.
Dimension screenDim = getDefaultToolkit().getScreenSize();
```

Fields

```
protected final Map     desktopProperties
protected final         PropertyChangeSupport desktopPropsSupport
```

Constructors

```
public    Toolkit()
```

Methods

```
protected abstract java.awt.peer.ButtonPeer      createButton(Button target)
protected abstract java.awt.peer.TextFieldPeer   createTextField
                                                       (TextField target)
protected abstract java.awt.peer.LabelPeer       createLabel(Label target)
protected abstract java.awt.peer.ListPeer        createList(List target)
protected abstract java.awt.peer.CheckboxPeer    createCheckbox(Checkbox
                                                       target)
protected abstract java.awt.peer.ScrollbarPeer   createScrollbar
                                                       (Scrollbar target)
protected abstract java.awt.peer.ScrollPanePeer  createScrollPane
                                                       (ScrollPane target)
protected abstract java.awt.peer.TextAreaPeer    createTextArea(TextArea
                                                       target)
protected abstract java.awt.peer.ChoicePeer      createChoice(Choice
                                                       target)
protected abstract java.awt.peer.FramePeer       createFrame(Frame target)
protected abstract java.awt.peer.CanvasPeer      createCanvas(Canvas
                                                       target)
protected abstract java.awt.peer.PanelPeer       createPanel(Panel target)
protected abstract java.awt.peer.WindowPeer      createWindow(Window
                                                       target)
protected abstract java.awt.peer.DialogPeer      createDialog(Dialog
```

protected abstract java.awt.peer.MenuBarPeer	**createMenuBar**(MenuBar target)
protected abstract java.awt.peer.MenuPeer	**createMenu**(Menu target)
protected abstract java.awt.peer.PopupMenuPeer	**createPopupMenu** (PopupMenu target)
protected abstract java.awt.peer.MenuItemPeer	**createMenuItem**(MenuItem target)
protected abstract java.awt.peer.FileDialogPeer	**createFileDialog** (FileDialog target)
protected abstract java.awt.peer. CheckboxMenuItemPeer	**createCheckboxMenuItem** (CheckboxMenuItem target)
protected java.awt.peer	**createComponentLightweightPeer** (Component target)
protected abstract java.awt.peer.FontPeer	**getFontPeer**(String name, int style)
protected void	**loadSystemColors** (int[] systemColors)
public abstract Dimension	**getScreenSize**()
public abstract int	**getScreenResolution**()
public abstract ColorModel	**getColorModel**()
public abstract String[]	**getFontList**()
public abstract FontMetrics	**getFontMetrics**(Font font)
public abstract void	**sync**()
public static Toolkit	**getDefaultToolkit**()
public abstract Image	**getImage**(String filename)
public abstract Image	**getImage**(URL url)
public abstract Image	**createImage**(String filename)
public abstract Image	**createImage**(URL url)
public abstract boolean	**prepareImage**(Image image, int width, int height, ImageObserver observer)
public abstract int	**checkImage**(Image image, int width, int height, ImageObserver observer)
public abstract Image	**createImage** (ImageProducer producer)
public Image	**createImage**(byte[] imagedata)
public abstract Image	**createImage**(byte[] imagedata, int imageoffset, int imagelength)
public abstract PrintJob	**getPrintJob**(Frame frame,

```
public abstract void                  beep()
public abstract Clipboard             getSystemClipboard()
public int                            getMenuShortcutKeyMask()
protected static Container            getNativeContainer
                                          (Component c)
public Cursor                         createCustomCursor
                                          (Image cursor,
                                          Point hotSpot,
                                          String name)
                                          throws
                                          IndexOutOfBoundsException
public Dimension                      getBestCursorSize
                                          (int preferredWidth,
                                          int preferredHeight)
public int                            getMaximumCursorColors()
public static String                  getProperty(String key,
                                          String defaultValue)
public final EventQueue               getSystemEventQueue()
protected abstract EventQueue         getSystemEventQueueImpl()
public abstract java.awt.dnd.peer     createDragSourceContextPeer
                                          (DragGestureEvent
                                          DragSourceContextPeer
                                          dge)
                                          throws
                                          InvalidDnDOperationException
public DragGestureRecognizer          createDragGestureRecognizer
                                          (Class
                                          abstractRecognizerClass,
                                          DragSource ds,
                                          Component c,
                                          int srcActions,
                                          DragGestureListener dgl)
public final Object                   getDesktopProperty
                                          (String propertyName)
protected final void                  setDesktopProperty
                                          (String name,
                                          Object newValue)
protected Object lazilyLoadDesktop    Property(String name)
protected void     initializeDesktop  Properties()
public void addPropertyChange         Listener(String name,
                                          PropertyChangeListener
                                          pcl)
public void removePropertyChange      Listener(String name,
                                          PropertyChangeListener
                                          pcl)
public void                           addAWTEventListener
                                          (AWTEventListener
                                          listener,
```

```
                                        long eventMask)
public void                         removeAWTEventListener
                                        (AWTEventListener
                                         listener)
```

Class Window

```
public class Window
               extends Container
```

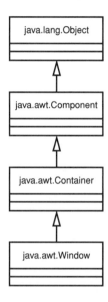

A Window is a top-level container. It is the parent class for Frame and Dialog. It has no border and no title bar. Generally, one does not directly instantiate a Window object.

Constructors

```
public      Window(Frame owner)
public      Window(Window owner)
```

Methods

```
protected void          finalize()
                            throws Throwable
public void             addNotify()
public void             pack()
public void             show()
public void             dispose()
public void             toFront()
public void             toBack()
public Toolkit          getToolkit()
public final String     getWarningString()
public Locale           getLocale()
public InputContext     getInputContext()
```

public Window	getOwner()
public Window[]	getOwnedWindows()
public void	addWindowListener(WindowListener l)
public void	removeWindowListener(WindowListener l)
protected void	processEvent(AWTEvent e)
protected void	processWindowEvent(WindowEvent e)
public Component	getFocusOwner()
public boolean	postEvent(Event e)
public boolean	isShowing()
public void	applyResourceBundle(ResourceBundle rb)
public void	applyResourceBundle(String rbName)

java.awt.datatransfer Interface and Class Details

This package contains interfaces and classes to support copy, cut, and paste operations between applications.

Interface ClipboardOwner

public abstract interface **ClipboardOwner**

This interface is used by classes that provide input to the system clipboard.

Methods

public void   **lostOwnership**(Clipboard clipboard, Transferable contents)

Interface FlavorMap

public abstract interface **FlavorMap**

This is used by implementing classes to map Native types to Mime types and associated DataFlavors.

Methods

public Map	getNativesForFlavors(DataFlavor[] flavors)
public Map	getFlavorsForNatives(String[] natives)

Interface Transferable

public abstract interface Transferable

This interface declares methods for use by classes that can transfer data.

Methods

public DataFlavor[]	getTransferDataFlavors()
public boolean	isDataFlavorSupported(DataFlavor flavor)
public Object	getTransferData(DataFlavor flavor)
	throws UnsupportedFlavorException, IOException

Class Clipboard

public class **Clipboard**
                extends Object

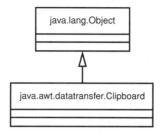

This class provides methods to copy, cut, and paste data. Listing 21.1 contains sample code you can use to provide the functionality of copy, cut, and paste in your program. This program is intended for you to copy, cut, and paste between the two TextAreas in one Frame. However, you can paste to the right-most window from other textual sources, such as a word processing program that is not in Java.

Listing 21.1   Copy, Cut, and Paste Using the Clipboard Class (EditableDriver.java)
```
// Program to demonstrate copy, cut, and paste
// using java.awt.datatransfer.
import java.awt.*;
import java.awt.event.*;
import java.awt.datatransfer.*;
import java.io.*;

class EditableGUI extends Frame
     {
      public TextArea sourceTA;
      public TextArea targetTA;
      Menu editMenu;
      MenuItem copyMI;
      MenuItem cutMI;
      MenuItem pasteMI;
      MenuBar mb;

      public EditableGUI()
         {
          sourceTA = new TextArea(60,10);
          targetTA = new TextArea(60,10);
          // Create two TextAreas to demonstrate
          // copy, cut and paste.
          Panel sourcePanel = new Panel();
          sourcePanel.setLayout(new BorderLayout());
          // Create a Panel with a BorderLayout.
          sourcePanel.add("North", new Label("Source"));
```

continues

Listing 21.1 continued

```java
            sourcePanel.add("Center", sourceTA);
            Panel targetPanel = new Panel();
            targetPanel.setLayout(new BorderLayout());
            targetPanel.add("North", new Label("Target"));
            targetPanel.add("Center", targetTA);
            // The above code creates two Panels to use for
            // copying and pasting between.

            // Now build the menus for copying,
            // cutting, and pasting.
            editMenu = new Menu("Edit");
            copyMI = new MenuItem("Copy");
            cutMI = new MenuItem("Cut");
            pasteMI = new MenuItem("Paste");
            mb = new MenuBar();
            editMenu.add(copyMI);
            editMenu.add(cutMI);
            editMenu.addSeparator();
            // You can easily add a separator line
            // in a Java menu.
            editMenu.add (pasteMI);
            mb.add(editMenu);
            setMenuBar(mb);
            // Set up to listen to menu clicks.
            MenuProcessor mp = new MenuProcessor(this);
            copyMI.addActionListener(mp);
            cutMI.addActionListener(mp);
            pasteMI.addActionListener(mp);
            // Add Panels to Frame.
            setLayout(new GridLayout(1,2));
            add(sourceTA);
            add(targetTA);
            // This makes two equal-sized Panels.

            setSize(600,400);
            setVisible(true);
            // You will need to implement a WindowListener
            // to be able to easily close the application.
        }
    } // End Class definition for EditableGUI.

// The following code could easily be modified so that
// you could copy, cut, and paste between a Java GUI and
// another program.
class MenuProcessor implements ActionListener,
                              ClipboardOwner
    // Implementing ClipboardOwner is needed for using the Clipboard.
    {
```

```java
// This class is for ActionEvents on MenuItems.
EditableGUI gui;
// Enable callbacks to GUI object.

public MenuProcessor(EditableGUI g)
    {
     gui = g;
    }

public void actionPerformed(ActionEvent e)
    {
     if ("Paste".equals(e.getActionCommand()))
        {
         Transferable tf =
             Toolkit.getDefaultToolkit().getSystemClipboard()
             ↪.getContents(this);
// Get the contents of the clipboard known to this
// AWT object.

            try
               {
                if (tf != null
                    && tf.isDataFlavorSupported
                           (DataFlavor.stringFlavor))
                   {
                    gui.targetTA.setBackground(Color.white);
                    gui.targetTA.setForeground(Color.black);
                    gui.targetTA.
                           replaceRange((String)tf.getTransferData
                             (DataFlavor.stringFlavor),
                              gui.targetTA.getSelectionStart(),
                              gui.targetTA.getSelectionEnd()));
                   }
               }
            catch (UnsupportedFlavorException ufe)
               {
                System.out.println(ufe.getMessage());
               }
            catch (IOException ioe)
               {
                ioe.printStackTrace();
               }
        }
     if ("Copy".equals(e.getActionCommand()))
        {
         setClipContents();   // User-defined method
        }
     if ("Cut".equals(e.getActionCommand()))
        {
```

continues

Listing 21.1 continued

```
            setClipContents();
            gui.sourceTA.replaceRange("",
                                gui.sourceTA.getSelectionStart(),
                                gui.sourceTA.getSelectionEnd());
        }
      }

   boolean setClipContents()
       {
        String selectedText = gui.sourceTA.getSelectedText();
        StringSelection sourceContents =
                                new StringSelection(selectedText);
        Toolkit.getDefaultToolkit().getSystemClipboard().
                                setContents(sourceContents, this);
        return true;
       }

   public void lostOwnership(Clipboard clip, Transferable transf)
       {
        System.out.println("Lost the clipboard ownership");
       }
  }

public class EditableDriver
     {
      public static void main(String args[])
          {
            EditableGUI gui = new EditableGUI();
          }

     }
```

Fields

```
protected ClipboardOwner      owner
protected Transferable        contents
```

Constructors

```
public    Clipboard(String name)
```

Methods

```
public String         getName()
public void           setContents(Transferable contents,
                          ClipboardOwner owner)
public Transferable   getContents(Object requestor)
```

Class DataFlavor

```
public class DataFlavor
            extends Object
            implements Externalizable, Cloneable
```

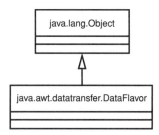

A `DataFlavor` represents the data format of data in the clipboard, during drag and drop, or in a file system. The main flavor currently available is `String`. See the code in Listing 21.1 for an example of using the `DataFlavor` class.

Fields

```
public static final DataFlavor    stringFlavor
public static final DataFlavor    plainTextFlavor
public static final String        javaSerializedObjectMimeType
public static final DataFlavor    javaFileListFlavor
public static final String        javaJVMLocalObjectMimeType
public static final String        javaRemoteObjectMimeType
```

Constructors

```
public    DataFlavor(Class representationClass,
              String humanPresentableName)
public    DataFlavor(String mimeType, String humanPresentableName)
public    DataFlavor(String mimeType, String humanPresentableName,
              ClassLoader classLoader)
              throws ClassNotFoundException
public    DataFlavor(String mimeType) throws ClassNotFoundException
public    DataFlavor()
```

Methods

```
protected static final Class tryToLoadClass(String
                               className, ClassLoader fallback)
                               throws ClassNotFoundException
public String          getMimeType()
public Class           getRepresentationClass()
public String          getHumanPresentableName()
public String          getPrimaryType()
public String          getSubType()
public String          getParameter(String paramName)
public void            setHumanPresentableName
                          (String humanPresentableName)
```

```
public boolean              equals(Object o)
public boolean              equals(DataFlavor dataFlavor)
public boolean              equals(String s)
public boolean              isMimeTypeEqual(String mimeType)
public final boolean        isMimeTypeEqual(DataFlavor dataFlavor)
public boolean              isMimeTypeSerializedObject()
public boolean              isRepresentationClassInputStream()
public boolean              isRepresentationClassSerializable()
public boolean              isRepresentationClassRemote()
public boolean              isFlavorSerializedObjectType()
public boolean              isFlavorRemoteObjectType()
public boolean              isFlavorJavaFileListType()
public void                 writeExternal(ObjectOutput os)
                                throws IOException
public void                 readExternal(ObjectInput is)
                                throws IOException,
                                ClassNotFoundException
public Object               clone()
                                throws CloneNotSupportedException
protected String            normalizeMimeTypeParameter(String
                                parameterName,
                                String parameterValue)
protected String            normalizeMimeType(String mimeType)
```

Class StringSelection

```
public class StringSelection
            extends Object
            implements Transferable, ClipboardOwner
```

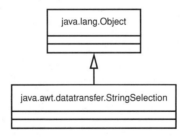

This class provides methods to transfer a String in plain text format. See Listing 21.1, the Clipboard class, for an example of using the StringSelection class.

Constructors

```
public    StringSelection(String data)
```

Methods

```
public DataFlavor[]   getTransferDataFlavors()
public boolean        isDataFlavorSupported(DataFlavor flavor)
public Object         getTransferData(DataFlavor flavor)
```

```
                        throws UnsupportedFlavorException, IOException
public void             lostOwnership(Clipboard clipboard,
                            Transferable contents)
```

Class SystemFlavorMap

```
public final class SystemFlavorMap
                        extends Object
                        implements FlavorMap
```

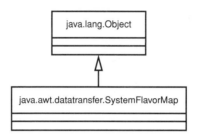

This class maps native platform data formats to Mime types and their associated Java types.

Methods

```
public static FlavorMap   getDefaultFlavorMap()
public Map                getNativesForFlavors(DataFlavor[] flavors)
public Map                getFlavorsForNatives(String[] natives)
public static String      encodeJavaMIMEType(String mimeType)
public static String      encodeDataFlavor(DataFlavor df)
public static boolean     isJavaMIMEType(String atom)
public static String      decodeJavaMIMEType(String atom)
public static DataFlavor  decodeDataFlavor(String atom)
                            throws ClassNotFoundException
```

java.awt.dnd Interface and Class Details

This package provides classes and interfaces to enable drag and drop between applications. Both Java and non-Java applications can be sources or targets. A Java program must be either the source or the target.

Interface Autoscroll

```
public abstract interface Autoscroll
```

The Autoscroll interface is used by classes that might be drop targets and have scrollable regions that might not be visible.

Methods

```
public Insets      getAutoscrollInsets()
public void        autoscroll(Point cursorLocn)
```

Interface DragGestureListener

public abstract interface **DragGestureListener**
                       extends EventListener

This interface should be implemented by any class that wants to receive notification of a drag-and-drop operation being initiated. Chapter 8, "GUI Programming I: Applications," discusses using drag and drop and gives a complete example of using the major interfaces and classes.

> **NOTE**
>
> This package has been undergoing significant work during 1999, so if you need to use this facility, you should be sure you are using the latest Java 2 SDK. As of November 1999, this is the Java 2 SDK Standard Edition Version 1.3 beta.

Methods

public void   **dragGestureRecognized**(DragGestureEvent dge)

Interface DragSourceListener

public abstract interface **DragSourceListener**
                       extends EventListener

This interface is implemented by classes that want to provide feedback to users on the state of a drag-and-drop gesture.

Methods

public void   **dragEnter**(DragSourceDragEvent dsde)
public void   **dragOver**(DragSourceDragEvent dsde)
public void   **dropActionChanged**(DragSourceDragEvent dsde)
public void   **dragExit**(DragSourceEvent dse)
public void   **dragDropEnd**(DragSourceDropEvent dsde)

Interface DropTargetListener

public abstract interface **DropTargetListener**
                       extends EventListener

This interface is used by classes to provide notification that drop targets have been moved or dropped.

Methods

public void   **dragEnter**(DropTargetDragEvent dtde)
public void   **dragOver**(DropTargetDragEvent dtde)
public void   **dropActionChanged**(DropTargetDragEvent dtde)
public void   **dragExit**(DropTargetEvent dte)
public void   **drop**(DropTargetDropEvent dtde)

Class DnDConstants

```
public final class DnDConstants
                extends Object
```

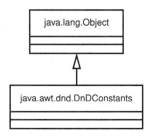

This class provides constants for drag-and-drop operations.

Fields

```
public static final int    ACTION_NONE
public static final int    ACTION_COPY
public static final int    ACTION_MOVE
public static final int    ACTION_COPY_OR_MOVE
public static final int    ACTION_LINK
public static final int    ACTION_REFERENCE
```

Class DragGestureEvent

```
public class DragGestureEvent
                extends EventObject
```

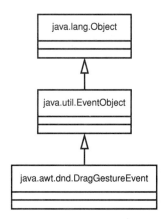

A `DragGestureEvent` is generated by a drag-and-drop gesture and is passed to an object that implements the `DragGestureListener` interface.

Constructors
public **DragGestureEvent**(DragGestureRecognizer dgr, int act, Point ori,
                    List evs)

Methods
public DragGestureRecognizer	getSourceAsDragRecognizer()
public Component	getComponent()
public DragSource	getDragSource()
public Point	getDragOrigin()
public Iterator	iterator()
public Object[]	toArray()
public Object[]	toArray(Object[] array)
public int	getDragAction()
public InputEvent	getTriggerEvent()

public void	**startDrag**(Cursor dragCursor,
	        Transferable transferable,
	        DragSourceListener dsl)
	        throws InvalidDnDOperationException

public void	**startDrag**(Cursor dragCursor,
	        Image dragImage, Point imageOffset,
	        Transferable transferable,
	        DragSourceListener dsl)
	        throws InvalidDnD OperationException

Class DragGestureRecognizer
public abstract class **DragGestureRecognizer**
                    extends Object

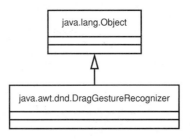

The DragGestureRecognizer class is an abstract class that is subclassed by listener classes that listen for a drag-and-drop gesture's initial moves.

Fields
protected DragSource	dragSource
protected Component	component
protected DragGestureListener	dragGestureListener
protected int	sourceActions
protected ArrayList	events

Constructors

protected	**DragGestureRecognizer**(DragSource ds, Component c, int sa, DragGestureListener dgl)
protected	**DragGestureRecognizer**(DragSource ds, Component c, int sa)
protected	**DragGestureRecognizer**(DragSource ds, Component c)
protected	**DragGestureRecognizer**(DragSource ds)

Methods

protected abstract void	**registerListeners**()
protected abstract void	**unregisterListeners**()
public DragSource	**getDragSource**()
public Component	**getComponent**()
public void	**setComponent**(Component c)
public int	**getSourceActions**()
public void	**setSourceActions**(int actions)
public InputEvent	**getTriggerEvent**()
public void	**resetRecognizer**()
public void	**addDragGestureListener**(DragGestureListener dgl) throws TooManyListenersException
public void	**removeDragGestureListener**(DragGesture Listener dgl)
protected void fireDragGesture	**Recognized**(int dragAction, Point p)
protected void	**appendEvent**(InputEvent awtie)

Class DragSource

public class **DragSource**
                extends Object

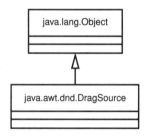

This class initiates a drag-and-drop gesture.

Fields

public static final Cursor	**DefaultCopyDrop**
public static final Cursor	**DefaultMoveDrop**
public static final Cursor	**DefaultLinkDrop**
public static final Cursor	**DefaultCopyNoDrop**
public static final Cursor	**DefaultMoveNoDrop**
public static final Cursor	**DefaultLinkNoDrop**

Constructors

```
public      DragSource()
```

Methods

```
public static DragSource      getDefaultDragSource()
public static boolean         isDragImageSupported()
public void                   startDrag(DragGestureEvent trigger,
                                  Cursor dragCursor, Image dragImage,
                                  Point imageOffset,
                                  Transferable transferable,
                                  DragSourceListener dsl,
                                  FlavorMap flavorMap)
                                  throws InvalidDnDOperationException
public void                   startDrag(DragGestureEvent trigger,
                                  Cursor dragCursor,
                                  Transferable transferable,
                                  DragSourceListener dsl,
                                  FlavorMap flavorMap)
                                  throws InvalidDnDOperationException
public void                   startDrag(DragGestureEvent trigger,
                                  Cursor dragCursor, Image dragImage,
                                  Point dragOffset,
                                  Transferable transferable,
                                  DragSourceListener dsl)
                                  throws InvalidDnDOperationException
public void                   startDrag(DragGestureEvent trigger,
                                  Cursor dragCursor,
                                  Transferable transferable,
                                  DragSourceListener dsl)
                                  throws InvalidDnDOperationException
protected DragSourceContext   createDragSourceContext
                                  (java.awt.dnd.peer.DragSourceContextPeer
                                  dscp, DragGestureEvent dgl,
                                  Cursor dragCursor, Image dragImage,
                                  Point imageOffset, Transferable t,
                                  DragSourceListener dsl)
public FlavorMap              getFlavorMap()
public DragGestureRecognizer  createDragGestureRecognizer
                                  (Class recognizerAbstractClass,
                                  Component c, int actions,
                                  DragGestureListener dgl)
public DragGestureRecognizer  createDefaultDragGestureRecognizer
                                  (Component c, int actions,
                                  DragGestureListener  dgl)
```

Class DragSourceEvent

```
public class DragSourceEvent
            extends EventObject
```

java.awt.dnd Interface and Class Details

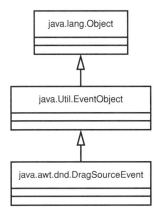

This is a base class for DragSourceEvent classes.

Constructors
public   **DragSourceEvent**(DragSourceContext dsc)

Methods
public DragSourceContext **getDragSourceContext**()

Class DropTarget

public class **DropTarget**
                extends Object
                implements DropTargetListener, Serializable

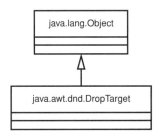

A DropTarget is a component that has something dropped on it through the completion of a DragGesture.

Constructors
```
public     DropTarget(Component c, int ops, DropTargetListener dtl,
               boolean act, FlavorMap fm)
public     DropTarget(Component c, int ops, DropTargetListener dtl,
               boolean act)
public     DropTarget()
public     DropTarget(Component c, DropTargetListener dtl)
public     DropTarget(Component c, int ops, DropTargetListener dtl)
```

Methods

public void	setComponent(Component c)
public Component	getComponent()
public void	setDefaultActions(int ops)
public int	getDefaultActions()
public void	setActive(boolean isActive)
public boolean	isActive()
public void	addDropTargetListener (DropTargetListener dtl) throws TooManyListenersException
public void	removeDropTargetListener (DropTargetListener dtl)
public void	dragEnter (DropTarget DragEvent dtde)
public void	dragOver (DropTarget DragEvent dtde)
public void	dropActionChanged (DropTargetDragEvent dtde)
public void	dragExit(DropTarget Event dte)
public void	drop(DropTarget DropEvent dtde)
public FlavorMap	getFlavorMap()
public void	setFlavorMap(FlavorMap fm)
public void	addNotify (java.awt.peer.ComponentPeer peer)
public void	removeNotify (java.awt.peer.ComponentPeer peer)
public DropTargetContext	getDropTargetContext()
protected DropTarget Context	createDropTargetContext()
protected DropTarget.DropTargetAutoScroller	createDropTargetAutoScroller (Component c, Point p)
protected void	initializeAutoscrolling (Point p)
protected void	updateAutoscroll (Point dragCursorLocn)
protected void	clearAutoscroll()

Class DropTargetEvent

```
public class DropTargetEvent
            extends EventObject
```

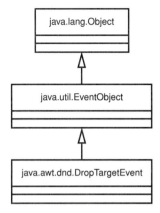

DropTargetEvent is the base class for all DropTargetEvent classes. It encapsulates a drag-and-drop operation, including DropTargetContext.

Fields
protected DropTargetContext **context**

Constructors
public   **DropTargetEvent**(DropTargetContext dtc)

Methods
public DropTargetContext   **getDropTargetContext**()

Class MouseDragGestureRecognizer
public abstract class **MouseDragGestureRecognizer**
                      extends DragGestureRecognizer
                      implements MouseListener, MouseMotionListener

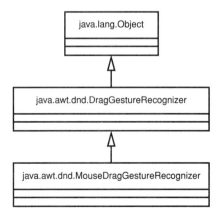

This class is for use in dealing with mouse-based drag-and-drop gestures through a DragGestureRecognizer.

Constructors

protected	**MouseDragGestureRecognizer**(DragSource ds, Component c, int act, DragGestureListener dgl)
protected	**MouseDragGestureRecognizer**(DragSource ds, Component c, int act)
protected	**MouseDragGestureRecognizer**(DragSource ds, Component c)
protected	**MouseDragGestureRecognizer**(DragSource ds)

Methods

protected void	**registerListeners**()
protected void	**unregisterListeners**()
public void	**mouseClicked**(MouseEvent e)
public void	**mousePressed**(MouseEvent e)
public void	**mouseReleased**(MouseEvent e)
public void	**mouseEntered**(MouseEvent e)
public void	**mouseExited**(MouseEvent e)
public void	**mouseDragged**(MouseEvent e)
public void	**mouseoved**(MouseEvent e)

java.awt.event Interface and Class Details

This package provides classes that define the event types for AWT events, such as Action events and mouse events.

Interface ActionListener

public abstract interface **ActionListener**
                         extends EventListener

Classes interested in processing ActionEvents must implement this interface. Such listeners are required to detect mouse clicks on Buttons, Menus, and several other objects.

Methods

public void	**actionPerformed**(ActionEvent e)

Interface AdjustmentListener

All known implementing classes:

public abstract interface	**AWTEventMulticaster**
public abstract interface	**AdjustmentListener**
	extends EventListener

The Adjustment interface must be implemented by listeners interested in AdjustmentEvents, which are generated by a user interacting with a scrollbar type of object. Many components, such as List, provide automatic scrolling. The ScrollPane class does automatic scrolling, making the use of the ScrollBar class largely unnecessary. If a program does use a ScrollBar, however, a listener implementing this interface is necessary. Fortunately, there is only one method to implement.

CAUTION

In previous versions of the Win32 JDK, the `ScrollBar` class had many problems. This is another reason to avoid it.

Methods

```
public void     adjustmentValueChanged(AdjustmentEvent e)
```

Interface FocusListener

```
public abstract interface FocusListener
                    extends EventListener
```

This interface should be implemented by listeners interested in keyboard-based focus events. To use this interface, you might do something like what is shown in the following code snippet.

In the GUI class:

```
Canvas can = new Canvas();
Can.addFocusListener(new CanvasFocusListener());
// A Canvas must get the focus before it can be modified by a user.
. . .
```

In the event-handling class:

```
class CanvasFocusListener implements FocusListener
    {
      public void focusGained(FocusEvent e)
         {
           // Let the user know she can work with the canvas now.
         }
      public void focusLost(FocusEvent e)
         {
           // Let the user know that she cannot modify the canvas now.
         }
    }
```

TIP

By itself, a `Canvas` or `Panel` cannot get the focus. You need to do something such as use a `MouseListener` object that can determine when the mouse is clicked on the `Canvas` or `Panel` and then call

can.requestFocus()

to get the focus on the `Canvas`, for instance.

Methods

```
public void     focusGained(FocusEvent e)
public void     focusLost(FocusEvent e)
```

Interface InputMethodListener

public abstract interface **InputMethodListener**
                                    extends EventListener

The `InputMethodListener` should be implemented by listeners interested in `InputMethod` events, such as listeners for text-editing components.

> **NOTE**
>
> The `InputMethod` framework is designed to let you use an English keyboard to enter characters of other alphabets, such as Kanji, which would otherwise need a very specialized keyboard and components.

Methods

public void   **inputMethodTextChanged**(InputMethodEvent event)
public void   **caretPositionChanged**(InputMethodEvent event)

Interface ItemListener

public abstract interface **ItemListener**
                                    extends EventListener

This interface should be implemented by classes used for listener objects that are interested in `ItemEvents`. This would include listeners registered on `Checkboxes` and `Lists`. The following code snippet shows the use of an `ItemListener`:

```
List subjectList = new List(5, false);
subjectList.add("History");
subjectList.add("Religion");
subjectList.add("Java Programming");
subjectList.add("Philosophy");
subjectList.add(new SubjectListener());
. . .
class SubjectListener implements ItemListener
    {
     public void itemStateChanged(ItemEvent ie)
         {
          System.out.println(ie.getSource());
         }
    }
```

> **TIP**
>
> The `itemStateChanged()` method is called only when an item in the `List` component is selected or deselected. If you do not need immediate notification and can wait for all data entry to be completed, you do not need to bother with an `ItemListener`.

Methods

public void   itemStateChanged(ItemEvent e)

Interface KeyListener

public abstract interface **KeyListener**
                        extends EventListener

The KeyListener interface should be implemented by any listener object interested in keyboard events.

Methods

public void   keyTyped(KeyEvent e)
public void   keyPressed(KeyEvent e)
public void   keyReleased(KeyEvent e)

Interface MouseListener

public abstract interface **MouseListener**
                        extends EventListener

The MouseListener interface is implemented by any objects that are interested in MouseEvents. This ranges from a mouse click event to a MouseEvent that is generated when the mouse enters a Component.

> **CAUTION**
>
> Be careful when using this interface to distinguish between a mouse click and a mouse press. If the user presses a mouse button but does not release it, and your MouseListener implementation only concerns itself with mouseClicked(), you will never be notified of user interaction with the mouse. A mouse press is totally different from a click.

Methods

public void   mouseClicked(MouseEvent e)
public void   mousePressed(MouseEvent e)
public void   mouseReleased(MouseEvent e)
public void   mouseEntered(MouseEvent e)
public void   mouseExited(MouseEvent e)

Interface MouseMotionListener

public abstract interface **MouseMotionListener**
                        extends EventListener

The MouseMotionListener interface is implemented by objects that want to process mouse motion events. This includes moving the mouse within a Component, as well as clicking and dragging the mouse within or outside of a Component. Events specifically related to mouse button events and a mouse entering or leaving a Component are handled by the MouseListener interface.

Methods

```
public void    mouseDragged(MouseEvent e)
public void    mouseMoved(MouseEvent e)
```

Interface TextListener

```
public abstract interface TextListener
                    extends EventListener
```

This interface is implemented by listener objects that want to receive text events. A text event occurs when text in a Component, such as a TextField or TextArea, is modified in some way.

Methods

```
public void    textValueChanged(TextEvent e)
```

Interface WindowListener

```
public abstract interface WindowListener
                    extends EventListener
```

This interface is implemented by listener objects that want to be notified of Window-related events, such as a window being minimized or closed. Of the methods here, the most important one to implement is windowClosing(). This method is called primarily when someone clicks the close box (in Win32), chooses the close option (Solaris), or clicks the title bar of a frame or a dialog.

Methods

```
public void    windowOpened(WindowEvent e)
public void    windowClosing(WindowEvent e)
public void    windowClosed(WindowEvent e)
public void    windowIconified(WindowEvent e)
public void    windowDeiconified(WindowEvent e)
public void    windowActivated(WindowEvent e)
public void    windowDeactivated(WindowEvent e)
```

Class ActionEvent

```
public class ActionEvent
            extends AWTEvent
```

An ActionEvent is instantiated whenever a Component-defined action event occurs, which is generally clicking a Button, selecting a MenuItem, or choosing a Checkbox. The following code snippet shows how to deal with Components that generate ActionEvents.

In the GUI class:

```
Button okButton = new Button("OK");
OkButton.addActionListener(new Buttonhandler(this));
```

java.awt.event Interface and Class Details 505

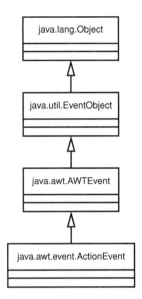

In the event-handling class:

```
class ButtonHandler implements ActionListener
    {
      GUI gui;
      public ButtonHandler(GUI g)
          {
            gui = g;
            // Save a reference to GUI for callback
            // purposes, such as accessing a TextField of
            // the GUI or calling a method of the GUI class.
          }
      public void actionPerformed(ActionEvent e)
          // Button clicks produce ActionEvents.
          {
            // Call tier 2 remote object.
            String book = gui.titleTF.getText();
            catalog.checkOut(book);
          }
    }
```

Fields

```
public static final int     SHIFT_MASK
public static final int     CTRL_MASK
public static final int     META_MASK
public static final int     ALT_MASK
public static final int     ACTION_FIRST
public static final int     ACTION_LAST
public static final int     ACTION_PERFORMED
```

Constructors

```
public      ActionEvent(Object source, int id, String command)
public      ActionEvent(Object source, int id, String command,
                 int modifiers)
```

Methods

```
public String      getActionCommand()
public int         getModifiers()
public String      paramString()
```

Class AdjustmentEvent

```
public class AdjustmentEvent
                 extends AWTEvent
```

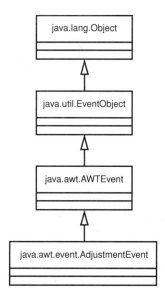

An AdjustmentEvent object is created when an adjustment event is created, generally by moving a scrollbar.

Fields

```
public static final int      ADJUSTMENT_FIRST
public static final int      ADJUSTMENT_LAST
public static final int      ADJUSTMENT_VALUE_CHANGED
public static final int      UNIT_INCREMENT
public static final int      UNIT_DECREMENT
public static final int      BLOCK_DECREMENT
public static final int      BLOCK_INCREMENT
public static final int      TRACK
```

Constructors

```
public     AdjustmentEvent(Adjustable source, int id, int type, int value)
```

Methods

```
public Adjustable   getAdjustable()
public int          getValue()
public int          getAdjustmentType()
public String       paramString()
```

Class FocusAdapter

```
public abstract class FocusAdapter
                      extends Object
                      implements FocusListener
```

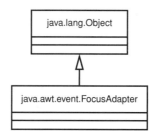

This Adapter class is a convenience class for processing focus events. All the methods have empty implementations.

Constructors

```
public     FocusAdapter()
```

Methods

```
public void     focusGained(FocusEvent e)
public void     focusLost(FocusEvent e)
```

Class FocusEvent

```
public class FocusEvent
             extends ComponentEvent
```

A FocusEvent is generated when the keyboard focus changes from one Component to another.

Fields

```
public static final int     FOCUS_FIRST
public static final int     FOCUS_LAST
public static final int     FOCUS_GAINED
public static final int     FOCUS_LOST
```

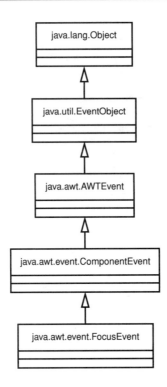

Constructors

```
public    FocusEvent(Component source, int id, boolean temporary)
public    FocusEvent(Component source, int id)
```

Methods

```
public boolean    isTemporary()
public String     paramString()
```

Class InputEvent

```
public abstract class InputEvent
                    extends ComponentEvent
```

This is the base class for all `InputEvent` classes. `InputEvent`s are events caught by listeners before the event is passed to the source component for processing. This allows a click on a button to be intercepted and consumed as an `InputEvent` before the button is activated by the mouse clock on the button.

Fields

```
public static final int     SHIFT_MASK
public static final int     CTRL_MASK
public static final int     META_MASK
public static final int     ALT_MASK
```

```
public static final int    ALT_GRAPH_MASK
public static final int    BUTTON1_MASK
public static final int    BUTTON2_MASK
public static final int    BUTTON3_MASK
```

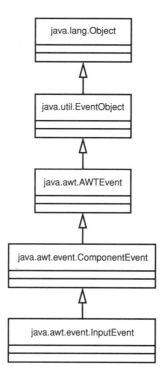

Methods

```
public boolean    isShiftDown()
public boolean    isControlDown()
public boolean    isMetaDown()
public boolean    isAltDown()
public boolean    isAltGraphDown()
public long       getWhen()
public int        getModifiers()
public void       consume()
public boolean    isConsumed()
```

Class ItemEvent

```
public class ItemEvent
              extends AWTEvent
```

510 Chapter 21: java.awt

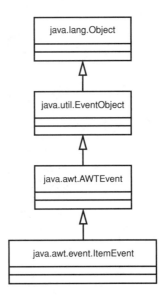

This event type is generated when an item is selected or deselected, such as when a Checkbox or an item in a List component is clicked. The event should be processed by a listener that implements the ItemListener interface. This means that the event will be processed in the itemStateChanged() method of the listener object. Normally you listen for only ItemEvents if you want to be immediately aware of a selection or deselection. Otherwise, it is simpler to interrogate such components all at once, such as when the user clicks the OK button.

Fields

```
public static final int     ITEM_FIRST
public static final int     ITEM_LAST
public static final int     ITEM_STATE_CHANGED
public static final int     SELECTED
public static final int     DESELECTED
```

Constructors

```
public      ItemEvent(ItemSelectable source, int id, Object item,
                int stateChange)
```

Methods

```
public ItemSelectable   getItemSelectable()
public Object           getItem()
public int              getStateChange()
public String           paramString()
```

Class KeyEvent

```
public class KeyEvent
            extends InputEvent
```

java.awt.event Interface and Class Details

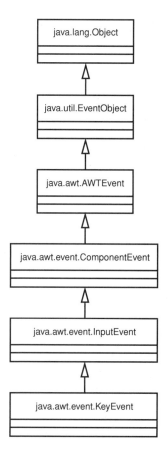

This event indicates that a keystroke occurred in a Component.

A KeyEvent is generated whenever a key is pressed or released. The key code returned is a virtual key code and might not correspond to the same character on every keyboard. You would listen for KeyEvents both to detect keystrokes to run the program and to detect what is typed within a TextField or another sort of Component. The following code snippet shows using a KeyEvent object passed to a KeyListener method implementation:

```
class GUI extends Jframe
    (
    JtextField patronID;
    public GUI()
        {
        // Check key strokes to be sure
        // the patron id is only numeric.
        patronID = new JtextField();
        patronID.addKeyListener(new KeyChecker());
. . .
        }
    }
```

Chapter 21: java.awt

In a `KeyListener` implementation:

```
class KeyChecker extends KeyAdapter
// While using an adapter class only saves typing
// (and typos), it is almost always beneficial to
// extend an adapter class rather than implement an
// event-listener interface. Note that adapter
// classes only exist for event-listener interfaces
// that contain multiple methods. There would be
// little point in an adapter class for only one method,
// since you wouldn't be able to avoid implementing that
// one method if you were interested in that event type.
    {
      public void keyPressed(KeyEvent e)
          {
           displayKey(e);
          }
       public void keyReleased(KeyEvent e)
          {
           displayKey(e);
          }
       public void keyTyped(KeyEvent e)
          {
           displayKey(e);
         }

       private void displayKey(KeyEvent e)
           {
            switch (e.getID())
                 {  // The ID is an int for the event type.
               case KeyEvent.KEY_TYPED:
                   {
                    System.out.print("The key typed is: " +
                        e.getKeyChar() +
                        "(" + (int)e.getKeyChar() + ")");
                    break;
                   }
               case KeyEvent.KEY_PRESSED:
                   {
                    System.out.print("Key pressed:   " +
                        e.getKeyChar() +
                        "(" + (int)e.getKeyChar() + ")");
                    break;
                   }
               case KeyEvent.KEY_RELEASED:
                   {
                    System.out.print("Key released:  " +
                        e.getKeyChar() +
                        "(" + (int)evt.getKeyChar() + ")");
                    break;
```

```
            }
        } // End Switch
    System.out.print
            ("The key code is: " + e.getKeyCode());
    }
}
```

Fields

public static final int	**KEY_FIRST**
public static final int	**KEY_LAST**
public static final int	**KEY_TYPED**
public static final int	**KEY_PRESSED**
public static final int	**KEY_RELEASED**
public static final int	**VK_ENTER**
public static final int	**VK_BACK_SPACE**
public static final int	**VK_TAB**
public static final int	**VK_CANCEL**
public static final int	**VK_CLEAR**
public static final int	**VK_SHIFT**
public static final int	**VK_CONTROL**
public static final int	**VK_ALT**
public static final int	**VK_PAUSE**
public static final int	**VK_CAPS_LOCK**
public static final int	**VK_ESCAPE**
public static final int	**VK_SPACE**
public static final int	**VK_PAGE_UP**
public static final int	**VK_PAGE_DOWN**
public static final int	**VK_END**
public static final int	**VK_HOME**
public static final int	**VK_LEFT**
public static final int	**VK_UP**
public static final int	**VK_RIGHT**
public static final int	**VK_DOWN**
public static final int	**VK_COMMA**
public static final int	**VK_MINUS**
public static final int	**VK_PERIOD**
public static final int	**VK_SLASH**
public static final int	**VK_0**
public static final int	**VK_1**
public static final int	**VK_2**
public static final int	**VK_3**
public static final int	**VK_4**
public static final int	**VK_5**
public static final int	**VK_6**
public static final int	**VK_7**
public static final int	**VK_8**
public static final int	**VK_9**
public static final int	**VK_SEMICOLON**
public static final int	**VK_EQUALS**
public static final int	**VK_A**

```java
public static final int    VK_B
public static final int    VK_C
public static final int    VK_D
public static final int    VK_E
public static final int    VK_F
public static final int    VK_G
public static final int    VK_H
public static final int    VK_I
public static final int    VK_J
public static final int    VK_K
public static final int    VK_L
public static final int    VK_M
public static final int    VK_N
public static final int    VK_O
public static final int    VK_P
public static final int    VK_Q
public static final int    VK_R
public static final int    VK_S
public static final int    VK_T
public static final int    VK_U
public static final int    VK_V
public static final int    VK_W
public static final int    VK_X
public static final int    VK_Y
public static final int    VK_Z
public static final int    VK_OPEN_BRACKET
public static final int    VK_BACK_SLASH
public static final int    VK_CLOSE_BRACKET
public static final int    VK_NUMPAD0
public static final int    VK_NUMPAD1
public static final int    VK_NUMPAD2
public static final int    VK_NUMPAD3
public static final int    VK_NUMPAD4
public static final int    VK_NUMPAD5
public static final int    VK_NUMPAD6
public static final int    VK_NUMPAD7
public static final int    VK_NUMPAD8
public static final int    VK_NUMPAD9
public static final int    VK_MULTIPLY
public static final int    VK_ADD
public static final int    VK_SEPARATER
public static final int    VK_SUBTRACT
public static final int    VK_DECIMAL
public static final int    VK_DIVIDE
public static final int    VK_DELETE
public static final int    VK_NUM_LOCK
public static final int    VK_SCROLL_LOCK
public static final int    VK_F1
public static final int    VK_F2
public static final int    VK_F3
```

```
public static final int    VK_F4
public static final int    VK_F5
public static final int    VK_F6
public static final int    VK_F7
public static final int    VK_F8
public static final int    VK_F9
public static final int    VK_F10
public static final int    VK_F11
public static final int    VK_F12
public static final int    VK_F13
public static final int    VK_F14
public static final int    VK_F15
public static final int    VK_F16
public static final int    VK_F17
public static final int    VK_F18
public static final int    VK_F19
public static final int    VK_F20
public static final int    VK_F21
public static final int    VK_F22
public static final int    VK_F23
public static final int    VK_F24
public static final int    VK_PRINTSCREEN
public static final int    VK_INSERT
public static final int    VK_HELP
public static final int    VK_META
public static final int    VK_BACK_QUOTE
public static final int    VK_QUOTE
public static final int    VK_KP_UP
public static final int    VK_KP_DOWN
public static final int    VK_KP_LEFT
public static final int    VK_KP_RIGHT
public static final int    VK_DEAD_GRAVE
public static final int    VK_DEAD_ACUTE
public static final int    VK_DEAD_CIRCUMFLEX
public static final int    VK_DEAD_TILDE
public static final int    VK_DEAD_MACRON
public static final int    VK_DEAD_BREVE
public static final int    VK_DEAD_ABOVEDOT
public static final int    VK_DEAD_DIAERESIS
public static final int    VK_DEAD_ABOVERING
public static final int    VK_DEAD_DOUBLEACUTE
public static final int    VK_DEAD_CARON
public static final int    VK_DEAD_CEDILLA
public static final int    VK_DEAD_OGONEK
public static final int    VK_DEAD_IOTA
public static final int    VK_DEAD_VOICED_SOUND
public static final int    VK_DEAD_SEMIVOICED_SOUND
public static final int    VK_AMPERSAND
public static final int    VK_ASTERISK
public static final int    VK_QUOTEDBL
```

```
public static final int     VK_LESS
public static final int     VK_GREATER
public static final int     VK_BRACELEFT
public static final int     VK_BRACERIGHT
public static final int     VK_AT
public static final int     VK_COLON
public static final int     VK_CIRCUMFLEX
public static final int     VK_DOLLAR
public static final int     VK_EURO_SIGN
public static final int     VK_EXCLAMATION_MARK
public static final int     VK_INVERTED_EXCLAMATION_MARK
public static final int     VK_LEFT_PARENTHESIS
public static final int     VK_NUMBER_SIGN
public static final int     VK_PLUS
public static final int     VK_RIGHT_PARENTHESIS
public static final int     VK_UNDERSCORE
public static final int     VK_FINAL
public static final int     VK_CONVERT
public static final int     VK_NONCONVERT
public static final int     VK_ACCEPT
public static final int     VK_MODECHANGE
public static final int     VK_KANA
public static final int     VK_KANJI
public static final int     VK_ALPHANUMERIC
public static final int     VK_KATAKANA
public static final int     VK_HIRAGANA
public static final int     VK_FULL_WIDTH
public static final int     VK_HALF_WIDTH
public static final int     VK_ROMAN_CHARACTERS
public static final int     VK_ALL_CANDIDATES
public static final int     VK_PREVIOUS_CANDIDATE
public static final int     VK_CODE_INPUT
public static final int     VK_JAPANESE_KATAKANA
public static final int     VK_JAPANESE_HIRAGANA
public static final int     VK_JAPANESE_ROMAN
public static final int     VK_CUT
public static final int     VK_COPY
public static final int     VK_PASTE
public static final int     VK_UNDO
public static final int     VK_AGAIN
public static final int     VK_FIND
public static final int     VK_PROPS
public static final int     VK_STOP
public static final int     VK_COMPOSE
public static final int     VK_ALT_GRAPH
public static final int     VK_UNDEFINED
public static final char    CHAR_UNDEFINED
```

Constructors

```
public    KeyEvent(Component source, int id, long when,
              int modifiers, int keyCode, char keyChar)
public    KeyEvent(Component source, int id, long when,
              int modifiers, int keyCode)
```

Methods

```
public int           getKeyCode()
public void          setKeyChar(char keyChar)
public void          setModifiers(int modifiers)
public char          getKeyChar()
public static String getKeyText(int keyCode)
public static String getKeyModifiersText(int modifiers)
public boolean       IsActionKey()
public String        paramString()
```

Class MouseEvent

```
public class MouseEvent
            extends InputEvent
```

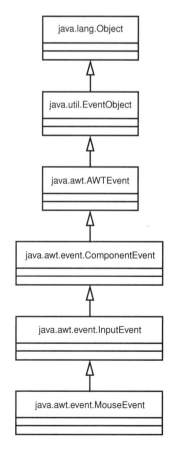

A `MouseEvent` is created for any mouse-related action. It covers events processed by both `MouseListeners` and `MouseMotionListeners`. Here's a code snippet that shows how to get some information regarding a mouse click:

In the GUI class:

```
class GUI extends Frame
    {
      int mouseX;
      int mouseY;
. . .
      public void paint(Graphics g)
          {
            g.setColor(new Color(mouseX, mouseY, 150));
            // Dynamically change the drawing color.
            fill3DRect(mouseX, mouseY, 20, 15, true);
            // Draw a 3D rectangle with its upper-left corner
            // where the mouse was clicked - that is,
            // 20 by 15 pixels and raised.
          }
    } // End GUI class snippet.
```

In the event-handling class:

```
class MouseTracker extends MouseAdapter
    {
      GUI gui;  // Callback object reference
                // to GUI instance, set in
                // MouseTracker constructor.
      public void mouseClicked(MouseEvent me)
          {
            gui.mouseX = me.getX();
            gui.mouseY = me.getY();
          }
    }
```

Fields

```
public static final int     MOUSE_FIRST
public static final int     MOUSE_LAST
public static final int     MOUSE_CLICKED
public static final int     MOUSE_PRESSED
public static final int     MOUSE_RELEASED
public static final int     MOUSE_MOVED
public static final int     MOUSE_ENTERED
public static final int     MOUSE_EXITED
public static final int     MOUSE_DRAGGED
```

Constructors

```
public    MouseEvent(Component source, int id, long when, int modifiers,
              int x, int y, int clickCount, boolean popupTrigger)
```

Methods

```
public int      getX()
public int      getY()
public Point    getPoint()
public void     translatePoint(int x, int y)
public int      getClickCount()
public boolean  isPopupTrigger()
public String   paramString()
```

Class PaintEvent

public class **PaintEvent**
        extends ComponentEvent

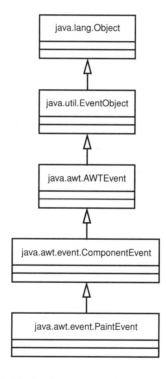

A `PaintEvent` is a special kind of event used with `paintUpdate` to be sure that `paintUpdate` calls are delivered properly along with other events from the event queue. It is not normally dealt with by application programs.

Fields

```
public static final int    PAINT_FIRST
public static final int    PAINT_LAST
public static final int    PAINT
public static final int    UPDATE
```

Constructors

public   **PaintEvent**(Component source, int id, Rectangle updateRect)

Methods

public Rectangle   **getUpdateRect**()
public void   **setUpdateRect**(Rectangle updateRect)
public String   **paramString**()

Class TextEvent

public class **TextEvent**
          extends AWTEvent

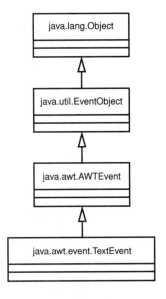

A TextEvent is generated whenever the text in a TextComponent, such as a TextField, is changed in any way. It is processed by an object that implements the TextListener interface. Here is a code snippet to show how you might handle a TextEvent that indicates the text has changed.

In the GUI class:

```
JtextArea bookNotes = new JtextArea();
bookNotes.addTextListener(new BookNoteListener(this));
```

In the event-handling class:

```
class BookNoteListener implements TextListener
    {
    GUI gui;
    public BookNoteListener(GUI g)
        {
        gui = g;
```

)
    public void textValueChanged(TextEvent e)
        {
         String text = gui.bookNotes.getText();
         saveNote(text);
        }

    public boolean saveNote(String ct)
        {
         // Write the String ct to a file.
        }
}
```

## Fields

```
public static final int     TEXT_FIRST
public static final int     TEXT_LAST
public static final int     TEXT_VALUE_CHANGED
```

Constructors

```
public     TextEvent(Object source, int id)
```

Methods

```
public String     paramString()
```

Class WindowAdapter

```
public abstract class WindowAdapter
                         extends Object
                         implements WindowListener
```

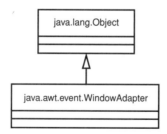

Like all adapter classes, WindowAdapter is a convenience class. It provides empty implementations of the methods in WindowListener. Although the use of an adapter class is optional, this is the most important of the adapter classes. It is quite unlikely that most programmers will ever deal with most of the WindowListener methods except for windowClosing(), so use of the WindowAdapter class is quite common and helpful. The following code snippet shows how to use the WindowAdapter. An application hardly ever needs to deal with any WindowEvent besides windowClosing, so this is definitely the time to use an adapter.
```

NOTE

You must implement `windowClosing()` to allow a user to close a window by clicking its close button or selecting Close from the window's system menu.

```
class GUI extends Frame
    {
    public GUI()
        {
        addWindowListener(new Terminator());
        }
    }
class Terminator extends WindowAdapter
    {
    public void windowClosing(WindowEvent e)
        {
        // You won't be back.
        System.exit(0);
        // Terminate the program and JVM.
        // Be sure to do any necessary cleanup
        // first, like closing streams.
        }
    }
```

Constructors

public   **WindowAdapter**()

Methods

public void	**windowOpened**(WindowEvent e)
public void	**windowClosing**(WindowEvent e)
public void	**windowClosed**(WindowEvent e)
public void	**windowIconified**(WindowEvent e)
public void	**windowDeiconified**(WindowEvent e)
public void	**windowActivated**(WindowEvent e)
public void	**windowDeactivated**(WindowEvent e)

Class WindowEvent

public class **WindowEvent**
              extends ComponentEvent

A `WindowEvent` is processed by an object that implements the `WindowListener` interface. A `WindowEvent` is generated whenever a window changes its status. For example, a `WindowEvent` is created when the user clicks the close button on the title bar of a `Frame`. Iconifying and deiconifying a window are handled in a default way by the JVM. Clicking the close button, although it produces a `WindowEvent`, does nothing unless a listener object implements the `windowClosing()` method.

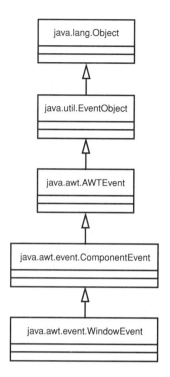

Fields

```
public static final int    WINDOW_FIRST
public static final int    WINDOW_LAST
public static final int    WINDOW_OPENED
public static final int    WINDOW_CLOSING
public static final int    WINDOW_CLOSED
public static final int    WINDOW_ICONIFIED
public static final int    WINDOW_DEICONIFIED
public static final int    WINDOW_ACTIVATED
public static final int    WINDOW_DEACTIVATED
```

Constructors

```
public     WindowEvent(Window source, int id)
```

Methods

```
public Window    getWindow()
public String    paramString()
```

java.awt.print Interface and Class Details

This package provides improved support (over JDK 1.0 and 1.1) for printing. It is built upon Java 2D support. This is a function of the fact that printing actually involves drawing a graphical image of the GUI to a printer.

Interface Pageable

public abstract interface **Pageable**

A Pageable object represents a set of pages. It also can provide page format and printable information on a specific page in the set of pages that the Pageable object represents. Prior to Java 2, there was no way to readily associate multiple pages.

Fields

public static final int **UNKNOWN_NUMBER_OF_PAGES**

Methods

public int   **getNumberOfPages**()
public PageFormat   **getPageFormat**(int pageIndex) throws
                            IndexOutOfBoundsException
public Printable   **getPrintable**(int pageIndex) throws
                            IndexOutOfBoundsException

Interface Printable

public abstract interface **Printable**

An object that implements Printable is used along with a PageFormat object to provide information to a printer to allow it to print a graphics image.

Fields

public static final int   **PAGE_EXISTS**
public static final int   **NO_SUCH_PAGE**

Methods

public int   **print**(Graphics graphics, PageFormat pageFormat,
                    int pageIndex)
                throws PrinterException

Interface PrinterGraphics

public abstract interface **PrinterGraphics**

This interface is implemented by Printable objects to provide a means to get a PrinterJob to print the target object. The PrinterJob provides a dialog to query the user regarding the page size, format, and printer to be used (in a platform-specific format).

Methods

public PrinterJob   **getPrinterJob**()

Class Book

public class **Book**
                extends Object
                implements Pageable

java.awt.print Interface and Class Details

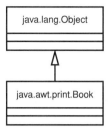

A Book object represents a collection of pages. These pages can be numbered and printed as a whole.

Constructors

```
public    Book()
```

Methods

```
public int         getNumberOfPages()
public PageFormat  getPageFormat(int pageIndex)
                        throws IndexOutOfBoundsException
public Printable   getPrintable(int pageIndex)
                        throws IndexOutOfBoundsException
public void        setPage(int pageIndex, Printable painter,
                        PageFormat page)
                        throws IndexOutOfBoundsException
public void        append(Printable painter, PageFormat page)
public void        append(Printable painter, PageFormat page,
                        int numPages)
```

Class PageFormat

```
public class PageFormat
              extends Object
              implements Cloneable
```

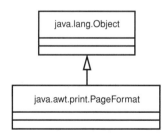

The format of a page, its size, and its orientation for printing, such as Landscape, is specified through a pageFormat object.

Fields
```
public static final int    LANDSCAPE
public static final int    PORTRAIT
public static final int    REVERSE_LANDSCAPE
```

Constructors
```
public     PageFormat()
```

Methods
```
public Object      clone()
public double      getWidth()
public double      getImageableX()
public double      getImageableY()
public double      getImageableWidth()
public double      getImageableHeight()
public Paper       getPaper()
public void        getPaper(Paper paper)
public void        setOrientation(int orientation)
                          throws IllegalArgumentException
public int         getOrientation()
public double[]    getMatrix()
```

Class PrinterJob
```
public abstract class PrinterJob
                          extends Object
```

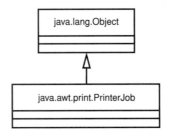

The PrinterJob class, which replaces the JDK 1.1 PrintJob class, is used by an application to control printing. It can optionally (and usually does) display a print dialog appropriate to the platform. It provides methods to control printing. The following code snippet shows the basic flow in an ActionEvent listener class for printing—that is, in response to the user's choosing a menu item for printing:

```
public void actionPerformed(ActionEvent e)
    {
    if (e.getSource() instanceof JButton)
        {
        PrinterJob pj = PrinterJob.getPrinterJob();
        // In order to print, you need a PrinterJob.
```

```
        // This logically connects your program to the printer.
        PageFormat pf = pj.pageDialog(pj.defaultPage());
        // Show a dialog that allows the user to format the page.
        pj.setPrintable(gui);
        if (pj.printDialog())
        // Display a print dialog.
           {
             try
                {
                  pj.print();
                }
             catch (Exception e)
                {
                  e.printStackTrace();
                }
           }
    }
```

Constructors
public **PrinterJob**()

Methods
public static PrinterJob	**getPrinterJob**()
public abstract void	**setPrintable**(Printable painter)
public abstract void	**setPrintable**(Printable painter, PageFormat format)
public abstract void	**setPageable**(Pageable document) throws NullPointerException
public abstract boolean	**printDialog**()
public abstract PageFormat	**pageDialog**(PageFormat page)
public abstract PageFormat	**defaultPage**(PageFormat page)
public PageFormat	**defaultPage**()
public abstract PageFormat	**validatePage**(PageFormat page)
public abstract void	**print**() throws PrinterException
public abstract void	**setCopies**(int copies)
public abstract int	**getCopies**()
public abstract String	**getUserName**()
public abstract void	**setJobName**(String jobName)
public abstract String	**getJobName**()
public abstract void	**cancel**()
public abstract boolean	**isCancelled**()

CHAPTER 22

java.beans

This chapter covers some of the most important classes and interfaces provided for creating and using JavaBeans. JavaBeans are generally client-side Components and usually, although not necessarily, visual Components. The classes in java.beans should not be confused with classes in javax.ejb packages. JavaBeans and Enterprise JavaBeans are totally separate entities that have little in common besides the notion of being Components.

The purpose of a JavaBean is to provide a client-side component or control that provides a complete function. For example, you might have a JavaBean that is a calendar, address book, phone dialer, or dictionary. Although it is possible to make a JavaBean that is simply a fancy button, the intention is that a JavaBean provide complete functionality.

Having created or obtained a JavaBean, a developer is expected to import the JavaBean into a development tool, such as Sun's Java Workshop. He would drag this new widget from the tool palette onto the GUI design screen. You can work with a JavaBean without using an IDE , but the primary intention is to use JavaBeans in the context of an IDE. You can also test your JavaBean using the BeanBox in the Bean Developer's Kit (BDK), a separate download available from the Javasoft Web site.

Many of the interfaces and classes you will see in the java.beans package relate to discovering or modifying properties of a JavaBean. A "property" in this context is not a Properties object. Rather, a property of a bean is simply a value that affects the appearance or behavior of a bean. For example, you might have a bean with a BackgroundColor property. When you import a JavaBean, the IDE uses *introspection* to find out the properties of the JavaBean and typically displays a *property sheet* to allow a developer to customize those properties. Then, when the bean is customized for the application, it can be saved to disk in that modified state with the changed properties, using object serialization.

To provide for these features, a JavaBean, which in reality might be several classes, must follow specific rules concerning method names for data members that are accessible properties. Given a property abc, you would use

```
public abc getabc()
public void setabc(some value)
```

In JDK 1.1, all the AWT components are made JavaBean-compliant in this way, and that might explain why many methods with names that do not match this pattern were deprecated.

Every property must have a get() method and a set() method that corresponds to the name of the property.

The developer of a JavaBean might also decide that the property sheet created by the IDE is insufficient and provide a special dialog for modifying properties. The IDE will then display this custom dialog instead of the default property sheet that it would have displayed based on introspection.

This all is performed at design time. At runtime, the properties have already been set, and users are not generally given the opportunity to interact with a JavaBean's properties in this way.

The introspection process just mentioned is based on the Reflection API. Under the covers, the introspection process interrogates a bean for its fields and methods. Again, the JavaBean specification requires that, for every property that can be accessed or modified externally, there must be a get() and set() method, except in the case of a boolean value, which can have an isabc() method that checks whether the property is set to true. The introspection mechanism assumes that a given bean follows this convention and will use getabc() and setabc() to manipulate the abc property of the JavaBean.

The following provides a quick view of the interfaces and classes in the java.beans package.

Package Name: java.beans

The java.beans package provides the basic framework for creating JavaBeans.

Interfaces

```
AppletInitializer
BeanInfo
Customizer
DesignMode
PropertyChangeListener
PropertyEditor
VetoableChangeListener
Visibility
```

Classes

```
BeanDescriptor
Beans
```

```
EventSetDescriptor
FeatureDescriptor
IndexedPropertyDescriptor
Introspector
MethodDescriptor
ParameterDescriptor
PropertyChangeEvent
PropertyChangeSupport
PropertyDescriptor
PropertyEditorManager
PropertyEditorSupport
SimpleBeanInfo
VetoableChangeSupport
```

Exceptions

```
IntrospectionException
PropertyVetoException
```

Package Name: java.beans.beancontext

A *bean context* is a container for one or more beans. It defines the execution environment for those beans.

Interfaces

```
BeanContext
BeanContextChild
BeanContextChildComponentProxy
BeanContextContainerProxy
BeanContextMembershipListener
BeanContextProxy
BeanContextServiceProvider
BeanContextServiceProviderBeanInfo
BeanContextServiceRevokedListener
BeanContextServices
BeanContextServicesListener
```

Classes

```
BeanContextChildSupport
BeanContextEvent
BeanContextMembershipEvent
BeanContextServiceAvailableEvent
BeanContextServiceRevokedEvent
BeanContextServicesSupport
BeanContextServicesSupport.BCSSServiceProvider
BeanContextSupport
BeanContextSupport.BCSIterator
```

java.beans Interface and Class Details

Interface AppletInitializer

public abstract interface **AppletInitializer**

The AppletInitializer interface provides the mechanism for initializing a JavaBean, which is also an applet, when the bean is instantiated by java.beans.Beans.instantiate().

Methods

```
public void       initialize(Applet newAppletBean, BeanContext bCtxt)
public void       activate(Applet newApplet)
```

Interface BeanInfo

public abstract interface **BeanInfo**

This interface is implemented by Bean providers to supply basic information about a Bean, including an icon for the Bean to place in a toolbar or similar Component.

Fields

```
public static final int       ICON_COLOR_16x16
public static final int       ICON_COLOR_32x32
public static final int       ICON_MONO_16x16
public static final int       ICON_MONO_32x32
```

Methods

```
public BeanDescriptor          getBeanDescriptor()
public EventSetDescriptor[]    getEventSetDescriptors()
public int                     getDefaultEventIndex()
public PropertyDescriptor[]    getPropertyDescriptors()
public int                     getDefaultPropertyIndex()
public MethodDescriptor[]      getMethodDescriptors()
public BeanInfo[]              getAdditionalBeanInfo()
public Image                   getIcon(int iconKind)
```

Interface Customizer

public abstract interface **Customizer**

This interface is implemented by a class so that the class can serve as a custom GUI to set the properties of a Bean. The implementing class should have a null constructor and inherit from java.awt.Component so that it can be added to a Container, like a Dialog.

Methods

```
public void       setObject(Object bean)
public void       addPropertyChangeListener(PropertyChangeListener listener)
public void       removePropertyChangeListener(PropertyChangeListener listener)
```

Interface PropertyChangeListener

```
public abstract interface PropertyChangeListener
                         extends EventListener
```

This interface is implemented by objects that want to be listeners for changes to bound Bean properties. A *bound* property is a property that, when changes occur, causes notification to be sent to interested parties. The class PropertyChangeSupport serves as a convenience class to provide methods to add and remove PropertyChangeListener objects, and code to fire PropertyChangeEvents to those listener objects when the bound property is changed. A JavaBean can inherit from this convenience class or use it as an inner class.

To implement a bound property, your bean needs to

- Import the java.beans package
- Instantiate a PropertyChangeSupport object, like this:
  ```
  private PropertyChangeSupport pcs =
                 new PropertyChangeSupport(this);
  ```
- Implement methods to add and remove PropertyChangeListener objects. Because PropertyChangeSupport provides these, your methods simply wrap them.
- Modify the set() method for the bound property to call firePropertyChange() so that a PropertyChangeEvent is sent to registered PropertyChangeListener objects for the change. The values you supply to the firePropertyChange() method are the old and new values of the property. These are put into a PropertyChangeEvent, which is then used as the parameter for calling propertyChange() (done for you). This passes the PropertyChangeEvent to each registered listener. This method is the one method in the PropertyChangeListener interface.
- Implement the propertyChange() method in the listener class. Do whatever is appropriate for a change to the bound property.

For further information, see the classes PropertyChangeSupport and PropertyChangeEvent.

Method

```
public void     propertyChange (PropertyChangeEvent evt)
```

Interface PropertyEditor

```
public abstract interface PropertyEditor
```

This interface is implemented by a Bean developer so that users can edit Bean properties. It supports multiple ways to display and edit those properties, although typically only a subset of those possibilities will be used by one PropertyEditor.

Methods

```
public void        setValue (Object value)
public Object      getValue()
public boolean     isPaintable()
public void        paintValue(Graphics gfx, Rectangle box)
```

```
public String         getJavaInitializationString()
public String         getAsText()
public void           setAsText(String text)
                           throws IllegalArgumentException
public String[]       getTags()
public Component      getCustomEditor()
public boolean        supportsCustomEditor()
public void           addPropertyChangeListener
                           (PropertyChangeListener listener)
public void           removePropertyChangeListener
                           (PropertyChangeListener listener)
```

Interface VetoableChangeListener

```
public abstract interface VetoableChangeListener
                          extends EventListener
```

By default, there are no restrictions outside a Bean regarding its properties. It is possible, however, to use another object to constrain property changes in a Bean by giving another object the power to veto a change to a Bean's property. To do this, the other object has to implement this interface so that it listens for VetoableChanges to a Bean.

Methods

```
public void    vetoableChange (PropertyChangeEvent evt)
                    throws PropertyVetoException
```

Class BeanDescriptor

```
public class BeanDescriptor
             extends FeatureDescriptor
```

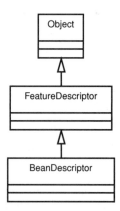

A BeanDescriptor object is returned by a BeanInfo object to provide global information about a Bean, such as the Bean's classname.

A BeanDescriptor returns descriptors for properties, methods, and events. This provides an equivalent, more powerful version of Reflection. You can use it to learn about the JavaBean. You can use this information in your program. Builder tools use this information for creating property sheets and the like in an IDE.

Constructors
```
public   BeanDescriptor (Class beanClass)
public   BeanDescriptor(Class beanClass, Class customizerClass)
```

Methods
```
public Class    getBeanClass()
public Class    getCustomizerClass()
```

Class Beans
```
public class Beans
            extends Object
```

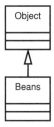

This class provides methods for general-purpose creation and manipulation of a Bean.

Constructors
```
public   Beans()
```

Methods
```
public static Object    instantiate (ClassLoader cls, String beanName)
                            throws IOException, ClassNotFoundException
public static Object    instantiate(ClassLoader cls, String beanName,
                            BeanContext beanContext)
                            throws IOException, ClassNotFoundException
public static Object    instantiate(ClassLoader cls, String beanName,
                            BeanContext beanContext,
                            AppletInitializer initializer)
                            throws IOException, ClassNotFoundException
public static Object    getInstanceOf(Object bean, Class targetType)
public static boolean   isInstanceOf(Object bean, Class targetType)
public static boolean   isDesignTime()
public static boolean   isGuiAvailable()
public static void      setDesignTime(boolean isDesignTime)
                            throws SecurityException
public static void      setGuiAvailable(boolean isGuiAvailable)
                            throws SecurityException
```

Class IndexedPropertyDescriptor

```
public class IndexedPropertyDescriptor
              extends PropertyDescriptor
```

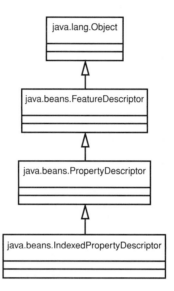

A Bean may have a property that is in the form of an array of property values. This class provides methods for accessing specific values of that property array.

Constructors

```
public  IndexedPropertyDescriptor (String propertyName, ClassbeanClass)
           throws IntrospectionException
public  IndexedPropertyDescriptor(String propertyName, Class
           beanClass, String getterName,
           String setterName, String indexedGetterName, String
           indexedSetterName)
           throws IntrospectionException
public  IndexedPropertyDescriptor(String propertyName, Method getter,
           Method setter, Method indexedGetter, Method indexedSetter)
           throws IntrospectionException
```

Methods

```
public Method   getIndexedReadMethod()
public void     setIndexedReadMethod(Method getter)
                    throws IntrospectionException
public Method   getIndexedWriteMethod()
public void     setIndexedWriteMethod(Method setter)
                    throws IntrospectionException
public Class    getIndexedPropertyType()
```

Class Introspector

```
public class Introspector
            extends Object
```

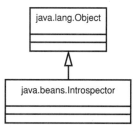

This class is used to provide tools with information about the properties, events, and methods of a JavaBean. The Introspection class can be used in place of Reflection, even with a class that does not represent a JavaBean. It is much easier to use than Reflection, so if you need to interrogate an object or class, consider using this instead of the Reflection APIs in this way:

```
Class c = Class.getClass(myObject);
BeanInfo bInfo = Introspection.getBeaninfo();
```

Fields

```
public static final int        USE_ALL_BEANINFO
public static final int        IGNORE_IMMEDIATE_BEANINFO
public static final int        IGNORE_ALL_BEANINFO
```

Methods

```
public static BeanInfo         getBeanInfo (Class beanClass)
                                   throws IntrospectionException
public static BeanInfo         getBeanInfo(Class beanClass, int flags)
                                   throws IntrospectionException
public static BeanInfo         getBeanInfo(Class beanClass, Class stopClass)
                                   throws IntrospectionException
public static String           decapitalize(String name)
public static String[]         getBeanInfoSearchPath()
public static void             setBeanInfoSearchPath(String[] path)
public static void             flushCaches()
public static void             flushFromCaches(Class clz)
```

Class PropertyChangeEvent

```
public class PropertyChangeEvent
            extends EventObject
```

Whenever a bound or constrained property changes, a PropertyChangeEvent is fired. To process this event, an object must implement the PropertyChangeListener interface or the VetoableChangeListener.

538 Chapter 22: java.beans

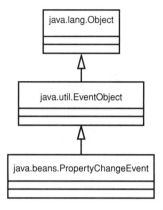

Constructors

```
public  PropertyChangeEvent (Object source, String propertyName,
           Object oldValue, Object newValue)
```

Methods

```
public String     getPropertyName()
public Object     getNewValue()
public Object     getOldValue()
public void       setPropagationId(Object propagationId)
public Object     getPropagationId()
```

Class PropertyDescriptor

```
public class PropertyDescriptor
              extends FeatureDescriptor
```

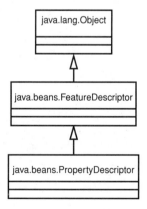

A `PropertyDescriptor` is an object that is used to describe a JavaBean property so that the property can be interpreted and manipulated.

Constructors
```
public  PropertyDescriptor (String propertyName, Class beanClass)
            throws IntrospectionException
public  PropertyDescriptor(String propertyName, Class beanClass,
            String getterName, String setterName)
            throws IntrospectionException
public  PropertyDescriptor(String propertyName, Method getter,
            Method setter)
            throws IntrospectionException
```

Methods
```
public Class     getPropertyType()
public Method    getReadMethod()
public void      setReadMethod(Method getter)
                     throws IntrospectionException
public Method    getWriteMethod()
public void      setWriteMethod(Method setter)
                     throws IntrospectionException
public boolean   isBound()
public void      setBound(boolean bound)
public boolean   isConstrained()
public void      setConstrained(boolean constrained)
public void      setPropertyEditorClass(Class propertyEditorClass)
public Class     getPropertyEditorClass()
```

Class SimpleBeanInfo
```
public class SimpleBeanInfo
                extends Object
                implements BeanInfo
```

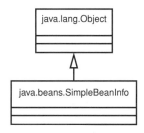

This is a basic class for a Bean to use to provide information through the methods specified in the BeanInfo interface. The methods by default return a hoop value, so any method that a developer wants to use must be overridden in a subclass. When the introspector sees the hoop value, it automatically performs low-level introspection to analyze the target bean.

Constructors
```
public SimpleBeanInfo()
```

Methods

public BeanDescriptor	**getBeanDescriptor**()
public PropertyDescriptor[]	**getPropertyDescriptors**()
public int	**getDefaultPropertyIndex**()
public EventSetDescriptor[]	**getEventSetDescriptors**()
public int	**getDefaultEventIndex**()
public MethodDescriptor[]	**getMethodDescriptors**()
public BeanInfo[]	**getAdditionalBeanInfo**()
public Image	**getIcon**(int iconKind)
public Image	**loadImage**(String resourceName)

CHAPTER 23

java.io

There are several Stream, Reader, and Writer classes. They are all included here. This chapter provides a quick view of the interfaces and classes in the IO package.

Package Name: java.io

This package provides Java support for doing both byte-oriented IO (Stream classes) and Unicode-oriented (Reader and Writer) input and output. In addition to Streams, Readers, and Writers, this package defines various File classes. In JDK 1.0, only Stream-oriented classes were available. Those classes, in large part, are now considered deprecated. Because Java natively uses Unicode, it makes more sense to use Reader and Writer classes that do their work based on Unicode characters instead of mere bytes. If bytes are used, Java has to translate Unicode characters into ASCII characters to write them out and back into Unicode characters when it reads them.

This package also provides support for object serialization. This is a mechanism for sending an object across the network and then re-creating the object on the receiving end of the serialized object. For example, this would allow you to send a Customer object across the network to a remote object or to write an object to a file. This could even be used to create a primitive object database. Serialization is a key technology in Java, and it's used with JavaBeans and RMI.

Interfaces

```
DataInput
DataOutput
Externalizable
FileFilter
FilenameFilter
ObjectInput
ObjectInputValidation
```

ObjectOutput
ObjectStreamConstants
Serializable

Classes

BufferedInputStream
BufferedOutputStream
BufferedReader
BufferedWriter
ByteArrayInputStream
ByteArrayOutputStream
CharArrayReader
CharArrayWriter
DataInputStream
DataOutputStream
File
FileDescriptor
FileInputStream
FileOutputStream
FilePermission
FileReader
FileWriter
FilterInputStream
FilterOutputStream
FilterReader
FilterWriter
InputStream
InputStreamReader
LineNumberInputStream
LineNumberReader
ObjectInputStream
ObjectInputStream.GetField
ObjectOutputStream
ObjectOutputStream.PutField
ObjectStreamClass
ObjectStreamField
OutputStream
OutputStreamWriter
PipedInputStream
PipedOutputStream
PipedReader
PipedWriter
PrintStream
PrintWriter
PushbackInputStream
PushbackReader
RandomAccessFile
Reader
SequenceInputStream
SerializablePermission

StreamTokenizer
StringBufferInputStream
StringReader
StringWriter
Writer

Exceptions
CharConversionException
EOFException
FileNotFoundException
InterruptedIOException
InvalidClassException
InvalidObjectException
IOException
NotActiveException
NotSerializableException
ObjectStreamException
OptionalDataException
StreamCorruptedException
SyncFailedException
UnsupportedEncodingException
UTFDataFormatException
WriteAbortedException

Interface and Class Details

Interface Externalizable

```
public abstract interface Externalizable
                        extends Serializable
```

The Externalizable interface is implemented by classes that want to have complete control over the process of serialization. Under this scenario, only the class name is serialized by the JVM. Everything else has to be done by the object itself.

> **NOTE**
>
> Before deciding to use this interface, developers should consider overriding readObject and writeObject while still using normal serialization. Making an Externalizable class is a very complex process.

Methods

```
public void     writeExternal (ObjectOutput out)
                    throws IOException
public void     readExternal(ObjectInput in)
                    throws IOException, ClassNotFoundException
```

Interface FileFilter

public abstract interface **FileFilter**

An object implementing the `FileFilter` interface uses its methods to select the type of files to display in a `FileDialog`.

> **NOTE**
> This hasn't worked in previous versions of Sun's JVM in Win32 environments. You couldn't filter files correctly.

Methods

public boolean   **accept** (File pathname)

Interface FilenameFilter

The interface `FilenameFilter` is implemented by objects to filter files based on filenames. The interface is

public abstract interface **FilenameFilter**

Methods

public boolean   **accept** (File dir, String name)

Interface Serializable

public abstract interface **Serializable**

Object serialization is a key feature in Java, used by RMI and other mechanisms in Java. It is the process of converting an object into a format that can be sent over a network and converted back into an object at the other end of the connection. The serialized object is passed as a byte array. This conversion process is normally performed by the JVM without any coding required. The only exception occurs when a field should not be copied. In this case, the field can be marked as `transient`. This will cause Java to put a bookmark in the serialized object where the field would have been. Similarly, static fields are not copied. The serialization mechanism is intelligent enough to make only one copy of a duplicated object in the serialized form. The `Serializable` interface is easy to implement in a class, as it has no methods. Therefore, a class signature that says it "implements `Serializable`" is essentially signaling the JVM that the object is eligible for serialization. Not all objects can be serialized. If they are not defined as implementing `Serializable`, such as the class `Thread`, attempting to write them as an object will fail.

Fields

public static final long   **serialVersionUID**

Class BufferedInputStream

public class BufferedInputStream
            extends FilterInputStream

Interface and Class Details

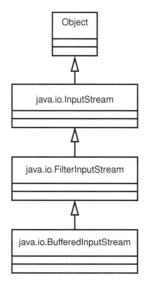

A `BufferedInputStream` provides a wrapper around a byte-level stream such as a `FileInputStream`. It allows for much more efficient I/O by permitting you to buffer the input.

> **TIP**
>
> You should always use buffering when doing I/O in Java, no matter what class you are using. Reading or writing data one byte or one character at a time is grossly inefficient. You should always try to do I/O in large chunks. The optimal size of the chunk may vary from operating system to operating system, but a page (1024 or 2048 bytes) would not be a bad choice in most situations.

Fields

```
protected byte[]    buf
protected int       count
protected int       pos
protected int       markpos
protected int       marklimit
```

Constructors

```
public      BufferedInputStream(InputStream in)
public      BufferedInputStream(InputStream in, int size)
```

Methods

```
public int      read()
                    throws IOException
public int      read(byte[] b, int off, int len)
                    throws IOException
public long     skip(long n)
```

```
public int          available()
                         throws IOException
public void         mark(int readlimit)
public void         reset()
                         throws IOException
public boolean      markSupported()
public void         close()
                         throws IOException
```

Class BufferedOutputStream

```
public class BufferedOutputStream
             extends FilterOutputStream
```

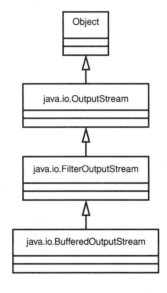

This class provides a stream to wrap a byte-oriented output stream, such as FileOutputStream, so that an object can perform buffered IO, which is much more efficient than a non-buffered IO operation. Buffering data can significantly improve application performance in Java.

The same caveat applies here as with BufferedInputStream. It is vital that you buffer output as well as input.

Fields

```
protected byte[]    buf
protected int       count
```

Constructors

```
public          BufferedOutputStream(OutputStream out)
public          BufferedOutputStream(OutputStream out, int size)
```

```
public void     write(int b)
                    throws IOException
public void     write(byte[] b, Int off, int len)
                    throws IOException
public void     flush()
                    throws IOException
```

Class BufferedReader

```
public class BufferedReader
            extends Reader
```

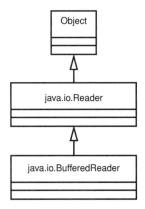

The BufferedReader provides the same facilities that a BufferedInputStream does, except that as a Reader subclass, it performs buffered input operations on Unicode characters, not merely bytes. One could use this class's readLine() method to read a line of input from the command-line as a Unicode-based String object. Here's what you would do:

```
InputStreamReader isr = new InputStreamReader(System.in);
// Convert from byte stream class to Reader class.
BufferedReader br = new BufferedReader(isr);
String input = br.readLine();
```

Constructors

```
public BufferedReader (Reader in, int sz)
public BufferedReader(Reader in)
```

Methods

```
public int      read()
                    throws IOException
public int      read(char[] cbuf, int off, int len)
                    throws IOException
public String   readLine()
                    throws IOException
public long     skip(long n)
                    throws IOException
```

```
public boolean  ready()
                    throws IOException
public boolean  markSupported()
public void     mark(int readAheadLimit)
                    throws IOException
public void     reset()
                    throws IOException
public void     close()
                    throws IOException
```

Class BufferedWriter

```
public class BufferedWriter
            extends Writer
```

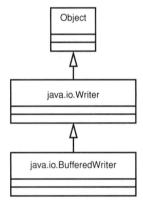

The BufferedWriter class provides for writing buffered output, as does the BufferedOutputStream, but has the additional benefit of writing data as Unicode characters, reflecting Java's internal character representation. Again, buffering data for I/O is critical for application performance.

Constructors

```
public      BufferedWriter (Writer out)
public      BufferedWriter(Writer out, int sz)
```

Methods

```
public void     write(int c)
                    throws IOException
public void     write(char[] cbuf, int off, int len)
                    throws IOException
public void     write(String s, int off, int len)
                    throws IOException
public void     newLine()
                    throws IOException
public void     flush()
                    throws IOException
```

```
public void    close()
                    throws IOException
```

Class ByteArrayInputStream

```
public class ByteArrayInputStream
                extends InputStream
```

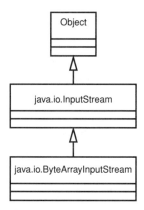

A ByteArrayInputStream is a stream which holds data in the form of a byte array. A very useful application of this is for a ByteArrayOutputStream to be used for concatenating multiple, disparate data elements into one contiguous byte array, which can then be retrieved with a ByteArrayInputStream. This stream can be used to hold data in memory.

Fields

```
protected byte[]   buf
protected int      pos
protected int      mark
protected int      count
```

Constructors

```
public     ByteArrayInputStream (byte[] buf)
public     ByteArrayInputStream(byte[] buf, int offset, int length)
```

Methods

```
public int      available()
public int      read()
public int      read(byte[] b, int off, int len)
public long     skip(long n)
public void     mark(int readAheadLimit)
public boolean  markSupported()
public void     reset()
public void     close()                       throws IOException
```

Class ByteArrayOutputStream

public class **ByteArrayOutputStream**
               extends OutputStream

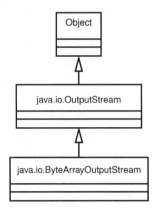

A ByteArrayOutputStream stores data in an array of bytes internally. It can be used to store disparate data elements as a byte array that can be retrieved from a ByteArrayInputStream. These two streams can be used in concert in memory to concatenate disparate data elements together in a ByteArrayOutputStream and then to read them back as a byte array or string using a ByteArrayInputStream.

Fields

```
protected byte[]   buf
protected int      count
```

Constructors

```
public    ByteArrayOutputStream()
public    ByteArrayOutputStream(int size)
```

Methods

```
public void    write(int b)
public void    write(byte[] b, int off, int len)
public void    writeTo(OutputStream out)
                   throws IOException
public void    reset()
public byte[]  toByteArray()
public int     size()
public String  toString()
public String  toString(String enc)
                   throws UnsupportedEncodingException
public String  toString(int hibyte)
public void    close()
                   throws IOException
```

Class CharArrayReader

```
public class CharArrayReader
                extends Reader
```

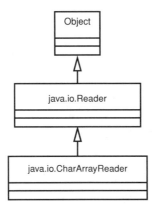

This class can read an array of Unicode characters, generally those created with a CharArrayWriter. It is similar to a ByteArrayInputStream except that a CharArrayReader functions at the level of characters, not bytes.

Fields

```
protected char[]    buf
protected int       pos
protected int       markedPos
protected int       count
```

Constructors

```
public      CharArrayReader(char[] buf)
public      CharArrayReader(char[] buf, int offset, int length)
```

Methods

```
public int      read()
                    throws IOException
public int      read(char[] b, int off, int len)
                    throws IOException
public long     skip(long n)
                    throws IOException
public boolean  ready()
                    throws IOException
public boolean  markSupported()
public void     mark(int readAheadLimit)
                    throws IOException
public void     reset()
                    throws IOException
public void     close()
```

Class CharArrayWriter

public class **CharArrayWriter**
                extends Writer

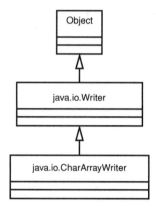

This class is for writing an array of Unicode characters. It can be used to create an array of characters to be read by a `CharArrayReader`.

Fields

```
protected char[]    buf
protected int       count
```

Constructors

```
public    CharArrayWriter()
public    CharArrayWriter(int initialSize)
```

Methods

```
public void      write(int c)
public void      write(char[] c, int off, int len)
public void      write(String str, int off, int len)
public void      writeTo(Writer out)
                     throws IOException
public void      reset()
public char[]    toCharArray()
public int       size()
public String    toString()
public void      flush()
public void      close()
```

Class DataInputStream

public class **DataInputStream**
                extends FilterInputStream
                implements DataInput

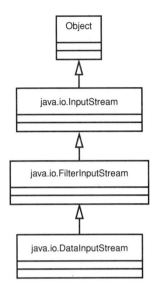

A DataInputStream is a byte-oriented stream that can read Java primitive data types. It can also be used to send any string as a UTF string. It is very common to wrap a more primitive stream in a DataInputStream for reading from a stream. This class can also be used to read unsigned numeric data into Java ints, which are, of course, signed. You use a DataInputStream by "wrapping" an InputStream. This is a very common technique in Java for doing I/O. Here's a brief example:

```
FileInputStream fis = new FileInputStream("Books.txt");
DataInputStream dis = new DataInputStream(fis);
String s = dis.readUTF();
```

Constructors
public   **DataInputStream**(InputStream in)

Methods

```
public final int          read(byte[] b)
                              throws IOException
public final int          read(byte[] b, int off, int len)
                              throws IOException
public final void         readFully(byte[] b)
                              throws IOException
public final void         readFully(byte[] b, int off, int len)
                              throws IOException
public final int          skipBytes(int n)
                              throws IOException
public final boolean      readBoolean()
                              throws IOException
public final byte         readByte()
                              throws IOException
```

public final int	**readUnsignedByte**()
	throws IOException
public final short	**readShort**()
	throws IOException
public final int	**readUnsignedShort**()
	throws IOException
public final char	**readChar**()
	throws IOException
public final int	**readInt**()
	throws IOException
public final long	**readLong**()
	throws IOException
public final float	**readFloat**()
	throws IOException
public final double	**readDouble**()
	throws IOException
public final String	**readLine**()
	throws IOException
public final String	**readUTF**()
	throws IOException
public static final String	**readUTF**(DataInput in)
	throws IOException

Class DataOutputStream

```
public class DataOutputStream
               extends FilterOutputStream
               implements DataOutput
```

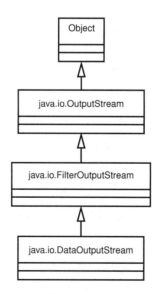

The DataOutputStream class is used to write Java primitives to a stream, such as char, boolean, and long, rather than having to put separate bytes together.

You use a DataOutputStream by wrapping it around a more basic OutputStream. Here's an example:

```
FileOutputStream fos = new FileOutputStream("CallNoFile");
DataOutputStream dos = new DataOutputStream(fos);
dos.writeInt(2234);
```

Fields

protected int   **written**

Constructors

DataOutputStream (OutputStream out)

Methods

public void	**write**(int b) throws IOException
public void	**write**(byte[] b, int off, int len) throws IOException
public void	**flush**() throws IOException
public final void	**writeBoolean**(boolean v) throws IOException
public final void	**writeByte**(int v) throws IOException
public final void	**writeShort**(int v) throws IOException
public final void	**writeChar**(int v) throws IOException
public final void	**writeInt**(int v) throws IOException
public final void	**writeLong**(long v) throws IOException
public final void	**writeFloat**(float v) throws IOException
public final void	**writeDouble**(double v) throws IOException
public final void	**writeBytes**(String s) throws IOException
public final void	**writeChars**(String s) throws IOException
public final void	**writeUTF**(String str) throws IOException
public final int	**size**()

Class File

```
public class File
            extends Object
            implements Serializable, Comparable
```

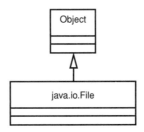

The class File represents a File object. It does not represent a physical file, though it may be associated with a physical file or a directory. That is, it is perfectly possible to call a File constructor to make an instance of a File object that contains the name of a non-existent file. This will not cause an error when the File object is created. It will only cause an error when a program attempts to use the File object to read the non-existent file.

Unlike file handling in other languages such as C, a file represented by a File object is not explicitly opened. It is implicitly opened when the File name or File object is supplied to a Stream, Reader, or Writer class constructor or method. For output operations, the physical file is created by this action. When a physical file is opened or created for a File object, there is no provision to specify any attributes, such as opening for read-only.

Also, the same file cannot be written on two separate occasions and maintain the original contents. If a program writes to the physical file Test.txt, closes the file, and exits, the next Java program that tries to write to this file will get an empty file. If a program needs the contents to persist, it must open the file as a RandomAccessFile object.

You can make a file lots of ways. Here's how you would create a File object based on a directory/filename combination:

```
//First make a File object representing a directory.
File dir = new File("/export");
File theFile = new File(dir, "BookCatalog.dat");
```

Fields

```
public static final char    separatorChar
public static final String  separator
public static final char    pathSeparatorChar
public static final String  pathSeparator
```

Constructors

```
public    File (String pathname)
public    File(String parent, String child)
public    File(File parent, String child)
```

Methods

```
public String    getName()
public String    getParent()
public File      getParentFile()
public String    getPath()
```

```
public boolean         isAbsolute()
public String          getAbsolutePath()
public File            getAbsoluteFile()
public String          getCanonicalPath()
                           throws IOException
public File            getCanonicalFile()
                           throws IOException
public URL             toURL()
                           throws MalformedURLException
public boolean         canRead()
public boolean         canWrite()
public boolean         exists()
public boolean         isDirectory()
public boolean         isFile()
public boolean         isHidden()
public long            lastModified()
public long            length()
public boolean         createNewFile()
                           throws IOException
public boolean         delete()
public void            deleteOnExit()
public String[]        list()
public String[]        list(FilenameFilter filter)
public File[]          listFiles()
public File[]          listFiles(FilenameFilter filter)
public File[]          listFiles(FileFilter filter)
public boolean         mkdir()
public boolean         mkdirs()
public boolean         renameTo(File dest)
public boolean         setLastModified(long time)
public boolean         setReadOnly()
public static File[]   listRoots()
public static File     createTempFile(String prefix, String suffix,
                           File directory)
                           throws IOException
public static File     createTempFile(String prefix, String suffix)
                           throws IOException
public int             compareTo(File pathname)
public int             compareTo(Object o)
public boolean         equals(Object obj)
public int             hashCode()
public String          toString()
```

Class FileInputStream

```
public class FileInputStream
            extends InputStream
```

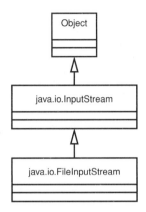

A `FileInputStream` reads input from a stream one byte at a time. It is essentially the lowest-level of abstraction among the concrete classes in java.io. This a very primitive stream class and probably is not useful for much except for wrapping inside another class. For example:

```
FileInputStream fis = new FileInputStream("BookObj.dat");
ObjectInputStream ois = new ObjectInputStream(fis);
Book b = (Book)ois.readObject();
```

Constructors

```
public  FileInputStream (String name)
            throws FileNotFoundException
public  FileInputStream(File file)
            throws FileNotFoundException
public  FileInputStream(FileDescriptor fdObj)
```

Methods

```
public int                   read()
                                 throws IOException
public int                   read(byte[] b)
                                 throws IOException
public int                   read(byte[] b, int off, int len)
                                 throws IOException
public long                  skip(long n)
                                 throws IOException
public int                   available()
                                 throws IOException
public void                  close()
                                 throws IOException
public final FileDescriptor  getFD()
                                 throws IOException
protected void               finalize()
                                 throws IOException
```

Class FileOutputStream

```
public class FileOutputStream
            extends OutputStream
```

Interface and Class Details 559

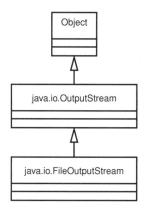

A FileOutputStream is a stream for writing bytes, generally to a file. It is the lowest level of abstraction among the concrete classes in java.io. Like a FileInputStream, a FileOutputStream is a fairly primitive object and not nearly as useful as other I/O classes. Therefore, it is better to wrap a FileOutputStream in another stream. For example:

```
FileOutputStream fos = new FileOutputStream("BookObj.dat");
ObjectOutputStream oos = new ObjectOutputStream(fos);
Book b = new Book("Lewis, C.S.", "Out of the Silent Planet");
oos.writeObject(b);
```

Constructors

```
public     FileOutputStream (String name)
                throws FileNotFoundException
public     FileOutputStream(String name, boolean append)
                throws FileNotFoundException
public     FileOutputStream(File file)
                throws IOException
public     FileOutputStream(FileDescriptor fdObj)
```

Methods

```
public void                    write(int b)
                                   throws IOException
public void                    write(byte[] b)
                                   throws IOException
public void                    write(byte[] b, int off, int len)
                                   throws IOException
public void                    close()
                                   throws IOException
public final FileDescriptor    getFD()
                                   throws IOException
protected void                 finalize()
                                   throws IOException
```

Class FilePermission

```
public final class FilePermission
                   extends Permission
                   implements Serializable
```

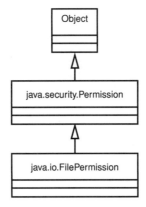

A `FilePermission` object represents a pathname and the actions that can be performed upon it.

Constructors
public   **FilePermission** (String path, String actions)

Methods
```
public boolean              implies(Permission p)
public boolean              equals(Object obj)
public int                  hashCode()
public String               getActions()
public PermissionCollection newPermissionCollection()
```

Class FileReader
public class **FileReader**
            extends InputStreamReader

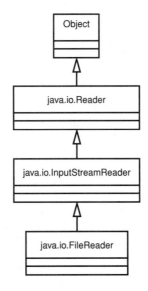

The class `FileReader` is a basic `Reader` class that reads input data at the character level from a file or other source. It assumes valid character mapping.

Constructors
```
public    FileReader (String fileName)
               throws FileNotFoundException
public    FileReader(File file)
               throws FileNotFoundException
public    FileReader(FileDescriptor fd)
```

Class FileWriter
```
public class FileWriter
               extends OutputStreamWriter
```

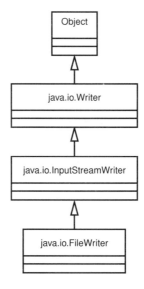

The `FileWriter` class can write characters out to a file or other data store. It is a low-level of abstraction among the `Writer` subclasses.

Constructors
```
public    FileWriter (String fileName)
               throws IOException
public    FileWriter(String fileName, boolean append)
               throws IOException
public    FileWriter(File file)
               throws IOException
public    FileWriter(FileDescriptor fd)
```

Class InputStream
```
public abstract class InputStream
                    extends Object
```

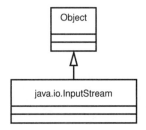

`InputStream` is the base class for all the input stream classes. It is abstract itself and must be subclassed to make a class that can be instantiated. It provides the basic methods shared by all input streams, such as read and mark. You do not directly use this abstract class as a general rule.

Constructors
```
public    InputStream()
```

Methods
```
public abstract int    read()
                           throws IOException
public int             read(byte[] b)
                           throws IOException
public int             read(byte[] b, int off, int len)
                           throws IOException
public long            skip(long n)
                           throws IOException
public int             available()
                           throws IOException
public void            close()
                           throws IOException
public void            mark(int readlimit)
public void            reset()
                           throws IOException
public boolean         markSupported()
```

Class InputStreamReader
```
public class InputStreamReader
              extends Reader
```

An `InputStreamReader` is a basic `Reader` class and can be used by other `Reader` classes. It is useful for going from a byte stream to a character reader object. For example, you can wrap `System.in` in an `InputStreamReader` and wrap that in a `BufferedReader` to read lines of text from the keyboard, like this:

```
InputStreamReader isr = new InputStreamReader(System.in);
BufferedReader br = new BufferedReader(isr);
String input = br.readLine();
```

Interface and Class Details 563

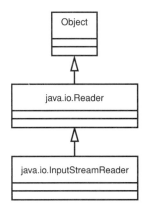

Constructors

```
public      InputStreamReader (InputStream in)
public      InputStreamReader(InputStream in, String enc)
                throws UnsupportedEncodingException
```

Methods

```
public String       getEncoding()
public int          read()
                        throws IOException
public int          read(char[] cbuf, int off, int len)
                        throws IOException
public boolean      ready()
                        throws IOException
public void         close()
                        throws IOException
```

Class LineNumberReader

```
public class LineNumberReader
                extends BufferedReader
```

A `LineNumberReader` object reads input from a character-oriented stream and provides line numbers for the input. A line is demarcated by a line feed, carriage return, or a combination of both.

Constructors

```
public      LineNumberReader(Reader in)
public      LineNumberReader(Reader in, int sz)
```

Methods

```
public void         setLineNumber(int lineNumber)
public int          getLineNumber()
public int          read()
                        throws IOException
public int          read(char[] cbuf, int off, int len)
                        throws IOException
```

```
public String     readLine()
                      throws IOException
public long       skip(long n)
                      throws IOException
public void       mark(int readAheadLimit)
                      throws IOException
public void       reset()
                      throws IOException
```

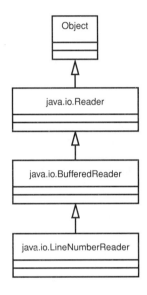

Class ObjectInputStream

```
public class ObjectInputStream
            extends InputStream
            implements ObjectInput, ObjectStreamConstants
```

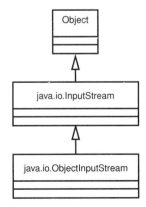

The `ObjectInputStream` class can be used to read objects and primitives from a stream. In general, its use is for deserializing serialized objects. This deserialization is automatic unless a subclass overrides `readObject` or implements `Externalizable`. This class provides the highest level of abstraction for an input stream. There is no `Reader`-based equivalent. You could use it to get an object from elsewhere, such as an object sent across a socket. Here's a simple example:

```
FileInputStream fis = new FileInputStream("BookObj.dat");
ObjectInputStream ois = new ObjectInputStream(fis);
Book b = (Book)ois.readObject();
```

Constructors

```
public        ObjectInputStream(InputStream in)
                  throws IOException, StreamCorruptedException
protected     ObjectInputStream()
                  throws IOException, SecurityException
```

Methods

```
public final Object              readObject()
                                     throws OptionalDataException,
                                     ClassNotFoundException, IOException
protected Object                 readObjectOverride()
                                     throws OptionalDataException,
                                     ClassNotFoundException, IOException
public void                      defaultReadObject()
                                     throws IOException,
                                     ClassNotFoundException,
                                     NotActiveException
public ObjectInputStream.GetField readFields()
                                     throws IOException,
                                     ClassNotFoundException,
                                     NotActiveException
public void                      registerValidation
                                     (ObjectInputValidation obj, int prio)
                                     throws NotActiveException,
                                     InvalidObjectException
protected Class                  resolveClass(Object StreamClass v)
                                     throws IOException,
                                     ClassNotFoundException
protected Object                 resolveObject(Object obj)
                                     throws IOException
protected boolean                enableResolveObject(boolean enable)
                                     throws SecurityException
protected void                   readStreamHeader()
                                     throws IOException,
                                     StreamCorruptedException
public int                       read()
public int                       read(byte[] b, int off, int len)
                                     throws IOException
```

public int	available()
public void	close()
	throws IOException
public boolean	readBoolean()
	throws IOException
public byte	readByte()
	throws IOException
public int	readUnsignedByte()
	throws IOException
public short	readShort()
	throws IOException
public int	readUnsignedShort()
	throws IOException
public char	readChar()
	throws IOException
public int	readInt()
	throws IOException
public long	readLong()
	throws IOException
public float	readFloat()
	throws IOException
public double	readDouble()
	throws IOException
public void	readFully(byte[] data)
	throws IOException
public void	readFully(byte[] data, int offset, int size)
	throws IOException
public int	skipBytes(int len)
	throws IOException
public String	readLine()
	throws IOException
public String	readUTF()
	throws IOException

Class ObjectOutputStream

```
public class ObjectOutputStream
            extends OutputStream
            implements ObjectOutput, ObjectStreamConstants
```

An ObjectOutputStream is a stream that operates at a high level of abstraction. It can be used to write objects and primitives to a stream. It also has a header that is sent first and must be read first from an ObjectInputStream. This stream would be used to write serialized objects so that they can be sent to another object or stored in a file.

Interface and Class Details

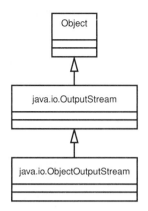

 TIP

You might use this for writing a Vector to a Socket that contains customer information for an e-commerce application. By using a Vector, you reduce network round trips, because you don't have to send several discrete data items.

Here's a simple example:

```
FileOutputStream fos = new FileOutputStream("BookObj.dat");
ObjectOutputStream oos = new ObjectOutputStream(fos);
Book b = new Book("Lewis,C.S.", "That Hideous Strength");
oos.writeObject(b);
```

Constructors

```
public        ObjectOutputStream(OutputStream out)
                      throws IOException
protected     ObjectOutputStream()
                      throws IOException, SecurityException
```

Methods

```
protected void                      writeObjectOverride(Object obj)
                                            throws IOException
public void                         useProtocolVersion(int version)
                                            throws IOException
public final void                   writeObject(Object obj)
                                            throws IOException
public void                         defaultWriteObject()
                                            throws IOException
public ObjectOutputStream.PutField  putFields()
                                            throws IOException
public void                         writeFields()
                                            throws IOException
public void                         reset()
                                            throws IOException
```

protected void	**annotateClass**(Class cl) 　　throws IOException
protected Object	**replaceObject**(Object obj) 　　throws IOException
protected boolean	**enableReplaceObject**(boolean enable) 　　throws SecurityException
protected void	**writeStreamHeader**() 　　throws IOException
public void	**write**(int data) 　　throws IOException
public void	**write**(byte[] b) 　　throws IOException
public void	**write**(byte[] b, int off, int len) 　　throws IOException
public void	**flush**() 　　throws IOException
protected void	**drain**() 　　throws IOException
public void	**close**() 　　throws IOException
public void	**writeBoolean**(boolean data) 　　throws IOException
public void	**writeByte**(int data) 　　throws IOException
public void	**writeShort**(int data) 　　throws IOException
public void	**writeChar**(int data) 　　throws IOException
public void	**writeInt**(int data) 　　throws IOException
public void	**writeLong**(long data) 　　throws IOException
public void	**writeFloat**(float data) 　　throws IOException
public void	**writeDouble**(double data) 　　throws IOException
public void	**writeBytes**(String data) 　　throws IOException
public void	**writeChars**(String data) 　　throws IOException
public void	**writeUTF**(String data) 　　throws IOException

Class OutputStream

```
public abstract class OutputStream
                extends Object
```

Interface and Class Details

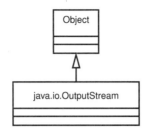

This is an abstract class, which is the superclass for all out stream classes. It defines the basic methods used for all output streams, such as flush() and write(). You generally do not want to use this class, because it is too primitive.

Constructors
```
public    OutputStream()
```

Methods
```
public abstract void    write(int b)
                            throws IOException
public void             write(byte[] b)
                            throws IOException
public void             write(byte[] b, int off, int len)
                            throws IOException
public void             flush()
                            throws IOException
public void             close()
                            throws IOException
```

Class PipedInputStream
```
public class PipedInputStream
            extends InputStream
```

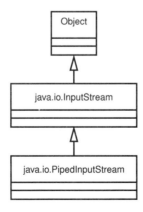

A `PipedInputStream` is used to read data from a `PipedOutputStream`. Typically, piped streams are used for communication between threads. One thread will generally write data to a `PipedOutputStream` and another thread will read data from a `PipedInptStream` connected to the `PipedOutputStream`. Generally, one thread should not use both of these two streams connected together. Otherwise, a deadlock can be created.

Fields

```
protected static final int      PIPE_SIZE
protected byte[]                buffer
protected int                   in
protected int                   out
```

Constructors

```
public          PipedInputStream(PipedOutputStream src)
                    throws IOException
public          PipedInputStream()
```

Methods

```
public void         connect(PipedOutputStream src)
                        throws IOException
protected void      receive(int b)
                        throws IOException
public int          read()
                        throws IOException
public int          read(byte[] b, int off, int len)
                        throws IOException
public int          available()
                        throws IOException
public void         close()
                        throws IOException
```

Class PipedOutputStream

```
public class PipedOutputStream
            extends OutputStream
```

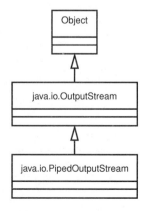

A `PipedOutputStream` can be used with a `PipedInputStream` to provide for communication between threads. One thread writes to a `PipedOutputStream` and another thread reads that data by connecting to the `PipedOutputStream` with a `PipedInputStream`.

Constructors

```
public     PipedOutputStream(PipedInputStream snk)
                throws IOException
public     PipedOutputStream()
```

Methods

```
public void    connect(PipedInputStream snk)
                   throws IOException
public void    write(int b)
                   throws IOException
public void    write(byte[] b, int off, int len)
                   throws IOException
public void    flush()
                   throws IOException
public void    close()
                   throws IOException
```

Class PrintStream

```
public class PrintStream
                extends FilterOutputStream
```

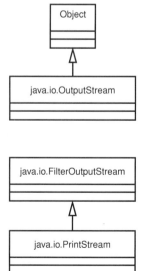

PrintStream is a convenient class for printing output, either to files or to standard out. This class has multiple overloaded methods to print a variety of data types. Unlike most other IO classes, PrintStream does not generally throw any exceptions.

You can use this in your code for putting in debugging statements like

```
System.out.println("Got this far");
```

You can also use it to write data as lines of text. For example:

```
String s1 = textfield1.getText();
String s2 = textfield2.getText();
PrintStream ps = new PrintStream(new FileOutputStream("Text.dat"));
ps.println(s1);
ps.println(s2);
ps.close();
```

Constructors

```
public      PrintStream(OutputStream out)
public      PrintStream(OutputStream out, boolean autoFlush)
```

Methods

```
public void       flush()
public void       close()
public boolean    checkError()
protected void    setError()
public void       write(int b)
public void       write(byte[] buf, int off, int len)
public void       print(boolean b)
public void       print(char c)
public void       print(int i)
public void       print(long l)
public void       print(float f)
public void       print(double d)
public void       print(char[] s)
public void       print(String s)
public void       print(Object obj)
public void       println()
public void       println(boolean x)
public void       println(char x)
public void       println(int x)
public void       println(long x)
public void       println(float x)
public void       println(double x)
public void       println(char[] x)
public void       println(String x)
public void       println (Object x)
```

Class PrintWriter

```
public class PrintWriter
              extends Writer
```

Interface and Class Details

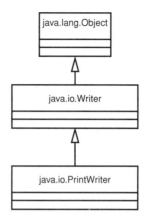

The PrintWriter class is similar to the PrintStream class except that it is used for writing Unicode characters, as opposed to raw bytes. Like a PrintStream, a PrintWriter can write to a file. The benefit of using a PrintWriter is that Java does not need to translate between characters and bytes in order to write to the file. It can simply write out Unicode characters.

Fields

protected Writer   **out**

Constructors

public	**PrintWriter**(Writer out)
public	**PrintWriter**(Writer out, boolean autoFlush)
public	**PrintWriter**(OutputStream out)
public	**PrintWriter**(OutputStream out, boolean autoFlush)

Methods

public void	**flush**()
public void	**close**()
public boolean	**checkError**()
protected void	**setError**()
public void	**write**(int c)
public void	**write**(char[] buf, int off, int len)
public void	**write**(char[] buf)
public void	**write**(String s, int off, int len)
public void	**write**(String s)
public void	**print**(boolean b)
public void	**print**(char c)
public void	**print**(int i)
public void	**print**(long l)
public void	**print**(float f)
public void	**print**(double d)
public void	**print**(char[] s)

```
public void          print(String s)
public void          print(Object obj)
public void          println()
public void          println(boolean x)
public void          println(char x)
public void          println(int x)
public void          println(long x)
public void          println(float x)
public void          println(double x)
public void          println(char[] x)
public void          println(String x)
public void          println (Object x)
```

Class RandomAccessFile

```
public class RandomAccessFile
            extends Object
            implements DataOutput, DataInput
```

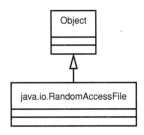

A RandomAccessFile provides a file object that supports reading from and writing to specific positions in the file, as well as appending to the end of the file. This is significantly different from a basic File object. If you attempt to write to a pre-existing physical file mapped to a File object, its contents are erased and replaced by the new output. To avoid this, a RandomAccessFile must be used. Because the RandomAccessFile class provides no support for buffering data, it is advisable to subclass this class with one that provides buffering of input and output. This can significantly improve performance.

Constructors

```
public      RandomAccessFile(String name, String mode)
                throws FileNotFoundException
public      RandomAccessFile(File file, String mode)
                throws IOException
```

Methods

```
public final FileDescriptor    getFD()
                                   throws IOException
public int                     read()
                                   throws IOException
```

Interface and Class Details

```
public int              read(byte[] b, int off, int len)
                            throws IOException
public int              read(byte[] b)
                            throws IOException
public final void       readFully(byte[] b)
                            throws IOException
public final void       readFully(byte[] b, int off, int len)
                            throws IOException
public int              skipBytes(int n)
                            throws IOException
public void             write(int b)
                            throws IOException
public void             write(byte[] b)
                            throws IOException
public void             write(byte[] b, int off, int len)
                            throws IOException
public long             getFilePointer()
                            throws IOException
public void             seek(long pos)
                            throws IOException
public long             length()
                            throws IOException
public void             setLength(long newLength)
                            throws IOException
public void             close()
                            throws IOException
public final boolean    readBoolean()
                            throws IOException
public final byte       readByte()
                            throws IOException
public final int        readUnsignedByte()
                            throws IOException
public final short      readShort()
                            throws IOException
public final int        readUnsignedShort()
                            throws IOException
public final char       readChar()
                            throws IOException
public final int        readInt()
                            throws IOException
public final long       readLong()
                            throws IOException
public final float      readFloat()
                            throws IOException
public final double     readDouble()
                            throws IOException
public final String     readLine()
                            throws IOException
public final String     readUTF()
                            throws IOException
```

```
public final void          writeBoolean(boolean v)
                                        throws IOException
public final void          writeByte(int v)
                                        throws IOException
public final void          writeShort(int v)
                                        throws IOException
public final void          writeChar(int v)
                                        throws IOException
public final void          writeInt(int v)
                                        throws IOException
public final void          writeLong(long v)
                                        throws IOException
public final void          writeFloat(float v)
                                        throws IOException
public final void          writeDouble(double v)
                                        throws IOException
public final void          writeBytes(String s)
                                        throws IOException
public final void          writeChars(String s)
                                        throws IOException
public final void          writeUTF(String str)
                                        throws IOException
```

Class Reader

```
public abstract class Reader
                        extends Object
```

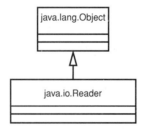

The Reader class is the abstract superclass of all the character-oriented input stream classes, or readers. It provides the minimum set of methods, similar to what the InputStream class defines for byte-oriented input streams, for character data.

Fields

```
protected Object      lock
```

Constructors

```
protected      Reader()
protected      Reader(Object lock)
```

Methods

```
public int              read()
                            throws IOException
public int              read(char[] cbuf)
                            throws IOException
public abstract int     read(char[] cbuf, int off, int len)
                            throws IOException
public long             skip(long n)
                            throws IOException
public boolean          ready()
                            throws IOException
public boolean          markSupported()
public void             mark(int readAheadLimit)
                            throws IOException
public void             reset()
                            throws IOException
public abstract void    close()
                            throws IOException
```

Class SequenceInputStream

```
public class SequenceInputStream
            extends InputStream
```

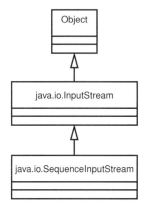

A SequenceInputStream object provides the capability to read multiple streams as one stream, in order of their specification.

Constructors

```
public    SequenceInputStream(Enumeration e)
public    SequenceInputStream(InputStream s1, InputStream s2)
```

Methods

```
public int      available()
                    throws IOException
```

```
public int      read()
                    throws IOException
public int      read(byte[] b, int off, int len)
                    throws IOException
public void     close()
                    throws IOException
```

Class StreamTokenizer

```
public class StreamTokenizer
                extends Object
```

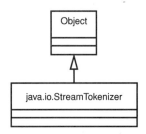

The StreamTokenizer provides a means to read a stream as a series of tokens, read (or rather, returned) one at a time. A file in which fields are separated by colons, for example, could be read one field at a time, using the colon as the divider between tokens.

Fields

```
public int                  ttype
public static final int     TT_EOF
public static final int     TT_EOL
public static final int     TT_NUMBER
public static final int     TT_WORD
public String               sval
public double               nval
```

Constructors

```
public      StreamTokenizer(InputStream is)
public      StreamTokenizer(Reader r)
```

Methods

```
public void     resetSyntax()
public void     wordChars(int low, int hi)
public void     whitespaceChars(int low, int hi)
public void     ordinaryChars(int low, int hi)
public void     ordinaryChar(int ch)
public void     commentChar(int ch)
public void     quoteChar(int ch)
public void     parseNumbers()
public void     eolIsSignificant(boolean flag)
public void     slashStarComments(boolean flag)
```

```
public void     slashSlashComments(boolean flag)
public void     lowerCaseMode(boolean fl)
public int      nextToken()
                    throws IOException
public void     pushBack()
public int      lineno()
public String   toString()
```

Class StringBufferInputStream

```
public class StringBufferInputStream
            extends InputStream
```

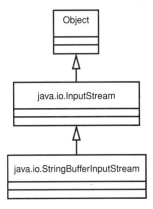

This is a byte-oriented stream which provides for reading data from a String as a stream. Only the lower eight bits of a character are used by this stream class. This entire class is deprecated because of this feature. A StringReader should always be used instead of a StringBufferInputStream.

Fields

```
protected String    buffer
protected int       pos
protected int       count
```

Constructors

```
public      StringBufferInputStream(String s)
```

Methods

```
public int      read()
public int      read(byte[] b, int off, int len)
public long     skip(long n)
public int      available()
public void     reset()
```

Class StringReader

public class **StringReader**
              extends Reader

The `StringReader` class is a character-based stream designed for reading `String`s from an input source.

Constructors
public   **StringReader**(String s)

Methods
```
public int        read()
                      throws IOException
public int        read(char[] cbuf, Int off, int len)
                      throws IOException
public long       skip(long ns)
                      throws IOException
public boolean    ready()
                      throws IOException
public boolean    markSupported()
public void       mark(int readAheadLimit)
                      throws IOException
public void       reset()
                      throws IOException
public void       close()
```

Class StringWriter

public class **StringWriter**
              extends Writer

The `StringWriter` class is a character-based stream that provides for writing characters from a buffer to a `String`.

Interface and Class Details 581

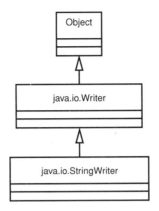

Constructors
```
public      StringWriter()
public      StringWriter(int initialSize)
```

Methods
```
public void             write(int c)
public void             write(char[] cbuf, int off, int len)
public void             write(String str)
public void             write(String str, int off, int len)
public String           toString()
public StringBuffer     getBuffer()
public void             flush()
public void             close()
                            throws IOException
```

Class Writer

```
public abstract class Writer
                        extends Object
```

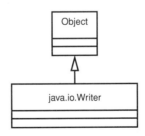

The Writer class is the abstract base class for all other Writer, or character-oriented streams.

Fields
```
protected Object     lock
```

Constructors

```
protected     Writer()
protected     Writer(Object lock)
```

Methods

```
public void              write(int c)
                             throws IOException
public void              write(char[] cbuf)
                             throws IOException
public abstract void     write(char[] cbuf, int off, int len)
                             throws IOException
public void              write(String str)
                             throws IOException
public void              write(String str, int off, Int len)
                             throws IOException
public abstract void     flush()
                             throws IOException
public abstract void     close()
                             throws IOException
```

CHAPTER 24

java.lang

This chapter provides a quick reference for the interfaces, classes, and methods in java.lang. This is the core package in the Java 2 SDK, and it defines the basic pieces that all other classes depend on, whether they are part of the Java 2 SDK, or user-defined classes. This package has many classes and interfaces which are used frequently, such as String, Class, Thread, Exception, and System. The System class is the basic class for console output. To use it, type

```
System.out.println(some primitive or object);
```

The class Class is used to interrogate other classes and to help load classes dynamically into memory (for example, a JDBC driver). The String class is used to represent character strings. The System class provides several useful methods, such as arraycopy(), provides access to the Runtime object, and defines standard in, standard out, and standard err. The class Object is the base class of all other classes and objects in Java, including arrays.

Interfaces

Cloneable
Comparable
Runnable

Classes

Boolean
Byte
Character
Character.Subset
Character.UnicodeBlock
Class
ClassLoader
Compiler

Double
Float
InheritableThreadLocal
Integer
Long
Math
Number
Object
Package
Process
Runtime
RuntimePermission
SecurityManager
Short
String
StringBuffer
System
Thread
ThreadGroup
ThreadLocal
Throwable
Void

Exceptions

ArithmeticException
ArrayIndexOutOfBoundsException
ArrayStoreException
ClassCastException
ClassNotFoundException
CloneNotSupportedException
Exception
IllegalAccessException
IllegalArgumentException
IllegalMonitorStateException
IllegalStateException
IllegalThreadStateException
IndexOutOfBoundsException
InstantiationException
InterruptedException
NegativeArraySizeException
NoSuchFieldException
NoSuchMethodException
NullPointerException
NumberFormatException
RuntimeException
SecurityException
StringIndexOutOfBoundsException
UnsupportedOperationException

Errors
```
AbstractMethodError
ClassCircularityError
ClassFormatError
Error
ExceptionInInitializerError
IllegalAccessError
IncompatibleClassChangeError
InstantiationError
InternalError
LinkageError
NoClassDefFoundError
NoSuchFieldError
NoSuchMethodError
OutOfMemoryError
StackOverflowError
ThreadDeath
UnknownError
UnsatisfiedLinkError
UnsupportedClassVersionError
VerifyError
VirtualMachineError
```

Interface and Class Details

Interface Cloneable
`public abstract interface Cloneable`

This interface is used to indicate that the class can have its instances cloned. The clone() method, inherited from Object, is valid, although typically a user-defined class will need to define its own version of clone() to provide the behavior desired for copying an entire object with a deep copy. A deep copy is the process of copying all the fields of all the dependent objects of a given object being copied. If you have a class that contains a GregorianCalendar object, a deep copy would copy the object, instantiate a new GregorianCalendar object for the copied object, and copy all the fields from the GregorianCalendar object that is being copied. In general, if an object has no clone() method defined that does a deep copy, the JVM does a shallow copy, copying object references and not actually copying dependent objects contained within the cloned object. If you attempt to clone() an object whose class does not implement Cloneable, you will receive a CloneNotSupportedException. This interface has no methods.

Interface Comparable
`public abstract interface Comparable`

This interface is used to order objects based on the class's natural order, which is generally ascending order. It shows up most visibly in the Collection framework classes in java.util, but it is valid for any class to implement this method. The class is then required to implement a `compareTo()` method, which compares objects based on the natural order of the class. Lists and other `Collection` implementations can use the `Comparable` interface for sorting through the `Collections.sort()` method.

Methods
int   **compareTo** (Object o)

Interface Runnable
public abstract interface **Runnable**

This interface is used for multithreading. Implementers of this interface provide a `run()` method, which is then used by a thread. The only code a thread will run is one coded in a `run()` method. A common place to see this interface implemented is in an Applet. The Applet provides a `run()` method so that the Applet can use `MediaTracker` to monitor the downloading of images in a separate thread of execution. In this way, the GUI part of the Applet can continue functioning while image downloading is taking place. Any Applet that needs to download several images should use this technique in order to get the user interface painted and functioning as soon as possible.

Methods
void   **run**()

Class Boolean
public final class **Boolean**
                extends Object
                implements Serializable

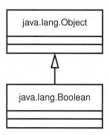

This is a wrapper class for `boolean` primitives. It is useful for passing a `boolean` primitive as a parameter to a method that accepts only an instance of `Object` or a subclass of `Object`, such as the methods of `Vector`.

Fields
static Boolean **FALSE**
static Boolean **TRUE**
static Class   **TYPE**

Constructors
Boolean(boolean value)
Boolean(String s)

Methods
boolean	booleanValue()
boolean	equals(Object obj)
static boolean	getBoolean(String name)
int	hashCode()
String	toString()
static Boolean	valueOf(String s)

Class Byte
public final class **Byte**
                extends Number
                implements Comparable

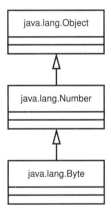

This is a wrapper class for byte primitives. It is useful for passing a byte primitive as a parameter to a method that accepts only an instance of Object or a subclass of Object, such as the methods of Vector.

Fields
static byte	MAX_VALUE
static byte	MIN_VALUE
static Class	TYPE
static byte	MAX_VALUE
static byte	MIN_VALUE
static Class	TYPE

Constructors
Byte(byte value)
Byte(String s)

Methods

byte	**byteValue**()
int	**compareTo**(Byte anotherByte)
int	**compareTo**(Object o)
static Byte	**decode**(String nm)
double	**doubleValue**()
boolean	**equals**(Object obj)
float	**floatValue**()
int	**hashCode**()
int	**intValue**()
long	**longValue**()
static byte	**parseByte**(String s)
static byte	**parseByte**(String s, int radix)
short	**shortValue**()
String	**toString**()
static String	**toString**(byte b)
static Byte	**valueOf**(String s)
static Byte	**valueOf**(String s, int radix)

Class Character

public final class **Character**
                    extends Object
                    implements Serializable, Comparable

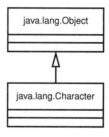

The Character class provides a wrapper class for char primitives. It is useful for passing a char primitive as a parameter to a method that accepts only an instance of Object or a subclass of Object, such as the methods of Vector.

> **NOTE**
>
> The character attribute tables for specific versions of Unicode are available at
>
> ftp://ftp.unicode.org/Public/

Fields

static byte	**COMBINING_SPACING_MARK**
static byte	**CONNECTOR_PUNCTUATION**
static byte	**CONTROL**
static byte	**CURRENCY_SYMBOL**

static byte	DASH_PUNCTUATION
static byte	DECIMAL_DIGIT_NUMBER
static byte	ENCLOSING_MARK
static byte	END_PUNCTUATION
static byte	FORMAT
static byte	LETTER_NUMBER
static byte	LINE_SEPARATOR
static byte	LOWERCASE_LETTER
static byte	MATH_SYMBOL
static int	MAX_RADIX
static char	MAX_VALUE
static int	MIN_RADIX
static char	MIN_VALUE
static byte	MODIFIER_LETTER
static byte	MODIFIER_SYMBOL
static byte	NON_SPACING_MARK
static byte	OTHER_LETTER
static byte	OTHER_NUMBER
static byte	OTHER_PUNCTUATION
static byte	OTHER_SYMBOL
static byte	PARAGRAPH_SEPARATOR
static byte	PRIVATE_USE
static byte	SPACE_SEPARATOR
static byte	START_PUNCTUATION
static byte	SURROGATE
static byte	TITLECASE_LETTER
static Class	TYPE
static byte	UNASSIGNED
static byte	UPPERCASE_LETTER

Constructors

Character (char value)

Methods

char	**charValue**()
int	**compareTo**(Character anotherCharacter)
int	**compareTo**(Object o)
static int	**digit**(char ch, int radix)
boolean	**equals**(Object obj)
static char	**forDigit**(int digit, int radix)
static int	**getNumericValue**(char ch)
static int	**getType**(char ch)
int	**hashCode**()
static boolean	**isDefined**(char ch)
static boolean	**isDigit**(char ch)
static boolean	**isIdentifierIgnorable**(char ch)
static boolean	**isISOControl**(char ch)
static boolean	**isJavaIdentifierPart**(char ch)
static boolean	**isJavaIdentifierStart**(char ch)
static boolean	**isJavaLetter**(char ch) (deprecated)

```
static boolean      isJavaLetterOrDigit(char ch) (deprecated)
static boolean      isLetter(char ch)
static boolean      isLetterOrDigit(char ch)
static boolean      isLowerCase(char ch)
static boolean      isSpace(char ch) (deprecated)
static boolean      isSpaceChar(char ch)
static boolean      isTitleCase(char ch)
static boolean      isUnicodeIdentifierPart(char ch)
static boolean      isUnicodeIdentifierStart(char ch)
static boolean      isUpperCase(char ch)
static boolean      isWhitespace(char ch)
static char         toLowerCase(char ch)
String              toString()
static char         toTitleCase(char ch)
static char         toUpperCase(char ch)
```

Class Class

```
public final class Class
                extends Object
                implements Serializable
```

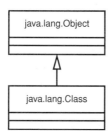

The class Class can be used to provide information about an object or class definition. It can also be used to dynamically load a class using the forName() method in this way:

```
Class.forName("Myjdbcdriver");
```

You can also get information using this class. For example, here is how to get the name of another class:

```
String className = anObject.getClass().getName();
```

Class Class provides numerous methods used in reflection for interrogating an object or class definition for fields, modifiers, constructors, and methods.

Methods

```
static Class        forName(String className)
static Class        forName(String name, boolean initialize,
                        ClassLoader loader)
Class[]             getClasses()
ClassLoader         getClassLoader()
```

Class	getComponentType()
Constructor	getConstructor(Class[] parameterTypes)
Constructor[]	getConstructors()
Class[]	getDeclaredClasses()
Constructor	getDeclaredConstructor(Class[] parameterTypes)
Constructor[]	getDeclaredConstructors()
Field	getDeclaredField(String name)
Field[]	getDeclaredFields()
Method	getDeclaredMethod(String name, Class[] parameterTypes)
Method[]	getDeclaredMethods()
Class	getDeclaringClass()
Field	getField(String name)
Field[]	getFields()
Class[]	getInterfaces()
Method	getMethod(String name, Class[] parameterTypes)
Method[]	getMethods()
int	getModifiers()
String	getName()
Package	getPackage()
ProtectionDomain	getProtectionDomain()
URL	getResource(String name)
InputStream	getResourceAsStream(String name)
Object[]	getSigners()
Class	getSuperclass()
boolean	isArray()
boolean	isAssignableFrom(Class cls)
boolean	isInstance(Object obj)
boolean	isInterface()
boolean	isPrimitive()
Object	newInstance()
String	toString()

Class ClassLoader

public abstract class **ClassLoader**
                 extends Object

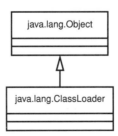

ClassLoader is the abstract base class for all class loaders, both those defined in the Java 2 SDK and custom, user-defined class loaders. The purpose of a custom class loader is to help control the loading of classes. It is used when your application requires help in addition to that offered by the facilities defined in the primordial class loader. Most applications do not need a custom class loader. It is needed less often in Java 2 than it is in previous Java versions, in part due to the Extension mechanism.

Constructors
```
protected      ClassLoader()
protected      ClassLoader(ClassLoader parent)
```

Methods
```
protected Class        defineClass(byte[] b, int off, int len) (deprecated)
protected Class        defineClass(String name, byte[] b, int off, int len)
protected Class        defineClass(String name, byte[] b, int off, int len,
                           ProtectionDomain protectionDomain)
protected Package      definePackage(String name, String specTitle,
                           String specVersion, String specVendor,
                           String implTitle, String implVersion,
                           String implVendor, URL sealBase)
protected Class        findClass(String name)
protected String       findLibrary(String libname)
protected Class        findLoadedClass(String name)
protected URL          findResource(String name)
protected Enumeration  findResources(String name)
protected Class        findSystemClass(String name)
protected Package      getPackage(String name)
protected Package[]    getPackages()
ClassLoader            getParent()
URL                    getResource(String name)
InputStream            getResourceAsStream(String name)
Enumeration            getResources(String name)
static ClassLoader     getSystemClassLoader()
static URL             getSystemResource(String name)
static InputStream     getSystemResourceAsStream(String name)
static Enumeration     getSystemResources(String name)
Class                  loadClass(String name)
protected Class        loadClass(String name, boolean resolve)
protected void         resolveClass(Class c)
protected void         setSigners(Class c, Object[] signers)
```

Class Compiler
```
public final class Compiler
                  extends Object
```

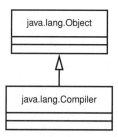

The Compiler class does nothing but serve as a placeholder for Java to native code compilers, such as a JIT (just-in-time) compiler.

Methods

```
static Object    command(Object any)
static boolean   compileClass(Class clazz)
static boolean   compileClasses(String string)
static void      disable()
static void      enable()
```

Class Double

```
public final class Double
                    extends Number
                    implements Comparable
```

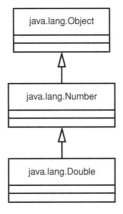

The Double class is a wrapper for double primitives. It is useful for passing a double primitive as a parameter to a method that accepts only an instance of Object or a subclass of Object, such as the methods of Vector.

Fields

```
static double    MAX_VALUE
static double    MIN_VALUE
static double    NaN
static double    NEGATIVE_INFINITY
static double    POSITIVE_INFINITY
static Class     TYPE
```

Constructors

```
Double(double value)
Double(String s)
```

Methods

byte	**byteValue**()
int	**compareTo**(Double anotherDouble)
int	**compareTo**(Object o)
static long	**doubleToLongBits**(double value)
double	**doubleValue**()
boolean	**equals**(Object obj)
float	**floatValue**()
int	**hashCode**()
int	**intValue**()
boolean	**isInfinite**()
static boolean	**isInfinite**(double v)
boolean	**isNaN**()
static boolean	**isNaN**(double v)
static double	**longBitsToDouble**(long bits)
long	**longValue**()
static double	**parseDouble**(String s)
short	**shortValue**()
String	**toString**()
static String	**toString**(double d)
static Double	**valueOf**(String s)

Class Float

public final class **Float**
                extends Number
                implements Comparable

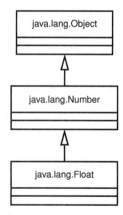

The Float class is a wrapper class for float primitives. It is useful for passing a byte primitive as a parameter to a method that accepts only an instance of Object or a subclass of Object, such as the methods of Vector. The Float class also provides methods which are useful for converting command-line or GUI input from string data that represents floating point data into a float primitive.

Fields

static float	**MAX_VALUE**
static float	**MIN_VALUE**
static float	**NaN**
static float	**NEGATIVE_INFINITY**
static float	**POSITIVE_INFINITY**
static Class	**TYPE**

Constructors

Float(double value)
Float(float value)
Float(String s)

Methods

byte	**byteValue**()
int	**compareTo**(Float anotherFloat)
int	**compareTo**(Object o)
double	**doubleValue**()
boolean	**equals**(Object obj)
static int	**floatToIntBits**(float value)
float	**floatValue**()
int	**hashCode**()
static float	**intBitsToFloat**(int bits)
int	**intValue**()
boolean	**isInfinite**()
static boolean	**isInfinite**(float v)
boolean	**isNaN**()
static boolean	**isNaN**(float v)
long	**longValue**()
static float	**parseFloat**(String s)
short	**shortValue**()
String	**toString**()
static String	**toString**(float f)
static Float	**valueOf**(String s)

Class Integer

```
public final class Integer
                extends Number
                implements Comparable
```

The Integer class is a wrapper class for int primitives. Note that, unlike other wrapper classes, the name of this class does not match the name of the primitive data type. It is useful for passing an int primitive as a parameter to a method that accepts only an instance of Object or a subclass of Object, such as the methods of Vector.

596 Chapter 24: java.lang

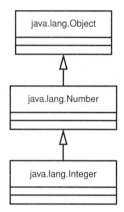

The `Integer` class and other wrapper classes also are used for data conversion. When a user types data into a `TextField`, for example, the `getText()` method retrieves the data as a `String`. If the value is supposed to be numeric, maybe an `int` for some value or a `float` for money, you need to convert it. To convert the `String` to an `int`, you can code

```
int value = Integer.parseInt(textfld.getText());
```

This will convert the `String` in the `TextField` into an `int` called `value`.

Fields

```
static int        MAX_VALUE
static int        MIN_VALUE
static Class      TYPE
```

Constructors

```
Integer(int value)
Integer(String s)
```

Methods

```
byte              byteValue()
int               compareTo(Integer anotherInteger)
int               compareTo(Object o)
static Integer    decode(String nm)
double            doubleValue()
boolean           equals(Object obj)
float             floatValue()
static Integer    getInteger(String nm)
static Integer    getInteger(String nm, int val)
static Integer    getInteger(String nm, Integer val)
int               hashCode()
```

int	**intValue**()
long	**longValue**()
static int	**parseInt**(String s)
static int	**parseInt**(String s, int radix)
short	**shortValue**()
static String	**toBinaryString**(int i)
static String	**toHexString**(int i)
static String	**toOctalString**(int i)
String	**toString**()
static String	**toString**(int i)
static String	**toString**(int i, int radix)
static Integer	**valueOf**(String s)
static Integer	**valueOf**(String s, int radix)

Class Long

```
public final class Long
                    extends Number
                    implements Comparable
```

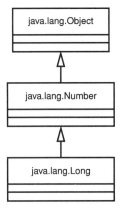

The Long class provides a wrapper class for long primitives. It is useful for passing a long primitive as a parameter to a method that accepts only an instance of Object or a subclass of Object, such as the methods of Vector.

Fields
static long	**MAX_VALUE**
static long	**MIN_VALUE**
static Class	**TYPE**

Constructors
Long (long value)
Long(String s)

Methods
byte	**byteValue**()
int	**compareTo**(Long anotherLong)

```
int          compareTo(Object o)
static Long  decode(String nm)
double       doubleValue()
boolean      equals(Object obj)
float        floatValue()
static Long  getLong(String nm)
static Long  getLong(String nm, long val)
static Long  getLong(String nm, Long val)
int          hashCode()
int          intValue()
long         longValue()
static long  parseLong(String s)
static long  parseLong(String s, int radix)
short        shortValue()
static String toBinaryString(long i)
static String toHexString(long i)
static String toOctalString(long i)
String       toString()
static String toString(long i)
static String toString(long i, int radix)
static Long  valueOf(String s)
static Long  valueOf(String s, int radix)
```

Class Math

```
public final class Math
                 extends Object
```

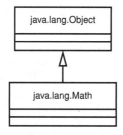

The Math class provides several functions for doing mathematical calculations, such as min, max, absolute value, square root, sine, cosines, and the like. Most of these methods are static. Static methods are used because you do not really want to create an instance of this class. You simply want to put a value into a formula and get a result back. Therefore, the Math class provides methods that act as mathematical functions to call with a value and from which you get a value back.

Fields

```
static double  E
static double  PI
```

Methods

```
static double    abs(double a)
static float     abs(float a)
static int       abs(int a)
static long      abs(long a)
static double    acos(double a)
static double    asin(double a)
static double    atan(double a)
static double    atan2(double a, double b)
static double    ceil(double a)
static double    cos(double a)
static double    exp(double a)
static double    floor(double a)
static double    IEEEremainder(double f1, double f2)
static double    log(double a)
static double    max(double a, double b)
static float     max(float a, float b)
static int       max(int a, int b)
static long      max(long a, long b)
static double    min(double a, double b)
static float     min(float a, float b)
static int       min(int a, int b)
static long      min(long a, long b)
static double    pow(double a, double b)
static double    random()
static double    rint(double a)
static long      round(double a)
static int       round(float a)
static double    sin(double a)
static double    sqrt(double a)
static double    tan(double a)
static double    toDegrees(double angrad)
static double    toRadians(double angdeg)
```

Class Object

public class **Object**

```
java.lang.Object
```

Object is the base class of all classes in Java, both those in the Java 2 SDK and all user-defined classes. Having Object at the top of all class hierarchies allows for flexible coding like this:

```
public boolean doSomething(Object obj)
{
if(obj instanceof someClass)
```

    {
        // Do something appropriate.
    }
}

This method can take an object of any class. Inside the method, if it matters, you can determine the exact class type. If the exact type doesn't matter, you just use the `obj` parameter as is. This makes for much more flexible code that will be much easier to use than code with separate methods for every data type in your program.

This class also provides many methods used by all other classes, such as `wait()` and `notify()`, used in multithreaded programs, and `equals()` to compare two objects.

Constructors
Object ()

Methods

protected Object	clone()
boolean	equals(Object obj)
protected void	finalize()
Class	getClass()
int	hashCode()
void	notify()
void	notifyAll()
String	toString()
void	wait()
void	wait(long timeout)
void	wait(long timeout, int nanos)

Class Runtime
public class **Runtime**
          extends Object

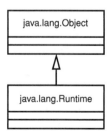

A Runtime object represents the runtime environment of your program. You can use the Runtime object, but it is a singleton, and you cannot make your own instance of it. You can call `getRuntime()` to get the Runtime object. You can use the object for calling the methods of this class, such as

Runtime.getRuntime().gc()

which is a request to run garbage collection. Note that this is a request. Garbage collection runs as a low priority thread. If and when the CPU is idle, the Garbage Collector might run. Garbage collection also takes place when there is no more memory available in the JVM.

You can also query the environment like this:

```
Runtime.getRuntime().totalMemory();
```

This returns total memory. Another useful, but a platform-dependent method is exec(). You can use this to run a command or program on the same system. Windows users should note that you cannot simply say

```
Runtime.getRuntime().exec("dir");
```

Instead, you must do an exec() on Command.com and pass it a parameter that is the command you want to execute.

Methods

Process	**exec**(String command)
Process	**exec**(String[] cmdarray)
Process	**exec**(String[] cmdarray, String[] envp)
Process	**exec**(String command, String[] envp)
void	**exit**(int status)
long	**freeMemory**()
void	**gc**()
InputStream	**getLocalizedInputStream**(InputStream in) (deprecated)
OutputStream	**getLocalizedOutputStream**(OutputStream out) (deprecated)
static Runtime	**getRuntime**()
void	**load**(String filename)
void	**loadLibrary**(String libname)
void	**runFinalization**()
static void	**runFinalizersOnExit**(boolean value) (deprecated)
long	**totalMemory**()
void	**traceInstructions**(boolean on)
void	**traceMethodCalls**(boolean on)

Class RuntimePermission

```
public final class RuntimePermission
                extends BasicPermission
```

The RuntimePermission class represents permissions granted to your program, usually in a policy file. A RuntimePermission contains a category, such as FilePermission, and a target name, which might be a file or an absolute path to a file specified as a URL. It might also represent all files. The target name is tied to the type or category of permission. You can grant permission of type RuntimePermission or other permission classes, such as ReflectionPermission, in a policy file The default permissions available in Java 2 can be seen in the policytool.

602 Chapter 24: java.lang

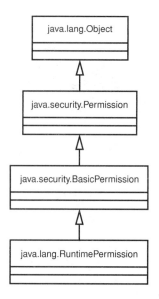

Constructors

`RuntimePermission`(String name)
`RuntimePermission`(String name, String actions)

Class SecurityManager

```
public class SecurityManager
                extends Object
```

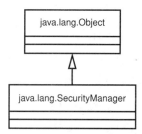

The `SecurityManager` class is the base class for program security. By default, Java only grants permissions that have been specifically given. Browsers generally instantiate a `SecurityManager` object, which does not allow Applets to read or write to the client system, change `ThreadGroup` properties, read certain system properties, or connect to a host besides the one it came from. Applications generally (with the notable exception of RMI) do not run with a `SecurityManager` installed in memory. After a `SecurityManager` object is instantiated in a JVM, it cannot be replaced. In Java 2, the behavior of the `SecurityManager` has changed, so that now, when a given operation such as creating a `FileInputStream` is requested, the `SecurityManager` object (or an instance of a subclass instance) checks the permissions granted to that code to decide if the operation will be allowed.

Interface and Class Details 603

> **NOTE**
>
> For more information about `SecurityManager` changes made in Java 2 and advice regarding porting of 1.1-style security managers, see the release documentation at
>
> java.sun.com/products/jdk/1.2/docs/guide/security/index.html

Fields

```
protected boolean       inCheck (deprecated)
```

Constructors

```
SecurityManager ()
```

Methods

```
void                checkAccept(String host, int port)
void                checkAccess(Thread t)
void                checkAccess(ThreadGroup g)
void                checkAwtEventQueueAccess()
void                checkConnect(String host, int port)
void                checkConnect(String host, int port, Object context)
void                checkCreateClassLoader()
void                checkDelete(String file)
void                checkExec(String cmd)
void                checkExit(int status)
void                checkLink(String lib)
void                checkListen(int port)
void                checkMemberAccess(Class clazz, int which)
void                checkMulticast(InetAddress maddr)
void                checkMulticast(InetAddress maddr, byte ttl)
void                checkPackageAccess(String pkg)
void                checkPackageDefinition(String pkg)
void                checkPermission(Permission perm)
void                checkPermission(Permission perm, Object context)
void                checkPrintJobAccess()
void                checkPropertiesAccess()
void                checkPropertyAccess(String key)
void                checkRead(FileDescriptor fd)
void                checkRead(String file)
void                checkRead(String file, Object context)
void                checkSecurityAccess(String target)
void                checkSetFactory()
void                checkSystemClipboardAccess()
boolean             checkTopLevelWindow(Object window)
void                checkWrite(FileDescriptor fd)
void                checkWrite(String file)
protected int       classDepth(String name) (deprecated
protected int       classLoaderDepth() (deprecated)
protected ClassLoader  currentClassLoader() (deprecated)
protected Class     currentLoadedClass() (deprecated)
```

```
protected Class[]      getClassContext()
boolean                getInCheck() (deprecated)
Object                 getSecurityContext()
ThreadGroup            getThreadGroup()
protected boolean      inClass(String name) (deprecated)
protected boolean      inClassLoader() (deprecated)
```

Class Short

```
public final class Short
                    extends Number
                    implements Comparable
```

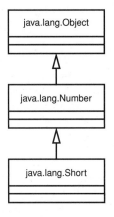

The Short class is a wrapper class for short primitives. This is useful for passing a short primitive to a method, such as the methods of a Vector, which only take instances of classes, not primitives.

Fields

```
static short    MAX_VALUE
static short    MIN_VALUE
static Class    TYPE
```

Constructors

Short(short value)
Short(String s)

Methods

```
byte            byteValue()
int             compareTo(Object o)
int             compareTo(Short anotherShort)
static Short    decode(String nm)
double          doubleValue()
boolean         equals(Object obj)
float           floatValue()
```

```
int             hashCode()
int             intValue()
long            longValue()
static short    parseShort(String s)
static short    parseShort(String s, int radix)
short           shortValue
String          toString()
static String   toString(short s)
static Short    valueOf(String s)
static Short    valueOf(String s, int radix)
```

Class String

```
public final class String
                extends Object
                implements Serializable, Comparable
```

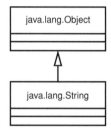

The String class represents a character string. There are several methods to convert other kinds of data, such as a byte array, into a String. Strings live in two places, depending upon how they are created:

- The String literal pool
- The heap

If you create a String like this:

```
String author1 = "Lewis, C.S.";
```

the String is placed in the String literal pool. If you create a String like this:

```
String author2 = new String("Lewis, C.S.");
```

this String is placed in the heap. This distinction is important because this code

```
if(author1 == author2)
```

will return false. In contrast,

```
if(author1.equalsIgnoreCase(author2))
```

returns true. The first tests for the equality of object references. The equals() method or equalsIgnoreCase, however, tests for equality of String contents. If you code this:

```
String author3 = "Lewis, C.S.";
if(author2 == author3)
```

it will return true. When a String needs to be put in the String literal pool, Java first checks to see if it is already there. If it is, the object reference is simply returned—in this case easily to author3. If it is not, a duplicate copy is placed in the String literal pool. You can create duplicate Strings with the new String() approach, however, because new causes separate memory to be allocated for the String.

The memory used for a String is special. A String, once defined, cannot be changed directly. If you attempt to change a String, such as concatenating to it, Java in fact creates a new buffer, copies the String into it, and adds the piece you are concatenating. The original String's memory area is then discarded. This plugs several security holes so that no one can dynamically change the contents of a String by merely manipulating memory. The definition of String is also *final*. You cannot override or subclass the class to change this immutability.

Fields

```
static Comparator     CASE_INSENSITIVE_ORDER
```

Constructors

```
String()
String(byte[] bytes)
String(byte[] ascii, int hibyte) (deprecated)
String(byte[] bytes, int offset, int length)
String(byte[] ascii, int hibyte, int offset, int count) (deprecated)
String(byte[] bytes, int offset, int length, String enc)
String(byte[] bytes, String enc)
String(char[] value)
String(char[] value, int offset, int count)
String(String value)
String(StringBuffer buffer)
```

Methods

```
char              charAt(int index)
int               compareTo(Object o)
int               compareTo(String anotherString)
int               compareToIgnoreCase(String str)
String            concat(String str)
static String     copyValueOf(char[] data)
static String     copyValueOf(char[] data, int offset, int count)
boolean           endsWith(String suffix)
boolean           equals(Object anObject)
boolean           equalsIgnoreCase(String anotherString)
byte[]            getBytes()
void              getBytes(int srcBegin, int srcEnd, byte[] dst, int dstBegin)
                      (deprecated)
byte[]            getBytes(String enc)
void              getChars(int srcBegin, int srcEnd, char[] dst, int dstBegin)
int               hashCode()
int               indexOf(int ch)
int               indexOf(int ch, int fromIndex)
```

```
int             indexOf(String str)
int             indexOf(String str, int fromIndex)
String          intern()
int             lastIndexOf(int ch)
int             lastIndexOf(int ch, int fromIndex)
int             lastIndexOf(String str)
int             lastIndexOf(String str, int fromIndex)
int             length()
boolean         regionMatches(boolean ignoreCase, int toffset, String other, int
                    offset, int len)
boolean         regionMatches(int toffset, String other, int ooffset, int len)
String          replace(char oldChar, char newChar)
boolean         startsWith(String prefix)
boolean         startsWith(String prefix, int toffset)
String          substring(int beginIndex)
String          substring(int beginIndex, int endIndex)
char[]          toCharArray()
String          toLowerCase()
String          toLowerCase(Locale locale)
String          toString()
String          toUpperCase()
String          toUpperCase(Locale locale)
String          trim()
static String   valueOf(boolean b)
static String   valueOf(char c)
static String   valueOf(char[] data)
static String   valueOf(char[] data, int offset, int count)
static String   valueOf(double d)
static String   valueOf(float f)
static String   valueOf(int i)
static String   valueOf(long l)
static String   valueOf(Object obj)
```

Class StringBuffer

```
public final class StringBuffer
                    extends Object
                    implements Serializable
```

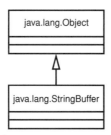

A `String` is an immutable, first-degree object. In fact, when you try to change it, Java creates a new area in memory to create the new version. A `StringBuffer` object, on the other hand, is mutable and allows you to change its contents in place. Therefore, if your program needs to do lots of `String` manipulation, as a word processing program might, you should use `StringBuffers` rather than `Strings` to save memory.

Constructors

StringBuffer()
StringBuffer(int length)
StringBuffer(String str)

Methods

StringBuffer	**append**(boolean b)
StringBuffer	**append**(char c)
StringBuffer	**append**(char[] str)
StringBuffer	**append**(char[] str, int offset, int len)
StringBuffer	**append**(double d)
StringBuffer	**append**(float f)
StringBuffer	**append**(int i)
StringBuffer	**append**(long l)
StringBuffer	**append**(Object obj)
StringBuffer	**append**(String str)
int	**capacity**()
char	**charAt**(int index)
StringBuffer	**delete**(int start, int end)
StringBuffer	**deleteCharAt**(int index)
void	**ensureCapacity**(int minimumCapacity)
void	**getChars**(int srcBegin, int srcEnd, char[] dst, int dstBegin)
StringBuffer	**insert**(int offset, boolean b)
StringBuffer	**insert**(int offset, char c)
StringBuffer	**insert**(int offset, char[] str)
StringBuffer	**insert**(int index, char[] str, int offset, int len)
StringBuffer	**insert**(int offset, double d)
StringBuffer	**insert**(int offset, float f)
StringBuffer	**insert**(int offset, int i)
StringBuffer	**insert**(int offset, long l)
StringBuffer	**insert**(int offset, Object obj)
StringBuffer	**insert**(int offset, String str)
int	**length**()
StringBuffer	**replace**(int start, int end, String str)
StringBuffer	**reverse**()
void	**setCharAt**(int index, char ch)
void	**setLength**(int newLength)
String	**substring**(int start)
String	**substring**(int start, int end)
String	**toString**()

Class System

public final class **System**
                    extends Object

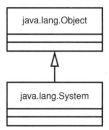

The System class is a singleton that provides several useful methods. It defines standard in, out and err. It allows you to get system properties, with getProperty() or getProperties(). It allows you to copy arrays with arraycopy(). It provides a means to get the system Runtime object.

Fields

static PrintStream	err
static InputStream	in
static PrintStream	out

Methods

static void	**arraycopy**(Object src, int src_position, Object dst, int dst_position, int length)
static long	**currentTimeMillis**()
static void	**exit**(int status)
static void	**gc**()
static String	**getenv**(String name) (deprecated)
static Properties	**getProperties**()
static String	**getProperty**(String key)
static String	**getProperty**(String key, String def)
static SecurityManager	**getSecurityManager**()
static int	**identityHashCode**(Object x)
static void	**load**(String filename)
static void	**loadLibrary**(String libname)
static String	**mapLibraryName**(String libname)
static void	**runFinalization**()
static void	**runFinalizersOnExit**(boolean value) (deprecated)
static void	**setErr**(PrintStream err)
static void	**setIn**(InputStream in)
static void	**setOut**(PrintStream out)
static void	**setProperties**(Properties props)
static String	**setProperty**(String key, String value)
static void	**setSecurityManager**(SecurityManager s)

Class Thread

public class **Thread**
              extends Object
              implements Runnable

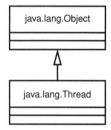

A Thread is a unit of work or execution context. It is used for accomplishing multiple tasks at one time. A Thread is not serializable. This makes sense, because you cannot use its context to set the environment from an object. A Thread has four states:

- Initialized, accomplished with a constructor
- Runnable, accomplished with start()—The start() method makes the Thread ready to execute, but the Thread is put into a queue, where it awaits its turn at the CPU. The started Thread will execute when the JVM or CPU schedules the Thread to run.
- Nonrunnable, accomplished with wait(), join(), suspend(), or yield()—A nonrunnable Thread can be made runnable again.
- Dead, accomplished with stop() or by completing its run() method—A dead Thread cannot be started or made runnable again.

Threads always run the code in a run() method defined in a class that implements the Runnable interface. This is the only way to create code that a Thread will execute, even if the run() method calls other methods.

Fields

static int   **MAX_PRIORITY**
static int   **MIN_PRIORITY**
static int   **NORM_PRIORITY**

Constructors

Thread()
Thread(Runnable target)
Thread(Runnable target, String name)
Thread(String name)
Thread(ThreadGroup group, Runnable target)
Thread(ThreadGroup group, Runnable target, String name)
Thread(ThreadGroup group, String name)

Methods

static int	**activeCount**()
void	**checkAccess**()
int	**countStackFrames**() (deprecated)
static Thread	**currentThread**()
void	**destroy**()
static void	**dumpStack**()
static int	**enumerate**(Thread[] tarray)
ClassLoader	**getContextClassLoader**()
String	**getName**()
int	**getPriority**()
ThreadGroup	**getThreadGroup**()
void	**interrupt**()
static boolean	**interrupted**()
boolean	**isAlive**()
boolean	**isDaemon**()
boolean	**isInterrupted**()
void	**join**()
void	**join**(long millis)
void	**join**(long millis, int nanos)
void	**resume**() (deprecated)
void	**run**()
void	**setContextClassLoader**(ClassLoader cl)
void	**setDaemon**(boolean on)
void	**setName**(String name)
void	**setPriority**(int newPriority)
static void	**sleep**(long millis)
static void	**sleep**(long millis, int nanos)
void	**start**()
void	**stop**() (deprecated)
void	**stop**(Throwable obj) (deprecated)
void	**suspend**() (deprecated)
String	**toString**()
static void	**yield**()

Class ThreadGroup

public class **ThreadGroup**
          extends Object

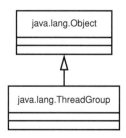

A Thread always runs as part of a ThreadGroup. You can modify several Threads by modifying the properties of the ThreadGroup to which the Threads belong.

Constructors
ThreadGroup(String name)
ThreadGroup(ThreadGroup parent, String name)

Methods

int	**activeCount**()
int	**activeGroupCount**()
boolean	**allowThreadSuspension**(boolean b) (dprecated)
void	**checkAccess**() (deprecated)
void	**destroy**()
int	**enumerate**(Thread[] list)
int	**enumerate**(Thread[] list, boolean recurse)
int	**enumerate**(ThreadGroup[] list)
int	**enumerate**(ThreadGroup[] list, boolean recurse)
int	**getMaxPriority**()
String	**getName**()
ThreadGroup	**getParent**()
void	**interrupt**()
boolean	**isDaemon**()
boolean	**isDestroyed**()
void	**list**()
boolean	**parentOf**(ThreadGroup g)
void	**resume**() (deprecated)
void	**setDaemon**(boolean daemon)
void	**setMaxPriority**(int pri)
void	**stop**() (deprecated)
void	**suspend**() (deprecated)
String	**toString**()
void	**uncaughtException**(Thread t, Throwable e)

Class Throwable

public class **Throwable**
        extends Object
        implements Serializable

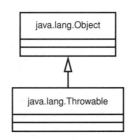

The Throwable class is the base class of all Error and Exception classes. Generally, programs do not deal with the Throwable class directly, but only with its subclasses. Other classes, however, can use the methods inherited from Throwable directly.

Constructors
Throwable()
Throwable(String message)

Methods

Throwable	**fillInStackTrace**()
String	**getLocalizedMessage**()
String	**getMessage**()
void	**printStackTrace**()
void	**printStackTrace**(PrintStream s)
void	**printStackTrace**(PrintWriter s)
String	**toString**()

CHAPTER 25

java.lang.reflect

This chapter provides a quick reference for the interfaces and classes in java.lang.reflect. The application programming interfaces (APIs) in this package are used to determine information about a class for which you have no class definition. Reflection would be most suitable for tools such as class browsers, GUI builders, and debuggers. You can use Reflection to find the name of a class, its fields, interfaces, methods, constructors, arrays, and modifiers. You can also use APIs in this package to execute methods or change the values of the data members of a class. This includes arrays. See Chapter 13, "Reflection," to learn how to use them.

TIP

You may find it more efficient to use the Introspection mechanism in JavaBeans to get the same information. Introspection uses Reflection under the covers.

NOTE

Most normal business applications never need to use these APIs. There are, however, methods in the class Class that are of general usefulness such as forName() and getName(). The first lets you load a class dynamically on demand, and the second lets you get at the object that sent an event, any kind if event. This method is much more general in application than a method such as getActionCommand(), if you want to determine the source of an ActionEvent.

The Reflection APIs were designed principally for Java Beans. Reflection enables a Java IDE, for example, to figure out what the fields and methods of an imported Java Bean class are, and enables a developer to set those fields, called *Properties* in the case of a Bean, through the IDE, even though the IDE has never previously seen the class definition.

Interfaces
Member

Classes
AccessibleObject
Array
Constructor
Field
Method
Modifier
ReflectPermission

Interface and Class Details

Interface Member
public abstract interface **Member**

This interface provides a mechanism for identifying information about a specific field (data member) method or constructor.

Fields
static int **DECLARED**
static int   **PUBLIC**

Methods
Class   **getDeclaringClass()**
int   **getModifiers()**
String   **getName()**

Class AccessibleObject
public class **AccessibleObject**
                extends Object

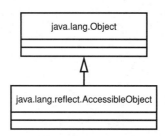

The AccessibleObject class is the base class for the Field, Constructor, and Method classes. It permits a program to set a flag to modify the accessibility of an object's data members, constructors, and methods from the default provided by the access control modifiers (such as package default, protected, and private).

> **CAUTION**
>
> Be aware of what Reflection permits. Unless your class prevents it, my program can inspect and execute methods in your object or modify its data members using Reflection. You should consider, therefore, whether you want to allow or restrict this privilege.

Constructors
```
protected     AccessibleObject()
```

Methods
```
boolean       isAccessible()
static void   setAccessible(AccessibleObject[] array, boolean flag)
void          setAccessible(boolean flag)
```

Class Array
```
public final class Array
                    extends Object
```

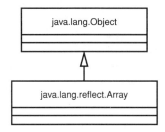

This class provides support for accessing Array information and for dynamically creating arrays.

Methods
```
static Object   get(Object array, int index)
static boolean  getBoolean(Object array, int index)
static byte     getByte(Object array, intI index)
static char     getChar(Object array, int index)
static double   getDouble(Object array, int index)
static float    getFloat(Object array, int index)
static int      getInt(Object array, int I index)
static int      getLength(Object array)
static long     getLong(Object array, int index)
static short    getShort(Object array, int index)
static Object   newInstance(Class componentType, int length)
static Object   newInstance(Class componentType, int[] dimensions)
```

```
static void    set(Object array, int index, Object value)
static void    setBoolean(Object array, int index, boolean z)
static void    setByte(Object array, int index, byte b)
static void    setChar(Object array, int index, char c)
static void    setDouble(Object array, int index, double d)
static void    setFloat(Object array, int index, float f)
static void    setInt(Object array, int index, int i)
static void    setLong(Object array, int index, long l)
static void    setShort(Object array, int index, short s)
```

Class Constructor

```
public final class Constructor
                  extends AccessibleObject
                  implements Member
```

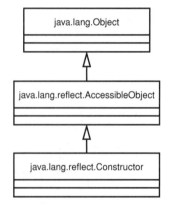

The constructor is used to obtain information about a class's constructor(s) and to call a constructor. The main methods for obtaining the constructors of a class are

```
getConstructors()
getConstructor()
getDeclaredConstructor()
getDeclaredConstructors()
```

They are all found in the class java.lang.Class.

Methods

```
boolean    equals(Object obj)
Class      getDeclaringClass()
Class[]    getExceptionTypes()
int        getModifiers()
String     getName()
Class[]    getParameterTypes()
int        hashCode()
Object     newInstance(Object[] initargs)
String     toString()
```

Class Field

public final class **Field**
                    extends AccessibleObject
                    implements Member

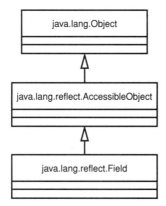

The Field class is used to get the Fields (data members) in a class or interface, and from those Field objects, the modifiers of each field. The values of a Field can also be set through get() and set() methods. A Field is obtained with one of the following methods from the class Class:

getField()
getDeclaredField()
getDeclaredFields()
getFields()

For an example, see Chapter 13, "Reflection."

Methods

```
boolean   equals(Object obj)
Object    get(Object obj)
boolean   getBoolean(Object obj)
byte      getByte(Object obj)
char      getChar(Object obj)
Class     getDeclaringClass()
double    getDouble(Object obj)
float     getFloat(Object obj)
int       getInt(Object obj)
long      getLong(Object obj)
int       getModifiers()
String    getName()
Class     getType()
int       hashCode()
void      set(Object obj, Object value)
void      setBoolean(Object obj, boolean z)
```

```
voidset    Byte(Object obj, byte b)
voidset    Char(Object obj, char c)
voidset    Double(Object obj, double d)
voidset    Float(Object obj, float f)
voidset    Int(Object obj, int i)
voidset    Long(Object obj, long l)
voidset    Short(Object obj, short s)
String     toString()
```

Class Method

```
public final class Method
                    extends AccessibleObject
                    implements Member
```

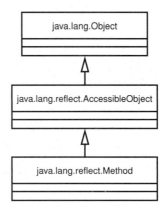

The Method class is used to obtain the names, modifiers, and parameters of the methods of a class. You can get the methods through one of the following methods in the class Class:

```
getMethods(),
getMethod(String, Class[]),
getDeclaredMethods(),
getDeclaredMethod(String, Class[])
```

A method discovered through Reflection can be executed with the invoke() method.

Methods

```
boolean    equals(Object obj)
Class      getDeclaringClass()
Class[]    getExceptionTypes()
int        getModifiers()
String     getName()
Class[]    getParameterTypes()
Class      getReturnType()
int        hashCode()
Object     invoke(Object obj, Object[] args)
String     toString()
```

Class Modifier

public class **Modifier**
           extends Object

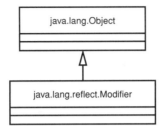

The Modifier class is used to discover the modifiers for a class or member using

Class.getModifiers()
Member.getModifiers()

The Modifier class contains several public final static int data members that can be used to compare the modifiers of a class or member. They can be used to determine if a class is abstract, for example. When you get the Modifier object for a class, you essentially get an int that includes all the modifier information. You can test this int to see if it includes a specific value, or simply print all the modifiers with the toString() method.

Fields

static int	ABSTRACT
static int	FINAL
static int	INTERFACE
static int	NATIVE
static int	PRIVATE
static int	PROTECTED
static int	PUBLIC
static int	STATIC
static int	STRICT
static int	SYNCHRONIZED
static int	TRANSIENT
static int	VOLATILE

Constructors

Modifier ()

Methods

static boolean	isAbstract(int mod)
static boolean	isFinal(int mod)
static boolean	isInterface(int mod)
static boolean	isNative(int mod)
static boolean	isPrivate(int mod)

static boolean	**isProtected**(int mod)
static boolean	**isPublic**(int mod)
static boolean	**isStatic**(int mod)
static boolean	**isStrict**(int mod)
static boolean	**isSynchronized**(int mod)
static boolean	**isTransient**(int mod)
static boolean	**isVolatile**(int mod)
static String	**toString**(int mod)

Class ReflectPermission

public final class **ReflectPermission**
                        extends BasicPermission

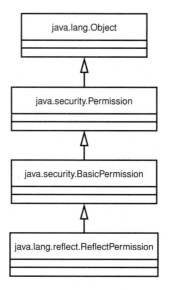

The `ReflectPermission` is the `Permission` class for Reflection. `ReflectPermission` has no actions, and the only name defined is `suppressAccessChecks`, which suppresses access checking by reflected objects. If this permission is set in a policy file, the consequence is that an object reflecting the data members and methods of another object can see all the data members and methods, whether the access for these members or methods is public, protected, private, or package-level default.

CAUTION

The ability to interrogate and manipulate an object using `ReflectPermission` is a powerful feature. It should only be granted with an understanding of the consequences of this permission. It allows one object to read all the private data of another object. This not only violates encapsulation, but can also pose severe security risks for sensitive data. Outside of debugging code, grant this Permission with great care. I cannot stress enough that `ReflectPermission` discards the default behavior of the JVM for access permission.

Table 25.1, based on the Java API documentation, shows what permission ReflectPermission grants and the consequences of that permission.

Table 25.1 What ReflectPermission Grants and the Attendant Risks

Permission Target Name	What the Permission Grants	Potential Risks of Allowing Permission
SuppressAccessChecks	Access to all fields and the capability to invoke constructors and methods regardless of access modifiers	Sensitive data accessible by malicious code

Constructors

ReflectPermission (String name)
ReflectPermission(String name, String actions)

CHAPTER 26

java.math

The java.math package has only two classes, BigDecimal and BigInteger. These two classes exist principally to allow for arbitrary precision numbers. This allows you to use these classes and not lose precision. Although these classes can be used anywhere, they serve especially to help with SQL data types that do not map numbers directly to any Java primitive data type.

Classes

BigDecimal
BigInteger

Class Details

Class BigDecimal

```
public class BigDecimal
              extends Number
              implements Comparable
```

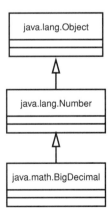

A `BigDecimal` object is an immutable, arbitrary precision, signed, decimal number. A `BigDecimal` has two components:

- An arbitrary precision, integer, unscaled value
- A nonnegative 32-bit integer scale that represents the number of digits to the right of the decimal point

You can perform arithmetic on a `BigDecimal`, as well as scaling and rounding. You have complete control over rounding. Here is a code snippet showing the use of a `BigDecimal` being used with a `PreparedStatement` for an SQL call:

```
PreparedStatement prepstmt = conn.prepareStatement
        ("UPDATE EMPLOYEE_TABLE " +
         SET SALARY = ? WHERE EMPNUM = ?");
  prepstmt.setBigDecimal(1, 276672.00);
    // Arbitrary-precision decimal number
  prepstmt.setInt(2, 77539);
```

Fields

static int	ROUND_CEILING
static int	ROUND_DOWN
static int	ROUND_FLOOR
static int	ROUND_HALF_DOWN
static int	ROUND_HALF_EVEN
static int	ROUND_HALF_UP
static int	ROUND_UNNECESSARY
static int	ROUND_UP

Constructors

BigDecimal(BigInteger val)
BigDecimal(BigInteger unscaledVal, int scale)
BigDecimal(double val)
BigDecimal(String val)

Methods

BigDecimal	**abs**()
BigDecimal	**add**(BigDecimal val)
int	**compareTo**(BigDecimal val)
int	**compareTo**(Object o)
BigDecimal	**divide**(BigDecimal val, int roundingMode)
BigDecimal	**divide**(BigDecimal val, int scale, int roundingMode)
double	**doubleValue**()
boolean	**equals**(Object x)
float	**floatValue**()
int	**hashCode**()
int	**intValue**()
long	**longValue**()
BigDecimal	**max**(BigDecimal val)
BigDecimal	**min**(BigDecimal val)
BigDecimal	**movePointLeft**(int n)

```
BigDecimal            movePointRight(int n)
BigDecimal            multiply(BigDecimal val)
BigDecimal            negate()
int                   scale()
BigDecimal            setScale(int scale)
BigDecimal            setScale(int scale, int roundingMode) int signum()
BigDecimal            subtract(BigDecimal val)
BigInteger            toBigInteger()
String                toString()
BigInteger            unscaledValue()
static BigDecimal     valueOf(long val)
static BigDecimal     valueOf(long unscaledVal, int scale)
```

Class BigInteger

```
public class BigInteger
               extends Number
               implements Comparable
```

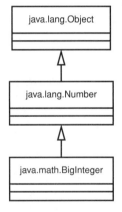

The BigInteger class provides immutable, arbitrary precision integers. All operations on a BigInteger object function as if the BigInteger were in two's complement form, like a primitive int. In addition, any of the operations defined in java.lang.Math may be performed on a BigInteger, as well as all the operations that can be done on an int primitive. Other operations may be performed on a BigInteger as well, such as GCD computations and bit manipulations, among others. Unlike an int primitive, operations on BigIntegers do not overflow. Instead, the result is made as large as necessary to hold the correct value.

Fields

```
static BigInteger     ONE
static BigInteger     ZERO
```

Constructors

```
BigInteger (byte[] val)
BigInteger(int signum, byte[] magnitude)
```

```
BigInteger(int bitLength, int certainty, Random rnd)
BigInteger(int numBits, Random rnd)
BigInteger(String val)
BigInteger(String val, int radix)
```

Methods

BigInteger	**abs**()
BigInteger	**add**(BigInteger val)
BigInteger	**and**(BigInteger val)
BigInteger	**andNot**(BigInteger val)
int	**bitCount**()
int	**bitLength**()
BigInteger	**clearBit**(int n)
int	**compareTo**(BigInteger val)
int	**compareTo**(Object o)
BigInteger	**divide**(BigInteger val)
BigInteger[]	**divideAndRemainder**(BigInteger val)
double	**doubleValue**()
boolean	**equals**(Object x)
BigInteger	**flipBit**(int n)
float	**floatValue**()
BigInteger	**gcd**(BigInteger val)
int	**getLowestSetBit**()
int	**hashCode**()
int	**intValue**()
boolean	**isProbablePrime**(int certainty)
long	**longValue**()
BigInteger	**max**(BigInteger val)
BigInteger	**min**(BigInteger val)
BigInteger	**mod**(BigInteger m)
BigInteger	**modInverse**(BigInteger m)
BigInteger	**modPow**(BigInteger exponent, BigInteger m)
BigInteger	**multiply**(BigInteger val)
BigInteger	**negate**()
BigInteger	**not**()
BigInteger	**or**(BigInteger val)
BigInteger	**pow**(int exponent)
BigInteger	**remainder**(BigInteger val)
BigInteger	**setBit**(int n)
BigInteger	**shiftLeft**(int n)
BigInteger	**shiftRight**(int n)
int	**signum**()
BigInteger	**subtract**(BigInteger val)
boolean	**testBit**(int n)
byte[]	**toByteArray**()
String	**toString**()
String	**toString**(int radix)
static BigInteger	**valueOf**(long val)
BigInteger	**xor**(BigInteger val)

CHAPTER 27

java.net

This chapter provides a quick reference of interfaces and classes in java.net, which provides support for performing networking in Java. There's support for TCP sockets, UDP sockets, and UDP multicast sockets. The class java.net.INetAddress provides methods to obtain IP addresses from host names as well as host names from IP addresses. It also provides the getLocalHost() method to obtain an INetAddress object (which contains the host address and host name) for the local host, like so:

```
InetAddress thisComputer = InetAddress.getLocalHost();
```

In addition, java.net provides classes for making connections to a URL—for example, the URLConnection and HttpURLConnection classes. These two classes may be used to communicate from a Java applet or application to a CGI script or a servlet. These two classes can call get() method and post() method routines as well as calling getOutputStream() and then writing to this stream to a middle-tier program. The getOutputStream() method may be used get a stream for passing an object from an application, usually on tier 1, to a servlet on tier 2 instead of just String data, as you would pass in a get() or post() request.

Interfaces

ContentHandlerFactory
FileNameMap
SocketImplFactory
SocketOptions
URLStreamHandlerFactory

Classes

Authenticator
ContentHandler
DatagramPacket
DatagramSocket
DatagramSocketImpl

HttpURLConnection
InetAddress
JarURLConnection
MulticastSocket
NetPermission
PasswordAuthentication
ServerSocket
Socket
SocketImpl
SocketPermission
URL
URLClassLoader
URLConnection
URLDecoder
URLEncoder
URLStreamHandler

Exceptions
BindException
ConnectException
MalformedURLException
NoRouteToHostException
ProtocolException
SocketException
UnknownHostExcetion
UnknownServiceException

Interface and Class Details

Interface ContentHandlerFactory
public abstract interface **ContentHandlerFactory**

This interface is used for a concrete factory (in design-pattern terminology) in creating content-handler objects for specific MIME types. It's used by the class URLStreamHandler to create ContentHandler instances for MIME types. Generally, application programs do not explicitly create ContentHandler objects directly.

> **NOTE**
>
> The ContentHandler is factory created by a concrete factory. You can have an abstract factory or a concrete factory. An abstract factory provides a factory method, like getSomeObject() in an abstract class. You don't ever instantiate the factory; you only use its factory method. URLStreamHandler is an abstract class. A concrete factory in this situation would be a concrete class (one you can instantiate) that subclasses the abstract class URLStreamHandler and provides a method for creating concrete ContentHandler objects. The goal here of using both abstract and concrete factories is to allow you to have a way to organize related concrete factories—in this case, for all the kinds of content handlers that might be needed for various MIME types.

Methods

ContentHandler   `createContentHandler`(String mimetype)

Interface SocketImplFactory

public abstract interface **SocketImplFactory**

This interface defines a concrete factory implemented by the classes `ServerSocket` and `Socket` to create implementations of these socket classes.

Methods

SocketImpl   `createSocketImpl`()

Interface SocketOptions

public abstract interface **SocketOptions**

This interface declares methods for setting or getting socket options in a `Socket`, `ServerSocket`, or `MulticastSocket`. Use this interface if the default properties of a given socket implementation are not suitable for your application but you don't need to create a custom socket implementation.

> **NOTE**
> You will not directly use `SocketOptions` methods or data members if you are not subclassing `SocketImpl` or `DatagramSocketImpl`.

Fields

static int	**IP_MULTICAST_IF**
static int	**SO_BINDADDR**
static int	**SO_LINGER**
static int	**SO_RCVBUF**
static int	**SO_REUSEADDR**
static int	**SO_SNDBUF**
static int	**SO_TIMEOUT**
static int	**TCP_NODELAY**

Methods

Object   `getOption`(int optID)
void   `setOption`(int optID, Object value)

Class ContentHandler

public abstract class **ContentHandler**
                        extends Object

The abstract class `ContentHandler` is the superclass of all classes that read an object from a `URLConnection`.

632 Chapter 27: java.net

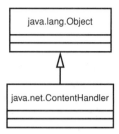

An application doesn't generally call the getContent method in this class directly. Instead, an application calls the getContent() method in class URL or URLConnection. The application's content-handler factory—an instance of a class that implements the interface ContentHandlerFactory set up by a call to setContentHandler()—is called with a String that gives the MIME type of the object being received on the socket. The factory returns an instance of a subclass of ContentHandler, and its getContent method is called to create the object.

Constructors
ContentHandler ()

Methods
abstract Object   **getContent**(URLConnection urlc)

Class DatagramPacket
public final class **DatagramPacket**
                extends Object

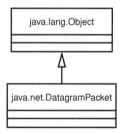

The DatagramPacket class implements a datagram packet, which is used to send information from one datagram socket to another. Datagram sockets and packets provide for connectionless communication, which is less reliable than TCP connections.

When you construct a DatagramPacket object, you must first decide if it will be used for sending or receiving UDP. Here is a code snippet that shows how to do each (although there are more constructors than these two for DatagramPacket):

```
byte[199] recvBuffer;
byte[199] sendBuffer;
// Make a DatagramPacket to receive data
Datagram receiver = new DatagramPacket(recvBuffer, recvBuffer.length);
```

```
// Make a DatagramPacket to send data
Datagram sender = new DatagramPacket(sendBuffer, sendBuffer.length,
                                     "rumba", 12553);
```

Notice that the main difference between these two constructor calls is that a DatagramPacket for sending requires a logical address, which consists of the host and port number of where the packet should be sent.

Constructors

DatagramPacket(byte[] buf, int length)
DatagramPacket(byte[] buf, int length, InetAddress address, int port)
DatagramPacket(byte[] buf, int offset, int length)
DatagramPacket(byte[] buf, int offset, int length, InetAddress address,
            int port)

Methods

InetAddress	**getAddress**()
byte[]	**getData**()
int	**getLength**()
int	**getOffset**()
int	**getPort**()
void	**setAddress**(InetAddress iaddr)
void	**setData**(byte[] buf)
void	**setData**(byte[] buf, int offset, int length)
void	**setLength**(int length)
void	**setPort**(int iport)

Class DatagramSocket

public class **DatagramSocket**
                extends Object

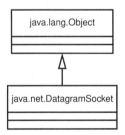

This class represents a socket for sending and receiving datagram packets. There's no concept, as in TCP sockets, of a Socket and ServerSocket. Instead, you either create a DatagramSocket bound to a specific host and port, or you leave out the host and port and the system chooses an arbitrary port for you on the requesting host. Here is a simple code snippet to show the key pieces of using a DatagramSocket (although there is more involved, as shown in Chapter 14, "Java Network Programming"):

```
DatagramSocket socket = new DatagramSocket(5555);
try
```

```
{
DatagramPacket recvPacket = new
                   DatagramPacket(inBuffer, inBuffer.length);
  // Create a DatagramPacket to receive client requests.
  socket.receive(recvPacket);
  // Wait for a client request. This code blocks until it gets input.
  clientAddress = recvPacket.getAddress();
     clientPort = recvPacket.getPort();
     String text = new String(recvPacket.getData(),
                        0,recvPacket.getLength());
}
```

This snippet shows the creation of a DatagramSocket object and a DatagramPacket object. Then you use the socket to get the packet from a sender (not a caller). The code blocks until it gets a packet. Then the contents of the package are accessed.

TIP

Using DatagramPackets and DatagramSockets you can create a simple, asynchronous messaging system for applications that do not need instant responses, such as a workflow engine or inventory control system.

Constructors

DatagramSocket ()
DatagramSocket(int port)
DatagramSocket(int port, InetAddress laddr)

Methods

void	close()
void	connect(InetAddress address, int port)
void	disconnect()
InetAddress	getInetAddress()
InetAddress	getLocalAddress()
int	getLocalPort()
int	getPort()
int	getReceiveBufferSize()
int	getSendBufferSize()
int	getSoTimeout()
void	receive(DatagramPacket p)
void	send(DatagramPacket p)
void	setReceiveBufferSize(int size)
void	setSendBufferSize(int size)
void	setSoTimeout(int timeout)

Class HttpURLConnection

public abstract class **HttpURLConnection**
                        extends URLConnection

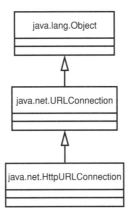

This is a URLConnection with support for HTTP-specific features. It would be an appropriate choice if you wanted to use an applet to communicate over HTTP to a Web server—either to a CGI script or, better still, a servlet. Using a servlet on the server side, you can even send objects from the applet to the server by using getOutputStream() and then wrapping it in an ObjectOutputStream.

Fields

static int	HTTP_ACCEPTED
static int	HTTP_BAD_GATEWAY
static int	HTTP_BAD_METHOD
static int	HTTP_BAD_REQUEST
static int	HTTP_CLIENT_TIMEOUT
static int	HTTP_CONFLICT
static int	HTTP_CREATED
static int	HTTP_ENTITY_TOO_LARGE
static int	HTTP_FORBIDDEN
static int	HTTP_GATEWAY_TIMEOUT
static int	HTTP_GONE
static int	HTTP_INTERNAL_ERROR
static int	HTTP_LENGTH_REQUIRED
static int	HTTP_MOVED_PERM
static int	HTTP_MOVED_TEMP
static int	HTTP_MULT_CHOICE
static int	HTTP_NO_CONTENT
static int	HTTP_NOT_ACCEPTABLE
static int	HTTP_NOT_AUTHORITATIVE
static int	HTTP_NOT_FOUND
static int	HTTP_NOT_MODIFIED
static int	HTTP_OK
static int	HTTP_PARTIAL
static int	HTTP_PAYMENT_REQUIRED
static int	HTTP_PRECON_FAILED
static int	HTTP_PROXY_AUTH
static int	HTTP_REQ_TOO_LONG
static int	HTTP_RESET

```
static int              HTTP_SEE_OTHER
static int              HTTP_SERVER_ERROR
static int              HTTP_UNAUTHORIZED
static int              HTTP_UNAVAILABLE
static int              HTTP_UNSUPPORTED_TYPE
static int              HTTP_USE_PROXY
static int              HTTP_VERSION
protected String        method
protected int           responseCode
protected String        responseMessage
```

Constructors

```
protected     HttpURLConnection(URL u)
```

Methods

```
abstract void           disconnect()
InputStream             getErrorStream()
static boolean          getFollowRedirects()
Permission              getPermission()
String                  getRequestMethod()
int                     getResponseCode()
String                  getResponseMessage()
static void             setFollowRedirects(boolean set)
void                    setRequestMethod(String method)
abstract boolean        usingProxy()
```

Class InetAddress

```
public final class InetAddress
                   extends Object
                   implements Serializable
```

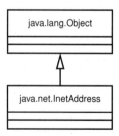

The InetAddress class represents an IP address for a host. You can use methods of this class to obtain the identity of the current host—getLocalHost(), get the name of a host based on its IP address—getHostname(), get an IP address using the host name—getHostByName(), and so forth. Here is a sample of some of what you can do with this class:

```
InetAddress theHost = InetAddress.getLocalHost();
System.out.println("Local host: " + theHost);
String hostName = theHost.getHostName();
```

```
String hostAddress = theHost.getHostAddress();
System.out.println("Host Name:    " + hostName);
System.out.println("Host Address: " + hostAddress);
System.out.println("Host address by host name: " +
                   InetAddress.getByName(hostName));
```

This code must be wrapped in a try block.

Methods

```
boolean                  equals(Object obj)
byte[]                   getAddress()
static InetAddress[]     getAllByName(String host)
static InetAddress       getByName(String host)
String                   getHostAddress()
String                   getHostName()
static InetAddress       getLocalHost()
int                      hashCode()
boolean                  isMulticastAddress()
String                   toString()
```

Class JarURLConnection

```
public abstract class JarURLConnection
                      extends URLConnection
```

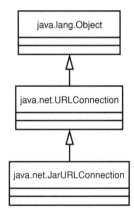

The JarURLConnection class represents a URLConnection to a jar file. You can use a JarURLConnection object to read a jar file as a URL. Here's the format of a jar URL:

jar:<url>!/{entry}

A JarURLConnection class could be used to extract or read a single file from a given jar file. You could, therefore, read a single class from a jar file on the local host, or an applet could read a single class from a jar file on a Web server on demand.

Here are some examples of getting a single jar entry, a whole jar file, or a jar directory. In the examples, !/ serves as a separator.

Jar entry:

jar:http://www.dantooine.com/ecommerce/buy.jar!/COM/dantooine/Catalog.class

Jar file:

jar:http://www.dantooine.com/ecommerce/buy.jar!/

Jar directory:

jar:http://www.dantooine.com//boy.jar!/COM/dantooine/

Once you have the JarURLConnection, you can access the jar file or enter like any other URLConnection object or use the specific java.util classes that support dealing with jar files.

Fields
protected URLConnection   jarFileURLConnection

Constructors
protected   JarURLConnection(URL url)

Methods

Attributes	getAttributes()
Certificate[]	getCertificates()
String	getEntryName()
JarEntry	getJarEntry()
abstract JarFile	getJarFile()
URL	getJarFileURL()
Attributes	getMainAttributes()
Manifest	getManifest()

Class MulticastSocket
public class **MulticastSocket**
        extends DatagramSocket

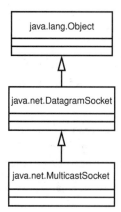

A `Socket` in Java can communicate to one host and port. A UDP `DatagramSocket` can communicate to one host and port at a time. A `MulticastSocket` can send a `DatagramPacket` to multiple ports on multiple hosts at one time. This could allow for broadcasting a message, for example, and would be useful in a messaging or publish/subscribe architecture.

Like a regular UDP `DatagramSocket`, a UDP `MulticastSocket` is less reliable than a TCP `Socket`, but it's more flexible. Here is a simple code snippet showing you the basics of using a `MulticastSocket` object. When you use this class, you need to add recipients to a group. All the members of the group then get whatever is sent from the `MulticastSocket` object:

```
// Create data for the socket to send.
 byte[] msg = {'S', 'U', 'N', 'W', ' ', '9', '3', '.', '5'};
 InetAddress groupAddr = InetAddress.getByName("225.3.3.8");
 // There is a specific range reserved for multicast sockets.
 MulticastSocket multiSock = new MulticastSocket(9953);
 multiSock.joinGroup(groupAddr);
 DatagramPacket stockQuote = new DatagramPacket(msg,
                                                msg.length,
                                                groupAddr,
                                                9953);
 // The DatagramPacket constructor specifies the data,
 // its length, the group's IP address, and port of the
 // MulticastSocket.
 multiSock.send(stockQuote);
 // Get group responses!
 byte[] response = new byte[1000];
 DatagramPacket receiver = new DatagramPacket(response,
                                              response.length);
 multiSock.receive(receiver);
 // You can also leave the group.
 multiSock.leaveGroup(groupAddr);
```

Using the `MulticastSocket` class, you can build your own publish-subscribe application.

Constructors

MulticastSocket ()
MulticastSocket(int port)

Methods

InetAddress	**getInterface**()
int	**getTimeToLive**()
byte	**getTTL**() (Deprecated)
void	**joinGroup**(InetAddress mcastaddr)
void	**leaveGroup**(InetAddress mcastaddr)
void	**send**(DatagramPacket p, byte ttl)
void	**setInterface**(InetAddress inf)
void	**setTimeToLive**(int ttl)
void	**setTTL**(byte ttl) (Deprecated)

Class PasswordAuthentication

public final class **PasswordAuthentication**
                    extends Object

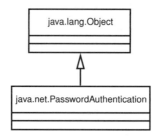

The `PasswordAuthentication` class is used by an authenticator to authenticate a user. The `PasswordAuthentication` object merely holds a user ID and password.

Constructors
PasswordAuthentication (String userName, char[] password)

Methods
char[] **getPassword**()
String **getUserName**()

Class ServerSocket

public class **ServerSocket**
                    extends Object

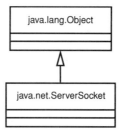

A `ServerSocket` object is the server-side socket used in a TCP/IP client/server application. When you create a `ServerSocket`, you specify a particular port and then use an `accept()` on that port. Here's an example:

```
ServerSocket ss = new ServerSocket(7777);
ss.accept();
```

The `accept()` call blocks until a client connects to it.

You can also use a `ServerSocket` to prevent more than one copy of your program from being run on a given host. If you create a `ServerSocket` on a given port, even if you never use the ServerSocket, a second copy of the program, when attempting to connect to the same port, will throw an exception. Then you can catch that exception and tell the user that only one copy of the program may run on the given host.

Constructors

```
ServerSocket (int port)
ServerSocket(int port, int backlog)
ServerSocket(int port, int backlog, InetAddress bindAddr)
```

Methods

```
Socket            accept()
void              close()
InetAddress       getInetAddress()
int               getLocalPort()
int               getSoTimeout()
protected void    implAccept(Socket s)
static void       setSocketFactory(SocketImplFactory fac)
void              setSoTimeout(int timeout)
String            toString()
```

Class Socket

public class **Socket**
           extends Object

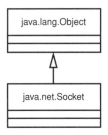

A Socket object is a TCP socket, used for communicating between two hosts. A Socket is created generally with the host name and port address of the application to which you need to connect. When a client-side Socket connects to a ServerSocket, the accept() method of the ServerSocket returns a Socket object. These Socket objects are more reliable than UDP sockets because they make a real connection between hosts. Therefore, if it's imperative for a method to successfully send data to another host, TCP sockets should be chosen over UDP sockets. If it doesn't matter much—for example, for sports scores that will be re-sent 30 seconds later, or for an atomic clock value that will not be valid later—the lower overhead of UDP sockets is preferable for network bandwidth.

Constructors

```
protected     Socket()
protected     Socket(InetAddress address, int port)
protected     Socket(InetAddress host, int port, boolean stream)
                  (Deprecated)
```

protected	**Socket**(InetAddress address, int port, InetAddress, localAddr, int localPort)
protected	**Socket**(SocketImpl impl)
protected	**Socket**(String host, int port)
protected	**Socket**(String host, int port, boolean stream) (Deprecated)
protected	**Socket**(String host, int port, InetAddress localAddr, int localPort)

Methods

void	**close**()
InetAddress	**getInetAddress**()
InputStream	**getInputStream**()
InetAddress	**getLocalAddress**()
int	**getLocalPort**()
OutputStream	**getOutputStream**()
int	**getPort**()
int	**getReceiveBufferSize**()
int	**getSendBufferSize**()
int	**getSoLinger**()
int	**getSoTimeout**()
boolean	**getTcpNoDelay**()
void	**setReceiveBufferSize**(int size)
void	**setSendBufferSize**(int size)
static void	**setSocketImplFactory**(SocketImplFactory fac)
void	**setSoLinger**(boolean on, int linger)
void	**setSoTimeout**(int timeout)
void	**setTcpNoDelay**(boolean on)
String	**toString**()

Class SocketImpl

public abstract class **SocketImpl**
                 extends Object
                 implements SocketOptions

SocketImpl is an abstract base class for all concrete socket implementations.

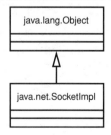

Fields

protected InetAddress	**address**
protected FileDescriptor	**fd**

```
protected int                    localport
protected int                    port
```

Constructors
```
SocketImpl ()
```

Methods
```
protected abstract void          accept(SocketImpl s)
protected abstract int           available()
protected abstract void          bind(InetAddress host, int port)
protected abstract void          close()
protected abstract void          connect(InetAddress address, int
                                     port)
protected abstract void          connect(String host, int port)
protected abstract void          create(boolean stream)
protected FileDescriptor         getFileDescriptor()
protected InetAddress            getInetAddress()
protected abstract InputStream   getInputStream()
protected int                    getLocalPort()
protected abstract OutputStream  getOutputStream()
protected int                    getPort()
protected abstract void          listen(int backlog)
String                           toString()
```

Class URL
```
public final class URL
                    extends Object
                    implements Serializable
```

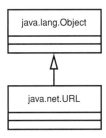

The URL class represents a Uniform Resource Locator, which is the "path" to a resource on the World Wide Web, such as a Web page, image, or class file.

Information on the types of URLs and their formats can be found at

`http://www.ncsa.uiuc.edu/demoweb/url-primer.html`

This is an example of a URL. A URL may contain several parts:

- Protocol—Specifies the protocol being used, such as http, ftp, file, or rmi.
- Domain name—This is the main location of the resource, which is frequently a Web server, such as www.sun.com.

- File component—This specifies additional information of where the resource is, including a directory structure and a filename, such as `index.html`.
- Port number—A URL may contain a specific port number. Generally, the port used for http is port 80, but this can be modified by an organization.
- Ref—An extra piece of information that generally refers to a location within a given Web page, specified with a pound sign (#) and a location name (for example, #openingfiles). This is appended to the end of the URL. Therefore, you could have a URL that looks like this:

  http://www.purejava.com/source/chapter45/ejb#creating

  Note that this URL is fictitious.

Constructors

```
URL (String spec)
URL(String protocol, String host, int port, String file)
URL(String protocol, String host, int port, String file,
    URLStreamHandler handler)
URL(String protocol, String host, String file)
URL(URL context, String spec)
URL(URL context, String spec, URLStreamHandler handler)
```

Methods

boolean	equals(Object obj)
Object	getContent()
String	getFile()
String	getHost()
int	getPort()
String	getProtocol()
String	getRef()
int	hashCode()
URLConnection	openConnection()
InputStream	openStream()
boolean	sameFile(URL other)
protected void	set(String protocol, String host, int port, String file, String ref)
static void	setURLStreamHandlerFactory(URLStreamHandlerFactory fac)
String	toExternalForm()
String	toString()

Class URLConnection

public abstract class **URLConnection**
                    extends Object

The `URLConnection` class is an abstract base class for all concrete URL connection subclasses, such as `HttpURLConnection`. This class provides several essential methods, such as `openConnection()` for creating a connection, `getContent`, `get()`, `post()`, and so on for getting or sending content over the connection, and several methods for interrogating the URL connection header information.

Interface and Class Details

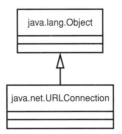

Fields

protected boolean	`allowUserInteraction`	
protected boolean	`connected`	
protected boolean	`doInput`	
protected boolean	`doOutput`	
protected long	`ifModifiedSince`	
protected URL	`url`	
protected boolean	`useCaches`	

Constructors

protected   **URLConnection**(URL url)

Methods

abstract void	`connect()`
boolean	`getAllowUserInteraction()`
Object	`getContent()`
String	`getContentEncoding()`
int	`getContentLength()`
String	`getContentType()`
long	`getDate()`
static boolean	`getDefaultAllowUserInteraction()`
static String	`getDefaultRequestProperty(String key)`
boolean	`getDefaultUseCaches()`
boolean	`getDoInput()`
boolean	`getDoOutput()`
long	`getExpiration()`
static FileNameMap	`getFileNameMap()`
String	`getHeaderField(int n)`
String	`getHeaderField(String name)`
long	`getHeaderFieldDate(String name, long Default)`
int	`getHeaderFieldInt(String name, int Default)`
String	`getHeaderFieldKey(int n)`
long	`getIfModifiedSince()`
InputStream	`getInputStream()`
long	`getLastModified()`
OutputStream	`getOutputStream()`
Permission	`getPermission()`
String	`getRequestProperty(String key)`
URL	`getURL()`

boolean	getUseCaches()
protected static String	guessContentTypeFromName(String fname)
static String	guessContentTypeFromStream(InputStream is)
void	setAllowUserInteraction(boolean allowuserinteraction)
static void	setContentHandlerFactory(ContentHandlerFactory fac)
static void	setDefaultAllowUserInteraction(boolean defaultallowuserinteraction)
static void	setDefaultRequestProperty(String key, String value)
void	setDefaultUseCaches(boolean defaultusecaches)
void	setDoInput(boolean doinput)
void	setDoOutput(boolean dooutput)
static void	setFileNameMap(FileNameMap map)
void	setIfModifiedSince(long ifmodifiedsince)
void	setRequestProperty(String key, String value)
void	setUseCaches(boolean usecaches)
String	toString()

Class URLStreamHandler

public abstract class **URLStreamHandler**
                extends Object

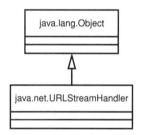

The class URLStreamHandler is the abstract base class for all protocol stream handlers. A *protocol stream handler* determines how to handle a specific network protocol and deal with specific data types on the stream.

Constructors

URLStreamHandler ()

Methods

protected abstract URLConnection	openConnection(URL u)
protected void	parseURL(URL u, String spec, int start, int limit)
protected void	setURL(URL u, String protocol, String host, int port, String file, String ref)
protected String	toExternalForm(URL u)

CHAPTER 28

java.rmi

This chapter provides a quick reference for the java.rmi package, the basic core pieces of Remote Method Invocation. In particular, this package defines the Remote interface, which is used by all RMI remote interfaces. This package also has the Naming class, which is used by code that creates remote objects to bind them to the RMIRegistry, and which is used by clients to find remote object stubs. This package also has the class RemoteException. Not only is this exception important in RMI, but it also appears elsewhere. For example, most methods of Enterprise JavaBeans classes must be declared as throwing a RemoteException.

Interfaces

Remote

Classes

MarshalledObject
Naming
RMISecurityManager

Exceptions

AccessException
AlreadyBoundException
ConnectException
ConnectIOException
MarshalException
NoSuchObjectException
NotBoundException
RemoteException
RMISecurityException
ServerError
ServerException
ServerRuntimeException
StubNotFoundException

UnexpectedException
UnknownHostException
UnmarshalException

Interface and Class Details

Interface Remote
public abstract interface Remote

The Remote interface must be extended by a remote interface. The Remote interface is the interface that defines the remotely accessible methods for a class. Generally that class implements the Remote interface and extends UnicastRemoteObject or extends Activatable, like this:

```
public interface Issueable extends Remote
    {
        // Remote method signatures.
    }
public LibraryCard extends UnicastRemoteObject
                    Implements Issueable
    {
     // Code to implement Issueable interface and do anything else
     // necessary, including specifying a constructor that throws
     // RemoteException.
    }
```

This is a flag to the JVM to say that the interface is a remote interface. Remote does not declare any methods.

Class MarshalledObject
public final class **MarshalledObject**
                extends Object

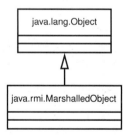

A MarshalledObject instance contains a serialized version of the object passed in the marshalled object's constructor. The serialized object is used in marshalling and unmarshalling remote method parameters. The serialized object may have a codebase URL associated with it in the MarshalledObject instance. A MarshalledObject is needed to provide data values for initializing an Activatable object because there's no way to pass values for data members in the constructor of an Activatable object.

All local objects used as parameters in remote object calls are marshalled with a `MarshalledObject`. In the following example, the `MarshalledObject` takes a single `String` parameter:

```
// Create a MarshalledObject to pass parameters
// to the Book constructor.
MarshalledObject mo = new MarshalledObject
                                ("How Shall We Then Live?");
```

Constructors
MarshalledObject (Object obj)

Methods
```
boolean    equals(Object obj)
Object     get()
int        hashCode()
```

Class Naming

```
public final class Naming
                        extends Object
```

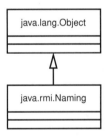

The `Naming` class provides methods for binding or unbinding an object in the `RMIRegistry` so that other objects outside the JVM doing the bind operation can find the object. `Naming` also provides the mechanism `Naming.lookup()` to locate a remote object. The result of doing a `lookup()` is a remote object reference to an object that implements the remote interface referred to in the `lookup()` call. Using the naming service in RMI is much simpler than in CORBA. Since everything in RMI is in Java, there is no need to narrow references, and you don't need to narrow the reference to the naming service, the `RMIRegistry`, either. Here are two examples of using the `Naming` class. When registering a remote object in the `RMIRegistry`, you write code like this:

```
Book remoteBook = new Book("How Shall We Then Live?");
             // Instantiate the remote object. To the caller
             // object, this is just another local object.
Naming.rebind("RemoteBook", remoteBook);
```

The name `RemoteBook` in quotes is the logical name by which a client can search for a remote reference to this object in the `RMIRegistry`. Its value can be anything you like, but it is helpful if it corresponds in some close way to the name of the class.

TIP

Although you could call `bind()` in the preceding code snippet, that is generally not done. You should use `rebind()`. The reason is that if the object was already bound and you call `bind()` again, you will get an exception for trying to bind an already bound object. If you call `rebind()`, you will not get this exception, no matter how many times you call `rebind()`.

NOTE

Technically, you do not have to bind an object to the `RMIRegistry` for it to be accessed as a remote object. If you have subclassed `UnicastRemoteObject`, you can instead do an `exportObject()` call. This is not the preferred method, but there are times when it is the best approach. In fact, in some cases, just the act of instantiating an object that extends `UnicastRemoteObject` is enough to make your object available for remote classes. However, this is somewhat more complicated than using the `RMIRegistry`.

Over on the client, you might call the `lookup()` method of the `Naming` class like this:

```
String server = "localhost";
String rmiUrl = "rmi://";
String remoteClass = "RemoteBook";
rmiUrl = rmiUrl + server + "/" + remoteClass;
Borrowable remoteBook = (Borrowable)Naming.lookup(rmiUrl);
```

Methods

static void	**bind**(String name, Remote obj)
static String[]	**list**(String name)
static Remote	**lookup**(String name)
static void	**rebind**(String name, Remote obj)
static void	**unbind**(String name)

Class RMISecurityManager

public class **RMISecurityManager**
                    extends SecurityManager

The `RMISecurityManager` is required to access remote methods and download stubs or activate remote objects. There are many limitations provided by the `RMISecurityManager` that are not provided for by the default `java.policy` file (JAVA_HOME/jre/lib/security). Generally, for RMI, you must create a policy file that grants more permissions. In particular, you must grant permission for seeing more system properties and for accessing a larger group of port numbers. You create an `RMISecurityManager` in your code by doing this:

```
System.setSecurityManager(new RMISecurityManager());
```

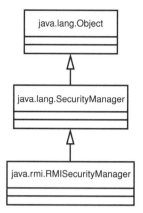

Constructors
RMISecurityManager()

Methods
void   **checkPackageAccess**(String pkgname)

CHAPTER 29

java.rmi.server and java.rmi.activation

This chapter provides a quick reference of classes and interfaces used in creating RMI remote objects. The package java.rmi.server has changed significantly from JDK 1.1. This gives rise to the incompatibility between JDK 1.1 RMI programs and Java 2 stubs. If you have JDK 1.1-based RMI programs, you need to recompile them because there have been significant changes in how stubs work, among other things.

The packages java.rmi.server and java.rmi.activation provide support for two approaches to remote object instantiation. Using java.rmi.server.UnicastRemoteObject, you can define a class for a remote object. This object is then instantiated by a program running generally on a server system. The classes and interfaces in java.rmi.activation, on the other hand, are used when a program on one host (generally a client or tier-two program) wants to instantiate an object on-the-fly, most commonly on another host. In the first situation, the "client" cannot run until the "server" creates the remote object instance. With activation, the client doesn't have to wait for a server-side program. Instead, the client can simply make a remote object on another system as needed.

Package Name: java.rmi.activation

Interfaces

ActivationInstantiator
ActivationMonitor
ActivationSystem
Activator

Classes

Activatable
ActivationDesc

ActivationGroup
ActivationGroupDesc
ActivationGroupDesc.CommandEnvironment
ActivationGroupID
ActivationID

Exceptions
ActivateFailedException
ActivationException
UnknownGroupException
UnknownObjectException

Package Name: java.rmi.server

Interfaces
LoaderHandler (deprecated)
RemoteCall (deprecated)
RemoteRef
RMIClientSocketFactory
RMIFailureHandler
RMIServerSocketFactory
ServerRef
Skeleton (deprecated)
Unreferenced

Classes
LogStream (deprecated)
ObjID
Operation (deprecated)
RemoteObject
RemoteServer
RemoteStub
RMIClassLoader
RMISocketFactory
UID
UnicastRemoteObject

Exceptions
ExportException
ServerCloneException
ServerNotActiveException
SkeletonMismatchException (deprecated)
SkeletonNotFoundException (deprecated)
SocketSecurityException

java.rmi.server Interface and Class Details

Interface RemoteRef

public abstract interface **RemoteRef**
                               extends Externalizable

A RemoteRef object is a handle to a remote object. It's used by a RemoteStub to call a method on a remote object.

Fields

```
static String      packagePrefix
static long        serialVersionUID
```

Methods

```
void            done(RemoteCall call) (Deprecated)
String          getRefClass(ObjectOutput out)
void            invoke(RemoteCall call) (Deprecated)
Object          invoke(Remote obj, Method method, Object[] params, long opnum)
RemoteCall      newCall(RemoteObject obj, Operation[] op, int opnum,
                    long hash) (Deprecated)
boolean         remoteEquals(RemoteRef obj)
int             remoteHashCode()
String          remoteToString()
```

Interface RMIClientSocketFactory

public abstract interface **RMIClientSocketFactory**

An RMIClientSocketFactory interface defines the method for creating an RMICLientSocket, which is passed to a client when it uses a remote reference to a remote object. The RMIClientSocket may be downloaded to the client.

> **NOTE**
>
> You can define your own custom socket factories. For example, you might want to use sockets that do compression or encryption. See http://java.sun.com/products/jdk/1.2/docs/guide/rmi/rmisocketfactory.doc.html for a tutorial on how to create custom RMI socket factories.

Methods

```
Socket     createSocket(String host, int port)
```

Interface RMIServerSocketFactory

public abstract interface **RMIServerSocketFactory**

An RMIServerSocketFactory interface is used to obtain server sockets for an RMI call to a remote object.

Methods
ServerSocket   createServerSocket(int port)

Interface ServerRef
```
public abstract interface ServerRef
                        extends RemoteRef
```

ServerRef provides a handle to server-side remote object references for use in remote object calls.

Fields
static long   serialVersionUID

Methods
RemoteStub   exportObject(Remote obj, Object data)
String   getClientHost()

Class RemoteObject
```
public abstract class RemoteObject
                        extends Object
                        implements Remote, Serializable
```

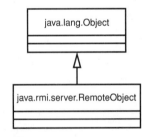

The class RemoteObject provides remote versions of the methods for java.lang.Object: toString(), equals(), and hashCode(). If you do not subclass UnicastRemoteObject in your remote objects, you need to implement remote versions of these methods yourself. Applications generally do not use RemoteObject directly.

Fields
protected RemoteRef   ref

Constructors
protected   RemoteObject()
protected   RemoteObject(RemoteRef newref)

Methods
boolean   equals(Object obj)
RemoteRef   getRef()
int   hashCode()
String   toString()
static Remote   toStub(Remote obj)

Class RMIClassLoader

public class **RMIClassLoader**
                extends Object

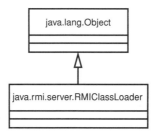

The class RMIClassLoader is a core piece of RMI and is involved in loading classes and stubs from one host to another. Applications generally do not use this class directly, but RMIClassLoader is involved in loading RMI classes into the JVM.

Methods

```
static String    getClassAnnotation(Class cl)
static Object    getSecurityContext(ClassLoader loader) (Deprecated)
static Class     loadClass(String name) (Deprecated)
static Class     loadClass(String codebase, String name)
static Class     loadClass(URL codebase, String name)
```

Class RemoteServer

public abstract class **RemoteServer**
                extends RemoteObject

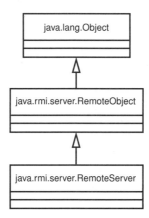

The class RemoteServer is the immediate, abstract superclass for Activatable and UnicastRemoteObject. RemoteServer provides the framework for crucial RMI activities such as creating and exporting remote objects. A remote object must be exported before it can be accessed remotely. This happens automatically when you subclass Activatable or UnicastRemoteObject. Applications generally do not use this class directly.

Constructors

protected	**RemoteServer**()
protected	**RemoteServer**(RemoteRef ref)

Methods

static String	**getClientHost**()
static PrintStream	**getLog**()
static void	**setLog**(OutputStream out)

Class UnicastRemoteObject

public class **UnicastRemoteObject**
           extends RemoteServer

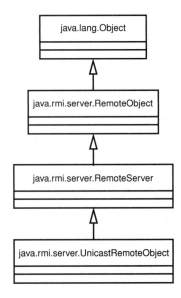

The class UnicastRemoteObject serves as the base class for most user-defined remote object classes. By subclassing UnicastRemoteObject, you obtain several important methods. If you do not extend UnicastRemoteObject, you must export your objects yourself and provide a remote implementation of hashCode(), equals(), and toString() because the versions inherited from java.lang.Object do not support remote objects. Here is a simple example of using this class:

```
class LibraryCard extends UnicastRemoteObject
      implements Issueable
   {
     // class definition goes here.
   }
```

Constructors

protected	**UnicastRemoteObject**()
protected	**UnicastRemoteObject**(int port)

```
protected      UnicastRemoteObject(int port, RMIClientSocketFactory csf,
                   RMIServerSocketFactory ssf)
```

Methods

```
Object              clone()
static RemoteStub   exportObject(Remote obj)
static Remote       exportObject(Remote obj, int port)
static Remote       exportObject(Remote obj, int port,
                        RMIClientSocketFactory csf,
                        RMIServerSocketFactory ssf)
static boolean      unexportObject(Remote obj, boolean force)
```

java.rmi.activation Class Details

Class Activatable

```
public abstract class Activatable
                    extends RemoteServer
```

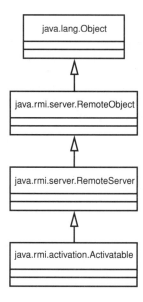

The Activatable class is the abstract base class you need to subclass to define a class that can have an instance remotely activated (that is, *instantiated*). The role of Activatable for a remote object is similar in this regard to the role of UnicastRemoteObject for a remote object. Here is a code snippet to show this class being used as a superclass:

```
public class ActivatableBook extends Activatable
                             implements Borrowable
{
    // Define class here.
}
```

You would make a class that extends Activatable, as opposed to UnicastRemoteObject, if it is important for a client to create remote objects on-the-fly without requiring one to already exist on the server system.

Constructors

protected	**Activatable**(ActivationID id, int port)
protected	**Activatable**(ActivationID id, int port, RMIClientSocketFactory csf, RMIServerSocketFactory ssf)
protected	**Activatable**(String location, MarshalledObject data, boolean restart, int port)
protected	**Activatable**(String location, MarshalledObject data, boolean restart, int port, RMIClientSocketFactory csf, RMIServerSocketFactory ssf)

Methods

static Remote	**exportObject**(Remote obj, ActivationID id, int port)
static Remote	**exportObject**(Remote obj, ActivationID id, int port, RMIClientSocketFactory csf, RMIServerSocketFactory ssf)
static ActivationID	**exportObject**(Remote obj, String location, MarshalledObject data, boolean restart, int port)
static ActivationID	**exportObject**(Remote obj, String location, MarshalledObject data, boolean restart, int port, RMIClientSocketFactory csf, RMIServerSocketFactory ssf)
protected ActivationID	**getID**()
static boolean	**inactive**(ActivationID id)
static Remote	**register**(ActivationDesc desc)
static boolean	**unexportObject**(Remote obj, boolean force)
static void	**unregister**(ActivativationID id)

Class ActivationDesc

public final class **ActivationDesc**
               extends Object
               implements Serializable

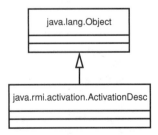

This class provides objects that describe "activatable" objects in terms of the information needed to activate them. Here's what an ActivationDesc instance contains:

- The activation group
- The class name
- The class file location
- A marshalled object. This can be used to initialize fields of the activated object. It's needed because the constructor for an Activatable object does not permit custom parameters.

Here is a code snippet showing how to create one:

```
ActivationDesc desc = new ActivationDesc
                         (actGrID, "ActivatableBook",
                       // Activation group, class name.
                         location, mo);
                       // Class file location and
                       // MarshalledObject instance.
// Give rmid enough info to instantiate
// the activatable object.
```

Constructors

ActivationDesc (ActivationGroupID groupID, String className, String location, MarshalledObject data)
ActivationDesc(ActivationGroupID groupID, String className, String location, MarshalledObject data, boolean restart)
ActivationDesc(String className, String location, MarshalledObject data)
ActivationDesc(String className, String location, MarshalledObject data, boolean restart)

Methods

boolean	**equals**(Object obj)
String	**getClassName**()
MarshalledObject	**getData**()
ActivationGroupID	**getGroupID**()
String	**getLocation**()
boolean	**getRestartMode**()
int	**hashCode**()

Class ActivationGroup

```
public abstract class ActivationGroup
                extends UnicastRemoteObject
                implements ActivationInstantiator
```

An `ActivationGroup` object is responsible for instantiating the `Activatable` classes in the group. It notifies an `ActivationMonitor` of the status of the attempt to create the instance. The following code snippet shows how to get an `ActivationGroup`:

```
ActivationGroup.createGroup(actGrID, bookGroup, 0);
                // This method takes three parms:
                //    ActivationGroupID id
                //    ActivationGroupDesc desc
                //    long incarnation
```

662 Chapter 29: java.rmi.server and java.rmi.activation

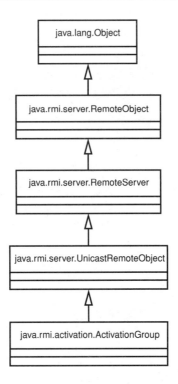

Constructors
protected   ActivationGroup(ActivationGroupID groupID)

Methods

protected void	**activeObject**(ActivationID id, MarshalledObject mobj)
abstract void	**activeObject**(ActivationID id, Remote obj)
static ActivationGroup	**createGroup**(ActivationGroupID id, ActivationGroupDesc desc, long incarnation)
static ActivationGroupID	**currentGroupID**()
static ActivationSystem	**getSystem**()
protected void	**inactiveGroup**()
boolean	**inactiveObject**(ActivationID id)
static void	**setSystem**(ActivationSystem system)

Class ActivationGroupDesc

```
public final class ActivationGroupDesc
                extends Object
                implements Serializable
```

An ActivationGroupDesc (activation group descriptor) object contains the information necessary to create an ActivationGroup instance.

java.rmi.activation Class Details

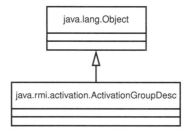

Here's what an `ActivationGroupDesc` contains:

- The class name for the `ActivationGroup`
- The location, or code source, for the `ActivationGroup`'s class definition
- A `MarshalledObject` instance that contains data for initializing the `ActivationGroup` object

Here is a code snippet showing how to make an `ActivationGroupDesc`:

```
ActivationGroupDesc.CommandEnvironment actCmdEnv = null;
ActivationGroupDesc bookGroup = new ActivationGroupDesc(sysProps, actCmdEnv);
```

The `ActivationGroup` is created by calling the `ActivationGroup.createGroup()` method, which invokes a constructor.

Constructors
ActivationGroupDesc (Properties overrides,
    ActivationGroupDesc.CommandEnvironment cmd)
ActivationGroupDesc(String className, String location, MarshalledObject data,
    Properties overrides, ActivationGroupDesc.CommandEnvironment cmd)

Methods

boolean	**equals**(Object obj)
String	**getClassName**()
ActivationGroupDesc.CommandEnvironment	**getCommandEnvironment**()
MarshalledObject	**getData**()
String	**getLocation**()
Properties	**getPropertyOverrides**()
int	**hashCode**()

Class ActivationID

```
public class ActivationID
            extends Object
            implements Serializable
```

An `ActivationID` (activation identifier) object contains data for identifying a remote object that can be activated. This includes a unique identifier for the `activatable` object and a remote reference to the object's activator. An `ActivationID` can be obtained in multiple ways, including

664 Chapter 29: java.rmi.server and java.rmi.activation

- Calling `Activatable.register()`
- Calling `Activatable.exportObject()`
- Calling the `Activatable` constructor, which both activates and exports an object

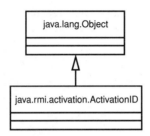

An `ActivationID` contains several pieces of data, including

- A remote reference to the activator for the object
- A unique identifier for the activatable object

Constructors
`ActivationID` (Activator activator)

Methods

```
Remote     activate(boolean force)
boolean    equals(Object obj)
int        hashCode()
```

CHAPTER 30

java.security

This chapter provides a quick reference of the interfaces in java.security and java.security.cert. There are several useful classes here—for example, MessageDigest, KeyStore, KeyPair, Permission, AllPermission, and Policy. If you want to use access control lists (ACLs), you should also consult java.security.acl. Note that the permissions granted through policies, and which instantiate classes in java.security, have absolutely nothing to do with the permissions provided through java.security.acl. Java 2 also provides support for creating self-signed certificates to authenticate signatures—primarily certificates that use the X.509 format.

Package Name: java.security

Interfaces

Certificate
Guard
Key
Principal
PrivateKey
PrivilegedAction
PrivilegedExceptionAction
PublicKey

Classes

AccessControlContext
AccessController
AlgorithmParameterGenerator
AlgorithmParameterGeneratorSpi
AlgorithmParameters
AlgorithmParametersSpi
AllPermission
BasicPermission
CodeSource

DigestInputStream
DigestOutputStream
GuardedObject
Identity
IdentityScope
KeyFactory
KeyFactorySpi
KeyPair
KeyPairGenerator
KeyPairGeneratorSpi
KeyStore
KeyStoreSpi
MessageDigest
MessageDigestSpi
Permission
PermissionCollection
Permissions
Policy
ProtectionDomain
Provider
SecureClassLoader
SecureRandom
SecureRandomSpi
Security
SecurityPermission
Signature
SignatureSpi
SignedObject
Signer
UnresolvedPermission

Exceptions
AccessControlException
DigestException
GeneralSecurityException
InvalidAlgorithmParameterException
InvalidKeyException
InvalidParameterException
KeyException
KeyManagementException
KeyStoreException
NoSuchAlgorithmException
NoSuchProviderException
PrivilegedActionException
ProviderException
SignatureException
UnrecoverableKeyException

Package Name: java.security.cert

Interfaces
X509Extension

Classes
Certificate
CertificateFactory
CertificateFactorySpi
CRL
X509Certificate
X509CRL
X509CRLEntry

Exceptions
CertificateEncodingException
CertificateException
CertificateExpiredException
CertificateNotYetValidException
CertificateParsingException
CRLException

java.security.cert Interface and Class Details

Interface Key

```
public abstract interface Key
                   extends Serializable
```

The Key interface is the base interface from which several subinterfaces extend. The Key interface is never implemented directly. This interface defines common features of all Key implementations. All Key implementations have the following items:

- An algorithm—The algorithm for generating the key
- An encoded form—The form of the key used for transmitting it outside of a JVM
- A format—The name of the format of the encoded key

Fields
```
static long    serialVersionUID
```

Methods
```
String    getAlgorithm()
byte[]    getEncoded()
String    getFormat()
```

Class AllPermission

```
public final class AllPermission
                    extends Permission
```

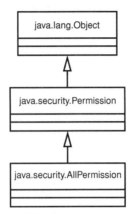

The `AllPermission` class is a permission that implies all other permissions. Although this may be convenient for testing, you probably don't want to use this in a production environment, because it grants to code various permissions, including `SocketPermission` for all sockets, `FilePermission` for all operations, `PropertyPermission` for all properties, and others. In general, you want a more finely tuned set of permissions. That's why protection domains with permissions exit. They permit finely tuned sets of permissions for specific programs, code signers, or code domains.

You normally set permissions in a policy file using `policytool`. However, it is possible to check for a given permission within your code. For example, you could write the following:

```
AllPermission ap = new AllPermission();
AccessController.checkPermission(ap);
// If the checkPermission method determines that All Permission
// is granted, it simply returns. If it determines that
// AllPermission is not granted, this method throws an
// AccessControlException.
```

Constructors

AllPermission ()
AllPermission(String name, String actions)

Methods

boolean	**equals**(Object obj)
String	**getActions**()
int	**hashCode**()
boolean	**implies**(Permission p)
PermissionCollection	**newPermissionCollection**()

Class CodeSource
public class **CodeSource**
            extends Object
            implements Serializable

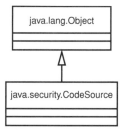

The CodeSource class describes a codebase that includes both code and the certificates of signers of that code, if any.

Constructors
CodeSource (URL url, Certificate[] certs)

Methods
boolean	**equals**(Object obj)
Certificate[]	**getCertificates**()
URL	**getLocation**()
int	**hashCode**()
boolean	**implies**(CodeSource codesource)
String	**toString**()

Class KeyPair
public final class **KeyPair**
            extends Object
            implements Serializable

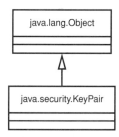

This class is a simple holder for a key pair, which consists of a public key and a private key. A KeyPair object provides no security for its contents, so if it's serialized, it should probably be enciphered or treated with care like a private key. You can generate a pair of keys in Java using the keytool program. You might invoke it like this:

670 Chapter 30: java.security

```
keytool -genkey -alias JavaMaster -keystore PureJava -storepass mykeys
```

This command tells Java to generate a key pair and store it in a key/certificate database called PureJava, which belongs to the alias JavaMaster and is password-protected with the password mykeys.

Constructors
KeyPair (PublicKey publicKey, PrivateKey privateKey)

Methods
PrivateKey	**getPrivate**()
PublicKey	**getPublic**()

Class KeyStore

```
public class KeyStore
              extends Object
```

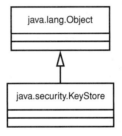

A `KeyStore` object, like its file-based counterpart (created with the keytool program), contains keys and certificates in memory. It has two types of entries:

- A key entry—An encryption key stored in protected format to prevent unauthorized access. Generally, this is a private key, which would be stored with an associated certificate. The key/certificate pair would be suitable for self-signed code. Generally, this code and its related key/certificate pair would be used within an organization rather than across the Internet, where a certificate from a certificate authority (such as Verisign) is much more common and more appropriate. Because a key relates to signing code and the certificate authenticates the digital signature, you should generally not accept a self-signed certificate as sufficient authentication, nor should you expect others outside your organization to do so, as a rule.
- A trusted certificate entry—This is typically a public key certificate (the certificate contains the public key) that is trusted. In other words, the certificate is trusted by the `keystore` owner.

Entries in a `keystore` are identified by an *alias,* which is what goes into the `signedBy` field when you're creating a policy file for signed code. There's no specification here regarding how to make a `KeyStore` object persistent. This means implementers have great flexibility to use varying secure techniques.

Constructors

protected   KeyStore(KeyStoreSpi keyStoreSpi, Provider provider,
             String type)

Methods

Enumeration	**aliases**()
boolean	**containsAlias**(String alias)
void	**deleteEntry**(String alias)
Certificate	**getCertificate**(String alias)
String	**getCertificateAlias**(Certificate cert)
Certificate[]	**getCertificateChain**(String alias)
Date	**getCreationDate**(String alias)
static String	**getDefaultType**()
static KeyStore	**getInstance**(String type)
static KeyStore	**getInstance**(String type, String provider)
Key	**getKey**(String alias, char[] password)
Provider	**getProvider**()
String	**getType**()
boolean	**isCertificateEntry**(String alias)
boolean	**isKeyEntry**(String alias)
void	**load**(InputStream stream, char[] password)
void	**setCertificateEntry**(String alias, Certificate cert)
void	**setKeyEntry**(String alias, byte[] key, Certificate[] chain)
void	**setKeyEntry**(String alias, Key key, char[] password, Certificate[] chain)
int	**size**()
void	**store**(OutputStream stream, char[] password)

Class MessageDigest

public abstract class **MessageDigest**
                 extends MessageDigestSpi

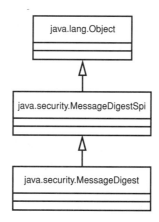

672 Chapter 30: java.security

The `MessageDigest` class implements a message digest. A message digest is essentially a hash value of a message sent across the Internet. Computationally, no two messages should create the same message digest (and it has been calculated that the sun will burn out before someone can determine the message content from the message digest). A message digest can be used to verify whether a message has been changed. If the recipient of the message creates a `MessageDigest` object in the same way and the message digest hash value is different from that sent in the message, you know the message was changed. It's entirely possible, however, that someone could intercept the message in transit, change it, and create a new message digest value. Therefore, by itself, a `MessageDigest` object is not a guarantee of message integrity. If you receive a message and then contact the sender and compare the sender's copy of the message digest with the message digest you received with the message, you can determine with confidence whether the original message was changed in transit. If both message digests match, the message was not changed. Here's a code snippet that shows the basics of making a digest for a pre-existing file:

```
MessageDigest md = MessageDigest.getInstance("md");
File theDoc = new File("MessageDoc.txt");
FileInputStream fis = new FileInputStream(theDoc);
byte[] document = new byte[(int)theDoc.length()];
fis.read(document);
md.update(document);
byte[] mdDigest = md.digest();
```

This creates a `MessageDigest` object for a document called MessageDoc.txt.

Constructors
protected   MessageDigest(String algorithm)

Methods
Object	**clone**()
byte[]	**digest**()
byte[]	**digest**(byte[] input)
int	**digest**(byte[] buf, int offset, int len)
String	**getAlgorithm**()
int	**getDigestLength**()
static MessageDigest	**getInstance**(String algorithm)
static MessageDigest	**getInstance**(String algorithm, String provider)
Provider	**getProvider**()
static boolean	**isEqual**(byte[] digesta, byte[] digestb)
void	**reset**()
String	**toString**()
void	**update**(byte input)
void	**update**(byte[] input)
void	**update**(byte[] input, int offset, int len)

Class Permission
```
public abstract class Permission
                extends Object
                implements Guard, Serializable
```

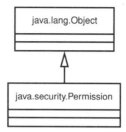

This is the abstract superclass of several other Permission classes, such as FilePermission. Permissions are objects that may, if appropriate, optionally include actions. A protection domain consists of code and its related permission objects. You can grant permissions through code in some cases, but in general you grant permissions defined by the Java 2 SDK through a policy file, generated by the policytool.

Constructors
Permission (String name)

Methods
void	checkGuard(Object object)
abstract boolean	equals(Object obj)
abstract String	getActions()
String	getName()
abstract int	hashCode()
abstract boolean	implies(Permission permission)
PermissionCollection	newPermissionCollection()
String	toString()

Class Policy
public abstract class **Policy**
                      extends Object

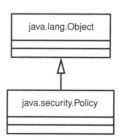

A Java Policy object represents the combination of permissions granted to an application in a specific protection domain. These permissions can be generated in a number of ways, including through the policytool, in which fine-grained permissions can be granted to all code, to a specific code domain, or to one or more code signers.

There's only one Policy object per JVM, and it affects all the code in that JVM. You can obtain the policy object for a protection domain, along with its permissions, by coding something like this, given the CodeSource object:

```
Policy policy = Policy.getPolicy();
PermissionCollection permissions =
                   policy.getPermissions(theCodeSource)
```

Constructors
Policy ()

Methods
abstract PermissionCollection	getPermissions(CodeSource codesource)
static Policy	getPolicy()
abstract void	refresh()
static void	setPolicy(Policy policy)

Class ProtectionDomain

public class **ProtectionDomain**
        extends Object

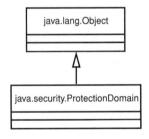

The ProtectionDomain class represents a group of classes and their associated permissions. Every program runs within its own protection domain.

Constructors
ProtectionDomain (CodeSource codesource, PermissionCollection permissions)

Methods
CodeSource	getCodeSource()
PermissionCollection	getPermissions()
boolean	implies(Permission permission)
String	toString()

java.security.cert Class Details

Class Certificate

public abstract class **Certificate**
        extends Object

java.security.cert Class Details

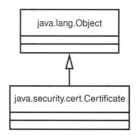

The Certificate class is an abstract base class for a number of concrete Certificate classes. A *certificate* serves to validate that a digital signature belongs to the alleged signer, such as an individual or company. Certificates can be self-generated or obtained from a certificate authority (CA). A self-generated certificate would be appropriate for an intranet application. For an applet from an external source, in general, you would only want to accept a certificate from a certificate authority. You should also be aware that a certificate may be of little or great worth. It's possible to buy a certificate from a CA for a very small amount based on supplying only an email address to verify the signer's identity. Other certificates, which cost much more, are much more reliable. Accepting a certificate as valid is a matter of trust.

Constructors
```
protected    Certificate(String type)
```

Methods
```
boolean              equals(Object other)
abstract byte[]      getEncoded()
abstract PublicKey   getPublicKey()
String               getType()
int                  hashCode()
abstract String      toString()
abstract void        verify(PublicKey key)
abstract void        verify(PublicKey key, String sigProvider)
```

Class CRL
```
public abstract class CRL
                 extends Object
```

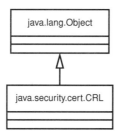

The CRL class is the abstract base class for all concrete Certificate Revocation List (CRL) classes, such as X509CRL.

Most developers won't need to use this unless they're specifically involved in validating and invalidating certificates.

Constructors
protected   CRL(String type)

Methods
String   getType()
abstract boolean   isRevoked(Certificate cert)
abstract String   toString()

Class X509Certificate
public abstract class **X509Certificate**
                         extends Certificate
                         implements X509Extension

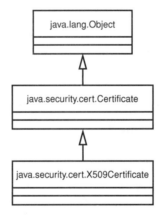

The X509Certificate class is an abstract class that prescribes the methods for interacting with an X.509 certificate. This is a very common certificate format used for authenticating digital signatures. An X.509 contains several elements, including the signature, signature identifier, and signature algorithm. An X.509 certificate would be provided by someone or some company that digitally signed code or documents and sent them across the Internet, among other uses. This would also be the normal certificate type to use in an intranet for signed code or internally signed documents to verify the signature.

The X509Certificate object is generated with a CertificateFactory.

Constructors
protected   **X509Certificate**()

Methods

abstract void	checkValidity()
abstract void	checkValidity(Date date)
abstract int	getBasicConstraints()
abstract Principal	getIssuerDN()
abstract boolean[]	getIssuerUniqueID()
abstract boolean[]	getKeyUsage()
abstract Date	getNotAfter()
abstract Date	getNotBefore()
abstract BigInteger	getSerialNumber()
abstract String	getSigAlgName()
abstract String	getSigAlgOID()
abstract byte[]	getSigAlgParams()
abstract byte[]	getSignature()
abstract Principal	getSubjectDN()
abstract boolean[]	getSubjectUniqueID()
abstract byte[]	getTBSCertificate()
abstract int	getVersion()

Class X509CRL

```
public abstract class X509CRL
                     extends CRL
                     implements X509Extension
```

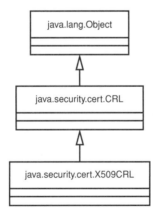

The X509CRL abstract class provides support for an X.509 Certificate Revocation List. An X509CRL object is a list with a timestamp of revoked X.509 certificates, signed by a certificate authority. You use a factory to create these like this:

```
FileInputStream fis = new FileInputStream("X509-CRList.dat");
CertificateFactory certFactory =
 CertificateFactory.getInstance("X.509");
X509CRL x509CRL =
 (X509CRL)certFactory.generateCRL(fis);
fis.close();
```

Constructors

```
protected    X509CRL()
```

Methods

```
boolean                equals(Object other)
abstract byte[]        getEncoded()
abstract Principal     getIssuerDN()
abstract Date          getNextUpdate()
abstract X509CRLEntry  getRevokedCertificate(BigInteger serialNumber)
abstract Set           getRevokedCertificates()
abstract String        getSigAlgName()
abstract String        getSigAlgOID()
abstract byte[]        getSigAlgParams()
abstract byte[]        getSignature()
abstract byte[]        getTBSCertList()
abstract Date          getThisUpdate()
abstract int           getVersion()
int                    hashCode()
abstract void          verify(PublicKey key)
abstract void          verify(PublicKey key, String sigProvider)
```

CHAPTER 31

java.sql

This chapter provides a quick reference of all the interfaces and classes in java.sql. The package java.sql provides the framework for JDBC programming, which is the mechanism for working with databases in Java. This package consists primarily of interfaces implemented by vendors. This allows a Java developer to write code that's quite independent of a specific database system, because the implementation classes are all hidden from the JDBC code.

Interfaces

```
Array
Blob
CallableStatement
Clob
Connection
DatabaseMetaData
Driver
PreparedStatement
Ref
ResultSet
ResultSetMetaData
SQLData
SQLInput
SQLOutput
Statement
Struct
```

Classes

```
Date
DriverManager
DriverPropertyInfo
Time
Timestamp
Types
```

Exceptions

BatchUpdateException
DataTruncation
SQLException
SQLWarning

Interface and Class Details

Interface Blob

public abstract interface **Blob**

This interface provides the method definition for a Blob. This is the Java version of the SQL data type Blob, which maps a *binary large object* to a column in a relational table.

Blobs can be useful in Java when you're working with a relational table to store an entire object. A Blob in Java differs from most SQL data types in that it stores a pointer to the data, rather than the data itself, in the column. The Blob is only valid during the transaction that created it. You can access a method through getBlob() and setBlob() in ResultSet, PreparedStatement, and CallableStatement.

Methods

InputStream	**getBinaryStream**()
byte[]	**getBytes**(long pos, int length)
long	**length**()
long	**position**(Blob pattern, long start)
long	**position**(byte[] pattern, long start)

Interface CallableStatement

public abstract interface **CallableStatement**
                          extends PreparedStatement

This interface declares the methods that can be used in JDBC to work with stored procedures. A *stored procedure* is one or more SQL statements (usually) stored in the database in a compiled form. When you create a CallableStatement object, you use this object to call the stored procedure, just as you would a method.

CallableStatement indicates parameters in a stored procedure using the ? symbol. These parameters are numbered left to right, starting at 1. You use set*xxx*() methods to set the values of the parameters, and you use get*xxx*() methods to get back values from parameters of type OUT and from a result set, if CallableStatement returns one. JDBC supports IN and OUT parameters but not INOUT parameters. In the following code snippet, a stored procedure will be created and stored in the Books table of a library's RDBMS and then executed using a CallableStatement:

```
String storedProc = "create procedure SHOW_LEWIS_BOOKS" +
                    "as " +
                    "select TITLE, PUBLISHER, DATE " +
                            "from BOOKS" +
```

```
                              "where AUTHOR = " +
                              "'Lewis, C.S.'";
Statement stmt = conn.createStatement();
stmt.executeUpdate(storedProc);
CallableStatement cs = con.prepareCall
                 ("{call SHOW_LEWIS_BOOKS}");
ResultSet rs = cs.executeQuery();
// First, create the contents of a stored procedure, in this
// case a SQL statement. Then put it in the database with
// the executeUpdate() call. Then execute the stored
// procedure by calling executeQuery on the
// resulting CallableStatement.
```

Methods

```
Array         getArray(int i)
BigDecimal    getBigDecimal(int parameterIndex)
BigDecimal    getBigDecimal(int parameterIndex, int scale) (Deprecated)
Blob          getBlob(int i)
boolean       getBoolean(int parameterIndex)
byte          getByte(int parameterIndex)
byte[]        getBytes(int parameterIndex)
Clob          getClob(int i)
Date          getDate(int parameterIndex)
Date          getDate(int parameterIndex, Calendar cal)
double        getDouble(int parameterIndex)
float         getFloat(int parameterIndex)
int           getInt(int parameterIndex)
long          getLong(int parameterIndex)
Object        getObject(int parameterIndex)
Object        getObject(int i, Map map)
Ref           getRef(int i)
short         getShort(int parameterIndex)
String        getString(int parameterIndex)
Time          getTime(int parameterIndex)
Time          getTime(int parameterIndex, Calendar cal)
Timestamp     getTimestamp(int parameterIndex)
Timestamp     getTimestamp(int parameterIndex, Calendar cal)
void          registerOutParameter(int parameterIndex, int sqlType)
void          registerOutParameter(int parameterIndex, int sqlType, int scale)
void          registerOutParameter(int paramIndex, int sqlType String typeName)
boolean       wasNull()
```

Interface Connection

```
public abstract interface Connection
```

The Connection interface provides method declarations for a database connection. A connection is required to communicate with a database. The normal means of getting an object that implements the Connection interface is

```
Connection conn = DriverManager.getConnection(dbURL)
```

where dbURL is a URL that describes the information needed by the DriverManager object to locate an appropriate database JDBC driver and provides sufficient information for the driver to connect to the database system.

It's critical that you be aware of the fact that, by default, a Connection object commits work after every single call. To prevent this—which you ought to do—and commit when you think it's appropriate, call setAutoCommit(false). You should also be sure to set the isolation level by calling the following:

```
TheConnection.setTransactionIsolation
                (TRANSACTION_REPEATABLE_READ);
// Set the transaction isolation level to Repeatable Read,
// which means that dirty reads and nonrepeatable reads are
// disallowed, but you may still get phantom rows.
```

Fields

static int	TRANSACTION_NONE
static int	TRANSACTION_READ_COMMITTED
static int	TRANSACTION_READ_UNCOMMITTED
static int	TRANSACTION_REPEATABLE_READ
static int	TRANSACTION_SERIALIZABLE

Methods

void	clearWarnings()
void	close()
void	commit()
Statement	createStatement()
Statement	createStatement(int resultSetType, int resultSetConcurrency)
boolean	getAutoCommit()
String	getCatalog()
DatabaseMetaData	getMetaData()
int	getTransactionIsolation()
Map	getTypeMap()
SQLWarning	getWarnings()
boolean	isClosed()
boolean	isReadOnly()
String	nativeSQL(String sql)
CallableStatement	prepareCall(String sql)
CallableStatement	prepareCall(String sql, int resultSetType, int resultSetConcurrency)
PreparedStatement	prepareStatement(String sql)
PreparedStatement	prepareStatement(String sql, int resultSetType, int resultSetConcurrency)
void	rollback()
void	setAutoCommit(boolean autoCommit)
void	setCatalog(String catalog)
void	setReadOnly(boolean readOnly)
void	setTransactionIsolation(int level)
void	setTypeMap(Map map)

Interface Driver
public abstract interface **Driver**

The `Driver` interface specifies the methods a JDBC driver should implement. A JDBC driver is normally created and registered with `DriverManager`, like this:

`Class.forName("MyDriver");`

This causes the class definition to be loaded. As a rule, and in conformance with JDBCspecification, a `Driver` implementation class uses a static initializer to instantiate itself and register itself with `DriverManager` using the `registerDriver()` method.

The use of the `Driver` interface allows a program to stay completely independent of the implementation of a `Driver` implementation class, so the class can be modified or even replaced by a different class without the program being changed at all, except possibly the `Driver` implementation classname. The `Driver` implementation is not specified and may vary greatly from vendor to vendor, both in logic and performance. JDBC drivers are of one of four types, and you should choose a driver based in part on this:

- Type 1—JDBC-ODBC bridge. This is not recommended for a commercial program.
- Type 2—JDBC native driver. This type uses C APIs to communicate directly with the DBMS.
- Type 3—A vendor-neutral, network-based protocol.
- Type 4—Java calls are made directly to the database. This type is generally supplied by a DBMS vendor.

More information can be found in the JDBC 2.0 specification.

Methods
```
boolean                 acceptsURL(String url)
Connection              connect(String url, Properties info)
int                     getMajorVersion()
int                     getMinorVersion()
DriverPropertyInfo[]    getPropertyInfo(String url, Properties info)
boolean                 jdbcCompliant()
```

Interface PreparedStatement
public abstract interface **PreparedStatement**
                        extends Statement

A `PreparedStatement` object represents a SQL prepared statement. When a SQL statement is submitted to a DBMS, it must be parsed, compiled, optimized, and have a query plan generated. A `PreparedStatement` improves your program's performance, if you need to submit the same statement many times using different parameters, by creating and caching a compiled version of a SQL statement so that the statement does not need to be parsed, compiled, and optimized every single time it's executed. You build a `PreparedStatement` like this:

```
PreparedStatement ps = conn.createPreparedStatement
                ("select * from Employee where LastName = ? and Division =
                 ?");
ps.setString(1, "Smith");
ps.setInt(2, 100);
ResultSet rs = ps.executeQuery();
```

Here, ? stands for a modifiable value in the SQL statement. You set the value with a set*xxx*() method, which specifies a parameter number and a value. Then, the PreparedStatement is submitted to the Driver object. Generally, you would use the set*xxx*() methods and execute the PreparedStatement inside a loop, getting the parameter values from another table or from a file.

Methods

void	addBatch()
void	clearParameters()
boolean	execute()
ResultSet	executeQuery()
int	executeUpdate()
ResultSetMetaData	getMetaData()
void	setArray(int i, Array x)
void	setAsciiStream(int parameterIndex, InputStream x, int length)
void	setBigDecimal(int parameterIndex, BigDecimal x)
void	setBinaryStream(int parameterIndex, InputStream x, int length)
void	setBlob(int i, Blob x)
void	setBoolean(int parameterIndex, boolean x)
void	setByte(int parameterIndex, byte x)
void	setBytes(int parameterIndex, byte[] x)
void	setCharacterStream(int parameterIndex, Reader reader, int length)
void	setClob(int i, Clob x)
void	setDate(int parameterIndex, Date x)
void	setDate(int parameterIndex, Date x, Calendar cal)
void	setDouble(int parameterIndex, double x)
void	setFloat(int parameterIndex, float x)
void	setInt(int parameterIndex, int x)
void	setLong(int parameterIndex, long x)
void	setNull(int parameterIndex, int sqlType)
void	setNull(int paramIndex, int sqlType, String typeName)
void	setObject(int parameterIndex, Object x)
void	setObject(int parameterIndex, Object x, int targetSqlType)
void	setObject(int parameterIndex, Object x, int targetSqlType, int scale)
void	setRef(int i, Ref x)
void	setShort(int parameterIndex, short x)
void	setString(int parameterIndex, String x)
void	setTime(int parameterIndex, Time x)

void	setTime(int parameterIndex, Time x, Calendar cal)
void	setTimestamp(int parameterIndex, Timestamp x)
void	setTimestamp(int parameterIndex, Timestamp x, Calendar cal)
void	setUnicodeStream(int parameterIndex, InputStream x, int length) (Deprecated)

Interface ResultSet

public abstract interface **ResultSet**

ResultSet represents an object that contains the rows and columns returned from a query. With a JDBC 1.0–style ResultSet, you can advance forward through the ResultSet using next() and then extract column values with one of a number of get*xxx*() methods. Using a JDBC 2.0 scrollable ResultSet, you can also move backwards in a ResultSet, go to the top of the ResultSet, jump to a specific row, and so forth. For example, assume a table with four columns: String Author, String Title, Date PubDate, and int numCopies. Here is a query that creates and processes a ResultSet for the query:

```
Statement stmt = conn.createStatement();
ResultSet rs = stmt.executeQuery("select * from Books");
While(rs.next() == true)
    {
      System.out.println("Author: " + rs.getString("Author"));
      // Specify the data type in the getxxx() method, like
      // getString(), and specify the column name or,
      // less desirably, the column number, to obtain
      // the contents of this column from this row.
      System.out.println("Title: " + rs.getString("Title"));
      System.out.println("Number of copies: " +
                        Rs.getInt("numCopies"));
    }
```

Fields

static int	CONCUR_READ_ONLY
static int	CONCUR_UPDATABLE
static int	FETCH_FORWARD
static int	FETCH_REVERSE
static int	FETCH_UNKNOWN
static int	TYPE_FORWARD_ONLY
static int	TYPE_SCROLL_INSENSITIVE
static int	TYPE_SCROLL_SENSITIVE

Methods

boolean	absolute(int row)
void	afterLast()
void	beforeFirst()
void	cancelRowUpdates()
void	clearWarnings()

void	**close**()
void	**deleteRow**()
int	**findColumn**(String columnName)
boolean	**first**()
Array	**getArray**(int i)
Array	**getArray**(String colName)
InputStream	**getAsciiStream**(int columnIndex)
InputStream	**getAsciiStream**(String columnName)
BigDecimal	**getBigDecimal**(int columnIndex)
BigDecimal	**getBigDecimal**(int columnIndex, int scale) (Deprecated)
BigDecimal	**getBigDecimal**(String columnName)
BigDecimal	**getBigDecimal**(String columnName, int scale) (Deprecated)
InputStream	**getBinaryStream**(int columnIndex)
InputStream	**getBinaryStream**(String columnName)
Blob	**getBlob**(int i)
Blob	**getBlob**(String colName)
boolean	**getBoolean**(int columnIndex)
boolean	**getBoolean**(String columnName)
byte	**getByte**(int columnIndex)
byte	**getByte**(String columnName)
byte[]	**getBytes**(int columnIndex)
byte[]	**getBytes**(String columnName)
Reader	**getCharacterStream**(int columnIndex)
Reader	**getCharacterStream**(String columnName)
Clob	**getClob**(int i)
Clob	**getClob**(String colName)
int	**getConcurrency**()
String	**getCursorName**()
Date	**getDate**(int columnIndex)
Date	**getDate**(int columnIndex, Calendar cal)
Date	**getDate**(String columnName)
Date	**getDate**(String columnName, Calendar cal)
double	**getDouble**(int columnIndex)
double	**getDouble**(String columnName)
int	**getFetchDirection**()
int	**getFetchSize**()
float	**getFloat**(int columnIndex)
float	**getFloat**(String columnName)
int	**getInt**(int columnIndex)
int	**getInt**(String columnName)
long	**getLong**(int columnIndex)
long	**getLong**(String columnName)
ResultSetMetaData	**getMetaData**()
Object	**getObject**(int columnIndex)
Object	**getObject**(int i, Map map)
Object	**getObject**(String columnName)
Object	**getObject**(String colName, Map map)
Ref	**getRef**(int i)
Ref	**getRef**(String colName)
int	**getRow**()

short	**getShort**(int columnIndex)
short	**getShort**(String columnName)
Statement	**getStatement**()
String	**getString**(int columnIndex)
String	**getString**(String columnName)
Time	**getTime**(int columnIndex)
Time	**getTime**(int columnIndex, Calendar cal)
Time	**getTime**(String columnName)
Time	**getTime**(String columnName, Calendar cal)
Timestamp	**getTimestamp**(int columnIndex)
Timestamp	**getTimestamp**(int columnIndex, Calendar cal)
Timestamp	**getTimestamp**(String columnName)
Timestamp	**getTimestamp**(String columnName, Calendar cal)
int	**getType**()
InputStream	**getUnicodeStream**(int columnIndex) (Deprecated)
InputStream	**getUnicodeStream**(String columnName) (Deprecated)
SQLWarning	**getWarnings**()
void	**insertRow**()
boolean	**isAfterLast**()
boolean	**isBeforeFirst**()
boolean	**isFirst**()
boolean	**isLast**()
boolean	**last**()
void	**moveToCurrentRow**()
void	**moveToInsertRow**()
boolean	**next**()
boolean	**previous**()
void	**refreshRow**()
boolean	**relative**(int rows)
boolean	**rowDeleted**()
boolean	**rowInserted**()
boolean	**rowUpdated**()
void	**setFetchDirection**(int direction)
void	**setFetchSize**(int rows)
void	**updateAsciiStream**(int columnIndex, InputStream x, int length)
void	**updateAsciiStream**(String columnName, InputStream x, int length)
void	**updateBigDecimal**(int columnIndex, BigDecimal x)
void	**updateBigDecimal**(String columnName, BigDecimal x)
void	**updateBinaryStream**(int columnIndex, InputStream x, int length)
void	**updateBinaryStream**(String columnName, InputStream x, int length)
void	**updateBoolean**(int columnIndex, boolean x)
void	**updateBoolean**(String columnName, boolean x)
void	**updateByte**(int columnIndex, byte x)
void	**updateByte**(String columnName, byte x)
void	**updateBytes**(int columnIndex, byte[] x)
void	**updateBytes**(String columnName, byte[] x)

void	**updateCharacterStream**(int columnIndex, Reader x, int length)
void	**updateCharacterStream**(String columnName, Reader reader, int length)
void	**updateDate**(int columnIndex, Date x)
void	**updateDate**(String columnName, Date x)
void	**updateDouble**(int columnIndex, double x)
void	**updateDouble**(String columnName, double x)
void	**updateFloat**(int columnIndex, float x)
void	**updateFloat**(String columnName, float x)
void	**updateInt**(int columnIndex, int x)
void	**updateInt**(String columnName, int x)
void	**updateLong**(int columnIndex, long x)
void	**updateLong**(String columnName, long x)
void	**updateNull**(int columnIndex)
void	**updateNull**(String columnName)
void	**updateObject**(int columnIndex, Object x)
void	**updateObject**(int columnIndex, Object x, int scale)
void	**updateObject**(String columnName, Object x)
void	**updateObject**(String columnName, Object x, int scale)
void	**updateRow**()
void	**updateShort**(int columnIndex, short x)
void	**updateShort**(String columnName, short x)
void	**updateString**(int columnIndex, String x)
void	**updateString**(String columnName, String x)
void	**updateTime**(int columnIndex, Time x)
void	**updateTime**(String columnName, Time x)
void	**updateTimestamp**(int columnIndex, Timestamp x)
void	**updateTimestamp**(String columnName, Timestamp x)
boolean	**wasNull**()

Interface Statement

public abstract interface **Statement**

The Statement interface is implemented by objects used to execute dynamic (not prepared) SQL statements, especially for queries that return a ResultSet object.

Methods

void	**addBatch**(String sql)
void	**cancel**()
void	**clearBatch**()
void	**clearWarnings**()
void	**close**()
boolean	**execute**(String sql)
int[]	**executeBatch**()
ResultSet	**executeQuery**(String sql)
int	**executeUpdate**(String sql)
Connection	**getConnection**()
int	**getFetchDirection**()

Interface and Class Details 689

```
int              getFetchSize()
int              getMaxFieldSize()
int              getMaxRows()
boolean          getMoreResults()
int              getQueryTimeout()
ResultSet        getResultSet()
int              getResultSetConcurrency()
int              getResultSetType()
int              getUpdateCount()
SQLWarning       getWarnings()
void             setCursorName(String name)
void             setEscapeProcessing(boolean enable)
void             setFetchDirection(int direction)
void             setFetchSize(int rows)
void             setMaxFieldSize(int max)
void             setMaxRows(int max)
void             setQueryTimeout(int seconds)
```

Class DriverManager

public class **DriverManager**
              extends Object

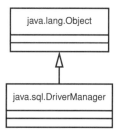

The DriverManager class exists as a singleton in the JVM and is responsible for managing JDBC drivers. The DriverManager maintains a list of drivers and their subprotocols. When an object requests a database connection with the getConnection() method, the DriverManager object finds a suitable driver in the internal list it maintains, if there is a suitable driver, and delegates to that driver the job of getting a connection and returning a Connection object to the caller.

JDBC drivers get into the DriverManager's driver list in one of two ways:

- By calling registerDriver() in the driver's code
- By being named in the jdbc.drivers property, like this:

    java -Djdbc.drivers=driver1.class, driver2.class

Methods

```
static void              deregisterDriver(Driver driver)
static Connection        getConnection(String url)
static Connection        getConnection(String url, Properties info)
static Connection        getConnection(String url, String user, String password)
```

static Driver	**getDriver**(String url)
static Enumeration	**getDrivers**()
static int	**getLoginTimeout**()
static PrintStream	**getLogStream**() (Deprecated)
static PrintWriter	**getLogWriter**()
static void	**println**(String message)
static void	**registerDriver**(Driver driver)
static void	**setLoginTimeout**(int seconds)
static void	**setLogStream**(PrintStream out) (Deprecated)
static void	**setLogWriter**(PrintWriter out)

Class Timestamp

public class **Timestamp**
      extends Date

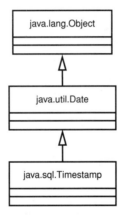

This class is a wrapper for `java.util.Date` that lets a `java.sql.TimeStamp` object represent a SQL timestamp.

Constructors

Timestamp (int year, int month, int date, int hour, int minute,
  int second, int nano) (Deprecated)
Timestamp(long time)

Methods

boolean	**after**(Timestamp ts)
boolean	**before**(Timestamp ts)
boolean	**equals**(Object ts)
boolean	**equals**(Timestamp ts)
int	**getNanos**()
void	**setNanos**(int n)
String	**toString**()
static Timestamp	**valueOf**(String s)

CHAPTER 32

java.text

The java.text package is useful for formatting numbers, dates, and times in multiple forms. This is particularly important for internationalization or localization of applications.

Interfaces

AttributedCharacterIterator
CharacterIterator

Classes

Annotation
AttributedCharacterIterator.Attribute
AttributedString
BreakIterator
ChoiceFormat
CollationElementIterator
CollationKey
Collator
DateFormat
DateFormatSymbols
DecimalFormat
DecimalFormatSymbols
FieldPosition
Format
MessageFormat
NumberFormat
ParsePosition
RuleBasedCollator
SimpleDateFormat
StringCharacterIterator

Exception

ParseException

Class Details

Class ChoiceFormat

```
public class ChoiceFormat
               extends NumberFormat
```

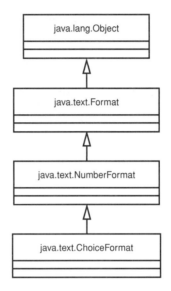

The ChoiceFormat class is useful for formatting a range of numbers. It is often used in a MessageFormat for dealing with plurals. The choices are specified with a list of doubles in ascending order. The ChoiceFormat class differs from the other formatting classes in this package because it requires the use of a constructor, rather than a factory method, such as getInstance(). A ChoiceFormat is specified with two formats: limits and values. Here's a short code snippet that you could make part of a program:

```
double[] limitArray = {1,2,3,4,5,6};
String[] formatArray = {"Jan","Feb","Mar","Apr","May","Jun"};
ChoiceFormat choiceForm = new ChoiceFormat(limitArray,
                                           formatArray);
 ParsePosition parsed = new ParsePosition(0);
   for (double i = 0.0; i <= 8.0; ++i)
      {
        parsed.setIndex(0);
        System.out.println(i + " -> " + choiceForm.format(i) +
                    " -> " +
            choiceForm.parse(choiceForm.format(i),parsed));
      }
```

Constructors

ChoiceFormat(double[] limits, String[] formats)
ChoiceFormat(String newPattern)

Methods

void	**applyPattern**(String newPattern)
Object	**clone**()
boolean	**equals**(Object obj)
StringBuffer	**format**(double number, StringBuffer toAppendTo, FieldPosition status)
StringBuffer	**format**(long number, StringBuffer toAppendTo, FieldPosition status)
Object[]	**getFormats**()
double[]	**getLimits**()
int	**hashCode**()
static double	**nextDouble**(double d)
static double	**nextDouble**(double d, boolean positive)
Number	**parse**(String text, ParsePosition status)
static double	**previousDouble**(double d)
void	**setChoices**(double[] limits, String[] formats)
String	**toPattern**()

Class DateFormat

public abstract class **DateFormat**
                          extends Format

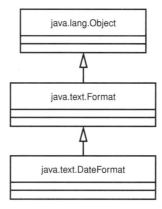

The DateFormat class is an abstract base class for classes that format and parse dates and times in a locale-independent way, such as SimpleDateFormat. You use them with a specific locale to get the date format you need. This formatting is illustrated in Chapter 18, "Text." DateFormat primarily provides factory methods for getting formatting objects and putting dates in specific formats. You can use these formatting objects to turn a Date object into a nicely formatted string such as

September 15, 1999 1:49 PM PST

Fields

static int	**AM_PM_FIELD**
protected Calendar	**calendar**

```
static int              DATE_FIELD
static int              DAY_OF_WEEK_FIELD
static int              DAY_OF_WEEK_IN_MONTH_FIELD
static int              DAY_OF_YEAR_FIELD
static int              DEFAULT
static int              ERA_FIELD
static int              FULL
static int              HOUR_OF_DAY0_FIELD
static int              HOUR_OF_DAY1_FIELD
static int              HOUR0_FIELD
static int              HOUR1_FIELD
static int              LONG
static int              MEDIUM
static int              MILLISECOND_FIELD
static int              MINUTE_FIELD
static int              MONTH_FIELD
protected NumberFormat  numberFormat
static int              SECOND_FIELD
static int              SHORT
static int              TIMEZONE_FIELD
static int              WEEK_OF_MONTH_FIELD
static int              WEEK_OF_YEAR_FIELD
static int              YEAR_FIELD
```

Constructor

```
protected     DateFormat()
```

Methods

```
Object                  clone()
boolean                 equals(Object obj)
String                  format(Date date)
abstract StringBuffer   format(Date date, StringBuffer toAppendTo,
                               FieldPosition fieldPosition)
StringBuffer            format(Object obj, StringBuffer toAppendTo,
                               FieldPosition fieldPosition)
static Locale[]         getAvailableLocales()
Calendar                getCalendar()
static DateFormat       getDateInstance()
static DateFormat       getDateInstance(int style)
static DateFormat       getDateInstance(int style, Locale aLocale)
static DateFormat       getDateTimeInstance()
static DateFormat       getDateTimeInstance (int dateStyle, int timeStyle)
static DateFormat       getDateTimeInstance (int dateStyle, int timeStyle,
                               Locale aLocale)
static DateFormat       getInstance()
NumberFormat            getNumberFormat()
static DateFormat       getTimeInstance()
static DateFormat       getTimeInstance(int style)
static DateFormat       getTimeInstance(int style, Locale aLocale)
TimeZone                getTimeZone()
```

Class Details 695

```
int                     hashCode()
boolean                 isLenient()
Date                    parse(String text)
abstract Date           parse(String text, ParsePosition pos)
Object                  parseObject(String source, ParsePosition pos)
void                    setCalendar(Calendar newCalendar)
void                    setLenient(boolean lenient)
void                    setNumberFormat(NumberFormat newNumberFormat)
void                    setTimeZone(TimeZone zone)
```

Class DecimalFormat
public class **DecimalFormat**
            extends NumberFormat

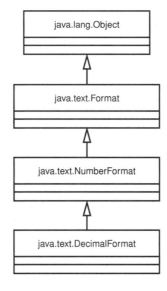

The DecimalFormat class is used to perform custom formatting of numeric data, using special characters to determine what separates digits, what (if anything) replaces zero in a number, and so forth.

Constructors
DecimalFormat()
DecimalFormat(String pattern)
DecimalFormat(String pattern,
DecimalFormatSymbols symbols)

Methods
```
void                    applyLocalizedPattern(String pattern)
void                    applyPattern(String pattern)
Object                  clone()
boolean                 equals(Object obj)
StringBuffer            format(double number, StringBuffer result,
```

	FieldPosition fieldPosition)
StringBuffer	**format**(long number, StringBuffer result, FieldPosition fieldPosition)
DecimalFormatSymbols	**getDecimalFormatSymbols()**
int	**getGroupingSize()**
int	**getMultiplier()**
String	**getNegativePrefix()**
String	**getNegativeSuffix()**
String	**getPositivePrefix()**
String	**getPositiveSuffix()**
int	**hashCode()**
boolean isDecimalSeparator	**AlwaysShown()**
Number	**parse**(String text, ParsePosition parsePosition)
void setDecimalFormat	**Symbols**(DecimalFormatSymbols newSymbols)
void setDecimalSeparator	**AlwaysShown**(boolean newValue)
void	**setGroupingSize**(int newValue)
void	**setMaximumFractionDigits**(int newValue)
void	**setMaximumIntegerDigits**(int newValue)
void	**setMinimumFractionDigits**(int newValue)
void	**setMinimumIntegerDigits**(int newValue)
void	**setMultiplier**(int newValue)
void	**setNegativePrefix**(String newValue)
void	**setNegativeSuffix**(String newValue)
void	**setPositivePrefix**(String newValue)
void	**setPositiveSuffix**(String newValue)
String	**toLocalizedPattern()**
String	**toPattern()**

Class MessageFormat

public class **MessageFormat**
                extends Format

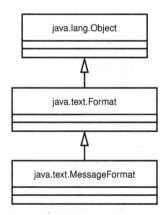

The MessageFormat class is used for formatting textual messages. It is particularly useful for dealing with complex messages that need varying position values for different languages.

Constructors
`MessageFormat` (String pattern)

Methods
```
void            applyPattern(String newPattern)
Object          clone()
boolean         equals(Object obj)
StringBuffer    format(Object[] source, StringBuffer result,
                    FieldPosition ignore)
StringBuffer    format(Object source, StringBuffer result, FieldPosition ignore)
static String   format(String pattern, Object[] arguments)
Format[]        getFormats()
Locale          getLocale()
int             hashCode()
Object[]        parse(String source)
Object[]        parse(String source, ParsePosition status)
Object          parseObject(String text, ParsePosition status)
void            setFormat(int variable, Format newFormat)
void            setFormats(Format[] newFormats)
void            setLocale(Locale theLocale)
String          toPattern()
```

Class NumberFormat
public abstract class **NumberFormat**
                    extends Format

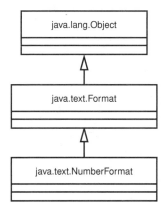

The `NumberFormat` class is the abstract base class for all number formatting classes. It provides several basic methods for formatting numbers in both standard locale-independent ways and custom ways.

Fields
```
static int     FRACTION_FIELD
static int     INTEGER_FIELD
```

Constructors
NumberFormat()

Methods

Object	clone()
boolean	equals(Object obj)
String	format(double number)
abstract StringBuffer	format(double number, StringBuffer toAppendTo, FieldPosition pos)
String	format(long number)
abstract StringBuffer	format(long number, StringBuffer toAppendTo, FieldPosition pos)
StringBuffer	format(Object number, StringBuffer toAppendTo, FieldPosition pos)
static Locale[]	getAvailableLocales()
static NumberFormat	getCurrencyInstance()
static NumberFormat	getCurrencyInstance(Locale inLocale)
static NumberFormat	getInstance()
static NumberFormat	getInstance(Locale inLocale)
int	getMaximumFractionDigits()
Int	getMaximumIntegerDigits()
int	getMinimumFractionDigits()
int	getMinimumIntegerDigits()
static NumberFormat	getNumberInstance()
static NumberFormat	getNumberInstance(Locale inLocale)
static NumberFormat	getPercentInstance()
static NumberFormat	getPercentInstance(Locale inLocale)
int	hashCode()
boolean	isGroupingUsed()
boolean	isParseIntegerOnly()
Number	parse(String text)
abstract Number	parse(String text, ParsePosition pPos)
Object	parseObject(String source, ParsePosition pPos)
void	setGroupingUsed(boolean newValue)
void	setMaximumFractionDigits(int newValue)
void	setMaximumIntegerDigits(int newValue)
void	setMinimumFractionDigits(int newValue)
void	setMinimumIntegerDigits(int newValue)
void	setParseIntegerOnly(boolean value)

Class SimpleDateFormat

public class **SimpleDateFormat**
          extends DateFormat

The SimpleDateFormat class enables you to format and parse dates in a locale-independent way and represent them according to a specific locale on-the-fly. For example, using the same Date object, you can print a short version of a date, such as 09/15/99, or a long version, such as September 15, 1999. You can also print a version of the date for a specific locale other than the United States, such as the form used in England: 15/9/99, in which the day precedes the month.

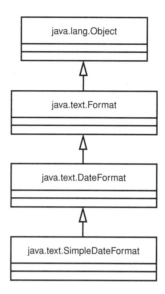

You can use several different symbols, as shown in Table 32.1.

Table 32.1 Date Formatting Symbols

Symbol	Meaning	Presentation	Example
G	Era designator	(Text)	AD
y	Year	(Number)	1996
M	Month in year	(Text & Number)	July & 07
d	Day in month	(Number)	10
h	Hour in am/pm (1–12)	(Number)	12
H	Hour in day (0–23)	(Number)	0
m	Minute in hour	(Number)	30
s	Second in minute	(Number)	55
S	Millisecond	(Number)	978
E	Day in week	(Text)	Tuesday
D	Day in year	(Number)	189
F	Day of week in month	(Number)	2 (2nd Wed in July)
w	Week in year	(Number)	27
W	Week in month	(Number)	2
a	Am/pm marker	(Text)	PM
k	Hour in day (1–24)	(Number)	24
K	Hour in am/pm (0–11)	(Number)	0
z	Time zone	(Text)	Pacific Standard Time
'	Escape for text	(Delimiter)	
''	Single quote	(Literal)	'

The number of symbols in the pattern determines the format of the date. For an example, see Table 32.2.

Table 32.2 Samples of Formatting Symbol Use

Format Pattern Example	Result
`"yyyy.MM.dd G 'at' hh:mm:ss z"`	1999.98.15 AD at 16:12:16 PDT
`"EEE, MMM d, ''yy"`	Wed, September 15, '98

Constructors

```
SimpleDateFormat()
SimpleDateFormat(String pattern)
SimpleDateFormat(String pattern, DateFormatSymbols formatData)
SimpleDateFormat(String pattern, Locale loc)
```

Methods

void	`applyLocalizedPattern(String pattern)`
void	`applyPattern(String pattern)`
Object	`clone()`
boolean	`equals(Object obj)`
StringBuffer	`format(Date date, StringBuffer toAppendTo, FieldPosition pos)`
Date	`get2DigitYearStart()`
DateFormatSymbols	`getDateFormatSymbols()`
int	`hashCode()`
Date	`parse(String text, ParsePosition pos)`
void	`set2DigitYearStart(Date startDate)`
void	`setDateFormatSymbols(DateFormatSymbols newForSym)`
String	`toLocalizedPattern()`
String	`toPattern()`

CHAPTER 33

java.util

This chapter provides a quick reference of the classes in java.util. Several of these classes are very common and very important. The java.util package contains the Collection framework (with Set, List, and Map implementations), Vector (which is now part of the Collection framework), Date, GregorianCalendar, and Properties, just to name a few of the more important classes.

Interfaces

Collection
Comparator
Enumeration
EventListener
Iterator
List
ListIterator
Map
Map.Entry
Observer
Set
SortedMap
SortedSet

Classes

AbstractCollection
AbstractList
AbstractMap
AbstractSequentialList
AbstractSet
ArrayList
Arrays
BitSet
Calendar
Collections
Date

Dictionary
EventObject
GregorianCalendar
HashMap
HashSet
Hashtable
LinkedList
ListResourceBundle
Locale
Observable
Properties
PropertyPermission
PropertyResourceBundle
Random
ResourceBundle
SimpleTimeZone
Stack
StringTokenizer
TimeZone
TreeMap
TreeSet
Vector
WeakHashMap

Exceptions

ConcurrentModificationException
EmptyStackException
MissingResourceException
NoSuchElementException
TooManyListenersException

Interface and Class Details

Interface Collection

public abstract interface **Collection**

The Collection interface is the base interface for all Collection interfaces and the basis of all Collection classes in the Collection framework. Collection is simply a set of objects that can be treated as individual items or as a group. The Collection interface specifies methods for dealing with individual objects, such as add(), and for dealing with a whole Collection at once, such as removeAll().

Methods

boolean	**add**(Object o)
boolean	**addAll**(Collection c)
void	**clear**()
boolean	**contains**(Object o)
boolean	**containsAll**(Collection c)
boolean	**equals**(Object o)

Interface and Class Details

```
int        hashCode()
boolean    isEmpty()
Iterator   iterator()
boolean    remove(Object o)
boolean    removeAll(Collection c)
boolean    retainAll(Collection c)
int        size()
Object[]   toArray()
Object[]toArray(Object[] a)
```

Interface Iterator

public abstract interface **Iterator**

The Iterator interface specifies the methods for an object that can be used to iterate or step through a Collection. Here is a code snippet showing how you might iterate through a collection and remove from it any element that matches some condition:

```
public boolean filterOutJunk(Collection bookColl)
    {
     for (Iterator I = bookColl.iterator();
                        i.hasNext(); )
        {
        if (isJunkyBook(i.next()))
            i.remove();
     return true;
    }
```

Methods

```
boolean    hasNext()
Object     next()
void       remove()
```

Interface List

public abstract interface **List**
                    extends Collection

The List interface specifies the methods for a Collection implemented as a list. A List implementation provides for a Collection that's ordered and allows duplicate objects. The following is a small code fragment that shows how to create, populate, and extract from a List. This code uses the Collections.shuffle() method, which rearranges the elements in the list in a random fashion. Therefore, the contents come out in random order.

```
public boolean shuffleAuthors(String authors[])
    {
    // This method accepts a String array of authors.
    List authorList = new ArrayList();
    // Create an object that implements the List interface.
    for (int i=0; i<authors.length; i++)
```

```
        authorList.add(authors[i]);
    Collections.shuffle(authorList, new Random());
    System.out.println(authorList);
    Return true;
}
```

Methods

void	**add**(int index, Object element)
boolean	**add**(Object o)
boolean	**addAll**(Collection c)
boolean	**addAll**(int index, Collection c)
void	**clear**()
boolean	**contains**(Object o)
boolean	**containsAll**(Collection c)
boolean	**equals**(Object o)
Object	**get**(int index)
int	**hashCode**()
int	**indexOf**(Object o)
boolean	**isEmpty**()
Iterator	**iterator**()
int	**lastIndexOf**(Object o)
ListIterator	**listIterator**()
ListIterator	**listIterator**(int index)
Object	**remove**(int index)
boolean	**remove**(Object o)
boolean	**removeAll**(Collection c)
boolean	**retainAll**(Collection c)
Object	**set**(int index, Object element)
int	**size**()
List	**subList**(int fromIndex, int toIndex)
Object[]	**toArray**()
Object[]	**toArray**(Object[] a)

Interface Map

public abstract interface **Map**

The Map interface specifies the methods for a Collection implemented as a Map. A Map is not technically a Collection in a normal sense. A Map implementation object consists of key/value pairs. A Map may not contain duplicate key values. By default, a Map has no ordering. A TreeMap, on the other hand, is an implementation that provides for ordering. The following is a code snippet that shows how to create a map object, add to it, and then determine the frequency of various values in it. In general, you do not want a Map to contain duplicate items, but this is semantically valid. It's a performance issue if a Map contains duplicate items.

```
public boolean getFrequency(String authors[])
    {
    Map map = new HashMap();
    // Initialize frequency table
```

```
      for (int i=0; i<authors.length; i++)
          {
            Integer frequency =
                      (Integer) map.get(authors[i]);
            map.put(authors[i], (frequency == null ? ONE :
                      new Integer(freq.intValue() + 1)));
          }
      System.out.println(map.size()+
                      " distinct authors detected:");
      System.out.println(map);
      return true;
    }
```

Methods
```
void         clear()
boolean      containsKey(Object key)
boolean      containsValue(Object value)
Set          entrySet()
boolean      equals(Object o)
Object       get(Object key)
int          hashCode()
boolean      isEmpty()
Set          keySet()
Object       put(Object key, Object value)
void         putAll(Map t)
Object       remove(Object key)
int          size()
Collection   values()
```

Interface Observer
```
public abstract interface Observer
```

The Observer interface specifies the methods for the "observer" participant in the Observer/Observable design pattern. This design pattern refers to an object-oriented scheme for having any number of objects passively observe an observable object. The observers want to know when the observable object performs one or more activities. Generally, the observable object notifies the observers that some event has occurred.

Although the method names and exact framework are different, you can see this design pattern at work when using Java beans. When one of a bean's properties changes, the bean notifies any registered PropertyChangeListener.

Methods
```
void    update(Observable o, Object arg)
```

Interface Set
```
public abstract interface Set
                    extends Collection
```

Set specifies the methods for a Collection, which is unordered but allows no duplicates. Here is a code snippet showing how to create and add an element to a HashSet:

```java
public boolean buildSet(Book[] newBooks)
    {
     Set bookSet = new HashSet();
     // Returns an object that implements the Set interface.
     for (int i=0; i<newBooks.length; i++)
         if (!bookSet.add(newBooks[i]))
             System.out.println("Duplicate detected: " +
                         newBooks[i]);
     System.out.println(bookSet.size()+
                 " distinct new books: "+ bookSet);
     return true;
    }
```

Methods

boolean	**add**(Object o)
boolean	**addAll**(Collection c)
void	**clear**()
boolean	**contains**(Object o)
boolean	**containsAll**(Collection c)
boolean	**equals**(Object o)
int	**hashCode**()
boolean	**isEmpty**()
Iterator	**iterator**()
boolean	**remove**(Object o)
boolean	**removeAll**(Collection c)
boolean	**retainAll**(Collection c)
int	**size**()
Object[]	**toArray**()
Object[]	**toArray**(Object[] a)

Class ArrayList

```
public class ArrayList
            extends AbstractList
            implements List, Cloneable, Serializable
```

An ArrayList object implements the List interface in the form of a "growable" array. In fact, you can create an array from an ArrayList, and vice versa.

Constructors

ArrayList ()
ArrayList(Collection c)
ArrayList(int initialCapacity)

Interface and Class Details

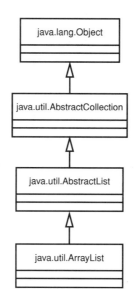

Methods

void	**add**(int index, Object element)
boolean	**add**(Object o)
boolean	**addAll**(Collection c)
boolean	**addAll**(int index, Collection c)
void	**clear**()
Object	**clone**()
boolean	**contains**(Object elem)
void	**ensureCapacity**(int minCapacity)
Object	**get**(int index)
int	**indexOf**(Object elem)
boolean	**isEmpty**()
int	**lastIndexOf**(Object elem)
Object	**remove**(int index)
void	**removeRange**(int fromIndex, int toIndex)
Object	**set**(int index, Object element)
int	**size**()
Object[]	**toArray**()
Object[]	**toArray**(Object[] a)
void	**trimToSize**()

Class BitSet

```
public class BitSet
             extends Object
             implements Cloneable, Serializable
```

Chapter 33: java.util

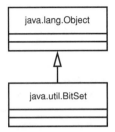

A `BitSet` object is a vector of bits that can be stepped through with nonnegative integers. You may want to use a `BitSet` to store bit information rather than using AND, OR, or XOR operations on bits in an `int`.

Constructors
BitSet ()
BitSet(int nbits)

Methods
void	**and**(BitSet set)
void	**andNot**(BitSet set)
void	**clear**(int bitIndex)
Object	**clone**()
boolean	**equals**(Object obj)
boolean	**get**(int bitIndex)
int	**hashCode**()
int	**length**()
void	**or**(BitSet set)
void	**set**(int bitIndex)
int	**size**()
String	**toString**()
void	**xor**(BitSet set)

Class Calendar
public abstract class **Calendar**
                    extends Object
                    implements Serializable, Cloneable

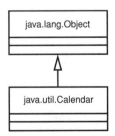

Interface and Class Details

The Calendar class is the base class for working with calendar-type information. The difference between Calendar and Date is that Date is for a specific moment in time, whereas Calendar is meant for actual dates. You should use a subclass of Calendar, because Calendar is an abstract class and cannot therefore be instantiated. The only one currently in the SDK is GregorianCalendar. If you need to create your own calendar class that doesn't use Gregorian dates, you should still try to subclass Calendar in order to get common data members and at least some methods. The Calendar class provides locale-specific support. For example, if you ask what the first day of the week is, the Calendar class returns "Sunday" for the U.S. but "Monday" for France.

Fields

static int	AM
static int	AM_PM
static int	APRIL
protected boolean	areFieldsSet
static int	AUGUST
static int	DATE
static int	DAY_OF_MONTH
static int	DAY_OF_WEEK
static int	DAY_OF_WEEK_IN_MONTH
static int	DAY_OF_YEAR
static int	DECEMBER
static int	DST_OFFSET
static int	ERA
static int	FEBRUARY
static int	FIELD_COUNT
protected int[]	fields
static int	FRIDAY
static int	HOUR
static int	HOUR_OF_DAY
protected boolean[]	isSet
protected boolean	isTimeSet
static int	JANUARY
static int	JULY
static int	JUNE
static int	MARCH
static int	MAY
static int	MILLISECOND
static int	MINUTE
static int	MONDAY
static int	MONTH
static int	NOVEMBER
static int	OCTOBER
static int	PM
static int	SATURDAY
static int	SECOND
static int	SEPTEMBER
static int	SUNDAY
static int	THURSDAY

protected long	**time**
static int	**TUESDAY**
static int	**DECEMBER**
static int	**WEDNESDAY**
static int	**WEEK_OF_MONTH**
static int	**WEEK_OF_YEAR**
static int	**YEAR**
static int	**ZONE_OFFSET**

Constructors

protected	**Calendar**()
protected	**Calendar**(TimeZone zone, Locale aLocale)

Methods

abstract void	**add**(int field, int amount)
boolean	**after**(Object when)
boolean	**before**(Object when)
void	**clear**()
void	**clear**(int field)
Object	**clone**()
protected void	**complete**()
protected abstract void	**computeFields**()
protected abstract void	**computeTime**()
boolean	**equals**(Object obj)
int	**get**(int field)
int	**getActualMaximum**(int field)
int	**getActualMinimum**(int field)
static Locale[]	**getAvailableLocales**()
int	**getFirstDayOfWeek**()
abstract int	**getGreatestMinimum**(int field)
static Calendar	**getInstance**()
static Calendar	**getInstance**(Locale aLocale)
static Calendar	**getInstance**(TimeZone zone)
static Calendar	**getInstance**(TimeZone zone, Locale aLocale)
abstract int	**getLeastMaximum**(int field)
abstract int	**getMaximum**(int field)
int	**getMinimalDaysInFirstWeek**()
abstract int	**getMinimum**(int field)
Date	**getTime**()
protected long	**getTimeInMillis**()
TimeZone	**getTimeZone**()
int	**hashCode**()
protected int	**internalGet**(int field)
boolean	**isLenient**()
boolean	**isSet**(int field)
abstract void	**roll**(int field, boolean up)
void	**roll**(int field, int amount)
void	**set**(int field, int value)
void	**set**(int year, int month, int date)
void	**set**(int year, int month, int date, int hour, int minute)

```
void                    set(int year, int month, int date,
                            int hour, int minute, int second)
void                    setFirstDayOfWeek(int value)
void                    setLenient(boolean lenient)
void                    setMinimalDaysInFirstWeek(int value)
void                    setTime(Date date)
protected void          setTimeInMillis(long millis)
void                    setTimeZone(TimeZone value)
String                  toString()
```

Class Collections

```
public class Collections
             extends Object
```

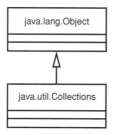

The Collections class provides a number of methods for working with any kind of collection. It provides collection views (which allow you to extract elements from a collection) such as a KeySet, which is just the key values from a Map implementation. This class also provides a number of wrappers for Collection objects, such as a synchronized wrapper, to make a Collection implementation (which does not use synchronization) behave in a synchronized fashion.

Fields

```
static List         EMPTY_LIST
static Set          EMPTY_SET
```

Methods

```
static int          binarySearch(List list, Object key)
static int          binarySearch(List list, Object key, Comparator c)
static void         copy(List dest, List src)
static Enumeration  enumeration(Collection c)
static void         fill(List list, Object o)
static Object       max(Collection coll)
static Object       max(Collection coll, Comparator comp)
static Object       min(Collection coll)
static Object       min(Collection coll, Comparator comp)
static List         nCopies(int n, Object o)
static void         reverse(List l)
static Comparator   reverseOrder()
```

static void	**shuffle**(List list)
static void	**shuffle**(List list, Random rnd)
static Set	**singleton**(Object o)
static void	**sort**(List list)
static void	**sort**(List list, Comparator c)
static Collection	**synchronizedCollection**(Collection c)
static List	**synchronizedList**(List list)
static Map	**synchronizedMap**(Map m)
static Set	**synchronizedSet**(Set s)
static SortedMap	**synchronizedSortedMap**(SortedMap m)
static SortedSet	**synchronizedSortedSet**(SortedSet s)
static Collection	**unmodifiableCollection**(Collection c)
static List	**unmodifiableList**(List list)
static Map	**unmodifiableMap**(Map m)
static Set	**unmodifiableSet**(Set s)
static SortedMap	**unmodifiableSortedMap**(SortedMap m)
static SortedSet	**unmodifiableSortedSet**(SortedSet s)

Class GregorianCalendar

public class **GregorianCalendar**
        extends Calendar

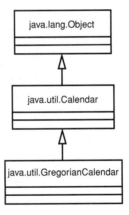

The GregorianCalendar class provides support for creating and manipulating calendar objects (that is, objects that represent a date and time). There are several fields—many from Calendar—that you can set, including time zones, daylight savings time, specific days and times to milliseconds, and so forth. Here's a code snippet to show how to create a GregorianCalendar object:

```
// Get time zone ids.
        String[] tzIds = TimeZone.getAvailableIDs(-8 * 60 * 60 * 1000);
// Create a Pacific Standard Time time zone.
        pdt = new SimpleTimeZone(-8 * 60 * 60 * 1000, tzIds[0]);
        // Set up rules for daylight savings time.
        pdt.setStartRule(Calendar.APRIL, 1, Calendar.SUNDAY,
                                        2 * 60 * 60 * 1000);
```

Interface and Class Details

```
        pdt.setEndRule(Calendar.OCTOBER, -1, Calendar.SUNDAY,
                                            2 * 60 * 60 * 1000);
        // Create a GregorianCalendar with the Pacific Daylight
        // time zone and the current date and time.
Calendar calendar = new GregorianCalendar(pdt);
        Date trialTime = new Date();
        calendar.setTime(trialTime);
        System.out.println("WEEK_OF_MONTH: " + TH));
```

This class would, of course, have to be instantiated from another object.

Fields
```
static int      AD
static int      BC
```

Constructors
GregorianCalendar ()
GregorianCalendar(int year, int month, int date)
GregorianCalendar(int year, int month, int date, int hour, int minute)
GregorianCalendar(int year, int month, int date, int hour,
    int minute, int second)
GregorianCalendar(Locale aLocale)
GregorianCalendar(TimeZone zone)
GregorianCalendar(TimeZone zone, Locale aLocale)

Methods
```
void            add(int field, int amount)
protected void  computeFields()
protected void  computeTime()
boolean         equals(Object obj)
int             getActualMaximum(int field)
int             getActualMinimum(int field)
int             getGreatestMinimum(int field)
Date            getGregorianChange()
int             getLeastMaximum(int field)
int             getMaximum(int field)
int             getMinimum(int field)
int             hashCode()
boolean         isLeapYear(int year)
void            roll(int field, boolean up)
void            roll(int field, int amount)
void            setGregorianChange(Date date)
```

Class HashMap
```
public class HashMap
            extends AbstractMap
            implements Map, Cloneable, Serializable
```

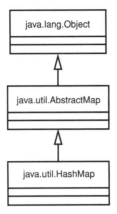

The HashMap class uses a hash table implementation to implement a Map, with keys and values ordered according to how the keys are hashed.

Constructors
```
HashMap()
HashMap(int initialCapacity)
HashMap(int initialCapacity, float loadFactor)
HashMap(Map t)
```

Methods

void	**clear**()
Object	**clone**()
boolean	**containsKey**(Object key)
boolean	**containsValue**(Object value)
Set	**entrySet**()
Object	**get**(Object key)
boolean	**isEmpty**()
Set	**keySet**()
Object	**put**(Object key, Object value)
void	**putAll**(Map t)
Object	**remove**(Object key)
int	**size**()
Collection	**values**()

Class HashSet

```
public class HashSet
            extends AbstractSet
            implements Set, Cloneable, Serializable
```

The HashSet class implements the Set interface, which is a collection of unordered objects that have no duplicate elements. HashSet is built on a hash table (actually a HashMap).

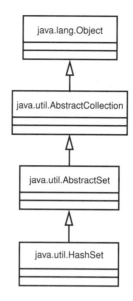

Constructors

HashSet()
HashSet(Collection c)
HashSet(int initialCapacity)
HashSet(int initialCapacity, float loadFactor)

Methods

```
boolean    add(Object o)
void       clear()
Object     clone()
boolean    contains(Object o)
boolean    isEmpty()
Iterator   iterator()
boolean    remove(Object o)
int        size()
```

Class Locale

public final class **Locale**
                    extends Object
                    implements Cloneable, Serializable

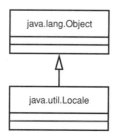

The `Locale` class provides support for representing specific geographical, political, or cultural regions. It does not merely represent a single language, but it can cover, for example, both the French language of France and the French dialect of Canada. You use a `Locale` object to access `ResourceBundle` objects to implement locale-specific values for text, numbers, and dates.

Fields

static Locale	CANADA
static Locale	CANADA_FRENCH
static Locale	CHINA
static Locale	CHINESE
static Locale	ENGLISH
static Locale	FRANCE
static Locale	FRENCH
static Locale	GERMAN
static Locale	GERMANY
static Locale	ITALIAN
static Locale	ITALY
static Locale	JAPAN
static Locale	JAPANESE
static Locale	KOREA
static Locale	KOREAN
static Locale	PRC
static Locale	SIMPLIFIED_CHINESE
static Locale	TAIWAN
static Locale	TRADITIONAL_CHINESE
static Locale	UK
static Locale	US

Constructors

Locale (String language, String country)
Locale(String language, String country, String variant)

Methods

Object	clone()
boolean	equals(Object obj)
static Locale[]	getAvailableLocales()
String	getCountry()
static Locale	getDefault()
String	getDisplayCountry()
String	getDisplayCountry(Locale inLocale)
String	getDisplayLanguage()
String	getDisplayLanguage(Locale inLocale)
String	getDisplayName()
String	getDisplayName(Locale inLocale)
String	getDisplayVariant()
String	getDisplayVariant(Locale inLocale)
String	getISO3Country()
String	getISO3Language()

```
static String[]    getISOCountries()
static String[]    getISOLanguages()
String             getLanguage()
String             getVariant()
int                hashCode()
static void        setDefault(Locale newLocale)
String             toString()
```

Class Observable

```
public class Observable
              extends Object
```

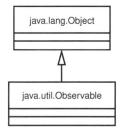

The Observable class represents an observable object, as described in the Observer interface. The Observable object has the responsibility of notifying interested observers of events. This is based on the Observer/Observable design pattern. Many developers take a different approach to implementing this design pattern and prefer an interface to define an Observable object so that the Observable object can subclass some other class.

Constructors
```
Observable ()
```

Methods
```
void              addObserver(Observer o)
protected void    clearChanged()
int               countObservers()
void              deleteObserver(Observer o)
void              deleteObservers()
boolean           hasChanged()
void              notifyObservers()
void              notifyObservers(Object arg)
protected void    setChanged()
```

Class Properties

```
public class Properties
              extends Hashtable
```

Chapter 33: java.util

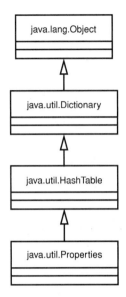

The Properties class provides for a set of properties built on key/value pairs. A Properties object is a special kind of HashTable. All the keys and values must be Strings. There are several system properties that contain helpful information. Those can be obtained like this:

```
Properties props = System.getProperties();
```

Alternatively, you can ask for a specific property like this:

```
String fileSep = Stem.getProperty("file.separator");
```

Properties can be very useful in creating configuration files. Windows users are probably accustomed to INI files or the Windows Registry. You can store similar information, such as the proper directory for a program to use, in a Properties object stored in a file. See the "Properties" section in Chapter 19, "Utility Classes," for a complete example of getting and changing properties and storing them on disk.

Fields

protected Properties **defaults**

Constructors

Properties ()
Properties(Properties defaults)

Methods

String	**getProperty**(String key)
String	**getProperty**(String key, String defaultValue)
void	**list**(PrintStream out)
void	**list**(PrintWriter out)
void	**load**(InputStream inStream)

```
Enumeration      propertyNames()
void             save(OutputStream out, String header) (Deprecated)
Object           setProperty(String key, String value)
void             store(OutputStream out, String header)
```

Class PropertyPermission

```
public final class PropertyPermission
                        extends BasicPermission
```

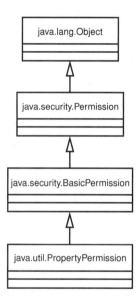

The PropertyPermission class represents permissions granted for accessing various system properties. These should be granted with care because some of them relate to a client machine's file system. The properties are primarily system properties, such as os.name and user.name. There are two actions allowed on a property: read and write. These determine, as their names suggest, the ability to access and update a property value, respectively.

Constructors
PropertyPermission (String name, String actions)

Methods
```
boolean                 equals(Object obj)
String                  getActions()
int                     hashCode()
boolean                 implies(Permission p)
PermissionCollection    newPermissionCollection()
```

Class ResourceBundle
public abstract class **ResourceBundle**
                    extends Object

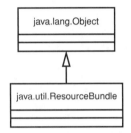

A ResourceBundle object maps variables in a program, such as the label on a button, to locale-specific values. For example, a ResourceBundle for U.S. English would map GOOD to *good,* whereas a French one would map GOOD to *bon,* and a German one would map GOOD to *gut.* See Chapter 18, "Text," for more examples.

Fields
protected ResourceBundle   **parent**

Constructors
ResourceBundle ()

Methods
static ResourceBundle	**getBundle**(String baseName)
static ResourceBundle	**getBundle**(String baseName, Locale locale)
static ResourceBundle	**getBundle**(String baseName, Locale locale, ClassLoader loader)
abstract Enumeration	**getKeys**()
Locale	**getLocale**()
Object	**getObject**(String key)
String	**getString**(String key)
String[]	**getStringArray**(String key)
protected abstract Object	**handleGetObject**(String key)
protected void	**setParent**(ResourceBundle parent)

Class StringTokenizer
public class **StringTokenizer**
                    extends Object
                    implements Enumeration

The StringTokenizer class provides a mechanism for breaking a string up into logical pieces based on tokens, such as a colon or blank space. This class is much easier to use than `StreamTokenizer`. Here's a code snippet showing how you might use the `StringTokenizer` class:

```
StringTokenizer strtok = new StringTokenizer
                ("Demonstrating the StringTokenizer class");
 while(strtok.hasMoreTokens())
    {
    println(strtok.nextToken());
    } // This will treat the blanks as delimiters of tokens
      // and print each word separately.
```

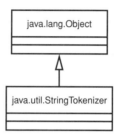

Constructors

StringTokenizer (String str)
StringTokenizer(String str, String delim)
StringTokenizer(String str, String delim, boolean returnTokens)

Methods

int	**countTokens**()
boolean	**hasMoreElements**()
boolean	**hasMoreTokens**()
Object	**nextElement**()
String	**nextToken**()
String	**nextToken**(String delim)

Class Vector

public class **Vector**
                extends AbstractList
                implements List, Cloneable, Serializable

The `Vector` class existed before Java 2 but has been made part of the `Collection` framework. Unlike other classes in the `Collection` framework, however, a `Vector`'s methods are still synchronized. `Vector` is a very useful class. It can grow dynamically, and you can put any kind of object (but not primitives) into it. You might use it, for example, to send e-commerce information from a client's system to a servlet, putting each distinct field in an element of a vector. Unless you need synchronized methods, however, you should use some other collection implementation, such as `HashSet`. Here's a code snippet to show how to create a `Vector` and add elements to it and then get its size.

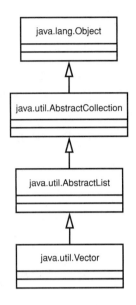

```
Vector vect = new Vector(50,5);
vect.addElement("Add a String");
vect.addElement(new Date());
vect.addElement(new Integer(50));
System.out.println("Size of vect is " + vect.size());
if(vect.isEmpty() == true)
    System.out.println("Vector is empty");
```

CAUTION

You should never create a `Vector` without giving it both an initial size and an increment amount. If you do not specify the latter, when Java needs to add an element, it first creates a `Vector` twice the size of the existing one. This is not too bad for a `Vector` with five `Integer` objects, but it's a serious problem for a `Vector` with 5,000 `GregorianCalendar` objects.

Fields

```
protected int         capacityIncrement
protected int         elementCount
protected Object[]    elementData
```

Constructors

Vector ()
Vector(Collection c)
Vector(int initialCapacity)
Vector(int initialCapacity, int capacityIncrement)

Methods

```
void         add(int index, Object element)
boolean      add(Object o)
boolean      addAll(Collection c)
boolean      addAll(int index, Collection c)
void         addElement(Object obj)
int          capacity()
void         clear()
Object       clone()
boolean      contains(Object elem)
boolean      containsAll(Collection c)
void         copyInto(Object[] anArray)
Object       elementAt(int index)
Enumeration  elements()
void         ensureCapacity(int minCapacity)
boolean      equals(Object o)
Object       firstElement()
Object       get(int index)
int          hashCode()
int          indexOf(Object elem)
int          indexOf(Object elem, int index)
void         insertElementAt(Object obj, int index)
boolean      isEmpty()
Object       lastElement()
int          lastIndexOf(Object elem)
int          lastIndexOf(Object elem, int index)
Object       remove(int index)
boolean      remove(Object o)
boolean      removeAll(Collection c)
void         removeAllElements()
boolean      removeElement(Object obj)
void         removeElementAt(int index)
void         removeRange(int fromIndex, int toIndex)
boolean      retainAll(Collection c)
Object       set(int index, Object element)
void         setElementAt(Object obj, int index)
void         setSize(int newSize)
int          size()
List         subList(int fromIndex, int toIndex)
Object[]     toArray()
Object[]     toArray(Object[] a)
String       toString()
void         trimToSize()
```

CHAPTER 34

java.util.jar

This chapter provides a quick reference for java.util.jar, which supports creating and manipulating a jar file programmatically. Using a jar file outside of a program is simple. You can create it like this:

```
jar cf MyJar.jar *.class *.gif
```

in which jar says to run the jar command. The cf flags tell the jar command to create a jar file (c is for create, and f is for file). MyJar.jar is the name of the jar file to create. This is followed by the list of files to put into the jar file. In this case, it is all Java class files and all the .gif files in the current directory.

A *jar file* is a Java platform-neutral version of a PKWare zip file. You can extract the contents of a jar file by typing this:

```
jar xvf MyJar.jar
```

The flags xvf tell the jar command to extract (x) from a file (f) in verbose mode (show on the screen what is happening). This is followed by the jar filename MyJar.jar.

Since a jar file is platform-neutral, you can create one and extract one any place there is a Sun-compliant JVM. As a side benefit, because jar files are related to zip files, you can use the jar command on a platform that does not support zip files, such as Solaris, to unzip a zip file, like this:

```
jar xvf Myfiles.zip
```

This will treat Myfiles.zip like a jar file and extract it, restoring the original directory structure.

You can also execute a jar file from the command line or from a script. You specify the jar file in a URL and then use the JarRunner command to execute the jar file. Here is an example:

```
java JarRunner http://www.Vaporware.com/NetMonitor.jar
```

Using this mechanism, you can execute the program that is contained in NetMonitor.jar, which means that the jar file itself is executable, and not just an archive file.

Classes

```
Attributes
Attributes.Name
JarEntry
JarFile
JarInputStream
JarOutputStream
Manifest
```

Exceptions

```
JarException
```

Class Details

Class JarEntry

public class **JarEntry**
                extends ZipEntry

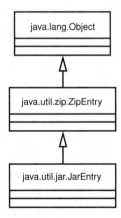

This class represents a jar file entry, such as a class or jpeg file. The following code snippet shows how to get the entries in a jar file and query them.

```
JarFile jf = new JarFile("SomeJarFile.jar");
// Create a JarFile object from the file SomeJarFile.jar.
Enumeration jarEnum = jf.entries();
while(jarEnum.hasMoreElements())
    {
    JarEntry je = (JarEntry)enumJar.nextElement();
    // Create a JarEntry from a jar entry in the jar file.
    Attributes jarAttr = je.getAttributes();
```

Class Details 727

```
    Set keys = jarAttr.keySet();
    // Get keys of Attributes as a KeySet.
 Collection values = jarAttr.values();
    // Get values that go with keys as a Collection.
    // Next, you could iterate through keys and values
    // or whatever you want to do with them.
```

Constructors
JarEntry (JarEntry je)
JarEntry(String name)
JarEntry(ZipEntry ze)

Methods
Attributes	**getAttributes**()
Certificate[]	**getCertificates**()

Class JarFile

public class	**JarFile**
extends	**ZipFile**

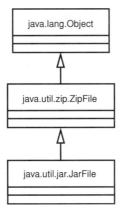

The class JarFile provides for reading the contents of a jar file, or any file that can be accessed as a RandomAccessFile. A JarFile object can also read an optional Manifest entry because it extends java.util.zip.ZipFile. A Manifest file contains information about the jar file, or meta data about the jar file. Here is a code snippet to show some basic things you can do with a JarFile object:

```
JarFile jf = new JarFile(someFileObject);
Enumberation jarEnum = jf.entries();
JarEntry je = jf.getJarEntry("BookJpeg");
// Get a specific jar file entry.
Manifest man = jf.getManifest();
// Retrieve the manifest for this jar file.
```

NOTE

Since `JarFile` extends `ZipFile`, there are also methods here and in `JarEntry` for processing zip file entries.

Fields

static String   MANIFEST_NAME

Constructors

JarFile (File file)
JarFile(File file, boolean verify)
JarFile(String name)
JarFile(String name, boolean verify)

Methods

Enumeration	**entries**()
ZipEntry	**getEntry**(String name)
InputStream	**getInputStream**(ZipEntry ze)
JarEntry	**getJarEntry**(String name)
Manifest	**getManifest**()

Class JarInputStream

public class **JarInputStream**
                 extends ZipInputStream

JarInputStream is a special kind of FilterInputStream that provides methods for reading the contents of a jar file, including the Manifest entry, if present. You might want to read one or more entries from a jar file yourself. For example, you might want to extract an image from a jar file. Here's a code snippet showing how to read individual entries as a stream:

```
try
    {
    JarInputStream jis = new JarInputStream
        (new FileInputStream("SomeJarFile.jar"));
    JarEntry je = null;
    while ((je = jis.getNextJarEntry()) != null)
        {
        // Process jar entry, such as
        // converting bytes into a jpeg Image object.
        jis.closeEntry();
        // Close the entry as you would a stream.
        }
    jis.close();
    // Close the JarInputStream.
```

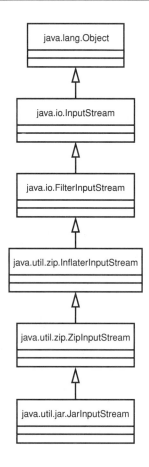

Constructors
JarInputStream (InputStream in)
JarInputStream(InputStream in, boolean verify)

Methods
protected	**ZipEntry createZipEntry**(String name)
Manifest	**getManifest**()
ZipEntry	**getNextEntry**()
JarEntry	**getNextJarEntry**()
int	**read**(byte[] b, int off, int len)

Class JarOutputStream
public class **JarOutputStream**
            extends ZipOutputStream

730 Chapter 34: java.util.jar

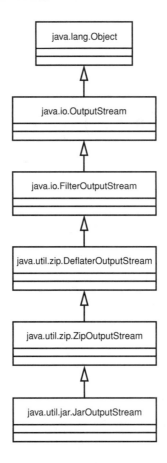

The JarOutputStream class provides methods for writing an entry in a jar file, including a Manifest entry.

Constructors
JarOutputStream (OutputStream out)
JarOutputStream(OutputStream out, Manifest man)

Methods
void **putNextEntry**(ZipEntry ze)

Class Manifest
```
public class Manifest
            extends Object
            implements Cloneable
```

Class Details 731

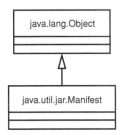

The `Manifest` class provides methods to work with `Manifest` entry names and attributes of the `Manifest` itself and the individual entries. The following code snippet shows the use of a `Manifest` object:

```
Manifest man = theJarFile.getManifest();
FileInputStream fis = new FileInputStream
                  ("AjarFile.jar");
man.read(fis);
// Read in a Manifest file from the specified
// InputStream. The current Manifest contents are
// merged with the contents of the file. The read() and
// write() methods might be useful for examining the
// deployment descriptor of an Enterprise JavaBean.
Attributes manAttr = man.getMainAttributes();
Map manEntries = man.getEntries();
Attributes entryAttr = man.getAttributes("jarEntry");
```

Constructors

Manifest ()
Manifest(InputStream is)
Manifest(Manifest man)

Methods

void	**clear**()
Object	**clone**()
boolean	**equals**(Object o)
Attributes	**getAttributes**(String name)
Map	**getEntries**()
Attributes	**getMainAttributes**()
int	**hashCode**()
void	**read**(InputStream is)
void	**write**(OutputStream out)

INDEX

SYMBOLS

< > (angle brackets), 63
* (asterisk) arithmetic operator, 88
\ (back slash), 322
| bitwise operator, 92-93
~ bitwise operator, 96
, (comma), 85
{ } (curly braces), 28, 31, 85-85
/ (forward slash), 88, 322
- (minus sign) arithmetic operator, 87
== operator, 89
( ) (parentheses), 85
% (percent sign), arithmetic operator, 88
+ (plus sign) arithmetic operator, 87
? (question mark), 90, 341, 680
; (semicolon), 31, 85
! operator, 89
!/ separator, 637
!= operator, 89
|= operator, 88
& bitwise operator, 91, 92
&= operator, 88
&& bitwise operator, 87
<, 63
<=, 89
<< operator, 89
<< left shift bitwise operator, 94-95
<<= operator, 88
> operator, 89
>= operator, 89
>> right shift bitwise operator, 95
>>> unsigned right shift bitwise operator, 95-96
>>>= operator, 88

^ bitwise operator, 93-94
^= operator, 88
2D geometric objects, classes and interfaces, 417

A

abc property, methods, 530
absolute positioning
    code, running on platforms, 110
    components, GUI (graphical user interface), code, 107-110
    No LayoutManager, code, 107-108
    setBounds() method, 109
abstract classes, 47-50
abstract factory, 630
abstract methods, interfaces, 83
Abstract Windowing Toolkit. *See* AWT
accept() method, 640-641
Access, JDBC (Java Database Connectivity), 338
access modifiers, 67
Accessibility, APIs (Application Programming Interfaces)
    assistive technologies, 131
    federal requirements, 19
    GUI (graphical user interface), AccessibleText, 136
    JFC (Java Foundation classes), 131
    code, 132-135
AccessibleObject class, 616-617
AccessibleText, Accessibility APIs (Application Programming Interfaces), 136
ActionEvent, 79
ActionListener interface, 80
ACTION_COPY (drag action), 149
ACTION_LINK (drag action), 149
ACTION_MOVE (drag action), 149
ACTION_REFERENCE (drag action), 149
Activatable class, 659-660
ActivationDesc class, 660-661
ActivationGroup class, 661-662
ActivationGroup.createGroup() method, 663
ActivationGroupDesc class, 662-663

ActivationID class, 663-664
ActiveEvent interface, methods, 419
Adapter classes, 137-138
    Delegation event handling, code, 138-148
Add New Permission dialog box, 314
addAll() method, 382
addAnAppt method, multiple threads calling, 72
addImage() method, 188
addresses, IP (Internet Protocol), 258-261
addxxxListener() method, 137
Adjustable interface, fields or methods, 419
Affine transforms, 19
algorithms, 387
aliases, entries, 670
aligning { } (curly braces), 86
AllPermission class, , 668
AND bitwise operator, 87, 91-92
APIs (Application Programming Interfaces), 19, 615
    documentation, methods throwing exceptions, 191
    JDBC 2.0, 349
        batch updates, 355
        ResultSet, limiting size, 361
        ResultSet, modifying, 355
        ResultSet, scrolling, 350
        ResultSet, scrolling code, 350-355
        ResultSet, updating code, 356-361
    new features
        accessibility, 19
        graphics, 19-20
    Reflection, 615
Applet class, 409-411
AppletContext interface, methods, 408
AppletInitializer interface, methods, 532
applets. *See also* java.applet
    .au file format, 175
    coding, 165
    destroy() method, 168
    dialog boxes, 166
    Frame class, 166
    GUI components, 407
    images (single) displaying, 178

init() method, 167
MediaTracker, 586
    methods, 180
    multiple images, downloading, 181
menus, 166
methods
    destroy(), 168
    init(), 167
    MediaTracker, 180
    paint(), 167
    start(), 167
    stop(), 168
numbering, 173
paint() method, 167
parameters, setting values, 175
programming
    code, 171-172
    images (displaying multiple), code, 180-188
    images (displaying single), code, 178-180
    images, code, 177-178
    parameters, code, 173-174
    sound, code, 175-177
running, 169
    code, 168
    with AppletViewer, 170-171
    with Java plug-in, 170-171
in sandbox, activity restrictions, 166-167
security, 166-167
sound, playing, 175
    in AppletViewer, 177
start() method, 167
stop() method, 168

appletsSwing, 171
AppletStub interface, 408
AppletViewer
    applets, running, 170-171
    sound, playing, 177
application programming GUI (graphical user interface), 105-107
    absolute positioning of components, code, 107-110

Accessibility APIs, 131
    code, 132-135
Adapter classes, 137-138
    Delegation event handling code, 138-148
Delegation event-handling, 136-137
    code, 138-148
drag and drop, 148-150
    code, 150-162
Frame, 106
JFC (Java Foundation classes), 126-127
layout managers, 107
positioning components
    BorderLayout, code, 113-117
    CardLayout, code, 117-120
    FlowLayout, code, 111-113
    GridBagLayout, code, 122-125
    GridLayout, code, 120-122
    layout managers, 110-111
Swing, code, 127-131
Application Programming Interfaces. *See* **APIs**
applications
    applets, coding as, 165
    data, transferring between, 415
    i18n, 365-369
    methods, 31-32
    ServerSockets, 261
    Sockets, using, 259
    TCP client and server, creating, 261-269
architecture, RMI (Remote Method Invocation), 279-280, 291
arguments, createStatement() method, 350-351
arithmetic
    floating point, 37
    operators, 87-88
Array class, methods, 617-618
arraycopy() method, 609
ArrayList class, 387, 706-707
arrays of objects, 59, 61-62
assistive technologies, 131
asterisk (*) arithmetic operator, 88
asymmetric keys, 319
attributes of classes, discovering, 246

.au file format, 175
audio. *See* sound
AudioClip
    interface, 409
    object, creating, 175
authenticating users, 640
autoCommit, turning off, 362
AWT (Abstract Windowing Toolkit)
    components
        class hierarchy, 106
        lightweight, 106
        JDK 1.1, 530
        peers, 105
    GUI event handling, 416
    layout manager classes, inheritance, 111
    lightweight components, 106
    Pure JFC Swing, 413
    Swing
        comparing, 18, 126
        moving to, 126
AWTEvent class, 422-423
AWTEventMulticaster class, 423, 426

B

back slash (\), 322
batches, updating, 355
BDK (Bean Developer's Kit), 529
Bean class, 536
bean context, 531
BeanDescriptor class, 534-535
BeanInfo interface, fields or methods, 532
Beans class, 529, 534-535
behavior of objects, 9
BigDecimal class, 625-627
BigInteger class, 627-628
bin directory, 15
binary large objects, 680
bind() method, 285, 650
BitSet class, 96, 707-708
bitwise operators, 90
    & (ampersand), 91-92
    &&, 87
    ^ (caret), 93-94
    | (pipe symbol), 92-93
    ~ (tilde), 96

<< left shift, 94-95
\>> right shift, 95
\>>> unsigned right shift, 95-96
AND, 87, 91-92
complement, 96
OR, 92-93
XOR, 93-94
Blob (binary large object), interface or methods, 680
Book class, 244
BookCatalog table, 338
BookQuery class, 268
Boolean class, 586-587
boolean primitive data type, 33-34
BorderLayout class, 115-116, 426-427
borders, containers, 460
bound properties, implementing, 533
Break statement, 101-102
browsers, applets, coding , 165
BufferedInputStream class, 544-546
BufferedOutputStream class, 546
BufferedReader class, 239-240, 547-548
BufferedWriter class, 240, 548
buffering, 545
business logic methods, 282
Button class, 427-428
ButtonGroup, JRadioButtons, 131
Buttons, clickable, 428
Byte class, 587-588
byte level, 91
byte primitives, 594
    data type, 33-36
byte-level, I/O, performing, 231, 233-234
ByteArrayInputStream class, 549
ByteArrayOutputStream class, 224, 550
bytecode, 8

C

C programming language, Java,
    comparing, 11
CA (certificate authority), 318, 675
Calendar class, 57-58, 294, 708-711
calendar systems, classes, creating, 394
calendars, GregorianCalendar class, 394
    code, 395-399

classes

CallableStatement, 341
    code, 348-349
    interface, 680-681
calling remote objects
    methods, 253
    with parameters, code, 292-298
canonical objects, Web site, 244
Canvas class, 428-429
CardLayout class, 429
    components, code to display, 117-119
    constructors, 430
    methods, 430
    show() method, 120
case sensitivity, 27
Catalog class, static method, 66
catch blocks, 191, 193
    try-catch, nesting, 194
cells, laying out, code, 120-121
certificate authority (CA), 318, 675
Certificate class, 674-675
Certificate Revocation List (CRL) class, 675-676
certificates
    default expiration period, 321
    digital signatures, 675-676
    fingerprints, 321
    sending, 320
    X.509, 676-677
cf flags, jar command, 725
char primitives, 588
    data type, 33-35
character attribute tables, Unicode FTP site, 588
Character class, 589-590
CharArrayReader class, 551
CharArrayWriter class, 552
Checkbox class, 430-431
CheckboxGroup class, 431-432
checkOut() method, 69
Choice class, 432-433
ChoiceFormat class, 692-693
Class class, 54-55, 583
    methods, 590-591, 615
Class object, 246-248
Class.forName method, 246

.class suffix, 246
classes, 37
    { } curly braces, 31
    abstract, 38, 47-50
    AccessibleObject, 616-617
    Activatable, 659-660
    ActivationDesc, 660-661
    ActivationGroup, 661-662
    ActivationGroupDesc, 662-663
    ActivationID, 663-664
    Adapter, 137-138
        Delegation event handling, code, 138-148
    AllPermission, 668
    Applet, 409-411
    Array, methods, 617-618
    ArrayList, 706-707
    Attributes, 246-248
    AWT, GUI event handling, 416
    AWTEvent, 422-423
    AWTEventMulticaster, 423-426
    Bean, 536
    BeanDescriptor, 534-535
    Beans, 535
    BigDecimal, 625-627
    BigInteger, 627-628
    BitSet, 96, 707-708
    Book, 244
    BookQuery, 268
    Boolean, 586-587
    BorderLayout, 426-427
    BufferedInputStream, 544-546
    BufferedOutputStream, 546
    BufferedReader, 239-240, 547-548
    BufferedWriter, 240, 548
    Button, 427-428
    Byte, 587-588
    ByteArrayInputStream, 549
    ByteArrayOutputStream, 550
    Calendar, 57-58, 394, 708-711
    Canvas, 428-429
    CardLayout, 120, 429-430
    Catalog, static method, 66
    Certificate, 674-675
    Character, 588-590

CharArrayReader, 551
CharArrayWriter, 552
Checkbox, 430-431
CheckboxGroup, 431-432
Choice, 432-433
ChoiceFormat, 692-693
Class, 54-55, 583, 590-591, 615
class keyword, 38
ClassLoader, 591-592
CodeSource, 669
Collection Framework, iterator() method, 384
Collections, 387, 711-712
Color, 433-435
Compiler, 592-593
Component, 39, 106, 435-439
Constructor, 616, 618
constructors, 40-45
    code to obtain information, 249-251
    methods, 618
Container, 40, 113, 439-441
ContentHandler, 631-632
CRL (Class Revocation List), 675-676
Cursor, 441-442
DatagramPacket, 632-633
DatagramSocket, 633-634
DataInputStream, 552-554
DataOutputStream, 554-555
Date, 53-54
DateFormat, 373-377, 693-695
DateFormatSymbols, 378
DecimalFormat, 370-373, 695-696
DecimalFormatSymbols, 370-372, 378
defining, 38
definitions, 28
    LibraryCard, code, 294-295
    punctuation, 85
    remote classes, code, 284-285
    remote object class, code, 294-295
Dialog, 442-444
Double, 593-594
driver, main method, 109
DriverManager, 332, 689-690

Error, 189, 613
Event Listener, Delegation event handling, code, 138-148
EventObject, 379
Exception, 189, 613
    catch blocks, 191
    code for declaring methods that throw exceptions, 197-198
    code to create, 198-199
    creating, 200-201
    FileNotFoundException, 194
    finally clause code, 195-197
    handling or declaring, 201
    non-RuntimeExceptions, 190
    RuntimeExceptions, 190
    try-catch, 193-194
    try-catch code, 191-193
    try-catch-finally, 190-191
    user-defined code, 198-199
extends keyword, 39-40
Field, 616, 619-620
File, 226-229, 555-557
FileDialog, 444-445
FileDriver6, 244
FileInputStream, 557-558
FileOutputStream, 558-559
FilePermission, 559-560
FileReader, 560-561
FileWriter, 561
final, 50
Float, 594-595
FlowLayout, 445-446
Font, 446-449
for calendar systems, creating, 394
Frame, 40, 166, 449-451
functions in java.text package, 365
GidBagConstraints, 455
Graphics, 451-453
Graphics2D, 453-455
GregorianCalendar, 394-399, 712-713
GridBagConstraints, 456-457
GridBagLayout, 457-458
GridLayout, 458-459
HashMap, 713-714
HashSet, 714-715

hierarchy, AWT components, 106
HttpURLConnection, 634-636
Image, 459-460
implementation, 383-384
IndexedPropertyDescriptor, 536
InetAddress, 260-261, 636-637
InputStream, 561-562
InputStreamReader, 562-563
Insets, 460-461
Integer, 595-597
interfaces, 79
introspection, Reflection, 537
Introspector, 537
Iterator, 382
JarEntry, 726-727
JarFile, 727-728
JarInputStream, 728-729
JarOutputStream, 729-730
JarURLConnection, 637-638
Java 2D, new features, 19-20
java.applet, 408-411
java.awt, 413-415
java.awt.datatransfer, 415
java.awt.dnd, 415-416
java.awt.event, 416-417
java.awt.font, 417
java.awt.geom, 417-418
java.awt.Graphics, 174, 180
java.awt.print, 418
java.beans, 530-531
    BeanDescriptor, 534-535
    Beans, 535
    IndexedPropertyDescriptor, 536
    Introspector, 537
    PropertyChangeEvent, 537-538
    PropertyDescriptor, 538-539
    SimpleBeanInfo, 539-540
java.beans.beancontext, 531
java.io, 542-543
    BufferedInputStream, 544-546
    BufferedOutputStream, 546
    BufferedReader, 547-548
    BufferedWriter, 548
    ByteArrayInputStream, 549
    ByteArrayOutputStream, 550

    CharArrayReader, 551
    CharArrayWriter, 552
    DataInputStream, 552-554
    DataOutputStream, 554-555
    File, 555-557
    FileInputStream, 557-558
    FileOutputStream, 558-559
    FilePermission, 559-560
    FileReader, 560-561
    FileWriter, 561
    InputStream, 561-562
    InputStreamReader, 562-563
    LineNumberReader, 563
    ObjectInputStream, 564-566
    ObjectOutputStream, 566-568
    OutputStream, 568-569
    PipedInputStream, 569-570
    PipedOutputStream, 570-571
    PrintStream, 571-572
    PrintWriter, 572-574
    RandomAccessFile, 574-576
    Reader, 576-577
    SequenceInputStream, 577
    StreamTokenizer, 578-579
    StringBufferInputStream, 579
    StringReader, 580
    StringWriter, 580-581
    Writer, 581-582
java.lang, 29, 583-584
    Boolean, 586-587
    Byte, 587-588
    Character, 588-590
    Class, 590-591
    ClassLoader, 591-592
    Compiler, 592-593
    Double, 593-594
    Float, 594-595
    Integer, 595-597
    Long, 597-598
    Math, 598-599
    Object, 599-600
    Runtime, 600-601
    RuntimePermission, 601
    SecurityManager, 602-604
    Short, 604-605

740 classes

    String, 605-607
    StringBuffer, 607-608
    System, 609
    Thread, 610-611
    ThreadGroup, 611-612
    Throwable, 612-613
java.lang.Object, 29
java.lang.reflect
    AccessibleObject, 616-617
    Array, 617-618
    Constructor, 618
    Field, 619-620
    Method, 620
    Modifier, 621-622
    ReflectPermission, 622-623
java.math
    BigDecimal, 625-627
    BigInteger, 627-628
java.net, 629-630
    ContentHandler, 631-632
    DatagramPacket, 632-633
    DatagramSocket, 633-634
    HttpURLConnection, 634-636
    InetAddress, 636-637
    JarURLConnection, 637-638
    MulticastSocket, 638-639
    PasswordAuthentication, 640
    ServerSocket, 640-641
    Socket, 641-642
    SocketImpl, 642-643
    URL, 643-644
    URLConnection, 644-646
    URLStreamHandler, 646
java.net.InetAddress, 259, 261
java.rmi, 647
    MarshalledObject, 648-649
    Naming, 649-650
    RMISecurityManager, 650-651
java.rmi.activation, 653
    Activatable, 659-660
    ActivationDesc, 660-661
    ActivationGroup, 661-662
    ActivationGroupDesc, 662-663
    ActivationID, 663-664

java.rmi.server, 654
    RemoteObject, 656
    RemoteServer, 657-658
    RMIClassLoader, 657
    UnicastRemoteObject, 658-659
java.security, 665-666
java.security.cert
    AllPermission, 668
    Certificate, 674-675
    CodeSource, 669
    CRL (Class Revocation List),
        675-676
    KeyPair, 669-670
    KeyStore, 670-671
    MessageDigest, 671-672
    Permission, 672-673
    Policy, 673-674
    ProtectionDomain, 674
    X509Certificate, 676-677
    X509CRL, 677-678
java.sql, 679
    DriverManager, 689-690
    Timestamp, 690
java.text package, 691
java.util, 701-702
    ArrayList, 706-707
    BitSet, 707-708
    Calendar, 708-711
    Collections, 711-712
    GregorianCalendar, 712-713
    HashMap, 713-714
    HashSet, 714-715
    Locale, 715-717
    Observable, 717
    Properties, 717-718
    PropertyPermission, 719
    ResourceBundle, 720
    StringTokenizer, 720-721
    Vector, 721-723
java.util.jar
    JarEntry, 726-727
    JarFile, 727-728
    JarInputStream, 728-729
    JarOutputStream, 729-730
    Manifest, 730-731

classes 741

JFC (Java Foundation classes), 17-18, 125-131
KeyPair, 669-670
KeyStore, 670-671
Keywords, 38-39
Label, 461
layout manager, inheritance, 111
libraries, Java, 7
LineNumberReader, 563
List, 462-463
Listener, implementing, 137
Locale, 367-369, 715-717
locale-sensitive, code to check, 369
Long, 597-598
Manifest, 730-731
manipulating, code, 253, 255-256
MarshalledObject, 648-649
Math, 598-599
MediaTracker, 464-465
Menu, 465-466
MenuBar, 467
MenuItem, 468
MenuShortcut, 469
MessageDigest, 671-672
MessageFormat, 696-697
Method, 616, 620
methods, 65
    code to obtain information, 249-251
    overriding illegally, code, 77-78
    overriding, code, 78
    package-level access, 70
    throwing exceptions, code, 76-77
Modifier, 621-622
MulticastSocket, 638-639
names, code to obtain, 246-248
naming, 30, 285, 649-650
native methods, code, 71
non-RuntimeExceptions, 190
NumberFormat, 370-372, 697-698
Object, 39, 46, 54, 583, 599-600
ObjectInputStream, 564-566
ObjectOutputStream, 566-568
Objects, serializing, 66
Observable, 717

OutputStream, 224, 568-569
Panel, 469-470
PasswordAuthentication, 640
Permission, 672-673
    ReflectPermission, 622
PipedInputStream, 569, 570
PipedOutputStream, 570-571
Point, 470-471
Policy, 673-674
PopupMenu, 471
PrintJob, 472-473
PrintStream, 239, 571-572
PrintWriter, 239, 572-574
private methods, code, 69
Properties, 57, 717-718
PropertyChangeEvent, 533, 537-538
PropertyChangeListener, 533
PropertyChangeSupport, 533
PropertyDescriptor, 538-539
PropertyPermission, 719
protected methods, code, 68
ProtectionDomain, 674
public keyword, 38
public methods, code, 67, 69
RandomAccessFile, 574-576
Reader, 225, 234, 576-577
Rectangle, 473-475
Reflection, java.lang.reflect, 245
ReflectPermission, 622-623
remote, class definitions, code, 284-285
RemoteObject, 656
RemoteServer, 657-658
ResourceBundle, 720
    code to internationalize applications, 367-369
resources, changing incorrectly, code, 72
RMIClassLoader, 657
RMISecurityManager, 650-651
Runtime, 55-56, 600-601
RuntimeExceptions, 190
RuntimePermission, 601
ScrollPane, 19, 475-476
SDK (Software Development Kit), 14
SecurityManager, 21, 309-310, 603-604
SequenceInputStream, 577

742 classes

ServerSocket, 640-641
setup, creating, 301-304
Short, 604-605
signed, 310
SimpleBeanInfo, 539-540
SimpleDateFormat, 373-378, 698-700
Socket, 641-642
SocketImpl, 642-643
static methods, code, 66
stream, 223
StreamTokenizer, 578-579
String, 51-53, 583, 605-607
StringBuffer, 607-608
StringBufferInputStream, 579
StringReader, 580
StringTokenizer, 720-721
StringWriter, 580-581
superclasses, 39
Swing, GUI event handling, 416
synchronized keyword, code, 73
System, 55, 66, 583, 609
TextArea, 476
Thread, 58-59, 203, 610-611
ThreadGroup, 611-612
Throwable, 189-201, 612-613
Timestamp, 690
TransferableString, drag and drop, code, 161-162
Transparency, 422
UnicastRemoteObject, 283, 658-659
URL, 643-644
URLConnection, 644-646
URLs (uniform resource locators), accessing, 275-277
URLStreamHandler, 646
Vector, 56-57, 721-723
wrapper, primitives, mapping between, 59
Writer, 225, 234, 581-582
X509Certificate, 676-677
X509CRL, 677-678
ClassLoader class, 591-592
classLoaders, 332-333
clauses, finally, code, 195-197
clear() method, 399

clickable buttons, 428
client-side components, 529
clients, 258
BookQuery class, 268
definition of, 279
implementing, code, 288-291
ObjectInputStream, 262
ObjectOutputStream, 262
remote object parameters, code, 295-297
RMI, Naming.lookup() method, code, 289-291
running, 292
servers, order between, 262
TCP (Transmission Control Protocol)
applications, creating, 261-269
programs, sockets, 265-266
UDP (User Datagram Protocol), Datagram sockets and packets, 271-273
clone() method, 585
Cloneable interface, 585
close() method, 224-225
code. *See also* **syntax**
absolute positioning, No LayoutManager, 107-108
Accessibility APIs, JFC (Java Foundation classes), 132-135
applets, 165
images (displaying multiple), programming, 180-188
images (displaying single), programming, 178-180
images, programming, 177-178
parameters, programming, 173-174
programming, 171-172
sound, programming, 175-177
AWTEventMulticaster class, 424
BookQuery class, used by clients and servers, 267-268
BorderLayout class, 115-116, 427
bytecode, 8
CallableStatement, 348-349
CardLayout, components, displaying, 117-119

Catalog class, static method, 66
cells, laying out, 120-121
Checkbox class, 431
Choice class, 432
classes
    attributes, obtaining, 246-248
    manipulating, 253-256
    names, obtaining, 246-248
    resources, changing
        incorrectly, 72
    static methods, 66
    synchronized keyword, 73
clients, implementing, 288-291
constructors, obtaining information,
    249-251
databases, 334-341
dates, formatting, 373-377
declaring methods that throw exceptions,
    197-198
Delegation event handling, 138-148
Dialog class, 443
digital signing, 314-317
digitally signing, 318-323
drag and drop, 150-162
Exception class, 198-199
exceptions, user-defined, 199-200
File class, 226-229
filenames, 27
finally clause, 195-197
FlowLayout, components, sizing and
    positioning, 111-112
Frame class, 450
generic methods, 205
GregorianCalendar class, 395-399
GridBagConstraints class, 456
GridBagLayout class, 123-125, 458
GUI (graphical user interface), position-
    ing components
        absolute, 107-110
        BorderLayout, 113-117
        CardLayout, 117-120
        FlowLayout, 111-113
        GridBagLayout, 122-125
        GridLayout, 120-122
        Swing, 127-131

HashSet, 384-386
HTML (Hypertext Transfer Protocol),
    applets, running, 168
I/O (input/output), 231-237, 241-244
INetAddress class, host IP information,
    260-261
interfaces, 251-253
Issueable remote interfaces, 293-294
jar file entries, querying, 726-727
.java files, 27
java.lang.Thread, subclassing, 206-207
LibraryCard, class definitions, 294-295
LinkedList, 388-391
List, 387-391
List class, 462
Locale class, internationalizing applica-
    tions, 367-369
locales, locale-sensitive classes, 369
Map, 391-393
Menu class, 465
MenuShortcut class, 469
MessageDigest, 327-329
methods
    exceptions, throwing, 76-77
    obtaining information, 249-251
    overriding, 77-78
naming conventions, 30
native methods, classes, 71
notify() method, deadlocks, avoiding,
    218-221
numeric data, formatting, 370-372
numeric values, formatting
    DecimalFormat class, 370-372
    DecimalFormatSymbols class,
        370-372
    NumberFormat class, 370-372
Objects, 240, 253-256
one block of, synchronizing, 213
opcodes, 8
Panel class, 470
Permissions, user-defined, 324-326
PreparedStatement, 345-348
private methods, classes, 69
Properties files, internationalizing
    applications, 367-368

Properties object, 400-403
protected methods, classes, 68
public methods, classes, 67, 69
RandomAccessFile class, 229-231
Rectangle class, 473
remote activation, remote objects, creating from clients, 298-307
remote classes, class definitions, 284-285
remote factories, creating on servers, 285-288
remote interface, 282-283
remote objects
    class definitions, 283-285, 294-295
        creating with rebind() method, 287-288
        registering with rebind() method, 287-288
ResourceBundle class, internationalizing applications, 367-369
ResultSet, 341-345
    scrolling, 350-355
    updating, 356-361
ResultSetMetadata, 341-345
RMI clients, Naming.lookup() method, 289-291
running, static methods, 67
ScrollPane class, 475
signed policy files, 322
SQL (Structured Query Language), paring, 334
superclasses, methods, overriding, 75-76
Swing, 127-131
synchronized, object lock, 216
tables, creating, 334, 336-341
TCP (Transmission Control Protocol)
    client programs, sockets, 265-266
    server programs, sockets and ServerSockets, 263-265
text, reading or writing, 237-239
Thread object
    creating with Runnable objects, 204-205
    subclassing, 206-207

Threads, synchronizing, 213, 215-216
times, formatting, 373-377
try-catch, 191, 193
UDP (User Datagram Protocol), Datagram sockets and packets
    clients, 271-273
    servers, 269-271
Unicode, 223
URLs (uniform resource locators), accessing with URL and URLConnection classes, 275, 277
wait() method, deadlocks, avoiding, 218-221
writing, in JDBC (Java Database Connectivity), 332

CodeSource class, 669
Collection Framework, 379-380
    classes, iterator() method, 384
    implementations, 382
        classes, features, 383
        HashSet code, 384-386
        List, 387
        List code, 387-391
        Map, 391
        Map code, 391-393
        Set, 384
    Iterator, 384
    interfaces, 25, 380-382
    List implementations, 387
    Map implementations, 391
    methods, 381-384
    Set implementations
        HashSet code, 384-386
        List code, 387-391
        Map code, 391-393
Collection interface, 702
    Collections class, comparing, 387
    methods, 702-703
collections, JDBC 2, 25-26
Collections class, 711-712
    Collection interface, comparing, 387
Collections.binarySearch() method, 387
Collections.reverse() method, 387
Collections.shuffle() method, 387, 703
Collections.sort() method, 387, 586

Color class, 433-435
comma (,), 85
command lines, Strings, reading, 240
commands
    jar, cf and xvf flags, 725
    private key, 320
comments, 30
commit() method, 362
committing statements, 362
Comparable interface, 381, 585-586
Comparator interface, 381
compareTo() method, 586
comparing
    Java and C programming language, 11
    Swing and AWT, 18
Compiler class, 592-593
compilers
    inlining methods, 65
    Javac, 8
    JIT (just-in-time), 593
complement bitwise operator, 96
Component class
    constructors, 435
    fields, 435
    hierarchy, 39
    methods, 435-439
    subclasses, 106
components
    absolute positioning, code, 107-110
    arranging, 122
    arranging and sizing, 427
    AWT (Abstract Windowing Toolkit)
        class hierarchy, 106
        JDK 1.1, 530
        lightweight, 106
    BigDecimal class, 626
    CardLayout, code to display, 117-119
    client-side, 529
    constraints, defining, 456
    containers, unresizable, 113
    events, 136
    FlowLayout
        code, sizing and positioning, 111-112
        positioning, 112

heavyweight, Java, 18
lightweight, Swing, 18
listeners, registering, 137
positioning, 458
    BorderLayout, code, 113-117
    CardLayout, code, 117-120
    FlowLayout, code, 111-113
    GridBagLayout, code, 122-125
    GridLayout, code, 120-122
    layout managers, 110-111
sizing, 458
Swing
    code, 127-130
    lightweight, 18
Composite interface, 419
CompositeContext interface, 420
concrete factory
    ContentHandlerFactory class, 630
    SocketImplFactory class, 631
CONCUR_UPDATABLE, 356
Connection interface, 82, 333, 681-682
connection pools, 333
constraints, defining, 456
Constructor class, 616-618
Constructor object, 246
constructors
    AccessibleObject class, 617
    Activatable class, 660
    ActivationDesc class, 661
    ActivationGroup class, 662
    ActivationGroupDesc class, 663
    ActivationID class, 664
    AllPermission class, 668
    Applet class, 410
    ArrayList class, 706
    AWTEvent class, 423
    AWTEventMulticaster class, 424
    BeanDescriptor class, 535
    Beans class, 535
    BigDecimal class, 626
    BigInteger class, 627
    BitSet class, 708
    BorderLayout class, 427
    BufferedInputStream class, 545
    BufferedOutputStream class, 546

BufferedReader class, 547
BufferedWriter class, 548
Button class, 428
ByteArrayInputStream class, 549
ByteArrayOutputStream class, 550
Calendar class, 710
Canvas class, 429
CardLayout class, 430
Certificate class, 675
Character class, 589
CharArrayReader class, 551
CharArrayWriter class, 552
Checkbox class, 431
CheckboxGroup class, 432
Choice class, 433
classes, 40, 618
ClassLoader class, 592
CodeSource class, 669
Color class, 434
Component class, 435
Container class, 439
ContentHandler class, 632
CRL (Class Revocation List) class, 676
Cursor class, 442
DatagramSocket class, 634
DataInputStream class, 553
DataOutputStream class, 555
DateFormat class, 694
DecimalFormat class, 695
default, 42-43
Dialog class, 444
File class, 226, 556
FileDialog class, 444
FileInputStream class, 558
FileOutputStream class, 559
FilePermission class, 560
FileReader class, 561
FileWriter class, 561
FlowLayout class, 446
Font class, 447
Frame class, 451
Graphics class, 452
Graphics2D class, 454
GregorianCalendar class, 713
GridBagConstraints class, 456

GridBagLayout class, 457
GridLayout class, 459
HashMap class, 714
HttpURLConnection class, 636
Image class, 460
IndexedPropertyDescriptor class, 536
information, code to obtain, 249-251
InputStream class, 562
InputStreamReader class, 563
Insets class, 460
JarEntry class, 727
JarFile class, 728
JarInputStream class, 729
JarOutputStream class, 730
JarURLConnection class, 638
KeyPair class, 670
KeyStore class, 671
Label class, 461
LineNumberReader class, 563
List class, 462
Locale class, 716
Long class, 597
Manifest class, 731
MarshalledObject class, 649
MediaTracker class, 464
Menu class, 466
MenuBar class, 467
MenuItem class, 468
MenuShortcut class, 469
MessageDigest class, 672
MessageFormat class, 697
Modifier class, 621
MulticastSocket class, 639
NumberFormat class, 698
Object class, 600
ObjectInputStream class, 565
ObjectOutputStream class, 567
Observable class, 717
OutputStream class, 569
overloading, 43-44
Panel class, 470
parent, invoking, 44-45
PasswordAuthentication class, 640
Permission class, 673
PipedInputStream class, 570

data members 747

PipedOutputStream class, 571
Point class, 471
Policy class, 674
PopupMenu class, 471
PrintJob class, 472
PrintStream class, 572
PrintWriter class, 573
Properties class, 718
PropertyChangeEvent class, 538
PropertyDescriptor class, 539
PropertyPermission class, 719
ProtectionDomain class, 674
RandomAccessFile class, 574
Reader class, 576
Rectangle class, 474
ReflectPermission class, 623
RemoteObject class, 656
RemoteServer class, 658
ResourceBundle class, 720
RMISecurityManager class, 651
ScrollPane class, 475
SecurityManager class, 603
SequenceInputStream class, 577
ServerSocket class, 641
signature, 41, 191
SimpleBeanInfo class, 539
SimpleDateFormat class, 700
Socket class, 641
SocketImpl class, 643
static methods, 66
StreamTokenizer class, 578
StringBufferInputStream class, 579
StringReader class, 580
StringTokenizer class, 721
StringWriter class, 581
Timestamp class, 690
UnicastRemoteObject class, 658
URL class, 644
URLConnection class, 645
URLStreamHandler class, 646
Vector class, 722
Writer class, 582
X509Certificate class, 676
X509CRL class, 678

Container class, 40
    constructors, 439
    default layout managers, 113
    methods, 440-441
containers
    BorderLayout, 114
    borders, 460
    components, arranging and sizing, 427
    default layout managers, 113
    locations, 114
    unresizable, 113
ContentHandler class, 631-632
ContentHandlerFactory interface, 630-631
Continue statement, 101-102
control flow
    Break statement, 101-102
    Continue statement, 101-102
    Do-while loops, 98
    For loop, 99
    If-else statements, 96-97
    modifying, 101-102
    Switch statement, 100-101
    While loop, 98-99
coordinates, x and y, 470
copying objects, deep or shallow, 585
create() method, 229
createStatement() method, 356
    arguments, 350-351
CRL (Class Revocation List) class, 675-676
curly braces { }, 28, 31, 85
    aligning, 86
Cursor class, 441-442
cursors
    mouse, 441
    scrollable, 23
custom permissions, creating, 323-324, 326
Customizer interface, 532

D

data, applications, transferring between, 415
data entry screen, code, 123-125
data members
    interfaces, 83
    modifying, 253

data types, 33
   abstract classes, 47-50
   arrays of objects, 59-62
   boolean primitive data type, 34
   byte primitive data type, 35-36
   Calendar class, 57-58
   char primitive data type, 34-35
   Class class, 54-55
   classes, 37
      constructors, 40-45
      defining, 38
      extends keyword, 39-40
      final, 50
      wrapper, 59
   data members, initializing, 46-47
   Date classes, 53-54
   double primitive data type, 37
   final classes, 50
   float primitive data type, 36-37
   int primitive data type, 36
   long primitive data type, 36
   Object classes, 54
   objects
      arrays, 59-62
      creating with JVM (Java virtual machine), 45
      initializing, 46-47
   primitives, 33
      boolean, 34
      byte, 35-36
      char, 34-35
      double, 37
      float, 36-37
      int, 36
      I/O, 234-237
      long, 36
      short, 36
   Properties class, 57
   Runtime class, 55-56
   short primitive data type, 36
   String classes, 51-53
   System class, 55
   Thread class, 58-59
   Vector class, 56-57
   wrapper classes, 59

database management system (DBMS), 22
databases
   autoCommit, turning off, 362
   CallableStatement, code, 348-349
   connections
      code, 334-341
      creating, 332-334
      method declarations, 681
      pools, 333
   isolation levels, setting, 362-363
   JDBC (Java Database Connectivity), 331-332
   JDBC 2.0
      APIs, 349-350
      batch updates, 355
      ResultSet, scrolling code, 350-355
      ResultSet, updating code, 356-361
   keystore, 319
   PreparedStatement, code, 345-348
   programming java.sql package, 331
   ResultSet, code, 341-345
   ResultSetMetadata, code, 341-345
   tables
      BookCatalog, 338
      code to create, 334-341
      schema, 339
DataFlavor (drag and drop), 148
Datagram packets, 269-273
Datagram sockets and packets
   UDP clients, 271-273
   UDP servers, 269-271
DatagramPacket class, 632-633
datagrams, sockets, sending and receiving, 633
DatagramSocket class, 633-634
DataInputStream class, 552
   constructors, 553
   I/O, code to perform, 234-237
   methods, 553-554
DataOutputStream class, 554-555
   I/O, code to perform, 234-237
Date classes, 53-54
Date objects, adding or removing, 216
dateArray object, dates, adding or removing, 216

DateFormat class, 373-377, 693-695
DateFormatSymbols class, 378
dates
    formatting, 373-377, 693, 698
    formatting symbols, 699-700
    GregorianCalendar class, 394-395
        code, 395-399
    i18n (internationalization), formatting, 373-378
    java.text package, 365
    parsing, 698
DBMS (database management system), 22
Dead state, 610
deadlocks
    avoiding, 217-221
    handling, 217
    notify() method, 217
        code, 218-221
    wait() method, 217
        code, 218-221
deadly embrace. *See* deadlocks
debugging tools, 16
DecimalFormat class
    constructors, 695
    format options, 373
    methods, 695-696
    numeric values, code to format, 370-372
    pattern options, 373
DecimalFormatSymbols class, 378
    numeric values, code to format, 370-372
decrement operators, 88-89
deep copies of objects, 585
defaults
    constructors, 42-43
    layout managers, containers, 113
    locales, finding, 370
    properties file, 369
defining
    classes, 28, 38
    interfaces, 82
    main method, 31
Delegation event handling, code, Adapter class or Event Listener class, 138-148
Delegation event-handling, 136-137
delete() method, 229

designs, patterns
    MVC (Model-View-Controller, 20
    objects, singletons, 67
    Observer/Observable, Observer interface, 705
destroy() method, 168
dialog boxes
    Add New Permission, 314
    in applets, 166
Dialog class, 442-444
digests
    message, 326-329
    MessageDigest, 672
        code, 327-329
digital signatures
    certificates, 675-676
    verifying, 318
digital signing, code, 314-323
directories, bin, 15
DNS (domain name service), 258
Do-while loops, 98
Documentation, SecurityManager class, Java Web site, 603
domain name service (DNS), 258
Double class
    fields, 593
    methods, 594
double primitives, 33, 37, 593
downloading
    multiple images with MediaTracker, 181
    stubs, 306-307, 650
drag and drop, 415
    ACTION_COPY, 149
    ACTION_LINK, 149
    ACTION_MOVE, 149
    ACTION_REFERENCE, 149
    code, 150-161
    DataFlavor, 148
    drag actions, 149
    DragSource, 148
    DropTarget, 148
    new features, 20
    screen after operation, 163
    screen before operation, 162
    TransferableString class, code, 161-162

DragGestureRecognizer, 149
dragging and dropping. *See* drag and drop
DragSource (drag and drop), 148
drawImage method, 180
drawing, Affine transforms, 19
drawString() method, 174
driver class, main method, 109
Driver interface, 683
DriverManager class, 332, 689-690
DriverManager.getConnection() method, 333
drivers, JDBC
    managing, 689
    methods, 683
    types, 683
DropTarget (drag and drop), 148

E

e-commerce, TCP sockets, 259
encapsulation, objects, 9
Enterprise JavaBeans, 529
entries, 670
environments, Java, 7
errors. *See also* exceptions
    java.awt, 415
    java.lang, 585
    pointer, 11
event dispatching, multicast, 424
event handlers, Delegation
    code, Adapter classes or Event Listener class, 138-148
    event-handling, 136-137
Event Listener class, Delegation event handling, code, 138-148
event-handling GUI (graphical user interface) interfaces, 79-83
EventObject class, 379
events
    ActionEvent, 79
    components, 136
Exception class, 189, 613
    catch blocks, 191
    code to create, 198-199
    code for declaring methods that throw exceptions, 197-198

creating, 200-201
FileNotFoundException, 194
finally clause code, 195-197
handling or declaring, 201
non-RuntimeExceptions, 190
RuntimeExceptions, 190
try-catch, 193-194
    code, 191-193
try-catch-finally, 190-191
user-defined, code, 198-199
exceptions. *See also* errors
    catch blocks, 193-194
    debugging, 193
    Error class, 189
    Exception class, 189
        code for declaring methods that throw exceptions, 197-198
        code to create, 198-199
        creating, 200-201
        FileNotFoundException, 194
        finally clause code, 195-197
        handling or declaring, 201
        non-RuntimeExceptions, 190
        RuntimeExceptions, 190
        try-catch, 190-194
    handling, 189
    InterruptedException, 206
    IOException, 193
    java.awt, 415
    java.awt.datatransfer, 415
    java.awt.dnd, 416
    java.awt.geom, 418
    java.awt.print, 418
    java.beans, 531
    java.io, 543
    java.lang, 584
    java.net, 630
    java.rmi, 647-648
    java.rmi.activation, 654
    java.rmi.server, 654
    java.security, 666
    java.security.cert, 667
    java.sql, 680
    java.text package, 691
    java.util, 702

fields 751

java.util.jar, 726
non-RuntimeExceptions class, 190
objects, instantiating, 201
RuntimeExceptions class, 190
stack trace, 201
stack traces, 193
throw keyword, 200
Throwable class, Error class, 189
Throwable class, Exception class, 189
    code for declaring methods that throw exceptions, 197-198
    code to create, 198-199
    creating, 200-201
    FileNotFoundException, 194
    finally clause code, 195-197
    handling or declaring, 201
    try-catch, 190-194
throwing
    API documentation, 191
    code, 76-77
try-catch, handling with, 201
user-defined code, 199-200

exec() method, 601
executeUpdate() method, 362
exportObject() method, 650
extends keyword, classes, 39-40
extensions
    Java, 10
    JDBC 2, 24-25
Externalizable interface, 543

F

factories
    abstract, 630
    concrete
        ContentHandlerFactory class, 630
        SocketImplFactory class, 631
    remote
        code to create on servers, 285-288
        object factories, turning into, 279
        programs, starting, 292
    sockets, RMI custom, Web site tutorial, 655
features, new. *See* **new features**
federal requirements for accessibility, 19

Field
    class, 616, 619-620
    object, 246
fields
    Adjustable interface, 419
    AWTEvent class, 423
    AWTEventMulticaster class, 424
    BeanInfo interface, 532
    BigDecimal class, 626
    BigInteger class, 627
    Boolean class, 586
    BorderLayout class, 427
    BufferedInputStream class, 545
    BufferedOutputStream class, 546
    Byte class, 587
    ByteArrayInputStream class, 549
    ByteArrayOutputStream class, 550
    Calendar class, 709-710
    Character class, 588-589
    CharArrayReader class, 551
    CharArrayWriter class, 552
    Collections class, 711
    Color class, 434
    Component class, 435
    Connection interface, 682
    Cursor class, 441-442
    DataOutputStream class, 555
    DateFormat class, 693-694
    Double class, 593
    File class, 556
    FileDialog class, 444
    Float class, 595
    FlowLayout class, 446
    Font class, 447
    Frame class, 451
    GregorianCalendar class, 713
    GridBagConstraints class, 456
    GridBagLayout class, 457
    HttpURLConnection class, 635-636
    Image class, 459
    Insets class, 460
    Integer class, 596
    Introspector class, 537
    JarFile class, 728
    JarURLConnection class, 638

Key interface, 667
Label class, 461
Locale class, 716
Long class, 597
Math class, 598
MediaTracker class, 464
Member interface, 616
Modifier class, 621
NumberFormat class, 697
in objects, transient or
  unserializable, 241
PipedInputStream class, 570
Point class, 470
PrintWriter class, 573
Properties class, 718
Reader class, 576
Rectangle class, 474
RemoteObject class, 656
RemoteRef interface, 655
ResourceBundle class, 720
ResultSet interface, 685
ScrollPane class, 475
SecurityManager class, 603
Serializable interface, 544
ServerRef interface, 656
Short class, 604
SocketImpl class, 642
SocketOptions interface, 631
StreamTokenizer class, 578
String class, 606
StringBufferInputStream class, 579
System class, 609
Thread class, 610
transient, 241
Transparency interface, 422
URLConnection class, 645
Vector class, 722
Writer class, 581
File class, 555
  code, 226-229
  constructors, 226, 556
  fields, 556
  methods, 556-557
file objects, 556
FileDialog class, 444-445

FileDriver6 class, 244
FileFilter interface, 544
FileInputStream class, 557
  constructors, 558
  I/O, code to perform, 231-234
  methods, 558
FilenameFilter interface, 544
filenames, 27
FileNotFoundException, 194
FileOutputStream class, 558
  constructors, 559
  I/O, code to perform, 231-234
  methods, 559
FilePermission class, 559-560
FilePermissions, granting, 323
FileReader class, 560-561
files
  .au format, 175
  .gif, images, creating, 459
  .java, 27
  .jpeg, images, creating, 459
  File object, 225-226
  jar
    creating, 319, 725
    entries, code to query, 726-727
    entries, writing, 730
    JarURLConnection class, 637
    reading, 727-728
    signing, 320
    unjarring, 15
  policy
    applets, overcoming activity
      restrictions, 167
    creating, 312-314
    finding, 311
    information, Java Web site, 312
    installing, 312
    keystores for signed code, 322
    permissions, adding, 313
    RMI.jp, 292
    role, 311
  Properties, 366
    code to internationalize
      applications, 367-368
    default .properties file, 369

MessageBundle_de_DE.
    properties, 368
MessageBundle_en_US.
    properties, 368
Properties, setting up in InstantDB, 337
RandomAccessFile object, 225-226
source
    import statements, 29
    main method defined, 31
zip, unzipping, 15
FileWriter class, 561
final classes, 50
final methods, 65
finally clause, code, 195-197
finding
    policy files, 311
    remote objects, 281-282
fingerprints in certificates, 321
firewalls, UDP (User Datagram Protocol) packets, 259
flags, 90
    jar command, cf or xvf, 725
Float class, 594-595
float primitives, 33, 36-37, 594
floating point arithmetic, 37
FlowLayout class, 111-113, 445-446
flush() method, 224-225
Font class, 446-449
fonts, interrogating or manipulating, 417
For loop, 99
formats
    DecimalFormat class, options, 373
    files, .au, 175
formatting
    dates, 693, 698
        code, 373-377
        internationalizing, 373-378
        SimpleDateFormat class, code, 373-377
        symbols, 699-700
    numbers, 692, 697
    numeric data
        code, 370-372
        internationalizing, 370-373
    DecimalFormat, pattern options, 373

numeric values, code, 370-372
SimpleDateFormat class symbols, 377-378
text, 696-370
times, 373-3
forName() method, 333, 590, 615
forward slash (/), 88, 322
Frame class, 40, 449—451
    applets, 166
Frame object, 40
    show() method, 106, 109, 120
Frames, novice mistakes, 108
FTP (File Transfer Protocol) sites, Unicode, character attribute tables, 588
functions, executing with static methods, 67

G

garbage collection, 14
generic methods, coding, 205
geometric objects2D, classes and interfaces, 417
get method, 256
get() method, 530, 629
getabc() method, 530
getActionCommand() method, 615
getByName() method, 261
getBytes() method, 229
getClass() method, 246, 248
getConnection() method, 332
getConstructors() method, 249, 251
getContent() method, 632
getCurrencyInstance() method, 372
getDefault() method, 370
getFields() method, 248
getFloat() method, 339
getHostByName() method, 636
getHostName() method, 261
getImage() call, asynchronous, 188
getInt() method, 344
getLocalHost() method, 629, 636
getMessage() method, 193
getMethods() method, 249, 251
getModifiers() method, 248, 251
getName() method, 248, 615

getObject() method, 344
getOutputStream() method, 635
getParameterTypes() method, 251
getProperties() method, 66, 609
getProperty() method, 399, 403, 609
getReturnType() method, 251
getRuntime() method, 600
getSomeObject() method, 630
getString() method, 366
getSuperclass() method, 248
getType() method, 248
getxxx() methods, 339, 680
GidBagConstraints class, 455
.gif files, images, creating, 459
goto keyword, 87
graphics, Affine transforms, 19
granting
  FilePermissions, 323
  permissions, 312
graphical user interfaces. *See* GUIs
graphics, APIs (Application Programming Interfaces), 19-20
Graphics class, 451
  constructors, 452
  methods, 452-453
Graphics2D class, 453
  constructors, 454
  methods, 454-455
green threads, 206
GregorianCalendar class, 394, 712
  code, 395-399
  constructors, 713
  fields, 713
  methods, 713
  quirks, 395
GregorianCalendar object, 585
  values, modifying, 399
GridBagConstraints class
  code, 456
  constructors, 456
  fields, 456
  methods, 457
  parameters, 122
  RELATIVE parameter, 122
  REMAINDER parameter, 122

GridBagLayout class, 457
  constructors, 457
  data entry screen, code, 123-125
  fields, 457
  methods, 457-458
gridHeight parameter, 122
GridLayout class
  cells, laying out, code, 120-121
  code, 458
  components, arranging, 122
  constructors, 459
  methods, 459
grids, components, positioning or sizing, 458
gridWidth parameter, 122
gridY parameter, 122
GUIs (graphical user interfaces), 17, 105-107. *See also* **Swing**
  absolute positioning
    code, running on platforms, 110
    No LayoutManager, code, 107-108
    setBounds() method, 109
  Accessibility APIs
    AccessibleText, 136
    assistive technologies, 131
    code, 132-135
  Adapter classes, 137-138
    Delegation event handling, code, 138-148
  applets, 407
  application programming, 105-107
    absolute positioning of components, code, 107-110
    Accessibility APIs, 131
    Accessibility APIs, code, 132-135
    Adapter classes, 137-138
    Adapter classes, Delegation event handling code, 138-148
    BorderLayout, positioning components, code, 113-117
    CardLayout, positioning components, code, 117-120
    Delegation event-handling, 136-137

drag and drop, 148-150
drag and drop, code, 150-162
FlowLayout, positioning components, code, 111-113
Frame, 106
GridBagLayout, positioning components, code, 122-125
GridLayout, positioning components, code, 120-122
JFC (Java Foundation classes), 126-127
layout managers, 107
layout managers, positioning components, 110-111
Swing, code, 127-131
AWT (Abstract Windowing Toolkit), 105
BorderLayout, code, 115-116
CardLayout, components, code to display, 117-119
Component class, subclasses, 106
components, events, 136
containers, 114
Delegation event-handling, 136-137
drag and drop, 148-149
    code, 150-161
    screen after operation, 163
    screen before operation, 162
    TransferableString class, code, 161-162
event handling, AWT and Swing classes, 416
FlowLayout, components, positioning, 112
Frame, 106, 109
Frames, novice mistakes, 108
GridBagConstraints, parameters, 122
GridBagLayout, data entry screen, code, 123-125
GridLayout
    cells, code to layout, 120-121
    components, arranging, 122
interfaces, event-handling, 79-83
JFC (Java Foundation classes), 126-127
    Accessibility APIs, 131
    Accessibility APIs, code, 132-135

Swing, 125-127
Swing, code, 127-131
layout manager classes, inheritance, 111
layout managers, 107
main method, 109
methods, main, 109
positioning components
    BorderLayout, code, 113-117
    CardLayout, code, 117-120
    FlowLayout, code, 111-113
    GridBagLayout, code, 122-125
    GridLayout, code, 120-122
    layout managers, 110-111
    components, code, 127-130

H

HasA relationship, objects, 39
HashMap class, 713
    constructors, 714
    methods, 383, 714
HashSet
    class, 714-715
    implementation class, 384
hasNext() method, 382, 384
heavyweight components, Java, 18
hierarchies, inheritance, Collection or Map interfaces, 380
hoop values, methods, 539
hosts
    client, 258
    IP (Internet Protocol)
        addresses, 258
        InetAddress class, 260-261
    naming, 258-261
    port numbers, 258-259
    servers, 258
    sockets, creating, 259
HotJava, RMIRegistry, binding to, 286
Hotspot, compilers, inlining methods, 65
HTML (Hypertext Markup Language), code, running applets, 168
HTTP (Hypertext Transfer Protocol), 257
HttpURLConnection class, 634-636

756 I/O (input/output)

I

I/O (input/output)
   buffering, 545
   File class, code, 226-229
   File object, 225-226
   code, 227-228
      File object, 225-226
      RancomAccessFile class,
         code, 229-231
      RandomAccessFile object,
         225-226
   InputStream class, 224
   java.io package, 223
   Object serialization, 240-241
   objects, reading and writing, 240
   performing
      byte-level, 231-234
      DataInputStream, code, 234-237
      DataOutputStream, code, 234-237
      FileInputStream, code, 231-234
      FileOutputStream, code, 231-234
      Object serialization, 240-241
      ObjectInputStream, code,
         241-244
      ObjectOutputStream, code,
         241-244
      objects, reading and writing, 240
      primitive data types, 234-237
      text, reading and writing, 237-239
   RandomAccessFile class, code, 229-231
   RandomAccessFile object, 225-226
   Reader class, 225
   streams, 223-225
   text, reading and writing, 237-239
   Writer class, 225
i18n (internationalization)
   applications, code, 365-369
   dates, formatting, 373-378
   numeric data, formatting, 370-373
   text, formatting, 369-370
   times, formatting, 373-378
IDE (Integrated Development Environment), JavaBeans, introspection, 529

identifiers, punctuation, 85
identity, objects, 9
If statement, ?: operator, 90
If-else statements, 96-97
IFC (Internet Foundation Classes), 17
illegally overriding methods, 77-78
Image class, 459-460
ImageIcon, 131
ImageObserver interface, 180
images
   in applets, code, 177-178
   creating from .gif and .jpeg files, 459
   multiple, displaying in applets, code, 180-188
   single, displaying in applets, code, 178-180
   MediaTracker, 181
   registering with MediaTracker, 188
imageUpdate() method, 180
implementation classes
   class names, 383
   Collection Framework, 383
   HashSet, 384
   TreeSet, 384
implementations
   Collection Framework, 382-383
      HashSet code, 384-386
      interfaces, 381
      List code, 387-391
      Map code, 391-393
      Set, 384
   List, 387
   Map, 381, 391
   Set
      HashSet code, 384-386
      List code, 387-391
      Map code, 391-393
import statements, 28-29
increment operators, 88-89
IndexedPropertyDescriptor class, 536
InetAddress class, 636
INetAddress class
   host IP information, 260-261
   methods, 637

interfaces

inheritance
    classes, extends keyword, 39-40
    hierarchy, Collection or Map
        interfaces, 380
    layout manager classes, 111
    multiple, 11
    objects, 9
init() method, 167, 410
Initialized state, 610
Initializing data members or objects, 46-47
inlining methods, 65
input and output. *See* **I/O**
InputStream class, 224, 561-562
InputStreamReader class, 562-563
insertRow() method, 356
Insets class, 460-461
installing policy files, 312
InstantDB
    properties files, setting up, 337
    ResultSets, updating, 355
    Web site, 334, 338
instantiating
    classes, constructors, 40-45
    exception objects, 201
int level, 91
int primitives, 33, 36 595
Integer class, 595-596
integers, BigInteger Class, 627
Integrated Development Environment (IDE), 529
interfaces
    { } curly braces, 31
    abstract methods, 83
    ActionListener, 80
    ActiveEvent, 419
    Adjustable, 419
    AppletContext, 408
    AppletInitializer, 532
    AppletStub, 408
    AudioClip, 409
    BeanInfo, 532
    Blob, 680
    CallableStatement, 680-681
    Class object, 246-248
    classes, 79

    Cloneable, 585
    Collection
        Collections class, comparing, 387
        inheritance hierarchy, 380
        methods, 702-703
    Collection Framework, 25, 380-383
    Comparable, 381, 585-586
    Comparator, 381
    Composite, 419
    CompositeContext, 420
    Connection, 82, 333, 681-682
    ContentHandlerFactory, 630-631
    contents, 83-84
    Customizer, 532
    data members, 83
    defining, 82
    Driver, 683
    Externalizable, 543
    FileFilter, 544
    FilenameFilter, 544
    GUIs (graphical user interfaces), event handling, 79-83
    ImageObserver, 180
    information, code to obtain, 251-253
    interrogating, code, 251-253
    ItemSelectable, 420
    Iterator, 703
    java.applet, 407-409
    java.awt, 413
    java.awt.datatransfer, 415
    java.awt.dnd, 415
    java.awt.event, 416
    java.awt.font, 417
    java.awt.geom, 417
    java.awt.print, 418
    java.beans, 530-534
    java.beans.beancontext, 531
    java.io, 541-544
    java.lang, 583, 586
    java.lang.reflect, 616
    java.net, 629-631
    java.rmi, 647-648
    java.rmi.activation, 653
    java.rmi.Remote, 282
    java.rmi.server, 654-656

758 interfaces

java.security, 665
java.security.cert, 667
java.sql, 679
    Blob, 680
    CallableStatement, 680-681
    Connection, 681-682
    Driver, 683
    PreparedStatement, 683-685
    ResultSet, 685-688
    Statement, 688-689
java.text package, 691
java.util, 701
    Collection, 702-703
    Iterator, 703
    List, 703-704
    Map, 704-705
    Observer, 705
    Set, 705-706
javax.sql, 340
JNI (Java Native Interface), 70
Key, 667
LayoutManager, 420
LayoutManager2, 420
List, 381, 703-704
Logging, 82-84
Map, 380-381, 704-705
Member, 616
MenuContainer, 421
naming, 30
Observer, 705
Paint, 421
PaintContext, 421
PreparedStatement, 683
PrintGraphics, 421
PropertyChangeListener, 533
PropertyEditor, 533-534
Remote, 648
remote
    code to create, 282-283
    Issueable, code, 293-294
RemoteRef, 655
ResultSet, 685-688
RMIClientSocketFactory, 655
RMIServerSocketFactory, 655-656
Runnable, 81, 586

Serializable, 241, 544
ServerRef, 656
Set, 381, 705-706
Shape, 421-422
signature, 80
SocketImplFactory, 631
SocketOptions, 631
Statement, 688-689
Transparency, 422
TreeMap, 704
variables, 83
VetoableChangeListener, 534
internationalization. *See* **i18n**
Internet Foundation Classes (IFC), 17
Interrogating interfaces, code, 251-253
InterruptedException, 206
introspection, JavaBeans, 529, 615
Introspection class, 537
Introspector class, 537
invoking parent constructors, 44-45
IOException, 193
IP (Internet Protocol)
    addresses, 258-259, 261
    INetAddress class, 260-261, 636
IsA relationship, objects, 39
Isabc() method, 530
isDirectory() method, 229
isolation levels, setting, 362-363
Issueable remote interfaces, code, 293-294
ItemSelectable interface, 420
Iterator, 383
    class, 382
    elements, adding, 391
    hasNext() method, 384
    interface, 703
iterator() method, 382, 384
Iterators, 383

J

jar command, cf or xvf flags, 725
jar files
    creating, 319, 725
    entries
        querying, code, 726-727
        writing, 730

JarURLConnection class, 637
    reading, 727-728
    signing, 320
    unjarring, 15
JarEntry class, 726-727
JarFile class, 727-728
JarInputStream class, 728-729
JarOutputStream class, 729-730
JarURLConnection class, 637-638
Java
    C programming language, comparing, 11
    class library, 7
    components, heavyweight, 18
    Developer's Connection Web site, 384
    environment, 7
    extensions, 10
    garbage collection, 14
    heavyweight components, 18
    JRE (Java Runtime Environment), 14
    JVM (Java virtual machine), 7, 13-14
    multithreading, 13
    networks, 10
    object-oriented language, 8-10
    platform neutral, 8
    plug-ins, 170-171
        aprogramming language, 7
    SDK (Software Development Kit), 14-16
    security, 11-12
    virtual machine. *See* JVM
    Web site
        policy file information, 312
        RMI (Remote Method Invocation) information, 282
        SecurityManager class documentation, 603
Java 2D, classes, new features, 19-20
Java Database Connectivity. *See* **JDBC**
.java files, 27, 459
Java Foundation Classes (JFC), 17-18, 125-131
Java Native Interface (JNI), 70
Java Remote Method Protocol (JRMP), 280
Java Runtime Environment (JRE), 14

java-beans, JavaBeans, client-side components, 529
java.applet
    Applet class, 409-411
    AppletContext interfaces, 408
    AppletStub interfaces, 408
    AudioClip interfaces, 409
    class, 408
    classes, Applet, 409-411
    interfaces, 407
        AppletContext, 408
        AppletStub, 408
        AudioClip, 409
    methods
        AppletContext interface, 408
        AppletStub interface, 408
java.awt, 413
    ActiveEvent interface, 419
    Adjustable interface, 419
    AWTEvent class, 422-423
    AWTEventMulticaster class, 423-426
    BorderLayout class, 426-427
    Button class, 427-428
    Canvas class, 428-429
    CardLayout class, 429-430
    Checkbox class, 430-431
    CheckboxGroup class, 431-432
    Choice class, 432-433
    classes, 413-415
        AWTEvent, 422-423
        AWTEventMulticaster, 423-426
        BorderLayout, 426-427
        Button, 427-428
        Canvas, 428-429
        CardLayout, 429-430
        Checkbox, 430-431
        CheckboxGroup, 431-432
        Choice, 432-433
        Color, 433-435
        Component, 435-439
        Container, 439-441
        Cursor, 441-442
        Dialog, 442-444
        FileDialog, 444-445
        FlowLayout, 445-446

760 java.awt

    Font, 446-449
    Frame, 449-451
    Graphics, 451-453
    Graphics2D, 453-455
    GridBagConstraints, 455-457
    GridBagLayout, 457-458
    GridLayout, 458-459
    Image, 459-460
    Label, 461
    List, 462-463
    MediaTracker, 464-465
    Menu, 465-466
    MenuBar, 467
    MenuItem, 468
    MenuShortcut, 469
    Panel, 469-470
    Point, 470-471
    PopupMenu, 471
    PrintJob, 472-473
    Rectangle, 473-475
    ScrollPane, 475-476
    TextArea, 476
Color class, 433-435
Component class, 435-439
Composite interface, 419
CompositeContext interface, 420
Container class, 439-441
Cursor class, 441-442
Dialog class, 442-444
errors, 415
exceptions, 415
FileDialog class, 444-445
FlowLayout class, 445-446
Font class, 446-449
Frame class, 449-451
Graphics class, 451-453
Graphics2D class, 453-455
GridBagConstraints class, 455-457
GridBagLayout class, 457
GridLayout class, 458-459
Image class, 459-460
Insets class, 460-461
interfaces, 413

    ActiveEvent, 419
    Adjustable, 419
    Composite, 419
    CompositeContext, 420
    ItemSelectable, 420
    LayoutManager, 420
    LayoutManager2, 420
    LayoutManager2, methods, 420
    MenuContainer, 421
    Paint, 421
    PaintContext, 421
    PrintGraphics, 421
    Shape, 421-422
    Transparency, 422
ItemSelectable interface, 420
Label class, 461
LayoutManager interface, 420
LayoutManager2 interface, 420
List class, 462-463
MediaTracker class, 464-465
Menu class, 465-466
MenuBar class, 467
MenuContainer interface, 421
MenuItem class, 468
MenuShortcut class, 469
Paint interface, 421
PaintContext interface, 421
Panel class, 469-470
Point class, 470-471
PopupMenu class, 471
PrintGraphics interface, 421
PrintJob class, 472-473
Rectangle class, 473-475
ScrollPane class, 475-476
Shape interface, 421-422
TextArea class, 476
Transparency interface, 422

java.awt.datatransfer, 415
java.awt.dnd, 415-416
java.awt.event, 416-417
java.awt.font, 417
java.awt.geom, 417-418
java.awt.Graphics class, 174, 180
java.awt.print, 418
java.beans, 529

AppletInitializer interface, 532
Bean class, 536
bean context, 531
BeanDescriptor, 534
BeanDescriptor class, 534-535
BeanInfo interface, 532
Beans class, 534-535
bound properties, implementing, 533
classes, 530-531
    Bean, 536
    BeanDescriptor, 534-535
    Beans, 535
    IndexedPropertyDescriptor, 536
    Introspector, 537
    PropertyChangeEvent, 537-538
    PropertyDescriptor, 538-539
    SimpleBeanInfo, 539-540
constructors
    BeanDescriptor class, 535
    Beans class, 535
    IndexedPropertyDescriptor
      class, 536
    PropertyChangeEvent class, 538
    PropertyDescriptor class, 539
    SimpleBeanInfo class, 539
Customizer interface, 532
exceptions, 531
fields
    BeanInfo interface, 532
    Introspector class, 537
hoop values, methods, 539
IndexedPropertyDescriptor class, 536
interfaces, 530
    AppletInitializer, 532
    BeanInfo, 532
    Customizer, 532
    PropertyChangeListener, 533
    PropertyEditor, 533-534
    VetoableChangeListener, 534
Introspection class, Reflection, 537
Introspector class, 537
JavaBean properties, 529
methods
    AppletInitializer interface, 532
    BeanDescriptor class, 535

BeanInfo interface, 532
Beans class, 535
Customizer interface, 532
hoop values, 539
IndexedPropertyDescriptor
    class, 536
Introspector class, 537
PropertyChangeEvent class, 538
PropertyChangeListener
    interface, 533
PropertyDescriptor class, 539
PropertyEditor interface, 533-534
SimpleBeanInfo class, 540
VetoableChangeListener
    interface, 534
properties, bound, implementing, 533
PropertyChangeEvent class, 537-538
PropertyChangeListener interface, 533
PropertyDescriptor class, 538-539
PropertyEditor interface, 533-534
Reflection, Introspection class, 537
SimpleBeanInfo class, 539-540
VetoableChangeListener interface, 534
java.beans.beancontext, 531
java.beans.Beans.instantiate(), 532
java.io, 541
    BufferedInputStream class, 544-546
    BufferedOutputStream class, 546
    BufferedReader class, 547-548
    BufferedWriter class, 548
    ByteArrayInputStream class, 549
    ByteArrayOutputStream class, 550
    CharArrayReader class, 551
    CharArrayWriter class, 552
    classes, 542-543
        BufferedInputStream, 544-546
        BufferedOutputStream, 546
        BufferedReader, 547-548
        BufferedWriter, 548
        ByteArrayInputStream, 549
        ByteArrayOutputStream, 550
        CharArrayReader, 551
        CharArrayWriter, 552
        DataInputStream, 552-554
        DataOutputStream, 554-555

File, 555-557
FileOutputStream, 558-559
FilePermission, 559-560
FileReader, 560-561
FileWriter, 561
InputStream, 561-562
InputStreamReader, 562-563
LineNumberReader, 563
ObjectInputStream, 564-566
ObjectOutputStream, 566-568
OutputStream, 568-569
PipedInputStream, 569-570
PipedOutputStream, 570-571
PrintStream, 571-572
PrintWriter, 572-574
RandomAccessFile, 574-576
Reader, 576-577
SequenceInputStream, 577
StreamTokenizer, 578-579
StringBufferInputStream, 579
StringReader, 580
StringWriter, 580-581
Writer, 581-582
constructors
   BufferedInputStream class, 545
   BufferedOutputStream class, 546
   BufferedReader class, 547
   BufferedWriter class, 548
   ByteArrayInputStream class, 549
   ByteArrayOutputStream class, 550
   CharArrayReader class, 551
   CharArrayWriter class, 552
   DataInputStream class, 553
   DataOutputStream class, 555
   File class, 556
   FileInputStream class, 558
   FileOutputStream class, 559
   FilePermission class, 560
   FileReader class, 561
   FileWriter class, 561
   InputStream class, 562
   InputStreamReader class, 563
   LineNumberReader class, 563
   ObjectInputStream class, 565
   ObjectOutputStream class, 567

   OutputStream class, 569
   PipedInputStream class, 570
   PipedOutputStream class, 571
   PrintStream class, 572
   PrintWriter class, 573
   RandomAccessFile class, 574
   Reader class, 576
   SequenceInputStream class, 577
   StreamTokenizer class, 578
   StringBufferInputStream class, 579
   StringReader class, 580
   StringWriter class, 581
   Writer class, 582
DataInputStream class, 552-554
DataOutputStream class, 554-555
exceptions, 543
Externalizable interface, 543
fields
   BufferedInputStream class, 545
   BufferedOutputStream class, 546
   ByteArrayInputStream class, 549
   ByteArrayOutputStream class, 550
   CharArrayReader class, 551
   CharArrayWriter class, 552
   DataOutputStream class, 555
   File class, 556
   PipedInputStream class, 570
   PrintWriter class, 573
   Reader class, 576
   Serializable interface, 544
   StreamTokenizer class, 578
   StringBufferInputStream class, 579
   Writer class, 581
File class, 555-557
FileFilter interface, 544
FileInputStream class, 557-558
FilenameFilter interface, 544
FileOutputStream class, 558-559
FilePermission class, 559-560
FileReader class, 560-561
FileWriter class, 561
InputStream class, 561-562

InputStreamReader class, 562-563
interfaces, 541
    Externalizable, 543
    FileFilter, 544
    FilenameFilter, 544
    Serializable, 544
LineNumberReader class, 563
methods
    BufferedInputStream class, 545-546
    BufferedReader class, 547-548
    BufferedWriter class, 548
    ByteArrayInputStream class, 549
    ByteArrayOutputStream class, 550
    CharArrayReader class, 551
    CharArrayWriter class, 552
    DataInputStream class, 553-554
    DataOutputStream class, 555
    Externalizable interface, 543
    File class, 556-557
    FileFilter interface, 544
    FileInputStream class, 558
    FilenameFilter interface, 544
    FileOutputStream class, 559
    FilePermission class, 560
    InputStream class, 562
    InputStreamReader class, 563
    LineNumberReader class, 563
    ObjectInputStream class, 565-566
    ObjectOutputStream class, 567-568
    OutputStream class, 569
    PipedInputStream class, 570
    PipedOutputStream class, 571
    PrintStream class, 572
    PrintWriter class, 573-574
    RandomAccessFile class, 574-576
    Reader class, 577
    SequenceInputStream class, 577
    StreamTokenizer class, 578-579
    StringBufferInputStream class, 579
    StringReader class, 580
    StringWriter class, 581
    Writer class, 582

ObjectInputStream class, 564-566
ObjectOutputStream class, 566-568
OutputStream class, 568-569
PipedInputStream class, 569-570
PipedOutputStream class, 570-571
PrintStream class, 571-572
PrintWriter class, 572-574
RandomAccessFile class, 574-576
Reader class, 576-577
SequenceInputStream class, 577
Serializable interface, 544
StreamTokenizer class, 578
StringBufferInputStream class, 579
StringReader class, 580
StringWriter class, 580-581
Writer class, 581-582

java.lang, 583
    Boolean class, 586-587
    Byte class, 587-588
    Character class, 588-580
    Class class, 590-591
    classes, 583-584
        Boolean, 586-587
        Byte, 587-588
        Character, 588-590
        Class, 590-591
        ClassLoader, 591-592
        Compiler, 592-593
        Double, 593-594
        Float, 594-595
        Integer, 595-597
        Long, 597-598
        Math, 598-599
        Object, 599-600
        Runtime, 600-601
        SecurityManager, 602-604
        Short, 604-605
        String, 605-607
        StringBuffer, 607-608
        System, 609
        Thread, 610-611
        ThreadGroup, 611-612
        Throwable, 612-613
    ClassLoader class, 591-592
    Cloneable interface, 585

764 java.lang

Comparable interface, 585-586
Compiler class, 592-593
constructors
    Character class, 589
    ClassLoader class, 592
    Long class, 597
    Object class, 600
    SecurityManager class, 603
Double class, 593-594
errors, 585
exceptions, 584
fields
    Boolean class, 586
    Byte class, 587
    Character class, 588-589
    Double class, 593
    Float class, 595
    Integer class, 596
    Long class, 597
    Math class, 598
    SecurityManager class, 603
    Short class, 604
    String class, 606
    System class, 609
    Thread class, 610
Float class, 594-595
Integer class, 595-597
interfaces, 583
    Cloneable, 585
    Comparable, 585
    Comparable, methods, 586
    Runnable, 586
    Runnable, methods, 586
Long class, 597-598
Math class, 598-599
methods
    Boolean class, 587
    Byte class, 588
    Character class, 589-590
    Class class, 590-591
    ClassLoader class, 592
    Comparable interface, 586
    Compiler class, 593
    Double class, 594
    Float class, 595

Integer class, 596-597
Long class, 597-598
Math class, 599
Object class, 600
Runnable interface, 586
Runtime class, 601
SecurityManager class, 603-604
Short class, 604-605
String class, 606-607
StringBuffer class, 608
System class, 609
Thread class, 611
ThreadGroup class, 612
Throwable class, 613
Object class, 599-600
Runnable interface, 586
Runtime class, 600-601
RuntimePermission class, 601
SecurityManager class, 602-604
Short class, 604-605
String class, 605-607
StringBuffer class, 607-608
System class, 609
Thread class, 610-611
ThreadGroup class, 611-612
Throwable class, 612-613
java.lang class, 29
java.lang.Object class, 29
    RemoteObject class, methods, 656
java.lang.reflect, 615
    AccessibleObject class, 616-617
    Array class, 617-618
    classes, 616
        AccessibleObject, 616-617
        Array, 617-618
        Constructor, 618
        Field, 619-620
        Method, 620-622
        ReflectPermission, 622-623
    Constructor class, 618
    constructors
        AccessibleObject class, 617
        Modifier class, 621
        ReflectPermission class, 623
    Field class, 619-620

fields
    Member interface, 616
    Modifier class, 621
interfaces, 616
Member interface, 616
Method class, 620
methods
    AccessibleObject class, 617
    Array class, 617-618
    Constructor class, 618
    Field class, 619-620
    Member interface, 616
    Method class, 620
    Modifier class, 621-622
Modifier class, 621-622
ReflectPermission class, 622-623

java.lang.reflect, 245

java.lang.Thread, subclassing, code, 206-207

java.math
BigDecimal class, 625-627
BigInteger class, 627-628
classes
    BigDecimal, 625-627
    BigInteger, 627-628
    BigInteger, methods, 628
constructors
    BigDecimal class, 626
    BigInteger class, 627
fields
    BigDecimal class, 626
    BigInteger class, 627
methods
    BigDecimal class, 626-627
    BigInteger class, 628

java.net
classes, 629-630
    ContentHandler, 631-632
    DatagramPacket, 632-633
    DatagramSocket, 633-634
    HttpURLConnection, 634-636
    InetAddress, 636-637
    JarURLConnection, 637-638
    MulticastSocket, 638-639
    PasswordAuthentication, 640
    ServerSocket, 640-641
    Socket, 641-642
    SocketImpl, 642-643
    URL, 643-644
    URLConnection, 644-646
    URLStreamHandler, 646
constructors
    ContentHandler class, 632
    DatagramSocket class, 634
    HttpURLConnection class, 636
    JarURLConnection class, 638
    MulticastSocket class, 639
    PasswordAuthentication class, 640
    ServerSocket class, 641
    Socket class, 641
    SocketImpl class, 643
    URL class, 644
    URLConnection class, 645
    URLStreamHandler class, 646
ContentHandler class, 631-632
ContentHandlerFactory interface, 630-631
DatagramPacket class, 632-633
DatagramSocket class, 633-634
exceptions, 630
fields
    HttpURLConnection class, 635-636
    JarURLConnection class, 638
    SocketImpl class, 642
    SocketOptions interface, 631
    URLConnection class, 645
HttpURLConnection class, 634-636
InetAddress class, 636-637
interfaces, 629
    ContentHandlerFactory, 630-631
    SocketImplFactory, 631
    SocketOptions, 631
JarURLConnection class, 637-638
methods
    ContentHandler class, 632
    ContentHandlerFactory interface, 631
    DatagramPacket class, 633

766 java.net

DatagramSocket class, 634
HttpURLConnection class, 636
InetAddress class, 637
JarURLConnection class, 638
MulticastSocket class, 639
PasswordAuthentication
 class, 640
ServerSocket class, 641
Socket class, 642
SocketImpl class, 643
SocketImplFactory interface, 631
SocketOptions interface, 631
URL class, 644
URLConnection class, 645-646
URLStreamHandler class, 646
MulticastSocket class, 638-639
PasswordAuthentication class, 640
ServerSocket class, 640-641
Socket class, 641-642
SocketImpl class, 642-643
SocketImplFactory interface, 631
SocketOptions interface, 631
URL class, 643-644
URLConnection class, 644-646
URLStreamHandler class, 646

java.net.InetAddress class, 259-261

java.rmi

classes, 647
 MarshalledObject, 648-649
 Naming, 649-650
 RMISecurityManager, 650-651
constructors
 MarshalledObject class, 649
 RMISecurityManager class, 651
exceptions, 647-648
interfaces, 647-648
MarshalledObject class, 648-649
methods
 MarshalledObject class, 649
 Naming class, 650
 RMISecurityManager class, 651
Naming class, 649-650
Remote interface, 648
RMISecurityManager class, 650-651

java.rmi.activation

Activatable class, 659-660
ActivationDesc class, 660-661
ActivationGroup class, 661-662
ActivationGroupDesc class, 662-663
ActivationID class, 663-664
classes, 653
 Activatable, 659-660
 ActivationDesc, 660-661
 ActivationGroup, 661-662
 ActivationGroupDesc, 662-663
 ActivationID, 663-664
constructors
 Activatable class, 660
 ActivationDesc class, 661
 ActivationGroup class, 662
 ActivationGroupDesc class, 663
 ActivationID class, 664
exceptions, 654
interfaces, 653
methods
 Activatable class, 660
 ActivationDesc class, 661
 ActivationGroup class, 662
 ActivationGroupDesc class, 663
 ActivationID class, 664

java.rmi.Remote interface, 282

java.rmi.server, 653

classes, 654
 RemoteObject, 656
 RemoteServer, 657
 RemoteServer, constructors, 658
 RMIClassLoader, 657
 UnicastRemoteObject, 658-659
constructors
 RemoteObject class, 656
 RemoteServer class, 658
 UnicastRemoteObject class, 658
exceptions, 654
fields
 RemoteObject class, 656
 RemoteRef interface, 655
 ServerRef interface, 656
interfaces, 654
 RemoteRef, 655
 RMIClientSocketFactory, 655

RMIServerSocketFactory, 655-656
ServerRef, 656
methods
    RemoteObject class, 656
    RemoteRef interface, 655
    RemoteServer class, 658
    RMIClassLoader class, 657
    RMIClientSocketFactory interface, 655
    RMIServerSocketFactory interface, 656
    ServerRef interface, 656
    UnicastRemoteObject class, 659
RemoteObject class, 656
RemoteRef interface, 655
RemoteServer class, 657-658
RMIClassLoader class, 657
RMIClientSocketFactory interface, 655
RMIServerSocketFactory interface, 655-656
ServerRef interface, 656
UnicastRemoteObject class, 658-659

java.security
classes, 665-666
exceptions, 666
interfaces, 665

java.security.cert
AllPermission class, 668
Certificate class, 674-675
classes, 667
    AllPermission, 668
    Certificate, 674-675
    CodeSource, 669
    CRL (Class Revocation List), 675-676
    KeyPair, 669-670
    KeyStore, 670-671
    MessageDigest, 671-672
    Permission, 672-673
    Policy, 673-674
    ProtectionDomain, 674
    X509Certificate, 676-677
    X509CRL, 677-678
CodeSource class, 669
constructors
    AllPermission class, 668
    Certificate class, 675
    CodeSource class, 669
    CRL (Class Revocation List) class, 676
    KeyPair class, 670
    KeyStore class, 671
    MessageDigest class, 672
    Permission class, 673
    Policy class, 674
    ProtectionDomain class, 674
    X509Certificate class, 676
    X509CRL class, 678
CRL (Class Revocation List) class, 675-676
exceptions, 667
fields, Key interface, 667
interfaces, Key, 667
Key interface, 667
KeyPair class, 669-670
KeyStore class, 670-671
MessageDigest class, 671-672
methods
    AllPermission class, 668
    Certificate class, 675
    CodeSource class, 669
    CRL (Class Revocation List) class, 676
    Key interface, 667
    KeyPair class, 670
    KeyStore class, 671
    MessageDigest class, 672
    Permission class, 673
    Policy class, 674
    ProtectionDomain class, 674
    X509Certificate class, 677
    X509CRL class, 678
Permission class, 672-673
Policy class, 673-674
ProtectionDomain class, 674
X509Certificate class, 676-677
X509CRL class, 677-678

768 java.sql

java.sql
    Blob interface, 680
    CallableStatement interface, 680-681
    classes, 679
        DriverManager, 689-690
        Timestamp, 690
    Connection interface, 681-682
    Constructors, Timestamp class, 690
    database programming, 331
    Driver interface, 683
    DriverManager class, 689-690
    exceptions, 680
    fields
        Connection interface, 682
        ResultSet interface, 685
    interfaces, 679
        Blob, 680
        CallableStatement, 680-681
        Connection, 681-682
        Driver, 683
        PreparedStatement, 683-685
        ResultSet, 685-688
        Statement, 688-689
    methods
        Blob interface, 680
        CallableStatement interface, 681
        Connection interface, 682
        Driver interface, 683
        DriverManager class, 689-690
        PreparedStatement interface, 684-685
        ResultSet interface, 685, 687-688
        Statement interface, 688-689
        Timestamp class, 690
    PreparedStatement interface, 683-685
    ResultSet interface, 685-688
    Statement interface, 688-689
    Timestamp class, 690

java.text
    ChoiceFormat class, 692-693
    class functions, 365
    classes, 691
    DateFormat class, 693, 695
    DecimalFormat class, 695-696
    exceptions, 691

    interfaces, 691
    MessageFormat class, 696
    NumberFormat class, 697-698
    SimpleDateFormat class, 698-700

java.util, 379
    ArrayList class, 706-707
    BitSet class, 707-708
    Calendar class, 708-711
    classes, 701-702
        ArrayList, 706-707
        BitSet, 707-708
        Calendar, 708-711
        Collections, 711-712
        GregorianCalendar, 712-713
        HashMap, 713-714
        HashSet, 714-715
        Locale, 715-717
        Observable, 717
        Properties, 717-718
        PropertyPermission, 719
        ResourceBundle, 720
        StringTokenizer, 720-721
        Vector, 721-723
    Collection Framework, 379
        implementations, 382-384
        interfaces, 380-382
        List implementations, 387
        Map implementations, 391
        Set implementations, 384-393
    Collection interface, 702-703
    Collections class, 711-712
    constructors
        ArrayList class, 706
        BitSet class, 708
        Calendar class, 710
        GregorianCalendar class, 713
        HashMap class, 714
        Locale class, 716
        Observable class, 717
        Properties class, 718
        PropertyPermission class, 719
        ResourceBundle class, 720
        StringTokenizer class, 721
        Vector class, 722
    exceptions, 702

fields
    Calendar class, 709-710
    Collections class, 711
    GregorianCalendar class, 713
    Locale class, 716
    Properties class, 718
    ResourceBundle class, 720
    Vector class, 722
GregorianCalendar class, 394-399, 712-713
HashMap class, 713-714
HashSet class, 714-715
interfaces, 701
    Collection, 702-703
    Iterator, 703
    List, 703-704
    Map, 704-705
    Observer, 705
    Set, 705-706
Iterator interface, 703
List interface, 703-704
Locale class, 715-717
Map interface, 704-705
methods
    ArrayList class, 707
    BitSet class, 708
    Calendar class, 710-711
    Collection interface, 702-703
    Collections class, 711-712
    GregorianCalendar class, 713
    HashMap class, 714
    HashSet class, 715
    Iterator interface, 703
    List interface, 704
    Locale class, 716-717
    Map interface, 705
    Observable class, 717
    Observer interface, 705
    Properties class, 718
    PropertyPermission class, 719
    ResourceBundle class, 720
    Set interface, 706
    StringTokenizer class, 721
    Vector class, 723
Observable class, 717
Observer interface, 705
Properties class, 717-718
Properties object, 399-403
PropertyPermission class, 719
ResourceBundle class, 720
Set interface, 705-706
StringTokenizer class, 720-721
Vector class, 721-723

java.util.jar, 725
classes
    JarEntry, 726-727
    JarFile, 727-728
    JarInputStream, 728-729
    JarOutputStream, 729-730
    Manifest, 730-731
constructors
    JarEntry class, 727
    JarFile class, 728
    JarInputStream class, 729
    JarOutputStream class, 730
    Manifest class, 731
exceptions, 726
fields, JarFile class, 728
JarEntry class, 726-727
JarFile class, 727-728
JarInputStream class, 728-729
JarOutputStream class, 729-730
Manifest class, 730-731
methods
    JarEntry class, 727
    JarFile class, 728
    JarInputStream class, 729
    JarOutputStream class, 730
    Manifest class, 731

JavaBeans
abc property, methods, 530
bean context, 531
client-side components, 529
IDE (Integrated Development Environment), 529
introspection, 529, 615
Isabc() method, 530
JDK 1.1, AWT components, 530
methods, Isabac(), 530
properties, 529-530

purpose, 529
Reflection API, 530
Javac compiler, 8
javadoc utility, 15
javax.ejb packages, 529
javax.sql, interfaces, 340
javax.swing package, 17
jdb (debugging tool), 16
JDBC (Java Database Connectivity), 331-332
    AutoCommit, turning off, 362
    CallableStatement, 341, 348-349
    code, writing, 332
    databases
        autoCommit, turning off, 362
        CallableStatement, code, 348-349
        connection pools, 333
        connections, code, 334-341
        connections, creating, 332-333
        isolation levels, setting, 362-363
        PreparedStatement, code, 345-348
        ResultSet, code, 341-345
        ResultSetMetadata, code, 341-345
        tables, code to create, 334-341
    drivers, 683, 689
    InstantDB Web site, 334, 338
    isolation levels, setting, 362-363
    javax.sql, interfaces, 340
    Microsoft Access, 338
    PreparedStatement, 340-341, 345-348
    ResultSet
        code, 341-345
        objects, passing, 338
    ResultSetMetadata,
        code, 341-345
        tables, schema, 339
    SQL (Structured Query Language)
        statements, supporting, 340
JDBC 2.0
    APIs, 349-350
    batch updates, 355
    collections, 25-26
    extensions, 24-25
    new features, 22-26
    package versioning, 24

reference objects, 24
ResultSet
    modifying, 355
    ResultSet, scrolling, 350
    scrolling code, 350-355
    size, limiting, 361
    updating code, 356-361
sound, 26
jdbc.drivers property, 689
JDK 1.1, AWT components, 530
JFC (Java Foundation Classes), 17-18, 125-131
JIT (just-in-time) compiler, 593
JNI (Java Native Interface), 70
join() method, 208, 610
JradioButtons, ButtonGroup, 131
JRE (Java Runtime Environment), 14
JRMP (Java Remote Method Protocol), 280
just-in-time (JIT) compiler, 593
JVM (Java virtual machine), 7
    garbage collection, 14
    Java, 13-14
    objects, creating, 45

K

kernel thread, 206
Key interface, 667
key/value pairs, Properties class, 718
KeyPair class, 669-670
keys
    asymmetric, 319
    keypass option, 320
    private, 319-320
    public, 319
    storepass option, 320
    symmetric, 319
KeyStore class, 670-671
keystore databases, 319
KeyStore object, entries, 670
keystores, 322
keytool, 319
keywords
    abstract, 38
    class, 38

extends, 39
goto, 87
public, 38
synchronized, code, 73
syntax, 86-87
throw, 200
throws, 200

L

Label class, 461
languages, object-oriented. *See* Java
layers, Transport Layer, 280
layout managers
    classes, inheritance, 111
    components, arranging and sizing, 427
    default, containers, 113
    GUIs (graphical user interfaces), 107
    No LayoutManager, absolute positioning, code, 107-108
LayoutManager interface, 420
LayoutManager2 interface, 420
left shift (<<) bitwise operator, 94-95
libraries, class, Java, 7
LibraryCard, class definitions, code, 294-295
lightweight components, 18, 106
LineNumberReader class, 563
LinkedList, code, 388-391
List class, 462-463
List interface, 381, 703-704
list() method, 229, 286
Listener class, implementing, 137
listeners on components, registering, 137
lists
    ArrayList, 387
    LinkedList, code, 388-391
    mailing, RMI-USERS subscribing to, 307
    scrollable, 462
Litwak, Ken, 312
load() method, 403
local objects, versus remote objects, 281
Locale class, 715-717
    internationalizing applications, code, 367-369

Locale.getDisplayName method, 369
locales
    default, finding, 370
    locale-sensitive classes, code to check, 369
locations, containers, 114
locks, object
    releasing, 217
    synchronized code, 216
Logging interface, 82-84
logical operators, 87
Long class, 597-598
long primitives, 33, 36, 597
lookup() method, 649-650
loops
    Do-while, 98
    For, 99
    While, 98-99

M

magic numbers, 12
mailing lists, RMI-USERS, subscribing to, 307
main method, 13, 31-32, 109
MalformedURLException, 274
Manifest class, 730-731
Map interface, 380-381, 704-705
mapping between primitives and wrapper classes, 59
mark() method, 224-225
marshal, 280
MarshalledObject class, 648-649
math, integers, BigInteger Class, 627
Math class, 598-599
MediaTracker, 586
    downloading, multiple images, 181
    Images, registering, 188
MediaTracker class, 464-465
MediaTracker methods, 180
Member interface, 616
Menu class, 465-466
MenuBar class, 467
MenuContainer interface, 421
MenuItem class, 468
menus in applets, 166

MenuShortcut class, 469
message digests, 326-329
MessageBundle_de_DE.properties, 368
MessageBundle_en_US.properties, 368
MessageDigest class, 327-329, 671-672
MessageFormat class, 696-697
Method class, 616, 620
Method object, 246
methods
    { } curly braces, 31
    abc property, 530
    abstract, interfaces, 83
    accept(), 640-641
    access modifiers, 67
    AccessibleObject class, 617
    Activatable class, 660
    ActivationDesc class, 661
    ActivationGroup class, 662
    ActivationGroup.createGroup(), 663
    ActivationGroupDesc class, 663
    ActivationID class, 664
    ActiveEvent interface, 419
    addAll(), 382
    addAnAppt, multiple threads calling, 72
    addImage(), 188
    addxxxListener(), 137
    Adjustable interface, 419
    AllPermission class, 668
    Applet class, 410-411
    AppletContext interface, 408
    AppletInitializer interface, 532
    of applets, 167-168
    AppletStub interface, 408
    Array class, 617-618
    arraycopy(), 609
    ArrayList, 387
    ArrayList class, 707
    AWTEvent class, 423
    AWTEventMulticaster class, 424-426
    BeanDescriptor class, 535
    BeanInfo interface, 532
    Beans class, 535
    BigDecimal class, 626-627
    BigInteger class, 628
    bind(), 285, 650

BitSet class, 708
Blob interface, 680
Boolean class, 587
BorderLayout class, 427
BufferedInputStream class, 545-546
BufferedReader class, 547-548
BufferedWriter class, 548
business logic, 282
Button class, 428
Byte class, 588
ByteArrayInputStream class, 549
ByteArrayOutputStream class, 550
Calendar class, 710-711
CallableStatement interface, 681
calling, 253
calls to remote objects, path, 280
Canvas class, 429
CardLayout class, 430
Certificate class, 675
Character class, 589-590
CharArrayReader class, 551
CharArrayWriter class, 552
Checkbox class, 431
CheckboxGroup class, 432
checkOut(), 69
Choice class, 433
ChoiceFormat class, 693
class, 65
Class class, 590-591, 615
Class.forName, 246
classes, 72, 285
ClassLoader class, 592
clear(), 399
close(), 224-225, 585
CodeSource class, 669
Collection Framework, 381-384
Collection interface, 702-703
Collections class, 711-712
Collections.binarySearch(), 387
Collections.reverse(), 387
Collections.shuffle(), 387, 703
Collections.sort(), 387, 586
Color class, 434-435
commit(), 362
Comparable interface, 586

compareTo(), 586
Compiler class, 593
Component class, 435-439
Composite interface, 419
CompositeContext interface, 420
Connection interface, 682
Constructor class, 618
constructors of classes, 618
Container class, 440-441
ContentHandler class, 632
ContentHandlerFactory interface, 631
create(), 229
createStatement(), 350-351, 356
CRL (Class Revocation List) class, 676
Cursor class, 442
Customizer interface, 532
DatagramPacket class, 633
DatagramSocket class, 634
DataInputStream class, 553-554
DataOutputStream class, 555
DateFormat class, 694-695
DecimalFormat class, 695-696
declarations, database connections, 681
declaring that throw exceptions, code, 197-198
definitions, punctuation, 85
delete(), 229
destroy(), 168
Dialog class, 444
Double class, 594
drawImage, 180
drawString(), 174
Driver interface, 683
DriverManager class, 689-690
DriverManager.getConnection(), 333
Exceptions, 76-77, 191
exec(), 601
executeUpdate(), 362
exportObject(), 650
Externalizable interface, 543
Field class, 619-620
File class, 556-557
FileDialog class, 445
FileFilter interface, 544
FileInputStream class, 558

FilenameFilter interface, 544
FileOutputStream class, 559
FilePermission class, 560
final, 65
Float class, 595
FlowLayout class, 446
flush(), 224-225
Font class, 447, 449
forName(), 333, 590, 615
Frame class, 451
generic, coding, 205
get, 256
get(), 530, 629
getabc(), 530
getActionCommand(), 615
getByName(), 261
getBytes(), 229
getClass(), 246, 248
getConnection(), 332
getConstructors(), 249, 251
getContent(), 632
getCurrencyInstance(), 372
getDefault(), 370
getFields(), 248
getFloat(), 339
getHostByName(), 636
getHostName(), 261
getInt(), 344
getLocalHost(), 629, 636
getMessage(), 193
getMethods(), 249, 251
getModifiers(), 248, 251
getName(), 248, 615
getObject(), 344
getOutputStream(), 635
getParameterTypes(), 251
getProperties(), 66, 609
getProperty(), 399, 403, 609
getReturnType(), 251
getRuntime(), 600
getSomeObject(), 630
getString(), 366
getSuperclass(), 248
getType(), 248
getxxx(), 339, 680

Graphics class, 452-453
Graphics2D class, 454-455
GregorianCalendar class, 713
GridBagConstraints class, 457
GridBagLayout class, 457-458
GridLayout class, 459
HashMap class 383, 714
HashSet class, 715
hasNext(), 382, 384
hoop values, 539
HttpURLConnection class, 636
Image class, 460
imageUpdate(), 180
IndexedPropertyDescriptor class, 536
InetAddress class, 637
Information, code to obtain, 249-251
init(), 167, 410
inlining, 65
InputStream class, 224, 562
InputStreamReader class, 563
insertRow(), 356
Insets class, 461
Integer class, 596-597
Introspector class, 537
Isabac(), 530
isDirectory(), 229
ItemSelectable interface, 420
Iterator interface, 703
iterator(), 382, 384
JarEntry class, 727
JarFile class, 728
JarInputStream class, 729
JarOutputStream class, 730
JarURLConnection class, 638
JDBC driver, 683
join(), 208, 610
Key interface, 667
KeyPair class, 670
KeyStore class, 671
Label class, 461
LayoutManager interface, 420
LayoutManager2 interface, 420
LineNumberReader class, 563
List class, 463
List interface, 704

list(), 229, 286
load(), 403
Locale class, 716-717
Locale.getDisplayName, 369
Long class, 597-598
lookup(), 649-650
main, 13, 31-32, 109
Manifest class, 731
Map interface, 705
mark(), 224-225
MarshalledObject class, 649
Math class, 599
MediaTracker class, 180, 464-465
Member interface, 616
Menu class, 466
MenuBar class, 467
MenuContainer interface, 421
MenuItem class, 468
MenuShortcut class, 469
MessageDigest class, 672
MessageFormat class, 697
Method class, 620
Modifier class, 621-622
modifiers
    access, 67
    final, 65
    native, 70-71
    private, 68
    protected, 68
    public, 67-68
    static, 65-67
    synchronized, 71-74
moveToInsertRow(), 356
MulticastSocket class, 639
naming, 30
Naming class, 650
Naming.lookup(), RMI clients, code,
    289-291
native, 70-71
next(), 339
notify(), deadlocks, avoiding, 217-221
notifyAll(), 218
NumberFormat class, 698
Object class, 600
ObjectInputStream class, 565-566

ObjectOutputStream class, 567-568
Observable class, 717
Observer interface, 705
open(), 229
openConnection(), 274
OutputStream class, 224, 569
overloading, 74-75
overriding, 75-78
pack(), 108
package-level access, 70
Paint interface, 421
paint(), 167, 175, 188
PaintContext interface, 421
Panel class, 470
parameters, naming, 63-64
PasswordAuthentication class, 640
Permission class, 673
PipedInputStream class, 570
PipedOutputStream class, 571
Point class, 471
Policy class, 674
pop(), 216, 222
PopupMenu class, 471
post(), 629
PreparedStatement interface, 684-685
printf(), 239
PrintGraphics interface, 421
PrintJob class, 473
println(), 239
printStackTrace(), 193
PrintStream class, 572
PrintWriter class, 573-574
private, 68
Properties class, 718
PropertyChangeEvent class, 538
PropertyChangeListener interface, 533
PropertyDescriptor class, 539
PropertyEditor interface, 533-534
PropertyPermission class, 719
protected, 68
ProtectionDomain class, 674
public, 31, 67-68
push(), 216, 222
RandomAccessFile class, 574-576
read(), 224-225

read(byte[ ] b), 224
read(char[ ] c), 225
readLine(), 240
Reader class, 225, 577
readUTF(), 234
rebind(), 287-288, 650
rebind(), 285
Rectangle class, 474-475
registerDriver(), 332, 689
registerOutParameter(), 341
remote
    accessing, 650
    java.lang.Object, 656
    parameters, 280-281
of remote objects, calling, 282-292
RemoteObject class, 656
RemoteRef interface, 655
RemoteServer class, 658
remove(), 382
removeAll(), 382
repaint(), 175
required, 31-32
reset(), 224-225
ResourceBundle class, 720
ResultSet, 339
ResultSet interface, 685, 687-688
RMIClassLoader class, 657
RMIClientSocketFactory interface, 655
RMISecurityManager class, 651
RMIServerSocketFactory interface, 656
rollback(), 362
run (), 205-206(), 586, 610
Runnable interface, 586
Runtime class, 601
save(), 403
ScrollPane class, 476
SecurityManager class, 309-310, 603-604
seek(), 229
SequenceInputStream class, 577
ServerRef interface, 656
ServerSocket class, 641
set, 256
Set interface, 706
set(), 530

setabc(), 530
setAutoCommit(false), 362, 682
setBounds(), absolute positioning, 109
setSize(), 108
setVisible (true)(), 108
setWeekdays(), 378
setxxx(), 340, 680, 684
Shape interface, 422
Short class, 604-605
show(), 120
signatures, 63, 191
SimpleBeanInfo class, 540
SimpleDateFormat class, 700
sleep(), 206
Socket class, 642
SocketImpl class, 643
SocketImplFactory interface, 631
SocketOptions interface, 631
start(), 167, 175, 206, 610
Statement interface, 688-689
static, 31, 65-67
stop(), 168, 175, 610, 409
store(), 403
StreamTokenizer class, 578-579
String class, 606-607
StringBuffer class, 608
StringBufferInputStream class, 579
StringReader class, 580
StringTokenizer class, 721
StringWriter class, 581
suspend(), 209, 610
synchronizing, 71-74, 216
System class, 609
talk(), 10
this (object reference), 64
Thread class, 611
Thread object, 207-209
ThreadGroup class, 612
Throwable class, 613
throws keyword, 200
Timestamp class, 690
toString(), 39, 244, 369
Transparency interface, 422
UnicastRemoteObject class, 659
updatexxx(), 356

URL class, 644
URLConnection class, 645-646
URLStreamHandler class, 646
validateBorrower(), 69
Vector class, 383, 723
VetoableChangeListener interface, 534
void, 31
wait(), 206, 217-222, 610
wash(), 10
write(), 224-225
write(byte[ ] b), 224
write(char[ ] c)), 225
writeLog(), 83
Writer class, 225, 582
writeUTF(), 234
X509Certificate class, 677
X509CRL class, 678
yield(), 610

Microsoft Access, JDBC (Java Database Connectivity), 338
minus sign (-), arithmetic operator, 87
Model-View-Controller (MVC) design pattern, 20
Modifier class, 621-622
modifiers of methods
    access, 67
    final, 65
    native, 70-71
    private, 68
    protected, 68
    public, 67-68
    static, 65-67
    synchronized, 71, 73-74
mouse
    cursors, 441
    drag and drop, 415
        ACTION_COPY, 149
        ACTION_LINK, 149
        ACTION_MOVE, 149
        ACTION_REFERENCE, 149
        code, 150-161
        DataFlavor, 148
        drag actions, 149
        DragSource, 148
        DropTarget, 148

Object serialization 777

screen after operation, 163
screen before operation, 162
TransferableString class, code, 161-162
moveToInsertRow() method, 356
multicast event dispatching, 424
MulticastSocket class, 638-639
multiple inheritance, 11
multiple threads, 203
    addAnAppt method, calling, 72
    resources, code changing incorrectly, 72
    synchronizing, 209-216
multithreading, Java, 13
MVC (Model-View-Controller) design pattern, 20

N

naming
    classes, 30, 246, 285
    examples, 30
    hosts, 258
    interfaces, 30
    methods, 30
    parameters, 63-64
    variables, 30, 64
Naming class, 649-650
Naming.lookup() method, RMI clients, code, 289-291
NaN (not a number), 37
nanoseconds parameter, 209
native methods, 70-71
native threads, 208
Netscape, IFC (Internet Foundation Classes), 17
networking concepts, 258-259
networks
    clients, 258
    hosts, 258-259
    IP (Internet Protocol), addresses, 258
    Java, 10
    objects, large or complex, sending, 269
    programming, 257-258
        Datagram packets, 269-273
        hosts names, 259-261
        java.net.InetAddress, 259,-261
        TCP client and server applications, 261-269
        UDP sockets, 269-273
        URLs (uniform resource locators), 273-277
    servers, 258
    sockets, creating, 259
    UDP (User Datagram Protocol) packets, firewalls, 259
new features
    APIs, 19-20
    drag and drop, 20
    Java 2D classes, 19-20
    JDBC 2, 22-26
    JFC (Java Foundation Classes), 17-18
    RMI (Remote Method Invocation), 21-22
    security, policy-based model, 21
    Swing, 17-20
next() method, 339
No LayoutManager, absolute positioning, code, 107-108
non-RuntimeExceptions class, 190
Nonrunnable state, 610
not a number (NaN), 37
notify() method, deadlocks, avoiding, 217-221
notifyAll() method, 218
NumberFormat class, 370-372, 697-698
numbering applets, 173
numbers
    formatting, 692, 697
    java.text package, 365
    magic, 12
numeric data, i18n (internationalization), 370-373
numeric values, formatting, 370-372

O

Object class, 39, 46, 54, 583, 599-600
object database management system (ODBMS), 70
object locks, 216-217
Object Query Language (OQL), 22
Object serialization, 240-241

object-oriented languages. *See* **Java**
ObjectInputStream class, 262, 564-566
   I/O, code to perform, 241-244
ObjectOutputStream class, 262
   I/O, code to perform, 241-244
objects. *See also* **RMI**
   2D geometric, classes and objects, 417
   activating in RMI (Remote Method Invocation), 299-306
   arrays, 59, 61-62
   AudioClip, creating, 175
   behavior, 9
   binary large objects, 680
   canonical, Web site, 244
   characteristics, 9-10
   Class, 246-248
   Constructor, 246
   creating, 45, 253-256
   Date, adding or removing, 216
   dateArray object, dates, adding or removing, 216
   deep copies, 585
   encapsulation, 9
   exceptions, instantiating, 201
   Field, 246
   fields, transient or unserializable, 241
   file, 556
   Frame, 40, 120
   GregorianCalendar, 399, 585
   HasA relationship, 39
   identity, 9
   inheritance, 9
   initializing, 46-47
   interrogating, 622
   IsA relationship, 39
   KeyStore, entries, 670
   large or complex, sending, 269
   local, versus remote objects, 281
   manipulating, 253-256, 622
   Method, 246
   Permission, creating, 314
   polymorphism, 10
   Properties, 399-403
   reading, 240
   reference, JDBC 2, 24
   Reflection, 245
   ReflectPermission class, 622
   remote
      activating, 650
      class definitions, code, 283-285, 294-295
      definition of, 281
      finding, 281-282, 286
      methods, calling, 280-292
      parameters, code to call, 292-298
      rebind() method, code to create or register, 287-288
      versus local objects, 281
   ResultSet, 23-24, 338
   RMIRegistry, 649-650
   Runnable, 204-206
   SecurityManager, 286, 311
   serializing, 66, 280, 544, 648
   shallow copies, 585
   singletons, 67
   sound clip, AudioClip interface, 409
   state, 9
   this (object reference), variable names, disambiguating, 64
   Thread, 203-209
   URLConnection, URLs (uniform resource locators), accessing, 274
   URLs (uniform resource locators), 274
   userProperties Properties object, reinitializing, 403
   Vectors, 240
   Window, 40
   writing, 240
Observable class, 717
Observer interface, 705
Observer/Observable design pattern, 705
ODBMS (object database management system), 70
opcodes, 8
open() method, 229
openConnection() method, 274
operators
   * (asterisk), 88
   ^ (caret), 93-94
   ^= , 88

/ (forward slash), 88
- (minus sign), 87
% (percent sign), 88
| (pipe symbol), 92-93
|= (pipe symbol and equals sign), 88
+ (plus sign), 87
~ (tilde), 96
==, 89
?:, 90
!, 89
!= , 89
&, 91-92
&&, 87
&=, 88
<=, 89
<<=, 88
<< left shift, 89, 94-95
>, 89
>> right shift, 95
>>> unsigned right shift, 95-96
>=, 89
>>=, 88
>>>=, 88
AND, 87, 91-92
arithmetic, 87-88
bitwise, 90
    ^ (caret), 93-94
    | (pipe symbol), 92-93
    ~ (tilde), 96
    & , 91-92
    &&, 87
    << left shift, 94-95
    >> right shift, 95
    >>> unsigned right shift, 95-96
    AND, 87, 91-92
    complement, 96
    OR, 92-94
complement, 96
decrement, 88-89
increment, 88-89
logical, 87
OR, 92-93
relational, 89-90
syntax, 87
XOR, 93-94

OQL (Object Query Language), 22
OR bitwise operator, 92-93
output, user-friendly, 369. *See also* **I/O**
OutputStream class, 224, 568-569
overloading
    constructors, 43-44
    methods, 74-75
overriding methods, 76-78

P

pack() method, 108
package statements, 28
package versioning, JDBC 2, 24
package-level access, methods, 70
packages. *See individual package names*
packets, UDP Datagram, 269-273
Paint interface, 421
paint() method, 167, 175, 188
PaintContext interface, 421
Panel class, 469-470
parameters
    of applets, 173-175
    GridBagConstraints, 122
    GridBagConstraints.RELATIVE, 122
    GridBagConstraints.REMAINDER, 122
    gridHeight, 122
    gridWidth, 122
    gridY, 122
    naming, 63-64
    nanoseconds, 209
    passing, 11
    procedures, stored, SQL (Structured Querey Language), 341
    punctuation, 85
    remote methods, 280-281
    remote objects, code to call, 292-298
parent constructors, invoking, 44-45
parentheses ( ), 85
parsing SQL (Structured Querey Language) code, 334
parsingdates, 698
passing parameters, 11
PasswordAuthentication class, 640
paths, method calls to remote objects, 280
patterns, DecimalFormat class, 373

peers, 105
percent sign (%), arithmetic operator, 88
Permission class, 622, 672-673
Permission object, creating, 314
permissions, 310-311
    AllPermission class, 668
    checking for, 318
    custom, creating, 323-326
    granting, 312
    policy files, adding to, 313
    PropertyPermission class, 719
    Reflection, 617
    RuntimePermission class, 601
    SecurityManager class, 310
    user-defined, code, 324-326
physically challenged, Accessibility APIs, 131-136
piped streams, theads, 570-571
PipedInputStream class, 569-570
PipedOutputStream class, 570-571
PLaF (Pluggable Look and Feel), 18
platforms, absolute positioning, 8, 110
playing sounds, 175
plug-ins, applets, running, 170-171
Pluggable Look and Feel (PLaF), 18
plus sign (+), arithmetic operator, 87
Point class, 470-471
pointer errors, 11
Policy class, 673-674
policy-based security, 21, 309-312
policy files
    applets, activity restrictions, overcoming, 167
    creating, 312-314
    finding, 311
    information, Java Web site, 312
    installing, 312
    keystores for signed code, 322
    permissions, adding, 313
    RMI.jp, 292
    role, 311
policy tool, 313, 668, 673
polymorphism, objects, 10
pop() method, 216, 222
PopupMenu class, 471

ports
    access, RMIRegistry, 286
    numbers, hosts, 258-259
    sockets, creating, 259
    specifying, 640
positioning components
    absolute, code, 107-110
    BorderLayout, code, 113-117
    CardLayout, code, 117-120
    FlowLayout, code, 111-113
    GridBagLayout, code, 122-125
    GridLayout, code, 120-122
    layout managers, 110-111
post() method, 629
PreparedStatement, 340-341
    code, 345-348
PreparedStatement interface, 683-685
primitive data types, 33
    boolean, 34
    byte, 35-36
    char, 34-35
    double, 37
    float, 36-37
    I/O, performing, 234-237
    int, 36
    long, 36
    short, 36
primitives, 11
    byte, 594
    char, 588
    double, 593
    float, 594
    int, 595
    long, 597
    short, 604
    wrapper classes, mapping between, 59
printf() method, 239
PrintGraphics interface, 421
printing
    problems, 20
    support for, 418
PrintJob class, 472-473
println() method, 239
printStackTrace() method, 193
PrintStream class, 239, 571-572

PrintWriter class, 239, 572-574
private keys, 319-320
private methods, 68-69
procedures, stored, 341, 680
programming
   applets
      code, 171-172
      images (displaying multiple),
        code, 180-188
      images (displaying single), code,
        178-180
      images, code, 177-178
      parameters, code, 173-174
      sound, code, 175-177
   applications. *See* application
    programming
   databases, java.sql package, 331
   networks, 257-258
      Datagram packets, 269-273
      host names, 259-261
      java.net.InetAddress, 259-261
      TCP client and server
        applications, 261-269
      UDP sockets, 269-273
      URLs (uniform resource
        locators), 273-277
programming languages. *See* **Java**
programs
   control flow
      Break statement, 101-102
      Continue statement, 101-102
      Do-while loops, 98
      For loop, 99
      If-else statements, 96-97
      modifying, 101-102
      Switch statement, 100-101
      While loop, 98-99
   hosts, port number, 258-259
   remote factories, starting, 292
   SecurityManager class, 602
properties
   abc, methods, 530
   beans, 529
   bound, 533
   code for getting, 400

   creating, 400
   examining, 399
   get() method, 530
   getting, 403
   Isabc() method, 530
   JavaBeans, 529
   jdbc.drivers, 689
   modifying, 400
   set() method, 530
Properties class, 57, 717-718
Properties files, 366
   default .properties file, 369
   internationalizing applications, code,
      367-368
   MessageBundle_de_DE.properties, 368
   MessageBundle_en_US.properties, 368
   setting up in InstantDB, 337
Properties object, 399-403
PropertyChangeEvent class, 533, 537-538
PropertyChangeListener class or
   interface, 533
PropertyChangeSupport class, 533
PropertyDescriptor class, 538-539
PropertyEditor interface, 533-534
PropertyPermission class, 719
protected methods, 68
protection domains, 311
ProtectionDomain class, 674
protocol stream handlers, 646
protocols
   HTTP (Hypertext Transfer
      Protocol), 257
   IP (Internet Protocol), 258
   JRMP (Java Remote Method
      Protocol), 280
   TCP (Transport Control Protocol), 257
   TCP/IP (Transmission Conrol
      Protocol/Internet Protocol), 257
   UDP (User Datagram Protocol), 257
public keys, 319
public method, 31, 67-69
punctuation, 31
   class definitions, 85
   identifiers, 85
   method definitions, 85

parameters, 85
statements, 85
syntax, 85-86
white space, 85
Pure JFC Swing, 413
push() method, 216, 222

Q-R

question mark (?), 341, 680

RandomAccessFile class, 574-576
read() method, 224-225
read(byte[ ] b) method, 224
read(char[ ] c) method, 225
Reader class, 225, 234, 576-577
reading
    jar files, 727-728
    objects, 240
    Strings, from command lines, 240
    text, 237-239
readLine() method, 240
readUTF() method, 234
rebind() method, 285, 650
    remote objects, code to create or register, 287-288
Rectangle class, 473-475
reference objects, JDBC 2, 24
Reflection
    APIs, 246, 615
    Class object, code to obtain, 246-248
    classes
        attributes, code to obtain, 246-248
        code to manipulate, 253-256
        java.lang.reflect package, 245
        names, code to obtain, 246-248
    constructor information, code to obtain, 249-251
    data members, modifying, 253
    interface information, code to obtain, 251-253
    interfaces, code to interrogate, 251-253
    Introspection class, 537
    method information, code to obtain, 249-251
    methods, calling, 253

    objects, 245
        code to create, 253-256
    permissions, 617
    ReflectPermission class, 622
Reflection API, JavaBeams, 530
ReflectPermission class, 622-623
registerDriver() method, 332, 689
registering
    listeners on components, 137
    remote objects, rebind() method, code, 287-288
registerOutParameter() method, 341
registries, RMIRegistry
    port access, 286
    remote objects, finding, 281-282
    starting, 292
reinitializing userProperties Properties object, 403
relational operators, 89-90
remote activation code, remote objects, creating from clients, 298-302, 304-307
remote classes, class definitions, code, 284-285
remote downloading, stubs, 306-307
remote factories
    object factories, turning into, 279
    programs, starting, 292
    server system on tier 2-n, 279
    on servers, code to create, 285-288
Remote interface, 648
remote interfaces, code
    creating, 282-283
    Issueable, 293-294
Remote Method Invocation. *See* **RMI**
remote methods
    accessing, 650
    parameters, 280-281
remote object class, class definitions, code, 294-295
remote objects
    activating, 650
    class definitions, code to implement, 283-285
    clients, creating from remote activation code, 298-307

RMI (Remote Method Invocation) 783

definition of, 281
finding, 281-282, 286
methods, calling, 280-292
parameters, code to call, 292-298
rebind() method, code to create or
register, 287-288
versus local objects, 281
Remote Reference Layer (RRL), 280
remote references, 280
RemoteObject class, 656
RemoteRef interface, 655
RemoteServer class, 657-658
remove() method, 382
removeAll() method, 382
repaint() method, 175
required methods, 31-32
reset() method, 224-225
ResourceBundle class, 720
    internationalizing applications, code, 367-369
ResultSet
    code, 341-345
    CONCUR_UPDATABLE, 356
    interface, 685-688
    methods, 339
    modifying, 355
    next() method, 339
    objects, passing, 23-24, 338
    ResultSetMetaData, tables, schema, 339
    scrolling, code, 350-355
    size, limiting, 361
    updating, 355-361
ResultSetMetadata
    code, 341-345
    Tables, schema, 339
revoked X.509 certificates, timestamp, 677
right shift >> bitwise operator, 95
    unsigned, >>> bitwise operator, 95-96
RMI (Remote Method Invocation), 21
    architecture, 279-280, 291
    business logic methods, 282
    clients
        code to implement, 288-291
        Naming.lookup() method, code, 289-291

remote object parameters, code, 295-297
running, 292
custom socket factories, Web site tutorial, 655
factories, remote, code to create on servers, 285-288
HotJava, RMIRegistry, binding to, 286
interfaces, remote, code to create, 282-283
Java Web site, 282
java.rmi.Remote interface, 282
JRMP (Java Remote Method Protocol), 280
marshal, 280
methods
    business logic, 282
    remote, parameters, 280-281
new features, 21-22
objects
    activating, 299-306
    remote versus local, 281
    remote, calling methods, 282-292
    remote, code to call with parameters, 292-298
    remote, code to implement class definitions, 283-285
    remote, finding, 281-282
    remote, remote activation code, 298-307
    serialized, 280
remote factory
    server system on tier 2-n, 279
    on servers, code to create, 285-288
    remote factory programs, starting, 292
remote interfaces, code to create, 282-283
remote methods, parameters, 280-281
remote objects
    class definitions, code to implement, 283-285
    creating from clients, remote activation code, 298-307

784 RMI (Remote Method Invocation)

finding, 281-282
methods, calling, 280-292
parameters, code to call, 292-298
rebind() method, code to create or register, 287-288
remote references, 280
RMI-USERS mailing list, subscribing to, 307
RMIRegistry
  HotJava, binding to, 286
  objects, 649-650
  port access, 286
  remote objects, finding, 281-282
  starting, 292
  URLs (uniform resource locators), 286
RRL (Remote Reference Layer), 280
SecurityManager object, 286
setup class, creating, 301-304
skeletons, 280, 291
stubs, 280, 291
  remote downloading, 306-307
Transport Layer, 280
UnicastRemoteObject class, 283
URLs (uniform resource locators)
  part of, 286
  remote objects, finding, 281
RMI.jp policy file, 292
RMIClassLoader class, 657
RMIClientSocketFactory interface, 655
RMISecurityManager class, 650-651
RMIServerSocketFactory interface, 655-656
rollback() method, 362
RRL (Remote Reference Layer), 280
run() method, 205-206, 586, 610
runnable Thread class, 208
Runnable
  interface, 81, 586
  objects, Thread object, creating, 204-206
Runnable state, 610
running
  applets, 168-171
  clients, 292
Runtime class, 55-56, 600-601

RuntimeExceptions class, 190
RuntimePermission class, 601

S

sandbox, 310
  applets, activity restrictions, 166-167
save() method, 403
saving, Properties object, 403
scheduling threads, 208
screens
  after drag and drop operation, 163
  before drag and drop operation, 162
  data entry, code, 123-125
  policy tool, 313
scrollable cursors, 23
scrollable lists, 462
scrolling ResultSet, code, 350-355
ScrollPane class, 19, 475-476
SDK (Software Development Kit)
  classes, 14
  tools, 15-16
  versions, 16
security
  applets, 166-167
  authenticating users, 640
  CA (certificate authority), 318
  certificates
    default expiration period, 321
    digital signatures, 675-676
    fingerprints, 321
    sending, 320
  code, digitally signing, 318-323
  digital signatures, verifying, 318
  ditigal signing, code, 314-315, 317
  FilePermissions, granting, 323
  final methods, 65
  jar files, signing, 320
  Java, 11-12
  keys, 319-320
  keystore databases, 319
  keystores, location, 322
  keytool, 319
  message digests, 326-329
  MessageDigest, code, 327-329
  new features, policy-based model, 21

Permission object, creating, 314
permissions, 310-311
    AllPermission class, 668
    checking for, 318
    creating, 323-326
    granting, 312
    policy files, adding to, 313
    user-defined, code, 324-326
policy-based, 21, 309-312
policy files
    creating, 312-314
    finding, 311
    information, Java Web site, 312
    installing, 312
    keystores for signed code, 322
    permissions, adding, 313
    role, 311
policy tool, screen, 313
protection domains, 311
revoked X.509 certificates, timestamp, 677
RMI (Remote Method Invocation), 21
sandbox, 310
SecurityManager class, 602
SecurityManager object, 286
Users, authenticating, 640
Verisign Web site, 318
X.509 certificates, 676

SecurityManager class, 21, 602
    constructors, 603
    documentation, Java Web site, 603
    fields, 603
    methods, 309-310, 603-604
    object, 286, 311
    permissions, 310
seek() method, 229
Select statement, 338
semicolon (;), 31, 85
separators (!/), 637
SequenceInputStream class, 577
Serializable interface, 241, 544
serialization, Object, 240-241
serializing objects, 66, 280, 544, 648
server system on tier 2-n, remote factory, 279

ServerRef interface, 656
servers, 258
    BookQuery class, 268
    clients, order between, 262
    definition of, 279
    ObjectInputStream, 262
    ObjectOutputStream, 262
    remote factories, code to create, 285-288
    TCP (Transmission Control Protocol)
        applications, creating, 261-269
        programs, sockets and ServerSockets, 263-265
    UDP (User Datagram Protocol), Datagram sockets and packets, 269-271
ServerSocket class, 640-641
ServerSockets, 261
    TCP server programs, 263-265
Set interface, 381, 705
    HashSet implementation class, 384
    methods, 706
    TreeSet implementation class, 384
set() method, 256, 530
setabc() method, 530
setAutoCommit(false) method, 362, 682
setBounds() method, absolute positioning, 109
setSize() method, 108
setup class, creating, 301-304
setVisible (true)() method, 108
setWeekdays() method, 378
setxxx() methods, 340, 680, 684
shallow copies of objects, 585
Shape interface, 421
Short class, 604-605
short primitives, 33, 36, 604
show() method, 120
signatures
    constructors, 41
    digital
        certificates, 675-676
        verifying, 318
    interfaces, 80
    methods, 63
    syntax, 63

signed class, 310
signed code, policy files, 322
signing
    code, digitally, 318-323
    digital code, 314-317
    jar files, 320
SimpleBeanInfo class, 539-540
SimpleDateFormat class, 698
    constructors, 700
    dates, code to format, 373-377
    formatting symbols, 377-378
    methods, 700
    time, code to format, 373-377
singletons, 67
sites, FTP (File Transfer Protocol), Unicode character attribute tables, 588
skeletons, 280
    RMI (Remote Method Invocation), 291
slashes, back (\) or forward (/), 322
sleep() method, 206
Socket class, 641-642
socket factories, RMI custom, Web site tutorial, 655
SocketImpl class, 642-643
SocketImplFactory interface, 631
SocketOptions interface, 631
sockets
    applications using, 259
    creating, 259
    datagrams, sending and receiving, 633
    networks, programming, 257-258
    options, setting or getting, 631
    ServerSockets, 261
    TCP (Transport Control Protocol), 257
        client programs, sockets, 265-266
        e-commerce, 259
        server programs, 263-265
    UDP (User Datagram Protocol), 257-259, 269-273
Sockets, Vectors, writing to, 567
Software Development Kit. *See* SDK
sound
    JDBC 2, 26
    playing, 175-177
    Web pages, 409

sound clip objects, AudioClip interface, 409
source files
    import statements, 29
    main method, defined, 31
SQL (Structured Query Language), 22
    auto-Commit, turning off, 362
    code, parsing, 334
    committing statements, 362
    procedures (stored), parameters, 341
    statements
        committing, 362
        supported by JDBC (Java Database Connectivity), 340
stack traces, 193, 201
start() method, 167, 206, 610
    applet sound, 175
starting remote factory programs or RMIRegistry, 292
Statement interface, 688-689
statements
    ; (semicolon), 31
    Break, 101-102
    CallableStatement, 341
        code, 348-349
    committing, 362
    Continue, 101-102
    If, ?: operator, 90
    If-else, 96-97
    import, 28-29
    package, 28
    PreparedStatement, 340-341
        code, 345-348
    punctuation, 85
    Select, 338
    SQL (Structured Query Language), supported by JDBC (Java Database Connectivity), 340
    Switch, 100-101
states, 9, 203, 610
static methods, 31
    Catalog class, 66
    class methods, 65
    code, 66-67
    constructors, 66
    functions, executing, 67

objects, serializing, 66
System class, 66
stop() method, 168, 610
  applet sound, 175
  sound on Web pages, 409
store() method, 403
stored procedures, 680
stream classes, 223
streams, 223-224
  files, 225-226
  piped, threads, 570-571
  protocol stream handlers, 646
  wrapping, 234, 237
StreamTokenizer class, 578-579
String class, 583, 605-607
String classes, 51-53
StringBuffer class, 607-608
StringBufferInputStream class, 579
StringReader class, 580
strings
  changing, 606
  reading from command lines, 240
  tokens, 720
  UTF, 234
StringTokenizer class, 720-721
StringWriter class, 580-581
structs, 9
Structured Query Language. *See* **SQL**
stubs, 280
  downloading, 650
  downloading remotely, 306-307
  RMI (Remote Method Invocation), 291
subclasses
  ByteArrayOutputStream class, 224
  Component class, 106
  InputStream class, 224
  Methods, overriding, 76
  OutputStream class, 224
  Reader class, 225
  Writer class, 225
Subclassing, java.lang.Thread or Thread object, code, 206-207
subscriptions, RMI-USERS mailing list, 307
suffixes, .class, 246
superclasses, 39, 75-76

suspend() method, 209, 610
Swing, 171. *See also* **GUIs**
  AWT (Abstract Windowing Toolkit), comparing, 18, 126
  components
    code, 127-130
    lightweight, 18
  JFC (Java Foundation classes), 125-127
    code, 127-131
  lightweight components, 18
  new features, 17
    MVC (Model-View-Controller) design pattern, 20
    PLaF (Pluggable Look and Feel), 18
Switch statement, 100-101
symmetric keys, 319
synchronization wrappers, Collection Framework methods, 384
synchronized code, object lock, 216
synchronized keyword, class illustrating use, code, 73
synchronized methods, 71-74
synchronizing
  code, one block of, 213
  methods, 216
  Threads
    code, 213-216
    multiple, 209-213
syntax. *See also* **code**
  ?: operators, 90
  arithmetic operators, 87-88
  bitwise operators, 90
    ^ (caret), 93-94
    | (pipe symbol), 92-93
    ~ (tilde), 96
    &, 91-92
    &&, 87
    << left shift, 94-95
    >> right shift, 95
    >>> unsigned right shift, 95-96
    AND, 87, 91-92
    complement, 96
    OR, 92-93
    XOR, 93-94

control flow, 96
    Break statement, 101-102
    Continue statement, 101-102
    Do-while loops, 98
    For loop, 99
    If-else statements, 96-97
    Switch statement, 100-101
    While loop, 98-99
decrement operators, 88-89
increment operators, 88-89
keywords, 86-87
logical operators, 87
operators, 87
    ^ (caret), 93-94
    | (pipe symbol), 92-93
    ~ (tilde), 96
    &, 91-92
    &&, 87
    ?:, 90
    << left shift, 94-95
    >> right shift, 95
    >>> unsigned right shift, 95-96
    AND, 87, 91-92
    arithmetic, 87-88
    bitwise, 90-96
    complement, 96
    decrement, 88-89
    increment, 88-89
    logical, 87
    OR, 92-93
    relational, 89-90
    XOR, 93-94
punctuation, 85-86
relational operators, 89-90
signatures, 63
try-catch-finally, 190
System class, 55, 66, 583, 609
system properties, code for getting, 400

T

tables
    BookCatalog, 338
    character attributes, 588
    creating, code, 334-341
    schema, 339

talk() method, 10
TCP (Transport Control Protocol)
    client and server applications, creating, 261-269
    client programs, sockets, 265-266
    server programs, sockets and ServerSockets, 263-265
    sockets, 257-259
TCP/IP (Transmission Copntrol Protocol/Internet Protocol), 257
technologiesassistive, 131
templates, 11
text
    formatting, 696
    i18n (internationalization)
        applications, 365
        formatting, 369-370
    java.text package, 365
    reading, 237-239
    writing, 237-239
TextArea class, 476
this (object reference), 64
Thread class, 58-59, 203
    fields, 610
    methods, 611
    runnable, 208
    states, 610
Thread object
    creating, 204-206
    methods, 207-209
    states, 203
    subclassing, code, 206-207
    suspend () method, 209
    threads, relationship, 206
ThreadGroup class, 611-612
threads
    deadlocks, avoiding, 217-221
    green, 206
    kernel, 206
    multiple, 72, 203, 209-216
    native, 208
    object locks, releasing, 217
    piped streams, 570-571
    scheduling, 208
    Thread object, relationship, 206

throw keyword, 200
Throwable class, 612
    Error class, 189
    Exception class, 189
        code for declaring methods that
            throw exceptions, 197-198
            creating, 200-201
            FileNotFoundException, 194
            finally clause code, 195-197
            handling or declaring, 201
            try-catch, 190-194
    methods, 613
throwing exceptions, code, 76-77
throws keyword, 200
throws someException, 191
time, formatting, 373-378
timestamp, revoked X.509 certificates, 677
Timestamp class, 690
tokens, Strings, 720
tools
    debugging, jdb, 16
    keytool, 319
    policy, screen, 313
    policytool, 668, 673
    SDK (Software Development Kit), 15-16
toString() method, 39, 244, 369
TransferableString class, drag and drop, code, 161-162
transient fields, 241
Transparency interface, 422
Transport Layer, 280
TreeMap interface, 704
TreeSet implementation class, 384
try blocks, variable, declaring, 196
try-catch, 194
    code, 191-193
    exceptions, handling, 201
try-catch-finally, 190-191

U

UCS (Universal Character Set), 234
UCS Transformation Format (UTF), 234
UDP (User Datagram Protocol)
    clients, Datagram sockets and packets, 271-273
    packets, firewalls, 259
    servers, Datagram sockets and packets, 269-271
    sockets, 257, 269-273
UnicastRemoteObject class, 283, 658-659
Unicode, 223, 588
uniform resource locators. *See* **URLs**
Universal Character Set (UCS), 234
unjarring jar files, 15
unsigned right shift >>> bitwise operator, 95-96
unzipping zip files, 15
updatexxx() methods, 356
updating
    batches, 355
    ResultSet, 355-361
URL class, 643-644
URLConnection class, 644-646
    URLs (uniform resource locators), accessing, 275-277
URLConnection object, URLs (uniform resource locators), accessing, 274
URLs (uniform resource locators), 273-277, 286
    / (forward slash), 322
    accessing with URL and URLConnection classes, 275-277
    keystores, location, 322
    objects, 274, 281, 286
    parts of, 286, 643-644
    types of, Web site, 643
    URLConnection object, accessing through, 274
URLStreamHandler class, 646
user-defined
    Exception class, code, 198-199
    exceptions, code, 199-200
    permissions, code, 324-326
user-friendly output, 369
userProperties Properties object, reinitializing, 403
users, authenticating, 640
UTF (UCS Transformation Format), 234
utilities. *See also* **Collection Framework; java.util**

GregorianCalendar class, 394-395
   code, 395-399
   javadoc, 15
   Properties object, 399-400
   code, 400-403

V

validateBorrower() method, 69
values, accessing, 366
variables
   delcaring in try blocks, 196
   interfaces, 83
   names, disambiguating, 64
   naming, 30
Vector class, 56-57, 383, 721-723
vectors, 262
   objects, 240
   sizing, 722
   writing to Sockets, 567
verifying digital signatures, 318
Verisign Web site, 318
VetoableChangeListener interface, 534
viewing Map interface, 381
void method, 31

W

wait() method, 206, 610
   deadlocks, avoiding, 217-221
   push() method and pop() method, 222
wash() method, 10
Web pages, sound, 409
Web sites
   canonical objects, 244
   InstantDB, 334, 338
   Java
      Developer's Connection, 384
      policy file information, 312
      RMI (Remote Method Invocation)
         information, 282
      RMI custom socket factories
         tutorial, 655
      SecurityManager class
         documentation, 603

RMI custom socket factories
   tutorial, 655
URLs (uniform resource locators), 643
Verisign, 318
While loop, 98-99
white space, syntax punctuation, 85
whitespace, 31
Window object, 40
wrapper classes, 59
wrappers, synchronizing, Collection
   Framework methods, 384
wrapping, 234, 237
write() method, 224-225
write(byte[ ] b) method, 224
write(char[ ] c)) method, 225
writeLog() method, 83
Writer class, 225, 234, 581-582
writeUTF() method, 234
writing
   code in JDBC (Java Database
      Connectivity), 332
   entries for jar files, 730
   objects, 240
   text, 237-239

X-Y-Z

x and y coordinates, 470
X.509 certificates, 676-677
X509Certificate class, 676-677
X509CRL class, 677-678
XOR bitwise operator, 93-94
xvf flags, jar command, 725

yield() method, 610

zip files, unzipping, 15

The IT site you asked for...

It's Here!

InformIT is a complete online library delivering information, technology, reference, training, news and opinion to IT professionals, students and corporate users.

Find IT Solutions Here!

www.informit.com

InformIT is a trademark of Macmillan USA, Inc.
Copyright © 1999 Macmillan USA, Inc.

Other Related Titles

Developing Java Servlets
James Goodwill
0-672-31600-5
$29.99 US/$44.95 CAN

Java Thread Programming
Paul Hyde
0-672-31585-8
$34.99 US/$52.95 CAN

Java GUI Development
Vartan Piroumian
0-672-31546-7
$34.99 US/$52.95 CAN

Java Distributed Objects
Bill McCarty and Luke Cassady-Dorion
0-672-31537-8
$49.99 US/$71.95 CAN

Java 2 for Professional Developers
Mike Morgan
0-672-31697-8
$34.99 US/$52.95 CAN

Pure JavaScript
R. Allen Wyke
0-672-31547-5
$34.99 US/$52.95 CAN

Pure Visual Basic
Dan Fox
0-672-31598-X
$24.99 US/$37.95 CAN

Pure C++
Eric Gufford
0-672-31511-4
$24.99 US/$37.95 CAN

Pure JFC Swing

Satyaraj Pantham
0-672-31423-1
$19.99 US/$28.95 CAN

Pure JFC 2D Graphics and Imaging

Satyaraj Pantham

0-672-31669-2
$24.99 US/$37.95 CAN

www.samspublishing.com

All prices are subject to change.